D0708916

FRANK WOOD'S
Business Accounting 1

We work with leading authors to develop the strongest educational materials in business and finance, bringing cutting-edge thinking and best learning practice to a global market.

Under a range of well-known imprints, including Financial Times Prentice Hall, we craft high quality print and electronic publications which help readers to understand and apply their content, whether studying or at work.

To find out more about the complete range of our publishing, please visit us on the World Wide Web at: **www.pearsoneduc.com**

FRANK WOOD'S

Business Accounting 1
NINTH EDITION

Frank Wood BSc (Econ), FCA

and

Alan Sangster BA, MSc, Cert TESOL, CA

FINANCIAL TIMES

Prentice Hall

An imprint of **Pearson Education**

Harlow, England · London · New York · Reading, Massachusetts · San Francisco · Toronto · Don Mills, Ontario · Sydney
Tokyo · Singapore · Hong Kong · Seoul · Taipei · Cape Town · Madrid · Mexico City · Amsterdam · Munich · Paris · Milan

Pearson Education Limited

Edinburgh Gate
Harlow
Essex CM20 2JE

and Associated Companies throughout the world.

Visit us on the World Wide Web at
www.pearsoneduc.com

First edition published in 1967
Second edition published under the
Longman imprint in 1972
Third edition published in 1979
Fourth edition published in 1984
Fifth edition published in 1989
Sixth edition published in 1993
Seventh edition published in 1996
Eighth edition published under the
Financial Times Pitman Publishing imprint in 1999
Ninth edition published in 2002

© Frank Wood 1967
© Longman Group UK Limited 1972, 1979, 1984, 1989, 1993
© Pearson Professional Limited 1996
© Financial Times Professional Limited 1999
© Pearson Education Limited 2002

ISBN 0 273 65552 3

British Library Cataloguing-in-Publication Data
A catalogue record for this book is available from the British Library

Library of Congress Cataloging-in-Publication Data
Wood, Frank.
  Frank Wood's business accounting 1 / Frank Wood and Alan Sangster.-- 9th ed.
    p. cm.
  Includes index.
  ISBN 0–273–65552–3 (alk. paper)
    1. Accounting. I. Title: Business accounting 1. II. Title: Business accounting one. III.
  Sangster, Alan. IV. Title.

  HF5635 .W863 2002
  657--dc21   2001056920

10 9 8 7 6 5 4 3 2
07 06 05 04 03

Typeset in 10/11.5 pt Sabon by 35.
Printed and bound in China
SWTC/02

Contents

Notes for teachers and lecturers

This textbook has been written so that a very thorough introduction to accounting is covered in two volumes. The split into two volumes is a recognition of the fact that many students will find all that they require contained in Volume 1. Volume 2 will then carry the studies of the remainder of the readers to a more advanced stage.

This textbook is ideal for anyone who wants to obtain a good grounding in financial accounting, for whatever purpose. In particular, it can be said to be very suitable for students who are starting to study the subject for A level, Scottish Higher Grade, or General Certificate of Secondary Education examinations, and for those embarking on their studies with the Open University Certificate in Accounting, Association of Accounting Technicians, the Institute of Secretaries and Administrators, or any of the six UK and Irish Chartered Accountancy bodies. The financial accounting requirements for National Vocational Qualifications are also fully covered.

Some improvements have been made to the pedagogical devices used in this new edition:

1 Each chapter:
   - starts with Learning Objectives (these have been completely revised in the new edition);
   - contains Activities designed to broaden and reinforce students' understanding of the concepts being covered and, in some cases, to introduce new concepts in such a way that they do not come as a surprise when introduced formally later in the book;
   - ends with Learning Outcomes that can be mapped back to the Learning Objectives, so reinforcing the major topics and concepts covered in the chapter;
   - contains answers to all the Activities immediately after the Learning Outcomes.
2 The book now has an alphabetical Glossary (Appendix 3) of all the significant terms introduced. Each entry is referenced back to the chapter in which it appeared.
3 Five sets of 20 Multiple Choice Questions are now positioned in the book (in Chapters 6, 13, 27, 33, and 45) at the point they should be attempted rather than as a group at the end of the book. The answers are all at the back of the book in Appendix 2.
4 A set of Notes for Students has been added at the front of the book. This covers how to use this book, how to tackle the end of chapter Review Questions, and how to study for and sit examinations. It should be read by students before they start working through the main text.
5 Use of a second colour has been introduced to enhance readability and bring out key points in the text.

The 46 chapters that remain from the eighth edition continue to cover the same topics as before. Some changes have been made to the content of the book in order to make it more relevant in today's accounting environment:

- Two new chapters have been added: Chapter 23, *Computerised Accounting Systems*, and Chapter 48, *An Introduction to Management Accounting*.
- Two chapters (40, *Bills of Exchange* and 41, *Consignment Accounts*) have been removed from the book and will be available on the Frank Wood website www.booksites.net/wood.
- Chapter 1, *The accounting equation and the balance sheet*, has been completely revised to remove horizontal financial statements and use the more common form of the accounting equation, Capital = Assets − Liabilities (the one previously used now being described as the 'alternate form').

- Chapters 7, *Trading and Profit and Loss Accounts*, and 8, *Balance Sheets*, have been rewritten to eliminate horizontal layouts.
- Horizontal financial statements have been removed from the rest of the book.
- Chapter 10, *Accounting Concepts*, has been updated, including the replacement of SSAP 2 with FRS 18. Review Questions have been added to the end of the chapter.
- The use of the term 'Journal' has been replaced with 'Day Book' when referring to the books of original entry for Purchases, Sales, Returns Inwards and Returns Outwards.
- Chapter 12, *The Banking System*, has been completely updated and now includes extensive material on plastic cards.
- Throughout the book, payment by means other than cash or cheque has been included where appropriate.
- 'Provision for doubtful debts' is now consistently used throughout the book (rather than 'Bad debt provision').
- 'Columnar' has replaced 'Analysis' when referring to columnar day books.
- Sales Ledger, Purchases Ledger and General Ledger are now consistently used throughout the book.
- Chapter 19, *Value Added Tax*, has been extensively revised.
- Chapter 22, *Computers and Accounting*, has been expanded and updated and some material has been moved to a new Chapter (23, *Computerised Accounting Systems*).
- In Chapter 26, *Depreciation of Fixed Assets*, a two-stage alternative to the way depreciation entries may be recorded has been added (as many students find this easier to understand and use than the one-stage method used in the 8th edition; the one-stage method is still included).
- In Chapter 28, *Accruals and Prepayments and Other Adjustments for Financial Statements* (amended title) an alternative way to record accruals and prepayments is offered (as many students find it easier to understand and use than the method used in the 8th edition; that method has been retained also). The term 'Worksheet' has been replaced with the more appropriate term 'Extended Trial Balance'.
- Thoughout the book, the term 'Financial Statements' has replaced 'Final Accounts', as many reviewers felt it was more appropriate.
- In Chapter 29, *The Valuation of Stock*, periodic stock valuation has been added.
- In Chapter 30, *Bank Reconciliation Statements*, reconciliation to the balance sheet amount has been added and recommended as the most appropriate approach to take at the end of the accounting period.
- Chapter 33, *Suspense Accounts and Errors*, is more clearly slanted against the use of suspense accounts, as they should no longer be very relevant in an age of computerised accounting systems. The material in this chapter could be usefully used to explore students' understanding of the need for accuracy in accounting records and to develop their understanding of double entry.
- The term 'non-profit-oriented' has replaced 'non-profit-making' wherever it is used.
- In Chapter 37, *Manufacturing Accounts*, the term 'indirect manufacturing costs' has replaced the less appropriate term 'factory overhead expenses'.
- Chapter 40, *Joint Venture Accounts*, has been extended. This topic is generally ignored but it serves as probably the best bridge between sole trader and partnership accounts and we would strongly recommend that it is included in that vein when about to introduce partnership accounts. It is also more relevant these days than it has been for many years, as FRS 9 makes clear.
- Chapter 47, *An Introduction to the Analysis and Interpretation of Accounting Statements*, has been extensively revised. The accounting standards at the end have been updated.
- Chapter 48, *An Introduction to Management Accounting*, summarises the role of the management accountant and the relationship between financial accounting and management accounting, so as to improve students' ability to contextualise accounting within organisations.

We hope that you find these changes helpful and appropriate and would welcome comments on these and any other changes you feel ought to be made in future editions. You can contact Alan Sangster by email at alan@sangster.co.uk or by letter via the publishers.

We would like to thank all those teachers and lecturers who gave us their advice as to the changes they would like to see incorporated in this edition. We are especially grateful to Mary Bishop, Mike Brookes, John Dunn, Mike Hoskins, Chris McMahon, Mak Yeun Teen, Stuart Mansen, John Morely, Roger Newman, Gideon Nyatuame, Steve Selijko, Rob Triggs, Wan Fadzilah Wan Yusoff and, of course, Michael Siaw Jun Choi and Muhammad Hanif Ghanghi for their insightful suggestions. There are many others too numerous to mention to whom we are indebted, and we trust that they will not be offended by our inability to list them all here.

We wish to acknowledge the permission to use past examination papers granted by the Association of Accounting Technicians, Oxford, Cambridge and RSA Examinations (Midland Examining Group questions), the Assessment and Qualifications Alliance (Northern Examinations and Assessment Board, Associated Examining Board and Southern Examining Group questions), Edexcel, the Scottish Qualifications Authority, the Association of Chartered Certified Accountants, the Institute of Chartered Secretaries and Administrators, and the Institute of Chartered Accountants in England and Wales.

We should point out that all answers to questions are the product of our own work and have not been supplied by any of the examining bodies.

Frank Wood and Alan Sangster

Notes for students

This textbook is organised so as to provide you with what has been found to be the most appropriate sequencing of topics as you build the foundations of your accounting knowledge. You will find that a number of features of the book, properly used, will enhance your understanding and extend your ability to cope with what will possibly appear, at first, to be a mystifying array of rules and procedures.

In order to make best use of this resource, you should consider the following as being a proven path to success:

- At the start of each chapter, read the Learning Objectives. Then, while you work through the material, try to detect when you have achieved each of these objectives.
- At the end of each chapter check what you have learnt against the Learning Outcomes that follow the main text.
- If you find that you cannot say 'yes, I have learnt that' to any of the Learning Outcomes, look back through the chapter and reread the topic you have not yet learnt.
- Learn the meaning of each new term as it appears. Do not leave learning what terms mean until you are revising for an exam. Accounting is best learnt as a series of building blocks. If you don't remember what terms mean, your knowledge and ability to 'do' accounting will be very seriously undermined, in much the same way as a wall built without mortar is likely to collapse the first time someone leans against it.
- Attempt each of the Activities in the book *at the point at which they appear.* This is *very* important. They will reinforce your learning and help set in context some of the material that may otherwise appear very artificial and distant from the world you live in. The answers are at the end of each chapter. Do not look at the answers before you attempt the questions, you'll just be cheating yourself. Once you have answered one, check your answer against the answer provided in the book and be sure you understand it before moving on.
- Attempt each of the sets of multiple choice questions when you reach them in the book. There are five sets of twenty questions, one at the end of each of Chapters 6, 13, 27, 33, and 45. The answers are in Appendix 2 at the back of the book. Do not look at the answers before you attempt the questions, you'll just be cheating yourself. If you get any wrong, be sure you understand why before moving on to new material.
- Learn the *accounting equation* when you first come across it in Chapter 1. It is *the* key to understanding many of the aspects of accounting that students find difficult. Make sure that you learn it in both the forms presented to you or that you can rearrange it to produce the alternate form when appropriate.
- Do not be disillusioned by the mystery of double entry. The technique has been in common use for over 500 years and is probably the most tried and trusted technique for doing anything you are ever likely to encounter. It really is not difficult, so long as you remember the accounting equation and can distinguish between things that you own and things that you owe. Like riding a bike, once you understand it, you'll never forget it and, the more you do it, the easier it gets.
- Because of time pressure, some teachers and lecturers will need to omit Chapter 40 (*Joint Venture Accounts*). Make sure that you work through it on your own before you look at the material in Chapter 41, the first chapter on accounting for partnerships. This is very important, as accounting for joint ventures bridges the gap between accounting for sole

traders and accounting for partnerships and will make it much easier for you to understand the differences between them.

- Above all, remember that accounting is a vehicle for providing financial information in a form that assists decision-making. Work hard at presenting your work as neatly as possible and remember that pictures (in this case, financial figures) only carry half the message. When you are asked for them, words of explanation and insight are essential in order to make an examiner appreciate what you know and that you actually understand what the figures mean.

There are two subjects we would like you to consider very carefully – making best use of the end of chapter Review Questions, and your examination technique.

Review questions: the best approach

We have set review questions at the end of most chapters for you to gauge how well you understand and can apply what you have learnt. If you simply read the text without attempting the questions then we can tell you now that you will not pass your examinations. You should first attempt each question, then check your answer fully against the answers at the back of the book.

What you should not do is perform a 'ticking' exercise. By this we mean that you should not simply compare the question with the answer and tick off the bits of the answer against the relevant part of the question. No one ever learnt to do accounting properly that way. It is tempting to save time in so doing but, believe us, you will regret it eventually. We have deliberately had the answers printed using a different page layout to try to stop you indulging in a 'ticking' exercise.

Need for practice

You should also try to find the time to answer as many exercises as possible. Our reasons for saying this are as follows:

1 Even though you may think you understand the text, when you come to answer the questions you may often find your understanding incomplete. The true test of understanding is whether or not you can tackle the questions competently.

2 It is often said that practice makes perfect, a sentiment we don't fully agree with. There is, however, enough sense in it in that, if you don't do quite a lot of accounting questions, you will almost certainly not become good at accounting.

3 You simply have to get up to a good speed in answering questions: you will always fail accounting examinations if you are a very slow worker. The history of accountancy examinations so far has always been that a ridiculously large amount of work has been expected from a student during a short time. However, examining boards maintain that the examination could be completed in the time by an adequately prepared student. You can take it for granted that *adequately prepared students* are those who not only have the knowledge, but have also been trained to work quickly and, at the same time, maintain accuracy and neatness.

4 Speed itself is not enough. You also have to be neat and tidy, and follow all the proper practices and procedures while working at speed. Fast but really scruffy work can also mean failing the exam. Why is this so? At this level the examiner is very much concerned with your practical ability in the subject. Accounting is a practical subject, and your practical competence is about to be tested. The examiner will, therefore, expect the answers to be neat and well set out. Untidy work with figures spread over the page in a haphazard

way, badly written figures, and columns of figures in which the vertical columns are not set down in straight lines, will incur the examiner's displeasure.

5 Appropriate presentation of information is important. Learn how to present the various financial statements you may need to produce in an examination. Examiners expect to see the items in trading and profit and loss accounts, balance sheets, and cash flow statements in the correct order and will probably deduct marks if you don't do this. Practice by writing down examples of these statements without any numbers until you always get the layout correct. One exam trick most students overlook is that the layout of a financial statement is often included in an examination paper as part of one question while another question asks you to produce a financial statement. The one you need to produce will contain different numbers but the general layout should be very similar.

Need for headings

The next thing is that work should not only be neat and well laid out. Headings should always be given, and any dates needed should be inserted. The test you should apply is to imagine that you are a partner in a firm of professional accountants and you are away on holiday for a few weeks. During that time your assistants have completed all sorts of work including reports, drafting final accounts, various forms of other computations and so on. All of this work is deposited on your desk while you are away. When you return you look at each item in the pile awaiting your attention. Suppose the first item looks like a balance sheet as at 31 December in respect of one of your clients. When you look at it you can see that it is a balance sheet, but you don't know for which client, neither do you know which year it is for. Would you be annoyed with your staff? Of course you would. So, in an examination, why should the examiner accept as a piece of your work a balance sheet answer without the date or the name of the business or the fact that it is a balance sheet written clearly across the top? If proper headings are not given you will lose a lot of marks. Always put in the headings properly. Don't wait until your examination to start this correct practice. Similar attention should be paid to sub-totals which need showing, e.g. for Fixed assets or for Current assets.

We will be looking at examination technique in the next section.

The examiner

What you should say to yourself is: 'Suppose I were in charge of an office, doing this type of accounting work, what would I say if one of my assistants put on my desk a sheet of paper with accounting entries on it written in the same manner as my own efforts in attempting this question?' Just look at some of the work you have done in the past. Would you have told your assistant to go back and do the work again because it is untidy? If you say that about your own work, why should the examiner think any differently?

Anyone who works in accounting knows that untidy work leads to completely unnecessary errors. Therefore, the examiner's insistence on clear, tidy, well laid out work is not an outdated approach. Examiners want to ensure that you are not going to mess up the work of an accounting department. Imagine going to the savings bank and the manager saying to you: 'We don't know whether you've got £5 in the account or £5,000. You see, the work of our clerks is so untidy that we can never sort out exactly how much is in anybody's account.' We would guess that you would not want to put a lot of money into an account at that bank. How would you feel if someone took you to court for not paying a debt of £100 when, in fact, you owed them nothing? This sort of thing would happen all the time if we simply allowed people to keep untidy accounts. The examiner is there to ensure that the person to whom they give a certificate will be worthy of it, and will not continually mess up the work of any firm at which they may work in the future.

We can imagine quite a few of you groaning at all this, and if you do not want to pass the examination please give up reading here. If you do want to pass, and your work is untidy, what can you do about it? Well, the answer is simple enough: start right now to be neat and orderly in your work. Quite a lot of students have said to us over the years: 'I may be giving you untidy work now but, when I actually get into the exam room, I will then do my work neatly enough.' This is as near impossible as anything can be. You cannot suddenly become able to do accounting work neatly, and certainly not when you are under the stress and strain of an examination. Even the neatest worker may well find in an examination that their work may not be of its usual standard as nervousness will cause them to make mistakes. If this is true, and you are an untidy worker now, your work in an examination is likely to be even more untidy. Have we convinced you yet?

The structure of the questions

We have tried to build up the review questions in a structured way, starting with the easiest and then going on to more difficult ones. We would like to have omitted all the difficult questions, on the basis that you may well spend a lot of time doing them without adding very much to your knowledge about accounting. However, if all the questions were straightforward, the shock of meeting more complicated questions for the first time in an examination could lead you to fail it. We have, therefore, tried to include a mixture of straightforward and complicated questions to give you the maximum benefit.

The answers

At the back of the book, you will find answers to approximately half of the Review Questions. The answers to the other review questions (indicated by the letter 'A' after the question number) are only available to you from your teacher or lecturer. Don't worry if you are studying this subject on your own. There are still more than sufficient review questions to ensure you know and understand the material in the book.

▌ Examination technique

As authors, we can use the first person here, as we want to put across to you a message about examinations, and we want you to feel that we are writing this for you as an individual rather than simply as one of the considerable number of people who have read this book.

By the time you sit your first examination, you will have spent a lot of hours trying to master such things as double entry, balance sheets, final adjustments, and goodness knows what else. Learning accounting/bookkeeping does demand a lot of discipline and practice. Compared with the many hours learning the subject, most students spend very little time actually considering in detail how to tackle the examination. You may be one of them, and we would like you to start planning now for that day when you will need to be able to demonstrate what you have learnt and understood, and can apply, the material in this book.

Understanding examiners

Let's start by saying that if you want to understand anything about examinations then you have got to understand examiners, so let us look together at what these peculiar creatures get up to in an examination. The first thing is that when they set an examination they are looking at it on the basis that they want good students to get a pass mark. Obviously anyone who doesn't achieve the pass mark will fail, but the object of the exercise is to find those who will pass, not find the failures. This means that if you have done your work properly, and if you are not sitting for an examination well above your intellectual capabilities, you should manage to get a pass mark. It is important for us to stress this before we get down to the details of setting about the task.

There are, however, quite a large number of students who will fail, not because they haven't put in enough hours on their studies, nor because they are unintelligent, but simply because they throw away marks unnecessarily by poor examination technique. If you can read the rest of this piece, and then say honestly that you wouldn't have committed at least one of the mistakes that we are going to mention, then you are certainly well outside the ordinary range of students.

Punctuality

Before thinking about the examination paper itself, let us think about how you are going to get to the examination room. If it is at your own college then you have no problems as to how you will get there. On the other hand, it may be an external centre. Do you know exactly where the place is? If not, you had better have a trip there if possible. How are you going to get there? If you are going by bus or train, do you know which bus or train to catch? Will it be the rush hour when it may well take you much longer than if it were held at midday?

Quite a large proportion of students lose their way to the examination room, or else arrive, breathless and flustered, at the very last minute. They then start off the attempt at the examination in a somewhat nervous state, a recipe for disaster for a lot of students. So plan how you are going to get there and give yourself enough time.

Last minute learning for your examination will be of little use to you. The last few days before the examination should not be spent cramming. You can look at past examination papers and rework some of them. This is totally different from trying to cram new facts into your head.

On your way to the examination, if you can, try relaxation exercises. Deep breathing exercises in particular will put you into a relaxed mood. If you can't do anything like this, try reading the newspaper. Granted, you will need some adrenalin to spur you into action when you actually start answering the examination paper, but you do not want to waste it before the examination instead and then put yourself into a highly nervous state.

Read the rubric carefully and follow its instructions

The rubric appears at the start of the examination paper, and says something such as:

> 'Attempt five questions only: the *three* questions in Section A and *two* from Section B.'

That instruction from the examiner is to be followed exactly. The examinee (i.e. you) cannot change the instruction – it means what it says.

Now you may think that is so simple that it is not worthwhile our forcibly pointing it out to you. We wish that was the case for all students. However, you would be amazed at the quite high percentage of students who do not follow the instructions given in the rubric. Having been examiners for many years for examining bodies all over the world we can assure you that we are not overstating the case. Let us look at two typical examples where students have ignored the rubric above:

(a) A student answered *two* questions from Section A and *three* from Section B. Here the examiner will mark the two Section A answers plus the first two answers shown on the examinee's script in respect of Section B. He will not read any part of the third displayed answer to Section B. The student can therefore only get marks for four answers.

(b) A student answered *three* questions from Section A and *three* from Section B. Here he will mark the three answers to Section A plus the first two displayed answers to Section B. He will not look at the third answer to Section B.

In the case of (*b*), the student may have done it that way deliberately, thinking that the examiner would mark all three Section B answers, and then award the student the marks from the best two answered questions. Most examiners will not waste time marking an extra answer. Students have argued that examiners would do that, but they are simply deluding themselves.

If you have time and want to give an extra answer, thinking that you will get better marks than one answered previously, then do so. If you do, make certain that the examiner is fully aware that you have deleted the answer that you do not want to have marked. Strike lines right through it, and also state that you wish to delete it. Otherwise it is possible that the first answers only will be marked and your new answer ignored.

Always remember in examinations that you should try to make life easier for the examiner. Give the examiner what he/she wants, in the way that he/she wants it. If you do, you will get better marks. Make their job harder than it needs to be and you will suffer. Examiners are only human beings after all!

Time planning

We must now look at the way in which you should tackle the examination paper. One of the problems with bookkeeping/accounting examinations is that students are expected to do a lot of work in a relatively short time. We have campaigned against this attitude, but the tradition is longstanding and here to stay. It will be the same for every other student taking your examination, so it is not unfair so far as any one student is concerned. Working at speed does bring various disadvantages, and makes the way you tackle the examination of even greater importance than for examinations where the pace is more leisurely.

Time per question

The marks allotted to each question will indicate how long you should take in tackling the question. Most examinations are of three hours' duration, i.e. 180 minutes. This means that in a normal examination, with 100 marks in total, a 20-mark question should be allocated 20 per cent of the time, i.e. 20% × 180 = 36 minutes. Similarly, a question worth 30 marks should take up 30 per cent of the time, i.e. 30% × 180 = 54 minutes, and so on. Alternatively it is 1.8 minutes for each mark awarded for the question.

If the question is in parts, and the marks awarded are shown against each part, then that will give you a clue as to the time to be spent on each part. If part of the question asks for a description, for instance, and only 3 marks are awarded to that part, then you should not spend twenty minutes on a long and detailed description. Instead a brief description, taking about five minutes, is what is required.

Do the easiest questions first

Always tackle the easiest question first, then the next easiest question and so on. Leave the most difficult question as the last one to be attempted. Why is this good advice? The fact is, most examiners usually set what might be called 'warm-up' questions. These are usually fairly short, and not very difficult questions, and the examiner will expect you to tackle these first.

You may be able to do the easiest question in less than the time allocated. The examiner is trying to be kind to you. The examiner knows that there is a certain amount of nervousness on the part of a student taking an examination, and wants to give you the chance to calm down by letting you tackle these short, relatively easy questions first of all, and generally settle down to your work.

Even where all the questions are worth equal marks, you are bound to find some easier than others. It is impossible for an examiner to set questions which are equally as difficult as each other. So, remember, start with the easiest question. This will give you a feeling of confidence. It is very desirable to start off in this way.

Do not expect that these 'warm-up' questions will be numbered 1 and 2 on your examination paper. Most accounting examinations start off with a rather long question, worth quite a lot of marks, as question number 1 on the paper. Over the years we have advised students not to tackle these questions first. A lot of students are fascinated by the fact that such a question is number 1, that it is worth a lot of marks, and their thinking runs: 'If I do this question first, and make a good job of it, then I am well on the way to passing the examination.'

There is no doubt that a speedy and successful attempt at such a question could possibly lead to a pass. The trouble is that this doesn't usually happen, and many students have admitted afterwards that their failure could be put down to simply ignoring this advice. What happens very often is that the student starts off on such a question, things don't go very well, a few mistakes are made, the student then looks at the clock and sees that they are not 'beating the clock' in terms of possible marks, and then panic descends on them. Leaving that question very hastily, the student then proceeds to the next question, which normally might have been well attempted but, because of the state of mind, a mess is made of that one as well, and so students fail an examination which they had every right to think they could pass.

Attempt every required question

The last point concerning time allocation which we want to get through is that you should attempt each and every question as required. On each question the first few marks are the easiest to get. For instance, on an essay question it is reasonably easy to get, say, the first 5 marks in a 20-mark question. Managing to produce a perfect answer to get the last 5 marks, from 15 to 20, is extremely difficult. This applies also to computational questions.

This means that in an examination of, say, five questions with 20 marks possible for each question, there is not much point in tackling three questions only and trying to make a good job of them. The total possible marks would be 60 marks, and if you had not achieved full marks for each question, in itself extremely unlikely, you could easily fall below the pass mark of, say, 50 marks. It is better to leave questions unfinished when your allotted time, calculated as shown earlier, has expired, and to then go on immediately to the other questions. It is so easy, especially in an accounting examination, to find that one has exceeded the time allowed for a question by a considerable margin. So, although you may find it difficult to persuade yourself to do so, move on to the next question when your time for a question has expired.

Computations

When you sit an examination, you should be attempting to demonstrate how well you know the topics being examined. In accounting examinations, there are three things in particular to remember. If you fail to do so, you will probably earn less marks than your knowledge deserves. One of these things has already been mentioned – be neat and tidy. The other two have to do with computations: *show all your workings* and *don't worry if your balance sheet does not balance.*

Workings

One golden rule which should *always* be observed is to show all of your workings. Suppose you have been asked to work out the Cost of Goods Sold, not simply as part of a Trading Account but for some other reason. On a scrap of paper you work out the answers below:

	£
Opening stock	4,000
Add Purchases	11,500
	15,500
Less Closing stock	(3,800)
	12,700

You put down the answer as £12,700. The scrap of paper with your workings on it is then crumpled up by you and thrown in the wastepaper basket as you leave the room. You may have noticed in reading this that in fact the answer should have been 11,700 and not 12,700 (the arithmetic was incorrect). The examiner may well have allocated, say, 4 marks for this bit of the question. What will he do when he simply sees your answer as £12,700? Will he say: 'I should imagine that the candidate mis-added to the extent of £1,000 and, as I am not unduly penalising for arithmetic, I will give the candidate 3½ marks'? I'm afraid the examiner cannot do this. The candidate got the wrong answer, there is no supporting evidence, and so the examiner gives marks as nil. If you had only attached the workings to your answer, then we have no doubt that you would have got 3½ marks at least.

It is often better to put the workings on the face of the final accounts, if appropriate. For instance, if rent paid is £1,900 and £300 of it has been paid in advance, you can show it on the face of the profit and loss account as:

Rent (1,900 – 300)   £1,600

By showing the workings in brackets you are demonstrating that you realise that they would not be shown on the published accounts. It also makes it easier for the examiner to mark.

Do balance sheets have to balance?

Many students ask: 'What should I do if my balance sheet doesn't balance?' The answer is quite simple: leave it alone and get on with answering the rest of the examination paper.

One of the reasons for this is to try and ensure that you answer the required number of questions. You might take 20 minutes to find the error, which might save you 1 mark. In that time you might have gained, say, 10 marks if, instead, you had tackled the next question, for which you would not have had time if you had wasted it by searching for the error(s). That assumes that you actually find the error(s)! Suppose you don't, you have spent 20 minutes looking for it, have not found it, so how do you feel now? The answer is, of course: quite terrible. You may make an even bigger mess of the rest of the paper than you would have done if you had simply ignored the fact that the balance sheet did not balance. In any case, it is quite possible to get, say, 29 marks out of 30 even though the balance sheet does not balance. The error may be a very minor case for which the examiner deducts one mark only.

Of course, if you have finished all the questions, then by all means spend the rest of your time tracing the error and correcting it. Be certain, however, that your corrections are carried out neatly. Untidy crossings-out can result in the loss of marks. So, sometimes, an error found can get back one mark, which is then lost again because the corrections make an untidy mess of your paper, and examiners often deduct marks, quite rightly so, for untidy work. It might be better to write against the error 'see note', indicating exactly where the note is shown. You can then illustrate to the examiner that you know what the error is and how to correct it.

Essay questions

Until a few years ago, there were not many essay questions in accounting examinations at this level. This has changed, and you therefore need to know the approach to use in answering such questions.

Typical questions

Before discussing these, we want you to look at two recent examination questions. Having done that, visualise carefully what you would write in answer to them. Here they are:

(a) You are employed as a bookkeeper by G Jones, a trader. State briefly what use you would make of the following documents in relation to your bookkeeping records.
(i) A bank statement.
(ii) A credit note received to correct an overcharge on an invoice.
(iii) A pay-in slip.
(iv) A petty cash voucher.

(b) Explain the term 'depreciation'. Name and describe briefly two methods of providing for depreciation of fixed assets.

Now we can test whether or not you would have made a reasonably good attempt at the questions. With question (a) a lot of students would have written down what a bank statement is, what a pay-in slip is, what a petty cash voucher is, and so on. Marks gained by you for an answer like that would be . . . virtually nil. Why is this? Well, you simply have not read the question properly. The question asked what *use* you would make of the documents, not *to describe* what the documents were. The bank statement would be used to check against the bank column in the Cash Book or cash records to see that the bank's entries and your own are in accordance with one another, with a bank reconciliation statement being drawn up to reconcile the two sets of records. The petty cash voucher would be used as a basis for entering up the payments columns in the Petty Cash Book. The *use* of the items was asked for, not the *descriptions* of the items.

Let us see if you have done better on question (b). Would you have written down how to calculate two methods of depreciation, probably the reducing balance method and the straight line method? But have you remembered that the question also asked you to *explain the term depreciation*? In other words, what is depreciation generally? A fair number of students will have omitted that part of the question. Our guess is that far more students would have made perhaps a poor attempt at question (a) rather than doing question (b).

Underline the key words

We have already illustrated that a large percentage of students fail to answer the question set, instead answering the question they imagine it to be. Too many students write down everything they know about a topic, rather than what the examiner has asked for.

To remedy this defect, *underline the key words* in a question. This brings out the meaning so that it is difficult to misunderstand the question. For instance, let us look at the following question:

'Discuss the usefulness of departmental accounts to a business.'

Many students will write down all they know about departmental accounts, how to draw them up, how to apportion overheads between departments, how to keep columnar sales and purchases journals to find the information, etc.

Number of marks gained . . . virtually nil.

Now underline the key words. They will be:

<u>Discuss</u> <u>usefulness</u> <u>departmental accounts</u>

The question is now seen to be concerned not with *describing* departmental accounts, but instead discussing the *usefulness* of departmental accounts.

Lastly, if the question says 'Draft a report on . . .' then the answer should be in the form of a *report*; if it says 'List the . . .' then the answer should consist of a *list*. Similarly 'Discuss . . .' asks for a *discussion*. 'Describe . . .' wants you to *describe* something, and so on.

You should therefore ensure that you are going to give the examiner

(*i*) What he is asking for *plus*
(*ii*) In the way that he wants it.

If you do not comply with (*i*) you may lose all the marks. If you manage to fulfil (*i*) but do not satisfy the examiner on (*ii*) you will still lose a lot of marks.

It is also just as important in computational questions to underline the key words to get at the meaning of a question, and then answer it in the manner required by the examiner. With computational questions it is better to look at what is required first before reading all of the rest of the question. That way, when you are reading the rest of the question, you are able to decide how to tackle it.

Never write out the question

Often – too often – students spend time writing out the text of essay questions before they set about answering them. This is a complete waste of time. It will not gain marks and should never be done.

Running out of time?

If your plans don't work out, you may find yourself with a question you could answer, but simply do not have the time to do it properly. It is better to write a short note to the examiner to that effect, and put down what you can of the main points in an abbreviated fashion. This will show that you have the knowledge and should gain you some marks.

Summary

Remember:

(*a*) Read the rubric, i.e. the instructions.
(*b*) Plan your time before you start.
(*c*) Tackle the easiest questions first.
(*d*) Finish off answering each question when your time allocation for the question is up.
(*e*) Hand in all your workings.
(*f*) Do remember to be neat, also include all proper headings, dates, sub-totals, etc. A lot of marks can be lost here.
(*g*) Only answer as many questions as you are asked to tackle by the examiner. Extra answers will not normally be marked and certainly won't get credit.
(*h*) Underline the *key* words in each question to ensure that you answer the question set, and not the question you wrongly take it to be.
(*i*) Never write out the text of essay questions.

Best of luck with your examination. We hope you get the rewards you deserve!

Frank Wood and Alan Sangster

**A Companion Website accompanies
BUSINESS ACCOUNTING VOLUME 1, 9th edition
by Frank Wood and Alan Sangster**

Visit the **Business Accounting** Companion Website at
www.booksites.net/wood to find valuable teaching and
learning material including:

For Students:
- Study material designed to help you improve your results
- Multiple-choice questions to test your knowledge
- Weblinks to sites of interest
- Accounting standards updates
- Extra material from the eighth edition of the textbook
- A fully searchable glossary

For Lecturers:
- A secure, password-protected site with material designed to help you teach
- *Solutions Manual*
- Downloadable OHP PowerPoints of learning objectives and selected diagrams
  from the book
- Direct email feedback to the author

PART 1

Introduction to double entry bookkeeping

Introduction

This part is concerned with the basic principles underlying the double entry system of bookkeeping.

CHAPTER 1

The accounting equation and the balance sheet

Learning objectives

After you have studied this chapter, you should be able to:
- explain what accounting is about
- explain the relationship between bookkeeping and accounting
- list the main users of accounting information and what accounting information they are interested in
- present and explain the accounting equation
- explain the relationship between the accounting equation and the layout of the balance sheet
- explain the meaning of the terms assets, capital, liabilities, debtors, and creditors
- describe how accounting transactions affect the items in the accounting equation
- draw up balance sheets after different accounting transactions have occurred

1.1 What is accounting?

People and businesses

Accounting is something that affects people in their personal lives just as much as it affects very large businesses. We all use accounting ideas when we plan what we are going to do with our money. We have to plan how much of it we will spend and how much we will save. We may write down a plan, known as a **budget**, or we may simply keep it in our minds.

Recording accounting data

However, when people talk about accounting, they are normally referring to accounting as used by businesses and other organisations. They cannot keep all the details in their minds so they have to keep records of it.

Organisations not only record cash received and paid out. They will also record goods bought and sold, items bought to use rather than to sell, and so on. This part of accounting is usually called the *recording of data*.

Classifying and summarising

When the data is being recorded it has to be organised so as to be most useful to the business. This is known as *classifying* and *summarising* data.

Following such classifications and summaries it will be possible to work out how much profit or loss has been made by the business during a particular period. It will also be possible to show what resources are owned by the business, and what is owed by it, on the closing date of the period.

Communicating information

From the data, people skilled in accounting should be able to tell whether or not the business is performing well financially. They should be able to ascertain the strengths and weaknesses of the business.

Finally, they should be able to tell or *communicate* their results to the owners of the business, or to others allowed to receive this information.

Accounting is, therefore, concerned with:

- recording data;
- classifying and summarising data;
- communicating what has been learned from the data.

1.2   What is bookkeeping?

The part of accounting that is concerned with recording data is often known as **bookkeeping**. Until about one hundred years ago all accounting data was recorded manually in books, hence the term 'bookkeeping'.

Nowadays, although hand-written books may be used (particularly by smaller organisations), most accounting data is recorded electronically and stored electronically using computers.

Bookkeeping is the process of recording data relating to accounting transactions in the accounting books.

1.3   Accounting is concerned with . . .

Accounting is concerned with the uses which accountants might make of the bookkeeping information given to them. This book will cover many such uses.

1.4   Users of accounting information

Possible users of accounting information include:

- *Owner(s) of the business.* They want to be able to see whether or not the business is profitable. In addition they want to know what the financial resources of the business are.
- *A prospective buyer.* When the owner wants to sell a business the buyer will want to see such information.
- *The bank.* If the owner wants to borrow money for use in the business, then the bank will need such information.
- *Tax inspectors.* They need it to be able to calculate the taxes payable.
- *A prospective partner.* If the owner wants to share ownership with someone else, then the would-be partner will want such information.
- *Investors*, either existing ones or potential ones. They want to know whether or not to invest their money in the business.

There are many other users of accounting unformation – suppliers and employees, for example. One obvious fact is that without properly recorded accounting data a business would have many difficulties providing the information these various users (often referred to as 'stakeholders') require.

1.5 The accounting equation

By adding up what the accounting records say belongs to a business and deducting what they say the business owes, you can identify what a business is worth according to those accounting records. The whole of financial accounting is based upon this very simple idea. It is known as the *accounting equation*.

It can be explained by saying that if a business is to be set up and start trading, it will need resources. Let's assume first that it is the owner of the business who has supplied all of the resources. This can be shown as:

$$\text{Resources supplied by the owner} = \text{Resources in the business}$$

In accounting, special terms are used to describe many things. The amount of the resources supplied by the owner is called **capital**. The actual resources that are then in the business are called **assets**. This means that when the owner has supplied all of the resources, the accounting equation can be shown as:

$$\text{Capital} = \text{Assets}$$

Usually, however, people other than the owner have supplied some of the assets. **Liabilities** is the name given to the amounts owing to these people for these assets. The accounting equation has now changed to:

$$\text{Capital} = \text{Assets} - \text{Liabilities}$$

This is the most common way in which the accounting equation is presented. It can be seen that the two sides of the equation will have the same totals. This is because we are dealing with the same thing from two different points of view – the value of the owners' investment in the business and the value of what is owned by the owners.

Activity 1.1
What piece of useful information that is available from these three items is not directly shown by this equation? (*Hint*: you were introduced to it at the start of this section.)

Unfortunately, with this form of the accounting equation, we can no longer see at a glance what value is represented by the resources in the business. You can see this more clearly if you switch assets and capital around to produce the alternate form of the accounting equation:

$$\text{Assets} = \text{Capital} + \text{Liabilities}$$

This can then be replaced with words describing the resources of the business:

> Resources: what they are = Resources: who supplied them
> (Assets)   (Capital + Liabilities)

It is a fact that no matter how you present the accounting equation, the totals of both sides will *always* equal each other, and that this will *always* be true no matter how many transactions there may be. The actual assets, capital and liabilities may change, but the total of the assets will always equal the total of capital + liabilities. Or, reverting to the more common form of the accounting equation, the capital will always equal the assets of the business minus the liabilities.

Assets consist of property of all kinds, such as buildings, machinery, stocks of goods and motor vehicles. Other assets include debts owed by customers and the amount of money in the bank account.

Liabilities include amounts owed by the business for goods and services supplied to the business and for expenses incurred by the business that have not yet been paid for. They also include funds borrowed by the business.

Capital is often called the owner's **equity** or net worth. It comprises the funds invested in the business by the owner plus any profits retained for use in the business less any share of profits paid out of the business to the owner.

Activity 1.2

What else would affect capital? (*Hint*: this item causes the value of capital to fall.)

1.6   The balance sheet and the effects of business transactions

The accounting equation is expressed in a financial position statement called the **balance sheet**.

Activity 1.3

Without looking back, write down the commonly used form of the accounting equation.

The balance sheet shows the financial position of an organisation at a point in time. In other words, it presents a snapshot of the organisation at the date for which it was prepared. The balance sheet is not the first accounting record to be made, nor the first that you will learn how to do, but it is a convenient place to start to consider accounting.

Let's now look at how a series of transactions affect the balance sheet.

1 The introduction of capital

On 1 May 20X7, B Blake started in business and deposited £5,000 into a bank account opened specially for the business. The balance sheet would appear:

B Blake
Balance Sheet as at 1 May 20X7

	£
Assets: Cash at bank	5,000
Capital	5,000

Note how the top part of the balance sheet contains the assets and the bottom part contains the capital. This is always the way the information is presented in a balance sheet.

2 The purchase of an asset by cheque

On 3 May 20X7, Blake buys a building for £3,000 paying by cheque. The effect of this transaction on the balance sheet is that the cash at the bank is decreased and the new asset, building, is added:

B Blake
Balance Sheet as at 3 May 20X7

	£
Assets	
Building	3,000
Cash at bank	2,000
	5,000
Capital	5,000

Note how the two parts of the balance sheet 'balance'. That is, their totals are the same. This is always the case with balance sheets.

3 The purchase of an asset and the incurring of a liability

On 6 May 20X7, Blake buys some goods for £500 from D Smith, and agrees to pay for them some time within the next two weeks. The effect of this is that a new asset, **stock** of goods, is acquired, and a liability for the goods is created. A person to whom money is owed for goods is known in accounting language as a **creditor**. The balance sheet becomes:

B Blake
Balance Sheet as at 6 May 20X7

	£
Assets	
Building	3,000
Stock of goods	500
Cash at bank	2,000
	5,500
Less: Creditor	(500)
	5,000
Capital	5,000

Note how the liability (the creditor) is shown as a deduction from the assets. This is exactly the same calculation as is presented in the most common form of the accounting equation.

Activity 1.4
Why do you think the £500 value for creditors is shown in brackets?

Now, let's return to our example.

4 Sale of an asset on credit

On 10 May 20X7, goods which cost £100 were sold to J Brown for the same amount, the money to be paid later. The effect is a reduction in the stock of goods and the creation of a new asset. A person who owes the firm money is known in accounting language as a **debtor**. The balance sheet is now:

B Blake
Balance Sheet as at 10 May 20X7

Assets	£
Building	3,000
Stock of goods	400
Debtor	100
Cash at bank	2,000
	5,500
Less: Creditor	(500)
	5,000
Capital	5,000

5 Sale of an asset for immediate payment

On 13 May 20X7, goods which cost £50 were sold to D Daley for the same amount. Daley paid for them immediately by cheque. Here one asset, stock of goods, is reduced, while another asset, bank, is increased. The balance sheet becomes:

B Blake
Balance Sheet as at 13 May 20X7

Assets	£
Building	3,000
Stock of goods	350
Debtor	100
Cash at bank	2,050
	5,500
Less: Creditor	(500)
	5,000
Capital	5,000

6 The payment of a liability

On 15 May 20X7, Blake pays a cheque for £200 to D Smith in part payment of the amount owing. The asset of bank is therefore reduced, and the liability to the creditor is also reduced. The balance sheet is now:

B Blake
Balance Sheet as at 15 May 20X7

Assets	£
Building	3,000
Stock of goods	350
Debtor	100
Cash at bank	1,850
	5,300
Less: Creditor	(300)
	5,000
Capital	5,000

Note how the total of each part of the balance sheet has not changed. The business is still worth £5,000 to the owner.

7 Collection of an asset

J Brown, who owed Blake £100, makes a part payment of £75 by cheque on 31 May 20X7. The effect is to reduce one asset, debtor, and to increase another asset, bank. The balance sheet becomes:

B Blake
Balance Sheet as at 31 May 20X7

Assets	£
Building	3,000
Stock of goods	350
Debtor	25
Cash at bank	1,925
	5,300
Less: Creditor	(300)
	5,000
Capital	5,000

1.7 Equality of the accounting equation

It can be seen that every transaction has affected two items. Sometimes it has changed two assets by reducing one and increasing the other. In other cases, the effect has been different. However, in each case other than the very first (when the business was started by the owner injecting some cash into it), no change was made to the total of either section of the balance sheet and the equality between their two totals has been maintained. The accounting equation has held true throughout the example, and it always will. The effect of each of these seven accounting transactions upon the two sections of the balance sheet is shown below:

Number of transaction as above	Assets	Capital and Liabilities	Effect on balance sheet totals
1	+	+	Each side added to equally
2	+ −		A *plus* and a *minus* both on the assets side *cancelling out* each other
3	+	+	Each side has equal deductions
4	+ −		A *plus* and a *minus* both on the assets side *cancelling out* each other
5	+ −		A *plus* and a *minus* both on the assets side *cancelling out* each other
6	−	−	Each side has equal deductions
7	+ −		A *plus* and a *minus* both on the assets side *cancelling out* each other

These are not the only types of accounting transactions that can take place. Two other examples arise when the owner withdraws resources from the business for his or her own use; and where the owner pays a business expense personally.

A summary of the effect upon assets, liabilities and capital of each type of transaction you've been introduced to so far is shown below:

Example of transaction	Effect	
(1) Owner pays capital into the bank	↑ Increase asset (Bank)	↑ Increase capital
(2) Buy goods by cheque	↓ Decrease asset (Bank)	↑ Increase asset (Stock of goods)
(3) Buy goods on credit	↑ Increase asset (Stock of goods)	↑ Increase liability (Creditors)
(4) Sale of goods on credit	↓ Decrease asset (Stock of goods)	↑ Increase asset (Debtors)
(5) Sale of goods for cash (cheque)	↓ Decrease asset (Stock of goods)	↑ Increase asset (Bank)
(6) Pay creditor	↓ Decrease asset (Bank)	↓ Decrease liability (Creditor)
(7) Debtor pays money owing by cheque	↑ Increase asset (Bank)	↓ Decrease asset (Debtors)
(8) Owner takes money out of the business bank account for own use	↓ Decrease asset (Bank)	↓ Decrease capital
(9) Owner pays creditor from private money outside the firm	↓ Decrease liability (Creditor)	↑ Increase capital

These last two types of transactions do cause the totals of each part of the balance sheet to change (as did the very first, when capital was introduced to the business by the owner). When the capital changes, the totals of the two parts of the balance sheet both change.

1.8 More detailed presentation of the balance sheet

Let's now look at the balance sheet of B Blake as at 31 May 20X7, presented in line with how you will learn to present the information later in the book:

B Blake
Balance Sheet as at 31 May 20X7

	£	£
Fixed assets		
Buildings		3,000
Current assets		
Stock of goods	350	
Debtor	25	
Cash at bank	1,925	
	2,300	
Less Current liabilities		
Creditor	(300)	
		2,000
		5,000
Capital		5,000

You will have noticed in this balance sheet the terms 'fixed assets', 'current assets' and 'current liabilities'. Chapter 8 contains a full and proper examination of these terms. At this point we will simply say:

- **Fixed assets** are assets which have a long life bought with the intention to use them in the business and not with the intention to simply resell them, e.g. buildings, machinery, fixtures, motor vehicles.
- **Current assets** are assets consisting of cash, goods for resale or items having a short life. For example, the value of stock in hand goes up and down as it is bought and sold. Similarly, the amount of money owing to us by debtors will change quickly, as we sell more to them on credit and they pay their debts. The amount of money in the bank will also change as we receive and pay out money.
- **Current liabilities** are those liabilities which have to be paid within no more than a year from the date on the balance sheet, e.g. creditors for goods bought.

Don't forget that there is a Glossary of accounting terms at the back of the book.

Learning outcomes

You should now have learnt that:

1 Accounting is concerned with the recording and classifying and summarising of data, and then communicating what has been learned from it.

2 It may not only be the owner of a business who will need the accounting information; it may need to be shown to others, e.g. the bank or the Inspector of Taxes.

3 Accounting information can help the owner(s) of a business to plan for the future.

4 The accounting equation is: Capital = Assets − Liabilities.

5 The two side of the accounting equation are represented by the two parts of the balance sheet.

6 The totals of one part of the balance sheet should always be equal to the total of the other part.

7 Every transaction affects two items in the accounting equation. Sometimes that may involve the same item being affected twice, once positively (going up) and once negatively (going down).

8 Every transaction affects two items in the balance sheet.

Note: Generally, the values used in exhibits and exercises have been kept down to relatively small amounts. This has been done deliberately to make the work of the student that much easier. Constantly handling large figures does not add anything to the study of the principles of accounting. Instead, it simply wastes a lot of the student's time, and he/she will probably make far more errors if larger figures are used.

It could lead to the authors being accused of not being 'realistic' with the figures given, but we believe that it is far more important to make learning easier for the student.

Answers to activities

1.1   Who supplied the resources of the business.

1.2   Capital will be reduced if a business makes a loss. The loss means that assets have been reduced and capital is reduced by the same amount so as to maintain the balance in the accounting equation.

1.3   Capital = Assets − Liabilities

1.4   It is a negative number. In accounting, we *always* use brackets to indicate negative numbers.

REVIEW QUESTIONS

If you haven't already started answering them, you now have a set of graded review questions to try. 'Graded' means that they get more difficult as you go through them. Ideally, they should be done in the sequence they appear. *However, don't forget that the questions with an 'A' after the question number do not have any answers provided in this book.* Your teacher or lecturer will be able to provide you with the answers to those questions but be sure to attempt them first before asking for the answers! The answers to the other questions can be found at the back of the book.

We realise that you would like to have *all* the answers in the book. However, teachers and lecturers would not then be able to test your knowledge with questions from this book, as you would already possess the answers. It is impossible to please everyone, and the compromise reached is that of putting a large number of review questions in the book.

This means that appropriate reinforcement of what you have learnt can take place, even if you are studying on your own and have to miss out all the 'A' questions because you have no access to the answers.

Multiple choice questions. In addition to these review questions, there are questions relating to the material in this chapter among a bank of multiple choice questions at the end of Chapter 6. You should wait and attempt them when you reach them, not before.

1.1 Complete the gaps in the following table:

	Assets	Liabilities	Capital
	£	£	£
(a)	12,500	1,800	?
(b)	28,000	4,900	?
(c)	16,800	?	12,500
(d)	19,600	?	16,450
(e)	?	6,300	19,200
(f)	?	11,650	39,750

1.2A Complete the gaps in the following table:

	Assets	Liabilities	Capital
	£	£	£
(a)	55,000	16,900	?
(b)	?	17,200	34,400
(c)	36,100	?	28,500
(d)	119,500	15,400	?
(e)	88,000	?	62,000
(f)	?	49,000	110,000

1.3 Which of the items in the following list are liabilities and which of them are assets?

(a) Office machinery
(b) Loan from C Shirley
(c) Fixtures and fittings
(d) Motor vehicles
(e) We owe a supplier for goods
(f) Bank balance

1.4A Classify the following items into liabilities and assets:

(a) Motor vehicles
(b) Premises
(c) Creditors for goods
(d) Stock of goods
(e) Debtors
(f) Owing to bank
(g) Cash in hand
(h) Loan from D Jones
(i) Machinery

1.5   State which of the following are wrongly classified:

Assets	Liabilities
Loan from C Smith	Stock of goods
Cash in hand	Debtors
Machinery	Money owing to bank
Creditors	
Premises	
Motor vehicles	

1.6A   Which of the following are shown under the wrong headings?

Assets	Liabilities
Cash at bank	Loan from J Graham
Fixtures	Machinery
Creditors	Motor vehicles
Building	
Stock of goods	
Debtors	
Capital	

1.7   A Smart is setting up a new business. Before actually selling anything, he bought a motor vehicle for £2,000, premises for £5,000 and a stock of goods for £1,000. He did not pay in full for his stock of goods and still owes £400 in respect of them. He borrowed £3,000 from D Bevan. After the events just described, and before trading starts, he has £100 cash in hand and £700 cash at bank. Calculate the amount of his capital.

1.8A   T Charles is starting a business. Before actually starting to sell anything, he bought fixtures for £2,000, a motor vehicle for £5,000 and a stock of goods for £3,500. Although he has paid in full for the fixtures and the motor vehicle, he still owes £1,400 for some of the goods. J Preston lent him £3,000. Charles, after the above, has £2,800 in the business bank account and £100 cash in hand. You are required to calculate his capital.

1.9   Draw up A Foster's balance sheet from the following information as at 31 December 20X8:

	£
Capital	23,750
Debtors	4,950
Motor vehicles	5,700
Creditors	2,450
Fixtures	5,500
Stock of goods	8,800
Cash at bank	1,250

1.10A   Draw up M Kelly's balance sheet as at 30 June 20X6 from the following items:

	£
Capital	15,000
Office machinery	9,000
Creditors	900
Stock of goods	1,550
Debtors	275
Cash at bank	5,075

1.11   Complete the columns to show the effects of the following transactions:

		Effect upon	
	Assets	*Liabilities*	*Capital*

(a)   We pay a creditor £70 in cash.
(b)   Bought fixtures £200 paying by cheque.
(c)   Bought goods on credit £275.
(d)   The proprietor introduces another £500 cash into the firm.
(e)   J Walker lends the firm £200 in cash.
(f)   A debtor pays us £50 by cheque.
(g)   We return goods costing £60 to a supplier whose bill we had not paid.
(h)   Bought additional shop premises paying £5,000 by cheque.

1.12A   Complete the columns to show the effects of the following transactions:

		Effect upon	
	Assets	*Liabilities*	*Capital*

(a)   Bought a motor van on credit £500.
(b)   Repaid by cash a loan owed to P Smith £1,000.
(c)   Bought goods for £150 paying by cheque.
(d)   The owner puts a further £5,000 cash into the business.
(e)   A debtor returns to us £80 goods. We agree to make an allowance for them.
(f)   Bought goods on credit £220.
(g)   The owner takes out £100 cash for his personal use.
(h)   We pay a creditor £190 by cheque.

1.13   C Sangster has the following items in his balance sheet as on 30 April 20X8:

Capital £20,900; Creditors £1,600; Fixtures £3,500; Motor vehicle £4,200; Stock of goods £4,950; Debtors £3,280; Cash at bank £6,450; Cash in hand £120.

During the first week of May 20X8

(a)   He bought extra stock of goods £770 on credit.
(b)   One of the debtors paid him £280 in cash.
(c)   He bought extra fixtures by cheque £1,000.

You are to draw up a balance sheet as on 7 May 20X8 after the above transactions have been completed.

1.14A   F Dale has the following assets and liabilities as on 30 November 20X9:

Creditors £3,950; Equipment £11,500; Motor vehicle £6,290; Stock of goods £6,150; Debtors £5,770; Cash at bank £7,280; Cash in hand £40.

The capital at that date is to be deduced by you.

During the first week of December 20X9

(a)   Dale bought extra equipment on credit for £1,380.
(b)   Dale bought extra stock by cheque £570.
(c)   Dale paid creditors by cheque £790.
(d)   Debtors paid Dale £840 by cheque and £60 by cash.
(e)   Dale put in an extra £250 cash as capital.

You are to draw up a balance sheet as on 7 December 20X9 after the above transactions have been completed.

CHAPTER 2

The double entry system for assets, liabilities and capital

After you have studied this chapter, you should be able to:

- explain what is meant by 'double entry'
- explain how the double entry system follows the rules of the accounting equation
- explain why each transaction is recorded into individual accounts
- describe the layout of a 'T-account'
- explain what is meant by the terms debit and credit
- explain the phrase 'debit the receiver and credit the giver'
- prepare a table showing how to record increases and decreases of assets, liabilities and capital in the accounts
- enter a series of transactions into T-accounts

2.1 Nature of a transaction

In Chapter 1, you saw how various events had changed two items in the balance sheet. Events which result in such changes are known as 'transactions'. This means that if the proprietor asks the price of some goods, but does not buy them, then there is no transaction. If the proprietor later asks the price of some other goods, and then buys them, then there would be a transaction, and two balance sheet items would then have to be altered.

2.2 The double entry system

We have seen that every transaction affects two items. We need to show these effects when we first record each transaction. That is, when we enter the data relating to the transaction in the accounting books we need to ensure that we do so in a way that ensures that the items that were affected by the transaction, and only those items, are shown as having changed. This is the bookkeeping stage of accounting and the process we use is called **double entry**. You will often hear it referred to as **double entry bookkeeping**. Either term is correct.

Activity 2.1
Why do you think it is called 'double entry'?

If we want to show the double effect of every transaction when we are doing our bookkeeping, we have to show the effect of each transaction on each of the two items it affects. For each transaction this means that a bookkeeping entry will have to be made to show an increase or decrease of one item, and another entry to show the increase or decrease of the other item. From this description, you will probably see that the term 'double entry bookkeeping' is a good one, as each entry is made twice (double entry).

At this point, you may be wondering why you can't just draw up a new balance sheet after each transaction, and so provide all the information required.

Activity 2.2
Why can't we just adjust the balance sheet and forget about making entries in any of the accounting books?

Instead of constantly drawing up balance sheets after each transaction what we have instead is the 'double entry' system. The basis of this system is that the transactions which occur are entered in a set of **accounts** within the accounting books. An account is a place where all the information referring to a particular asset or liability, or to capital, is recorded.

Thus, there will be an account where all the information concerning office equipment will be entered. Similarly, there will be an account for buildings, where all the information concerned with buildings will be shown. This will be extended so that every asset, every liability and capital will each have its own account for transactions involving that item.

2.3 The accounts for double entry

Each account should be shown on a separate page in the accounting books. The double entry system divides each page into two halves. The left-hand side of each page is called the **debit** side, while the right-hand side is called the **credit** side. The title of each account is written across the top of the account at the centre.

This is the layout of a page of an accounts book:

Title of account written here	
Left-hand side of the page This is the 'debit' side.	*Right-hand side of the page* This is the 'credit' side.

Do you see how the shape resembles a 'T'? Not surprisingly, these are commonly referred to as **T-accounts**:

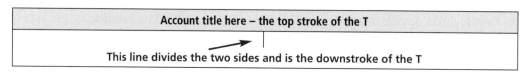

Account title here – the top stroke of the T
This line divides the two sides and is the downstroke of the T

Many students find it very difficult to make correct entries in the accounts because they forget that *debit* and *credit* have special accounting meanings. Don't fall into that trap. You must not confuse any other meanings you know for these two terms with the accounting ones.

You describe the entries in the accounts by saying something like 'debit account "x" with £z and credit account "y" with £z', inserting the names of the accounts and the actual amount in place of x, y, and z. So, for example, if you paid £10 by cheque for a kettle, you could say 'debit the kettle account with £10 and credit the bank account with £10'.

To actually make this entry, you enter £10 on the left-hand (i.e. debit) side of the kettle account and on the right-hand (i.e. credit) side of the bank account.

You learnt in Chapter 1 that transactions increase or decrease assets, liabilities or capital. In terms of the assets, liabilities, and capital:

- to **increase** an **asset** we make a DEBIT entry
- to **decrease** an **asset** we make a CREDIT entry
- to **increase** a **liability/capital** account we make a CREDIT entry
- to **decrease** a **liability/capital** account we make a DEBIT entry.

Placing these in a table organised by type of item, the double entry rules for bookkeeping are:

Accounts	To record	Entry in the account
Assets	an increase a decrease	Debit Credit
Liabilities	an increase a decrease	Credit Debit
Capital	an increase a decrease	Credit Debit

Let's look once again at the accounting equation:

	Capital =	Assets −	Liabilities
To increase each item	Credit	Debit	Credit
To decrease each item	Debit	Credit	Debit

The double entry rules for liabilities and capital are the same, but they are the opposite of those for assets. Looking at the accounts the rules will appear as:

Capital account		Any asset account		Any liability account	
Decreases	Increases	Increases	Decreases	Decreases	Increases
−	+	+	−	−	+

In a real business, at least one full page would be taken for each account in the accounting books. However, as we have not enough space in this textbook to put each account on a separate page, we will list the accounts under each other.

2.4 Worked examples

The entry of a few transactions can now be attempted.

1 The proprietor starts the business with £1,000 in cash on 1 August 20X8.

The effects of this transaction are entered as follows:

Effect	Action
1 Increases the *asset* of cash	Debit the cash account
2 Increases the capital	Credit the capital account

Cash

20X8		£	
Aug 1		1,000	

Capital

		20X8		£
		Aug 1		1,000

The date of the transaction has already been entered. (Never forget to enter the date of each transaction.) Now there remains the description (often referred to as the 'narrative') which is to be entered alongside the amount. This is completed by a cross-reference to the title of the other account in which the double entry is completed. The double entry to the item in the cash account is completed by an entry in the capital account. Therefore the word 'Capital' will appear as the narrative in the cash account:

Cash

20X8		£	
Aug 1 Capital		1,000	

Similarly, the double entry to the item in the capital account is completed by an entry in the cash account, so the word 'Cash' will appear in the capital account:

Capital

		20X8		£
		Aug 1 Cash		1,000

2 A van is bought for £275 cash on 2 August 20X8.

Effect	Action
1 Increases the *asset* of van	Debit the van account
2 Decreases the *asset* of cash	Credit the cash account

Van

20X8		£	
Aug 2 Cash		275	

Cash

		20X8		£
		Aug 2 Van		275

3 Fixtures (e.g. shelves) are bought on credit from Shop Fitters for £115 on 3 August 20X8.

Effect	Action
1 Increases the *asset* of fixtures	Debit the fixtures account
2 Increases the *liability* to Shop Fitters	Credit the Shop Fitters account

Fixtures

20X8		£	
Aug 3 Shop Fitters		115	

Shop Fitters

			20X8			£
			Aug	3	Fixtures	115

Note how the liability of creditors is split in the accounting books so that a separate account is maintained for each creditor.

4 Paid the amount owing in cash to Shop Fitters on 17 August 20X8.

Effect	Action
1 Decreases the *liability* to Shop Fitters 2 Decreases the *asset* of cash	Debit the Shop Fitters account Credit the cash account

Shop Fitters

20X8			£		
Aug	17	Cash	115		

Cash

			20X8			£
			Aug	17	Shop Fitters	115

5 Transactions to date.
Combining all four of these transactions, the accounts will now contain:

Cash

20X8			£	20X8			£
Aug	1	Capital	1,000	Aug	2	Van	275
				''	17	Shop Fitters	115

Capital

				20X8			£
				Aug	1	Cash	1,000

Van

20X8			£		
Aug	2	Cash	275		

Shop Fitters

20X8			£	20X8			£
Aug	17	Cash	115	Aug	3	Fixtures	115

Fixtures

20X8			£		
Aug	3	Shop Fitters	115		

Note how you enter each transaction in the account in date order.

Before you read further, work through Review Questions 2.1 and 2.2.

2.5   A further worked example

Have you noticed how each column of figures is headed by a '£' sign? This is important. You always need to indicate what the figures represent. In this case, it is £s, in other cases you will meet during this book, the figures may be thousands of pounds (represented by '£000') or they could be in a different currency altogether. Always include appropriate column headings.

Now you have actually made some entries in accounts, go carefully through the following example. Make certain you can understand every entry and, if you have any problems, reread the first four sections of this chapter until you are confident that you know and understand what you are doing.

First, here is a table showing a series of transactions, their effects and the double entry action to take:

Transactions	Effect	Action
19X8 May 1 Started an engineering business putting £1,000 into a business bank account.	↑ Increases *asset* of bank. ↑ Increases *capital* of owner.	Debit bank account. Credit capital account.
'' 3 Bought works machinery on credit from Unique Machines £275.	↑ Increases *asset* of machinery. ↑ Increases *liability* to Unique Machines.	Debit machinery account. Credit Unique Machines account.
'' 4 Withdrew £200 cash from the bank and placed it in the cash box.	↑ Increases *asset* of cash. ↓ Decreases *asset* of bank.	Debit cash account. Credit bank account.
May 7 Bought a van paying in cash £180.	↑ Increases *asset* of van. ↓ Decreases *asset* of cash.	Debit van account. Credit cash account.
'' 10 Sold some of the machinery for £15 on credit to B Barnes.	↑ Increases *asset* of money owing from B Barnes. ↓ Decreases *asset* of machinery.	Debit B Barnes account. Credit machinery account.
'' 21 Returned some of the machinery, value £27, to Unique Machines.	↓ Decreases *liability* to Unique Machines. ↓ Decreases *asset* of machinery.	Debit Unique Machines. Credit machinery account.
'' 28 B Barnes pays the firm the amount owing, £15, by cheque.	↑ Increases *asset* of bank. ↓ Decreases *asset* of money owing by B Barnes.	Debit bank account. Credit B Barnes account.
'' 30 Bought another van paying by cheque £420.	↑ Increases *asset* of vans. ↓ Decreases *asset* of bank.	Debit van account. Credit bank account.
'' 31 Paid the amount of £248 to Unique Machines by cheque.	↓ Decreases *liability* to Unique Machines. ↓ Decreases *asset* of bank.	Debit Unique Machines. Credit bank account.

You may find it worthwhile trying to enter all these transactions in T-accounts before reading any further. You will need to know that, similarly to creditors, the asset of debtors is split in the accounting books so that a separate account is maintained for each debtor. You will need accounts for Bank, Cash, Capital, Machinery, Vans, Unique Machines, and B Barnes.

In account form this is shown:

Bank

20X8			£	20X8			£
May	1	Capital	1,000	May	4	Cash	200
''	28	B Barnes	15	''	30	Van	420
				''	31	Unique Machines	248

Cash

20X8			£	20X8			£
May	4	Bank	200	May	7	Van	180

Capital

20X8				20X8			£
				May	1	Bank	1,000

Machinery

20X8			£	20X8			£
May	3	Unique Machines	275	May	10	B Barnes	15
				''	21	Unique Machines	27

Vans

20X8			£				
May	7	Cash	180				
''	30	Bank	420				

Unique Machines

20X8			£	20X8			£
May	21	Machines	27	May	3	Machinery	275
''	31	Bank	248				

B Barnes

20X8			£	20X8			£
May	10	Machinery	15	May	28	Bank	15

If you tried to do this before looking at the answer, be sure you understand any mistakes you made before going on.

2.6 Abbreviation of 'limited'

In this book, when we come across transactions with limited companies the letters 'Ltd' are used as the abbreviation for 'Limited Company'. Thus you will know that, if you see the name of a firm as 'W Jones Ltd', that business will be a limited company. In our accounting books, transactions with W Jones Ltd will be entered in the same way as for any other customer or supplier. It will be seen later that some limited companies use plc instead of Ltd.

Learning outcomes

You should now have learnt:

1 That double entry follows the rules of the accounting equation.
2 That double entry maintains the principle that every debit has a corresponding credit entry.
3 That double entries are made in accounts in the accounting books.
4 Why each transaction is entered into accounts rather than directly into the balance sheet.
5 How transactions cause increases and decreases in asset, liability and capital accounts.
6 How to record transactions in T-accounts.

Answers to activities

2.1 Each transaction is entered twice. In an accounting transaction, something always 'gives' and something 'receives' and both aspects of the transaction must be recorded. In other words, there is a double entry in the accounting books – each transaction is entered twice.

2.2 A balance sheet is a financial statement that summarises the financial position of an organisation at a point in time. It does not present enough information about the organisation to make it appropriate to enter each transaction directly on to the balance sheet. It does not, for instance, tell who the debtors are and how much each one of them owes the organisation, nor who the creditors are and the details of the amounts owing to each of them. We need to maintain a record of each individual transaction so that (a) we know what occurred and (b) we can check to see that it was correctly recorded.

REVIEW QUESTIONS

2.1 Complete the following table:

	Account to be debited	Account to be credited
(a) Bought office machinery on credit from D Isaacs Ltd.		
(b) The proprietor paid a creditor, C Jones, from his private monies outside the firm.		
(c) A debtor, N Fox, paid us in cash.		
(d) Repaid part of loan from P Exeter by cheque.		
(e) Returned some of office machinery to D Isaacs Ltd.		
(f) A debtor, N Lyn, pays us by cheque.		
(g) Bought van by cash.		

2.2A Complete the following table:

	Account to be debited	Account to be credited
(a) Bought lorry for cash.		
(b) Paid creditor, T Lake, by cheque.		
(c) Repaid P Logan's loan by cash.		
(d) Sold lorry for cash.		
(e) Bought office machinery on credit from Ultra Ltd.		
(f) A debtor, A Hill, pays us by cash.		
(g) A debtor, J Cross, pays us by cheque.		
(h) Proprietor puts a further amount into the business by cheque.		
(i) A loan of £200 in cash is received from L Lowe.		
(j) Paid a creditor, D Lord, by cash.		

2.3   Write up the asset and liability and capital accounts to record the following transactions in the records of G Powell.

20X7
July	1	Started business with £2,500 in the bank.
''	2	Bought office furniture by cheque £150.
''	3	Bought machinery £750 on credit from Planers Ltd.
''	5	Bought a van paying by cheque £600.
''	8	Sold some of the office furniture – not suitable for the firm – for £60 on credit to J Walker & Sons.
''	15	Paid the amount owing to Planers Ltd £750 by cheque.
''	23	Received the amount due from J Walker & Sons £60 in cash.
''	31	Bought more machinery by cheque £280.

2.4   You are required to open the asset and liability and capital accounts and record the following transactions for June 20X8 in the records of C Williams.

20X8
June	1	Started business with £2,000 in cash.
''	2	Paid £1,800 of the opening cash into a bank account for the business.
''	5	Bought office furniture on credit from Betta-Built Ltd for £120.
''	8	Bought a van paying by cheque £950.
''	12	Bought works machinery from Evans & Sons on credit £560.
''	18	Returned faulty office furniture costing £62 to Betta-Built Ltd.
''	25	Sold some of the works machinery for £75 cash.
''	26	Paid amount owing to Betta-Built Ltd £58 by cheque.
''	28	Took £100 out of the bank.
''	30	J Smith lent us £500 – giving us the money by cheque.

2.5A   Write up the asset, capital and liability accounts in the books of C Walsh to record the following transactions:

20X9
June	1	Started business with £5,000 in the bank.
''	2	Bought van paying by cheque £1,200.
''	5	Bought office fixtures £400 on credit from Young Ltd.
''	8	Bought van on credit from Super Motors £800.
''	12	Took £100 out of the bank and put it into the cash till.
''	15	Bought office fixtures paying by cash £60.
''	19	Paid Super Motors a cheque for £800.
''	21	A loan of £1,000 cash is received from J Jarvis.
''	25	Paid £800 of the cash in hand into the bank account.
''	30	Bought more office fixtures paying by cheque £300.

2.6A   Write up the accounts to record the following transactions:

20X7
March	1	Started business with £1,000 cash.
''	2	Received a loan of £5,000 from M Chow by cheque, a bank account being opened and the cheque paid into it.
''	3	Bought machinery for cash £60.
''	5	Bought display equipment on credit from Betterview Machines £550.
''	8	Took £300 out of the bank and put it into the cash till.
''	15	Repaid part of Chow's loan by cheque £800.
''	17	Paid amount owing to Betterview Machines £550 by cheque.
''	24	Repaid part of Chow's loan by cash £100.
''	31	Bought additional machinery, this time on credit from D Smith for £500.

The asset of stock

After you have studied this chapter, you should be able to:

- explain why it is inappropriate to use a stock account to record increases and decreases in stock
- describe the two causes of stock increasing
- describe the two causes of stock decreasing
- explain the difference between a purchase account and a returns inwards account
- explain the difference between a sales account and a returns outwards account
- explain how to record increases and decreases of stock in the appropriate accounts
- explain the meanings of the terms 'purchases' and 'sales' as used in accounting
- explain the differences in recording purchases on credit as compared to recording purchases that are paid for immediately in cash
- explain the differences in recording sales on credit as compared to recording sales that are paid for immediately in cash

3.1 Stock movements

In the examples in Chapter 1, goods were sold at the same price at which they were bought. This is, of course, extremely unusual. In fact, any new business doing this wouldn't last terribly long. Businesses need to make profits to survive, as many 'dot.com' Internet companies discovered in 2000 when their bubble burst and all the losses they had been making took effect.

Normally, goods and services are sold above cost price, the difference being **profit**. As you know, when goods and services are sold for less than their cost, the difference is a **loss**.

Activity 3.1

Let's think about the double entry implications if all sales were at cost price. Fill in the blanks in the following:

As we did in Chapter 1, it would be possible to have a stock account with goods purchased being _____ to the stock account (as purchases represent __ _____ in the asset, stock) and goods sold being _____ to it (as sales represent __ _____ in the asset, stock).

The difference between the two sides of the stock account would then represent the cost of the goods unsold at that date. (We'll ignore things like wastage and losses of stock for now.) However, most sales are not priced at cost and, therefore, the sales figures include elements of profit or loss. Because of this, in most cases, the difference between the two sides of the stock account would not represent the stock of goods. Maintaining a stock account on this basis would therefore serve no useful purpose.

To address this, we subdivide the way stock is reported into several accounts, each one showing a movement of stock. Firstly, we must distinguish between transactions that cause stock to increase and those that cause stock to decrease. Let's deal with each of these in turn.

1 **Increase in stock**. This can be due to one of two causes:

(*a*) The purchase of additional goods.
(*b*) The return in to the business of goods previously sold. The reasons for this are numerous. The goods may have been the wrong type; they may, for example, have been surplus to requirements or faulty.

To distinguish the two aspects of the increase of stocks of goods, two accounts are opened:

(*i*) **a Purchases Account** – in which purchases of goods are entered; and
(*ii*) **a Returns Inwards Account** – in which goods being returned in to the business are entered. (This is also known as the **Sales Returns Account**.)

So, for *increases* in stock, we need to choose which of these two accounts to use to record the *debit* side of the transaction.

2 **Decrease in stock**. Ignoring things like wastage and theft, this can be due to one of two causes:

(*a*) The sale of goods.
(*b*) Goods previously bought by the business now being returned to the supplier.

Once again, in order to distinguish the two aspects of the decrease of stocks of goods, two accounts are opened:

(*i*) **a Sales Account** – in which sales of goods are entered; and
(*ii*) **a Returns Outwards Account** – in which goods being returned out to a supplier are entered. (This is also known as the **Purchases Returns Account**.)

So, for *decreases* in stock, we need to choose which of these two accounts to use to record the *credit* side of the transaction.

As stock is an asset, and these four accounts are all connected with this asset, the double entry rules are those used for assets.

Activity 3.2
What are the double entry rules for assets?

Accounts	To record	Entry in the account
Assets	an increase a decrease	_____ _____

We shall now look at some entries in the following sections.

3.2 Purchase of stock on credit

On 1 August 20X8, goods costing £165 are bought on credit from D Henry. First, the twofold effect of the transaction must be considered so that the bookkeeping entries can be worked out.

1 The asset of stock is increased. An increase in an asset needs a debit entry in an account. Here the account is one designed for this type of stock movement. It is clearly a 'purchase' movement so that the account to use must be the purchases account.

2 There is an increase in a liability. This is the liability of the business to D Henry because the goods bought have not yet been paid for. An increase in a liability needs a credit entry. In this case, it would be a credit entry to D Henry's account.

These two entries appear in the acounts as:

Purchases

20X8		£	
Aug 1 D Henry		165	

D Henry

		20X8	£
		Aug 1 Purchases	165

Note that these entries look identical to those you would make if you were using a stock account rather than a purchases account.

3.3   Purchases of stock for cash

On 2 August 20X8, goods costing £22 are bought, cash being paid for them immediately.

1 As before, it is the asset of stock that is increased, so a debit entry will be needed. The movement of stock is that of a 'purchase', so the purchases account needs to be debited.

2 The asset of cash is decreased. To reduce an asset a credit entry is called for, and the asset is cash, so we need to credit the cash account.

Purchases

20X8		£	
Aug 2 Cash		22	

Cash

		20X8	£
		Aug 2 Purchases	22

3.4   Sales of stock on credit

On 3 August 20X8, goods were sold on credit for £250 to J Lee.

1 An asset account is increased. The increase in the asset of debtors requires a debit and the debtor is J Lee, so that the account concerned is that of J Lee.

2 The asset of stock is decreased. For this a credit entry to reduce an asset is needed. The movement of stock is clearly the result of a 'sale' and so it is the sales account that needs to be credited.

J Lee

20X8		£	
Aug 3 Sales		250	

Sales

		20X8	£
		Aug 3 J Lee	250

3.5 Sales of stock for cash

On 4 August 20X8, goods are sold for £55, cash being received immediately upon sale.

1 The asset of cash is increased, so the cash account must be debited.
2 The asset of stock is reduced. The reduction of an asset requires a credit and the movement of stock is represented by 'sales'. Thus the entry needed is a credit in the sales account.

Cash

20X8		£			
Aug 4 Sales		55			

Sales

			20X8		£
			Aug 4 Cash		55

So far, so good. Apart from replacing the stock account with the purchases account for stock increases and the sales account for stock decreases, you've done nothing different in your entries to the accounts compared with what you learnt in Chapters 1 and 2. Now let's look at the other stock-related transactions that cause stocks to increase and decrease – returns inwards (sales that are being returned) and returns outwards (purchases that are being returned to the supplier).

3.6 Returns inwards

On 5 August 20X8, goods which had been previously sold to F Lowe for £29 are now returned *to the business*. This could be for various reasons such as:

● we sent goods of the wrong size, the wrong colour or the wrong model;
● the goods may have been damaged in transit;
● the goods are of poor quality.

1 The asset of stock is increased by the goods returned. Thus, a debit representing an increase of an asset is needed. This time, the movement of stock is that of 'returns inwards'. The entry required is a debit in the returns inwards account.
2 There is a decrease in an asset. The debt of F Lowe to the business is now reduced. A credit is needed in F Lowe's account to record this.

Returns Inwards

20X8		£			
Aug 5 F Lowe		29			

F Lowe

			20X8		£
			Aug 5 Returns inwards		29

(Remember, another name for the returns inwards account is the 'sales returns account'.)

3.7 Returns outwards

On 6 August 20X8, goods previously bought for £96 are returned *by the business* to K Howe.

1 The liability of the business to K Howe is decreased by the value of the goods returned. The decrease in a liability needs a debit, this time in K Howe's account.

2 The asset of stock is decreased by the goods sent out. Thus, a credit representing a reduction in an asset is needed. The movement of stock is that of 'returns outwards' so the entry will be a credit in the returns outwards account.

K Howe

20X8		£			
Aug 6	Returns outwards	96			

Returns Outwards

			20X8		£
			Aug 6	K Howe	96

(Remember, another name for the returns outwards account is the 'purchases returns account'.)

You're probably thinking this is all very straighforward. Well, let's look at another example and see what you think once you've looked at it.

3.8 A worked example

20X9

May	1	Bought goods on credit £68 from D Small.
''	2	Bought goods on credit £77 from A Lyon & Son.
''	5	Sold goods on credit to D Hughes for £60.
''	6	Sold goods on credit to M Spencer for £45.
''	10	Returned goods £15 to D Small.
''	12	Goods bought for cash £100.
''	19	M Spencer returned £16 goods to us.
''	21	Goods sold for cash £150.
''	22	Paid cash to D Small £53.
''	30	D Hughes paid the amount owing by him £60 in cash.
''	31	Bought goods on credit £64 from A Lyon & Son.

You may find it worthwhile trying to enter all these transactions in T-accounts before reading any further. You will need the following accounts: Purchases, Sales, Returns Outwards, Returns Inwards, D Small, A Lyon & Son, D Hughes, M Spencer, and Cash.

Purchases

20X9			£			
May	1	D Small	68			
''	2	A Lyon & Son	77			
''	12	Cash	100			
''	31	A Lyon & Son	64			

Sales

				20X9			£
				May	5	D Hughes	60
				''	6	M Spencer	45
				''	21	Cash	150

Returns Outwards

				20X9			£
				May	10	D Small	15

Returns Inwards

20X9			£	
May	19	M Spencer	16	

D Small

20X9			£	20X9			£
May	10	Returns outwards	15	May	1	Purchases	68
″	22	Cash	53				

A Lyon & Son

				20X9			£
				May	2	Purchases	77
				″	31	Purchases	64

D Hughes

20X9			£	20X9			£
May	5	Sales	60	May	30	Cash	60

M Spencer

20X9			£	20X9			£
May	6	Sales	45	May	19	Returns inwards	16

Cash

20X9			£	20X9			£
May	21	Sales	150	May	12	Purchases	100
″	30	D Hughes	60	″	22	D Small	53

If you tried to do this before looking at the answer, be sure you understand any mistakes you made before going on.

3.9 Special meaning of 'sales' and 'purchases'

You need to remember that 'sales' and 'purchases' have a special meaning in accounting when compared to ordinary language usage.

Purchases in accounting means the *purchase of those goods which the business buys with the prime intention of selling*. Obviously, sometimes the goods are altered, added to, or used in the manufacture of something else, but it is the element of resale that is important. To a business that deals in computers, for instance, computers constitute purchases.

If something else is bought *which it is not intended to sell*, such as a van, such an item cannot be called 'purchases', even though in ordinary language you would say that a van has been purchased. The prime intention of buying the van is for usage and *not* for resale.

Similarly, **sales** means the *sale of those goods in which the business normally deals and which were bought with the prime intention of resale*. The word 'sales' must never be given to the disposal of other items, such as vans or buildings that were purchased to be used and *not* to be sold.

If we did not keep to these meanings, we would find it very difficult to identify which of the items in the purchases and sales accounts were stock and which were assets that had been bought to be used.

Let's now look at another of the small complications accountants need to deal with – the differences between the treatment of cash and credit transactions.

3.10 Comparison of cash and credit transactions for purchases and sales

As you saw in the last example, when goods are purchased for cash, the entries are:

- Debit the purchases account
- Credit the cash account.

On the other hand the complete set of entries for the purchase of goods on credit can be broken down into two stages: first, the purchase of the goods, and second, the payment for them.

The first part is:

- Debit the purchases account
- Credit the supplier's account.

The second part is:

- Debit the supplier's account
- Credit the cash account.

Activity 3.3

What is the difference between the treatment of cash and credit purchases?

A study of cash sales and credit sales reveals a similar difference in treatment:

Cash Sales	Credit Sales

Complete entry:
    Debit cash account
    Credit sales account
	First part:
	    Debit customer's account
	    Credit sales account
	Second part:
	    Debit cash account
	    Credit customer's account

Learning outcomes

You should now have learnt:

1 That it is *not* appropriate to use a stock account to record increases and decreases in stock because stock is normally sold at a price greater than its cost.

2 That stock increases either because some stock has been purchased or because stock that was sold has been returned by the buyer.

3 That stock decreases either because some stock has been sold or because stock previously purchased has been returned to the supplier.

4 That a purchase account is used to record purchases of stock (as debit entries in the account) and that a returns inwards account is used to record stock returned by customers (as debit entries in the account).

5 That a sales account is used to record sales of stock (as credit entries in the account) and that a returns outwards account is used to record stock returned to suppliers (as credit entries in the account).

6 How to record increases and decreases of stock in the appropriate accounts.

7 That in accounting, the term 'purchases' refers to purchases of stocks. Acquisitions of any other assets, such as vans, equipment and buildings, are *never* described as purchases.

8 That in accounting, the term 'sales' refers to sales of stocks. Disposals of any other assets, such as vans, equipment and buildings, are *never* described as sales.

9 That purchases for cash are *never* entered in the supplier's account.

10 That purchases on credit are *always* entered in the supplier's (creditor's) account.

11 That sales for cash are *never* entered in the customer's account.

12 That sales on credit are *always* entered in the customer's (debtor's) account.

Answers to activities

3.1 As we did in Chapter 1, it would be possible to have a stock account with goods purchased being DEBITED to the stock account (as purchases represent AN INCREASE in the asset, stock) and goods sold being CREDITED to it (as sales represent A DECREASE in the asset, stock).

3.2

Accounts	To record	Entry in the account
Assets	an increase	Debit
	a decrease	Credit

3.3 With cash purchases, no entry is made in the supplier's account. This is because cash passes immediately and therefore there is no need to keep a check of how much money is owing to that supplier. On the other hand, with credit purchases, the records should show to whom money is owed until payment is made and so an entry is always made in the supplier's (creditor's) account.

REVIEW QUESTIONS

3.1 Complete the following table:

*Account to   Account to
be debited   be credited*

(a) Goods bought on credit from J Reid.
(b) Goods sold on credit to B Perkins.
(c) Vans bought on credit from H Thomas.
(d) Goods sold, a cheque being received immediately.
(e) Goods sold for cash.
(f) Goods purchased by us returned to supplier, H Hardy.
(g) Machinery sold for cash.
(h) Goods sold returned to us by customer, J Nelson.
(i) Goods bought on credit from D Simpson.
(j) Goods we returned to H Forbes.

3.2A   Complete the following table:

	Account to be debited	*Account to be credited*
(a) Goods bought on credit from T Morgan.		
(b) Goods returned to us by J Thomas.		
(c) Machinery returned to L Jones Ltd.		
(d) Goods bought for cash.		
(e) Van bought on credit from D Davies Ltd.		
(f) Goods returned by us to I Prince.		
(g) D Picton paid us his account by cheque.		
(h) Goods bought by cheque.		
(i) We paid creditor, B Henry, by cheque.		
(j) Goods sold on credit to J Mullings.		

3.3   You are to write up the following in the books:

20X8
July	1	Started business with £500 cash.
''	3	Bought goods for cash £85.
''	7	Bought goods on credit £116 from E Morgan.
''	10	Sold goods for cash £42.
''	14	Returned goods to E Morgan £28.
''	18	Bought goods on credit £98 from A Moses.
''	21	Returned goods to A Moses £19.
''	24	Sold goods to A Knight £55 on credit.
''	25	Paid E Morgan's account by cash £88.
''	31	A Knight paid us his account in cash £55.

3.4A   Enter the following transactions in the appropriate accounts:

20X6
Aug	1	Started business with £1,000 cash.
''	2	Paid £900 of the opening cash into the bank.
''	4	Bought goods on credit £78 from S Holmes.
''	5	Bought a van by cheque £500.
''	7	Bought goods for cash £55.
''	10	Sold goods on credit £98 to D Moore.
''	12	Returned goods to S Holmes £18.
''	19	Sold goods for cash £28.
''	22	Bought fixtures on credit from Kingston Equipment Co £150.
''	24	D Watson lent us £100 paying us the money by cheque.
''	29	We paid S Holmes his account by cheque £60.
''	31	We paid Kingston Equipment Co by cheque £150.

3.5   Enter the following transactions in the accounts of E Sangster:

20X7
July	1	Started business with £10,000 in the bank.
''	2	T Cooper lent us £400 in cash.
''	3	Bought goods on credit from F Jones £840 and S Charles £3,600.
''	4	Sold goods for cash £200.
''	6	Took £250 of the cash and paid it into the bank.
''	8	Sold goods on credit to C Moody £180.
''	10	Sold goods on credit to J Newman £220.
''	11	Bought goods on credit from F Jones £370.
''	12	C Moody returned goods to us £40.
''	14	Sold goods on credit to H Morgan £190 and J Peat £320.
''	15	We returned goods to F Jones £140.

	17	Bought van on credit from Manchester Motors £2,600.
	18	Bought office furniture on credit from Faster Supplies Ltd £600.
	19	We returned goods to S Charles £110.
	20	Bought goods for cash £220.
	24	Goods sold for cash £70.
	25	Paid money owing to F Jones by cheque £1,070.
	26	Goods returned to us by H Morgan £30.
	27	Returned some of office furniture costing £160 to Faster Supplies Ltd.
	28	E Sangster put a further £500 into the business in the form of cash.
	29	Paid Manchester Motors £2,600 by cheque.
	31	Bought office furniture for cash £100.

3.6A Enter the following transactions in the accounts:

20X9
May 1 Started business with £2,000 in the bank.

	2	Bought goods on credit from C Shaw £900.
	3	Bought goods on credit from F Hughes £250.
	5	Sold goods for cash £180.
	6	We returned goods to C Shaw £40.
	8	Bought goods on credit from F Hughes £190.
	10	Sold goods on credit to G Wood £390.
	12	Sold goods for cash £210.
	18	Took £300 of the cash and paid it into the bank.
	21	Bought machinery by cheque £550.
	22	Sold goods on credit to L Moore £220.
	23	G Wood returned goods to us £140.
	25	L Moore returned goods to us £10.
	28	We returned goods to F Hughes £30.
	29	We paid Shaw by cheque £860.
	31	Bought machinery on credit from D Lee £270.

CHAPTER 4

The effect of profit or loss on capital and the double entry system for expenses and revenues

Learning objectives

After you have studied this chapter, you should be able to:

- calculate profit by comparing revenue with expenses
- explain how the accounting equation is used to show the effects of changes in assets and liabilities upon capital after goods or services have been traded
- explain why separate accounts are used for each type of expense and revenue
- explain why an expense is entered as a debit in the appropriate expense account
- explain why an item of revenue is entered as a credit in the appropriate revenue account
- enter a series of expense and revenue transactions into the appropriate T-accounts
- explain how the use of business cash for the owner's own purposes is dealt with in the accounting books

4.1 The nature of profit or loss

To an accountant, **profit** means the amount by which **revenues** are greater than **expenses** for a set of transactions. The term **revenues** means the sales value of goods and services that have been supplied to customers. The term **expenses** means the cost value of all the assets that have been used up to obtain those revenues.

If, therefore, we supplied goods and services valued for sale at £100,000 to customers, and the expenses incurred by us in order to supply those goods and services amounted to £70,000 the result would be a profit of £30,000:

		£
Revenues:	goods and services supplied to our customers for the sum of	100,000
Less Expenses:	value of all the assets used up to enable us to supply these goods and services	(70,000)
Profit is therefore:		30,000

On the other hand, it is possible for our expenses to exceed our revenues for a set of transactions. In this case the result is a **loss**. For example, a loss would be incurred given the following:

		£
Revenues:	what we have charged to our customers in respect of all the goods and services supplied to them	60,000
Less Expenses:	value of all the assets used up to supply these goods and services to our customers	(80,000)
Loss is therefore:		(20,000)

Activity 4.1

In each of these two examples, a different explanation was given for the terms 'revenues' and 'expenses'. What is the difference between the two explanations given for 'revenue'? What is the difference between the two explanations given for 'expenses'?

4.2 The effect of profit and loss on capital

Businesses exist to make profits and so increase their capital. Let's look at the relationship between profits and capital in an example.

On 1 January the assets and liabilities of a business are:

Assets: Fixtures £10,000; Stock £7,000; Cash at the bank £3,000.
Liabilities: Creditors £2,000.

The capital is found from the accounting equation:

$$\boxed{\text{Capital} = \text{Assets} - \text{Liabilities}}$$

In this case, capital is £10,000 + £7,000 + £3,000 − £2,000 = £18,000.

During January, the whole of the £7,000 stock is sold for £11,000 cash. On 31 January the assets and liabilities have become:

Assets: Fixtures £10,000, Stock nil, Cash at the bank £14,000.
Liabilities: Creditors £2,000.

The capital is now:

Assets £10,000 + £14,000 − Liabilities £2,000 = £22,000

So capital has increased by £4,000 from £18,000 to £22,000. It has increased by £4,000 increase because the £7,000 stock was sold at a profit of £4,000 for £11,000. Profit, therefore, increases capital:

$$\boxed{\text{Old capital} + \text{Profit} = \text{New capital}}$$

£18,000 + £4,000 = £22,000

A loss, on the other hand, would reduce the capital:

$$\boxed{\text{Old capital} - \text{Loss} = \text{New capital}}$$

4.3 Profit or loss and sales

Profit will be made when goods or services are sold at more than cost price, while the opposite will mean a loss.

(You will learn later that there are different types of profit, some of which you may have heard of, such as 'gross profit' and 'net profit'. For now, we're not going to complicate things by going into that level of detail so, whatever you may already know about these different types of profit, try to focus for the time being on the simple definition of profit presented here.)

4.4 Profit or loss and expenses

Once profits or losses have been calculated, you can alter the capital account. How often this will be done will depend on the business. Some only attempt to calculate their profits and losses once a year. Others do it at much more frequent intervals. Generally speaking, the larger the business, the more frequently profits are calculated.

In order to calculate profits and losses, revenues and expenses must be entered into appropriate accounts. All the expenses could be charged to one Expenses Account, but you would be able to understand the calculations of profit better if full details of each type of expense were shown in those profit calculations. The same applies to each type of revenue.

For this reason, a separate account is opened for each type of expense and for each type of revenue. For example, accounts in use may include:

Commissions Account	Subscriptions Account	Rent Account
Bank Interest Account	Motor Expenses Account	Postages Account
Royalties Receivable Account	Telephone Account	Stationery Account
Rent Receivable Account	General Expenses Account	Wages Account
Overdraft Interest Account	Audit Fees Account	Insurance Account

It is purely a matter of choice in a business as to the title of each expense or revenue account. For example, an account for postage stamps could be called 'Postage Stamps Account', 'Postages Account', 'Communication Expenses Account', and so on. Also different businesses amalgamate expenses, some having a 'Rent and Telephone Account', others a 'Rent, Telephone and Insurance Account', etc. Infrequent or small items of expense are usually put into a 'Sundry Expenses Account' or a 'General Expenses Account'.

Most organisations use names for their accounts that make it obvious which accounts are for revenue and which accounts are for expenses. However, some don't. When in doubt as to whether an account is for revenue or expenses, you have two obvious indicators to consult. The first is on which side the entries are mainly appearing. If, for example, it is the debit side, the account is almost certainly an expense account. The other indicator is the nature of the business. A commission account in the accounting books of a firm of stockbrokers is almost certainly a revenue account.

> ### Activity 4.2
> Identify which of the accounts listed above are expense accounts and which ones are revenue accounts.

4.5 Debit or credit

You need to know whether expense accounts should be debited or credited with the amounts involved. You know that assets involve expenditure by the business and are shown as debit entries. Expenses also involve expenditure by the business and should, therefore, also be debit entries. Why? Because assets and expenses must ultimately be paid for. This payment involves a credit to the bank account (or to the cash account) so the original entry in the asset account or in the expense account must be a debit.

Even where an expense is incurred on credit, the creditor must eventually be paid. The first entry will be to credit the supplier's (i.e. creditor's) account and debit the expense account. When payment is made to the supplier, the bank account is credited and the supplier's account is debited.

For example, if you pay rent of £500 in cash, the asset cash is decreased by £500. The accounting equation tells you that this means that the capital is reduced by each expense – if assets decrease, so does capital; if liabilities increase, capital decreases (otherwise the accounting equation won't balance). Expense accounts contain debit entries for expenses. The second part of the entry will either be a credit against an asset account, such as cash, or it will be a credit against a liability account, such as creditors.

Activity 4.3

Some students find this explanation involving the capital account very difficult to understand, so try this example to ensure you have followed it. Write down the accounting equation and see if you can work out what happens to it if (a) a business spends £30 in cash hiring a van for a day and (b) if a business hires a van for a day at a cost of £30 and is given 1 month to pay the bill. Assume in each case that the business has assets of £200, liabilities of £80 and capital of £120 before the transaction. What happens to capital in each case?

Revenue is the opposite of expenses and is, therefore, treated in the opposite way – revenue entries appear on the credit side of the revenue accounts. You've already seen this when you've entered sales figures as credits into the sales account. Thus, revenue is collected together in appropriately named accounts, where it is shown as a credit until it is transferred to the profit calculations at the end of the period.

Consider too the use of funds to pay for expenses which are used up in the short term, or assets which are used up in the long term, both for the purpose of winning revenue. Both of these forms of transactions are entered on the debit side of the appropriate accounts (expense accounts or asset accounts respectively), while the revenue which has been won is shown on the credit side of the appropriate accounts.

So, to summarise, profit belongs to the owners. Revenues increase profits, so they increase capital, and that makes them credits. Expenses decrease profits, so they reduce capital, and that makes them debits. The treatment of expenses is the same as the treatment of assets. Increases result in debit entries to the appropriate expense accounts, while decreases (such as refunds for overpayment of an electricity bill) result in credit entries to those same accounts. Revenue is treated the same as liabilities. Increases in revenue are credited to the appropriate revenue accounts, while decreases are debited to the same accounts.

4.6 Double entries for expenses and revenues

Let's look at some examples that demonstrate the double entry required:

1 Rent of £200 is paid in cash.
  Here the twofold effect is:

  (a) The total of the expenses of rent is increased. As expense entries are shown as debits, and the expense is rent, the action required is to debit the rent account with £200.

(b) The asset of cash is decreased. This means the cash account must be credited with £200 to show the decrease of the asset.

Summary: Debit the *rent account* with £200.
Credit the *cash account* with £200.

2 Motor expenses of £355 are paid by cheque.
The twofold effect is:

(a) The total of the motor expenses paid is increased. The amount in expense accounts is increased through debit entries, so the action required is to debit the motor expenses account with £355.
(b) The asset of funds in the bank is decreased. This means the bank account must be credited with £355 to show the decrease of the asset.

Summary: Debit the *motor expenses account* with £355.
Credit the *bank account* with £355.

3 £60 cash is received for commission earned by the business.

(a) The asset of cash is increased. This needs a debit entry of £60 in the cash account to increase the asset.
(b) The revenue account, commissions received, is increased. Revenue is shown by a credit entry, so, to increase the revenue account, the commissions received account is credited with £60.

Summary: Debit the *cash account* with £60.
Credit the *commissions received account* with £60.

Now look at some more transactions and their effect upon the accounts in the following table:

		Increase	Action	Decrease	Action
June 1	Paid for postage stamps by cash £50	Expenses of postages	Debit postages account	Asset of cash	Credit cash account
'' 2	Paid for electricity by cheque £229	Expense of electricity	Debit electricity account	Asset of bank	Credit bank account
'' 3	Received rent in cash £138	Asset of cash	Debit cash account	No decrease to record	No action to take
		Revenue of rent	Credit rent received account		
'' 4	Paid insurance by cheque £142	Expense of insurance	Debit insurance account	Asset of bank	Credit bank account

Entering these four examples into the appropriate accounts results in:

Cash

	£		£
June 3 Rent received	138	June 1 Postages	50

Bank

			£
	June 2	Electricity	229
	'' 4	Insurance	142

Electricity

	£	
June 2 Bank	229	

Insurance

	£	
June 4 Bank	142	

Postages

	£	
June 1 Cash	50	

Rent Received

			£
	June 3	Cash	138

4.7 Drawings

Sometimes the owners will want to take cash out of the business for their private use. This is known as **drawings**. Any money taken out as drawings will reduce capital. Drawings are never expenses of a business. However, like expenses, an increase in drawings is a debit entry with the credit being against an asset account, such as cash or bank.

In theory, the debit entry should be made in the capital account (as drawings decrease capital). However, to prevent the capital account becoming full of lots of small transactions, drawings are not entered in the capital account. Instead, a *drawings account* is opened, and the debits are entered there rather than in the capital account.

The following example illustrates the entries for drawings:

On 25 August, the owner takes £50 cash out of the business for his own use.

Effect	Action
1 Capital is decreased by £50	Debit the drawings account £50
2 Cash is decreased by £50	Credit the cash account £50

Drawings

	£	
Aug 25 Cash	50	

Cash

			£
	Aug 25	Drawings	50

Sometimes goods are taken for private use. These are also known as drawings. Entries for such transactions will be described later in this book.

You should now have learnt:

1 How to calculate profit by comparing revenue with expenses.

2 That the accounting equation is central to any explanation of the effect of trading upon capital.

3 Why every different type of expense is shown in a separate expense account.

4 Why every different type of revenue is shown in a separate revenue account.

5 Why an expense is shown as a debit entry in the appropriate expense account.

6 Why revenue is shown as a credit entry in the appropriate revenue account.

7 How to enter a series of expense and revenue transactions into the appropriate T-accounts.

8 What is meant by the term 'drawings'.

9 That drawings are *always* a reduction in capital and *never* an expense of a business.

10 How to record drawings of cash in the accounting books.

Answers to activities

4.1   There is no difference between either the two meanings given for revenues or the two meanings given for expenses. In each case, you are being given a slightly different wording so as to help you understand what the two terms mean.

4.2   *Expense Accounts*

Expense Accounts	*Revenue Accounts*
Rent Account	Subscriptions Account
Postages Account	Rent Receivable Account
Commissions Account	Royalties Receivable Account
Stationery Account	
Wages Account	
Insurance Account	
Bank Interest Account	
Motor Expenses Account	
Telephone Account	
General Expenses Account	
Overdraft Interest Account	
Audit Fees Account	

Note that the answer has assumed that *unless* words like 'received' or 'receivable' follow the name of an account, the account is an expense. For example, the Commission Account and the Bank Interest Account could easily be for revenue rather than expenses. However, accounting practice is that as most accounts are for expenses, where there may be some confusion as to whether an account is for revenue or expenses, the name of the revenue account should make it clear that it is for revenue, not expenses. You can see an example in this question if you compare the names of the two rent accounts. Accounts like Subscriptions tend to appear mainly in the accounting books of clubs and societies and so there is no need in that case to indicate in the name that it is a revenue account. You can tell whether subscriptions are revenue or expenditure items from the type of organisation whose accounting books you are looking at. The same would apply, but even more so, to Audit Fees which are only ever revenue accounts in the accounting books of a firm of accountants. In all other cases, they are expense accounts.

4.3   The accounting equation is Capital = Assets – Liabilities. In this example, it starts as £120 = £200 – £80. Each transaction is entered twice. In both cases, the debit entry is £30 to a van hire expense account. The credit in (a) is to the cash account. In (b) it is to the car hire company's account (the creditor's account). In order for the accounting equation to balance, in (a) an asset (i.e. cash) has been reduced by £30 so capital must be reduced by the same amount, £30. In the case of (b) liabilities (i.e. the van hire company's account) have increased by £30 and so capital must be also be reduced by that amount, £30. In the case of (a) the accounting equation becomes £90 = £170 − £80. In (b) it becomes £90 = £200 − £110. The effect on capital in both cases is that it decreases by the amount of the expense.

REVIEW QUESTIONS

4.1   Enter the following transactions, completing the double entry in the books for the month of May 20X7.

20X7
May   1   Started business with £2,000 in the bank.
 ''   2   Purchased goods £175 on credit from M Mills.
 ''   3   Bought fixtures and fittings £150 paying by cheque.
 ''   5   Sold goods for cash £275.
 ''   6   Bought goods on credit £114 from S Waites.
 ''   10   Paid rent by cash £15.
 ''   12   Bought stationery £27, paying in cash.
 ''   18   Goods returned to M Mills £23.
 ''   21   Let off part of the premises receiving rent by cheque £5.
 ''   23   Sold goods on credit to U Henry for £77.
 ''   24   Bought a van paying by cheque £300.
 ''   30   Paid the month's wages by cash £117.
 ''   31   The proprietor took cash for his own personal use £44.

4.2   Write up the following transactions in the books of L Thompson:

20X8
March   1   Started business with cash £1,500.
 ''   2   Bought goods on credit from A Hanson £296.
 ''   3   Paid rent by cash £28.
 ''   4   Paid £1,000 of the cash of the business into a bank account.
 ''   5   Sold goods on credit to E Linton £54.
 ''   7   Bought stationery £15 paying by cheque.
 ''   11   Cash sales £49.
 ''   14   Goods returned by us to A Hanson £17.
 ''   17   Sold goods on credit to S Morgan £29.
 ''   20   Paid for repairs to the building by cash £18.
 ''   22   E Linton returned goods to us £14.
 ''   27   Paid Hanson by cheque £279.
 ''   28   Cash purchases £125.
 ''   29   Bought a van paying by cheque £395.
 ''   30   Paid motor expenses in cash £15.
 ''   31   Bought fixtures £120 on credit from A Webster.

4.3A   Prepare the double entries (*not* the T-accounts) for the following transactions:

July   1   Started business with £8,000 in the bank.
 ''   2   Bought stationery by cheque £30.
 ''   3   Bought goods on credit from I Walsh £900.
 ''   4   Sold goods for cash £180.
 ''   5   Paid insurance by cash £40.
 ''   7   Bought machinery on credit from H Morgan £500.
 ''   8   Paid for machinery expenses by cheque £50.
 ''   10   Sold goods on credit to D Small £320.

July	11	Returned goods to I Walsh £70.
''	14	Paid wages by cash £70.
''	17	Paid rent by cheque £100.
''	20	Received cheque £200 from D Small.
''	21	Paid H Morgan by cheque £500.
''	23	Bought stationery on credit from Express Ltd £80.
''	25	Sold goods on credit to N Thomas £230.
''	31	Paid Express Ltd by cheque £80.

4.4A Write up the following transactions in the records of D DaSilva:

Feb	1	Started business with £3,000 in the bank and £500 cash.
''	2	Bought goods on credit: T Small £250; C Todd £190; V Ryan £180.
''	3	Bought goods for cash £230.
''	4	Paid rent in cash £10.
''	5	Bought stationery paying by cheque £49.
''	6	Sold goods on credit: C Crooks £140; R Rogers £100; B Grant £240.
''	7	Paid wages in cash £80.
''	10	We returned goods to C Todd £60.
''	11	Paid rent in cash £10.
''	13	R Rogers returns goods to us £20.
''	15	Sold goods on credit to: J Burns £90; J Smart £130; N Thorn £170.
''	16	Paid rates by cheque £130.
''	18	Paid insurance in cash £40.
''	19	Paid rent by cheque £10.
''	20	Bought van on credit from C White £600.
''	21	Paid motor expenses in cash £6.
''	23	Paid wages in cash £90.
''	24	Received part of amount owing from B Grant by cheque £200.
''	28	Received refund of rates £10 by cheque.
''	28	Paid by cheque: T Small £250; C Todd £130; C White £600.

4.5 From the following statements which give the cumulative effects of individual transactions, you are required to state as fully as possible what transaction has taken place in each case. There is no need to copy out the table.

Transaction:		A	B	C	D	E	F	G	H	I
Assets	£000	£000	£000	£000	£000	£000	£000	£000	£000	£000
Land and buildings	450	450	450	450	575	575	275	275	275	275
Motor vehicles	95	100	100	100	100	100	100	100	100	100
Office equipment	48	48	48	48	48	48	48	48	48	48
Stock	110	110	110	110	110	110	110	110	110	93
Debtors	188	188	188	188	188	108	108	108	108	120
Bank	27	22	22	172	47	127	427	77	77	77
Cash	15	15	11	11	11	11	11	11	3	3
	933	933	929	1,079	1,079	1,079	1,079	729	721	716
Liabilities										
Capital	621	621	621	621	621	621	621	621	621	616
Loan from Lee	200	200	200	350	350	350	350	–	–	–
Creditors	112	112	108	108	108	108	108	108	100	100
	933	933	929	1,079	1,079	1,079	1,079	729	721	716

Note: the sign *£000* means that all the figures shown underneath it are in thousands of pounds, e.g. Office Equipment book value is £48,000. It saves constantly writing out 000 after each figure, and is done to save time and make comparison easier.

4.6A The following table shows the cumulative effects of a succession of separate transactions on the assets and liabilities of a business.

Transaction:		A	B	C	D	E	F	G	H	I
Assets	£000	£000	£000	£000	£000	£000	£000	£000	£000	£000
Land and buildings	500	500	535	535	535	535	535	535	535	535
Equipment	230	230	230	230	230	230	230	200	200	200
Stocks	113	140	140	120	120	120	120	120	119	119
Trade debtors	143	143	143	173	160	158	158	158	158	158
Prepaid expenses*	27	27	27	27	27	27	27	27	27	27
Cash at bank	37	37	37	37	50	50	42	63	63	63
Cash on hand	9	9	9	9	9	9	9	9	9	3
	1,059	1,086	1,121	1,131	1,131	1,129	1,121	1,112	1,111	1,105
Liabilities										
Capital	730	730	730	740	740	738	733	724	723	717
Loan	120	120	155	155	155	155	155	155	155	155
Trade creditors	168	195	195	195	195	195	195	195	195	195
Accrued expenses*	41	41	41	41	41	41	38	38	38	38
	1,059	1,086	1,121	1,131	1,131	1,129	1,121	1,112	1,111	1,105

Required:
Identify clearly and as fully as you can what transaction has taken place in each case. Give two possible explanations for transaction I. Do not copy out the table but use the reference letter for each transaction.

(Association of Accounting Technicians)

Authors' note: You have not yet been introduced to the terms 'prepaid expenses' and 'accrued expenses'. Prepaid expenses are expenses that have been paid in advance, the benefits of which will only be felt by the business in a later accounting period. Because the benefit of having incurred the expense will not be received until a future time period, the expense is not included in the calculation of profit for the period in which it was paid. As it was not treated as an expense of the period when profit was calculated, the debit in the account is treated as an asset when the balance sheet is prepared, hence the appearance of the term 'prepaid expenses' among the assets in the question. Accrued expenses, on the other hand, are expenses that have not yet been paid for benefits which have been received. In F, £8,000 was paid out of the bank account of which £3,000 was used to pay off some of the accrued expenses.

CHAPTER 5

Balancing off accounts

After you have studied this chapter, you should be able to:

- close accounts when appropriate
- balance off accounts at the end of a period and bring down the opening balance to the next period
- distinguish between a debit balance and a credit balance
- describe and prepare accounts in three-column format

Introduction

In this chapter, you'll learn how to discover what the amount outstanding on an account is at a particular point in time. You'll also learn how to close accounts that are no longer needed and how to record appropriate entries in accounts at the end and beginning of periods. Finally, you'll learn that T-accounts are not the only way to record accounting transactions.

5.1 Accounts for debtors

Where debtors have paid their accounts

So far you have learnt how to record transactions in the accounting books by means of debit and credit entries. At the end of each accounting period the figures in each account are examined in order to summarise the situation they present. This will often, but not always, be a year if you are calculating profit. It will be at least once a month if you want to see what is happening with respect to particular accounts. Probably the most obvious reason for this is to find out how much our customers owe us for goods we have sold to them. In most businesses this is done at the end of each month.

Activity 5.1

Why do you think we would want to look at the debtor accounts in the accounting books as often as once a month?

Let's look at the account of one of our customers, K Tandy, for transactions in August 20X6:

K Tandy

20X6			£	20X6			£
Aug	1	Sales	144	Aug	22	Bank	144
Aug	19	Sales	300	Aug	28	Bank	300

If you add up the figures on each side, you will find that they both sum to £444. In other words, during the month we sold a total of £444 watch of goods to Tandy, and have been paid a total of £444 by her. This means that at the end of August she owes us nothing. As she owes us nothing, we do not need her account to prepare the balance sheet (there is no point in showing a figure for debtors of zero in the balance sheet). We can, therefore, **close off** her account on 31 August 20X6. This is done by inserting the totals on each side:

K Tandy

20X6			£	20X6			£
Aug	1	Sales	144	Aug	22	Bank	144
Aug	19	Sales	300	Aug	28	Bank	300
			444				444

Notice that totals in accounting are always shown with a single line above them, and a double line underneath. As shown in the following completed account for C Lee, totals on accounts at the end of a period are always shown on a level with one another, even when there are less entries on one side than on the other.

C Lee

20X6			£	20X6			£
Aug	11	Sales	177	Aug	30	Bank	480
Aug	19	Sales	203				
Aug	22	Sales	100				
			480				480

In this account, C Lee also owed us nothing at the end of August 20X6, as he had paid us for all the sales we made to him.

> *Note*: In handwritten accounts, you will often see this layout enhanced by two intersecting lines, one horizontal and one diagonal on the side which has less entries. If this were done, C Lee's account would look like this:
>
> ### C Lee
>
> | 20X6 | | | £ | 20X6 | | | £ |
> |---|---|---|---|---|---|---|---|
> | Aug | 11 | Sales | 177 | Aug | 30 | Bank | 480 |
> | Aug | 19 | Sales | 203 | | | | |
> | Aug | 22 | Sales | 100 | | | | |
> | | | | 480 | | | | 480 |
>
> We won't use this layout in this book, but your teacher or lecturer may want you to use it whenever you are preparing T-accounts.

Activity 5.2

Why do you think we would want to draw these two extra lines onto the hand-written account?

If an account contains only one entry on each side and they are equal, you don't need to include totals. For example:

K Wood

20X6			£	20X6			£
Aug	6	Sales	214	Aug	12	Bank	214

Now let's look at what happens when the two sides do not equal each other.

Where debtors still owe for goods

It is unlikely that everyone will have paid the amounts they owe us by the end of the month. In these cases, the totals of each side would not equal one another. Let's look at the account of D Knight for August 20X6:

D Knight

20X6			£	20X6			£
Aug	1	Sales	158	Aug	28	Bank	158
Aug	15	Sales	206				
Aug	30	Sales	118				

If you add the figures you will see that the debit side adds up to £482 and the credit side adds up to £158. You should be able to see what the difference of £324 (i.e. £482 – £158) represents. It consists of the last two sales of £206 and £118. They have not been paid for and so are still owing to us on 31 August 20X6.

In double entry, we only enter figures as totals if the totals on both sides of the account agree. We do, however, want to **balance off** the account for August showing that Knight owes us £324. (While there would be nothing wrong in using the term 'close off', 'balance off' is the more appropriate term to use when there is a difference between the two sides of an account.)

If Knight owes us £324 at close of business on 31 August 20X6, then the same amount will be owed to us when the business opens on 1 September 20X6.

Balancing the accounts is done in five stages:

1 Add up both sides to find out their totals. Note: do not write anything in the account at this stage.
2 Deduct the smaller total from the larger total to find the balance.
3 Now enter the balance on the side with the smallest total. This now means the totals will be equal.
4 Enter totals on a level with each other.
5 Now enter the balance on the line below the totals on the *opposite* side to the balance shown above the totals.

Against the balance above the totals, complete the date column by entering the last day of that period – for August, this will always be '31' even if the business was shut on that date because it fell on a weekend or was a holiday. Below the totals, show the first day of the next period against the balance – this will always be the day immediately after the last day of the previous period, in this case, September 1. The balance above the totals is described as the **balance *carried down*** (often this is abbreviated to 'balance c/d'). The balance below the total is described as the **balance *brought down*** (often abbreviated to 'balance b/d').

Knight's account when 'balanced off' will appear as follows:

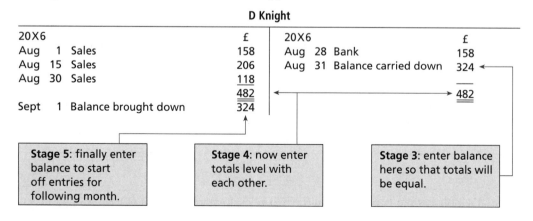

D Knight

20X6			£	20X6			£
Aug	1	Sales	158	Aug	28	Bank	158
Aug	15	Sales	206	Aug	31	Balance carried down	324
Aug	30	Sales	118				
			482				482
Sept	1	Balance brought down	324				

Stage 5: finally enter balance to start off entries for following month.

Stage 4: now enter totals level with each other.

Stage 3: enter balance here so that totals will be equal.

Note for students

- From now on, we will use the abbreviations 'c/d' and 'b/d'.
- The date given to balance c/d is the last day of the period which is finishing, and balance b/d is given the opening date of the next period.
- As the total of the debit side originally exceeded the total of the credit side, the balance is said to be a debit balance. This being a personal account (for a person), the person concerned is said to be a debtor – the accounting term for anyone who owes money to the business.

Just as when the two sides each have only one entry and the two sides are equal, if an account contains only one entry it is unnecessary to enter the total after entering the balance carried down (because the balance becomes the only entry on the other side and it is equal to the other entry). A double line ruled under the entry will mean that the entry is its own total. For example:

B Walters

20X6			£	20X6			£
Aug	18	Sales	51	Aug	31	Balance c/d	51
Sept	1	Balance b/d	51				

Note: T-accounts should *always* be closed off at the end of each period, even when they contain only one entry.

5.2 Accounts for creditors

Exactly the same principles will apply when the balances are carried down to the credit side. We can look at two accounts of our suppliers which are to be balanced off:

E Williams

20X6			£	20X6			£
Aug	21	Bank	100	Aug	2	Purchases	248
				Aug	18	Purchases	116

K Patterson

20X6			£	20X6			£
Aug	14	Returns outwards	20	Aug	8	Purchases	620
Aug	28	Bank	600	Aug	15	Purchases	200

We now add up the totals and find the balance, i.e. stages 1 and 2. When balanced off these will appear as:

E Williams

20X6			£	20X6			£
Aug	21	Bank	100	Aug	2	Purchases	248
Aug	31	Balance c/d	264	Aug	18	Purchases	116
			364				364
				Sept	1	Balance b/d	264

Stage 3: enter balance here so that totals will be equal.

Stage 4: now enter totals level with each other.

Stage 5: finally enter balance to start off entries for following month.

K Patterson

20X6			£	20X6			£
Aug	14	Returns outwards	20	Aug	8	Purchases	620
Aug	28	Bank	600	Aug	15	Purchases	200
Aug	31	Balance c/d	200				
			820				820
				Sept	1	Balance b/d	200

Before you read further attempt Review Questions 5.1 and 5.2.

5.3 Three-column accounts

Through the main part of this book, the type of account used is the T-account, where the left-hand side of the account is the debit side, and the right-hand side is the credit side. However, when computers are used the style of the ledger account is sometimes different. It appears as three columns of figures, one column for debit entries, another column for credit entries, and the last column for the balance. If you have a current account at a bank your bank statements will normally be shown using this three-column format method.

The accounts used in this chapter will now be redrafted to show the ledger accounts drawn up in this way.

K Tandy

			Debit	Credit	Balance (and whether debit or credit)	
20X6			£	£	£	
Aug	1	Sales	144		144	Dr
Aug	19	Sales	300		444	Dr
Aug	22	Bank		144	300	Dr
Aug	28	Bank		300	0	

C Lee

			Debit	Credit	Balance	
20X6			£	£	£	
Aug	11	Sales	177		177	Dr
Aug	19	Sales	203		380	Dr
Aug	22	Sales	100		480	Dr
Aug	30	Bank		480	0	

K Wood

			Debit	Credit	Balance	
20X6			£	£	£	
Aug	6	Sales	214		214	Dr
Aug	12	Bank		214	0	

D Knight

			Debit	Credit	Balance	
20X6			£	£	£	
Aug	1	Sales	158		158	Dr
Aug	15	Sales	206		364	Dr
Aug	28	Bank		158	206	Dr
Aug	31	Sales	118		324	Dr

B Walters

20X6		Debit £	Credit £	Balance £	
Aug	18	Sales	51		51	Dr

E Williams

20X6			Debit £	Credit £	Balance £	
Aug	2	Purchases		248	248	Cr
Aug	18	Purchases		116	364	Cr
Aug	21	Bank	100		264	Cr

K Patterson

20X6			Debit £	Credit £	Balance £	
Aug	8	Purchases		620	620	Cr
Aug	14	Returns	20		600	Cr
Aug	15	Purchases		200	800	Cr
Aug	28	Bank	600		200	Cr

Note how the balance is calculated after every entry. This can be done quite simply when using a computer because the software can automatically calculate the new balance as soon as an entry is made.

However, when manual methods are being used it is often too much work to have to calculate a new balance after each entry. Also, the greater the number of calculations, the greater the possibility of errors. For these reasons, it is usual for students to use two-sided accounts *except* when required to do so in an exam! However, it is important to note that there is no difference in principle – the final balances are the same using either method.

Learning outcomes

You should now have learnt:

1 How to close of accounts upon which there is no balance oustanding.

2 How to balance off accounts at the end of a period.

3 How to bring down the opening balance on an account at the start of a new period.

4 That when an opening balance on an account is a debit, that account is said to have a debit balance. It is also a debit balance during a period whenever the total of the debit side exceeds the total of the credit side.

5 That when an opening balance on an account is a credit, that account is said to have a credit balance. It is also a credit balance during a period whenever the total of the credit side exceeds the total of the debit side.

6 That 'debtors' are people or organisations whose account in your accounting books has a greater value on the debit side. They owe you money.

7 That 'creditors' are people or organisations whose account in your accounting books has a greater value on the credit side. You owe them money.

8 That both T-accounts and three-column accounts disclose the same balance, given identical information about transactions.

9 That three-column accounts update and show the balance on the account after every transaction.

10 How to prepare three-column accounts.

Answers to activities

5.1   In order to survive, business must, in the long term, make profits. However, even profitable businesses go 'bust' if they do not have enough funds to pay their bills when they are due. Debtors represent a resource that is not yet in the form of funds (e.g. cash) that can be used to pay bills. By regularly monitoring the position on the account of each debtor, a business can tell which debtors are being slow to pay and, very importantly, do something about it.

5.2   The purpose is to prevent any more entries being made in the account. The entries would *always* be made in ink, so as to prevent their being erased and replaced with different entries. In a computerised accounting system, there is no need for measures such as these as the controls and checks built into the computerised system prevent these things from happening.

REVIEW QUESTIONS

5.1   Enter the following items in the appropriate debtors' accounts (i.e. your customers' accounts) only; do *not* write up other accounts. Then balance off each of these personal accounts at the end of the month. (Keep your answer; it will be used as a basis for question 5.3.)

20X6
May	1	Sales on credit to H Harvey £690, N Morgan £153, J Lindo £420.
''	4	Sales on credit to L Masters £418, H Harvey £66.
''	10	Returns inwards from H Harvey £40, J Lindo £20.
''	18	N Morgan paid us by cheque £153.
''	20	J Lindo paid us £400 by cheque.
''	24	H Harvey paid us £300 by cash.
''	31	Sales on credit to L Masters £203.

5.2   Enter the following in the appropriate creditors' accounts (i.e. your suppliers' accounts) only. Do *not* write up the other accounts. Then balance off each of these personal accounts at the end of the month. (Keep your answer; it will be used as the basis for question 5.4.)

20X8
June	1	Purchases on credit from J Young £458, L Williams £120, G Norman £708.
''	3	Purchases on credit from L Williams £77, T Harris £880.
''	10	We returned goods to G Norman £22, J Young £55.
''	15	Purchases on credit from J Young £80.
''	19	We paid T Harris by cheque £880.
''	28	We paid J Young by cash £250.
''	30	We returned goods to L Williams £17.

5.3   Redraft each of the accounts given in your answer to 5.1 in three-column ledger style accounts.

5.4   Redraft each of the accounts given in your answer to 5.2 in three-column ledger style accounts.

5.5   Enter the following in the personal accounts (i.e. the creditor and debtor accounts) only. Do *not* write up the other accounts. Balance off each personal account at the end of the month. After completing this, state which of the balances represent debtors and which represent creditors.

20X8
Sept	1	Sales on credit to D Williams £458, J Moore £235, G Grant £98.
''	2	Purchases on credit A White £77, H Samuels £231, P Owen £65.
''	8	Sales on credit to J Moore £444, F Franklin £249.
''	10	Purchases on credit from H Samuels £12, O Oliver £222.
''	12	Returns inwards from G Grant £9, J Moore £26.
''	17	We returned goods to H Samuels £24, O Oliver £12.
''	20	We paid A White by cheque £77.

" 24 D Williams paid us by cheque £300.
" 26 We paid O Oliver by cash £210.
" 28 D Williams paid us by cash £100.
" 30 F Franklin pays us by cheque £249.

5.6A Enter the following transactions in personal accounts only. Bring down the balances at the end of the month. After completing this, state which of the balances represent debtors and which are creditors.

20X7

May 1 Credit sales B Flynn £241, R Kelly £29, J Long £887, T Fryer £124.
" 2 Credit purchases from S Wood £148, T DuQuesnay £27, R Johnson £77, G Henriques £108.
" 8 Credit sales to R Kelly £74, J Long £132.
" 9 Credit purchases from T DuQuesnay £142, G Henriques £44.
" 10 Goods returned to us by J Long £17, T Fryer £44.
" 12 Cash paid to us by T Fryer £80.
" 15 We returned goods to S Wood £8, G Henriques £18.
" 19 We received cheques from J Long £500, B Flynn £241.
" 21 We sold goods on credit to B Flynn £44, R Kelly £280.
" 28 We paid by cheque the following: S Wood £140, G Henriques £50, R Johnson £60.
" 31 We returned goods to G Henriques £4.

5.7A Redraft each of the accounts given in your answer to 5.6A in three-column style accounts.

CHAPTER 6

The trial balance

Learning objectives

After you have studied this chapter, you should be able to:
- prepare a trial balance from a set of accounts
- explain why the debit and credit trial balance totals should equal one another
- explain why some of the possible errors that can be made when double entries are being entered in the accounts do not prevent the trial balance from 'balancing'
- describe uses for a trial balance other than to check for double entry errors

Introduction

In this chapter, you'll learn how to prepare a trial balance from the accounts in the accounting books. You'll discover that the alternate version of the accounting equation can be a useful gude to understanding why a trial balance must balance if all the double entries in the accounts are correct. You'll also learn that the trial balance is no guarantee that the double entries have all been recorded correctly. Finally, you'll have the opportunity to do twenty multiple choice questions covering the material in Chapters 1–6.

6.1 Total debit entries = Total credit entries

You've learnt that under double entry bookkeeping
- for each debit entry there is a credit entry
- for each credit entry there is a debit entry.

Activity 6.1

Do you remember the alternate form of the accounting equation you were shown in Chapter 1? What does it tell you has happened when it does not balance?

All the items recorded in all the accounts on the debit side should equal in *total* all the items recorded on the credit side of the accounts. We need to check that for each debit entry there is also an equal credit entry. In order to do so, we prepare something called a **trial balance**.

A type of trial balance could be drawn up by listing all the accounts and then entering the total of all the debit entries in each account in one column and the total of all the credit entries in each account into another column. Finally, you would add up the two columns of figures and ensure they are equal. Using the worked exercise in Section 3.8, this trial balance would be:

Trial Balance as at 31 May 20X9		
	Dr	Cr
	£	£
Purchases	309	
Sales		255
Returns outwards		15
Returns inwards	16	
D Small	68	68
A Lyon & Son		141
D Hughes	60	60
M Spencer	45	16
Cash	210	153
	708	708

6.2 Total debit balances = Total credit balances

The method described in Section 6.1 is not the accepted method of drawing up a trial balance, but it is the easiest to understand at first. The form of trial balance used by accountants is a list of account balances arranged according to whether they are debit balances or credit balances.

Let's balance off the accounts you saw in Section 3.8. The new entries are highlighted so that you can see the entries required to arrive at the closing balances that are used in the trial balance.

You may find it worthwhile trying to balance these accounts yourself before reading any further.

Purchases

20X9			£	20X9			£
May	1	D Small	68	May	31	Balance c/d	309
''	2	A Lyon & Son	77				
''	12	Cash	100				
''	31	A Lyon & Son	64				
			309				309
June	1	Balance b/d	309				

Sales

20X9			£	20X9			£
May	31	Balance c/d	255	May	5	D Hughes	60
				''	6	M Spencer	45
				''	21	Cash	150
			255				255
				June	1	Balance b/d	255

Returns Outwards

20X9			£	20X9			£
May	31	Balance c/d	15	May	10	D Small	15
				June	1	Balance b/d	15

Returns Inwards

20X9			£	20X9			£
May	19	M Spencer	16	May	31	Balance c/d	16
June	1	Balance b/d	16				

D Small

20X9			£	20X9			£
May	10	Returns outwards	15	May	1	Purchases	68
''	22	Cash	53				
			68				68

A Lyon & Son

20X9			£	20X9			£
May	31	Balance c/d	141	May	2	Purchases	77
				''	31	Purchases	64
			141				141
				June	1	Balance b/d	141

D Hughes

20X9			£	20X9			£
May	5	Sales	60	May	30	Cash	60

M Spencer

20X9			£	20X9			£
May	6	Sales	45	May	19	Returns inwards	16
				''	31	Balance c/d	29
			45				45
June	1	Balance b/d	29				

Cash

20X9			£	20X9			£
May	21	Sales	150	May	12	Purchases	100
''	30	D Hughes	60	''	22	D Small	53
				''	31	Balance c/d	57
			210				210
June	1	Balance b/d	57				

If you tried to do this before looking at the answer, be sure you understand any mistakes you made before going on.

If the trial balance was drawn up using the closing account balances, it would appear as follows:

Trial Balance as at 31 May 20X9		
	Dr £	Cr £
Purchases	309	
Sales		255
Returns outwards		15
Returns inwards	16	
A Lyon & Son		141
M Spencer	29	
Cash	57	
	411	411

The trial balance always has the date of the *last* day of the accounting period to which it relates. It is a snapshot of the balances on the ledger accounts at that date.

Just like the trial balance you saw in Section 6.1, the two sides of this one also 'balance'. However, the totals are lower. This is because the £68 in D Small's account, £60 in

D Hughes' account, £16 in M Spencer's account and £153 in the cash account have been cancelled out from each side of these accounts by taking only the *balances* instead of *totals*. As equal amounts have been cancelled from each side, £297 in all, the new totals should still equal one another, as in fact they do at £411.

This form of trial balance is the easiest to extract when there are more than a few transactions during the period and it is the one accountants use.

Note that a trial balance can be drawn up at any time. However, it is normal practice to prepare one at the end of an accounting period before preparing a 'profit and loss account' and balance sheet. The profit and loss account shows what profit has been earned in a period. (You will be looking at profit and loss accounts in the next chapter.) The balance sheet shows what the assets and liabilities of a business are at the end of the period. (You were introduced to the balance sheet in Chapter 1.)

Activity 6.2

What advantages are there in preparing a trial balance when you are about to prepare a profit and loss account and balance sheet?

As you've just learnt from Activity 6.2. trial balances are not just done to find errors.

6.3 Trial balances and errors

Many students new to accounting assume that when the trial balance 'balances', the entries in the accounts must be correct. **This assumption is incorrect.** While it means that certain types of error have not been made (such as forgetting to enter the credit side of a transaction), there are several types of error that will not affect the balancing of a trial balance – omitting a transaction altogether, for example.

Examples of the errors which would be revealed, provided there are no compensating errors which cancel them out, are addition errors, using one figure for the debit entry and another figure for the credit entry, and entering only one side of a transaction. We shall consider these in greater detail in later chapters.

6.4 Multiple choice self-test questions

A growing practice of examining boards is to set multiple choice questions in accounting. In fact, this has become so popular with examiners that all the largest professional accounting bodies now use them, particularly in their first level examinations.

Multiple choice questions give an examiner the opportunity to cover large parts of the syllabus briefly, but in detail. Students who omit to study areas of the syllabus will be caught out by an examiner's use of multiple choice questions. It is no longer possible to say that it is highly probable a certain topic will not be tested – the examiner can easily cover it with a multiple choice question.

We have deliberately included sets of twenty multiple choice questions at given places in this textbook, rather than a few at the end of each chapter. Such questions are relatively easy to answer a few minutes after reading the chapter. Asking the questions later is a far better test of your powers of recall and understanding. It also gives you practice at answering questions covering a range of topics in one block, as in an examination.

Each multiple choice question has a 'stem' (a part which poses the problem), a 'key' (which is the one correct answer), and a number of 'distractors', i.e. incorrect answers. The key plus the distractors are known as the 'options'.

If you do not know the answer, you should guess. You may be right by chance, or you may remember something subconsciously. In any event, unless the examiner warns otherwise, you will be expected to guess if you don't know the answer.

Read through the Learning Outcomes for this chapter and then attempt Multiple Choice Set 1.

Answers to all the multiple choice questions are given in Appendix 2 at the end of this book.

Learning outcomes

You should now have learnt:

1 How to prepare a trial balance.

2 That trial balances are one form of checking the accuracy of entries in the accounts.

3 That errors can be made in the entries to the accounts that will not be shown up by the trial balance.

4 That the trial balance is used as the basis for preparing profit and loss accounts and balance sheets.

Answers to activities

6.1   The alternate form of the accounting equation is Assets = Capital + Liabilities. All the accounts with debit balances are assets and all the accounts with credit balances are either capital or liabilities. This means that so long as you enter a debit for every credit, the alternate accounting equation must always balance. If the alternate accounting equation does not balance, you've made an error somewhere, either in your double entries, or in your arithmetic within the individual accounts. Virtually all occurrences where the accounting equation does not balance that arise in practice are the result of double entry errors.

6.2   Firstly, you can verify whether the total of the debit balances equals the total of the credit balances. They need to be equal, or your profit and loss account and balance sheet will be incorrect and your balance sheet will not balance. (That is, the accounting equation will not balance.) Secondly, you need to know what the balance is on every account so that you can enter the appropriate figures into the profit and loss account and balance sheet. If you don't prepare a trial balance, you will find it much more difficult to prepare these two accounting statements.

MULTIPLE CHOICE QUESTIONS: SET 1

Each of these multiple choice questions has four suggested answers, (A), (B), (C) and (D). You should read each question and then decide which choice is best, either (A) or (B) or (C) or (D). *Write down your answers on a separate piece of paper.* You will then be able to redo the set of questions later without having to try to ignore your answers.

MC1   Which of the following statements is **incorrect**?

(A)   Assets – Capital = Liabilities
(B)   Liabilities + Capital = Assets
(C)   Liabilities + Assets = Capital
(D)   Assets – Liabilities = Capital

MC2   Which of the following is **not** an asset?

(A)   Buildings
(B)   Cash balance
(C)   Debtors
(D)   Loan from K Harris

MC3   Which of the following is a liability?

(A)   Machinery
(B)   Creditors for goods
(C)   Motor Vehicles
(D)   Cash at Bank

MC4   Which of the following is **incorrect?**

	Assets	Liabilities	Capital
	£	£	£
(A)	7,850	1,250	6,600
(B)	8,200	2,800	5,400
(C)	9,550	1,150	8,200
(D)	6,540	1,120	5,420

MC5   Which of the following statements is correct?

		Effect upon	
		Assets	Liabilities
(A)	We paid a creditor by cheque	–Bank	–Creditors
(B)	A debtor paid us £90 in cash	+Cash	+Debtors
(C)	J Hall lends us £500 by cheque	+Bank	–Loan from Hall
(D)	Bought goods on credit	+Stock	+Capital

MC6   Which of the following are correct?

	Accounts	To record	Entry in the account
(i)	Assets	an increase	Debit
		a decrease	Credit
(ii)	Capital	an increase	Debit
		a decrease	Credit
(iii)	Liabilities	an increase	Credit
		a decrease	Debit

(A)   (i) and (ii)
(B)   (ii) and (iii)
(C)   (i) and (iii)
(D)   (i), (ii) and (iii)

MC7   Which of the following are correct?

		Account to be debited	Account to be credited
(i)	Bought office furniture for cash	Office furniture	Cash
(ii)	A debtor, P Sangster, pays us by cheque	Bank	P Sangster
(iii)	Introduced capital by cheque	Capital	Bank
(iv)	Paid a creditor, B Lee, by cash	B Lee	Cash

(A)   (i), (ii) and (iii) only
(B)   (ii), (iii) and (iv) only
(C)   (i), (ii) and (iv) only
(D)   (i) and (iv) only

MC8 Which of the following are **incorrect**?

		Account to be debited	Account to be credited
(i)	Sold van for cash	Cash	Van
(ii)	Returned some of Office Equipment to Suppliers Ltd	Office Equipment	Suppliers Ltd
(iii)	Repaid part of loan from C Charles by cheque	Loan from C Charles	Bank
(iv)	Bought machinery on credit from Betterways Ltd	Betterways Ltd	Machinery

(A) (ii) and (iv) only
(B) (iii) and (iv) only
(C) (ii) and (iii) only
(D) (i) and (iii) only

MC9 Which of the following best describes the meaning of 'Purchases'?

(A) Items bought
(B) Goods bought on credit
(C) Goods bought for resale
(D) Goods paid for

MC10 Which of the following should not be called 'Sales'?

(A) Office fixtures sold
(B) Goods sold on credit
(C) Goods sold for cash
(D) Sale of item previously included in 'Purchases'

MC11 Of the following, which are correct?

		Account to be debited	Account to be credited
(i)	Goods sold on credit to R Williams	R Williams	Sales
(ii)	S Johnson returns goods to us	Returns inwards	S Johnson
(iii)	Goods bought for cash	Cash	Purchases
(iv)	We returned goods to A Henry	A Henry	Returns inwards

(A) (i) and (iii) only
(B) (i) and (ii) only
(C) (ii) and (iv) only
(D) (iii) and (iv) only

MC12 Which of the following are **incorrect**?

		Account to be debited	Account to be credited
(i)	Goods sold for cash	Cash	Sales
(ii)	Goods bought on credit from T Carter	Purchases	T Carter
(iii)	Goods returned by us to C Barry	C Barry	Returns outwards
(iv)	Van bought for cash	Purchases	Cash

(A) (i) and (iii) only
(B) (iii) only
(C) (ii) and (iv) only
(D) (iv) only

MC13 Given the following, what is the amount of Capital? Assets: Premises £20,000; Stock £8,500; Cash £100. Liabilities: Creditors £3,000; Loan from A Adams £4,000

(A) £21,100
(B) £21,600
(C) £32,400
(D) £21,400

MC14   Which of the following is correct?

(A)   Profit does not alter capital
(B)   Profit reduces capital
(C)   Capital can only come from profit
(D)   Profit increases capital

MC15   Which of the following are correct?

		Account to be debited	Account to be credited
(i)	Received commission by cheque	Bank	Commission received
(ii)	Paid rates by cash	Rates	Cash
(iii)	Paid motor expenses by cheque	Motor expenses	Bank
(iv)	Received refund of insurance by cheque	Insurance	Bank

(A)   (i) and (ii) only
(B)   (i), (ii) and (iii) only
(C)   (ii), (iii) and (iv) only
(D)   (i), (ii) and (iv) only

MC16   Of the following, which are **incorrect**?

		Account to be debited	Account to be credited
(i)	Sold van for cash	Cash	Sales
(ii)	Bought stationery by cheque	Stationery	Bank
(iii)	Took cash out of business for private use	Cash	Drawings
(iv)	Paid general expenses by cheque	General expenses	Bank

(A)   (ii) and (iv) only
(B)   (i) and (ii) only
(C)   (i) and (iii) only
(D)   (ii) and (iii) only

MC17   What is the balance on the following account on 31 May 20X5?

C De Freitas

20X5			£	20X5			£
May	1	Sales	205	May	17	Cash	300
''	14	Sales	360	''	28	Returns	50
''	30	Sales	180				

(A)   A credit balance of £395
(B)   A debit balance of £380
(C)   A debit balance of £395
(D)   There is a nil balance on the account

MC18   What would have been the balance on the account of C De Freitas in MC17 on 19 May 20X5?

(A)   A debit balance of £265
(B)   A credit balance of £95
(C)   A credit balance of £445
(D)   A credit balance of £265

MC19   Which of the following best describes a trial balance?

(A)   Shows the financial position of a business
(B)   It is a special account
(C)   Shows all the entries in the books
(D)   It is a list of balances on the books

MC20   Is it true that the trial balance totals should agree?

(A)   No, there are sometimes good reasons why they differ
(B)   Yes, except where the trial balance is extracted at the year end
(C)   Yes, always
(D)   No, because it is not a balance sheet

REVIEW QUESTIONS

6.1   You are to enter up the necessary accounts for the month of May from the following information relating to a small printing firm. Then balance off the accounts and extract a trial balance as at 31 May 20X6.

20X6
May	1	Started firm with capital in cash of £250.
''	2	Bought goods on credit from the following persons: D Ellis £54; C Mendez £87; K Gibson £25; D Booth £76; L Lowe £64.
''	4	Sold goods on credit to: C Bailey £43; B Hughes £62; H Spencer £176.
''	6	Paid rent by cash £12.
''	9	Bailey paid us his account by cheque £43.
''	10	H Spencer paid us £150 by cheque.
''	12	We paid the following by cheque: K Gibson £25; D Ellis £54.
''	15	Paid carriage by cash £23.
''	18	Bought goods on credit from C Mendez £43; D Booth £110.
''	21	Sold goods on credit to B Hughes £67.
''	31	Paid rent by cheque £18.

6.2   Enter the following transactions of a computer repair shop in the accounts and extract a trial balance as at 31 March 20X6.

20X6
March	1	Started business with £800 in the bank.
''	2	Bought goods on credit from the following persons: K Henriques £76; M Hyatt £27; T Braham £56.
''	5	Cash sales £87.
''	6	Paid wages in cash £14.
''	7	Sold goods on credit to: H Elliott £35; L Lane £42; J Carlton £72.
''	9	Bought goods for cash £46.
''	10	Bought goods on credit from: M Hyatt £57; T Braham £98.
''	12	Paid wages in cash £14.
''	13	Sold goods on credit to: L Lane £32; J Carlton £23.
''	15	Bought shop fixtures on credit from Betta Ltd £50.
''	17	Paid M Hyatt by cheque £84.
''	18	We returned goods to T Braham £20.
''	21	Paid Betta Ltd a cheque for £50.
''	24	J Carlton paid us his account by cheque £95.
''	27	We returned goods to K Henriques £24.
''	30	J King lent us £60 by cash.
''	31	Bought a van paying by cheque £400.

6.3A   Record the following details relating to a games software development business for the month of November 20X7 and extract a trial balance as at 30 November 20X7:

20X7
Nov	1	Started with £5,000 in the bank.
''	3	Bought goods on credit from: T Henriques £160; J Smith £230; W Rogers £400; P Boone £310.
''	5	Cash sales £240.

"	6	Paid rent by cheque £20.
"	7	Paid rates by cheque £190.
"	11	Sold goods on credit to: L Matthews £48; K Allen £32; R Hall £1,170.
"	17	Paid wages by cash £40.
"	18	We returned goods to: T Henriques £14; P Boone £20.
"	19	Bought goods on credit from: P Boone £80; W Rogers £270; D Diaz £130.
"	20	Goods were returned to us by: K Allen £2; L Matthews £4.
"	21	Bought van on credit from U Z Motors £500.
"	23	We paid the following by cheque: T Henriques £146; J Smith £230; W Rogers £300.
"	25	Bought another van, paying by cheque immediately £700.
"	26	Received a loan of £400 cash from A Williams.
"	28	Received cheques from: L Matthews £44; K Allen £30.
"	30	Proprietor brings a further £300 into the business, by a payment into the business bank account.

6.4A   Record the following transactions for the month of January of an antique shop, balance off all the accounts, and then extract a trial balance as at 31 January 20X8:

20X8

Jan	1	Started business with £3,500 cash.
"	2	Put £2,800 of the cash into a bank account.
"	3	Bought goods for cash £150.
"	4	Bought goods on credit from: L Coke £360; M Burton £490; T Hill £110; C Small £340.
"	5	Bought stationery on credit from Swift Ltd £170.
"	6	Sold goods on credit to: S Walters £90; T Binns £150; C Howard £190; P Peart £160.
"	8	Paid rent by cheque £55.
"	10	Bought fixtures on credit from Matalon Ltd £480.
"	11	Paid salaries in cash £120.
"	14	Returned goods to: M Burton £40; T Hill £60.
"	15	Bought van by cheque £700.
"	16	Received loan from J Henry by cheque £600.
"	18	Goods returned to us by: S Walters £20; C Howard £40.
"	21	Cash sales £90.
"	24	Sold goods on credit to: T Binns £100; P Peart £340; J Smart £115.
"	26	We paid the following by cheque: M Burton £450; T Hill £50.
"	29	Received cheques from: J Smart £115; T Binns £250.
"	30	Received a further loan from J Henry by cash £200.
"	30	Received £500 cash from P Peart.

PART 2

The financial statements of sole traders

Introduction

This part is concerned with preparing, from double entry records, the financial statements of sole traders.

CHAPTER 7

Trading and profit and loss accounts: an introduction

After you have studied this chapter, you should be able to:

- explain why profit is calculated
- calculate cost of goods sold, gross profit, and net profit
- explain the difference between gross profit and net profit
- explain the relationship between the trading account and the profit and loss account
- explain how to deal with closing stock when preparing a Trading and Profit and Loss Account
- close down the appropriate accounts and transfer the balances to the trading account
- close down the appropriate accounts and transfer the balances to the profit and loss account
- prepare a Trading and Profit and Loss Account from information given in a trial balance
- make appropriate double entries to incorporate net profit and drawings in the capital account

Introduction

In this chapter, you will learn how to close down revenue and expenditure accounts in order to calculate profit and prepare a Trading and Profit and Loss Account. You will learn how to adjust purchases with stock and arrive at the cost of goods sold, and will discover the difference between gross profit and net profit. You will learn how to prepare a Trading and Profit and Loss Account and, finally, you will learn how to transfer net profit and drawings to the capital account at the end of a period.

7.1 Purpose of trading and profit and loss accounts

The main reason why people set up businesses is to make profits. Of course, if the business is not successful, it may well incur losses instead. The calculation of such profits and losses is probably the most important objective of the accounting function. The owners will want to know how the actual profits compare with the profits they had hoped to make. Knowing what profits are being made helps businesses to do many things, including:

- planning ahead
- obtaining loans from banks, other businesses, or from private individuals

- telling prospective business partners how successful the business is
- telling someone who may be interested in buying the business how successful the business is
- calculating the tax due on the profits so that the correct amount of tax can be paid to the tax authorities.

Chapter 4 dealt with the grouping of revenue and expenses prior to bringing them together to compute profit. In the case of a trader (someone who is mainly concerned with buying and selling goods), the profits are calculated by drawing up a special account called a **Trading and Profit and Loss Account**. Nowadays this is often simply called the 'profit and loss account' but, for now, we'll use the full title.

You may find it easier at this point if you try to remember that the Trading and Profit and Loss Account is a *financial statement*. It is *not* an account in the sense that you have been using the term so far in this book.

7.2 Gross profit

One of the most important uses of trading and profit and loss accounts is that of comparing the results obtained with the results expected. In a trading organisation, a lot of attention is paid to how much profit is made, before deducting expenses, for every £1 of sales revenue. So that this can easily be seen in the profit calculation, the account in which profit is calculated is split into two sections – one in which the **gross profit** is found (this is the **Trading Account** part of the statement), and the next section in which the **net profit** is calculated (this is the 'Profit and Loss' part of the statement).

Gross profit is the excess of sales revenue over the **cost of goods sold**. Where the cost of goods sold is greater than the sales revenue, the result is a **gross loss**. By taking the figure of sales revenue less the cost of goods sold to generate that sales revenue, it can be seen that the accounting custom is to calculate a trader's profits only on goods that have been sold

> ### Activity 7.1
> What does this tell you about the costs and revenues that are included in the calculation of gross profit? (Hint: what do you not include in the calculation?)

To summarise:

Gross profit (calculated in the **Trading Account**)	Is the excess of sales revenue over the cost of goods sold in the period.

7.3 Net profit

Net profit, found in the **Profit and Loss Account**, consists of the gross profit plus any revenue other than that from sales, such as rents received or commissions earned, less the total costs used up during the period other than those already included in the 'cost of goods sold'. Where the costs used up exceed the gross profit plus other revenue, the result is said to be a **net loss**. Thus:

Net profit (calculated in the **Profit and Loss Account**)	Is what is left of the gross profit after all other expenses have been deducted.

7.4 Information needed

Before drawing up a trading and profit and loss account you should prepare the trial balance. This contains nearly all the information needed. (Later on in this book you will see that certain adjustments have to be made, but we will ignore these at this stage.)

We can now look at the trial balance of B Swift, drawn up as on 31 December 20X5 after the completion of his first year in business.

Exhibit 7.1

B Swift
Trial Balance as at 31 December 20X5

	Dr	Cr
	£	£
Sales		3,850
Purchases	2,900	
Rent	240	
Lighting expenses	150	
General expenses	60	
Fixtures and fittings	500	
Debtors	680	
Creditors		910
Bank	1,510	
Cash	20	
Drawings	700	
Capital		2,000
	6,760	6,760

Note: To make this easier to follow, we shall assume that purchases consist of goods that are resold without needing any further work. You'll learn later that these are known as 'finished goods' but, for now, we'll simply refer to them as 'goods'.

We have already seen that gross profit is calculated as follows:

Sales – Cost of Goods Sold = Gross Profit

It would be easier if all purchases in a period were always sold by the end of the same period. In that case, cost of goods sold would always equal purchases. However, this is not normally the case and so we have to calculate the cost of goods sold as follows:

What we bought in the period:	Purchases
Less Goods bought but not sold in the period:	Closing stock
	= Cost of goods sold

In Swift's case, there are goods unsold at the end of the period. However, there is no record in the accounting books of the value of this unsold stock. The only way that Swift can find this figure is by stocktaking at the close of business on 31 December 20X5. To do this he would have to make a list of all the unsold goods and then find out their value. The value he would normally place on them would be the cost price of the goods, i.e. what he paid for them. Let's assume that this is £300.

The cost of goods sold figure will be:

	£
Purchases	2,900
Less Closing stock	(300)
Cost of goods sold	2,600

Based on the sales revenue of £3,850 the gross profit can be calculated:

Sales – Cost of Goods Sold = Gross Profit
£3,850 – £2,600   = £1,250

We now have the information we need to complete the Trading part of the Trading and Profit and Loss Account statement. Next, we need to close off the sales and purchases accounts at the end of the period so that they start the next period with no balance. To do so, we need to create a trading account (this is *not* the same as the trading part of the Trading and Profit and Loss Account, though it does produce the same gross profit figure) and then make the following entries:

The balance of the sales account is transferred to the trading account by:

1 Debiting the sales account (thus closing it).
2 Crediting the trading account.

The balance of the purchases account is transferred to the trading account by:

1 Debiting the trading account.
2 Crediting the purchases account (thus closing it).

There is, as yet, no entry for the closing stock in the double entry accounts. This is achieved as follows:

1 Debit a closing stock account with the value of the closing stock.
2 Credit the trading account (thus completing the double entry).

The trading account will look like this:

Trading

20X5			£	20X5			£
Dec	31	Purchases	2,900	Dec	31	Sales	3,850
				''	31	Closing stock	300

We now close off the trading account in the normal way. In this case, revenues exceed costs so we describe the balance as 'gross profit'.

Trading

20X5			£	20X5			£
Dec	31	Purchases	2,900	Dec	31	Sales	3,850
''	31	Gross profit	1,250	''	31	Closing stock	300
			4,150				4,150

Note that the balance shown on the trading account is described as 'gross profit' rather than being described as a balance. Also, note that the balance (i.e. the gross profit) is not brought down to the next period. The other accounts used in these double entries appear as shown below. (Note that there is no detail of the entries prior to the end of the period as all the information we have been given is the closing balances. These closing balances are simply described here as 'balance'.)

Sales

20X5		£	20X5		£
Dec 31	Trading	3,850	Dec 31	Balance	3,850

Purchases

20X5		£	20X5		£
Dec 31	Balance	2,900	Dec 31	Trading	2,900

Closing Stock

20X5		£	20X5		£
Dec 31	Trading	300	Dec 31	Balance	300

The entry of the closing stock on the credit side of the trading account is, in effect, a deduction from the purchases on the debit side. As you will see when we look later at the Trading and Profit and Loss Account, the closing stock is shown as a deduction from the purchases and the figure then disclosed is described as 'cost of goods sold'.

It must be remembered that we are concerned here with the very first year of trading when, for obvious reasons, there is no opening stock. In Chapter 9, we will examine how to account for stock in the later years of a business.

We can now draw up a profit and loss account (as with the trading account we created, this is not the accounting statement of the same name, but an 'account' opened so that the end of period double entries can be completed). Double entries are then prepared, firstly transferring the gross profit from the trading account to the credit of the profit and loss account. To do this, you would change the entry in the trading account to read 'Gross profit transferred to profit and loss':

Trading

20X5		£	20X5		£
Dec 31	Purchases	2,900	Dec 31	Sales	3,850
'' 31	Gross profit transferred to				
	Profit and loss	1,250	'' 31	Closing stock	300
		4,150			4,150

Then, any revenue account balances, other than sales (which have already been dealt with in the trading account), are transferred to the credit of the profit and loss account. Typical examples are commissions received and rent received. In the case of B Swift, there are no such revenue accounts.

The costs used up in the year, in other words, the expenses of the year are then transferred to the debit of the profit and loss account. (It may also be thought, quite rightly, that as the fixtures and fittings have been used during the year with the subsequent deterioration of the assets, something should be charged for this use. The methods for doing this are left until Chapter 26.)

The profit and loss account will now appear as follows:

Profit and Loss

20X5		£	20X5		£
Dec 31	Rent	240	Dec 31	Gross profit transferred	
'' 31	Lighting expenses	150		from Trading	1,250
'' 31	General expenses	60			
'' 31	Net profit	800			
		1,250			1,250

The expense accounts closed off will now appear as:

Rent

20X5		£	20X5		£
Dec 31 Balance		240	Dec 31 Profit and loss		240

Lighting Expenses

20X5		£	20X5		£
Dec 31 Balance		150	Dec 31 Profit and loss		150

General Expenses

20X5		£	20X5		£
Dec 31 Balance		60	Dec 31 Profit and loss		60

You now have all the information you need in order to prepare the Trading and Profit and Loss Account for the year ending 31 December 20X5. It looks as follows:

Exhibit 7.2

B Swift
Trading and Profit and Loss Account for the year ended 31 December 20X5

	£	£
Sales		3,850
Less Cost of goods sold:		
Purchases	2,900	
Less Closing stock	(300)	
		(2,600)
Gross profit		1,250
Less Expenses		
Rent	240	
Lighting expenses	150	
General expenses	60	
		(450)
Net profit		800

7.5 Effect on the capital account

Although the net profit has been calculated at £800 and is shown as a balancing figure on the debit side of the profit and loss account, no credit entry has yet been made to complete the double entry. In other accounts, the credit entry would normally be the 'balance b/d' at the start of the next period. However, as net profit increases the capital of the owner, the credit entry must be made in the capital account. (You would change the entry in the profit and loss account from 'net profit' to read 'net profit transferred to capital'.)

The trading account and the profit and loss account, and, indeed, all the revenue and expense accounts, can thus be seen to be devices whereby the capital account is saved from being concerned with unnecessary detail. Every sale of a good at a profit increases the capital of the proprietor as does each item of revenue such as rent received. On the other hand, each sale of a good at a loss, or each item of expense, decreases the capital of the proprietor.

Instead of altering the capital after each transaction, the respective items of profit and loss, and of revenue and expense, are collected together using suitably described accounts. Then all the balances are brought together in one financial statement, the 'trading and profit and loss account', and the increase to the capital, i.e. the net profit, is determined. Alternatively, in the case of a net loss, the decrease in the capital is ascertained.

The fact that a separate drawings account has been in use can now also be seen to have been in keeping with the policy of avoiding unnecessary detail in the capital account. There will, therefore, only be one figure for drawings entered in the debit side of the capital account – the total of the drawings for the whole of the period.

The capital account, showing these transfers, and the drawings account now closed are as follows:

Capital

20X5		£	20X5			£
Dec 31	Drawings	700	Jan 1	Cash		2,000
" 31	Balance c/d	2,100	Dec 31	Net profit from		
				Profit and Loss		800
		2,800				2,800
			20X6			
			Jan 1	Balance b/d		2,100

Drawings

20X5		£	20X5		£
Dec 31	Balance	700	Dec 31	Capital	700

7.6 The balances still in our books

It should be noticed that not all the items in the trial balance have been used in the trading and profit and loss account. The remaining balances are assets or liabilities or capital, they are not expenses or sales. These will be used later when a balance sheet is drawn up. (You'll remember learning in Chapter 1 that assets, liabilities and capital are shown in balance sheets.)

Exhibit 7.3 shows the trial balance after the trading and profit and loss accounts have been prepared. All the accounts that were closed off when the trading and profit and loss account was prepared have been removed, and drawings and net profit have been transferred to the capital account. Notice also that the stock account, not originally in the trial balance, is in the redrafted trial balance, as the item was not created as a balance in the books until the trading account was prepared. We will be using this trial balance when we start to look at balance sheets in the next chapter.

Exhibit 7.3

B Swift		
Trial Balance as at 31 December 20X5		
(after the Trading Account and the Profit and Loss Accounts have been completed and the capital account adjusted for net profit and drawings)		
	Dr	*Cr*
	£	£
Fixtures and fittings	500	
Debtors	680	
Creditors		910
Stock	300	
Bank	1,510	
Cash	20	
Capital		2,100
	3,010	3,010

Answer to activity

7.1 You only include the costs that were incurred in creating those goods that were sold. These costs include the cost of buying those goods and any costs incurred in converting goods purchased into the goods that were sold – for example, the costs of converting raw materials into finished goods. The only costs you include are those that relate to the goods sold. The costs relating to goods that have not yet been sold are not included. You do not include other costs of the business, such as postage, motor expenses, office expenses, salaries of managers, and advertising costs. Nor do you include any costs relating to the purchase or use of any assets, such as motor vehicles, computers, machinery, fixtures and fittings, and buildings.

REVIEW QUESTIONS

7.1 From the following trial balance of B Webb, extracted after one year's trading, prepare a trading and profit and loss account for the year ended 31 December 20X6. A balance sheet is not required.

Trial Balance as at 31 December 20X6

	Dr	Cr
	£	£
Sales		18,462
Purchases	14,629	
Salaries	2,150	
Motor expenses	520	
Rent	670	
Insurance	111	
General expenses	105	
Premises	1,500	
Motor vehicles	1,200	
Debtors	1,950	
Creditors		1,538
Cash at bank	1,654	
Cash in hand	40	
Drawings	895	
Capital		5,424
	25,424	25,424

Stock at 31 December 20X6 was £2,548.

(Keep your answer; it will be used later in Question 8.1)

7.2 From the following trial balance of C Worth after his first year's trading, you are required to draw up a trading and profit and loss account for the year ended 30 June 20X8. A balance sheet is not required.

Trial Balance as at 30 June 20X8

	Dr	Cr
	£	£
Sales		28,794
Purchases	23,803	
Rent	854	
Lighting and heating expenses	422	
Salaries and wages	3,164	
Insurance	105	
Buildings	50,000	
Fixtures	1,000	
Debtors	3,166	
Sundry expenses	506	
Creditors		1,206
Cash at bank	3,847	
Drawings	2,400	
Vans	5,500	
Motor running expenses	1,133	
Capital		65,900
	95,900	95,900

Stock at 30 June 20X8 was £4,166.

(Keep your answer; it will be used later in Question 8.2)

7.3A From the following trial balance of F Chaplin drawn up on conclusion of his first year in business, draw up a trading and profit and loss account for the year ended 31 December 20X8. A balance sheet is not required.

Trial Balance as at 31 December 20X8

	Dr	Cr
	£	£
General expenses	210	
Rent	400	
Motor expenses	735	
Salaries	3,560	
Insurance	392	
Purchases	18,385	
Sales		26,815
Motor vehicle	2,800	
Creditors		5,160
Debtors	4,090	
Premises	20,000	
Cash at bank	1,375	
Cash in hand	25	
Capital		24,347
Drawings	4,350	
	56,322	56,322

Stock at 31 December 20X8 was £4,960.

(Keep your answer; it will be used later in Question 8.3A)

7.4A   Extract a trading and profit and loss account for the year ended 30 June 20X8 for F Kidd. The trial balance as at 30 June 20X8 after his first year of trading was as follows:

	Dr	Cr
	£	£
Rent	1,560	
Insurance	305	
Lighting and heating expenses	516	
Motor expenses	1,960	
Salaries and wages	4,850	
Sales		35,600
Purchases	30,970	
Sundry expenses	806	
Vans	3,500	
Creditors		3,250
Debtors	6,810	
Fixtures	3,960	
Buildings	28,000	
Cash at bank	1,134	
Drawings	6,278	
Capital		51,799
	90,649	90,649

Stock at 30 June 20X8 was £9,960.

(Keep your answer; it will be used later in Question 8.4A)

CHAPTER 8

Balance sheets

After you have studied this chapter, you should be able to:

- explain why balance sheets are not part of the double entry system
- explain why it is important that account balances are shown under appropriate headings in the balance sheet
- explain the meanings of the terms fixed asset, current asset, current liability, and long-term liability
- describe the sequence in which each of the five main categories of items appear in the balance sheet
- describe the sequence in which each fixed asset is entered in the balance sheet
- describe the sequence in which each current asset is entered in the balance sheet
- draw up a balance sheet from information given in a trial balance

Introduction

In this chapter, you'll learn how to present asset, liability, and capital balances in a balance sheet and of the importance of adopting a consistent and meaningful layout.

8.1 Contents of the balance sheet

In Chapter 1, you learnt that balance sheets contain details of assets, liabilities and capital. The items and amounts to be entered in the balance sheet are found in the accounting books. As shown in the last chapter, they comprise those **accounts with balances** that were *not* included in the trading and profit and loss account. All these accounts that continue to have balances must be assets, capital or liabilities.

Activity 8.1
Why have the accounts entered into the Trading and Profit and Loss Account been removed from the trial balance? (Hint: it is *not* just because they were entered in that statement.)

8.2 Drawing up a balance sheet

Let's look again at the post-Trading and Profit and Loss Account trial balance of B Swift (from Exhibit 7.3).

Exhibit 8.1

	Dr	Cr
B Swift **Trial Balance as at 31 December 20X5** (after the Trading Account and the Profit and Loss Accounts have been completed and the capital account adjusted for net profit and drawings)		
	£	£
Fixtures and fittings	500	
Debtors	680	
Creditors		910
Stock	300	
Bank	1,510	
Cash	20	
Capital		2,100
	3,010	3,010

You'll probably remember seeing examples of balance sheets in Chapter 1. If not, this would be a good time to spend a few minutes reading that chapter again.

Based on what you learnt in Chapter 1, let's now draw up the balance sheet for B Swift as at 31 December 20X5.

Exhibit 8.2

B Swift
Balance Sheet as at 31 December 20X5

	£
Assets	
Furniture and fittings	500
Stock	300
Debtors	680
Bank	1,510
Cash	20
	3,010
Less liabilities	
Creditors	(910)
	2,100
Capital	2,100

8.3 No double entry in balance sheets

After the way we used the double entry system in the last chapter to prepare the information we needed in order to draw up the Trading and Profit and Loss Account, it may seem very strange to you to learn that balance sheets are *not* part of the double entry system.

Activity 8.2
Why do you think it is that the balance sheet is not part of the double entry system?

When we draw up accounts such as a cash account, rent account, sales account, a trading account, or a profit and loss account, we are writing them up as part of the double entry system. We make entries on the debit side and the credit side of these accounts.

In drawing up a balance sheet, we do not enter anything in the various accounts. We do not actually transfer the fixtures and fittings balance or the creditors balance, or any of the other balances, to the balance sheet.

All we do is to *list* the asset, capital and liabilities balances so as to form a balance sheet. This means that none of these accounts have been closed off. *Nothing is entered in the ledger accounts.*

When the next accounting period starts, these accounts are still open and they all contain balances. As a result of future transactions, entries are then made in these accounts that add to, or deduct from these opening balances using double entry.

If you see the word 'account', you will know that what you are looking at is part of the double entry system and will include debit and credit entries. If the word 'account' is not used, it is not part of double entry. For instance, the following items are not 'accounts', and are therefore *not* part of the double entry:

Trial balance: this is simply a list of the debit and credit balances in the accounts.
Balance sheet: this is a list of balances arranged according to whether they are assets, capital or liabilities and so depict the financial situation on a specific date.

Note: The Trading and Profit and Loss Account is a special case. It is a financial statement and, itself, is not part of the double entry system. However, the Trading *account* and the Profit and Loss *account* which, together, provide the information that is presented in the Trading and Profit and Loss Account *are* individual accounts that *most definitely* lie within the double entry system.

8.4   Balance sheet layout

Have you ever gone into a shop and found that the goods you were interested in were all mixed up and not laid out in a helpful or consistent way? You can see an example of this in most large shops specialising in selling CDs. They mix up some of their stock, particularly anything on 'special offer', so that you need to search through everything in order to find what you want. In the process of doing so, the shop hopes that you will come across other things that you will buy that you would never have thought of buying otherwise. Some of Richard Branson's first Virgin record shops in the early 1970s used this technique and it seems to have developed from there as an effective way to sell music.

Unfortunately, this this mix-up presentation technique would be of no benefit to the users of the balance sheet. They would never find anything they didn't set out to find, but they would still have to go through the hassle of sorting through all the information in order to produce a meaningful balance sheet for themselves. Because the balance sheet is intended to be helpful and informative, rather than everyone having to do this for themselves, we take great care in ensuring that it portrays the information it contains in a consistent and meaningful way.

As a result, not only can a user who is only interested in looking at the balance sheet of one organisation find it easy to find information, other users who look at lots of different balance sheets, such as bank managers, accountants and investors, find it straightforward making comparisons between different balance sheets.

While the balance sheet layout used in Exhibit 8.2 could be considered useful, it can be improved. Let's look at a how we can do this. Firstly, we'll look at how assets could be presented in a more helpful and more meaningful way.

Assets

We are going to show the assets under two headings, fixed assets and current assets.

Fixed assets

Fixed assets are assets that

1 were not bought primarily to be sold; but
2 are to be used in the business; and
3 are expected to be of use to the business for a long time.

Examples: buildings, machinery, motor vehicles, fixtures and fittings.

Fixed assets are listed first in the balance sheet starting with those the business will keep the longest, down to those which will not be kept so long. For instance:

Fixed Assets
1 Land and buildings
2 Fixtures and fittings
3 Machinery
4 Motor vehicles

Current assets

Current assets are assets that are likely to change in the short term and certainly within twelve months of the balance sheet date. They include items held for resale at a profit, amounts owed by debtors, cash in the bank, and cash in hand.

These are listed in increasing order of liquidity. That is, starting with the asset furthest away from being turned into cash, finishing with cash itself. For instance:

Current Assets
1 Stock
2 Debtors
3 Cash at bank
4 Cash in hand

Some students feel that debtors should appear before stock because, at first sight, stock would appear to be more easily realisable (i.e. convertible into cash) than debtors. In fact, debtors could normally be more quickly turned into cash – you can often **factor** them by selling the rights to the amounts owed by debtors to a finance company for an agreed amount.

As all retailers would confirm, it is not so easy to quickly turn stock into cash. Another advantage of using this sequence is that it follows the order in which full realisation of the assets in a business takes place: before there is a sale, there must be a stock of goods which, when sold on credit, turns into debtors and, when payment is made by the debtors, turns into cash.

Liabilities

There are two categories of liabilities, current liabilities and long-term liabilities.

Current liabilities

Current liabilities are items that have to paid within a year of the balance sheet date.

Examples: bank overdrafts, amounts due to creditors for the purchase of goods for resale.

Long-term liabilities

Long-term liabilities are items that have to be paid more than a year after the balance sheet date.

Examples: bank loans, loans from other businesses.

8.5 A properly drawn up balance sheet

Exhibit 8.3 shows Exhibit 8.2 drawn up in better style. Also read the notes following the exhibit.

Exhibit 8.3

B Swift
Balance Sheet as at 31 December 20X5

	£	£
Fixed assets		
Furniture and fittings		500
Current assets		
Stock	300	
Debtors	680	
Bank	1,510	
Cash	20	
	2,510	
Less Current liabilities		
Creditors	(910)	
		1,600
		2,100
Capital		
Cash introduced		2,000
Add Net profit for the year		800
		2,800
Less Drawings		(700)
		2,100

Notes:
(a) There are four categories of entries shown in this balance sheet. In practice, the fifth, long-term liabilities, often appears. It is positioned after the current liabilities; and its total appears as a deduction under the figure depicting the difference between the totals of the fixed and current assets and the current liabilities. Exhibit 8.4 shows where this would be if B Swift had any long-term liabilities.
(b) The figure for each item within each category should be shown and a total for the category produced. An example of this is the £2,510 total of current assets. The figure for each asset is listed, and the total is shown below them.
(c) The total for current liabilities is subtracted from the total for current assets and the net figure is then placed under the figure for fixed assets.
   This net figure is an important one in accounting. It is known as **net current assets** or **working capital** and it shows the amount of resources the business has in a form that is readily convertible into cash.
(d) You do not write the word 'account' after each item.
(e) The owners will be most interested in their capital and the reasons why it has changed during the period. To show only the final balance of £2,100 means that the owners will not know how it was calculated. So we show the full details of the capital account.

(*f*) Look at the date on the balance sheet. Now compare it with the dates put on the top of the trading and profit and loss account in the last chapter. The balance sheet is a position statement – it is shown as being at one point in time, i.e. '*as at* 31 December 20X5'. The trading and profit and loss account is different. It is for a period of time, in this case for a whole year, and so it uses the phrase 'for the year ended 31 December 20X5'.

Exhibit 8.4

B Swift
Balance Sheet as at 31 December 20X5
(showing the position of long-term liabilities and net current assets)

	£	£
Fixed assets		
Furniture and fittings		500
Current assets		
Stock	300	
Debtors	680	
Bank	1,510	
Cash	20	
	2,510	
Less Current liabilities		
Creditors	(910)	
Net current assets		1,600
		2,100
Less Long-term liabilities		(–)
		2,100
Capital		
Cash introduced		2,000
Add Net profit for the year		800
		2,800
Less Drawings		(700)
		2,100

Learning outcomes

You should now have learnt:

1 That all balances remaining on a trial balance after the trading and profit and loss account for a period has been drawn up are displayed in a balance sheet dated 'as at' the last day of the period.

2 That the balance sheet is *not* part of double entry.

3 That the balance sheet starts with fixed assets at the top, then current assets, then current liabilities, then long-term liabilities, then capital.

4 The meanings of the terms fixed asset, current asset, current liability, and long-term liability.

5 That you list fixed assets in descending order starting with those that will remain in use in the business for the longest time.

6 That you list current assets top to bottom in increasing order of liquidity.

7 That current assets less current liabilities is known as 'net current assets' or 'working capital'.

8 Why net current assets is a very important figure.

Answers to activities

8.1   All these accounts should have been closed off when the trading and profit and loss account was completed. Only accounts with balances appear in a trial balance.

8.2   A balance sheet is a financial statement that summarises the position at the end of a period. It contains all the balances on the accounts held in the accounting books at that time. As it is prepared after the Trading and Profit and Loss Account, all the accounts have already been balanced off. All we do with the balance sheet is lift the balances carried forward from the accounts and place them in an appropriate position in the statement.

REVIEW QUESTIONS

8.1   Complete question 7.1 by drawing up a balance sheet as at 31 December 20X6.

8.2   Complete question 7.2 by drawing up a balance sheet as at 30 June 20X8.

8.3A   Complete question 7.3A by drawing up a balance sheet as at 31 December 20X8.

8.4A   Complete question 7.4A by drawing up a balance sheet as at 30 June 20X8.

CHAPTER 9

Trading and profit and loss accounts and balance sheets: further considerations

After you have studied this chapter, you should be able to:

- explain the terms returns inwards, returns outwards, carriage inwards, and carriage outwards
- record returns inwards and returns outwards in the Trading and Profit and Loss Account
- explain the difference between the treatment of carriage inwards and carriage outwards in the Trading and Profit and Loss Account
- explain why carriage inwards is treated as part of the cost of purchasing goods
- explain why carriage outwards is *not* treated as part of the cost of purchasing goods
- prepare a stock account showing the entries for opening and closing stock
- prepare a Trading and Profit and Loss Account and a Balance Sheet containing the appropriate adjustments for returns, carriage, and other items that affect the calculation of the cost of goods sold
- explain why the costs of putting goods into a saleable condition should be charged to the trading account

Introduction

This chapter contains material that *many* students get wrong in examinations. Take care as you work through it to understand and learn the points as they are presented to you.

In this chapter, you'll learn how to treat goods returned from customers and goods returned to suppliers in the trading account. You'll also learn how to deal with the costs of transporting goods into and out of a business. You will learn how to record stock in a stock account and then carry it forward in the account to the next period. You'll also learn how to enter opening stock in the trading account. You'll learn that there are other costs that must be added to the cost of goods in the trading account. Finally, you'll learn how to prepare a Trading and Profit and Loss Account and a Balance Sheet when any of these items are included in the list of balances at the end of a period.

9.1 Returns inwards and returns outwards

In Chapter 3, the idea of different accounts for different movements of stock was introduced. There are four accounts involved. The sales account and the **returns inwards account** deal with goods sold and goods returned by customers. The purchases account and the **returns outwards account** deal with goods purchased and goods returned to the supplier respectively. In our first look at the preparation of a trading account in Chapter 7, returns inwards and returns outwards were omitted. This was done deliberately. so that your first sight of trading and profit and loss accounts would be as straightforward as possible.

> **Activity 9.1**
>
> Why do you think organisations bother with the two returns accounts? Why don't they just debit sales returned to the sales account and credit purchases returned to the purchases account?

Just as you may have done yourself, a large number of businesses return goods to their suppliers (**returns outwards**) and will have goods returned to them by their customers (**returns inwards**). When the gross profit is calculated, these returns will have to come into the calculations. Suppose that in Exhibit 7.1 the trial balance of B Swift, rather than simply containing a sales account balance of £3,850 and a purchases account balance of £2,900 the balances showing stock movements had been:

Exhibit 9.1

B Swift Trial Balance as at 31 December 20X5 (extract)		
	Dr	*Cr*
	£	£
Sales		4,000
Purchases	3,120	
Returns inwards	150	
Returns outwards		220

Comparing the two situations (the one shown in Exhibit 7.1 and the one shown above) they do, in fact, amount to the same thing as far as gross profit is concerned. Sales were £3,850 in the original example. In the amended version, returns inwards should be deducted to get the correct figure for goods sold to customers and *kept* by them, i.e. £4,000 − £150 = £3,850. Purchases were originally shown as being £2,900. In the new version, returns outwards should be deducted to get the correct figure of purchases *kept* by Swift. Both the returns accounts are included in the calculation of gross profit, which now becomes:

> **(Sales less Returns Inwards) − (Cost of Goods Sold less Returns Outwards) = Gross Profit**

The gross profit is, therefore, unaffected and is, as calculated in Chapter 7, £1,250. The trading account will appear as in Exhibit 9.2:

Exhibit 9.2

B Swift
Trading and Profit and Loss Account for the year ended 31 December 20X5

	£	£
Sales		4,000
Less Returns inwards		(150)
		3,850
Less Cost of goods sold:		
Purchases	3,120	
Less Returns outwards	(220)	
	2,900	
Less Closing stock	(300)	
		(2,600)
Gross profit		1,250

9.2   Carriage

If you have ever purchased anything by mail order or over the Internet, you have probably been charged for 'postage and packing'. When goods are delivered by suppliers or sent to customers, the cost of transporting the goods is often an additional charge. In accounting, this charge is called 'carriage'. When it is charged for delivery of goods purchased, it is called **carriage inwards**. Carriage of goods out of a business to its customers is called **carriage outwards**.

When goods are purchased, the cost of carriage inwards may either be included as part of the price, or the business may have to pay separately for it. Suppose your business was buying exactly the same goods from two suppliers. One supplier might sell them for £100 and not charge anything for carriage. Another supplier might sell the goods for £95, but you would have to pay £5 to a courier for carriage inwards, i.e. a total cost of £100. In both cases, the same goods cost you the same total amount. It would not be appropriate to leave out the cost of carriage inwards from the 'cheaper' supplier in the calculation of gross profit, as the real cost to you having the goods available for resale is £100.

As a result, in order to ensure that the true cost of buying goods for resale is *always* included in the calculation of gross profit, carriage inwards is *always* added to the cost of purchases in the trading account.

Carriage outwards is not part of the selling price of our goods. Customers could come and collect the goods themselves, in which case there would be no carriage out expense for us to pay or to recharge to our customers. Carriage outwards is *always* entered in the profit and loss account. It is *never* included in the calculation of gross profit.

Suppose that in the illustration shown in this chapter, the goods had been bought for the same total figure of £3,120 but, in fact, £2,920 was the figure for purchases and £200 for carriage inwards. The trial balance would appear as in Exhibit 9.3.

Exhibit 9.3

B Swift Trial Balance as at 31 December 20X5 (extract)	Dr	Cr
	£	£
Sales		4,000
Purchases	2,920	
Returns inwards	150	
Returns outwards		220
Carriage inwards	200	

The Trading and Profit and Loss Account would then be as shown in Exhibit 9.4:

Exhibit 9.4

B Swift
Trading and Profit and Loss Account for the year ended 31 December 20X5

	£	£
Sales		4,000
Less Returns inwards		(150)
		3,850
Less Cost of goods sold:		
Purchases	2,920	
Less Returns outwards	(220)	
	2,700	
Carriage inwards	200	
	2,900	
Less Closing stock	(300)	
		(2,600)
Gross profit		1,250

It can be seen that the three versions of B Swift's trial balance have all been concerned with the same overall amount of goods bought and sold by the business, at the same overall prices. Therefore, in each case, the same gross profit of £1,250 has been found.

Before you proceed further, attempt Review Questions 9.1 and 9.2A.

9.3 | The second year of a business

At the end of his second year of trading, on 31 December 20X6, B Swift draws up another trial balance.

Exhibit 9.5

B Swift Trial Balance as at 31 December 20X6	Dr	Cr
	£	£
Sales		6,700
Purchases	4,260	
Lighting and heating expenses	190	
Rent	240	
Wages: shop assistant	520	
General expenses	70	
Carriage outwards	110	
Buildings	2,000	
Fixtures and fittings	750	
Debtors	1,200	
Creditors		900
Bank	120	
Cash	40	
Drawings	900	
Capital		3,100
Stock (at 31 December 20X5)	300	
	10,700	10,700

Adjustments needed for stock

So far, we have been looking at new businesses only. When a business starts, it has no stock brought forward. B Swift started in business in 20X5. Therefore, when we were preparing Swift's Trading and Profit and Loss Account for 20X5, there was only closing stock to worry about.

When we prepare the trading and profit and loss account for the second year we can see the difference. If you look back to the Trading and Profit and Loss Account in Exhibit 9.4, you can see there was closing stock of £300. This is the opening stock figure for 20X6 that we will need to incorporate in the trading account. It is also the figure for stock that you can see in the trial balance at 31 December 20X6.

The closing stock for one period is *always* brought forward as the opening stock for the next period.

Swift undertook a stocktake at 31 December 20X6 and valued the closing stock at that date at £550.

We can summarise the opening and closing stock account positions for Swift over the two years as follows:

Trading Account for period ———▶	Year to 31 December 20X5	Year to 31 December 20X6
Opening stock 1.1.20X5 Closing stock 31.12.20X5 Opening stock 1.1.20X6 Closing stock 31.12.20X6	None £300	 £300 £550

Stock account

Before going any further, let's look at the stock account for both years:

Stock

20X5		£	20X5		£
Dec 31	Trading	300	Dec 31	Balance c/d	300
20X6			20X6		
Jan 1	Balance b/d	300	Dec 31	Trading	300
Dec 31	Trading	550	'' 31	Balance c/d	550
		850			850

You can see that in 20X6 there is both a debit and a credit double entry made at the end of the period to the trading account. First, the stock account is credited with the opening stock amount of £300 and the trading account is debited with the same amount. Then, the stock account is debited with the closing stock amount of £550 and the trading account is credited with the same amount.

Thus, while the first year of trading only includes one stock figure in the trading account, for the second year of trading both opening and closing stock figures will be in the calculations.

Let's now calculate the cost of goods sold for 20X6:

	£
Stock of goods at start of year	300
Add Purchases	4,260
Total goods available for sale	4,560
Less What remains at the end of the year (i.e. closing stock)	(550)
Therefore the cost of goods that have been sold is	4,010

We can look at a diagram to illustrate this:

Exhibit 9.6

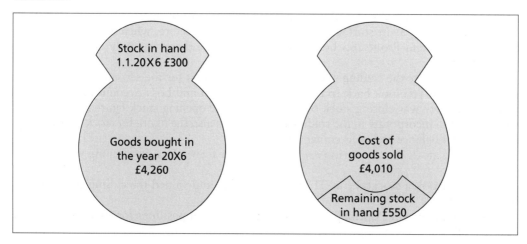

You can see that the left-hand container in the exhibit contains all the stock available to be sold during the year. In the right-hand container, the closing stock at the end of the year is now lying at the bottom and the empty space above it must, therefore, represent the stock that has been sold.

The calculation of gross profit can now be done. You know from the trial balance that sales were £6,700 and from the calculation above that the cost of goods sold was £4,010. Gross profit is, therefore, £2,690.

Now the trading and profit and loss account and the balance sheet can be drawn up, as shown in Exhibits 9.7 and 9.8.

Exhibit 9.7

B Swift
Trading and Profit and Loss Account for the year ended 31 December 20X6

	£	£
Sales		6,700
Less Cost of goods sold:		
Opening stock	300	
Add Purchases	4,260	
	4,560	
Less Closing stock	(550)	
		(4,010)
Gross profit		2,690
Less Expenses:		
Wages	520	
Lighting and heating expenses	190	
Rent	240	
General expenses	70	
Carriage outwards	110	
		(1,130)
Net profit		1,560

Exhibit 9.8

B Swift
Balance Sheet as at 31 December 20X6

	£	£
Fixed assets		
Buildings		2,000
Fixtures and fittings		750
		2,750
Current assets		
Stock	550	
Debtors	1,200	
Bank	120	
Cash	40	
	1,910	
Less Current liabilities		
Creditors	(900)	
		1,010
		3,760
Financed by:		
Capital: Balance at 1 January 20X6		3,100
Add Net profit for the year		1,560
		4,660
Less Drawings		(900)
		3,760

Financial statements

Financial statements is the term given to all the summary statements that accountants produce at the end of accounting periods. They used to be called **final accounts**, but this term is quite misleading (as none of the financial statements are really accounts in the accounting sense). Many people do, however, still refer to them as the 'final accounts' or simply as **the accounts** of a business. You will, therefore, need to be aware of these terms, just in case you read something that uses these terms, or your teacher or lecturer, or an examiner, uses them at some time.

Other expenses in the trading account

You already know that carriage inwards is added to the cost of purchases in the trading account. You also need to add to the cost of goods in the trading account any costs incurred in converting purchases into goods for resale. In the case of a trader, it is very unusual for any additional costs to be incurred getting the goods ready for sale.

> ### Activity 9.2
> What sort of costs do you think a trader may incur that would need to be added to the cost of the goods in the trading account?

For goods imported from abroad it is usual to find that the costs of import duty and insurance are treated as part of the cost of the goods, along with any costs incurred in repackaging the goods. Any such additional costs incurred in getting goods ready for sale are debited to the trading account.

Note: Students often find it difficult to remember how to treat returns and carriage in the Trading and Profit and Loss Account. You need to be sure you learn and remember that all returns, inwards and outwards, and carriage inwards appear in the calculation of gross profit. Carriage outwards appears as an expense in the profit and loss part of the statement.

9.4   A warning

Students lose a lot of marks on the topics covered in this chapter because they assume that the topics are easy and unlikely to be things that they will forget. Unfortunately, they are fairly easy to understand, and that is why they are easily forgotten and confused. You would be wise to make sure that you have understood and learnt everything presented to you in this chapter before you go any further in the book.

9.5   Review questions: the best approach

Before you attempt the review questions at the end of this chapter, you should read the section on review questions in the *Notes for Students* (pp. x–xix).

Learning outcomes

You should now have learnt:

1 That returns *inwards* should be deducted from sales in the *trading* account.

2 That returns *outwards* should be deducted from purchases in the *trading* account.

3 That carriage *inwards* is shown as an expense item in the *trading* account.

4 That carriage *outwards* is shown as an expense in the *profit and loss* account.

5 How to prepare the stock account and carry forward the balance from one period to the next.

6 That in the second and later years of a business, both opening and closing stocks are brought into the trading account.

7 That it is normal practice to show cost of goods sold as a separate figure in the trading account.

8 How to prepare a Trading and Profit and Loss Account that includes the adjustments for carriage inwards and both opening and closing stock in the trading part and carriage outwards as an expense in the profit and loss part.

9 That expense items concerned with getting goods into a saleable condition are charged in the trading account.

10 That where there is import duty or insurance charged on goods purchased, these costs are treated as part of the cost of goods sold.

Answers to activities

9.1 Organisations want to know how much they sold as a separate item from how much of those goods sold were returned. The same goes for purchases and the goods sent back to the supplier. It is useful to know what proportion of goods sold are returned and whether there is any pattern in which customers are returning them. On the purchases side, knowing how many times goods have been returned and the proportion of purchases from individual suppliers that are being returned helps with monitoring the quality of the goods being purchased. While this information could be gathered if returns accounts were not used, it would be a more messy task obtaining it. Most of all, however, the sales account is a revenue account. Entering returns inwards amounts in the sales account is contrary to the nature of the sales account. The same holds for the purchases account, which is an expense account, and returns outwards.

9.2 In the case of a trader, it is very unusual for any additional costs to be incurred getting the goods ready for sale. However, a trader who sells clocks packed in boxes might buy the clocks from one supplier, and the boxes from another. Both of these items would be charged in the trading account as purchases. In addition, if someone was paid to pack the clocks into the boxes, then the wages paid for that to be done would also be charged in the trading account as part of the cost of those goods. Be careful not to confuse this with the wages of shop assistants who sell the clocks. Those wages *must* be charged in the profit and loss account because they are selling costs rather than extra costs incurred getting the goods ready for sale. The wages of the person packing the clocks would be the only wages in this case that were incurred while 'putting the goods into a saleable condition'.

REVIEW QUESTIONS

9.1 From the following information, draw up the trading account of T Clarke for the year ended 31 December 20X7, which was his first year in business:

	£
Carriage inwards	670
Returns outwards	495
Returns inwards	890
Sales	38,742
Purchases	33,333
Stocks of goods: 31 December 20X7	7,489

9.2A The following information is available for the year ended 31 March 20X8. Draw up the trading account of K Taylor for that year.

	£
Stocks: 31 March 20X8	18,504
Returns inwards	1,372
Returns outwards	2,896
Purchases	53,397
Carriage inwards	1,122
Sales	54,600

9.3 From the following trial balance of R Graham, draw up a trading and profit and loss account for the year ended 30 September 20X9, and a balance sheet as at that date.

	Dr	Cr
	£	£
Stock 1 October 20X8	2,368	
Carriage outwards	200	
Carriage inwards	310	
Returns inwards	205	
Returns outwards		322
Purchases	11,874	
Sales		18,600
Salaries and wages	3,862	
Rent	304	
Insurance	78	
Motor expenses	664	
Office expenses	216	
Lighting and heating expenses	166	
General expenses	314	
Premises	5,000	
Motor vehicles	1,800	
Fixtures and fittings	350	
Debtors	3,896	
Creditors		1,731
Cash at bank	482	
Drawings	1,200	
Capital		12,636
	33,289	33,289

Stock at 30 September 20X9 was £2,946.

9.4   The following trial balance was extracted from the books of B Jackson on 30 April 20X7. From it, and the note about stock, prepare his trading and profit and loss account for the year ended 30 April 20X7, and a balance sheet as at that date.

	Dr	Cr
	£	£
Sales		18,600
Purchases	11,556	
Stock 1 May 20X6	3,776	
Carriage outwards	326	
Carriage inwards	234	
Returns inwards	440	
Returns outwards		355
Salaries and wages	2,447	
Motor expenses	664	
Rent	576	
Sundry expenses	1,202	
Motor vehicles	2,400	
Fixtures and fittings	600	
Debtors	4,577	
Creditors		3,045
Cash at bank	3,876	
Cash in hand	120	
Drawings	2,050	
Capital		12,844
	34,844	34,844

Stock at 30 April 20X7 was £4,998.

9.5A   The following is the trial balance of J Smailes as at 31 March 20X9. Draw up a set of financial statements for the year ended 31 March 20X9.

	Dr	Cr
	£	£
Stock 1 April 20X8	18,160	
Sales		92,340
Purchases	69,185	
Carriage inwards	420	
Carriage outwards	1,570	
Returns outwards		640
Wages and salaries	10,240	
Rent and rates	3,015	
Communication expenses	624	
Commissions payable	216	
Insurance	405	
Sundry expenses	318	
Buildings	20,000	
Debtors	14,320	
Creditors		8,160
Fixtures	2,850	
Cash at bank	2,970	
Cash in hand	115	
Drawings	7,620	
Capital		50,888
	152,028	152,028

Stock at 31 March 20X9 was £22,390.

9.6A   L Stokes drew up the following trial balance as at 30 September 20X8. You are to draft the trading and profit and loss account for the year ended 30 September 20X8 and a balance sheet as at that date.

	Dr	Cr
	£	£
Capital		30,955
Drawings	8,420	
Cash at bank	3,115	
Cash in hand	295	
Debtors	12,300	
Creditors		9,370
Stock 30 September 20X7	23,910	
Van	4,100	
Office equipment	6,250	
Sales		130,900
Purchases	92,100	
Returns inwards	550	
Carriage inwards	215	
Returns outwards		307
Carriage outwards	309	
Motor expenses	1,630	
Rent	2,970	
Telephone charges	405	
Wages and salaries	12,810	
Insurance	492	
Office expenses	1,377	
Sundry expenses	284	
	171,532	171,532

Stock at 30 September 20X8 was £27,475.

CHAPTER 10

Accounting concepts

Learning objectives

After you have studied this chapter, you should be able to:

- describe the assumptions which are made when recording accounting data
- explain why one set of accounts has to serve many purposes
- explain what is meant by objectivity and subjectivity
- explain what accounting standards are and why they exist
- explain the underlying concepts of accounting
- explain how the further overriding concepts of materiality, going concern, consistency, prudence, accruals, separate determination and substance over form affect the recording and adjustment of accounting data and the reporting of accounting information

Introduction

What you have been reading about so far has been concerned with the recording of transactions in the books. Such recording has been based on certain assumptions. Quite deliberately, these assumptions were not discussed in detail at the time. This is because it is much easier to look at them with a greater understanding *after* basic double entry has been covered. These assumptions are known as the *concepts of accounting*.

The trading and profit and loss accounts and balance sheets shown in the previous chapters were drawn up for the owner of the business. As shown later in the book, businesses are often owned by more than just one person and these accounting statements are for the use of all the owners.

If the financial statement were solely for the use of the owner(s), there would be no need to adopt a common framework for the preparation and presentation of the information contained within them. However, as you learnt at the start of this book, there are a lot of other people who may be interested in seeing these financial statements. It is for this reason that there has to be a commonly established practice concerning how the information in the financial statements is prepared and presented. In this chapter, you will learn about some of the agreed practices that underpin the preparation of accounting information, and about some of the regulations that have been developed to ensure that they are adhered to.

10.1 One set of final accounts for all purposes

If it had always been the custom to draft different kinds of financial statements for different purposes, so that one type was given to a banker, another type to someone wishing to buy the business, etc., then accounting would be very different from what it is today. However, this has not occurred. Identical copies of the financial statements are given to all the different stakeholders, irrespective of why they wish to look at them.

This means that the banker, the prospective buyer of the business, the owner and the other people all see the same trading and profit and loss account and balance sheet. This is not an ideal situation as the interests of each party are different and each party seeks different kinds of information from those wanted by the others. For instance, the bank manager would really like to know how much the assets would sell for if the business ceased trading. She could then see what the possibility would be of the bank obtaining repayment of its loan or the overdraft. Other people would also like to see the information in the way that is most useful to them.

Activity 10.1

This doesn't sound very ideal for anyone, does it? What benefits do you think there may be that outweigh these disadvantages of one set of financial statements for all?

Because everyone receives the same trading and profit and loss account and balance sheet, in order to be of any use, all the various stakeholders have to believe that the assumptions upon which the financial statements are based are valid and appropriate. If they don't, they won't trust the financial statements.

Assume that you are in a class of students and that you have the problem of valuing your assets, which consist of 10 textbooks. The first value you decide is based upon how much you could sell them for. Your own guess is £30, but the other members of your class may suggest they should be valued at anything from £15 to £50.

Suppose that you now decide to put a value on their use to you. You may well think that the use of these textbooks will enable you to pass your examinations and so you will get a good job. Another person may have the opposite idea concerning the use of the textbooks. The use value placed on the textbooks by others in the class will be quite different. Again, your value may be higher than those of some of your colleagues and lower than others.

Finally, you decide to value them by reference to cost. You take out the receipts you were given when you purchased the textbooks, which show that you paid a total of £60 for them. If the rest of the class does not think that you have altered the receipts, then they will all agree with you that the value, expressed at original cost, is £60. At last, you have found a way of valuing the textbooks where everyone agrees on the same figure. As this is the only valuation that you can all agree upon, each of you decides to use the idea of valuing the asset of textbooks at their cost price so that you can have a meaningful discussion about what you are worth (in terms of your assets, i.e. your textbooks) compared with everyone else in the class. It probably won't come as a surprise to you to learn that this is precisely the basis upon which the assets of a business are valued. Accountants call it the **historical cost concept**.

10.2 Objectivity and subjectivity

The use of a method which arrives at a value that everyone can agree to *because it is based upon a factual occurrence* – in the above example, the amount you paid for your textbooks – is said to be **objective**. Valuing assets at their cost to you is, therefore, objective – you are adhering to and accepting the facts. You are not placing your own interpretation on the facts. As a result, everyone else knows where the value came from and can see that there is very good evidence to support its adoption.

If, instead of being objective, you were **subjective**, you would use your own judgement to arrive at a cost. This often results in the value you arrive at being biased towards your own views and preferences – as in the example above when the usefulness of the textbooks to you for examinations was the basis of their valuation. Subjective valuations seem right to the person who makes them, but most other people would probably disagree with the value arrived at, because it won't appear to them to be objectively based.

The desire to provide the same set of financial statements for many different parties, and so provide a basis for measurement that is generally acceptable, means that objectivity is sought in financial accounting. If you are able to understand this desire for objectivity, then many of the apparent contradictions in accounting can be understood because it (objectivity) is at the heart of the financial accounting methods in use at the present time.

Financial accounting, therefore, seeks objectivity and it seeks consistency in how information is prepared and presented. To achieve this, there must be a set of rules which lay down the way in which the transactions of the business are recorded. These rules have long been known as 'accounting concepts'. A group of these have become known as 'fundamental accounting concepts' (also referred to as 'accounting principles') and have been enforced through their incorporation in accounting standards issued on behalf of the accountancy bodies and by their inclusion in the relevant legislation governing companies, the Companies Acts.

10.3 Accounting Standards and Financial Reporting Standards

At one time, there used to be quite wide differences in the ways that accountants calculated profits. In the late 1960s a number of cases led to a widespread outcry against this lack of uniformity in accounting practice.

In response, the accounting bodies formed the Accounting Standards Committee. It issued a series of accounting standards, called **Statements of Standard Accounting Practice** (SSAPs). The ASC was replaced in 1990 by the Accounting Standards Board, which also issued accounting standards, this time called **Financial Reporting Standards** (FRSs). Both forms of accounting standards are compulsory, enforced by company law.

By the end of 2001, nineteen FRSs had been issued and ten of the SSAPs were still in force. From time to time, the ASB also issues **Urgent Issue Task Force** Abstracts (UITFs). These are generally intended to be in force only while a standard is being prepared or an existing standard amended to cover the topic dealt with in the UITF. Of course, some issues do not merit a full standard and so most of the thirty UITFs issued to date are still in force. UITFs carry the same weight as accounting standards and their application is compulsory.

In November 1997, the ASB issued a third category of standard – the *Financial Reporting Standard for Smaller Entities* (FRSSE). SSAPs and FRSs had generally been developed with the larger company in mind. The FRSSE was the ASB's response to the view that smaller entities should not have to apply all the cumbersome rules contained in the SSAPs and FRSs. It is, in effect, a collection of some of the rules from virtually all the other accounting standards. Small entities can choose whether to apply it or, as seems unlikely, continue to apply all the other accounting standards.

The authority, scope and application of each document issued by the ASB is announced when the document is issued. Thus, even though each accounting standard and UITF must be applied by anyone preparing financial statements, in some cases certain classes of organisations are exempted from applying some or all of the rules contained within them. You can find out more about the work of the ASB and the standards and UITFs currently in issue at their website:

www.asb.org.uk/technical/statements.html

The use of accounting standards does not mean that two identical businesses will show exactly the same revenue, expenditure and profits year by year in their financial statements. It does, however, considerably reduce the possibilities of very large variations in financial reporting.

10.4 Accounting Standards and the legal framework

Accounting standards are drafted so that they comply with the laws of the United Kingdom and the Republic of Ireland. They also comply with European Union Directives. This is all to ensure that there is no conflict between the law and accounting standards. Anyone preparing financial statements which are intended to show a 'true and fair view' (i.e. truly reflect what has occurred and the financial position of the organisation) must observe the rules laid down in the accounting standards.

10.5 Underlying accounting concepts

A number of accounting concepts have been applied ever since financial statements were first produced for external reporting purposes. These have become second nature to accountants and are not generally reinforced, other than through custom and practice.

The historical cost concept

The need for this has already been described in the textbook valuation example. It means that assets are normally shown at cost price, and that this is the basis for valuation of the asset.

The money measurement concept

Accounting information has traditionally been concerned only with those facts covered by (*a*) and (*b*) which follow:

(*a*) it can be measured in monetary units, and
(*b*) most people will agree to the monetary value of the transaction.

This limitation is referred to as the **money measurement concept**, and it means that accounting can never tell you everything about a business. For example, accounting does not show the following:

(*c*) whether the business has good or bad managers,
(*d*) whether there are serious problems with the workforce,
(*e*) whether a rival product is about to take away many of the best customers,
(*f*) whether the government is about to pass a law which will cost the business a lot of extra expense in future.

The reason that (*c*) to (*f*) or similar items are not recorded is that it would be impossible to work out a monetary value for them which most people would agree to.

Some people think that accounting and financial statements tell you everything you want to know about a business. The above shows that this is not the case.

The business entity concept

The **business entity concept** implies that the affairs of a business are to be treated as being quite separate from the non-business activities of its owner(s).

The items recorded in the books of the business are, therefore, restricted to the transactions of the business. No matter what activities the proprietor(s) get up to outside the business, they are completely disregarded in the books kept by the business.

The only time that the personal resources of the proprietor(s) affect the accounting records of a business is when they introduce new capital into the business, or take drawings out of it.

The dual aspect concept

This states that there are two aspects of accounting, one represented by the assets of the business and the other by the claims against them. The concept states that these two aspects are always equal to each other. In other words, this is the alternate form of the accounting equation:

$$\boxed{\text{Assets} = \text{Capital} + \text{Liabilities}}$$

As you know, double entry is the name given to the method of recording transactions under the **dual aspect concept.**

The time interval concept

One of the underlying principles of accounting, the **time interval concept**, is that financial statements are prepared at regular intervals of one year. For internal management purposes they may be prepared far more frequently, possibly on a monthly basis or even more frequently.

10.6 Fundamental accounting concepts

These comprise a set of concepts considered so important that they have been enforced through accounting standards and/or through the Companies Acts. Five have been enforced through the Companies Act 1985, and a sixth through an accounting standard, FRS 5 (*Reporting the substance of transactions*).

The five enforced through the Companies Act are the going concern concept, the consistency concept, the prudence concept, the accruals concept, and the separate determination concept.

1 Going concern

The **going concern concept** implies that the business will continue to operate for the foreseeable future. It means that it is considered sensible to keep to the use of the historical cost concept when arriving at the valuations of assets.

Suppose, however, that a business is drawing up its final accounts at 31 December 20X8. Normally, using the historical cost concept, the assets would be shown at a total value of £100,000. It is known, however, that the business will be forced to close down in February 20X9, only two months later, and the assets are expected to be sold for only £15,000.

In this case it would not make sense to keep to the going concern concept, and so we can reject the historical cost concept for asset valuation purposes. In the balance sheet at 31 December 20X8 the assets will therefore be shown at the figure of £15,000. Rejection of the going concern concept is the exception rather than the rule.

Examples where the going concern assumption should be rejected are:

- if the business is going to close down in the near future;
- where shortage of cash makes it almost certain that the business will have to cease trading;
- where a large part of the business will almost certainly have to be closed down because of a shortage of cash.

2 Consistency

Even if we do everything already listed under the concepts, there will still be quite a few different ways in which items could be recorded. This is because there can be different interpretations as to the exact meaning of a concept.

Each business should try to choose the methods which give the most reliable picture of the business.

This cannot be done if one method is used in one year and another method in the next year, and so on. Constantly changing the methods would lead to misleading profits being calculated from the accounting records. Therefore the convention of consistency is used. The **consistency concept** says that when a business has once fixed a method for the accounting treatment of an item, it will enter all similar items that follow in exactly the same way.

However, it does not mean that the business has to follow the method until the business closes down. A business can change the method used, but such a change is not made without a lot of consideration. When such a change occurs and the profits calculated in that year are affected by a material amount (i.e. one that makes a noticeable difference to the figures shown in the financial statements) then, either in the profit and loss account itself or in one of the reports that accompany it, the effect of the change should be stated.

3 Prudence

Very often accountants have to use their judgement to decide which figure to take for an item. Suppose a debt has been owing for quite a long time, and no one knows whether it will ever be paid. Should the accountant be an optimist in thinking that it will be paid, or be more pessimistic?

It is the accountant's duty to see that people get the proper facts about a business. The accountant should make certain that assets are not valued too highly. Similarly, liabilities should not be shown at values that are too low. Otherwise, people might inadvisedly lend money to a business, which they would not do if they had been provided with the proper facts.

The accountant should always exercise caution when dealing with uncertainty while, at the same time, ensuring that the financial statements are neutral – that gains and losses are neither overstated nor understated – and this is known as **prudence**.

It is true that, in applying the prudence concept, an accountant will normally make sure that all losses are recorded in the books, but that profits and gains will not be anticipated by recording them before they should be recorded. Although it emphasises neutrality, many people feel that the prudence concept means that accountants will normally take the figure relating to unrealised profits and gains which will understate rather than overstate the profit for a period. That is, they believe that accountants tend to choose figures that will cause the capital of the business to be shown at a lower amount rather than at a higher amount.

Activity 10.2

Do you agree with this view that the prudence concept results in accountants producing financial statements that understate profits and gains and therefore present a value for capital that is lower than it should be? Justify your answer.

The recognition of profits at an appropriate time has long been recognised as being in need of guidelines and these have long been enshrined in what is known as the **realisation concept**. This is not so much a separate concept. Rather, it is a part of the broader concept of prudence. Its meaning was clarified by FRS 18, which was issued in 2000 and superseded SSAP 2, the accounting standard that first laid down most of the accounting concepts in use today.

The realisation concept holds to the view that profit and gains can only be taken into account when realisation has occurred and that realisation occurs only when the ultimate cash realised is capable of being assessed (i.e. determined) with reasonable certainty. Several criteria have to be observed before realisation can occur:

- goods or services are provided for the buyer;
- the buyer accepts liability to pay for the goods or services;
- the monetary value of the goods or services has been established;
- the buyer will be in a situation to be able to pay for the goods or services.

Notice that it is not the time

- when the order is received, or
- when the customer pays for the goods.

However, it is only when you can be reasonably certain as to how much will be received that you can recognise profits or gains.

Of course, recognising profits and gains now that will only be 100 per cent known in future periods is unlikely to ever mean that the correct amount has been recognised. Misjudgements can arise when, for example, profit is recognised in one period, only to discover later that this was incorrect because the goods involved have been returned in a later period because of some deficiency. Also, where services are involved rather than goods, the services might turn out to be subject to an allowance being given in a later period owing to poor performance.

Activity 10.3
What do you think the accountant should do about these possibilities when applying the realisation concept?

The accountant needs to take every possibility into account yet, at the same time, the prudence concept requires that the financial statements are 'neutral', that is, that neither gains nor losses should be overstated or understated.

As you will see if you take your studies to a more advanced stage, there are times other than on completion of a sale when profit may be recognised. These could include profits on long-term contracts spanning several years, such as the building of a hotel or a very large bridge. In this case, profit might be calculated for each year of the contract, even though the work is not finished at that date.

4 The accruals concept

The **accruals concept** says that net profit is the difference between revenues and the expenses incurred in generating those revenues, i.e.

$$\text{Revenues} - \text{Expenses} = \text{Net Profit}$$

Determining the expenses used up to obtain the revenues is referred to as *matching* expenses against revenues. The key to the application of the concept is that all income and charges relating to the financial period to which the financial statements relate should be taken into account without regard to the date of receipt or payment.

This concept is particularly misunderstood by people who have not studied accounting. To many of them, actual payment of an item in a period is taken as being matched against the revenue of the period when the net profit is calculated. The fact that expenses consist of the assets used up in a particular period in obtaining the revenues of that period, and that cash paid in a period and expenses of a period are usually different, as you will see later, comes as a surprise to a great number of them.

5 Separate determination

In determining the aggregate amount of each asset or liability, the amount of each individual asset or liability should be determined separately from all other assets and liabilities. For example, if you have three machines, the amount at which machinery is shown in the balance sheet should be the sum of the values calculated individually for each of the three machines. Only when individual values have been derived should a total be calculated.

This concept is, perhaps, best described in relation to potential gains and potential losses. If a business is being sued by a customer for £10,000 and there is a high probability that the business will lose the case, the prudence concept requires the £10,000 to be included as a liability in the financial statements. The same business may, itself, be suing a supplier for £6,000 and may have a good probability of winning the case. It might be tempting to offset the two claims, leaving a net liability of £4,000 to appear in the financial statements. Yet, this would be contrary to the realisation concept which would not allow the probable £6,000 gain to be realised until it was viewed with reasonable certainty that it was going to be received. The **separate determination concept** prohibits the netting-off of potential liabilities and potential gains. As a result, only the probable £10,000 expense would be recognised in the financial statements.

The remaining fundamental accounting concept, that of **substance over form**, was established by the issue of FRS 5.

6 Substance over form

It can happen that the legal form of a transaction can differ from its real substance. Where this happens, accounting should show the transaction in accordance with its real substance which is, basically, how the transaction affects the economic situation of the business. This means that accounting in this instance will not reflect the exact legal position concerning that transaction.

You have not yet come across the best and easiest illustration of this concept. Later in your studies you may have to learn about accounting for fixed assets being bought on hire purchase. We will take a car as an example.

- From a legal point of view, the car does not belong to the business until all the hire purchase instalments have been paid, and an option has been taken up whereby the business takes over legal possession of the car.
- From an economic point of view, you have used the car for business purposes, just as any other car owned by the business which was paid for immediately has been used. In this case, the business will show the car being bought on hire purchase in its ledger accounts and balance sheet as though it were legally owned by the business, but also showing separately the amount still owed for it.

In this way, therefore, the substance of the transaction has taken precedence over the legal form of the transaction.

10.7 Materiality

The accounting concepts already discussed have become accepted in the business world, their assimilation having taken place over many years. However, there is one overriding rule applied to anything that appears in a financial accounting statement – that of **materiality** – it should be 'material'. That is, it should be of interest to the stakeholders, those people who make use of financial accounting statements. It need not be material to every stakeholder, but it must be material to a stakeholder before it merits inclusion.

Accounting does not serve a useful purpose if the effort of recording a transaction in a certain way is not worthwhile. Thus, if a box of paper-clips was bought it would be used up over a period of time, and this cost is used up every time someone uses a paper-clip. It is possible to record this as an expense every time a paper-clip is used but, obviously, the price of a paper-clip is so small that it is not worth recording it in this fashion, nor is the entire box of paper-clips. The paper-clips are not a material item and, therefore, the box would be charged as an expense in the period it was bought, irrespective of the fact that it could last for more than one accounting period. In other words, do not waste your time in the elaborate recording of trivial items.

Similarly, the purchase of a cheap metal ashtray would also be charged as an expense in the period it was bought because it is not a material item, even though it may in fact last for twenty years. A lorry would, however, be deemed to be a material item in most businesses, and so, as will be seen in Chapter 26, an attempt is made to charge each period with the cost consumed in each period of its use.

> *Activity 10.4*
> Which fundamental accounting concept is what is being described in the previous paragraph an example of?

Businesses fix all sorts of arbitrary rules to determine what is material and what is not. There is no law that lays down what these should be – the decision as to what is material and what is not is dependent upon judgement. A business may well decide that all items under £100 should be treated as expenses in the period in which they were bought, even though they may well be in use in the business for the following ten years. Another business, especially a large one, may fix the limit at £1,000. Different limits may be set for different types of item.

It can be seen that the size and the type of business will affect the decisions as to which items are material. With individuals, an amount of £1,000 may well be more than you, as a student, possess. For a multi-millionaire, what is a material item and what is not will almost certainly not be comparable. Just as individuals vary, then, so do businesses. Some businesses have a great deal of machinery and may well treat all items of machinery costing less than £1,000 as not being material, whereas another business which makes about the same amount of profit, but has very little machinery, may well treat a £600 machine as being a material item as they have fixed their materiality limit at £250.

10.8 The assumption of the stability of currency

You don't have to be very old to remember that a few years ago many goods could be bought with less money than today. If you listen to any older relative, you are likely to hear many stories of how little this item or the other could be bought for x years ago. The currencies of the countries of the world are not stable in terms of what each unit of currency can buy over the years.

Accounting, however, uses the historical cost concept, which states that the asset is normally shown at its cost price. This means that accounting statements will be distorted because assets will be bought at different points in time at the price then ruling, and the figures totalled up to show the value of the assets in cost terms. For instance, suppose that you had bought a building twenty years ago for £20,000. You now decide to buy an identical additional building, but the price has now risen to £40,000. You buy it, and the buildings account now shows buildings at a figure of £60,000. One building is measured cost-wise in terms of the currency of twenty years ago, while the other is taken at today's currency value. The figure of a total of £60,000 is historically correct, but, other than that, the total figure cannot be said to be particularly valid for any other use.

This means that to make a correct assessment of accounting statements one must bear in mind the distorting effects of changing price levels upon the accounting entries as recorded. There are techniques for adjusting accounts so as to try and eliminate these distortions, but they fall outside the scope of this book and are dealt with in *Business Accounting 2*.

10.9 FRS 18

SSAP 2 was the first accounting standard to cover the disclosure of accounting policies which include accounting concepts. It dealt with four of the fundamental accounting concepts, going concern, accruals, consistency, and prudence. When FRS 18 was issued in 2000, it superseded SSAP 2. One change it brought concerned the clarification of what was meant by 'realisation' and so clarified the position concerning recognition of profits and gains. The other main change it introduced was to amend the SSAP 2 definition of prudence by stating that financial statements must be neutral. Various matters dealt with in this standard have not yet been examined, and are covered in later chapters. A fuller discussion of FRS 18 is left until Chapter 47.

10.10 Accounting concepts in action

This is too early a stage in your studies for you to be able to appreciate more fully how the concepts work in practice. It is far better left towards the end of this book and, therefore, we consider it in Chapter 47.

Learning outcomes

You should now have learnt:

1 Why one set of financial statements has to serve many purposes.
2 Why the need for general agreement has given rise to the concepts and conventions that govern accounting.
3 What is meant by objectivity and subjectivity.
4 What accounting standards are and why they exist.
5 The assumptions which are made when recording accounting data.
6 The underlying concepts of accounting.
7 How the further overriding concepts of materiality, going concern, consistency, prudence, accruals, separate determination and substance over form affect the recording and adjustment of accounting data and the reporting of accounting information.
8 That an assumption is made that monetary measures remain stable, i.e. that normally accounts are not adjusted for inflation or deflation.

Answers to activities

10.1 Although this is hardly ideal, at least everyone receives the same basic financial information concerning an organisation and, because all financial statements are prepared in the same way, comparison between them is reasonably straightforward. Also, some of the users of these financial statements have other sources of information, financial and otherwise, about a business – the banker, for example, will also have access to the accounts produced for use by the managers of the business. These 'management accounts' are considerably more detailed than the financial statements and most bankers insist upon access to them when large sums of money are involved. The banker will also have information about other businesses in the same industry and about the state of the market in which the business operates, and will thus be able to compare the performance of the business against those of its competitors.

10.2 Although accountants do include all the losses that have been identified in the financial statements, they also include all the gains that can be identified with reasonable certainty. In effect, by doing so, an accountant is being neutral and so, in practice, the amount of capital shown in the balance sheet should be a true reflection of the position as known when the financial statements were produced.

10.3 When applying the realisation concept, the accountant will endeavour to estimate as accurately as possible the returns or allowances that are reasonably likely to arise and will build that information into the calculation of the profit and gains to be recognised in the period for which financial statements are being prepared.

10.4 The accruals concept.

REVIEW QUESTIONS

10.1 What is meant by the 'money measurement concept'?

10.2 Explain the concept of prudence in relation to the recognition of profits and losses.

10.3 Explain the term 'materiality' as it is used in accounting.

PART 3

Books of original entry

Introduction

This part is concerned with the books into which transactions are first entered; it also includes chapters on VAT and on employees' pay, and two chapters on computers and computerised accounting systems.

CHAPTER 11

Books of original entry and ledgers

Learning objectives

After you have studied this chapter, you should be able to:

- justify the need for books of original entry
- explain what each book of original entry is used for
- describe the process of recording transactions in a book of original entry and then recording a summary of the transactions involving similar items in a ledger
- distinguish between personal and impersonal accounts
- list the ledgers most commonly used and distinguish between those that are used for personal accounts and those that are used for impersonal accounts
- explain the broader role of an accountant, the communicator role that lies beyond the recording and processing of data about transactions

Introduction

In this chapter, you will learn about the books in which details of accounting transactions are recorded. You will learn that Day Books and Journals are used to record all transactions made on credit and that the Cash Book is used to record all cash and bank transactions. Then, you will learn that these entries are transferred from the books of original entry to a set of books called Ledgers and that each Ledger is for a particular type of item and that, by having a set of Ledgers, entries in accounts of items of a similar nature are recorded in the same place.

11.1 The growth of the business

When a business is very small, all the double entry accounts can be kept in one book, which we would call a 'ledger'. As the business grows it would be impossible just to use one book, as the large number of pages needed for a lot of transactions would mean that the book would be too big to handle. Also, suppose we have several bookkeepers. They could not all do their work properly if there were only one ledger.

The answer to this problem is for us to use more books. When we do this, we put similar types of transactions together and have a book for each type. In each book, we will not mix together transactions which are different from one another.

11.2 Books of original entry

When a transaction takes place, we need to record as much as possible of the details of the transaction. For example, if we sold four computers on credit to a Mr De Souza for £1,000 plus VAT of £175 per computer, we would want to record that we sold four computers for £1,000 plus VAT of £175 each to Mr De Souza on credit. We would also want to record the address and contact information of Mr De Souza and the date of the transaction. Some businesses would also record information like the identity of the person who sold them to Mr De Souza and the time of the sale.

Books of original entry are the books in which we first record transactions, such as the sale of the four computers. We have a separate book for each kind of transaction.

Thus, the nature of the transaction affects which book it is entered into. Sales will be entered in one book, purchases in another book, cash in another book, and so on. We enter transactions in these books recording:

- the date on which each transaction took place – the transactions should be shown in date order;
- details relating to the sale (as listed in the computer example above) are entered in a 'details' column;
- a folio column entry is made cross-referencing back to the original 'source document', e.g. the invoice;
- the monetary amounts are entered in columns included in the books of original entry for that purpose.

11.3 Types of books of original entry

Books of original entry are known as either 'journals' or 'day books'. However, in the case of the last book of original entry shown below, it is always a 'journal' and the second last is always known as the 'cash book'. The term 'day book' is, perhaps, more commonly used, as it more clearly indicates the nature of these books of original entry – entries are made to them every day. The commonly used books of original entry are:

- **Sales Day Book** (or *Sales Journal*) – for credit sales.
- **Purchases Day Book** (or *Purchases Journal*) – for credit purchases.
- **Returns Inwards Day Book** (or *Returns Inwards Journal*) – for returns inwards.
- **Returns Outwards Day Book** (or *Returns Outwards Journal*) – for returns outwards.
- **Cash Book** – for receipts and payments of cash and cheques.
- General Journal (or **Journal** if the term 'Day Book' is used for the other books of original entry) – for other items.

Most students find it less confusing if 'Day Book' is used rather than 'Journal', as it makes it very clear what is meant when someone refers to 'The Journal'. During the remainder of this book, we will use the term 'Day Book'. However, never forget that the term 'day book' can always be substituted with the word 'journal'. Be sure to remember this. Examiners may use either term.

11.4 Using more than one ledger

Entries are made in the books of original entry. The entries are then summarised and the summary information is entered, using double entry, to accounts kept in the various ledgers of the business. One reason why a set of ledgers is used rather than just one big ledger is that this makes it easier to divide the work of recording all the entries between different bookkeepers.

Activity 11.1
Why else do you think we have more than one ledger?

11.5 Types of ledgers

The different types of ledgers most businesses use are:

- **Sales Ledger.** This is for customers' personal accounts.
- **Purchases Ledger.** This is for suppliers' personal accounts.
- **General Ledger.** This contains the remaining double entry accounts, such as those relating to expenses, fixed assets, and capital.

11.6 A diagram of the books commonly used

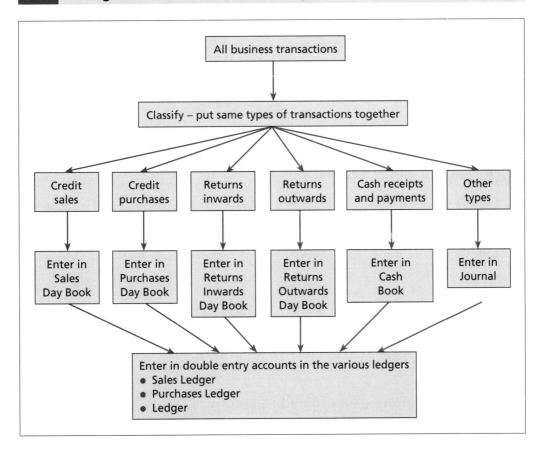

11.7 Description of books used

In the next few chapters we will look at the books used in more detail.

11.8 Types of accounts

Some people describe all accounts as personal accounts or as impersonal accounts.

- **Personal Accounts** – these are for debtors and creditors (i.e. customers and suppliers).
- **Impersonal Accounts** – divided between 'real' accounts and 'nominal' accounts:
  - **Real Accounts** – accounts in which possessions are recorded. Examples are buildings, machinery, fixtures and stock.
  - **Nominal Accounts** – accounts in which expenses, income and capital are recorded.

A diagram may enable you to follow this better:

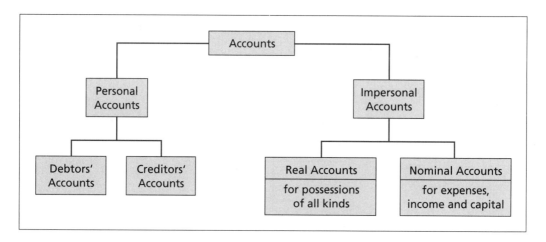

11.9 Nominal and private ledgers

The ledger in which the impersonal accounts are kept is known as the **Nominal** (or 'general') **Ledger**. In order to ensure privacy for the proprietor(s), the capital, drawings, and other similar accounts are sometimes kept in a **Private Ledger**. This prevents office staff from seeing details of items which the proprietors want to keep secret.

> ### Activity 11.2
> Why bother with *books of original entry*? Why don't we just enter transactions straight into the ledgers?

11.10 The accountant as a communicator

The impression is often given that all that an accountant does is produce figures arranged in various ways. This has led to a perception that accountants are boring, pragmatic people with no sense of humour. While it is true that such work does take up quite a lot of an accountant's time, it does not acount for all of a typical accountant's work. Accountants also need to be good communicators, not just in the way they present accounting information on paper, but also in how they verbally communicate the significance of the information they prepare.

An accountant can obviously arrange the financial figures so as to present the information in as meaningful a way as possible for the people who are going to use that information. That is, after all, what accountants are trained to do. If the financial figures are to be given to several people, all of whom are very knowledgeable about accounting, an accountant will simply apply all the conventions and regulations of accounting in order to present the information in the 'normal' accounting way, knowing full well that the recipients of the information will understand it.

On the other hand, accounting figures may well be needed by people who have absolutely no knowledge at all of accounting. In such a case, a typical accounting statement would be of little or no use to them. They would not understand it. In this case, an accountant might set out the figures in a completely different way to try to make it easy for them to grasp. For instance, instead of preparing a 'normal' trading and profit and loss account, the accountant might show the information as follows:

	£	£
In the year ended 31 December 20X9 you sold goods for		50,000
Now how much had those goods cost you to buy?		
At the start of the year you had stock costing	6,000	
+ You bought some more goods in the year costing	<u>28,000</u>	
So altogether you had goods available to sell that cost	34,000	
– At the end of the year, you had stock of goods unsold that cost	(<u>3,000</u>)	
So the goods you had sold in the year had cost you	<u>31,000</u>	
Let us deduct this from what you had sold the goods for		(31,000)
This means that you had made a profit on buying and selling goods, before any other expenses had been paid, amounting to		19,000

(We call this sort of profit the **gross** profit)

	£	£
But, during the year, you suffered other expenses such as wages, rent, and electricity. The amount of these expenses, not including anything you took for yourself, amounted to		(9,000)
So, in this year, your sales value exceeded all the costs involved in running the business, so that the sales could be made, by		£<u>10,000</u>

(We call this sort of profit the **net** profit)

An accountant is failing to perform his or her role appropriately and effectively if the figures are not arranged so as to make them meaningful to the recipient. The accountant's job is not just to produce figures for the accountant's own consumption, it is to communicate the results to other people, many of whom know nothing about accounting.

Activity 11.3

Reconcile this observation with the standardisation of the presentation of financial accounting information as contained in accounting standards and the Companies Acts.

Nowadays, communication skills are a very important part of the accountant's role. Very often, the accountant will have to talk to people in order to explain the figures, or send a letter or write a report about them. The accountant will also have to talk or write to people to find out exactly what sort of accounting information is needed by them, or to explain to them what sort of information could be provided.

If accounting examinations contained only computational type questions, they would not test the ability of candidates to communicate in any way other than writing down accounting figures and, as a result, the examinations would fail to examine these other important aspects of the job. In recent years much more attention has been paid by examining boards to these other aspects of an accountant's work.

Learning outcomes

You should now have learnt:

1 That transactions are classified and details about them are entered in the appropriate book of original entry.

2 That the books of original entry are used as a basis for posting the transactions in summary form to the double entry accounts in the various ledgers.

3 That there is a set of Books of Original Entry, each of which serves a specific purpose.

4 That there is a set of Ledgers, each of which serves a specific purpose.

5 That accountants need to be good communicators.

Answers to activities

11.1 The most important reason is to aid analysis by keeping similar items together.

11.2 Books of original entry contain all the important information relating to a transaction. Ledgers just contain a summary. In fact, some of the entries in the ledgers are often just one line entries covering an entire month of transactions.

11.3 There really is no conflict so far as financial information prepared for internal use is concerned. Financial statements produced for consumption by users outside the business do have to conform to the conventions relating to content and layout. However, those prepared for internal use do not. There is no reason why they could not be prepared along the lines of the Trading and Profit and Loss example shown on the previous page. External stakeholders will never receive their financial statements in this highly user-friendly form. It is simply too much work to customise the financial statement for every class of stakeholder.

CHAPTER 12

The banking system

Introduction

In this chapter, you'll learn about the current UK system for payment of money out of and into bank accounts. You'll learn about the range of plastic cards in use and about various alternatives to cheques that have arisen since the 1960s. You will also learn about the cheque clearing system and how to prepare cheques and bank pay-in slips.

12.1 Twenty-first-century banking

Until quite recently, if individuals wanted money out of their bank accounts, they had to go to their local branch and use a cheque to withdraw the amount they needed. Now they can go into their bank, hand over their **debit card** and withdraw money from their account. Alternatively, they can use virtually any cash machine to do the same thing.

This alternative to cheques first started in 1967 when Barclays Bank introduced the first 'automatic teller machines' (ATMs) or 'cash machines'. These early ATMs gave cash in exchange for tokens. In the early 1970s, **plastic cards** were introduced with magnetic strips that enabled the ATMs to read the account details and process transactions directly with the accounts held in the bank. This marked the start of the plastic card revolution in banking and transaction payment.

By the mid 1970s a number of banks had ATMs in the wall outside major branches where cash could be withdrawn using a **Personal Identification Number** or 'PIN'.

At that time, ATMs offered a very limited service – some, for example, only allowed you to withdraw £10, no matter how much you had in your bank account.

> ### Activity 12.1
> Why do you think they only offered a limited service at that time?

Gradually, cash machines became more common and by the mid 1980s the facilities they offered began to include the options to print a mini statement, provide a receipt, and vary the amount you wished to withdraw. However, you could only use the machines at some of the branches of your own bank.

ATM facilities now are very much better than thirty years ago. In addition to allowing withdrawal of funds and informing customers of the balance on their accounts, some ATMs also allow customers to order cheque books, change their PIN, request statements, pay bills, deposit funds and order mini statements; and most ATMs allow access to funds '24/7', i.e. 24 hours a day, 7 days a week. And, for some time, many banks and building societies have allowed their customers access to their accounts via cash machines owned by other institutions, principally through the Link network, of which 39 UK financial institutions are members.

It is hardly surprising that nearly half of all personal cash withdrawals from bank accounts are now done through an ATM and that over 75 per cent of all cash in circulation comes from an ATM. In fact, over 60 per cent of adults make an average of five withdrawals, each of an average of £55, from one of the UK's 30,000 ATMs each month. In a move towards widening accessibility, over a quarter of ATMs are *not* located at banks, but in places such as shopping centres, supermarkets, railway stations and airports where obtaining money quickly is important.

Outside the UK, customers of many UK banks can continue to use their plastic cards in ATMs through the Visa 'Plus' and Mastercard 'Cirrus' network.

Cash is still the most popular method of making payments, but use of debit and credit cards is growing, with 86 per cent of adults in the UK holding one or more plastic cards. **Direct debits** are the most popular form of non-cash payment and debit cards are the most popular form of payment by plastic card. The situation is changing rapidly, as can be seen by the way it changed between 1999 and 2000, as shown in Exhibit 12.1:

Exhibit 12.1

Payment transactions by medium	Number (billion)	% change on 1999
Debit card purchases	2.3	13.1
Credit and charge card purchases	1.5	8.0
Plastic card withdrawals at ATMs and branch counters	2.1	3.8
Direct debits, standing orders, direct credits and CHAPS	3.5	6.7
Cheques	2.7	(5.4)
Total non-cash (plastic card, automated and paper)	*12.2*	*4.4*
Cash payments (estimate)	27.9	
Others	0.8	(8.4)
TOTAL	40.9	

Activity 12.2

How many different forms of plastic cards do you think there are? Think about this for a minute and then list as many forms of plastic card as you can. (Note: this is *not* a question about how many different credit cards there are. It is about different forms of plastic cards, of which a credit card is but one example.)

Now let's look in more detail at some of the features of the UK banking and payments system.

12.2 Debit cards

The most basic debit cards have an ATM facility. However, many also serve as cheque guarantee cards and as **Switch** cards. Switch is a debit card system that is rapidly replacing cheques as a way to pay for in-store purchases. It allows holders to pay for purchases and, in some shops, withdraw cash at the checkout till. Similarly to cheques, the money spent is automatically withdrawn from the shopper's bank account within three days.

12.3 Direct Debits

Direct debits are the most popular form of non-cash payment and their use is forecast to double by the end of the decade. They were introduced as a paper-based system in 1967. The scheme is managed by BACS Limited, the UK's automated clearing house. They enable payments to be made automatically into a bank account for whatever amount the recipient requests. (This differs from another similar payment medium, the **standing order**, which pays only an amount agreed by the payer.)

12.4 Internet banking

Increasingly, people are making non-cash payments by using credit cards on the Internet. Individuals can also operate their bank accounts in this way, with many banks now offering a 24/7 facility to check account balances, set up standing orders, view direct debits, pay bills and transfer funds between current accounts and savings accounts.

12.5 Clearing

Clearing involves the transmission and settlement of cheque payments between accounts held at different banks and different branches of the same bank. Clearing generally takes three working days:

Day 1   Cheques are processed by the bank into which they were paid. Information about each cheque is then sent electronically through a secure data exchange network (the Inter Bank Data Exchange) to the clearing centre of the bank on which the cheque is drawn.

Day 2   Each cheque is physically delivered to an Exchange Centre, where each bank collects all the cheques drawn on accounts held with it.

Day 3   Bank staff review the cheques presented for payment and decide whether to authorise payment; and the banks pay each other the net value of the cheques transferred between them.

APACS

The Association for Payment Clearing Services was set up in 1985. It is the umbrella body for the UK payments industry and it oversees the major UK payment clearing systems and maintains their operational efficiency and financial integrity.

Cheque and Credit Clearing Company

The Cheque and Credit Clearing Company is responsible for the bulk clearing of cheques and paper credits throughout Great Britain. Cheque and credit payments in Northern Ireland are processed locally.

Members of the Cheque and Credit Clearing Company, under the umbrella of APACS, are individually responsible for processing cheques drawn by or credited to the accounts of their customers. In addition, several hundred other institutions, such as smaller building societies, provide cheque facilities for their customers and obtain indirect access to the cheque clearing mechanisms by means of commercially negotiated agency arrangements with one of the full members of APACS.

You can find further information about many of the topics so far covered in this chapter at the APACS website: www.apacs.org.uk/.

Let's look now at the types of bank account typically in use and at how cheque payments are made.

12.6 Types of account

There are two main types of bank account, current accounts and deposit accounts.

Current accounts

Current accounts may be used for regular payments into and out of a bank account. A **cheque book** will be given by the bank to the holder of the account. The cheque book will be used by the account holder to make payments out of the current account.

So that the account holder can pay money into his/her current account, the holder may also be given a pay-in book.

Holders of current accounts are usually also given a multiple use plastic card incorporating a cheque guarantee card, debit card and ATM card.

Many years ago, banks discovered that customers normally don't change banks once they have opened accounts. Their initial response in the 1970s was to encourage students to do so by offering free gifts, such as loose-leaf folders and note pads. Things have moved on a lot and they now offer reduced facility current accounts to children, young adults and students, often with free gifts such as toys, personal organisers, calculators, discount vouchers to be used in retail stores, and even cash.

Current accounts often earn little or no interest. To gain more interest on funds deposited in a bank, it is necessary to also open a **deposit account**.

Deposit accounts

These accounts generally earn more interest than current accounts and are intended for funds that will not be accessed on a frequent or regular basis. However, this is now changing with many banks linking current accounts to deposit accounts (also known as 'savings accounts') so that funds can be transferred from one to the other whenever it is appropriate.

Some banks operate this automatically but most leave it to the account holder to notify the bank, often by telephone, that a transfer should be made between the accounts.

12.7   Cheques

Use of cheques peaked in 1990, since when debit cards and direct debits have swiftly established themselves as favourite alternatives among private individuals. Nevertheless, they remain the most common form of payment used by businesses.

> *Activity 12.3*
> Why do you think businesses still prefer to use cheques?

The cheque system

1 When the bank has agreed to let someone open a current account it obtains a copy of the new customer's signature. This allows the bank to verify that cheques used are, in fact, signed by the customer. The bank then normally issues the new customer with a cheque book. (Note: some current accounts only offer a debit card and customers have to request a cheque book in addition if they intend writing cheques.)
2 The cheques can then be used to make payments out of the account. Account holders need to ensure that they do not make out a cheque for more than they have in their account – post-dating cheques (i.e. putting a future date on them when sufficient funds will be available) is not permitted and banks will not process such cheques. If a customer wishes to pay out more money than is available they should contact the bank first and request an **overdraft**. The bank is not obliged to grant an overdraft, though many grant all their customers a minimal one – perhaps £100 – when they open the current account that they can use if they wish. (Businesses often have very large overdrafts as this is a cheaper way of financing short-term borrowing than taking out a formal **bank loan**.)
3 The person filling in the cheque and using it for payment is known as the **drawer**. The person to whom the cheque is paid is known as the **payee**.

> *Activity 12.4*
> Why do you think an overdraft is cheaper than a bank loan?

The features of a cheque

Exhibit 12.2 shows a blank cheque before it is filled in.

Exhibit 12.2

On the face of the cheque are various sets of numbers. These are:

914234   Every cheque printed for the Cheshire Bank for your account will be given a different number, so that individual items can be traced.

09-07-99   Each branch of every bank in the United Kingdom has a different number given to it. Thus this branch has a 'code' number 09-07-99.

058899   Each account with the bank is given a different number. This particular number is kept only for the account of J Woodstock at the Stockport branch.

If a cheque has a counterfoil attached, it can be filled in at the same time as the cheque, showing the information that was entered on the cheque. The counterfoil is then kept as a note of what was paid, to whom, and when. (Many cheque books don't have counterfoils. Instead they contain separate pages where the details can be entered.)

We can now look at the completion of a cheque. Let's assume that we are paying seventy-two pounds and eighty-five pence to K Marsh on 22 May 20X5. Exhibit 12.3 shows the completed cheque.

Exhibit 12.3

In Exhibit 12.3, the drawer is J Woodstock, and the payee is K Marsh.

The two parallel lines across the face of the cheque are drawn as a safeguard. If this had not been done, the cheque would have been an 'uncrossed cheque'. If this cheque had not been crossed, a thief could have gone to the Stockport branch of the Cheshire Bank and obtained cash in exchange for the cheque. When the cheque is crossed it *must* be paid into a bank account. Normally, a more secure type of crossing is used.

Cheque crossings

Cheques can be further safeguarded by using a specific crossing, i.e. writing a form of instruction within the crossing on the cheques as shown in Exhibit 12.4:

Exhibit 12.4

These both mean the same thing. They are specific instructions to the banks about the use of the cheque. There is a third, more common crossing that also means the same thing, 'Account Payee'. As it is shorter, it is the one most commonly used. The use of any of these three crossings means the cheques should be paid only into the account of the payee named. If cheques are lost or stolen, the drawer must advise their bank immediately and confirm by letter. These cheques will be 'stopped', i.e. payment will not be made on these cheques, provided the drawer acts swiftly. If the cheque is lost or stolen it will be of no use to the thief or finder. This is because it is impossible for this cheque to be paid into any bank account other than that of the named payee. For obvious reasons, cheques are often printed with the 'Account Payee' crossing on them.

Cheque endorsements

Cheques with the above crossings can only be paid into the bank account of the payee. However, if the crossing does not contain any of these three terms, a cheque received by someone can be **endorsed** over to someone else. The person then receiving the cheque could bank it. This means that if Adam Smith receives a cheque from John Wilson, he can 'endorse' the cheque and hand it to Petra Jones as payment of money by Smith to Jones. Jones can then pay it into her bank account.

To endorse the cheque, Smith would write the words 'Pay P Jones or order' on the reverse side of the cheque and then sign underneath it. Jones would then usually bank the cheque, but she could endorse it over to someone else by adding yet another endorsement and signing it.

A cheque which has been paid to someone, and has passed through their bank account or been endorsed over by that person to someone else, is legal proof of the fact that payment had been made.

12.8 Pay-in slips

When we want to pay money into a current account, either cash or cheques, or both, we use a **pay-in slip**. When the payment is into an account held in a different bank, the form is called a **bank giro credit**. The two types of form are virtually identical. A bank giro credit can be used instead of a pay-in slip, but not the other way around, as the details of the other bank need to be entered on the bank giro credit. Exhibit 12.5 shows a completed bank giro credit:

Exhibit 12.5

Face of pay-in slip

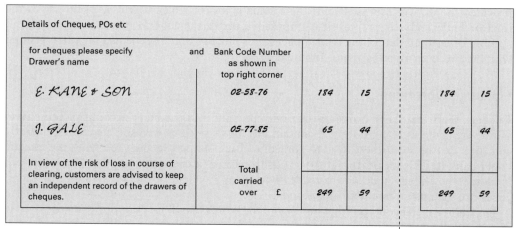

J Woodstock has banked the following items:

Four	£5 notes	
Three	£1 coins	
One	50p coin	
Other silver	30p	
Bronze coins	12p	
Cheques received from:		Code numbers:
E Kane & Son	£184.15	02-58-76
J Gale	£65.44	05-77-85

12.9 Cheque clearing

In Section 12.5, you learnt about the cheque clearing system. Let's now look at an example of how cheques paid from one person's bank account pass into another person's bank account. We'll use the cheque from Exhibit 12.3.

20X5
May 22   Woodstock, in Stockport, sends the cheque to K Marsh, who lives in Leeds. Woodstock enters the payment in his cash book.
May 23   Cheque received by Marsh. He banks it the same day in his bank account at Barclays Bank in Leeds. Marsh shows the cheque in his cash book as being received and banked on 23 May.
May 24   The Exchange Centre in London receives it, where the Cheshire Bank collects it. The Cheshire Bank sends the cheque to their Stockport branch.
May 25   Staff at the Stockport branch of the Cheshire Bank examine the cheque. If there is nothing wrong with it, the cheque can now be debited by the bank to J Woodstock's account.

In Chapter 30, we'll be looking at bank reconciliation statements. What we have looked at so far

20X5
May 22   the day on which Woodstock has made the entry in his cash book
May 25   the day when the bank makes an entry in Woodstock's account in respect of the cheque

will become an important part of your understanding of such statements.

Learning outcomes

You should now have learnt:

1 That the banking sector has been revolutionised by the developments in computers and information technology over the last 35 years.

2 That where previously payments could usually only be made by cash or cheque, there is now a wide range of alternatives, ranging from plastic cards to direct debits and direct transfers into bank accounts.

3 That the use of cheques is falling but that they are still a very common form of payment in business.

4 That cheque clearing is the way in which a cheque goes through the banking system and is credited to its rightful owner and charged against the drawer's bank account.

5 That it usually takes three days for a cheque payment to reach the account of the payee.

6 That it usually takes three days for a debit card payment to reach the account of the payee.

▶

7 That cash is still the most common form of medium for payments.

8 That holders of a current account will be normally be issued with a cheque book and a multiple use plastic card incorporating a cheque guarantee card, debit card and ATM card.

9 How to write a cheque.

10 That crossings on cheques indicate that they must be banked before cash can be collected for them.

11 That special crossings on cheques act as instructions to the banker, and are usually used to ensure that the cheque cannot be used by anyone other than its rightful owner.

12 That cheque endorsements enable the rightful owner of the cheque to give it to someone else.

13 How to make out a bank pay-in slip.

14 How to make out a bank giro credit.

Answers to activities

12.1 Computers were still very limited in what they could do, particularly in terms of the size of computer needed for even the smallest task. Without the sophisticated programming flexibility of modern computers, these first age cash machines could only have very limited facilities. There was also the fairly obvious point that cash machines were a new invention and no one knew at that time whether the general public would actually use them!

12.2 There are many varieties of plastic cards. A list based on one produced by the Association for Payment Clearing Services (APACS) is listed below:

- **Affinity Card.** A credit card where the card issuer makes a donation to an organisation (often a charity) every time the card is used.
- **ATM Card.** A plastic card used in an ATM for cash withdrawals and other bank services.
- **Business Card.** Also known as a company or corporate card. A card which companies issue to staff to pay for business expenses like travel costs.
- **Charge Card.** A payment card that requires the cardholder to settle the account in full at the end of a specified period, such as American Express and Diners cards. Holders have to pay an annual fee for the card. (Compare this to a credit card.)
- **Cheque Guarantee Card.** A card that guarantees settlement of cheques of up to a specified amount.
- **Credit Card.** A card enabling the holder to make purchases and to draw cash up to a pre-arranged limit. The credit granted in a period can be settled in full or in part by the end of a specified period. Many credit cards carry no annual fee. (Compare this to a charge card.)
- **Debit Card.** A card linked to a bank or building society account and used to pay for goods and services by debiting the holder's account. Debit cards are usually combined with other facilities such as ATM and cheque guarantee functions.
- **Electronic Purse.** Also known as a pre-payment card. This card has a stored cash value which can be used to purchase goods and services – it is an alternative to cash. The card can be disposable or re-loadable. Examples include Mondex and VisaCash.
- **Loyalty Card.** Cards issued by retailers to promote customer loyalty. Holders earn cash back, vouchers, or discounts. Examples include the Tesco Clubcard and the Boots Advantage card.
- **Payment Card.** A generic term for any plastic card (credit, debit, charge, etc.) which may be used on its own to pay for goods and services or to withdraw cash.
- **Purchasing Card.** A payment card issued to businesses, companies or government departments to make supplier and/or trade payments.

- **Smart Card**. A card that holds details on a computer chip instead of a traditional magnetic stripe. (This is expected to be the normal form of all credit and debit cards in the future.)
- **Shareholder Card**. A special form of store card issued to shareholders that operates like a credit card but gives the holder a discount off all purchases charged to the card. These cards can only be used in shops owned by the company that issued the card. An example is the Arcadia Group card.
- **Store Card**. Also known as a retailer card. A plastic payment card that can be used only in a specified retailer or group of retailers. An example is the John Lewis Partnership card.
- **Travel & Entertainment Card**. A plastic payment card which operates similarly to a charge card.

12.3 Businesses can't send employees round to all their suppliers with debit cards. Nor can they expect one-off suppliers to allow them to pay by direct transfer into the supplier's bank account. Cheques remain more convenient in many cases, though there is a definite shift towards more modern methods. The most obvious indicator of this is the attempt by many companies to encourage shareholders to accept their dividend payments as electronic transfers into the shareholders' bank accounts.

Customers also still often use cheques, particularly for postal payments for goods purchased by mail order and to send deposits on, for example, holidays – and to pay credit card bills!

12.4 It is not because the rate of interest is lower on overdrafts, it isn't, it is higher! It is because interest on overdrafts is charged daily on the amount of the overdraft on that date. Bank loans are for fixed amounts and interest is paid on the full amount each day whether or not the money has been spent. With an overdraft, customers have the freedom to use as much or as little of the overdraft as they wish (and so incur interest on the amount they are overdrawn). In many cases, they will never actually use the overdraft facility. Also, bank loans must be repaid on a stated date. Overdrafts are only payable to the bank when the bank demands repayment, which is rare, unless the individual or business looks likely to have problems paying back the overdraft at some future date. Thus, overdrafts are cheaper to use than bank loans, they are more flexible, and the borrower doesn't have to regularly look for other funds to replace them.

CHAPTER 13

Cash books

Learning objectives

After you have studied this chapter, you should be able to:

- explain the format of two-column and three-column Cash Books
- enter up and balance off Cash Books
- use folio columns for cross-referencing purposes
- make the entries for discounts allowed and discounts received both in the Cash Book and, at the end of a period, in the discount accounts in the General Ledger

Introduction

In this chapter, you'll learn how businesses record cash and cheque transactions in the Cash Book. You'll learn that a memorandum column, called the 'folio column' is included in the Cash Book; and you'll learn the reasons why this is done. You will learn how to make the necessary entries in the Cash Book and how to include entries for discounts received from creditors and allowed to debtors, both in the Cash Book and in the General Ledger.

13.1 Drawing up a cash book

The Cash Book consists of the cash account and the bank account put together in one book. We used to show these two accounts on different pages of the ledger. Now it is easier to put the two sets of account columns together. This means that we can record all money received and paid out on a particular date on the same page.

In the Cash Book, the debit column for cash is put next to the debit column for bank. The credit column for cash is put next to the credit column for bank.

Exhibit 13.1 shows how a cash account and a bank account would appear if they had been kept separately. In Exhibit 13.2, they are shown as if the transactions had, instead, been kept in a Cash Book.

The bank column contains details of the payments made by cheque and direct transfer from the bank account and of the money received and paid into the bank account. The bank will have a copy of the account in its own books.

Periodically, or on request from the business, the bank sends a copy of the account in its books to the business. This document is known as the **bank statement**. When the business receives the bank statement, it checks it against the bank columns in its Cash Book to ensure that there are no errors.

Exhibit 13.1

Cash

20X8			£	20X8			£
Aug	2	T Moore	33	Aug	18	Rent	20
''	5	K Charles	25	''	12	C Potts	19
''	15	F Hughes	37	''	28	Wages	25
''	30	H Howe	18	''	31	Balance c/d	49
			113				113
Sept	1	Balance b/d	49				

Bank

20X8			£	20X8			£
Aug	1	Capital	1,000	Aug	7	Rates	105
''	3	W P Ltd	244	''	12	F Small Ltd	95
''	16	K Noone	408	''	26	K French	268
''	30	H Sanders	20	''	31	Balance c/d	1,204
			1,672				1,672
Sept	1	Balance b/d	1,204				

Exhibit 13.2

Cash Book

20X8			Cash £	Bank £	20X8			Cash £	Bank £
Aug	1	Capital		1,000	Aug	7	Rates		105
''	2	T Moore	33		''	8	Rent	20	
''	3	W P Ltd		244	''	12	C Potts	19	
''	5	K Charles	25		''	12	F Small Ltd		95
''	15	F Hughes	37		''	26	K French		268
''	16	K Noone		408	''	28	Wages	25	
''	30	H Sanders		20	''	31	Balances c/d	49	1,204
''	30	H Howe	18						
			113	1,672				113	1,672
Sept	1	Balances b/d	49	1,204					

13.2 Cash paid into the bank

In Exhibit 13.2, the payments into the bank were cheques received by the business. They have been banked immediately upon receipt. We must now consider cash being paid into the bank.

1 Let's look at the position when customers pay their account in cash and, later, a part of this cash is paid into the bank. The receipt of the cash is debited to the cash column on the date received, the credit entry being in the customer's personal account. The cash banked has the following effect needing action:

Effect	Action
1 Asset of cash is decreased	Credit the asset account, i.e. the cash account which is represented by the cash column in the Cash Book.
2 Asset of bank is increased	Debit the asset account, i.e. the bank account which is represented by the bank column in the Cash Book.

A cash receipt of £100 from M Davies on 1 August 20X8 which was followed by the banking on 3 August of £80 of this amount would appear in the Cash Book as follows:

Cash Book						Cash	Bank
		Cash	*Bank*			*Cash*	*Bank*
20X8		£	£	20X8		£	£
Aug 1 M Davies		100		Aug 3 Bank		80	
'' 3 Cash			80				

The details column shows entries against each item stating the name of the account in which the completion of double entry has taken place. Against the cash payment of £80 appears the word 'bank', meaning that the debit £80 is to be found in the bank column, and the opposite applies.

2 Where the whole of the cash received is banked immediately the receipt can be treated in exactly the same manner as a cheque received, i.e. it can be entered directly into the bank column.

3 If the business requires cash, it may withdraw cash from the bank. Assuming this is done by use of a cheque, the business would write out a cheque to pay itself a certain amount in cash. The bank will give cash in exchange for the cheque over the counter. It could also be done using a cash card. The effect on the accounts is the same.

The twofold effect and the action required is:

Effect	Action
1 Asset of bank is decreased	Credit the asset account, i.e. the bank column in the Cash Book.
2 Asset of cash is increased	Debit the asset account, i.e. the cash column in the Cash Book.

A withdrawal of £75 cash on 1 June 20X8 from the bank would appear in the Cash Book as:

Cash Book					Cash	Bank
		Cash	*Bank*		*Cash*	*Bank*
20X8		£	£	20X8	£	£
June 1 Bank		75		June 1 Cash		75

Both the debit and credit entries for this item are in the same book. When this happens it is known as a **contra** item.

13.3 The use of folio columns

As you have already seen, the details column in an account contains the name of the account in which the other part of the double entry has been entered. Anyone looking through the books should, therefore, be able to find the other half of the double entry in the ledgers.

However, when many books are being used, just to mention the name of the other account may not be enough information to find the other account quickly. More information is needed, and this is given by using **folio columns**.

In each account and in each book being used, a folio column is added, always shown on the left of the money columns. In this column, the name of the other book and the number of the page in the other book where the other part of the double entry was made is stated against each and every entry. So as to ensure that the double entry is completed, the folio column should only be filled in when the double entry has been completed.

An entry for receipt of cash from C Kelly whose account was on page 45 of the sales ledger, and the cash recorded on page 37 of the Cash Book, would have the following folio column entries:

- in the Cash Book, the folio column entry would be SL 45
- in the Sales Ledger, the folio column entry would be CB 37.

Note how each of the titles of the books is abbreviated so that it can fit into the space available in the folio column. Each of any contra items (transfers between bank and cash) being shown on the same page of the Cash Book would use the letter 'C' (for 'contra') in the folio column. There is no need to also include a page number in this case.

The act of using one book as a means of entering transactions into the accounts, so as to perform or complete the double entry, is known as **posting**. For example, you 'post' items from the Sales Day Book to the appropriate accounts in the Sales Ledger and to the Sales Account and you 'post' items from the Cash Book to the appropriate accounts in the Sales Ledger.

Activity 13.1
Why do you think only one account is posted to from the Cash Book?

13.4 Advantages of folio columns

As described in 13.4, folio entries speed up the process of finding the other side of the double entry in the ledgers.

Activity 13.2
What other advantage can you think of for using a folio column?

13.5 Example of a cash book with folio columns

The following transactions are written up in the form of a Cash Book. The folio columns are filled in as though all the double entries had been completed to other accounts.

20X8				£
Sept	1	Proprietor puts capital into a bank account for the business.		940
"	2	Received cheque from M Boon.		115
"	4	Cash sales.		102
"	6	Paid rent by cash.		35
"	7	Banked £50 of the cash held by the business.		50
"	15	Cash sales paid direct into the bank.		40
"	23	Paid cheque to S Wills.		277
"	29	Withdrew cash from bank for business use.		120
"	30	Paid wages in cash.		118

Cash Book										(page 1)
		Folio	Cash	Bank				Folio	Cash	Bank
20X8			£	£	20X8				£	£
Sept	1 Capital	GL1		940	Sept	6 Rent	GL65	35	
''	2 M Boon	SL98		115	''	7 Bank	C	50	
''	4 Sales	GL87	102		''	23 S Wills	PL23		277
''	7 Cash	C		50	''	29 Cash	C		120
''	15 Sales	GL87		40	''	30 Wages	GL39	118	
''	29 Bank	C	120		''	30 Balances	c/d	19	748
			222	1,145				222	1,145
Oct	1 Balances	b/d	19	748					

The abbreviations used in the folio column are:

GL = General Ledger   SL = Sales Ledger   C = Contra   PL = Purchases Ledger

13.6 Cash discounts

Businesses prefer it if their customers pay their accounts quickly. A business may accept a smaller sum in full settlement if payment is made within a certain period of time. The amount of the reduction of the sum to be paid is known as a '*cash discount*'. The term 'cash discount' thus refers to the allowance given for quick payment. It is still called cash discount, even if the account is paid by cheque or by direct transfer into the bank account.

The rate of cash discount is usually stated as a percentage. Full details of the percentage allowed, and the period within which payment is to be made, are quoted on all sales documents by the seller. A typical period during which discount may be allowed is one month from the date of the original transaction.

Note: Cash discounts *always* appear in the profit and loss part of the Trading and Profit and Loss Account. They are not part of the cost of goods sold. Nor are they a deduction from selling price. Students often get this wrong in examinations – be careful!

13.7 Discounts allowed and discounts received

A business may have two types of cash discounts in its books. These are:

1 **Discounts allowed**: cash discounts allowed by a business to its customers when they pay their accounts quickly.
2 **Discounts received**: cash discounts received by a business from its suppliers when it pays what it owes them quickly.

We can now see the effect of discounts by looking at two examples.

Example 1

W Clarke owed us £100. He pays on 2 September 20X8 by cash within the time limit applicable for a 5 per cent cash discount. He will pay £100 – £5 = £95 in full settlement of his account.

Effect	Action
1 Of cash: Cash is increased by £95. Asset of debtors is decreased by £95.	Debit cash account, i.e. enter £95 in debit column of Cash Book. Credit W Clarke £95.
2 Of discounts: Asset of debtors is decreased by £5. (After the cash was paid there remained a balance of £5. As the account has been paid, this asset must now be cancelled.) Expenses of discounts allowed increased by £5.	Credit W Clarke £5. Debit discounts allowed account £5.

Example 2

The business owed S Small £400. It pays him on 3 September 20X8 by cheque within the time limit laid down by him for a 2$\frac{1}{2}$ per cent cash discount. The business will pay £400 − £10 = £390 in full settlement of the account.

Effect	Action
1 Of cheque: Asset of bank is reduced by £390. Liability of creditors is reduced by £390.	Credit bank, i.e. entry in the credit bank column for £390. Debit S Small's account £390.
2 Of discounts: Liability of creditors is reduced by £10. (After the cheque was paid, a balance of £10 remained. As the account has been paid the liability must now be cancelled.) Revenues of discounts received increased by £10.	Debit S Small's account £10. Credit discounts received account £10.

The accounts in the business's books would appear:

		Folio	Cash	Bank			Folio	Cash	Bank
Cash Book									*(page 32)*
20X8			£	£	20X8			£	£
Sept 2 W Clarke		SL12	95		Sept 3 S Small		PL75		390

Discounts Received   (General Ledger *page 18*)

		Folio	£
20X8			
Sept 2 S Small		PL75	10

Discounts Allowed   (General Ledger *page 17*)

	Folio	£
20X8		
Sept 2 W Clarke	SL12	5

	Folio	£			Folio	£
W Clarke					(Sales Ledger *page 12*)	
20X8			20X8			
Sept 1 Balance	b/d	100	Sept 2 Cash		CB32	95
			'' 2 Discount		GL17	5
		100				100

	Folio	£			Folio	£
S Small					(Purchases Ledger *page 75*)	
20X8			20X8			
Sept 3 Bank	CB32	390	Sept 1 Balance		b/d	400
'' 3 Discount	GL18	10				
		400				400

It is the accounting custom to enter the word 'Discount' in the personal accounts without stating whether it is a discount received or a discount allowed.

> ### Activity 13.3
> Why do you think it is accounting custom only to enter the word 'Discount' in the personal accounts?

13.8 Discounts columns in cash book

The *discounts allowed account* and the *discounts received account* are in the General Ledger along with all the other revenue and expense accounts. It has already been stated that every effort should be made to avoid too much reference to the General Ledger, hence the use of extra columns for discount in the Cash Book.

An extra column is added on each side of the Cash Book in which the amounts of discounts are entered. Discounts received are entered in the discounts column on the credit side of the Cash Book, and discounts allowed in the discounts column on the debit side of the Cash Book.

The Cash Book, if completed for the two examples so far dealt with, would be:

	Folio	Discount	Cash	Bank		Folio	Discount	Cash	Bank
Cash Book									*(page 32)*
20X8		£	£	£	20X8		£	£	£
Sept 2 W Clarke	SL12	5	95		Sept 3 S Small	PL75	10		390

There is no alteration to the method of showing discounts in the personal accounts.

To make entries in the discounts accounts in the General Ledger

Total of discounts column on receipts side of Cash Book } Enter on debit side of discounts allowed account

Total of discounts column on payments side of Cash Book } Enter on credit side of discounts received account

13.9 A worked example

				£
20X8				
May	1	Balances brought down from April:		
		Cash balance		29
		Bank balance		654
		Debtors accounts:		
			B King	120
			N Campbell	280
			D Shand	40
		Creditors accounts:		
			U Barrow	60
			A Allen	440
			R Long	100
''	2	B King pays us by cheque, having deducted 2½ per cent cash discount £3.		117
''	8	We pay R Long his account by cheque, deducting 5 per cent cash discount £5.		95
''	11	We withdrew £100 cash from the bank for business use.		100
''	16	N Campbell pays us his account by cheque, deducting 2½ per cent discount £7.		273
''	25	We paid wages in cash.		92
''	28	D Shand pays us in cash after having deducted 5 per cent cash discount.		38
''	29	We pay U Barrow by cheque less 5 per cent cash discount £3.		57
''	30	We pay A Allen by cheque less 2½ per cent cash discount £11.		429

Folio numbers have been included in the solution to make the example more realistic.

			Folio	Discount £	Cash £	Bank £				Folio	Discount £	Cash £	Bank £
Cash Book													**(page 64)**
20X8							20X8						
May	1	Balance	b/d		29	654	May	8	R Long	PL58	5		95
''	2	B King	SL13	3		117	''	11	Cash	C			100
''	11	Bank	C		100		''	25	Wages	GL77		92	
''	16	N Campbell	SL84	7		273	''	29	U Barrow	PL15	3		57
''	28	D Shand	SL91	2	38		''	30	A Allen	PL98	11		429
							''	31	Balances	c/d		75	363
				12	167	1,044					19	167	1,044
Jun	1	Balances	b/d		75	363							

Sales Ledger
B King (page 13)

20X8			Folio	£	20X8			Folio	£
May	1	Balance	b/d	120	May	2	Bank	CB64	117
					May	2	Discount	CB64	3
				120					120

N Campbell (page 84)

20X8			Folio	£	20X8			Folio	£
May	1	Balance	b/d	280	May	16	Bank	CB64	273
					May	16	Discount	CB64	7
				280					280

D Shand (page 91)

20X8			Folio	£	20X8			Folio	£
May	1	Balance	b/d	40	May	28	Cash	CB64	38
					May	28	Discount	CB64	2
				40					40

Purchases Ledger
U Barrow
(page 15)

20X8		Folio	£	20X8		Folio	£
May 29	Bank	CB64	57	May 1	Balance	b/d	60
May 29	Discount	CB64	3				
			60				60

R Long
(page 58)

20X8		Folio	£	20X8		Folio	£
May 8	Bank	CB64	95	May 1	Balance	b/d	100
May 8	Discount	CB64	5				
			100				100

A Allen
(page 98)

20X8		Folio	£	20X8		Folio	£
May 30	Bank	CB64	429	May 1	Balance	b/d	440
May 30	Discount	CB64	11				
			440				440

General Ledger
Wages
(page 77)

20X8		Folio	£				
May 25	Cash	CB64	92				

Discounts Received
(page 88)

				20X8		Folio	£
				May 31	Total for the month	CB64	19

Discounts Allowed
(page 89)

20X8		Folio	£				
May 31	Total for the month	CB64	12				

Is the above method of entering discounts correct?

You can easily check. See the following:

Discounts in Ledger Accounts	Debits		Credits	
		£		
Discounts Received	U Barrow	3	Discounts	
	R Long	5	Received	
	A Allen	11	Account	£19
		19		
				£
Discounts Allowed	Discounts		B King	3
	Allowed		N Campbell	7
	Account	£12	D Shand	2
				12

You can see that proper double entry has been carried out. Equal amounts, in total, have been entered on each side of the accounts.

13.10 Bank overdrafts

A business may borrow money from a bank by means of a **bank overdraft**. This means that the business is allowed to pay more out of its bank account than the total amount it has deposited in the account.

Up to this point, the bank balances have all been money at the bank, so they have all been assets, i.e. debit balances. When the bank account is overdrawn, the business owes money to the bank, so the account is a liability and the balance becomes a credit one.

Taking the cash book last shown, suppose that the amount payable to A Allen was £1,429 instead of £429. The amount in the bank account of £1,044, is exceeded by the amount withdrawn. We will take the discount for Allen as being £11. The cash book would appear as follows:

Cash Book									(page 64)
	Discount	*Cash*	*Bank*			*Discount*	*Cash*	*Bank*
20X8	£	£	£	20X8		£	£	£
May 1 Balances b/d		29	654	May 8 R Long		5		95
" 2 B King	3		117	" 11 Cash				100
" 11 Bank		100		" 25 Wages			92	
" 16 N Campbell	7		273	" 29 U Barrow		3		57
" 28 D Shand	2	38		" 30 A Allen		11		1,429
" 31 Balance c/d			637	" 31 Balance c/d			75	
	12	167	1,681			19	167	1,681
Jun 1 Balance b/d		75		Jun 1 Balance b/d				637

On a balance sheet, a bank overdraft will be shown as an item included under the heading 'current liabilities'.

13.11 Bank cash books

In the United Kingdom, except for very small organisations, three-column cash books are not usually used. All receipts, whether of cash or cheques, will be banked daily. A 'Petty Cash Book' will be used for payments of cash. As a result, there will be no need for cash columns in the Cash Book itself; however, the use of multiple-column cash books is widespread, their format being similar to that of an analytical Petty Cash Book (see Chapter 18).

This move away from three-column cash books is not yet evident in many other countries, especially where banking systems are not as developed or as efficient as in the UK.

Learning outcomes

You should now have learnt:

1 That a cash book consists of a cash account and a bank account put together into one book.

2 How to enter up and balance a two-column Cash Book, i.e. one containing a debit and a credit column for the bank account, and a debit and a credit column for the cash account.

3 That the bank columns in the Cash Book are for cheques and any other transfers of funds that have been made into or out of the bank account.

▶

4 That a folio column is included in the Cash Book so as to help trace entries made into accounts in the ledgers and so as to provide assurance that the double entries have been made.

5 That cash discounts are given to encourage people to pay their accounts within a stated time limit.

6 That 'cash discount' is the name given for discount for quick payment even where the payment was made by cheque or by direct transfer into the bank account, rather than by payment in cash.

7 That cash discounts appear in the profit and loss part of the Trading and Profit and Loss Account.

8 How to enter up and balance a three-column cash book, i.e. one containing a debit and a credit column for the bank account, a debit and a credit column for the cash account, and a debit and a credit column for discount.

9 That the discounts columns in the Cash Book make it easier to enter up the books. They act as a collection point for discounts allowed and discounts received, for which double entry into the General Ledger is completed when the totals are transferred to the discount accounts in the General Ledger, usually at the end of the month.

Answers to activities

13.1   Although the Cash Book is a book of original entry, it is also where the cash account and bank account are recorded. In effect, it is both a book of original entry and a ledger dedicated to those two accounts. As a result, each transaction in the Cash Book is only posted once to another account, the first part of the entry having been made when the transaction was recorded in the Cash Book.

13.2   If an entry has not been filled in, i.e. if the folio column is blank against an entry, the double entry has not yet been made. As a result, looking through the entry lines in the folio columns to ensure they have all been filled in helps detect such errors quickly.

13.3   It should be quite obvious whether discount is received or allowed. And, more importantly, the double entry is with the Cash Book columns for discount, not with either the discount allowed account or the discount received account in the General Ledger. At the end of the period (usually a month) the totals of the two discount columns in the Cash Book are posted to the discount allowed and discount received accounts in the General Ledger.

MULTIPLE CHOICE QUESTIONS: SET 2

Now attempt Set 2 of multiple choice questions. (Answers to all the multiple choice questions are given in Appendix 2 at the end of this book.)

Each of these multiple choice questions has four suggested answers, (A), (B), (C) and (D). You should read each question and then decide which choice is best, either (A) or (B) or (C) or (D). *Write down your answers on a separate piece of paper.* You will then be able to redo the set of questions later without having to try to ignore your answers.

MC21   Gross profit is

(A)   Excess of sales over cost of goods sold
(B)   Sales less Purchases

(C)   Cost of goods sold + Opening stock
(D)   Net profit less expenses of the period.

MC22   Net profit is calculated in the

(A)   Trading account
(B)   Profit and loss account
(C)   Trial balance
(D)   Balance sheet.

MC23   To find the value of closing stock at the end of a period we

(A)   do this by stocktaking
(B)   look in the stock account
(C)   deduct opening stock from cost of goods sold
(D)   deduct cost of goods sold from sales.

MC24   The credit entry for net profit is on the credit side of

(A)   The trading account
(B)   The profit and loss account
(C)   The drawings account
(D)   The capital account.

MC25   Which of these best describes a balance sheet?

(A)   An account proving the books balance
(B)   A record of closing entries
(C)   A listing of balances
(D)   A statement of assets.

MC26   The descending order in which current assets should be shown in the balance sheet is

(A)   Stock, Debtors, Bank, Cash
(B)   Cash, Bank, Debtors, Stock
(C)   Debtors, Stock, Bank, Cash
(D)   Stock, Debtors, Cash, Bank.

MC27   Which of these best describes fixed assets?

(A)   Are bought to be used in the business
(B)   Are items which will not wear out quickly
(C)   Are expensive items bought for the business
(D)   Are of long life and are not bought specifically for resale.

MC28   Carriage inwards is charged to the trading account because

(A)   It is an expense connected with buying goods
(B)   It should not go in the balance sheet
(C)   It is not part of motor expenses
(D)   Carriage outwards goes in the profit and loss account.

MC29   Given figures showing: Sales £8,200; Opening stock £1,300; Closing stock £900; Purchases £6,400; Carriage inwards £200, the cost of goods sold figure is

(A)   £6,800
(B)   £6,200
(C)   £7,000
(D)   Another figure.

MC30   The costs of putting goods into a saleable condition should be charged to

(A)   Trading account
(B)   Profit and loss account
(C)   Balance sheet
(D)   None of these.

MC31   Suppliers' personal accounts are found in the

(A)   Nominal ledger
(B)   General ledger
(C)   Purchases ledger
(D)   Sales ledger.

MC32   The Sales Day Book is best described as

(A)   Part of the double entry system
(B)   Containing customers' accounts
(C)   Containing real accounts
(D)   A list of credit sales.

MC33   Which of the following are personal accounts?

(*i*)   Buildings
(*ii*)   Wages
(*iii*) Debtors
(*iv*)   Creditors

(A)   (*i*) and (*iv*) only
(B)   (*ii*) and (*iii*) only
(C)   (*iii*) and (*iv*) only
(D)   (*ii*) and (*iv*) only.

MC34   When Lee makes out a cheque for £50 and sends it to Young, then Lee is known as

(A)   The payee
(B)   The banker
(C)   The drawer
(D)   The creditor.

MC35   If you want to make sure that your money will be safe if cheques sent are lost in the post, you should

(A)   Not use the postal service in future
(B)   Always pay by cash
(C)   Always take the money in person
(D)   Cross your cheques 'Account Payee only, Not Negotiable'.

MC36   When banking money in to your current account you should always use

(A)   A cheque book
(B)   A paying-in slip
(C)   A cash book
(D)   A general ledger.

MC37   A debit balance of £100 in a cash account shows that

(A)   There was £100 cash in hand
(B)   Cash has been overspent by £100
(C)   £100 was the total of cash paid out
(D)   The total of cash received was less than £100.

MC38   £50 cash taken from the cash till and banked is entered

(A)   Debit cash column £50: Credit bank column £50
(B)   Debit bank column £50: Credit cash column £50
(C)   Debit cash column £50: Credit cash column £50
(D)   Debit bank column £50: Credit bank column £50.

MC39   A credit balance of £200 on the cash columns of the cash book would mean

(A)   We have spent £200 more than we have received
(B)   We have £200 cash in hand
(C)   The bookkeeper has made a mistake
(D)   Someone has stolen £200 cash.

MC40   'Posting' the transactions in bookkeeping means

(A)   Making the first entry of a double entry transaction
(B)   Entering items in a cash book
(C)   Making the second entry of a double entry transaction
(D)   Something other than the above.

REVIEW QUESTIONS

13.1   Write up a two-column cash book for a marketing agency from the following details, and balance it off as at the end of the month:

20X8
May   1   Started business with capital in cash £100.
 ''   2   Paid rent by cash £10.
 ''   3   F Lake lent us £500, paid by cheque.
 ''   4   We paid B McKenzie by cheque £65.
 ''   5   Cash sales £98.
 ''   7   N Miller paid us by cheque £62.
 ''   9   We paid B Burton in cash £22.
 ''   11   Cash sales paid direct into the bank £53.
 ''   15   G Moores paid us in cash £65.
 ''   16   We took £50 out of the cash till and paid it into the bank account.
 ''   19   We repaid F Lake £100 by cheque.
 ''   22   Cash sales paid direct into the bank £66.
 ''   26   Paid motor expenses by cheque £12.
 ''   30   Withdrew £100 cash from the bank for business use.
 ''   31   Paid wages in cash £97.

13.2A   Write up a two-column cash book for a second-hand bookshop from the following:

20X9
Nov   1   Balance brought forward from last month: Cash £105; Bank £2,164.
 ''   2   Cash sales £605.
 ''   3   Took £500 out of the cash till and paid it into the bank.
 ''   4   J Matthews paid us by cheque £217.
 ''   5   We paid for postage stamps in cash £60.
 ''   6   Bought office equipment by cheque £189.
 ''   7   We paid J Lucas by cheque £50.
 ''   9   Received rates refund by cheque £72.
 ''   11   Withdrew £250 from the bank for business use.
 ''   12   Paid wages in cash £239.
 ''   14   Paid motor expenses by cheque £57.
 ''   16   L Levy lent us £200 in cash.

Nov   20   R Norman paid us by cheque £112.
"   28   We paid general expenses in cash £22.
"   30   Paid insurance by cheque £74.

13.3 A three-column cash book for a wine wholesaler is to be written up from the following details, balanced off, and the relevant discount accounts in the general ledger shown.

20X8
Mar   1   Balances brought forward: Cash £230; Bank £4,756.
"   2   The following paid their accounts by cheque, in each case deducting 5 per cent cash discounts: R Burton £140; E Taylor £220; R Harris £300 (all amounts are pre-discount).
"   4   Paid rent by cheque £120.
"   6   J Cotton lent us £1,000 paying by cheque.
"   8   We paid the following accounts by cheque in each case deducting a $2\frac{1}{2}$ per cent cash discount: N Black £360; P Towers £480; C Rowse £800 (all amounts are pre-discount).
"   10   Paid motor expenses in cash £44.
"   12   H Hankins pays his account of £77, by cheque £74, deducting £3 cash discount.
"   15   Paid wages in cash £160.
"   18   The following paid their accounts by cheque, in each case deducting 5 per cent cash discount: C Winston £260; R Wilson & Son £340; H Winter £460 (all amounts are pre-discount).
"   21   Cash withdrawn from the bank £350 for business use.
"   24   Cash Drawings £120.
"   25   Paid T Briers his account of £140, by cash £133, having deducted £7 cash discount.
"   29   Bought fixtures paying by cheque £650.
"   31   Received commission by cheque £88.

13.4A Enter the following in the three-column cash book of an office supply shop. Balance off the cash book at the end of the month and show the discount accounts in the general ledger.

20X8
June   1   Balances brought forward: Cash £97; Bank £2,186.
"   2   The following paid us by cheque in each case deducting a 5 per cent cash discount: R Harris £1,000; C White £280; P Peers £180; O Hardy £600.
"   3   Cash sales paid direct into the bank £134.
"   5   Paid rent by cash £88.
"   6   We paid the following accounts by cheque, in each case deducting $2\frac{1}{2}$ per cent cash discount: J Charlton £400; H Sobers £640; D Shallcross £200.
"   8   Withdrew cash from the bank for business use £250.
"   10   Cash sales £206.
"   12   D Deeds paid us their account of £89 by cheque less £2 cash discount.
"   14   Paid wages by cash £250.
"   16   We paid the following accounts by cheque: L Lucas £117 less cash discount £6; D Fisher £206 less cash discount £8.
"   20   Bought fixtures by cheque £8,000.
"   24   Bought lorry paying by cheque £7,166.
"   29   Received £169 cheque from D Steel.
"   30   Cash sales £116.
"   30   Bought stationery paying by cash £60.

CHAPTER 14

The sales day book and the sales ledger

Learning objectives

After you have studied this chapter, you should be able to:

- distinguish between a cash sale and a credit sale and between the way they are recorded in the accounting books
- explain why, when credit card payments are received at the time of sale, details of the customer are not recorded even though a debtor is created at the same time
- draw up a sales invoice
- explain why multiple copies are often made of each sales invoice
- make the appropriate entries relating to credit sales in a Sales Day Book
- make the correct postings from the Sales Day Book to the Sales Ledger and General Ledger
- explain how trade discounts differ from cash discounts, both in nature and in the way they are treated in the accounting books
- describe measures that may be taken to exercise credit control over debtors

Introduction

In Chapter 11, you learnt that, rather than having only one book of original entry and only one ledger, most businesses use a set of day books (or journals) and a set of ledgers. In this chapter, you'll learn more about the Sales Day Book (or Sales Journal) and the Sales Ledger. You'll also learn how cash and credit sales are entered in these books, and about trade discounts and how to record them.

14.1 Cash sales

As you have already learnt, when goods are paid for immediately they are described as 'cash sales', even where the payment has been made by cheque or transfer of funds from the customer's bank account into the seller's bank account. For accounting purposes, in such cases we do not need to know the names and addresses of customers nor what has been sold to them and, as a result, there is no need to enter such sales in the Sales Day Book. The Sales Day Book (and all the other day books) are only used for credit transactions.

Activity 14.1
Other than for accounting purposes, can you think of anything a business might want to record somewhere outside the accounting records concerning these transactions?

Credit card payments

When customers pay immediately by credit card, so far as recording details of the customer is concerned, this is treated as if it were a payment made by cash. No record is required for accounting purposes concerning the contact details of the customer. However, it is still a credit transaction and it does result in a debtor being created – the credit card company. The double entry would be a credit to the sales account and a debit to the credit card company's account in the Sales Ledger.

14.2   Credit sales

In all but the smallest business, most sales will be made on credit. In fact, the sales of many businesses will consist entirely of credit sales.

For each credit sale, the selling business will give or send a document to the buyer showing full details of the goods sold and the prices of the goods. This document is an 'invoice'. It is known to the buyer as a 'purchase invoice' and to the seller as a **sales invoice**. The seller will keep one or more copies of each sales invoice for his own use.

> **Activity 14.2**
> What uses would the seller have for these copies of the sales invoice?

Exhibit 14.1 is an example of an invoice.

Exhibit 14.1

Your Purchase Order 10/A/980	**INVOICE No 16554**	J Blake 7 Over Warehouse Leicester LE1 2AP 1 September 20X9	

To: D Poole & Co
   45 Charles Street
   Manchester M1 5ZN			

		Per unit	Total
		£	£
21 cases McBrand Pears		20	420
5 cartons Kay's Flour		4	20
6 cases Joy's Vinegar		20	120
			560
Terms 1¼% cash discount if paid within one month			

You must not think that all invoices will look exactly like the one shown in Exhibit 14.1. Each business will have its own design. All invoices will be uniquely numbered, usually sequentially, and they will contain the names and addresses of both the supplier and the customer. In this case, the supplier is J Blake and the customer is D Poole. (A 'purchase order' – there's one referred to in the top left-hand corner of this sales invoice – is the record or document drawn up by the customer that the customer referred to or gave the seller when the order was placed with the seller. It is used by the buyer to check the details of the order against the invoice and against the goods delivered.)

14.3 Copies of sales invoices

As soon as the sales invoices for the goods being sold have been made out, they are given or sent to the customer. The copies kept by the seller are created at the same time as the original.

14.4 Making entries in the sales day book

From the copy of the sales invoice, the seller enters up the transaction in the Sales Day Book. This book is merely a list of details relating to each credit sale:

- Date
- Name of customer
- Invoice number
- Folio column
- Final amount of invoice.

There is no need to show details of the goods sold in the Sales Day Book. This can be found by looking at copy invoices.

We can now look at Exhibit 14.2, which shows page 26 of a Sales Day Book, starting with the record of the sales invoice already shown in Exhibit 14.1. (These could have been on any page. In this example, we are assuming they have been entered on page 26 as pages 1–25 have been filled with details of earlier transactions.)

Exhibit 14.2

Sales Day Book				(page 26)
		Invoice No	Folio	Amount
20X9				£
Sept	1 D Poole	16554		560
ʺ	8 T Cockburn	16555		1,640
ʺ	28 C Carter	16556		220
ʺ	30 D Stevens & Co	16557		1,100
				3,520

14.5 Posting credit sales to the sales ledger

Instead of having one ledger for all accounts, we now have a separate Sales Ledger for credit sale transactions. This was described in Chapter 11.

1 The credit sales are now posted, one by one, to the debit side of each customer's account in the Sales Ledger.
2 At the end of each period the total of the credit sales is posted to the credit of the sales account in the General Ledger.

This is now illustrated in Exhibit 14.3.

Exhibit 14.3 Posting credit sales

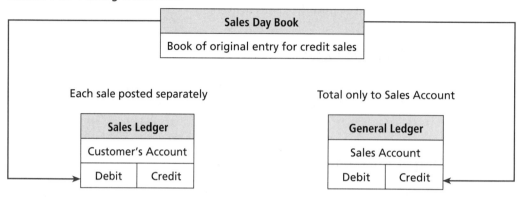

14.6 An example of posting credit sales

The Sales Day Book in Exhibit 14.2 is now shown again. This time, posting is made to the Sales Ledger and the General Ledger. Notice the completion of the folio columns with the reference numbers.

Sales Day Book			(page 26)
	Invoice No	*Folio*	*Amount*
20X9			£
Sept 1 D Poole	16554	SL 12	560
'' 8 T Cockburn	16555	SL 39	1,640
'' 28 C Carter	16556	SL 125	220
'' 30 D Stevens & Co	16557	SL 249	1,100
Transferred to Sales Account		GL 44	3,520

Sales Ledger

D Poole (page 12)

20X9		*Folio*	£		
Sept 1 Sales		SB 26	560		

T Cockburn (page 39)

20X9		*Folio*	£		
Sept 8 Sales		SB 26	1,640		

C Carter (page 125)

20X9		*Folio*	£		
Sept 28 Sales		SB 26	220		

D Stevens & Co (page 249)

20X9		*Folio*	£		
Sept 30 Sales		SB 26	1,100		

General Ledger

Sales (page 44)

		20X9		*Folio*	£
		Sept 30 Credit sales for the month		SB 26	3,520

Before you continue you should attempt Review Question 14.1.

14.7 Trade discounts

Suppose you are the proprietor of a business. You are selling to three different kinds of customer:

1 Traders who buy a lot of goods from you.
2 Traders who buy only a few items from you.
3 Direct to the general public.

The traders themselves have to sell the goods to the general public in their own areas. They have to make a profit to help finance their businesses, so they will want to pay you less than retail price (i.e. the price at which the goods are sold to the general public).

The traders who buy in large quantities will not want to pay as much as those traders who buy in small quantities. You want to attract large customers like these, so you are happy to sell to these traders at a lower price than the price you charge the other customers.

This means that your selling prices are at three levels:

1 to traders buying large quantities,
2 to traders buying small quantities, and
3 to the general public.

Let's use an example to illustrate this. You are selling a make of food mixing machine. The basic price is £200. The traders who buy in large quantities are given 25 per cent trade discount. The other traders are given 20 per cent, and the general public get no trade discount. The price paid by each type of customer would be:

		Trader 1		Trader 2	General Public
		£		£	£
Basic price		200		200	200
Less Trade discount	(25%)	(50)	(20%)	(40)	nil
Price to be paid by customer		150		160	200

You could deal with this by having three price lists, and many businesses do. However, some use trade discounts instead. This involves having only one price list but giving a **trade discount** to traders so that they are invoiced for the correct price.

Exhibit 14.4 is an example of an invoice for a food manufacturer and retailer that shows how trade discount is presented clearly and the trade discounted price easily identified. It is for the same items as were shown in Exhibit 14.1 as having been sold to D Poole. In that example, the seller operated a different price list for each category of customer. This time the seller is R Grant and trade discount is used to adjust the selling price to match the category of customer.

Exhibit 14.4

Your Purchase Order 11/A/G80	**INVOICE No 30756**	R Grant Higher Side Preston PR1 2NL 2 September 20X9	

To: D Poole & Co
    45 Charles Street
    Manchester M1 5ZN
		Tel (01703) 33122
		Fax (01703) 22331	

		Per unit	Total
		£	£
21 cases McBrand Pears		25	525
5 cartons Kay's Flour		5	25
6 cases Joy's Vinegar		25	150
			700
Less 20% trade discount			(140)
			560

By comparing Exhibits 14.1 and 14.4, you can see that the prices paid by D Poole were the same. It is simply the method of calculating the price that is different.

14.8 No double entry for trade discounts

As trade discount is simply a way of calculating sales prices, no entry for trade discount should be made in the double entry records, nor in the Sales Day Book. The recording of Exhibit 14.5 in R Grant's Sales Day Book and D Poole's personal account will be:

Sales Day Book			(page 87)
	Invoice No	Folio	Amount £
20X9			
Sept 2 D Poole	30756	SL 32	560

Sales Ledger
D Poole   (page 32)

20X9		Folio	£	
Sept 2 Sales		SB 87	560	

To compare with cash discounts:

● Trade discounts: *never* shown in double entry accounts, nor in the Trading and Profit and Loss Account.
● Cash discounts: *always* shown in double entry accounts and in the profit and loss part of the Trading and Profit and Loss Account.

Be very careful about this topic. Students often get confused between the treatment of trade discount and the treatment of cash discount. Remember, it is trade discount that is not entered anywhere in the accounts. Cash discount appears in the Cash Book and is always shown in the accounts.

14.9 Manufacturer's recommended retail price

Looking at an item displayed in a shop window, you will frequently see something like the following:

Wide Screen TV:	Manufacturer's Recommended Retail Price	£500
	less discount of 20 per cent	(100)
	You pay only	£400

Very often the manufacturer's recommended retail price is a figure above what the manufacturer would expect the public to pay for its product. In the case of the TV, the manufacturer would probably have expected the public to pay around £400 for the TV.

The inflated figure used for the 'manufacturer's recommended retail price' is simply a sales gimmick. Most people like to feel they are getting a bargain. Most people feel happier about making a purchase like this if they are told they are getting '20 per cent discount' and pay £400, than when they are told that the price is £400 and that they cannot get any discount.

14.10 Credit control

Any organisation which sells goods on credit should keep a close check to ensure that debtors pay their accounts on time. If this is not done properly, the amount of debtors can grow to a level that will make the business short of cash. Businesses that grow too short of cash will fail, no matter how profitable they may be.

The following procedures should be carried out:

1 A credit limit should be set for each debtor. Debtors should not be allowed to owe more than their credit limit. The amount of the limit will depend on the circumstances. Such things as the size of the customer's business and the amount of business done with it, as well as its past record of payments, will help guide the choice of credit limit. Credit rating agencies may be used to assess the credit worthiness of customers before credit is granted.

2 As soon as the payment date set by the seller has been reached, a check should be made to verify whether the debtor has paid the amount due. Failure to pay on time may trigger a refusal to supply any more goods to the customer until payment is received, even if the customer's credit limit has not been reached.

3 Where payment is not forthcoming, after investigation it may be necessary to take legal action to sue the customer for the debt. This will depend on the circumstances.

4 It is important that the customer is aware of what will happen if the amount due is not paid by the deadline set by the seller.

Learning outcomes

You should now have learnt:

1 That 'Sales Day Book' and 'Sales Journal' are different names for the same book.

2 That cash sales are not entered in the Sales Day Book.

3 That when credit card payments are received at the time of sale, details of the customer are not recorded even though a debtor is created at the same time.

4 That the Sales Day Book (or Sales Journal) contains information relating to each credit sale made in each period.

5 That the Sales Day Book is used for posting credit sales to the Sales Ledger.

6 That the total of the Sales Day Book for the period is posted to the credit of the sales account in the General Ledger.

7 How to make the appropriate entries relating to credit sales in a Sales Day Book and make the correct postings from it to the Sales Ledger and General Ledger.

8 How to prepare a sales invoice.

9 Why multiple copies are often made of each sales invoice.

10 That no entry is made for trade discounts in the double entry accounts.

11 That all businesses should operate a sound system of credit control over their debtors.

12 Some measures that may be taken to exercise credit control over debtors.

Answers to activities

14.1 A business may want to know the contact details of cash customers for marketing purposes. In fact, most businesses of any size would like to keep records in a database of all their cash customers for this reason. Businesses may also want to encourage cash customers to open credit accounts with the business so that they may be more likely to buy from the business in future. Also, where the goods sold are to be delivered to the customer, the customer's contact details will need to be recorded, but this will be in a record held elsewhere than in the accounting books.

14.2   Sellers keep copies of sales invoices for a number of reasons including: to prove that a sale took place; to enable the entries in the books to be correctly recorded and checked; to pass to the stock department so that the correct goods can be selected for shipping to the customer; to pass to the delivery department, so that the correct goods will be shipped to the customer and to the correct address, and to enable the goods to be shipped accompanied by a copy of the sales invoice so that the customer can acknowledge receipt of the correct goods.

REVIEW QUESTIONS

14.1   You are to enter up the Sales Day Book from the following details. Post the items to the relevant accounts in the Sales Ledger and then show the transfer to the sales account in the General Ledger.

20X6

Mar	1	Credit sales to J Gordon	£187
	3	Credit sales to G Abrahams	£166
''	6	Credit sales to V White	£12
''	10	Credit sales to J Gordon	£55
''	17	Credit sales to F Williams	£289
''	19	Credit sales to U Richards	£66
''	27	Credit sales to V Wood	£28
''	31	Credit sales to L Simes	£78

14.2A   Enter up the Sales Day Book from the following details. Post the items to the relevant accounts in the Sales Ledger and then show the transfer to the sales account in the General Ledger.

20X8

Mar	1	Credit sales to J Johnson	£305
	3	Credit sales to T Royes	£164
''	5	Credit sales to B Howe	£45
''	7	Credit sales to M Lee	£100
''	16	Credit sales to J Jakes	£308
''	23	Credit sales to A Vinden	£212
''	30	Credit sales to J Samuels	£1,296

14.3   F Benjamin of 10 Lower Street, Plymouth, is selling the following items at the recommended retail prices as shown: white tape £10 per roll, green felt at £4 per metre, blue cotton at £6 per sheet, black silk at £20 per dress length. He makes the following sales:

20X7

May	1	To F Gray, 3 Keswick Road, Portsmouth: 3 rolls white tape, 5 sheets blue cotton, 1 dress length black silk. Less 25 per cent trade discount.
''	4	To A Gray, 1 Shilton Road, Preston: 6 rolls white tape, 30 metres green felt. Less 33$\frac{1}{3}$ per cent trade discount.
''	8	To E Hines, 1 High Road, Malton: 1 dress length black silk. No trade discount.
''	20	To M Allen, 1 Knott Road, Southport: 10 rolls white tape, 6 sheets blue cotton, 3 dress lengths black silk, 11 metres green felt. Less 25 per cent trade discount.
''	31	To B Cooper, 1 Tops Lane, St Andrews: 12 rolls white tape, 14 sheets blue cotton, 9 metres green felt. Less 33$\frac{1}{3}$ per cent trade discount.

You are to (a) draw up a sales invoice for each of the above sales, (b) enter them up in the Sales Day Book and post to the personal accounts, and (c) transfer the total to the sales account in the General Ledger.

14.4A   J Fisher, White House, Bolton, is selling the following items at the retail prices as shown: plastic tubing at £1 per metre, polythene sheeting at £2 per length, vinyl padding at £5 per box, foam rubber at £3 per sheet. She makes the following sales:

20X9

June   1   To A Portsmouth, 5 Rockley Road, Worthing: 22 metres plastic tubing, 6 sheets foam rubber, 4 boxes vinyl padding. Less 25 per cent trade discount.

''   5   To B Butler, 1 Wembley Road, Colwyn Bay: 50 lengths polythene sheeting, 8 boxes vinyl padding, 20 sheets foam rubber. Less 20 per cent trade discount.

''   11   To A Gate, 1 Bristol Road, Hastings: 4 metres plastic tubing, 33 lengths of polythene sheeting, 30 sheets foam rubber. Less 25 per cent trade discount.

''   21   To L Mackeson, 5 Maine Road, Bath: 29 metres plastic tubing. No trade discount is given.

''   30   To M Alison, Daley Road, Box Hill: 32 metres plastic tubing, 24 lengths polythene sheeting, 20 boxes vinyl padding. Less $33\frac{1}{3}$ per cent trade discount.

Required:

(a) Draw up a sales invoice for each of the above sales, (b) enter them up in the Sales Day Book and post to the personal accounts, and (c) transfer the total to the sales account in the General Ledger.

CHAPTER 15

The purchases day book and the purchases ledger

Learning objectives

After you have studied this chapter, you should be able to:

- make the appropriate entries relating to credit purchases in a Purchases Day Book
- make the correct postings from the Purchases Day Book to the Purchases Ledger and General Ledger
- explain the differences between the processes of recording credit sales and credit purchases in the books

Introduction

In this chapter, you'll continue your look at the day books and ledgers by looking in more detail at the Purchases Day Book (or Purchases Journal) and the Purchases Ledger. Having already looked at the sales side of transactions in Chapter 14, you're now going to look at them from the side of purchases. Much of what you will learn in this chapter is virtually identical to what you learnt in Chapter 14. This shouldn't come as a surprise. After all, you're looking once more at how transactions are processed in day books and ledgers and the process ought to be similar as you move from the sales side to the purchases side of similar transactions. If it weren't, accounting would be a far more complex subject than it is.

15.1 Purchases invoices

An invoice is a **purchases invoice** when it is entered in the books of the buyer. As you learnt in Chapter 14, the same invoice from the perspective of the seller would be a sales invoice. For example, in Exhibit 14.1, the first invoice you looked at in Chapter 14,

- in the books of J Blake, the seller, it is a sales invoice, so
- in the books of D Poole, the buyer, it is a purchases invoice.

15.2 Making entries in the purchases day book

From the purchases invoices for goods bought on credit, the purchaser enters the details in the Purchases Day Book (or Purchases Journal).

Activity 15.1

Think back to what you learnt about the list of items contained in the Sales Day Book. What do you think is the list of items recorded in the Purchases Day Book?

There is no need to show details of the goods bought in the Purchases Day Book. This can be found by looking at the invoices themselves. Exhibit 15.1 is an example of a Purchases Day Book.

Exhibit 15.1

Purchases Day Book				(page 49)
		Invoice No	Folio	Amount
20X9				£
Sept	1	J Blake	9/101		560
″	8	B Hamilton	9/102		1,380
″	19	C Brown	9/103		230
″	30	K Gabriel	9/104		510
					2,680

Activity 15.2

Note the entry for 1 September and compare it to the entry on the same date shown in the Sales Day Book of J Blake in Exhibit 14.2. What differences are there between the entries in the two day books? Why do you think these differences arise?

15.3 Posting credit purchases to the purchases ledger

We now have a separate purchases ledger. The double entry is as follows:

1 The credit purchases are posted one by one, to the credit of each supplier's account in the Purchases Ledger.
2 At the end of each period the total of the credit purchases is posted to the debit of the purchases account in the General Ledger. This is now illustrated in Exhibit 15.2.

Exhibit 15.2 Posting credit purchases

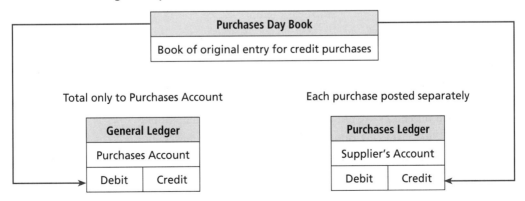

15.4 An example of posting credit purchases

The Purchases Day Book in Exhibit 15.1 is now shown again in Exhibit 15.3 but, this time, posting is made to the Purchases Ledger and the General Ledger. Note the completion of the folio columns indicating that the posting had been completed.

Exhibit 15.3

Purchases Day Book			(page 49)
	Invoice No	Folio	Amount
20X9			£
Sept 1 J Blake	9/101	PL 16	560
8 B Hamilton	9/102	PL 29	1,380
'' 19 C Brown	9/103	PL 55	230
'' 30 K Gabriel	9/104	PL 89	510
Transferred to Purchases Account		GL 63	2,680

Purchases Ledger
J Blake   (page 16)

		20X9		Folio	£
		Sept 1 Purchases		PB 49	560

B Hamilton   (page 29)

		20X9		Folio	£
		Sept 8 Purchases		PB 49	1,380

C Brown   (page 55)

		20X9		Folio	£
		Sept 19 Purchases		PB 49	230

K Gabriel   (page 89)

		20X9		Folio	£
		Sept 30 Purchases		PB 49	510

General Ledger
Purchases   (page 63)

20X9		Folio	£
Sept 30 Credit purchases for the month		PB 49	2,680

Learning outcomes

You should now have learnt:

1 That 'Purchases Day Book' and 'Purchases Journal' are different names for the same book.
2 That cash purchases are not entered in the Purchases Day Book.
3 That the Purchases Day Book is a list of all credit purchases.
4 That the Purchases Day Book is used to post the items to the personal accounts in the Purchases Ledger.

5 That the total of credit purchases for the period is posted from the Purchases Day Book to the debit of the purchases account in the General Ledger.

6 How to make the appropriate entries relating to credit purchases in a Purchases Day Book and make the correct postings from it to the Purchases Ledger and General Ledger.

7 That the process of making entries in the books of the purchaser is very similar to that of making those in the books of the seller.

Answers to activities

15.1 Similarly to the Sales Day Book, the Purchases Day Book is merely a list of details relating to each credit purchase. The list of items is virtually identical to those recorded in the Sales Day Book, the only differences being that it is the name of the supplier that is recorded, not the purchaser, and that the invoice number is replaced with the buyer's own internally generated reference number:

- date
- name of supplier
- the reference number of the invoice
- folio column
- final amount of invoice.

15.2 Apart from the name of the day books, there are two differences. Firstly, the description of the entry in each case contains the name of the other party to the transaction. This is the personal account in the respective ledger (sales or purchases) where details of the transaction will be entered. The second difference is in the entry in the Invoice Number column. In the case of the seller, Blake, the number entered in Chapter 14 was the number of the invoice that Blake gave to the invoice and is the invoice number shown on the invoice in Exhibit 14.1. In the case of the buyer, Poole, the invoice number is one Poole gave the invoice when it was received from the seller, Blake. As with the number assigned to it by the seller, the buyer also gives each purchase invoice a unique number relating to its place in the sequence of purchase invoices that the buyer has received so far in the period. '9/101' probably means 'month nine' (9), 'purchase invoice' (1) 'number one' (01).

REVIEW QUESTIONS

15.1 B Mann has the following purchases for the month of May 20X8:

20X8
May 1 From K King: 4 radios at £30 each, 3 music centres at £160 each. Less 25 per cent trade discount.
" 3 From A Bell: 2 washing machines at £200 each, 5 vacuum cleaners at £60 each, 2 dishwashers at £150 each. Less 20 per cent trade discount.
" 15 From J Kelly: 1 music centre at £300 each, 2 washing machines at £250 each. Less 25 per cent trade discount.
" 20 From B Powell: 6 radios at £70 each. Less 33$\frac{1}{3}$ per cent trade discount.
" 30 From B Lewis: 4 dishwashers at £200 each. Less 20 per cent trade discount.

Required:
(a) Enter up the purchases day book for the month.
(b) Post the transactions to the suppliers' accounts.
(c) Transfer the total to the purchases account.

15.2A   A Rowland has the following purchases for the month of June 20X9:

20X9
June   2   From C Lee: 2 sets golf clubs at £250 each, 5 footballs at £20 each. Less 25 per cent trade discount.
    ''   11   From M Elliott: 6 cricket bats at £20 each, 6 ice skates at £30 each, 4 rugby balls at £25 each. Less 25 per cent trade discount.
    ''   18   From B Wood: 6 sets golf trophies at £100 each, 4 sets golf clubs at £300. Less 33$\frac{1}{3}$ per cent trade discount.
    ''   25   From B Parkinson: 5 cricket bats at £40 each. Less 25 per cent trade discount.
    ''   30   From N Francis: 8 goal posts at £70 each. Less 25 per cent trade discount.

Required:
(a) Enter up the purchases day book for the month.
(b) Post the items to the suppliers' accounts.
(c) Transfer the total to the purchases account.

15.3   C Phillips, a sole trader specialising in material for Asian clothing, has the following purchases and sales for March 20X9:

Mar   1   Bought from Smith Stores: silk £40, cotton £80. All less 25 per cent trade discount.
  ''   8   Sold to Grantley: lycra goods £28, woollen items £44. No trade discount.
  ''   15   Sold to A Henry: silk £36, lycra £144, cotton goods £120. All less 20 per cent trade discount.
  ''   23   Bought from C Kelly: cotton £88, lycra £52. All less 25 per cent trade discount.
  ''   24   Sold to D Sangster: lycra goods £42, cotton £48. Less 10 per cent trade discount.
  ''   31   Bought from J Hamilton: lycra goods £270. Less 33$\frac{1}{3}$ per cent trade discount.

Required:
(a) Prepare the purchases and sales day books of C Phillips from the above.
(b) Post the items to the personal accounts.
(c) Post the totals of the day books to the sales and purchases accounts.

15.4A   A Henriques has the following purchases and sales for May 20X6:

20X6
May   1   Sold to M Marshall: brass goods £24, bronze items £36. Less 25 per cent trade discount.
  ''   7   Sold to R Richards: tin goods £70, lead items £230. Less 33 per cent trade discount.
  ''   9   Bought from C Clarke: tin goods £400. Less 40 per cent trade discount.
  ''   16   Bought from A Charles: copper goods £320. Less 50 per cent trade discount.
  ''   23   Sold to T Young: tin goods £50, brass items £70, lead figures £80. All less 20 per cent trade discount.
  ''   31   Bought from M Nelson: brass figures £100. Less 50 per cent trade discount.

Required:
(a) Write up the sales and purchases day books.
(b) Post the items to the personal accounts.
(c) Post the totals of the day books to the sales and purchases accounts.

CHAPTER 16

The returns day books

After you have studied this chapter, you should be able to:

- make the appropriate entries relating to returns outwards in the Returns Outwards Day Book
- make the appropriate entries relating to returns inwards in the Returns Inwards Day Book
- make the correct postings from the returns day books to the Purchases Ledger, Sales Ledger and General Ledger
- explain the differences between a credit note and a debit note
- describe how a debtor should use statements received from suppliers
- enter up the accounts for credit card transactions
- explain the need for internal checks on all sales and purchases invoices and credit notes
- describe what use may be made of factoring

Introduction

In this chapter, you'll continue your look at the day books and ledgers by looking in more detail at the two day books that are used to record returns – the Returns Inwards Day Book (or Returns Inwards Journal) and the Returns Outwards Day Book (or Returns Outwards Journal). Having already looked at the sales side of transactions in Chapter 14 and the purchases side in Chapter 15, you'll find that much of what you will learn in this chapter is very similar. In fact, postings from the returns day books to the personal accounts are the mirror image of the ones you learnt to make for sales and purchases.

16.1 Returns inwards and credit notes

You know that businesses allow customers to return goods they've bought. You've probably done so yourself at some time or other. Some retail businesses give every customer the right to do so within a few days of the sale and won't ask why they are being returned. It is a means of assuring the customer that the seller believes that the goods are of good quality and will do what the customer wants. Whatever the rights of return granted by the seller, in the UK there are also legal rights of return that permit retail customers to return goods for a refund should the goods prove to have been unfit for the purpose that was intended.

Businesses that deal with trade customers may operate a similar policy, but that would be more unusual and would normally include a proviso that the customer had a justifiable and reasonable reason for returning the goods.

> ### Activity 16.1
> List as many reasons as you can think of why (a) retail customers and (b) trade customers may return goods to the seller.

Sometimes sellers may agree to keep the goods returned, even when they don't normally do so, but won't provide a full refund. Sometimes buyers will agree to keep goods they had wanted to return if the seller offers to refund some of the price they paid.

When the seller agrees to take back goods and refund the amount paid, or agrees to refund part or all of the amount the buyer paid, a document known as a **credit note** will be sent to the customer, showing the amount of the allowance given by the seller.

It is called a credit note because the customer's account will be credited with the amount of the allowance, to show the reduction in the amount owed.

Referring back to Exhibit 14.4, if D Poole returns two of the cases of McBrand Pears, a credit note like the one shown in Exhibit 16.1 would be issued by R Grant, the seller.

Exhibit 16.1

		R Grant Higher Side Preston PR1 2NL

To: D Poole & Co
    45 Charles Street
    Manchester M1 5ZN
		8 September 20X9
		
		Tel (01703) 33122
		Fax (01703) 22331

	CREDIT NOTE No 9/37	
	Per unit	Total
	£ 25	£ 50
2 cases McBrand Pears *Less* 20% trade discount		(10) 40

To stop them being mistaken for invoices, credit notes are sometimes printed in red.

16.2 Returns inwards day book

The credit notes are listed in a Returns Inwards Day Book (or Returns Inwards Journal). This is then used for posting the items, as follows:

1 Sales Ledger: credit the amount of credit notes, one by one, to the accounts of the customers in the ledger.
2 General Ledger: at the end of the period the total of the Returns Inwards Day Book is posted to the debit of the returns inwards account.

16.3 Example of a returns inwards day book

Exhibit 16.2 presents an example of a Returns Inwards Day Book showing the items to be posted to the Sales Ledger and the General Ledger followed by the entries in the ledger accounts.

Exhibit 16.2

Returns Inwards Day Book			(page 10)
	Note No	Folio	Amount £
20X9			
Sept 8 D Poole	9/37	SL 12	40
'' 17 A Brewster	9/38	SL 58	120
'' 19 C Vickers	9/39	SL 99	290
'' 29 M Nelson	9/40	SL 112	160
Transferred to Returns Inwards Account		GL 114	610

Sales Ledger
D Poole   *(page 12)*

	20X9		Folio	£
	Sept 8 Returns inwards		RI 10	40

A Brewster   *(page 58)*

	20X9		Folio	£
	Sept 17 Returns inwards		RI 10	120

C Vickers   *(page 99)*

	20X9		Folio	£
	Sept 19 Returns inwards		RI 10	290

M Nelson   *(page 112)*

	20X9		Folio	£
	Sept 29 Returns inwards		RI 10	160

General Ledger
Returns Inwards   *(page 114)*

20X9		Folio	£	
Sept 30 Returns for the month		RI 10	610	

The Returns Inwards Day Book is sometimes known as the Sales Returns Day Book, because it is goods that were sold that are being returned.

16.4   Returns outwards and debit notes

If the supplier agrees, goods bought previously may be returned. When this happens a **debit note** is sent by the customer to the supplier giving details of the goods and the reason for their return.

The credit note received from the supplier will simply be evidence of the supplier's agreement, and the amounts involved.

Also, an allowance might be given by the supplier for any faults in the goods. Here also, a debit note should be sent to the supplier. Referring back to Exhibit 16.1, Exhibit 16.3 shows an example of the debit note that Poole, the buyer, may have sent to Grant, the seller.

Exhibit 16.3

	D Poole & Co
To: R Grant	**D Poole & Co**
Higher Side	**45 Charles Street**
Preston PR1 2NL	**Manchester M1 5ZN**

To: R Grant
    Higher Side
    Preston PR1 2NL

D Poole & Co
45 Charles Street
Manchester M1 5ZN
7 September 20X9

Tel (0161) 488 2142
Fax (0161) 488 2143

DEBIT NOTE No 9.22

	Per Unit	Total
	£	£
2 cases McBrand Pears damaged in transit	25	50
Less 20% trade discount		(10)
		40

Note the differences between this debit note and the credit note in Exhibit 16.1: the names and addresses have swapped places and the document is described as 'Debit Note No 9.22' rather than 'Credit Note No 9/37', because Poole uses its own debit note numbering sequence. Also, the dates are different. In this case, it is assumed that Poole raised the debit note on 7 September and sent it and the goods to Grant. Grant received the goods on 8 September and raised the credit note on that date. Finally, the reason for the return of the goods is given.

16.5 Returns outwards day book

The debit notes are listed in a Returns Outwards Day Book (or Returns Outwards Journal). This is then used for posting the items, as follows:

1 Purchases Ledger: debit the amounts of debit notes, one by one, to the personal accounts of the suppliers in the ledger.
2 General Ledger: at the end of the period, the total of the Returns Outwards Day Book is posted to the credit of the returns outwards account.

16.6 Example of a returns outwards day book

Exhibit 16.4 presents an example of a Returns Outwards Day Book showing the items to be posted to the Purchases Ledger and the General Ledger followed by the entries in the Ledger accounts.

Exhibit 16.4

Returns Outwards Day Book			(page 7)
	Note No	Folio	Amount
20X9			£
Sept 7 R Grant	9.22	PL 29	40
" 16 B Rose	9.23	PL 46	240
" 28 C Blake	9.24	PL 55	30
" 30 S Saunders	9.25	PL 87	360
Transferred to Returns Outwards Account		GL 116	670

Purchases Ledger
R Grant   *(page 29)*

20X9			Folio	£	
Sept	7	Returns outwards	RO 7	40	

B Rose   *(page 46)*

20X9			Folio	£	
Sept	16	Returns outwards	RO 7	240	

C Blake   *(page 55)*

20X9			Folio	£	
Sept	28	Returns outwards	RO 7	30	

S Saunders   *(page 87)*

20X9			Folio	£	
Sept	30	Returns outwards	RO 7	360	

General Ledger
Returns Outwards   *(page 116)*

				20X9			Folio	£
				Sept	30	Returns for the month	RO 7	670

The Returns Outwards Day Book is sometimes known as the Purchases Returns Day Book, because it is goods that were purchased that are being returned.

16.7 Double entry and returns

Exhibit 16.5 shows how double entry is made for both returns inwards and returns outwards.

Exhibit 16.5 Posting returns inwards and returns outwards

16.8 Statements

At the end of each month, a **statement** should be sent to each debtor who owes money on the last day of the month. It is really a copy of the debtor's account in the seller's books. It should show:

1 the amount owing at start of month;
2 the amount of each sales invoice sent to the debtor during the month;
3 credit notes sent to the debtor in the month;
4 cash and cheques received from the debtor during the month; and, finally,
5 the amount due from the debtor at the end of the month.

Exhibit 16.6 shows an example of a statement.

Exhibit 16.6

STATEMENT OF ACCOUNT

R GRANT
Higher Side
Preston PR1 2NL
Tel (01703) 33122
Fax (01703) 22331

Accounts Dept
D Poole & Co
45 Charles Street
Manchester M1 5ZN

Date	Details	Debit	Credit	Balance
20X9		£	£	£
Sept 1	Balance b/d			880
Sept 2	Invoice 30756	560		1,440
Sept 8	Returns 9/37		40	1,400
Sept 25	Bank		880	520
Sept 30	Balance owing c/d			520
All accounts due and payable within 1 month				

Debtors will check to see if the account in their accounting records agrees with the statement. If the statement shows they owe £520, but their records show a different amount due, they will investigate the difference in order to see whether either the statement or their records is incorrect. If they discover there has been an error in their books, they will correct it. If they find that there is an error in the statement, they will contact the seller.

Activity 16.2

What sort of things could result in the statement and the account held in the books of the debtor showing different balances?

Apart from enabling debtors to check the amount due, the statement also acts as a reminder to debtors that they owe the seller money, and shows the date by which they should make payment. Sellers who are contacted by a debtor querying a statement will benefit from having any errors identified in their records.

16.9   Sales and purchases via credit cards

Various banks, building societies and other financial institutions issue credit cards to their customers. The most common examples are Visa and MasterCard. The holder of the credit card purchases goods or services without giving cash or cheques, but simply signs a credit card voucher. The customer is given a copy and the other copy is filed by the seller. Such sales are very rarely sales to anyone other than the general public.

The seller is paid later by the credit card company for all the credit card transactions in the period since the last payment made to the seller. This payment is subject to a deduction of commission by the credit card company.

Once a month, the customer pays the credit card company for all of the payments charged to the credit card during the previous month.

As far as the purchaser is concerned, he has seen goods and has received them (or received the service he requested). In the eyes of the customer, they were paid for at the time of purchase and a loan has been granted by the credit card company in order to do so.

Once the customer has the goods, or has received the appropriate services, the customer does not become a debtor needing an entry in a Sales Ledger and so (as mentioned in Chapter 14) similarly to a cash sale, no ledger account is maintained for the customer. All the selling company is then interested in, from a recording point of view, is collecting the money from the credit card company.

The double entry needed is:

Sale of items via credit cards:	Dr: Credit card company
	Cr: Sales
Receipt of money from credit card company:	Dr: Bank
	Cr: Credit card company
Commission charged by credit card company:	Dr: Selling expenses
	Cr: Credit card company

Note: the commission is *not* a deduction from the selling price. It is treated in the same way as cash discounts. That is, it is a selling expense and is entered in the profit and loss part of the Trading and Profit and Loss Account.

16.10   Internal check

When sales invoices are prepared, they should be very carefully checked. A system is usually set up so that each stage of the preparation of an invoice is checked by someone other than the person whose job it is to send out the invoice.

> ### Activity 16.3
> What sort of things could occur that make checking of all invoices, both those for sales and those for purchases, something that all businesses should do?

A system should, therefore, be set up whereby invoices are checked at each stage by someone other than the person who sends out the invoices or is responsible for paying them.

For purchase invoices, checks should be established, such as using a rubber stamp to stamp each incoming invoice with a mini form with spaces for ticks as each stage of the check on them is completed. The spaces in the stamp will be filled in by the people responsible for making each of the checks on the purchase invoices received, e.g.:

- one person certifying that the goods were actually received
- a second person certifying that the goods were ordered
- a third person certifying that the prices and calculations on the invoice are correct, and in accordance with the order originally placed and agreed
- a fourth person certifying that the goods are in good condition and suitable for the purpose for which ordered.

Naturally, in a small business, simply because the office staff might be quite small, this cross-check may be in the hands of only one person other than the person who will pay the invoice.

A similar sort of check will be made in respect of sales invoices being sent out and on credit notes, both those being sent out and those being received.

16.11 Factoring

You've already learnt that one of the problems that many businesses face is the time taken by debtors to pay their accounts. Few businesses have so much cash available to them that they do not mind how long debtors takes to pay. It is a rather surprising fact that a lot of businesses which fail do so, not because the business is not making profits, but because the business has run out of cash funds. Once that happens, confidence in the business evaporates, and the business then finds that very few people will supply it with goods. It also cannot pay its employees. Closure of the business then happens fairly quickly in many cases.

As mentioned in Chapter 8, in the case of debtors, the cash flow problem may be alleviated by using the services of a financial intermediary called a **factor**.

Factoring is a financial service designed to improve the cash flow of healthy, growing companies, enabling them to make better use of management time and the money tied up in trade credit to customers.

In essence, factors provide their clients with three closely integrated services covering sales accounting and collection, credit management which can include protection against bad debts, and the availability of finance against sales invoices.

16.12 E&OE

On some invoices and other documents you will see 'E&OE' printed at the bottom. This abbreviation stands for 'Errors and Omissions Excepted'. Basically, this is a warning that there may possibly be errors or omissions which could mean that the figures shown could be incorrect, and that the recipient should check carefully the figures before taking any action concerning them.

Learning outcomes

You should now have learnt:

1 That 'Returns Inwards Day Book', 'Sales Journal' and 'Sales Returns Day Book' are different names for the same book.

2 That 'Returns Outwards Day Book', 'Purchases Journal' and 'Purchases Returns Day Book' are different names for the same book.

3 That goods returned by customers are all entered in a Returns Inwards Day Book.

4 That the Returns Inwards Day Book is used to post each item to the credit of the personal account of the customer in the Sales Ledger.

5 That the total of the Returns Inwards Day Book is debited at the end of the period to the returns inwards account in the General Ledger.

6 That goods returned to suppliers are all entered in a Returns Outwards Day Book.

7 What the difference is between a credit note and a debit note.

8 That the Returns Outwards Day Book is used to debit the personal account of each supplier in the Purchases Ledger.

9 That the total of the Returns Outwards Day Book is credited at the end of the period to the returns outwards account in the General Ledger.

10 How to make the appropriate entries relating to returns in the Returns Inwards and Returns Outwards day books and make the correct postings from them to the Purchases Ledger, Sales Ledger and General Ledger.

11 That the process of making entries for returns in the books of purchasers and sellers is the mirror image of those made in their books for purchases and sales.

12 That statements are used by debtors to check the entries made in their books.

13 Of a range of causes for differences that can arise between statements and the seller's account in the debtor's Purchases Ledger and that such differences may not all be the result of an error.

14 How credit card transactions are recorded in the books and how commission charged to sellers by the credit card companies is treated in the Trading and Profit and Loss Account.

15 Why an effective system of invoice checking should be used by all businesses.

16 Why factoring is an attractive option for some businesses.

Answers to activities

16.1 In either case, the reasons why goods may be returned include:
- they were of the wrong type (e.g. the wrong model number of replacement remote control for a TV)
- the item purchased was one that was already owned by the customer (e.g. a CD)
- they were the wrong colour (e.g. paint doesn't match the existing colour)
- they were the wrong size (e.g. a pair of trousers was too tight)
- they were faulty (e.g. a computer kept crashing)
- a customer bought more than was needed (newsagents returning unsold newspapers)
- a customer changed her mind (e.g. hire purchase agreement on a DVD player)
- a customer saw the same goods elsewhere at a cheaper price
- a customer found the goods too difficult to use (e.g. the instructions for setting up and operating a video recorder were too complicated)
- (for trade customers) a customer had returned a faulty item to them and they were now returning it to their supplier
- items received damaged by the customer (e.g. fruit delivered to a supermarket)
- the seller had asked all customers to return a specific item (e.g. when an electrical good or a child's toy is found to be dangerous).

16.2 Differences could be due to a number of things having occurred, including the following:
- a purchase had been omitted from the books of either the seller or the debtor
- a purchase had been incorrectly entered in the books of either the seller or the debtor
- a purchase had been made at the end of the month but only entered in the books of either the seller or the debtor in the following month
- goods returned had been entered in the books of the seller but not in the books of the debtor
- goods returned had been incorrectly entered in the books of either the seller or the debtor

- the debtor had entered goods as having been returned in the books when, in fact, the goods were not returned to the seller
- a purchase had been recorded in the books of the seller in the debtor's account when it should have been entered in the account of another customer
- a purchase had been recorded in the books of the debtor in the seller's account when it should have been entered in the account of another seller
- a payment made to the supplier and entered in the books of the debtor had not yet been received by the seller
- goods had been despatched by the seller and entered in the books of the seller but had not yet been received by the debtor.

16.3 If this were not done then it would be possible for someone inside a business to send out an invoice at a price less than the true price. Any difference could then be split between that person and the outside business. For example, if an invoice was sent to Ivor Twister & Co for £2,000 but the invoice clerk made it out deliberately for £200 then, if there was no cross-check, the difference of £1,800 could be split between the invoice clerk and Ivor Twister & Company.

Similarly, outside businesses could send invoices for goods which were never received by the business. This might be in collaboration with an employee within the business, but there are businesses sending false invoices which rely on the businesses receiving them being inefficient and paying for items never received. There have been cases of businesses sending invoices for such items as advertisements which have never been published. The cashier of the business receiving the invoice, if the business is an inefficient one, might possibly think that someone in the business had authorised the advertisements and would pay the bill. Besides these there are, of course, genuine errors that an invoice checking system helps to avoid.

REVIEW QUESTIONS

16.1 You are to enter up the Purchases Day Book and the Returns Outwards Day Book from the following details, then to post the items to the relevant accounts in the Purchases Ledger and to show the transfers to the General Ledger at the end of the month.

20X7

May	1	Credit purchase from H Lloyd £119.
"	4	Credit purchases from the following: D Scott £98; A Simpson £114; A Williams £25; S Wood £56.
"	7	Goods returned by us to the following: H Lloyd £16; D Scott £14.
"	10	Credit purchase from A Simpson £59.
"	18	Credit purchases from the following: M White £89; J Wong £67; H Miller £196; H Lewis £119.
"	25	Goods returned by us to the following: J Wong £5; A Simpson £11.
"	31	Credit purchases from: A Williams £56; C Cooper £98.

16.2A Enter up the Sales Day Book and the Returns Inwards Day Book from the following details. Then post to the customers' accounts and show the transfers to the General Ledger.

20X8

June	1	Credit sales to: A Simes £188; P Tulloch £60; J Flynn £77; B Lopez £88.
"	6	Credit sales to: M Howells £114; S Thompson £118; J Flynn £66.
"	10	Goods returned to us by: A Simes £12; B Lopez £17.
"	20	Credit sales to M Barrow £970.
"	24	Goods returned to us by S Thompson £5.
"	30	Credit sales to M Parkin £91.

16.3 You are to enter up the sales, purchases, returns inwards and returns outwards day books from the following details, then to post the items to the relevant accounts in the sales and purchase ledgers. The total of the day books are then to be transferred to the accounts in the General Ledger.

20X9

May	1	Credit sales: T Thompson £56; L Rodriguez £148; K Barton £145.
''	3	Credit purchases: P Potter £144; H Harris £25; B Spencer £76.
''	7	Credit sales: K Kelly £89; N Mendes £78; N Lee £257.
''	9	Credit purchases: B Perkins £24; H Harris £58; H Miles £123.
''	11	Goods returned by us to: P Potter £12; B Spencer £22.
''	14	Goods returned to us by: T Thompson £5; K Barton £11; K Kelly £14.
''	17	Credit purchases: H Harris £54; B Perkins £65; L Nixon £75.
''	20	Goods returned by us to B Spencer £14.
''	24	Credit sales: K Mohammed 57; K Kelly £65; O Green £112.
''	28	Goods returned to us by N Mendes £24.
''	31	Credit sales: N Lee £55.

16.4A   You are to enter the following items in the books, post to personal accounts, and show the transfers to the General Ledger.

20X9

July	1	Credit purchases from: K Hill £380; M Norman £500; N Senior £106.
''	3	Credit sales to: E Rigby £510; E Phillips £246; F Thompson £356.
''	5	Credit purchases from: R Morton £200; J Cook £180; D Edwards £410; C Davies £66.
''	8	Credit sales to: A Green £307; H George £250; J Ferguson £185.
''	12	Returns outwards to: M Norman £30; N Senior £16.
''	14	Returns inwards from: E Phillips £18; F Thompson £22.
''	20	Credit sales to: E Phillips £188; F Powell £310; E Lee £420.
''	24	Credit purchases from: C Ferguson £550; K Ennevor £900.
''	31	Returns inwards from: E Phillips £27; E Rigby £30.
''	31	Returns outwards to: J Cook £13; C Davies £11.

The journal

Introduction

In this chapter, you will learn about the book of original entry that sweeps up all the transactions that have not been entered fully in the other five books of original entry – the Journal. You'll learn about the sort of transactions that are entered in the Journal and how to make those entries. You'll also learn how to transfer those entries to the accounts in the ledgers. Finally, you will learn what the accounting cycle consists of and see how it links all the material you have learnt so far in this book.

17.1 Main books of original entry

We have seen in earlier chapters that most transactions are entered in one of the following books of original entry:

- Cash Book
- Sales Day Book
- Purchases Day Book
- Returns Inwards Day Book
- Returns Outwards Day Book.

These books are each devoted to a particular form of transaction. For example, all credit sales are in the Sales Day Book. To trace any of the transactions entered in these five books would be relatively easy, as we know exactly which book of original entry would contain the item.

17.2 The journal: the other book of original entry

The other items which do not pass through these five books are much less common, and sometimes much more complicated. It would be easy for a bookkeeper to forget the details of these transactions if they were made directly into the ledger accounts from the source documents and, if the bookkeeper left the business, it could be impossible to understand such bookkeeping entries.

Activity 17.1

If these five books are used to record all cash and bank transactions, and all credit purchase and sales items, what are these other items that need to be recorded in a sixth book of original entry?

What is needed is a form of diary to record such transactions, before the entries are made in the double entry accounts. This book is called the **Journal**. It will contain the following, for each transaction:

● the date
● the name of account(s) to be debited and the amount(s)
● the name of the account(s) to be credited and the amount(s)
● a description and explanation of the transaction (this is called a **narrative**)
● a folio reference to the source documents giving proof of the transaction.

The use of a journal makes fraud by bookkeepers more difficult. It also reduces the risk of entering the item once only instead of having double entry. Despite these advantages there are many businesses which do not have such a book.

17.3 Typical uses of the journal

Some of the main uses of the Journal are listed below. It must not be thought that this is a complete list.

● The purchase and sale of fixed assets on credit.
● The correction of errors in the ledger accounts.
● Writing off bad debts.
● Opening entries. These are the entries needed to open a new set of books.
● Adjustments to any of the entries in the ledgers.

The layout of the Journal is:

The Journal

Date	Details	Folio	Dr	Cr
	The name of the account to be debited. The name of the account to be credited. The narrative.			

On the first line in the entry is the account to be debited. The second line gives the account to be credited. It is indented so as to make it obvious that it is the credit part of the double entry. The final line is a description of what is being done and provides a permanent record of the reason(s) for the entry.

You should remember that the Journal is not a double entry account. It is a form of diary, just as are the Day Books you learnt about in Chapters 14 to 16. Entering an item in the Journal is not the same as recording an item in an account. Once the journal entry is made, the entry in the double entry accounts can then be made.

Note for students

The vertical lines have been included above in order to illustrate how the paper within the Journal may be printed. You may find it useful to rule your paper according to this layout when attempting examples and questions on this topic.

17.4   Journal entries in examination questions

If you were to ask examiners what type of bookkeeping and accounting questions are always answered badly by a lot of students they would certainly include 'questions involving journal entries'. This is not because they are difficult, but a lot of students seem to suffer some sort of mental block when doing such questions. The authors, who have been examiners for a large number of accounting bodies around the world, believe that this occurs because students fail to view the journal as a document containing instructions, three per transaction:

1 the account(s) to be debited,
2 the account(s) to be credited, and
3 a description of the transaction.

To help you avoid this sort of problem with journal entries, you'll first of all see what the entries are in the accounts, and then be shown how to write up the Journal for each of these entries. Let's now look at a few examples.

1 Purchase and sale on credit of fixed assets

1 A machine is bought on credit from Toolmakers Ltd for £550 on 1 July 20X8.

The transaction involves the acquisition of an asset matched by a new liability. From what you have learnt in earlier chapters, you will know that the acquisition of an asset is represented by a debit entry in the asset account. You will also know that a new liability is recorded by crediting a liability account. The double entries would be:

				Machinery		Folio	GL1
20X8				£			
July 1	Toolmakers Ltd	PL55	550				

	Toolmakers Ltd		Folio	PL55
	20X8			£
	July 1 Machinery		GL1	550

Activity 17.2

All the folio numbers have been entered in these ledger accounts. You do need to enter them at some time so that you can trace the other side of the entries, but why have they already been entered?

Now what we have to do is to record those entries in the journal. Remember, the journal is simply a kind of diary, not in account form but in ordinary written form. It says which account has to been debited, which account has been credited, and then gives the narrative which simply describes the nature of the transaction. For the transaction above, the journal entry will appear as follows:

Date	Details	Folio	Dr	Cr
20X8			£	£
July 1	Machinery	GL 1	550	
	Toolmakers Ltd	PL55		550
	Purchase of milling machine on credit,			
	Capital purchases invoice No 7/159			

2 Sale of stationery no longer required for £300 on credit to K Lamb on 2 July 20X8.

Here again it is not difficult to work out what entries are needed in the double entry accounts. They are as follows:

	K Lamb		Folio	SL79
20X8			£	
July 2 Stationery	GL51	300		

			Stationery			Folio	GL51
		20X8					£
		July 2 K Lamb			SL79		300

The journal entry will appear as follows:

Date	Details	Folio	Dr	Cr
20X8			£	£
July 2	K Lamb	SL79	300	
	Stationery	GL51		300
	Sales of stationery no longer required			
	See letter ref. KL3X8			

2 Bad debts

A debt of £78 owing to us from H Mander is written off as a bad debt on 31 August 20X8.

As the debt is now of no value we have to stop showing it as an asset. This means that we will credit H Mander to cancel it out of his account. A bad debt is an expense, and so we will debit it to a Bad Debts Account. The double entry for this is shown as:

	Bad Debts		Folio	GL16
20X8			£	
Aug 31 H Mander	SL99	78		

			H Mander			Folio	SL99
		20X8					£
		Aug 31 Bad debts			GL16		78

The journal entry is:

Date	Details	Folio	Dr	Cr
20X8			£	£
Aug 31	Bad debts	GL16	78	
	H Mander	SL99		78
	Debt written off as bad. See letter in file HM2X8			

Correction of errors

This is explained in detail in Chapters 32 and 33. However, the same procedures are followed as in the case of these other types of journal entries.

Opening entries

J Brew, after being in business for some years without keeping proper records, now decides to keep a double entry set of books. On 1 July 20X8 he establishes that his assets and liabilities are as follows:

Assets: Van £840, Fixtures £700, Stock £390,
Debtors – B Young £95, D Blake £45, Bank £80, Cash £20.
Liabilities: Creditors – M Quinn £129, C Walters £41.

The Assets therefore total £840 + £700 + £390 + £95 + £45 + £80 + £20 = £2,170; and the Liabilities total £129 + £41 = £170.

The Capital consists of Assets – Liabilities, £2,170 – £170 = £2,000.

1 July 20X8 will be the first day of the accounting period, as that is the date on which all the asset and liability values were established.

We start the writing up of the books on 1 July 20X8. To do this we:

1 Open asset accounts, one for each asset. Each opening asset is shown as a debit balance.
2 Open liability accounts, one for each liability. Each opening liability is shown as a credit balance.
3 Open an account for the capital. Show it as a credit balance.

The Journal records what you are doing, and why.
Exhibit 17.1 shows:

● The Journal
● The opening entries in the double entry accounts.

Exhibit 17.1

The Journal *(page 5)*

Date	Details	Folio	Dr	Cr
20X8			£	£
July 1	Van	GL1	840	
	Fixtures	GL2	700	
	Stock	GL3	390	
	Debtors – B Young	SL1	95	
	D Blake	SL2	45	
	Bank	CB1	80	
	Cash	CB1	20	
	Creditors – M Quinn	PL1		129
	C Walters	PL2		41
	Capital	GL4		2,000
	Assets and liabilities at this date			
	entered to open the books.		2,170	2,170

General Ledger

Van *(page 1)*

20X8		Folio	£	
July 1	Balance	J 5	840	

		Fixtures				*(page 2)*
20X8		*Folio*	£			
July 1 Balance		J 5	700			

		Stock				*(page 3)*
20X8		*Folio*	£			
July 1 Balance		J 5	390			

		Capital				*(page 4)*
		20X8		*Folio*	£	
		July 1 Balance		J 5	2,000	

Sales Ledger

		B Young				*(page 1)*
20X8		*Folio*	£			
July 1 Balance		J 5	95			

		D Blake				*(page 2)*
20X8		*Folio*	£			
July 1 Balance		J 5	45			

Purchases Ledger

		M Quinn				*(page 1)*
		20X8		*Folio*	£	
		July 1 Balance		J 5	129	

		C Walters				*(page 2)*
		20X8		*Folio*	£	
		July 1 Balance		J 5	41	

Cash Book

			Cash	Bank	*(page 1)*
			Cash	*Bank*	
20X8		*Folio*	£	£	
July 1 Balances		J 5	20	80	

Once these opening balances have been recorded in the books, the day-to-day transactions can be entered in the normal manner.

At the elementary level of examinations in bookkeeping, questions are often asked which entail opening a set of books and recording the day-by-day entries for the ensuing period.

Activity 17.3

Do you think you will ever need to do this again for this business? (Hint: think about the entries to be made at the start of the next accounting period.)

Other items

These can be of many types and it is impossible to write out a complete list. Several examples are now shown:

1 K Young, a debtor, owed £2,000 on 1 July. He was unable to pay his account in cash, but offers a car in full settlement of the debt. The offer is accepted on 5 July 20X9.

The personal account has now been settled and needs to be credited with the £2,000. On the other hand, the business now has an extra asset, a car, resulting in the car account needing to be debited with the £2,000 value that has been placed upon the new car.

The double entry recorded in the ledgers is:

			K Young					SL333
20X9			£	20X9				£
July 1	Balance b/d		2,000	July 5	Motor car		GL171	2,000

			Car		GL171
20X9			£		
July 5	K Young	SL333	2,000		

The journal entry is:

Date	Details	Folio	Dr	Cr
20X9			£	£
July 5	Car	GL171	2,000	
	K Young	SL333		2,000
	Accepted car in full settlement of debt			
	per letter dated 5/7/20X9			

2 T Jones is a creditor. On 10 July 20X9 his business is taken over by A Lee to whom the debt now is to be paid.

Here it is just one creditor being exchanged for another one. The action needed is to cancel the amount owing to T Jones by debiting his account, and to show it owing to Lee by opening an account for Lee and crediting it.

The entries in the ledger accounts are:

			T Jones				SL92
20X9			£	20X9			£
July 10	A Lee	SL244	150	July 1	Balance b/d		150

	A Lee			SL244
	20X9			£
	July 10	T Jones	SL92	150

The journal entry is:

Date	Details	Folio	Dr	Cr
20X9			£	£
July 10	T Jones	SL 92	150	
	A Lee	SL244		150
	Transfer of indebtedness as per letter ref G/1335			

3 We had not yet paid for an office printer we bought on credit for £310 when it was discovered to be faulty. On 12 July 20X9 we returned it to the supplier, RS Ltd. An

allowance of £310 was offered by the supplier and accepted. As a result, we no longer owe the supplier anything for the printer.

The double entry in the ledger accounts is:

RS Ltd							PL124
20X9				£	20X9		£
July 12 Office machinery		GL288	310		July 1 Balance b/d		310

	Office Machinery				GL288
			20X9		£
			July 12 RS Ltd	PL124	310

The journal entry is:

Date	Details	Folio	Dr	Cr
20X9			£	£
July 12	RS Ltd	PL124	310	
	Office machinery	GL288		310
	Faulty printer returned to supplier.			
	Full allowance given. See letter 10/7/20X9.			

17.5 Examination guidance

Later on in your studies, especially in *Business Accounting 2*, you may find that some of the journal entries become rather more complicated than those you have seen so far. The best plan for nearly all students is to follow this advice:

1 On your examination answer paper write a heading 'Workings'. Then show the double entry accounts under that heading.
2 Now put a heading 'Answer', and show the answer in the form of the Journal, as shown in this chapter.

If you are so good at the subject that you can manage without showing the workings, leave them out.

If the question asks for journal entries you must *not* fall into the trap of just showing the double entry accounts, as you could get no marks at all even though your double entry records are correct. The examiner wants to see the journal entries, and you *must* show that as your answer.

17.6 The basic accounting cycle

Now that we have covered all aspects of bookkeeping entries, we can show the whole **accounting cycle** in the form of the diagram in Exhibit 17.2.

Note that the 'accounting cycle' refers to the sequence in which data is recorded and processed until it becomes part of the financial statements at the end of the period.

Exhibit 17.2: The accounting cycle for a profit-making organisation

Source documents

Where original information
is to be found

- Sales and purchases invoices
- Debit and credit notes for returns
- Bank pay-in slips and cheque counterfoils
- Receipts for cash paid out and received
- Correspondence containing other financial
  information

Original entry

What happens to it

Classified and then entered in books of prime entry:

- The Cash Books*
- Sales and Purchases Day Books
- Returns Inwards and Outwards Day Books
- The Journal

Double entry

How the dual aspect of each
transaction is recorded

Double entry accounts

General Ledger	*Sales Ledger*	*Purchases Ledger*	*Cash Books**
Real and nominal accounts	Debtors' accounts	Creditors' accounts	Cash Book and Petty Cash Book

(*Note*: Cash Books fulfil both the roles of books
of original entry and double entry accounts)

Check arithmetic

Checking the arithmetical
accuracy of double entry
accounts

Trial balance

Profit or Loss

Calculation of profit or loss
for the accounting period

Trading and Profit and Loss Account

Closing financial position

Financial statement showing
liabilities, assets and capital at
the end of the accounting period

Balance sheet

Activity 17.4

What are the six books of original entry?

Learning outcomes

You should now have learnt:

1 What the Journal is used for.

2 That the Journal is the collection place for items that do not pass fully through the other five books of original entry.

3 That there is a range of possible types of transactions that must be entered in the Journal.

4 That the opening double entries made on starting a set of books for the first time are done using the Journal.

5 How to make the opening entries for a new set of books in the Journal and in the ledger accounts.

6 That the main parts of the accounting cycle are as follows:

 (*a*) Collect source documents.
 (*b*) Enter transactions in the books of original entry.
 (*c*) Post to ledgers.
 (*d*) Extract trial balance.
 (*e*) Prepare the trading and profit and loss account.
 (*f*) Draw up the balance sheet.

Answers to activities

17.1 All transactions relating to fixed assets. Also, entries have to be recorded somewhere when errors in the books have to be corrected, or when any figures in the ledger accounts need to be changed. Also, any transfers involving the Capital Account, such as when funds are set aside from the Capital Account in order to provide resources should a building need to be repaired or replaced.

17.2 You are looking at the ledger accounts after the details have been entered in them from the Journal and you always enter the folio numbers in ledger accounts as you make the entries, not afterwards. The check that the entries has been completed is made by only entering the folio numbers *in the Journal* as each entry is written in the appropriate ledger account. You could, therefore, see a journal entry in the Journal that has no folio numbers entered against it. This would signify that the journal entry has not yet been fully recorded in the appropriate ledger accounts. As mentioned above, you should *never* see this in a ledger account as the folio number is always entered *at the same time* as the rest of the details from the Journal are entered.

17.3 The need for opening entries will not occur very often. They will not be needed each year as the balances from the previous period will have been brought forward. They will only be required a second time if the business goes through a change in status, for example, if it becomes a limited company.

17.4 Cash Book, Sales Day Book, Purchases Day Book, Returns Inwards Day Book, Returns Outwards Day Book, and the Journal.

REVIEW QUESTIONS

17.1 You are to open the books of K Mullings, a trader, via the journal to record the assets and liabilities, and are then to record the daily transactions for the month of May. A trial balance is to be extracted as on 31 May 20X9.

20X9

May	1	*Assets*: Premises £2,000; Van £450; Fixtures £600; Stock £1,289. Debtors: N Hardy £40; M Nelson £180. Cash at bank £1,254; Cash in hand £45.
		Liabilities: Creditors: B Blake £60; V Reagan £200.
''	1	Paid rent by cheque £15.
''	2	Goods bought on credit from: B Blake £20; C Harris £56; H Gordon £38; N Lee £69.
''	3	Goods sold on credit to: K O'Connor £56; M Benjamin £78; L Staines £98; N Duffy £48; B Green £118; M Nelson £40.
''	4	Paid for motor expenses in cash £13.
''	7	Cash drawings by proprietor £20.
''	9	Goods sold on credit to: M Benjamin £22; L Pearson £67.
''	11	Goods returned to Mullings by: K O'Connor £16; L Staines £18.
''	14	Bought another van on credit from Better Motors Ltd £300.
''	16	The following paid Mullings their accounts by cheque less 5 per cent cash discount: N Hardy; M Nelson; K O'Connor; L Staines.
''	19	Goods returned by Mullings to N Lee £9.
''	22	Goods bought on credit from: J Johnson £89; T Best £72.
''	24	The following accounts were settled by Mullings by cheque less 5 per cent cash discount: B Blake; V Reagan; N Lee.
''	27	Salaries paid by cheque £56.
''	30	Paid rates by cheque £66.
''	31	Paid Better Motors Ltd a cheque for £300.

17.2 You are to show the journal entries necessary to record the following items:

(a) 20X8 May 1 Bought a van on credit from Kingston Garage for £6,790.

(b) 20X8 May 3 A debt of £34 owing from H Newman was written off as a bad debt.

(c) 20X8 May 8 Office furniture bought by us for £490 was returned to the supplier Unique Offices, as it was unsuitable. Full allowance will be given us.

(d) 20X8 May 12 We are owed £150 by W Charles. He is declared bankrupt and we received £39 in full settlement of the debt.

(e) 20X8 May 14 We take £45 goods out of the business stock without paying for them.

(f) 20X8 May 28 Some time ago we paid an insurance bill thinking that it was all in respect of the business. We now discover that £76 of the amount paid was in fact insurance of our private house.

(g) 20X8 May 28 Bought machinery £980 on credit from Systems Accelerated.

17.3A Show the journal entries necessary to record the following items:

20X7

Apr	1	Bought fixtures on credit from J Harper £1,809.
''	4	We take £500 goods out of the business stock without paying for them.
''	9	£28 of the goods taken by us on 4 April is returned back into stock by us. We do not take any money for the return of the goods.
''	12	K Lamb owes us £500. He is unable to pay his debt. We agree to take some office equipment from him at the value and so cancel the debt.
''	18	Some of the fixtures bought from J Harper, £65 worth, are found to be unsuitable and are returned to him for full allowance.
''	24	A debt owing to us by J Brown of £68 is written off as a bad debt.
''	30	Office equipment bought on credit from Super Offices for £2,190.

CHAPTER 18

The analytical petty cash book and the imprest system

After you have studied this chapter, you should be able to:

- explain why many organisations use a Petty Cash Book
- make entries in a Petty Cash Book
- transfer the appropriate amounts from the Petty Cash Book to the ledgers at the end of each period
- explain and operate the imprest system for petty cash
- explain why some organisations use a Bank Cash Book
- make entries in a Bank Cash Book

Introduction

You may remember that you learnt in Chapter 13 that there is a second type of cash book, called the **Petty Cash Book**, which many businesses use to record small amounts paid for in cash. (It was also included in the accounting cycle diagram in Chapter 17.) In this chapter, you'll learn of the type of items that are recorded in the Petty Cash Book, and how to make the entries to it. You'll also learn how to transfer financial data from the Petty Cash Book into the ledgers. Finally, you will learn about bank cash books and how they differ from the cash books you learnt about in Chapter 13.

18.1 Division of the cash book

As businesses continue to grow, some now having a commercial value in excess of that of many smaller countries, you have learnt that, for many, it has become necessary to have several books instead of just one ledger. In fact, nowadays all but the very smallest organisations use sets of ledgers and day books.

Activity 18.1
Why do we have day books? Why don't we just enter every transaction directly into the appropriate ledger accounts?

The Cash Book became a book of original entry so that all cash and bank transactions could be separated from the rest of the accounts in the General Ledger. It is for much the same reason that many organisations use a Petty Cash Book. Every business has a number of transactions of very small value which, were they all recorded in the Cash Book, would only serve to make it more difficult to identify the important transactions that businesses need to keep a close eye upon. Just like the Cash Book, the Petty Cash Book is both a book of original entry and a ledger account.

The advantages of using a Petty Cash Book can be summarised as follows:

- The task of handling and recording small cash payments can be given by the cashier (the person responsible for recording entries in the Cash Book) to a junior member of staff. This person is known as the 'Petty Cashier'. The cashier, who is a more senior and, consequently, higher paid member of staff would be saved from routine work.
- If small cash payments were entered into the main Cash Book, these items would then need posting one by one to the ledgers. For example, if travelling expenses were paid to staff on a daily basis, this could mean approximately 250 postings to the staff travelling expenses account during the year, i.e. 5 days per week × 50 working weeks per year. However, by using a Petty Cash Book, it would only be the monthly totals for each period that need posting to the General Ledger. If this were done, only twelve entries would be needed in the staff travelling expenses account instead of approximately 250.

When a petty cashier makes a payment to someone, then that person will have to fill in a voucher showing exactly what the payment was for. They usually have to attach bills, e.g. for petrol, to the petty cash voucher. They would sign the voucher to certify that their expenses had been received from the petty cashier.

18.2 The imprest system

It is all very well having a Petty Cash Book but, where does the money paid out from it come from? The **imprest system** is one where the cashier gives the petty cashier enough cash to meet the petty cash needs for the following period. Then, at the end of the period, the cashier finds out the amounts spent by the petty cashier, by looking at the entries in the Petty Cash Book. At the same time, the petty cashier may give the petty cash vouchers to the cashier so that the entries in the Petty Cash Book may be checked. The cashier then passes cash to the value of the amount spent on petty cash in the period to the petty cashier. In other words, the cashier tops up the amount remaining in petty cash to bring it back up to the level it was at when the period started. This process is the imprest system and this topped-up amount is known as the petty cash **float**.

Exhibit 18.1 shows an example of this method.

Exhibit 18.1

		£
Period 1	The cashier gives the petty cashier	100
	The petty cashier pays out in the period	(78)
	Petty cash now in hand	22
	The cashier now gives the petty cashier the amount spent	78
	Petty cash in hand at the end of period 1	100
Period 2	The petty cashier pays out in the period	(84)
	Petty cash now in hand	16
	The cashier now gives the petty cashier the amount spent	84
	Petty cash in hand at the end of period 2	100

It may be necessary to increase the petty cash float to be held at the start of each period. In the above case, if we had wanted to increase the float at the end of the second period to £120, then the cashier would have given the petty cashier an extra £20, i.e. £84 + £20 = £104.

In some small organisations, no Petty Cash Book is kept. Instead, at the end of each period, the amount left in petty cash is reconciled (i.e. checked and verified as correct) with the receipts held by the petty cashier. The amount spent is then given to the petty cashier in order to restore the float to its agreed level. However, this is not an ideal method to adopt. Businesses need to control the uses of all their resources, including petty cash, and so virtually every organisation that operates a petty cash float maintains a Petty Cash Book. The most common format adopted is the 'analytical petty cash book'.

18.3   Illustration of an analytical petty cash book

An analytical petty cash book is shown in Exhibit 18.2. This example shows one for an elementary school.

Exhibit 18.2

PETTY CASH BOOK   *(page 31)*

Receipts	Folio	Date		Details	Voucher No	Total	Motor Expenses	Staff Travelling Expenses	Postages	Cleaning	Ledger Folio	Ledger Accounts
£						£	£	£	£	£		£
300	CB 19	Sept	1	Cash								
		"	2	Petrol	1	16	16					
		"	3	J Green	2	23		23				
		"	3	Postages	3	12			12			
		"	4	D Davies	4	32		32				
		"	7	Cleaning	5	11				11		
		"	9	Petrol	6	21	21					
		"	12	K Jones	7	13		13				
		"	14	Petrol	8	23	23					
		"	15	L Black	9	5		5				
		"	16	Cleaning	10	11				11		
		"	18	Petrol	11	22	22					
		"	20	Postages	12	12			12			
		"	22	Cleaning	13	11				11		
		"	24	G Wood	14	7		7				
		"	27	C Brown	15	13					PL18	13
		"	29	Postages	16	12			12			
						244	82	80	36	33		13
							GL	GL	GL	GL		
244	CB 22	"	30	Cash			17	29	44	64		
		"	30	Balance	c/d	300						
544						544						
300		Oct	1	Balance	b/d							

The Receipts Column is the debit side of the Petty Cash Book. On giving £300 to the petty cashier on 1 September, the credit entry is made in the Cash Book while the debit entry is made in the Petty Cash Book. A similar entry is made on 30 September for the £244 paid by the headteacher to the petty cashier. As this amount covers all the expenses paid by the petty cashier, the float is now restored to its earlier level. The credit side is used to record all the payments made by the petty cashier.

The transactions that were recorded in the Petty Cash Book were:

20X8			£
Sept	1	The headteacher gives £300 as float to the petty cashier	
		Payments out of petty cash during September:	
''	2	Petrol: School bus	16
''	3	J Green – travelling expenses of staff	23
''	3	Postages	12
''	4	D Davies – travelling expenses of staff	32
''	7	Cleaning expenses	11
''	9	Petrol: School bus	21
''	12	K Jones – travelling expenses of staff	13
''	14	Petrol: School bus	23
''	15	L Black – travelling expenses of staff	5
''	16	Cleaning expenses	11
''	18	Petrol: School bus	22
''	20	Postages	12
''	22	Cleaning expenses	11
''	24	G Wood – travelling expenses of staff	7
''	27	Settlement of C Brown's account in the Purchases Ledger	13
''	29	Postages	12
''	30	The headteacher reimburses the petty cashier the amount spent in the month.	

The process followed during the period that led to these entries appearing in the Petty Cash Book as shown in Exhibit 18.2 is:

1 Enter the date and details of each payment. Put the amount paid in the Total column.
2 Put the same amount in the column for that type of expense.
3 At the end of each period, add up the Total column.
4 Add up each of the expense columns. The total found in step 3 should equal the total of all the expense columns. In Exhibit 18.2 this is £244.
5 Enter the amount reimbursed to make up the float in the Receipts column.
6 Balance off the Petty Cash Book, carrying down the petty cash in hand balance to the next period.

To complete the double entry for petty cash expenses paid:

1 The total of each expense column is debited to the appropriate expense account in the General Ledger.
2 The Folio Number of each expense account in the General Ledger is entered under the appropriate expense column in the Petty Cash Book. (This signifies that the double entry to the ledger account has been made.)
3 The last column in the Petty Cash Book is a Ledger column. It contains entries for items paid out of petty cash which need posting to a ledger other than the General Ledger. (This might arise, for example, if a Purchases Ledger account was settled out of petty cash.)

Activity 18.2

Where is the other side of the double entry for all these expense postings to the ledgers recorded?

The double entry for all the items in Exhibit 18.2 are shown in Exhibit 18.3.

Exhibit 18.3

Cash Book
(Bank and Folio columns only)   (page 19)

					20X8			Folio	£
					Sept	1	Petty cash	PCB 31	300
					''	30	Petty cash	PCB 31	244

General Ledger
School Bus Expenses   (page 17)

20X8			Folio	£	
Sept	30	Petty cash	PCB 31	82	

Staff Travelling Expenses   (page 29)

20X8			Folio	£	
Sept	30	Petty cash	PCB 31	80	

Postages   (page 44)

20X8			Folio	£	
Sept	30	Petty cash	PCB 31	36	

Cleaning   (page 64)

20X8			Folio	£	
Sept	30	Petty cash	PCB 31	33	

Purchases Ledger
C Brown   (page 18)

20X8			Folio	£	20X8				b/d	£
Sept	30	Petty cash	PCB 31	13	Sept	1	Balance		b/d	13

Note how the Folio column is used to enter 'b/d'. You may have noticed previously that this is done for both 'b/d' and 'c/d' in all ledger accounts and in the Cash Book.

18.4 Bank cash book

Nowadays, many businesses have only a small number of sales that are paid for with cash. The rest of the 'cash' sales are actually paid using credit cards, cheques, and direct transfers into the business bank account using systems like Switch (which is operated by UK banks and involves a customer's bank card being swiped into a special machine in the same way that credit card payments are processed). Switch is used in retail transactions and results in the payment being transferred from the customer's bank account into the business bank account.

Organisations which have only a small number of sales for cash may use a different form of Cash Book from the one you learnt about in Chapter 13. If they do, they will use a Petty Cash Book and a **Bank Cash Book**. The Bank Cash Book is given this name because *all* payments in cash are entered in the Petty Cash Book, and the Bank Cash Book contains *only* bank columns and discount columns.

In a Bank Cash Book (it could also be done in an 'ordinary' Cash Book), an extra column may be added. The extra column would show the details of the cheques and direct transfers banked, with just the total of the banking being shown in the total column.

Exhibit 18.4 shows the receipts side of a Bank Cash Book containing this extra column. The totals of the deposits made into the bank on each of the three days were £192, £381 and £1,218. The details column shows what the bankings are made up of.

Exhibit 18.4

Bank Cash Book (Receipts side)

Date 20X9	Details	Discount £	Items £	Total Banked £
May 14	G Archer	5	95	
" 14	P Watts	3	57	
" 14	C King		40	192
" 20	K Dooley	6	114	
" 20	Cash Sales		55	
" 20	R Jones		60	
" 20	P Mackie	8	152	381
" 31	J Young		19	
" 31	T Broome	50	950	
" 31	Cash Sales		116	
" 31	H Tiller	7	133	1,218

Learning outcomes

You should now have learnt:

1 That the Petty Cash Book saves (*a*) the Cash Book and (*b*) the ledger accounts from containing a lot of trivial detail.

2 That the use of the Petty Cash Book enables the cashier or a senior member of staff to delegate this type of work to a more junior member of staff.

3 That the cashier should periodically check the work performed by the petty cashier.

4 That all payments made by the petty cashier should have petty cash vouchers as evidence of proof of expense.

5 How to enter petty cash transactions into the Petty Cash Book.

6 How to transfer the totals for each expense recorded in the Petty Cash Book to the appropriate ledger accounts.

7 How to operate a float system for petty cash.

8 The difference between a Cash Book and a Bank Cash Book.

9 Why some organisations use a Bank Cash Book instead of a Cash Book.

Answers to activities

18.1 One reason why we have day books is to avoid too much detail being entered in the ledgers.

18.2 In the Petty Cash Book. Like the Cash Book, the Petty Cash Book is not only a book of original entry, it is also an account that would otherwise appear in the General Ledger.

REVIEW QUESTIONS

18.1   The following is a summary of the petty cash transactions of Jockfield Ltd for May 20X8.

May	1	Received from Cashier £300 as petty cash float	£
''	2	Postages	18
''	3	Travelling	12
''	4	Cleaning	15
''	7	Petrol for delivery van	22
''	8	Travelling	25
''	9	Stationery	17
''	11	Cleaning	18
''	14	Postage	5
''	15	Travelling	8
''	18	Stationery	9
''	18	Cleaning	23
''	20	Postage	13
''	24	Delivery van 5,000 mile service	43
''	26	Petrol	18
''	27	Cleaning	21
''	29	Postage	5
''	30	Petrol	14

You are required to:
(a) Rule up a suitable petty cash book with analysis columns for expenditure on cleaning, motor expenses, postage, stationery, travelling.
(b) Enter the month's transactions.
(c) Enter the receipt of the amount necessary to restore the imprest and carry down the balance for the commencement of the following month.
(d) State how the double entry for the expenditure is completed.

(*Association of Accounting Technicians*)

18.2

(a) Why do some businesses keep a petty cash book as well as a cash book?
(b) Kathryn Rochford keeps her petty cash book on the imprest system, the imprest being £25. For the month of April 20X9 her petty cash transactions were as follows:

			£
Apr	1	Petty cash balance	1.13
''	2	Petty cashier presented vouchers to cashier and obtained cash to restore the imprest	23.87
''	4	Bought postage stamps	8.50
''	9	Paid to Courtney Bishop, a creditor	2.35
''	11	Paid bus fares	1.72
''	17	Bought envelopes	0.70
''	23	Received cash for personal telephone call	0.68
''	26	Bought petrol	10.00

(i) Enter the above transactions in the petty cash book and balance the petty cash book at 30 April, bringing down the balance on 1 May.
(ii) On 1 May Kathryn Rochford received an amount of cash from the cashier to restore the imprest. Enter this transaction in the petty cash book.

(c) Open the ledger accounts to complete the double entry for the following:

(i) The petty cash analysis columns headed *Postage and Stationery* and *Travelling Expenses*;
(ii) The transactions dated 9 and 23 April 20X9.

(*Northern Examinations and Assessment Board: GCSE*)

18.3A Rule up a petty cash book with analysis columns for office expenses, motor expenses, cleaning expenses, and casual labour. The cash float is £350 and the amount spent is reimbursed on 30 June.

20X7			£
June	1	H Sangster – casual labour	13
''	2	Letterheadings	22
''	2	Unique Motors – motor repairs	30
''	3	Cleaning materials	6
''	6	Envelopes	14
''	8	Petrol	8
''	11	J Higgins – casual labour	15
''	12	Mrs Body – cleaner	7
''	12	Paper-clips	2
''	14	Petrol	11
''	16	Adhesive tape	1
''	16	Petrol	9
''	21	Motor taxation	50
''	22	T Sweet – casual labour	21
''	23	Mrs Body – cleaner	10
''	24	P Dennis – casual labour	19
''	25	Copy paper	7
''	26	Flat Cars – motor repairs	21
''	29	Petrol	12
''	30	J Young – casual labour	16

CHAPTER 19

Value added tax

Learning objectives

After you have studied this chapter, you should be able to:
- enter up VAT in all the necessary books and accounts
- distinguish between taxable businesses and other businesses
- make out sales invoices including charges for VAT
- fill in a VAT Return form

Introduction

In this chapter, you'll learn about the UK system of Value Added Tax. You will learn about how the concept that *the final consumer pays all* underlies the system and of how VAT is collected in stages as goods pass their way down the supply chain. You'll learn about the different rates of VAT and of the different ways VAT has to be recorded as a result. Finally, you will learn how to prepare a VAT Account and complete a VAT Return.

19.1 What is VAT?

Value Added Tax (VAT) is a tax charged on the supply of most goods and services in the United Kingdom. Some goods and services are not taxable, for example postal services. In addition some persons and businesses are exempted, such as those with low levels of turnover. Value Added Tax is administered in the UK by HM Customs and Excise.

The concept underlying VAT is that the tax is paid by the ultimate consumer of the goods or services *but* that everyone in the supply chain must account for and settle up the net amount of VAT they have received in the VAT tax period, usually three months. If they have received more in VAT than they have paid out in VAT, they must send that difference to HM Customs and Excise. If they have paid out more than they have received, they will be reimbursed the difference.

Goods typically pass through at lest two sellers (the manufacturer and the retailer) before they are finally sold to the consumer. These intermediate stage VAT payments will be cancelled out when the final stage in the chain is reached and the good or service is sold to its ultimate consumer.

Exhibit 19.1 shows, through an example, how the system works.

Exhibit 19.1

In the example in Exhibit 19.1,

1 a manufacturer sells a table to a retailer for £100 plus VAT of £17.50
2 the retailer pays the manufacturer £117.50 for the table
3 the VAT on that sale (£17.50) is sent by the manufacturer to the Customs and Excise
4 the retailer sells the goods to the consumer for £120 plus VAT of £21
5 the customer pays £141 to the retailer for the table
6 the amount of VAT paid for the goods by the retailer to the manufacturer (£17.50) is
   deducted from the VAT received by the retailer from the customer (£21) and the difference
   of £3.50 is then sent to Customs and Excise.

Only the ultimate consumer has actually paid any VAT. Unfortunately, everyone in the
chain has to send the VAT charged at the step when they were in the role of seller.

In theory, the amount received in stages by the Customs and Excise will equal the amount
of VAT paid by the the ultimate consumer in the final stage of the supply chain.

Activity 19.1

Can you think of any circumstances where this may not be the case?

19.2 Background

When VAT was first introduced in 1973 as a result of the entry of the UK into the EU, it
came as quite a shock to the business community and to many accountants. The previous

tax on goods, Purchase Tax, had only applied to manufacturers and wholesalers whose goods were liable to the tax. VAT, on the other hand, applied to virtually all goods and services and all but a few organisations suddenly found they had something extra to worry about.

Every entity responsible for accounting for VAT found that it had 'VAT Returns' to complete every quarter. Being late was not an option and they had to be accurate down to the last penny. As a result, some smaller businesses which lacked the necessary accounting expertise to do their VAT Returns themselves found their accountant's fees going up significantly.

The press of the day was full of horror stories of the impact upon people and businesses of a VAT inspector calling and many businesses were very worried that they would make a mistake in their VAT Return and end up being visited by the 'VAT man'.

Over the years, the initial panic has given way to acceptance that another piece of paper simply has to be processed and a debt outstanding settled or an amount receivable received. Accounting records and accounting systems now deal with VAT routinely and the additional work involved in all but the most complex businesses has now been absorbed and become largely unnoticeable as simply another part of the routine.

This is not to say that VAT is a simple tax to understand. While consumers hardly notice it (goods have to be sold clearly indicating the total price to pay), some organisations suffer at the hands of the complexity by virtue of their being involved in a mixture of goods and/or services, some of which are liable to VAT, some of which are not, and some of which are, but at a different rate of the tax.

Thankfully, this complexity is beyond the scope of this textbook. However, it is important that you know something about the nature of VAT and that, necessarily, means that you need to know something about the range of its application. Let's start with a brief look at the VAT rates and what they apply to.

19.3 VAT rates

The **standard rate** of VAT is decided by Parliament. It has been changed from time to time. At the time of writing it is 17.5 per cent. There is also currently a **reduced rate** of 8% on domestic fuel and power, one of 5% on the installation of some energy-saving materials, and a **zero rate** on items like food sold in a supermarket.

19.4 Standard-rated businesses

You've already seen an example in Exhibit 19.1 of what happens to the VAT when a manufacturer sells to a retailer who then sells to a consumer. Another common example involves a business selling its own product direct to the final consumer.

Imagine that Trader A takes raw materials she has grown and sells some to the general public.

Trader A sells goods to Jones for £100 + VAT of 17.5%:

		£
The sales invoice is for:	Price	100.00
	+ VAT 17.5%	17.50
	= Total price	117.50

Trader A will then pay the £17.50 she has collected to the Customs and Excise.

Note: VAT has to be recorded and included in the VAT Return to the penny.

In both this example and the one shown in Exhibit 19.1, you can see that the full amount of VAT has fallen on the person who finally buys the goods. The sellers have merely acted as unpaid collectors of the tax for HM Customs and Excise.

The value of goods sold and/or services supplied by a business is known as the **outputs**. VAT on such items is called **output tax**. The value of goods bought in and/or services supplied to a business is known as the **inputs**. The VAT on these items is, therefore, called **input tax**.

19.5 Exempted businesses

Some businesses are exempted from accounting for VAT. They do not add VAT to the amount at which they sell their products or supply their services, nor do they get a refund of the VAT they have themselves paid on goods and services bought by them.

The types of businesses exempted can be listed under two headings:

1 **Nature of business**. Various types of business do not have to add VAT to charges for goods or services. A bank, for instance, does not have to add VAT on to its bank charges, nor do credit card companies.
2 **Small businesses**. If small businesses do register for VAT then they will have to keep full VAT records in addition to charging out VAT. To save very small businesses the costs and effort of keeping such records, provided that their turnover is below a certain amount (currently £54,000), they don't need to register unless they want to. They can also deregister if their turnover falls below a certain level (currently £52,000).

> *Activity 19.2*
> Apart from not having to keep VAT records, what advantages might there be for a business that does not register for VAT?

19.6 Zero-rated businesses

This special category of business

1 does not have to add VAT on to the selling price of products, and
2 can obtain a refund of all VAT paid on the purchase of goods or services.

If, therefore, £100,000 of goods are sold by the business, nothing has to be added for VAT but, if £8,000 VAT had been paid by it on goods or services bought, then the business would be able to claim a full refund of the £8,000 paid.

It is **2** above which distinguishes it from an exempted business. A zero-rated business is, therefore, in a better position than an exempted business. Examples of zero-rated businesses are those selling young children's clothing and shoes.

19.7 Partly exempt businesses

Some businesses sell some goods which are exempt, some that are zero-rated, and others that are standard-rated. These traders will have to apportion their turnover accordingly, and follow the rules already described for each separate part of their turnover.

19.8 Different methods of accounting for VAT

If a business is exempted from registering for VAT (an **unregistered business**), it need not keep any VAT records. The amount it enters in its accounting records relating to expenditure would be the total amount paid to suppliers including any VAT. For example, if it purchased goods for £235 that included £35 for VAT, it would enter £235 in its purchases account and make no separate entries for the £35 VAT. It would not charge VAT on its sales. As a result, VAT will not appear anywhere in its accounting records or in its financial statements.

The VAT Account

All registered businesses must account for VAT on all the taxable supplies they make and all the taxable goods and services they receive. This includes standard-rated, reduced rate and zero-rated supplies. They must also keep records of any exempt supplies they make. They must also keep a summary (called a 'VAT Account') of the totals of input tax and output tax for each VAT tax period. All these records must be kept up to date.

Exhibit 19.2 shows an example of a 'VAT Account'[Note] in the format suggested by HM Customs and Excise.

Exhibit 19.2

20X3	£	20X3	£
Input Tax: January	1,000.10	Output Tax: January	1,645.40
February	1,240.60	February	2,288.15
March	845.85	March	1,954.80
	3,086.55		5,888.35
Net overclaim of input tax		Net understatement of output	
from previous returns	(130.65)	tax on previous returns	423.25
Bad debt relief	245.90		
Sub-total	3,201.80	Sub-total	6,311.60
Less: VAT on credits received		*Less:* VAT on credits allowed	
from suppliers	(18.20)	to customers	(14.90)
Total tax deductible	3,183.60	Total tax payable	6,296.70
		Less total tax deductible	(3,183.60)
		Payable to Customs and Excise	3,113.10

Note: Although this is described as a 'VAT Account' and it is set-out like a T-account, it is not ruled off in the way T-accounts are ruled off. It is a memorandum item and is not part of the double entry system.

VAT in the ledger accounts and financial statements

How VAT appears in the ledger accounts and in the financial statements depends on which of the following categories businesses fall into:

1 **Exempted businesses**: Do not record VAT. VAT does not appear in the financial statements.
2 **Standard-rated businesses**: Need to record all output and input VAT. VAT will not appear in the profit and loss account, though it will appear in the balance sheet among either current assets or current liabilities.
3 **Partially exempt businesses**: Need to record all output and input VAT. In the case of input VAT, they must distinguish between (a) expenditure relating to taxable supplies and (b) expenditure relating to exempt supplies. Only (a) can be reclaimed; (b) is added to the net cost to arrive at the cost of each item of expenditure of type (b) to enter in the financial statements.

VAT will not appear in the profit and loss account, though it will appear in the balance sheet among either current assets or current liabilities.

4 **Zero-rated businesses**: Need to record all *input* VAT. VAT will not appear as an expense in the profit and loss account, though it will appear in the balance sheet among the current assets.

The following discussion of the accounting entries needed will, therefore, distinguish between these two types of business: those which do not suffer VAT as an expense, and those to which VAT is an expense.

Note: For simplicity, all the remaining examples in this book use a VAT rate of 10 per cent.

19.9 Entries for businesses which can recover VAT paid

1 Standard-rated and reduced-rated businesses

Value Added Tax and sales invoices

These business will have to add VAT to the value of the sales invoices. It must be pointed out that this is based on the amount of the invoice *after* any trade discount has been deducted. Exhibit 19.3 is an invoice drawn up from the following details:

On 2 March 20X8, W Frank & Co, Hayburn Road, Stockport, sold the following goods to R Bainbridge Ltd, 267 Star Road, Colchester. Bainbridge's Order Number was A/4/559, for the following items:

200 Rolls T56 Black Tape at £6 per 10 rolls
600 Sheets R64 Polythene at £10 per 100 sheets
7,000 Blank Perspex B49 Markers at £20 per 1,000

All of these goods are subject to VAT at the rate of 10 per cent. A trade discount of 25 per cent is given by Frank & Co. The sales invoice is numbered 8851.

Exhibit 19.3

	W Frank & Co **Hayburn Road** **Stockport SK2 5DB** VAT No: 454 367 821	
To: R Bainbridge Ltd 267 Star Road Colchester CO1 1BT	**INVOICE No: 8851**	Date: 2 March 20X8 Your order no A/4/559

	£
200 Rolls T56 Black Tape @ £6 per 10 rolls	120
600 Sheets R64 Polythene @ £10 per 100 sheets	60
7,000 Blank Perspex B49 Markers @ £20 per 1,000	140
	320
Less Trade Discount 25%	(80)
	240
Add VAT 10%	24
	264

The Sales Day Book will normally have an extra column for the VAT contents of the sales invoice. This is needed to make it easier to account for VAT. The entry of several sales invoices in the Sales Day Book and in the ledger accounts can now be examined.

W Frank & Co sold the following goods during the month of March 20X8:

		Total of invoice, after trade discount deducted but before VAT is added	VAT 10%
20X8		£	£
March	2 R Bainbridge Ltd (*see Exhibit 19.3*)	240	24
''	10 S Lange & Son	300	30
''	17 K Bishop	160	16
''	31 R Andrews	100	10

Sales Day Book						(page 58)
		Invoice No	Folio	Net	VAT	Gross
20X8				£	£	£
March	2 R Bainbridge Ltd	8851	SL 77	240	24	264
''	10 S Lange & Son	8852	SL 119	300	30	330
''	17 K Bishop	8853	SL 185	160	16	176
''	31 R Andrews	8854	SL 221	100	10	110
Transferred to General Ledger				800	80	880
				GL76	GL90	

Now that the Sales Day Book has been written up, the next task is to enter the amounts of the invoices in the individual customers' accounts in the Sales Ledger. These are simply charged with the full amounts of the invoices including VAT.

As an instance of this, K Bishop will be shown as owing £176. When she pays her account she will pay £176. It is the responsibility of W Frank & Co to ensure that the figure of £16 VAT in respect of this item is included in the total amount payable to the Customs and Excise.

Sales Ledger
R Bainbridge Ltd (page 77)

20X8		Folio	£	
Mar 2 Sales		SB 58	264	

S Lange & Son (page 119)

20X8		Folio	£	
Mar 10 Sales		SB 58	330	

K Bishop (page 185)

20X8		Folio	£	
Mar 17 Sales		SB 58	176	

R Andrews (page 221)

20X8		Folio	£	
Mar 31 Sales		SB 58	110	

In total, therefore, the personal accounts have been debited with £880, this being the total of the amounts which the customers will have to pay. The actual 'sales' of the business are not £880, but £800. The other £80 is the VAT that W Frank & Co are collecting on behalf of HM Customs and Excise. The double entry is made in the General Ledger:

1 Credit the sales account with the sales content only, i.e. £800.
2 Credit the Value Added Tax account[Note] with the VAT content only, i.e. £80.

Note: This is *not* the same as the VAT Account required to be prepared by HM Customs and Excise.

These are shown as

General Ledger

Sales   (page 76)

		20X8		Folio	£
		Mar 31	Credit sales	SB 58	800

Value Added Tax   (page 90)

		20X8		Folio	£
		Mar 31	Sales Day Book:		
			VAT	SB 58	80

Value Added Tax and purchases invoices

In the case of a taxable business, it has to add VAT to its sales invoices, but it will *also* be able to get a refund of the VAT which it pays on its purchases.

As you saw in Exhibit 19.1, instead of paying VAT on sales to the Customs and Excise, and then claiming a refund of the VAT on purchases, the business sets-off the amount paid as VAT on purchases against the amount paid as VAT on sales. This means that only the difference has to be paid to the Customs and Excise. It is shown as:

	£
(a) VAT collected on sales invoices	xxx
(b) *Less* VAT paid on purchases	(xxx)
(c) Net amount to be paid to the Customs and Excise	xxx

In the (unusual) event that (a) is less than (b), it would be the Customs and Excise that would refund the difference (c) to the business. These settlements between businesses and the Customs and Excise normally takes place every three months, when the VAT Return is completed and submitted by the business to the Customs and Excise.

Activity 19.3

Why do you think it is rare for input VAT (i.e. VAT on purchases) to be greater than output VAT (i.e. VAT on sales)? When might this be most likely to occur?

The recording of purchases in the Purchases Book and Purchases Ledger follows a similar method to that of sales, but with the personal accounts being credited instead of debited.

We can now look at the records of purchases for the same business whose sales have been dealt with, W Frank & Co. The business made the following purchases for March 20X8:

	Total of invoice, after trade discount deducted but before VAT is added	VAT 10%
20X8	£	£
Mar 1 E Lyal Ltd (*see* Exhibit 19.4)	180	18
'' 11 P Portsmouth & Co	120	12
'' 24 J Davidson	40	4
'' 29 B Cofie & Son Ltd	70	7

Before looking at the recording of these in the purchases records, compare the first entry for E Lyal Ltd with Exhibit 19.4 to ensure that the correct amounts have been shown.

Exhibit 19.4

Date: 1/3/20X8
Your order no BB/667
 	
To: W Frank & Co
  Hayburn Road
  Stockport
	E Lyal Ltd
	College Avenue
	St Albans
	Hertfordshire ST2 4JA
	VAT No: 214 634 816
	INVOICE No K453/A Terms: Strictly net 30 days

	£
50 metres of BYC plastic 1 metre wide × £3 per metre	150
1,200 metal tags 500 mm × 10p each	120
	270
Less Trade discount at 33⅓%	(90)
	180
Add VAT 10%	18
	198

The Purchases Day Book entries can now be made:

Purchases Day Book				(page 38)
	Folio	Net £	VAT £	Gross £
20X8				
March 1 E Lyal Ltd	PL 15	180	18	198
'' 11 P Portsmouth	PL 70	120	12	132
'' 24 J Davidson	PL 114	40	4	44
'' 29 B Cofie Ltd	PL 166	70	7	77
Transferred to General Ledger		410	41	451
		GL 54	GL 90	

These are entered in the Purchases Ledger. Once again, there is no need for the VAT to be shown as separate amounts in the accounts of the suppliers.

Purchases Ledger

E Lyal Ltd   *(page 15)*

	20X8		Folio	£
	Mar 1 Purchases		PB 38	198

P Portsmouth   *(page 70)*

	20X8		Folio	£
	Mar 11 Purchases		PB 38	132

J Davidson   *(page 114)*

	20X8		Folio	£
	Mar 24 Purchases		PB 38	44

B Cofie Ltd   *(page 166)*

	20X8		Folio	£
	Mar 29 Purchases		PB 38	77

The personal accounts have been credited with a total of £451, this being the total of the amounts which W Frank & Co will have to pay to them.

The actual cost of purchases is not, however, £451. You can see that the correct amount is £410. The other £41 is the VAT which the various businesses are collecting for the

Customs and Excise. This amount is also the figure for VAT which is reclaimable from the Customs and Excise by W Frank & Co. The debit entry in the purchases account is, therefore, £410, as this is the actual cost of the goods to the business. The other £41 is entered on the debit side of the VAT account.

Notice that there is already a credit of £80 in the VAT account in respect of the VAT added to sales.

General Ledger
Purchases   *(page 54)*

20X8		*Folio*	£	
Mar 31	Credit purchases	PB 38	410	

Value Added Tax   *(page 90)*

20X8		*Folio*	£	20X8		*Folio*	£
Mar 31	Purchases Day Book: VAT	PB 38	41	Mar 31	Sales Day Book: VAT	SB 58	80
'' 31	Balance c/d		39				
			80				80
				Apr 1	Balance b/d		39

In the financial statements of W Frank & Co, the following entries would be made:

Trading Account for the month ended 31 March 20X8:
    Debited with £410 as a transfer from the Purchases account
    Credited with £800 as a transfer from the Sales account

Balance Sheet as at 31 March 20X8:
    The balance of £39 (credit) on the VAT account would be shown as a current liability, as it represents the amount owing to the Customs and Excise for VAT.

2 Zero-rated businesses

These businesses:

1 Do not have to include VAT on their sales invoices, as their rate of VAT is zero or nil.
2 They can, however, reclaim from the Customs and Excise any VAT paid on goods or services bought.

Accordingly, because of 1, no VAT is entered in the Sales Day Book. VAT on sales does not exist. Because of 2, the Purchases Day Book and Purchases Ledger will appear in exactly the same manner as for standard-rated businesses, as already shown in the case of W Frank & Co.

The VAT account will only have debits in it, being the VAT on purchases. Any balance on this account will be shown in the balance sheet as a debtor.

19.10 VAT and cash discounts

Where a cash discount is offered for speedy payment, VAT is calculated on an amount represented by the value of the invoice less such a discount. Even if the cash discount is lost because of late payment, the VAT will not change.

Exhibit 19.5 shows an example of such a sales invoice, assuming a cash discount offered of 2.5 per cent and the VAT rate at 10 per cent.

Exhibit 19.5

		£
Date: 1.3.20X8	ATC Ltd	
Your Order No: TS/778	18 High Street	
	London WC2 E9AN	
To: R Noble		
Belsize Road	VAT No: 967 425 735	
Edgeley		
Stockport	**INVOICE No ZT48910**	

	£
80 paper dispensers @ £20 each	1,600
Less Trade discount at 25%	400
	1,200
Add VAT 10%	117*
	1,317
Terms: Cash discount 2.5% if paid within 30 days	

* *Note*: The VAT has been calculated on the net price £1,200 less cash discount 2.5 per cent, i.e. £30, giving £1,170, 10% of which is £117.

19.11 Entries for businesses which cannot get refunds of VAT paid

As these businesses do not include VAT in the prices they charge, there is obviously no entry for VAT either in the Sales Day Book or in the Sales Ledger. They do not get a refund of VAT on purchases. This means that there will not be a VAT account. All that will happen is that VAT paid is included as part of the cost of the goods bought.

Assume that the only purchase made in a month was of goods for £120 + VAT £12 from D Oswald Ltd. The entries relating to it will appear as:

Purchases Day Book		*(page 11)*	
		Folio	£
20X8		PL 14	132
May 16 D Oswald Ltd			132
Transferred to General Ledger			
			GL 17

Purchases Ledger
D Oswald Ltd   *(page 14)*

			Folio	£
	20X8		PB11	132
	May 16 Purchases			

General Ledger
Purchases   *(page 17)*

20X8	*Folio*	£	
May 31 Purchases Day Book	PB11	132	

Trading Account for the month ended 31 May 20X8 (extract)

	£	£
Sales		xxx
Less Cost of goods sold		
Purchases	(132)	

19.12 VAT included in gross amount

You will often know only the gross amount of an item. This figure will, in fact, be made up of the net amount plus VAT. To find the amount of VAT which has been added to the net amount, a formula capable of being used with any rate of VAT can be used. It is:

$$\frac{\% \text{ rate of VAT}}{100 + \% \text{ rate of VAT}} \times \text{Gross amount} = \text{VAT}$$

Suppose that the gross amount of sales was £1,650 and the rate of VAT was 10 per cent. To find the amount of VAT and the net amount before VAT was added, you use the formula:

$$\frac{10}{100 + 10} \times £1,650 = \frac{10}{110} \times £1,650 = £150$$

Therefore, the net amount was £1,500 which, with VAT of £150 added, becomes £1,650 gross.

Given a VAT rate of 17.5 per cent, to find the amount of VAT in a gross price of £705, the calculation is:

$$\frac{17.5}{100 + 17.5} \times £705 = \frac{7}{47} \times £705 = £105$$

19.13 VAT on items other than sales and purchases

VAT is not just paid on purchases of raw materials and goods for resale. It is also payable on many expense items and on the purchase of fixed assets.

Businesses which *can* get refunds of VAT paid will not include VAT as part of the cost recorded in the ledger account of the expense or fixed asset. Businesses which *cannot* get refunds of VAT paid will include the VAT in the cost recorded in the ledger account of the expense or fixed asset. For example, two businesses buying similar items would treat the following items as shown:

	Business which can reclaim VAT		Business which cannot reclaim VAT	
Buys Machinery £200 + VAT £20	Debit Machinery	£200	Debit Machinery	£220
	Debit VAT Account	£20		
Buys Stationery £150 + VAT £15	Debit Stationery	£150	Debit Stationery	£165
	Debit VAT Account	£15		

19.14 Relief from VAT on bad debts

It is possible to claim relief on any debt which is more than six months old and has been written off in the accounts. You can see an example of this in the VAT Account shown in Exhibit 19.2. Should the debt later be paid, the VAT refunded will then have to be paid back to the Customs and Excise.

19.15 Purchase of cars

Normally, the VAT paid on a car bought for a business is not reclaimable.

19.16 VAT owing

VAT owing by or to the business can be included with debtors or creditors, as the case may be. There is no need to show the amount(s) owing as separate items.

19.17 Columnar day books and VAT

The use of columns for VAT in both sales and purchases day books is shown in Chapter 20.

19.18 Value added tax return forms

At the end of each VAT tax period, a 'Form VAT 100' has to be filled in and sent to the Customs and Excise. The most important part of the form is concerned with boxes 1 to 9 which are shown in Exhibit 19.6. For illustration, we have entered some figues in the form and have assumed a VAT rate of 10 per cent.

The contents of the boxes on form VAT 100 are now explained:

1 This box contains the VAT due on sales and other outputs. We have charged our customers £8,750 VAT on our sales invoices for the period.
2 This box would show the VAT due (but not paid) on all goods and related services acquired in this period from other EU member states. In this case there were no such transactions.
3 This box contains the total of Boxes 1 and 2. This is the total output tax due.
4 This box contains the total of the input tax you are entitled to reclaim for the period. We have made purchases and incurred expenses during the period on which we have been charged £6,250 VAT.
5 This is the difference between the figures in Boxes 3 and 4. If the amount in Box 3 is greater than the amount in Box 4, the amount in Box 5 is the amount payable to Customs and Excise. If the amount in Box 3 is less than the amount in Box 4, the amount in Box 5 is owing to you by HM Customs and Excise. As we have collected £8,750 VAT from our customers, but only suffered £6,250 on all purchases and expenses, we owe the Customs and Excise £2,500, i.e. £8,750 − £6,250.
6 In Box 6 you enter the total sales/outputs excluding any VAT. Our total value of sales for the period was £97,500.
7 In Box 7 you enter the total purchases/inputs excluding any VAT. Our total value of purchases and expenses was £71,900, but some of these expenses were not subject to a charge for VAT.
8 This box contains the total value of all supplies of goods to other EU member states. Of the sales included in Box 6, £10,000 was to other countries within the European Union. VAT was not charged on these sales.
9 This box contains the total value of all acquisitions of goods from other EU member states, including any goods acquired by you from another member state. Of the total purchases included in Box 7, £1,450 was from other countries within the European Union.

Exhibit 19.6

		£	
VAT due in this period on **sales** and other outputs	1	8,750	–
VAT due in this period on **acquisitions** from other **EU member states**	2	–	–
Total VAT due **(the sum of boxes 1 and 2)**	3	8,750	–
VAT reclaimed in this period on **purchases** and other inputs (including acquisitions from the EU)	4	6,250	–
Net VAT to be paid to Customs or reclaimed by you (difference between boxes 3 and 4)	5	2,500	–
Total value of **sales** and all other outputs excluding any VAT. **Include your box 8 figure**	6	97,500	–
Total value of **purchases** and all other inputs excluding any VAT. **Include your box 9 figure**	7	71,900	–
Total value of all supplies of goods and related services, excluding any VAT, to other **EU member states**	8	10,000	–
Total value of all acquisitions of goods and related services, excluding any VAT, from other **EU member states**	9	1,450	–

Only Boxes 1 to 5 actually refer to accounting for VAT. Boxes 6 to 9 are for statistical purposes so that the UK government can assess the performance of the economy and similar matters.

19.19 VAT on goods taken for private use

If a trader takes some goods out of his own business stock for his own private use, then he should be charged with any VAT incurred when the business acquired the goods.

For instance, suppose that Smith, a furniture dealer, takes a table and chairs out of stock for permanent use in his own home. In the business accounting records, both the net cost and VAT relating to the table and chairs were recorded and the VAT will have been reclaimed from HM Customs and Excise. You can't just charge the drawings account with the net cost of the table. That would mean that too much VAT had been reclaimed. You need to charge the proprietor's drawings with both the cost price of the goods *and* the VAT.

The double entry to be made if the table and chairs cost £1,000 + VAT at 10 per cent would, therefore, be:

	£	£
Dr Drawings	1,100	
Cr Purchases		1,000
VAT		100

There can sometimes be complicating circumstances, outside the scope of this book, which might influence the amount of VAT to be charged on such drawings.

19.20 HM Customs and Excise Notices

Alll the rules relating to VAT are contained in 'Notices' issued by HM Customs and Excise. These are all available at the HM Customs and Excise website: www.hmce.gov.uk/

One of the most useful Notices is the one that tells you all about the VAT system, *Notice 700, The VAT Guide* (www.hmce.gov.uk/notices/700conts.htm).

Learning outcomes

You should now have learnt:

1 That very small businesses with a low turnover (at the time of writing it is £54,000) do *not* have to register for VAT. They can, however, do so if they wish.

2 How to prepare a VAT Account as recommended by HM Customs and Excise.

3 That the VAT Account should show the balance owing to, or by, HM Customs and Excise.

4 That the VAT Account prepared for HM Customs and Excise is a memorandum item that is not part of the double entry system and is *not* the same as the ledger account for VAT.

5 That if a business cannot get a refund of VAT on its costs, then the VAT will be included in the costs transferred to the trading and profit and loss accounts, or be included in the cost of fixed assets in the balance sheet. VAT does not appear as a separate item in either financial statement.

6 That although businesses show VAT separately on sales invoices, the VAT is not regarded as part of the sales figure in the trading account.

7 That VAT is calculated on the sales value less any cash discount offered.

8 How to complete a VAT Return.

Answers to activities

19.1 Strictly speaking it should always work that way. Even if goods are never sold by the retailer and have to be scrapped, the system still works. The retailer becomes the final consumer. As a result, it is the retailer who ends up having to pay the full amount of VAT, albeit on the price paid to the manufacturer, rather than on the price at which the goods were being offered for sale.

19.2 The price consumers pay for goods and services from unregistered businesses should be lower than they pay registered businesses for the same items. This should help unregistered businesses compete against their larger competitors, which is good for the unregistered business and for the consumer. As a result, many unregistered businesses go to great lengths – some not exactly legal, such as doing work and being paid in cash so that nothing gets entered in the books – to ensure their turnover does not exceed the registration limit.

19.3 Goods and services are normally sold at a higher amount than was paid for them when purchased. Input VAT may be greater than output VAT when a business is new and has purchased a large amount of stock. It often takes time for a business to become established and for sales to reach their 'normal' level.

REVIEW QUESTIONS

19.1   On 1 May 20X7, D Wilson Ltd, 1 Hawk Green Road, Stockport, sold the following goods on credit to G Christie & Son, The Golf Shop, Hole-in-One Lane, Marple, Cheshire:

Order No A/496
3 sets 'Boy Michael' golf clubs at £270 per set.
150 Watson golf balls at £8 per 10 balls.
4 Faldo golf bags at £30 per bag.

Trade discount is given at the rate of 33$\frac{1}{3}$%.
All goods are subject to VAT at 10%.

(a) Prepare the sales invoice to be sent to G Christie & Son. The invoice number will be 10586.
(b) Show the entries in the personal ledgers of D Wilson Ltd and G Christie & Son.

19.2A   On 1 March 20X6, C Black, Curzon Road, Stockport, sold the following goods on credit to J Booth, 89 Andrew Lane, Stockport SK1 1AA, Order No 1697:

20,000 Coils Sealing Tape	@ £4.40 per 1,000 coils
40,000 Sheets Bank A5	@ £4.50 per 1,000 sheets
24,000 Sheets Bank A4	@ £4.25 per 1,000 sheets

All goods are subject to VAT at 10%.

(a) Prepare the sales invoice to be sent to J Booth.
(b) Show the entries in the personal ledgers of J Booth and C Black.

19.3   The following sales have been made by S Thompson Ltd during the month of June 20X9. All the figures are shown net after deducting trade discount, but before adding VAT at the rate of 10 per cent.

20X9
August	1	to M Sinclair & Co	£150
''	8	to M Brown & Associates	£260
''	19	to A Axton Ltd	£80
''	31	to T Christie	£30

You are required to enter up the Sales Day Book, Sales Ledger and General Ledger in respect of the above items for the month.

19.4   The following sales and purchases were made by R Colman Ltd during the month of May 20X6.

			Net	VAT added
20X6			£	£
May	1	Sold goods on credit to B Davies & Co	150	15
''	4	Sold goods on credit to C Grant Ltd	220	22
''	10	Bought goods on credit from:		
		G Cooper & Son	400	40
		J Wayne Ltd	190	19
''	14	Bought goods on credit from B Lugosi	50	5
''	16	Sold goods on credit to C Grant Ltd	140	14
''	23	Bought goods on credit from S Hayward	60	6
''	31	Sold goods on credit to B Karloff	80	8

Enter up the Sales and Purchases Day Books, Sales and Purchases Ledgers and the General Ledger for the month of May 20X6. Carry the balance down on the VAT account.

19.5A The credit sales and purchases for the month of December 20X7 in respect of C Dennis & Son Ltd were:

			Net, after trade discount £	VAT 10% £
20X7				
Dec	1	Sales to M Morris	140	14
''	4	Sales to G Ford Ltd	290	29
''	5	Purchases from P Hillman & Son	70	7
''	8	Purchases from J Lancia	110	11
''	14	Sales to R Volvo Ltd	180	18
''	18	Purchases from T Leyland & Co	160	16
''	28	Sales to G Ford Ltd	100	10
''	30	Purchases from J Lancia	90	9

Write up all of the relevant books and ledger accounts for the month.

19.6 Louise Baldwin commenced business as a wholesaler on 1 March 20X9.

Her sales on credit during March 20X9 were:

March 9 Neville's Electrical
4 computer monitors list price £180 each, less 20% trade discount
March 17 Maltby plc
20 computer printers list price £200 each, less 25% trade discount
March 29 Neville's Electrical
Assorted software list price £460, less 20% trade discount

All transactions are subject to Value Added Tax at 10%.

(a) Rule up a Sales Day Book and head the main columns as follows.

Date	Name and Details	List price less trade discount £-p	VAT £-p	Total £-p

Enter the above information in the Sales Day Book, totalling and ruling off at the end of March 20X9.
(b) Make the necessary postings from the Sales Day Book to the personal and nominal accounts in the ledger.
(c) Prepare a trial balance at 31 March 20X9.

(Edexcel Foundation, London Examinations: GCSE)

19.7A Mudgee Ltd issued the following invoices to customers in respect of credit sales made during the last week of May 20X7. The amounts stated are all net of Value Added Tax. All sales made by Mudgee Ltd are subject to VAT at 15%.

Invoice No	Date	Customer	Amount £
3045	25 May	Laira Brand	1,060.00
3046	27 May	Brown Bros	2,200.00
3047	28 May	Penfold's	170.00
3048	29 May	T Tyrrell	460.00
3049	30 May	Laira Brand	1,450.00
			£5,340.00

On 29 May Laira Brand returned half the goods (in value) purchased on 25 May. An allowance was made the same day to this customer for the appropriate amount.
    On 1 May 20X7 Laira Brand owed Mudgee Ltd £2,100.47. Other than the purchases detailed above Laira Brand made credit purchases (including VAT) of £680.23 from Mudgee Ltd on 15 May. On 21 May Mudgee Ltd received a cheque for £2,500 from Laira Brand.

Required:

(a) Show how the above transactions would be recorded in Mudgee Ltd's Sales Day Book for the week ended 30 May 20X7.

(b) Describe how the information in the Sales Day Book would be incorporated into Mudgee Ltd's double entry system.

(c) Reconstruct the personal account of Laira Brand as it would appear in Mudgee Ltd's ledger for May 20X7.

(*Association of Accounting Technicians*)

Columnar day books

After you have studied this chapter, you should be able to:

- explain why organisations use columnar day books
- decide which basis is to be used for the selection of analysis columns for columnar day books
- write up columnar day books for sales, purchases or for any other aspect of an organisation
- write up columnar day books that include a column for VAT
- explain the advantages of maintaining columnar day books compared to 'normal' day books
- explain why the advantages of maintaining day books far outweigh the disadvantages of doing so

Introduction

In this chapter, you'll learn why many organisations use columnar day books rather than the form of day book that you have learnt about in earlier chapters of this book. You'll learn how to prepare and make entries into columnar day books, and how to make the appropriate entries from them to the ledgers. In addition, you will learn about how to record VAT in columnar day books and of the advantages of using columnar day books rather than the form of day book you learnt about earlier.

20.1 Columnar purchases day books

So far, you may have assumed that the Purchases Day Book was solely for recording the original entry of purchases on credit and that all other expenditure was first entered in the Journal. There are many organisations which operate their Purchases Day Book in this way. However, many use only one book (the Purchases Day Book) to record all items obtained on credit. This will include transactions involving purchases, stationery, fixed assets, motor expenses, and so on. All credit invoices for any expense will be entered in this book.

However, although only one book is used, all of the various types of items are not simply lumped together. The business needs to know how much was for purchases, how much for stationery, how much for motor expenses, etc., so that the relevant ledger accounts can have the correct amount of expenditure entered in them. This is achieved by having a set of analysis columns in the book, in the same way as you have analysis columns in Cash Books and Petty Cash Books. All of the items are entered in a total column, but then they are analysed as between the different sorts of expenditure.

Exhibit 20.1 shows such a **Columnar Purchases Day Book** or 'Purchases Analysis Book', drawn up for a month from the following list of items obtained on credit:

20X9			£
May	1	Bought goods from D Watson Ltd on credit	296
,,	3	Bought goods on credit from W Donachie & Son	76
,,	5	Van repaired, received invoice from Barnes Motors Ltd	112
,,	6	Bought stationery from J Corrigan	65
,,	8	Bought goods on credit from C Bell Ltd	212
,,	14	Lorry serviced, received invoice from Barnes Motors Ltd	39
,,	23	Bought stationery on credit from A Hartford & Co	35
,,	26	Bought goods on credit from M Doyle Ltd	243
,,	30	Received invoice for carriage inwards on goods from G Owen	58

Exhibit 20.1

Columnar Purchases Day Book (page 105)

Date	Name of business	PL Folio	Total	Purchases	Stationery	Motor expenses	Carriage inwards
20X9			£	£	£	£	£
May 1	D Watson Ltd	129	296	296			
'' 3	W Donachie & Son	27	76	76			
'' 5	Barnes Motors Ltd	55	112			112	
'' 6	J Corrigan & Co	88	65		65		
'' 8	C Bell Ltd	99	212	212			
'' 14	Barnes Motors Ltd	55	39			39	
'' 23	A Hartford & Co	298	35		35		
'' 26	M Doyle Ltd	187	243	243			
'' 30	G Owen	222	58				58
			1,136	827	100	151	58
				GL 77	GL 97	GL 156	GL 198

Exhibit 20.1 shows that the figure for each item is entered in the Total column, and is then also entered in the column for the particular type of expense. At the end of the month the arithmetical accuracy of the additions can be checked by comparing the total of the Total column with the sum of totals of all of the other columns.

It can be seen that the total of purchases for the month of May was £827. This can be debited to the Purchases Account in the General Ledger. Similarly, the total of stationery bought on credit in the month can be debited to the Stationery Account in the General Ledger, and so on. The folio number of the page to which the relevant total has been debited is shown immediately under the total figure for each column, e.g. under the column for motor expenses is GL 156, meaning that this item has been entered on page 156 of the General Ledger.

Note for students

The vertical lines have been included above in order to illustrate how the paper within the purchases analysis book may be printed. You may find it useful to rule your paper according to this layout when attempting examples and questions on this topic. If you do, remember that the number of columns will vary according to the circumstances.

Activity 20.1

Think for a moment about a computerised accounting system – that is, one where all the entries are made on computer and the books are electronic documents. Can you think of any reason why the folio number in such cases would not represent a specific page in a ledger?

The entries in the ledgers can now be shown:

General Ledger
Purchases Account   *(page 77)*

20X9			£	
May	31	Purchases analysis 105	827	

Stationery   *(page 97)*

20X9			£	
May	31	Purchases analysis 105	100	

Motor Expenses   *(page 156)*

20X9			£	
May	31	Purchases analysis 105	151	

Carriage Inwards   *(page 198)*

20X9			£	
May	31	Purchases analysis 105	58	

The individual accounts of the creditors, whether they be for goods or for expenses such as stationery or motor expenses, can be kept together in a single Purchases Ledger. However, there is no need for the Purchases Ledger simply to have accounts only for creditors for purchases. Perhaps there is a slight misuse of the name Purchases Ledger where this happens, but it is common practice amongst a lot of businesses. Many businesses will give it the more correct title in that case of the **Bought Ledger**.

To carry through the double entry involved with Exhibit 20.1 the Purchases Ledger is now shown.

Purchases Ledger
W Donachie & Son   *(page 27)*

	20X9				£
	May	3	Purchases	PB 105	76

Barnes Motors Ltd   *(page 55)*

	20X9				£
	May	5	Purchases	PB 105	112
	''	14	''	PB 105	39

J Corrigan & Co   *(page 88)*

	20X9				£
	May	6	Purchases	PB 105	65

C Bell Ltd   *(page 99)*

	20X9				£
	May	8	Purchases	PB 105	212

D Watson Ltd   *(page 129)*

	20X9				£
	May	1	Purchases	PB 105	296

M Doyle Ltd   *(page 187)*

	20X9				£
	May	26	Purchases	PB 105	243

G Owen   *(page 222)*

		20X9				£
		May	30	Purchases	PB 105	58

A Hartford & Co   *(page 298)*

		20X9				£
		May	23	Purchases	PB 105	35

If the business were split up into departments or sections, instead of having one *Purchases* column it would be possible to have one column for *each* of the departments. In this way, the total purchases for each department for the accounting period could be ascertained. In fact, you could have as many columns as you wanted in this book. It all depends how extensively you want to analyse the credit expenditure recorded in the book. You might, for example, wish to keep all entries for credit purchases made from one supplier in one column dedicated to that supplier and so only post the total purchases from that supplier each month to the supplier's personal account in the Purchases Ledger.

20.2   Columnar sales day books

A similar approach can be adopted with the Sales Day Book. You may, for example, wish to know the sales for each section or department of the business. The 'normal' Sales Day Book shows only the total of sales for the accounting period. In this case, you could use a **Columnar Sales Day Book** (or Sales Analysis Book). For a business selling sports goods, household goods and electrical items, it might appear as in Exhibit 20.2.

Exhibit 20.2

Columnar Sales Day Book

Date	Name of business	SL Folio	Total	Sports Dept	Household Dept	Electrical Dept
20X9			£	£	£	£
May 1	N Coward Ltd	87	190		190	
'' 5	L Oliver	76	200	200		
'' 8	R Colman & Co	157	300	102		198
'' 16	Aubrey Smith Ltd	209	480			480
'' 27	H Marshall	123	220	110	45	65
'' 31	W Pratt	66	1,800		800	1,000
			3,190	412	1,035	1,743

Note for students

As with the Columnar Purchases Day Book, the vertical lines have been included above in order to illustrate how the paper within the Columnar Sales Day Book may be printed. You may find it useful to rule your paper according to this layout when attempting examples and questions on this topic. If you do, remember that the number of columns will vary according to the circumstances.

20.3   Columnar day books and VAT

In the UK, if a business is 'zero-rated' for Value Added Tax (VAT), it doesn't charge customers VAT and so does not add VAT on to the value of its sales invoices and cannot reclaim VAT on its purchases. Items that are zero-rated include most food (but not meals in restaurants and cafés or hot take-away food and drink), books and newspapers, young children's clothing and shoes, prescriptions, and many aids for disabled people.

(VAT was, of course, the subject of Chapter 19. You can also find out more about VAT at the UK Customs and Excise website: www.hmce.gov.uk)

Both Exhibits 20.1 and 20.2 have been prepared on the basis that the business is zero-rated. Let's imagine that the business in Exhibit 20.2 was not zero-rated. The Columnar Sales Day Book would need to include a column for VAT.

In Exhibit 20.3, the debtors are shown charged with the gross amounts (selling price net of VAT plus VAT), e.g. N Coward Ltd with £209 (i.e. £190 plus VAT of £19). The VAT account would be credited with £319 being the total of the VAT column. The sales account would be credited with the sales figures of £412, £1,035, and £1,743. (For ease of calculation, we're using a VAT rate of 10 per cent.)

Exhibit 20.3

Columnar Sales Day Book

Date	Name of business	SL Folio	Total	VAT	Sports Dept	Household Dept	Electrical Dept
20X9			£	£	£	£	£
May 1	N Coward Ltd	87	209	19		190	
" 5	L Oliver	76	220	20	200		
" 8	R Colman & Co	157	330	30	102		198
" 16	Aubrey Smith Ltd	209	528	48			480
" 27	H Marshall	123	242	22	110	45	65
" 31	W Pratt	66	1,980	180		800	1,000
			3,509	319	412	1,035	1,743

Note how all the columns to the right of the VAT column contain the same information as in the zero-rated VAT example in Exhibit 20.2.

Activity 20.2

Why is the total amount received for each sale not inserted in each of the department columns? Hint: students often suggest that the total amount relating to each transaction represents the value of the sale and so it is the total amount that needs to be recorded in the General Ledger in order that the figure for sales in the Trading and Profit and Loss Account is not understated.

Similarly, a Columnar Purchases Day Book could include a VAT column. In this case, the total of the VAT column would be debited to the VAT account. The total of the Purchases column would be debited to the Purchases Account with the total of each expense column debited to the various expense accounts in the General Ledger.

20.4 Advantages of columnar day books

The advantages of columnar day books are that they provide exactly the information an organisation needs, at the time when it is wanted, in a convenient and easy to find place, and they avoid cluttering up the ledgers with lots of detailed transaction data. Different businesses have different needs and, therefore, analyse their day books in different ways.

Columnar day books enable us to do such things as:

1 Calculate the profit or loss made by each part of a business.
2 Draw up control accounts for the sales and purchases ledgers (*see* Chapter 31).
3 Keep a check on the sales of each type of goods sold.

4 Keep a check on goods sold in different locations, departments, or sections.
5 Identify purchasers of each type of good offered for sale.

> **Activity 20.3**
>
> List as many things as you can that could be analysed in a separate column in a columnar day book that would enable an organisation to do something far more easily than when a 'normal' day book is used.

20.5 Books as collection points

You have learnt so far that the Sales and Purchases Day Books, and the day books for returns, are simply collection points for the data to be entered in the accounts of the double entry system. There is nothing by law or accounting standard that says that, for instance, a Sales Day Book has to be maintained. We could just look at the sales invoices and enter the debits in the customers' personal accounts from them. Then we could keep all the sales invoices together in a file. At the end of the month we could add up the amounts of the sales invoices, and then enter that total to the credit of the Sales Account in the General Ledger, but we wouldn't want to! Would we?

> **Activity 20.4**
>
> Spend one minute listing as many advantages as you can for *not* using books of original entry for purchases, sales, and returns transactions. Then spend another minute listing as many disadvantages as you can think of.

While, there is, strictly speaking, no need for columnar day books to be used if entries are made directly into the ledger accounts from the source documents, it is considered good practice to do so, particularly when the accounting records are not computerised.

Learning outcomes

You should now have learnt:

1 That columnar day books and analysis books are two names for the same thing.

2 That columnar day books are used in order to show the value of each of the various types of items bought and sold so that the relevant accounts may have the correct amount entered into them.

3 That the columns in a columnar day book are chosen on the basis of what type of information an organisation wishes to be highlighted as, for example, in the case of a department or a major supplier.

4 How to prepare a columnar day book for entry of the relevant data.

5 How to make entries in columnar day books and transfer the balances at the end of a period to the appropriate ledger accounts.

6 How to include VAT in a columnar day book.

7 That the advantages of maintaining day books far outweigh the disadvantages of doing so.

Answers to activities

20.1 This convention that the folio number represents a page in a ledger is really only applicable to hand-written manual accounting systems. In many organisations, the folio number is the number of the *account* in the ledger, rather than the *page* in the ledger. This is particularly the case in computerised accounting systems, when page numbers, as such, do not exist.

20.2 VAT does not increase sales revenue. It is a tax on sales and the money received in respect of it is passed directly to HM Customs and Excise. VAT does not appear in the Trading and Profit and Loss Account.

20.3 There are many other things columnar day books can enable an organisation to do far more easily than when a 'normal' day book is used. For example, they can be used to

- record the details of all sales to a major customer in a book other than the General Ledger
- record the details of all purchases from a major supplier in a book other than the General Ledger
- identify which supplier(s) each type of good offered for sale was purchased from
- identify which types of goods offered for sale are purchased by a particular supplier.

20.4 There is probably only one advantage of not using these day books – that no one needs to write entries in them if they don't exist. There are many, many disadvantages. The most obvious concerns what happens when an invoice is lost from the box before it is recorded in the ledger, or even after it has been recorded in the ledger. How can you verify the transaction took place or was for the amount of money entered in the ledger? And how can you tell what was actually bought or sold without the original (source) document? All businesses really ought to use day books.

REVIEW QUESTIONS

20.1 C Taylor, a wholesale dealer in electrical goods, has three departments: (*a*) Hi Fi, (*b*) TV, and (*c*) Sundries. The following is a summary of Taylor's sales invoices during the period 1 to 7 February 20X7:

	Customer	Invoice No	Department	List price less trade discount £	VAT £	Total invoice price £
Feb 1	P Small	586	TV	2,600	260	2,860
'' 2	L Goode	587	Hi Fi	1,800	180	1,980
'' 3	R Daye	588	TV	1,600	160	1,760
'' 5	B May	589	Sundries	320	Nil	320
'' 7	L Goode	590	TV	900	90	990
'' 7	P Small	591	Hi Fi	3,400	340	3,740

(*a*) Record the above transactions in a columnar book of original entry and post to the general ledger in columnar form.

(*b*) Write up the personal accounts in the appropriate ledger.
NB Do not balance off any of your ledger accounts.

The VAT rate was 10 per cent.

20.2   Enter up a columnar purchases day book with columns for the various expenses for M Barber for the month from the following information on credit items.

20X6			£
July	1	Bought goods from L Ogden	220
″	3	Bought goods from E Evans	390
″	4	Received electricity bill (lighting & heating from North Electricity Board)	88
″	5	Bought goods from H Noone	110

20X6			£
July	6	Lorry repaired, received bill from Kirk Motors	136
″	8	Bought stationery from Avon Enterprises	77
″	10	Van serviced, bill from Kirk Motors	55
″	12	Gas bill received from North Gas Board (lighting & heating)	134
″	15	Bought goods from A Dodds	200
″	17	Bought light bulbs (lighting & heating) from O Aspinall	24
″	18	Goods bought from J Kelly	310
″	19	Invoice for carriage inwards from D Adams	85
″	21	Bought stationery from J Moore	60
″	23	Goods bought from H Noone	116
″	27	Received invoice for carriage inwards from D Flynn	62
″	31	Invoice for motor spares supplied during the month received from Kirk Motors	185

20.3   Enter up the relevant accounts in the purchases and general ledgers from the columnar purchases day book you have completed for Question 20.2.

CHAPTER 21

Employees' pay

Learning objectives

After you have studied this chapter, you should be able to:

- explain the basic system of PAYE income tax
- explain the difference between employee's and employer's National Insurance Contributions
- calculate the net pay of an employee given details of his or her gross pay and PAYE income tax and other deductions
- calculate the amount of the employer's National Insurance Contribution that would have to be paid on behalf of an employee given details of the employee's gross pay and PAYE income tax and other deductions
- explain how basic pensions and additional pensions are determined

Introduction

In this chapter, you'll learn about the calculation of pay and the deductions that are made from it by an employer for tax and National Insurance. You'll also learn about two forms of state pensions that an employee may be eligible for upon retirement, and about a number of items that reduce an employee's liability to income tax. You'll learn about some benefits that employees can receive as a result of their having made National Insurance Contributions. Finally, you'll learn how to calculate the net payment received by employees after adjusting their gross pay by the reliefs available and deductions, both statutory and voluntary, that have to be made.

21.1 Pay

Employees are paid either a wage or a salary. If you see an advert for a job and it mentions that the rate of pay will be £4 per hour, that is an example of a wage. If, on the other hand, an advert refers to an annual amount, that is a salary. In the UK, we normally talk about wages per hour or per week, and salaries per year.

> *Activity 21.1*
> Write down what you think would be good definitions for the term 'wage' and the term 'salary'.

In the UK, every employee is taxed under a system called **PAYE** (**Pay As You Earn**). This means that for every employee, employers are required by law to make various deductions for tax and National Insurance (effectively a contribution towards some of the free benefits people who have made these contributions receive from the state, such as money paid by the state to someone who is out of work or retired). As a result, a distinction is made between

- **Gross pay,** which is the amount of wages or salary *before* deductions are made, and
- **Net pay,** which is the amount of wages or salary *after* deductions.

Many employees talk about 'take-home pay'. This is, in fact, the same as their net pay.

> ### Activity 21.2
> What other deductions might be made from gross pay by an employer?

21.2 Methods of calculating gross pay

The methods employers use to calculate gross pay vary widely, not just between employers but also for employees in the same organisation. The main methods are:

- a fixed amount per period of time, usually a year;
- piece rate: pay based on the number of units produced by the employee;
- commission: a percentage based on the value of sales made by the employee;
- basic hourly rate: a fixed rate multiplied by number of hours worked.

Arrangements for rewarding people for working overtime (time exceeding normal hours worked) will vary widely. The rate will usually be in excess of that paid during normal working hours. Many people who are being paid salaries are not paid for working overtime.

In addition, bonuses may be paid on top of these 'normal' earnings. Bonus schemes will also vary widely, and may depend on the amount of net profit made by the company, or on the amount of work performed, or on the quality of performance by the employee, or on production levels achieved, either by the whole company or by the department in which the employee works. In some cases, these bonuses can amount to many times an employee's 'normal' salary.

> ### Activity 21.3
> Can you think of any examples where these extremely high bonuses have been paid?

21.3 Income tax deductions

In the UK, the wages and salaries of all employees are liable to have income tax deducted from them. It does not mean that everyone will pay income tax – some may not earn enough to be liable for any tax. However, if income tax is found to be payable, under the PAYE system the employer deducts the tax due from the employee's wages or salary and sends it to the Inland Revenue, the government department in charge of the collection of income tax.

Each person in the UK is allowed to subtract various amounts called 'allowances' from their earnings when calculating how much they are liable to pay in income tax. Many people pay no tax because they earn less than their total allowance. The amounts given for each person depend upon his or her personal circumstances, but everyone is entitled to a personal allowance. For the Income Tax year ending on 5 April 2002, that allowance was £4,535.

An extra allowance is given to blind people. Anyone aged over 65 receives an additional allowance, as do married couples aged over 65. Other allowances available may depend on the type of job. For example, some people can claim allowances for special clothing they need for their job. The totals of these allowances are known as a person's 'personal reliefs' or **personal allowances**. Once these have been deducted, any balance of income remaining will have to suffer income tax. However, contributions to superannuation (or pension) schemes are also deducted before arriving at the amount upon which tax is due – you'll learn about superannuation contributions later in this chapter.

The calculation is, therefore:

	£
Gross pay	xxx
Less: reliefs	(xxx)
Pay which is taxable	xxx

Two people may, therefore, earn the same wages, but if one of them gets more allowances than the other, he or she will have less taxable pay, and so will pay less income tax than the other person.

Each year in the Budget, the Chancellor of the Exchequer announces what the rates of income tax are going to be for the following year, and also how much is to be deducted in respect of each allowance.

Because of the annual changes in tax rates and allowances, the rates of income tax shown from here onwards are for illustration only, and are not necessarily the actual rates of income tax at the time you are reading this book.

Let's assume that the rates of income tax (on the amount actually exceeding the allowances for each person) are:

On the first £3,000	Income Tax at 20%
On the next £24,000	Income Tax at 25%
On the remainder	Income Tax at 40%

The income tax payable by each of four people can now be calculated:

1 Miss Brown earns £3,800 per annum. Her personal reliefs amount to £4,000. Income tax payable = Nil.
2 Mr Green earns £8,760 per annum. His personal reliefs amount to £4,000. Income tax is therefore payable on the excess of £4,760. This amounts to:

		£
On first £3,000 at 20%	=	600
On remaining £1,760 at 25%	=	440
Total income tax for the year		1,040

3 Mr Black earns £10,700 per annum. His personal reliefs amount to £5,300. Income tax is therefore payable on the excess of £5,400. This amounts to:

		£
On first £3,000 at 20%	=	600
On remaining £2,400 at 25%	=	600
Total income tax for the year		1,200

4 Mr White earns £39,700 per annum. His personal allowances amount to £5,200. Income tax is therefore payable on the excess of £34,500. This amounts to:

		£
On first £3,000 at 20%	=	600
On next £24,000 at 25%	=	6,000
On remaining £7,500 at 40%	=	3,000
Total income tax for the year		9,600

Let's assume that Miss Brown and Mr Green are paid weekly, and Mr Black and Mr White are paid monthly. If each payment to them during the year was of equal amounts, then we can calculate the amount of PAYE deducted from each payment of earnings.

PAYE deducted on a weekly basis:

1 Miss Brown. Tax for year = nil. Tax each week = nil.
2 Mr Green. Tax for year = £1,040. Tax each week £1,040 ÷ 52 = £20.

PAYE deducted on a monthly basis:

3 Mr Black. Tax for year = £1,200. Tax each month £1,200 ÷ 12 = £100.
4 Mr White. Tax for year = £9,600. Tax each month £9,600 ÷ 12 = £800.

These examples were deliberately made easy to understand. In real life, earnings may change part-way through a tax year, the amounts paid each week or month may be different, etc. The Inland Revenue issues employers with tax tables to help calculate the PAYE code numbers used to deal with the different allowances employees may have, and we shall look at these next.

21.4 PAYE code numbers

We have already seen that personal reliefs, which are deducted from gross pay to find taxable pay, will vary between employees.

When employers come to use tax tables they need an easy method of knowing the amount of personal reliefs to which each of their employees is entitled. The Inland Revenue solve this for employers by giving each employee a tax code number and giving the employer books of tax code tables that show what tax to deduct.

The **tax code** will incorporate all the tax reliefs to which the employee is entitled. This means that should the worker receive extra reliefs for special clothing, or for being blind, these extra reliefs will be incorporated into the tax code.

To find the tax code, the total of all the reliefs is first calculated. The tax code will consist of the total reliefs excluding the final digit. The number will be followed by a letter. For example:

L means a code incorporating the basic personal allowance.
P is for a tax code with the full personal allowance for those aged 65–74.

In the case of the employees given in section 21.3

- Miss Brown's personal reliefs amounted to £4,000. Her tax code will be 400L.
- Mr Green's personal reliefs amounted to £4,000. His tax code will be 400L.
- Mr Black is aged 66. His personal tax reliefs amounted to £5,300. His tax code will be 530P.
- Mr White is aged 69. His personal tax reliefs amounted to £5,200. His tax code will be 520P.

21.5 National Insurance

In the UK, National Insurance Contributions have to be paid for and by each employee. In return, the employee may claim benefits from the state, if and when required, e.g. for retirement or when unemployment. The actual benefits available in return for these contributions are:

- Incapacity Benefit
- Jobseeker's Allowance
- Maternity Allowance
- Retirement Pension

- Widowed Mother's Allowance
- Widow's Payment
- Widow's Pension.

National Insurance Contributions are split into two parts:

(*a*) the part that employees have to suffer by it being deducted from their pay;
(*b*) the part that the employer has to suffer. This is not deductible from pay.

The rates change from time to time but, assuming a total national insurance rate of 19 per cent, of which the employee's contribution is 9 per cent and the employer's contribution 10 per cent, then £38 total contribution will have to be paid in respect of an employee who has earned £200 in the period, i.e. £200 × 19% = £38.

Of this, £18 (9%) can be deducted from the employee's pay, whilst £20 (10%) is a cost of the employer.

Pensions

Paying National Insurance Contributions results in employees receiving a state pension when they retire. Where an employee qualifies for a 'basic pension', the pension paid is based upon the number of years in which the 'minimum amount' of contributions were paid. This minimum amount is based on employees needing to have paid contributions on earnings of at least 52 times the weekly lower earnings limit during a tax year. If the weekly lower earnings limit is £100, the employee would need to have earned £5,200 in the year for that year to included in the calculation of the basic pension. The number of years when this occurred is then multiplied by the basic pension per year to arrive at the amount of basic pension the individual will receive.

Where employees pay more than the minimum amount required for a basic pension, they will be entitled to an extra pension on top of their basic pension. This is known as 'additional pension' (AP). It is based upon earnings during the employee's working life from the year 1978–79 to that ending before the one in which the employee reaches retirement age.

Where an employee belongs to a contracted-out (superannuation or) occupational pension scheme (one operated by or on behalf of their employer) or a personal pension scheme (one run by, for example, an insurance company to which the employee makes contributions out of net pay), that scheme will provide a pension wholly or partly in place of any additional pension the individual may have otherwise been eligible to receive.

21.6 Other deductions from pay

Pensions contributions

An employee may belong to a company's occupational pension scheme. The money paid into the fund will be paid partly by the company and partly by the employee. For example, in many cases the employee's contribution will be 6 per cent, with the company paying whatever is necessary to give the employee the agreed amount of pension.

The amount of the contribution payable by the employee will, therefore, be deducted in calculating the net pay due to them.

Voluntary contributions

These include items such as charitable donations, subscriptions to the business's social club, union subscriptions and payments under a 'Save as You Earn' (SAYE) Scheme.

21.7　Statutory Sick Pay and Statutory Maternity Pay

1 Statutory Sick Pay (SSP) is a payment made to employees when they are ill and absent from work. At present, it is not paid for the first three days of illness, and is limited to a total of 28 weeks' maximum.
2 Statutory Maternity Pay (SMP) is a payment made for up to 18 weeks to an employee away from work on maternity leave.

SSP and SMP are paid to employees in the same way as ordinary wages. They are both liable to have income tax and National Insurance deducted from them.

21.8　Calculation of net wages/salary payable

UK students who need to know how to use PAYE tax and National Insurance tables will need to study this further.

For general guidance for all readers, and for those who do not want to know about the use of income tax and National Insurance tables, we can look at two general examples of the calculation of net pay. The percentages used are for illustrative purposes only.

		£
(A) G Jarvis:	Gross earnings for the week ended 8 May 20X8	100
	Income tax: found by consulting tax tables and employee's code number	12
	National Insurance: 9% of gross pay	9

G Jarvis: Payslip week ended 8 May 20X8

	£	£
Gross pay for the week		100
Less Income tax	12	
National Insurance	9	
		(21)
Net pay		79

		£
(B) H Reddish:	Gross earnings for the month of May 20X8	800
	Income tax (from tax tables)	150
	Superannuation: 6% of gross pay	48
	National Insurance: 9% of gross pay	72

H Reddish: Payslip month ended 31 May 20X8

	£	£
Gross pay for the month		800
Less Income tax	150	
Superannuation	48	
National Insurance	72	
		(270)
Net pay		530

The total costs to the employer in each of the above cases will be as follows, assuming the employer's part of National Insurance Contributions to be £10 for Jarvis and £80 for Reddish:

	G Jarvis	H Reddish
	£	£
Gross pay	100	800
Employer's share of National Insurance	10	80
Total cost to the employer	110	880

It will be the figures of £110 and £880 that will be incorporated in the Trading and Profit and Loss Account as expenses shown under wages and salaries headings.

You can find out more about income tax and National Insurance Contributions at the Inland Revenue website: www.inlandrevenue.gov.uk

Learning outcomes

You should now have learnt:

1 That the PAYE system ensures that employees pay tax on their earnings.

2 That the amount of tax paid varies between employees and depends on their eligibility for the various reliefs available.

3 That tax codes are used by employers to calculate tax due by employees.

4 That National Insurance Contributions are deducted from earnings at the same time as income tax.

5 That superannuation (i.e. pension) contributions are deducted from earnings to find taxable pay.

6 That the level of state pension is dependent upon the individual having paid sufficient employee's National Insurance Contributions before reaching retirement age.

7 That employees who are members of a superannuation (or occupational pension) scheme pay lower levels of National Insurance Contributions.

8 That employers pay an employer's National Insurance Contribution on behalf of each employee.

9 How to calculate net pay given the gross pay, PAYE, and NIC amounts.

Answers to activities

21.1 There is no exact definition of 'wage' or of 'salary'. In general, it is accepted that wages are earnings paid on a weekly basis, whilst salaries are paid monthly. In accounting, you will see this distinction taken a step further when you look at types of costs in Chapter 47. In effect, accounting assumes that salaries are fixed amounts paid monthly and that people who are paid a salary do not receive any extra payment should they happen to work extra hours in the month. Those who earn wages are assumed to be paid extra when they work extra hours.

21.2 Other deductions include contributions to a superannuation scheme (i.e. a pension scheme), charitable contributions (where the employee has agreed to give some of the wage or salary to a charity and has asked the employer to deduct the money from the amount earned), and subscriptions to a trade union (where the employer has asked that this be done). None of these are compulsory, but they all affect the amount the employee is left with as 'take-home pay'.

21.3 People working as traders in the financial markets can earn huge amounts in bonus payments – figures in excess of £1 million are not unusual – if they or their business have had a particularly successful year. However, very few people perform this type of work, and some of those who do receive very small bonuses if, indeed, they receive any bonus at all.

REVIEW QUESTIONS

Note: These questions are for general use only. They have been designed to be able to be worked out without the use of tax and National Insurance tables. The National Insurance given is the employee's part only.

21.1 H Smith is employed at a rate of £5 per hour. During the week to 18 May 20X9 he worked his basic week of 40 hours. According to the requisite tables the income tax due on his wages was £27, and National Insurance £16. Calculate his net wages.

21.2 B Charles has a basic working week of 40 hours, paid at the rate of £4 per hour. For hours worked in excess of this he is paid 1½ times basic rate. In the week to 12 March 20X6 he worked 45 hours. The first £80 per week is free of income tax, on the next £50 he pays at the 20% rate and above that he pays at the 25% rate. National Insurance amounted to £17. Calculate his net wages.

21.3 B Croft has a job as a car salesman. He is paid a basic salary of £200 per month, with a commission extra of 2% on the value of his car sales. During the month of April 20X6 he sells £30,000 worth of cars. The first £450 per month is free of income tax, on the next £50 he pays at the 20% rate and above that he pays at the 25% rate. He also pays National Insurance for the month of £66. Calculate his net pay for the month.

21.4 T Penketh is an accountant with a salary of £2,000 per month plus bonus, which for May 20X6 was £400. He pays superannuation contributions of 5% of gross pay, and these are allowed as reliefs against income tax. In addition to this he has further reliefs (free pay) of £430. The taxable pay is taxed at the rate of 20% on the first £250, whilst the remainder suffers the 25% tax rate. In addition he pays National Insurance of £190. Calculate his net pay for the month.

21.5A K Blake is employed at the rate of £6 per hour. During the week to 25 May 20X6 he works 35 hours. According to the tax and National Insurance tables he should pay income tax £28 and National Insurance £18. Calculate his net wages.

21.6A R Kennedy is a security van driver. He has a wage of £200 per week, plus danger money of £2 per hour extra spent in transporting gold bullion. During the week ended 15 June 20X6 he spends 20 hours taking gold bullion to London Airport. The first £90 per week of his pay is free of income tax, whilst on the next £50 he pays at the 20% rate, and at the 25% rate above that figure. He pays National Insurance for the week of £19. Calculate his net pay for the week.

21.7A Mrs T Hulley is paid monthly. For part of April 20X6 she earns £860 and then goes on maternity leave, her maternity pay for April being £90. She has pay free of tax £320, whilst on the next £250 she pays at the 20% tax rate, and 25% above that. She pays £79 National Insurance. Calculate her net pay for the month.

21.8A P Urmston is paid monthly. For June 20X6 he earns £1,500 and also receives statutory sick pay of £150. He pays £90 superannuation which is allowed as a relief against income tax and he has further reliefs (free pay) of £350. The taxable pay is taxed at the rate of 20% on the first £250 and 25% thereafter. He pays National Insurance of £130 for the month. Calculate his net pay for the month.

CHAPTER 22

Computers and accounting

After you have studied this chapter, you should be able to:

- explain that different computer hardware configurations are used, depending largely upon company size
- explain why financial accounting packages tend to be bought 'off-the-shelf', possibly customised to the business, or the software (particularly in larger companies) may be commissioned from computer software specialists either within the business or from external agencies
- explain why accountants use spreadsheets to write many of their own computer programs, particularly for managerial accounting purposes
- explain that an accounting information system is just one part of the management information system
- describe the structure and flexibility of spreadsheets
- explain why a database package is a useful tool
- explain the importance of backing up data in a computerised environment
- explain the importance of and benefits of the use of passwords
- describe the requirements and implications of the Data Protection Act 1998

Introduction

In this chapter, you'll learn about how computers can be used for inputting and processing data to produce output from an accounting system for decision-making. You'll learn about how computers are linked together and of the differences between buying ready-made accounting software and writing the accounting program from scratch. You'll be introduced to spreadsheets and database packages and you will learn of the importance of backing up data and using passwords. Finally, you will learn about the regulations relating to the storage of personal data on computer.

22.1 Background

Nowadays, there are very few businesses which do not use a computer for at least some of their data processing tasks. In some cases, this may simply involve the accountant using a spreadsheet as an extended trial balance, the data being input having been obtained, in the first place, from the manually maintained ledgers. Once the final adjustments to the trial balance have been made, the spreadsheet would then be used to produce the financial statements. (You will be learning about these accounting activities in the next few chapters.)

In other cases, computers may be used for most or even all the accounting tasks. Whatever the level of use of computers in accounting, accountants need to be able to understand how data is being entered and processed so that they can understand and have faith in the reliability of the figures produced. It has been suggested, for example, that over 60 per cent of spreadsheet programs have errors. This is something accountants need to guard against.

Auditors have special computer programs designed to test the reliability of computerised accounting systems but it is obviously better to ensure that the computers are being used appropriately and correctly in the first place, rather than relying on an auditor to discover that some aspect of the system is not operting correctly – you would not, for example, wish to discover that for the previous year you have been giving all your customers a 10 per cent cash discount, even when they haven't paid you the amount they owe you! Thus, when computers are used in accounting, the accountant involved needs to ensure that they are being used appropriately and that the records they are creating and the output they produce is both valid and meaningful.

22.2 Large versus small systems

The technology when computers are used in an accounting system will vary in size to meet the volume of data processing required by the business. Very large businesses may use a large and extremely powerful central computer for handling bulk data and workstations and/or stand-alone PCs for a number of purposes such as data entry, producing departmental accounts and **financial modelling** (i.e. **forecasting** and **what if** or **sensitivity analysis**). Other businesses will use PCs for all accounting purposes.

Whatever the hardware used, where more than one person is using the computerised part of the accounting system some mechanism has to be in place to enable data to be entered and accessed by everyone who is responsible for that aspect of the system. This is unlikely to be done by sharing the same PC, so some appropriate organisation of the hardware is required.

Networks

When a central computer is used, the **workstations** used to interrogate the data held on the central computer may be **dumb terminals** – i.e. they have no processing capabilities of their own – or PCs. In either case, they need to be networked (i.e. linked together through wires that run from their workstations to the central computer or via phone lines over the Internet).

In some cases, these groupings of central computer with workstations will be a **local area network** (LAN) (i.e. internal to the location). In other cases, they will be part of a **wide area network** (WAN) (i.e. connected outwith the location of the workstation to, for example, a computer located at the business's head office in another city). It is quite common for a workstation to be connected to both a local area network and a wide area network.

Being linked together has the advantage that data and information can be passed directly from one computer to another. Thus, although they can operate independently of any other computer, PC-based systems may also be connected together on a local area network, and have links to wide area networks.

Special forms of these networks emerged over the last few years as a result of the extension of the Internet. It is now becoming increasingly common for businesses to have an 'Intranet', a network based on Internet technologies where data and information private to the business is made available to employees of the business. Some also have **Extranets**, where data and information private to the business is made available to a specific group of outsiders, for example making a company's stock records available on-line to major customers. Of course, most now have **websites** where they place information for the use of anyone who happens to want to look at it. In many cases, these contain copies of the latest financial statements of the business and a part of the website is devoted to promoting and selling goods and services.

Software

The software used may be developed in-house (by employees) or written under contract with an outside business or agency. Such systems are tailored to exactly what the business wants and are sometimes referred to as 'bespoke' systems. A large supermarket chain, for example, could have software developed incorporating the EPOS (electronic point of sale) system now common at supermarket check-outs. Not only do these check-out systems keep an accurate check on what is sold, in the form of an electronic Cash Book, but such information can be fed into the central computer to assist the process of reordering stock from warehouses, and to keep a check on cash sales. They also provide data for stock analysis and marketing purposes.

Expensive, specially designed software (often called 'customised' software) of this type will be used, generally, only by large businesses. Many medium-sized and smaller businesses will not require such special solutions, and will rely on 'off-the-shelf' software packages, most of which are flexible enough to be adapted to meet the major needs of most businesses.

Most financial accounting and bookkeeping programs are purchased off-the-shelf and then developed in-house, often by the accountants working, in the case of ledger systems, with their organisation's IT department.

Besides the main accounting system, the part used for recording transactions, adjustments and producing financial statements, accountants also use the accounting system to tackle other problems not yet discussed in this textbook. These will include matters such as forecasting the cash flows of a business, stock ordering, deciding on capital expenditure investment, how to find the sales volume at which the business moves into profit (breakeven analysis) and costing.

For such purposes, irrespective of the size of the business, accountants can use PC-based spreadsheets (see Section 22.5), such as Excel, and databases, such as Access. Such systems will change fairly rapidly over the years as new ones are developed.

The cost of computer hardware and software has been falling in real terms for many years – it has been suggested that had the same relative cost reduction applied to a Rolls-Royce car, it would now be cheaper to throw the car away once it ran out of petrol than to fill up the petrol tank! Consequently, computerisation is now affordable for all businesses. In fact, such has been the increase in data processing and power and range of analysis available as a result of businesses seeking to maximise the use of their computing power that many businesses now process such large volumes of data that they would find it impossible to revert to a manual system.

22.3 Benefits from computers

Time-saving with respect to transaction processing, increased accuracy and the production of a whole series of reports are obvious desirable and realistic benefits when computers are used for accounting. The basic principle of any accounting system is depicted in Exhibit 22.1:

Exhibit 22.1

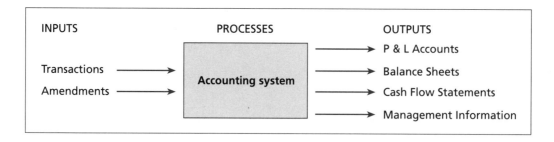

Computers can be used in all aspects of the accounting system. When computers are used for some or all of these activities they can do everything that can be done with a manual system, but computers often do them faster, more accurately, and more efficiently.

Increased job satisfaction

Increased job satisfaction and more effective use of operator time can be an added bonus of computerisation. For example, if a business computerises its stock records, an operator's job of keeping records properly maintained will be much the same as in the manual system. However, with instant reporting facilities available, such as a list of all stock items that may be in short supply, the operator can produce details almost instantly. This will allow an operator the facility of keeping a much closer check on stock levels. Also, if time can be saved in producing stock reports, the operator may have more time to 'chase up' suppliers who are not delivering on time or 'shop around' the market for better suppliers and products. Obviously, these are more interesting tasks than entering data into the accounting records and then ploughing through them in order to produce the reports.

> *Activity 22.1*
> Is it always going to be the case that employees experience greater satisfaction of working in a computerised environment?

Overall

Many more benefits of computerisation tend to become apparent as businesses develop their systems. It is worth noting that the extent of the benefits will vary from business to business, with each one deriving different benefits. It may well be the case that a business can derive no benefit at all from computerisation.

Some benefits bring problems of their own. For example, once computers are being used effectively in an accounting system, managers will often find themselves extracting reports that under a manual system could not be achieved within a timescale that would serve a useful purpose. The improved reporting and analysis that can be achieved by computerisation should improve the whole decision-making process within a business, but it can also lead to information overload as decision-makers suddenly find they have too much information for them to fully understand and apply.

22.4 Management information systems

All computer systems, whether purchased off-the-shelf or custom-made for a particular business, will need to supply information in a form that management can use to assist in its decision-making. Whether the output is on paper, via computer screens, on disk, or available on-line, the information system centred upon the computer is generally referred to as the 'management information system' (MIS). The MIS contains far more information than the accounting information system – production data and marketing statistics, for example, would be included in the MIS. The accounting information system is a component within the MIS, and must be capable of integration with the other functional information systems that together comprise the rest of the MIS.

Beyond standard reports, MISs are normally flexible enough to allow management to extract the kind of reports that may be unique to their business or department. These reports can be extracted in a very short time compared with that taken using a manual system, and they serve to enhance the control management have over their business.

However, two things should be emphasised, and they have not changed since the early days of computerised information systems:

1 The reports and information extracted from a computer can only be as good as the data placed into it – the well-known 'garbage in, garbage out' situation. If the full benefits of computerisation are to be enjoyed, regular checks need to be made to ensure that the data input is accurate and timely.
2 Computerisation allows infinite instant access to data. It is a straightforward matter designing and producing a new report, and it can be easier to print all possible types of reports across all functions than to limit the reports produced to those actually needed by the people they are sent to. If report generation is not controlled, information overload will occur and decision-makers may have difficulty seeing the wood because of all the trees.

22.5 Use of spreadsheets

The spreadsheet is the software tool most used by accountants. Spreadsheets first appeared in 1979 and within only a handful of years surveys were showing that of those accountants who had access to PCs, virtually 100 per cent were using them for some task or other. The name derives from the appearance of the computer *spreading* accounts on a *sheet*, allowing the user to directly enter numbers, formulae or text into the cells. Exhibit 22.2 shows an example of an empty spreadsheet.

Exhibit 22.2

Screen shot reprinted by permission from Microsoft Corporation.

As you can see, the screen is divided into vertical columns and horizontal rows to form a grid of cells. Each cell is referred to by its co-ordinate, like a map reference or point on a graph. For example, cell C12 is in column C row 12. Formulae can be entered to link cells. An example of linking cells is where a cell entry reads:

$$(=B5*C12)$$

(Note the use of an asterisk to represent a multiplication sign.)

This expression makes the value of the contents of the cell it is in equal to the value of cell B5 multiplied by the value of cell C12. Thus, if the formula was entered in cell D16 and B5 contained the number 6 and C12 contained the number 4, D16 would display the value 24. A spreadsheet is, effectively, a massively powerful screen-based calculator and report generator whose output, both text and graphs, can be printed or electronically transmitted to another computer.

Any figure can be changed at any time and the new results will instantly and automatically be shown. This makes it very easy to perform **what if** or **sensitivity analysis** (for example, what would the result be if sales were to increase by 10 per cent?) and has led to a far higher level of understanding of the effects of decisions than was ever possible when all such recalculations could involve anything up to days of work. It is this facility of being able to quickly recalculate formulae that makes the spreadsheet a powerful, useful and popular analytical tool.

Spreadsheets can be used in order to seek goals, such as specific profit figures. For example, spreadsheets can depict the sales and costs of a business and the goal seeking function can then be used to determine what selling price will be required in order to achieve a specific net profit.

Spreadsheets tend to be written by accountants for their own use, rather than by computer programmers. Some other examples of uses for spreadsheets include:

- financial plans and budgets can be represented as a table, with columns for time periods (e.g. months) and rows for different elements of the plan (e.g. costs and revenue);
- tax, investment and loan calculations can be made with ease;
- statistics using built-in functions such as averages, standard deviations, time series and regression analysis can be calculated;
- consolidation – merging branch or departmental accounts to form group (consolidated) accounts – is easy to produce;
- multi-dimensional spreadsheets can be created, enabling far deeper analysis of data – the 'sheet' tabs at the foot of the spreadsheet in Exhibit 22.2 can each be a 'dimension' that can be linked to other sheets, thus permitting views to be developed across various dimensions of a business activity. Even without this facility, the number of rows and columns available in a spreadsheet make this type of data modelling relatively simple for all but the most complex of scenarios;
- currency conversion is simple – useful for an organisation with overseas interests such as a multinational company;
- timetabling and roster planning of staff within organisations or departments can be performed.

It is hardly surprising that spreadsheets are so widely used by accountants.

Activity 22.2
Why do you think that accountants frequently write their own spreadsheet programs rather than having them written by an IT specialist?

22.6 Use of databases

Instead of being specifically designed for the types of tasks that accountants perform a lot, databases are designed for a more general purpose. A database is organised into a collection of related files into which go records. For example, a stock system could be developed where a stock file contains a record for each item of stock. The records are further broken down into fields. Hence, there could be a field for reference, one for description, a quantity, reordering level and so on. The system would then be developed to keep such records updated.

This application is favoured by many businesses as it tends to be more flexible than an accounting package and easier and cheaper to put together than a set of programs specifically written for the business.

Such database packages require a little more computing expertise and a sound knowledge of the accounting system in order to create something appropriate. In such instances, while many would be written by an accountant, it is possible that computing and accounting personnel would work together on the development, particularly where the accountant had no previous experience of using the database software.

22.7 Data back-ups

One of the most important principles in computing is the discipline of backing up data held on computer. Backing-up is now performed easily by simply copying the relevant files to another computer or onto a storage medium, such as a CD or even a floppy disk.

This serves the purpose that, if anything ever goes wrong with the data, then the business can always revert to a back-up copy of the data. If, for example, a company backs up its data at midday and there is a loss of data later that afternoon, then the worst that could happen is that the company has to restore the data from the midday back-up and then re-enter the data since that time. Clearly, therefore, the more often a business backs up its data, the less work is needed in the event of data loss.

Many of the software packages routinely used by accountants, such as spreadsheets, can be programmed to automatically back up work every few minutes so that it is not all lost should the computer or program crash.

22.8 Passwords

When computers are being used along with an accounting package, it is normally possible for passwords to be set up to restrict which personnel have access to certain parts of the computerised elements of the accounting system. This assists management in maintaining tighter control on the system and avoids over-complicating operations for operators. It ensures that operators do not have access to more parts of a wider system than they need in order to do their job adequately and avoids the risks inherent in exposing all parts of the system to all operators. As an extra benefit, if the functions available to operators are limited, it becomes easier and quicker to train the operators.

> ### Activity 22.3
> What has happened in recent years to make the use of passwords more important than ever?

22.9 Data security and the Data Protection Act 1998

Most businesses that make extensive use of computers for accounts, payroll, and any other applications that involve personal details of individuals, need to register with the **Office of the Information Commissioner.**

The Data Protection Act defines a **data controller** as someone who determines how and for which purposes **personal data** is used. A **data subject** is anyone on whom data is held on a computer that can be identified as relating to them. Such data on a computer has to be processed by the computer's software before it can serve the purpose of information. It is this information that the **Information Commissioner** wants to know about.

Essentially, data users must declare what information they have access to on data subjects and the uses they will put that information to. The main objective of the Act is to ensure that individuals are aware of what is being held about them on business computers and allow them access to this information.

If a business is only using the Sales Ledger or Purchases Ledger for preparing and sending invoices and statements and does not use the comment details for a contact name then registration may not be necessary. Also, if customers and suppliers are companies, and individuals cannot be identified in the data, registration is not necessary. In the same way, if all a business does with payroll data is to pay wages and prepare statutory returns, registration is not necessary.

If customer and supplier lists are used for sending out sales promotions, the business must register. Likewise, registration is required if a business uses data on the payroll for management information about staff sickness or any form of staff monitoring.

Forms for registration require the business to reveal the kind of data it holds on individuals and the purpose for which it wants to use it. The business must also give details on how data subjects can find out what data is held on computer about them.

In addition to the possible need to register, businesses must comply with certain practices with regard to holding personalised data on computer. Many of these legal requirements simply define good computing practice and should be applied, where applicable, to all data used on a computer. These legal principles are contained in Schedule I of the Act:

1 Personal data shall be processed fairly and lawfully and, in particular, shall not be processed unless certain conditions contained in Schedules 2 and 3 of the Act have been met.
2 Personal data shall be obtained only for one or more specified and lawful purposes, and shall not be further processed in any manner incompatible with that purpose or those purposes.
3 Personal data shall be adequate, relevant and not excessive in relation to the purpose or purposes for which they are processed.
4 Personal data shall be accurate and, where necessary, kept up to date.
5 Personal data processed for any purpose or purposes shall not be kept for longer than is necessary for that purpose or those purposes.
6 Personal data shall be processed in accordance with the rights of data subjects under this Act.
7 Appropriate technical and organisational measures shall be taken against unauthorised or unlawful processing of personal data and against accidental loss or destruction of, or damage to, personal data.
8 Personal data shall not be transferred to a country or territory outside the European Economic Area unless that country or territory ensures an adequate level of protection for the rights and freedoms of data subjects in relation to the processing of personal data.

The website of the Office of the Information Commissioner can be found at www.dataprotection.gov.uk/ and the text of the Data Protection Act 1998 can be found at www.hmso.gov.uk/acts/acts1998/19980029.htm

Learning outcomes

You should now have learnt that:

1 Computers can be and normally are linked together when they are used as part of the accounting system.
2 Software may be written from scratch or bought 'off-the-shelf'.
3 Software bought 'off-the-shelf' is often customised to fit the needs of the organisation.
4 Accounting information systems are just one part of an overall management information system.
5 Output can be excessive and cause information overload if not controlled to ensure it is useful to the person who receives it.
6 Spreadsheets are in general use by accountants who commonly develop their own software applications with them.
7 Databases are well suited to recording facts such as names, addresses, and stock levels.
8 Backing up data is an essential task in a computerised environment.
9 Use of passwords assists in limiting access to parts of an information system and to the system as a whole and should not be ignored, particularly as the Internet has opened up the possibility of information systems being penetrated by outsiders.
10 The Data Protection Act 1998 must be observed when personal data is held on computer.

Answers to activities

22.1 No, there are many negative impacts on individuals. For example, a job may have been interesting previously because it involved searching about for information. Now it is routine and, therefore, less interesting. Also, computers and software can have faults that make it frustrating to use them, such as a PC crash where all data entered is lost or a network failure that means no work can be done.

22.2 There are many reasons, including:

Pragmatic reasons:
- Accountants understand accounting better than IT specialists so may spend a lot of the time instructing IT specialists in how to perform accounting tasks rather than in telling them what is required.
- A spreadsheet written by an IT specialist may contain logic errors arising from a lack of knowledge of accounting.
- Accountants known what they want, IT specialists need to be told, and telling someone something does not necessarily mean (a) that they understand what you want, (b) that they agree with what you want to the extent that they think it is worthwhile providing it, and (c) that what they produce will actually be what was requested. (For example, an accountant may ask for a spreadsheet to prepare financial statements from a trial balance and the IT specialist may produce one where all the items within the balance sheet categories have been put in alphabetic order and some of the headings have been changed to make them more 'normal'.)
- All but the very complex spreadsheet programs can be written in a few hours, some in minutes. It may take longer to explain what is required than to actually write it.
- IT specialists have other work to do and it may take them days, weeks, even months, to produce the spreadsheet, by which time the accountant wants something else instead.
- Some spreadsheet applications that an accountant writes will be needed immediately and will not be used again. There is no time to brief anyone on what is required.

Risk aversion reasons:
- A lack of willingness on the part of the accountant to appear unable to perform what many accountants would consider to be a trivial skill effectively enough to produce their own spreadsheets.
- The '*not invented here syndrome*', whereby people do not generally like to use someone else's idea of what is required. They prefer to use one they made themselves, even if it is technically and operationally inferior, and takes more time and effort to do than can be justified by the benefits that result.
- A desire not to use a spreadsheet in the first place, possibly arising from a low level of personal IT literacy.

22.3 This has become a far more important aspect of information systems in recent years, because of the many ways in which outsiders can hack into company information systems through the company's Internet links.

REVIEW QUESTIONS

22.1 What are the legal principles underlying the protection of personal information kept on computers?

22.2 What benefits can flow from processing sales details on a computer?

22.3 For what type of activities in accounting is the use of spreadsheets particularly suitable?

CHAPTER 23

Computerised accounting systems

Learning objectives

After you have studied this chapter, you should be able to:

- explain how computerised accounting systems mimic manual accounting systems and can do everything that is done by a manual accounting system
- describe how computerised accounting systems automate most of the entries required in a manual accounting system including, in some cases, the initial entry for each transaction
- describe and explain the advantages and pitfalls of using a computerised accounting system
- explain the importance of fully integrating a computerised accounting system
- explain the importance of full compatibility between the various components of a computerised accounting system
- explain the need to take great care when converting from a manual accounting system to a computerised one

Introduction

In this chapter, you'll learn about the differences between manual and computerised accounting information systems and about the benefits of using computerised accounting systems to produce output for decision-making. You will also learn of the variety of output that can be produced by a computerised information system. In addition, you will learn of the importance of integration and compatibility of all the components of a computerised accounting system and of the need to take great care when switching from a manual system to a computerised one.

23.1 Background

Most businesses, except the very smallest, now use computers to handle their accounting data. When businesses switch to computerised accounting, they soon discover that book-keeping and accounting skills are more important than computing ones. This is because users of many computerised accounting systems have very little to learn in order to use them. In Windows-based software, as you can see from the entry screen of the *Sage Instant Accounting 2000* accounting package shown in Exhibit 23.1, the interfaces look fairly familiar – the file menu is usually in the top left, for example, and many of the icons are the same and have the same meanings across a whole range of software produced by different companies.

Exhibit 23.1

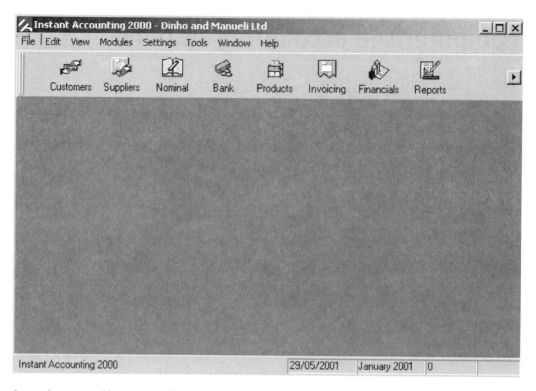

Screen shot reprinted by courtesy of the Sage Group plc.

Activity 23.1

Not very long ago, only the largest businesses used computers to handle their accounting data. Why do you think the situation is so different now?

The methods adopted in computer-based accounting adhere to the fundamental principles of accounting covered in this and other accounting textbooks. No matter how sophisticated and easy to use a computerised accounting system is, it will not overcome the need for book-keeping and accounting knowledge by those in control. Imagine, for example, how anyone who does not know how to prepare journal entries could correct an error in an original entry correctly from an accounting point of view and, just as importantly, understand why it is important not to erase the original entry.

Apart from a need for knowledge of accounting principles in order to best convert a business from manual to computer-based accounting, some accounting knowledge is required to help understand the significance of many of the outputs from a computerised accounting system, just as it is required in respect of output from a manual accounting system.

Thus, computerised accounting systems do not remove the need for some accounting knowledge among those responsible for key accounting tasks or from those who use the output from the accounting systems. In fact, some accountants working in practice would tell you that they believe there is an even greater need for accounting knowledge among those who record the transactions in a computerised accounting system than in a manual one.

Activity 23.2

What do you think? Is there an even greater need for accounting knowledge among those that record the transactions in a computerised accounting system? Why?/Why not?

23.2 Benefits of using a computerised accounting system

As you learnt in Chapter 22, there are many benefits from using a computerised accounting system. Overall, probably the greatest benefit comes from the fact that a computerised accounting system can do the same things as a manual system, but does them better. Thus all the features in a manual system, such as the one shown in Exhibit 23.2, can be replicated in a computerised accounting system which not only does them quicker, more accurately, and 100 per cent consistently, but can also do them more frequently *and* do other things as well.

Exhibit 23.2

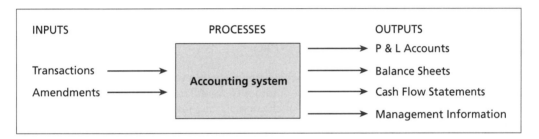

Let's look at some of these benefits in more detail.

Speed and accuracy

The main aim of computerising an accounting system is to perform the processing stage electronically, much more quickly, consistently and accurately than if it were done manually. However, transactions and amendment details have to be input into the process (1) in the correct form, (2) in the correct order, and (3) in a timely manner. Although there is scope to use electronic methods of entering some of this information (e.g. EPOS systems and document scanning), it requires a good deal of initiative and an organised way of doing things in order to do so. Nevertheless, improved accuracy is one of the more obvious benefits of any kind of computerised accounting system.

Further time-saving can be achieved by immediate output of reports, such as customer statements, purchase analysis, cash and bank statements, and details about whether the business is meeting sales targets. Such reports and statements can be produced both on request and, automatically, by the computer searching through information generated and saved within the accounting system and then producing whatever report is required.

Error detection

Effective reporting is often required in order to improve the decision-making process. For example, a computerised accounting system should be capable of detecting when a customer appears to be running up excessive debts with the business, so offering the chance for the credit controller to take remedial action.

Another area is the need to remain within budgets. Many business expenses can get out of hand if they are not checked at regular intervals. A computerised accounting system should be capable of an activity called **exception reporting**, a process of issuing a warning message to decision-makers when something unexpected is happening: for example, when expenditure against a budget is higher than it should be. In a manual accounting system, the situation can occur that errors or unwanted transactions go unnoticed until too late when the repercussions have already incurred unnecessary costs to the business.

Enhanced reporting

For many businesses, the task of producing reports on a regular basis, such as VAT Returns, payroll processing, cash flow analysis, and financial statements, can be time-consuming, tedious and unrewarding. The use of a computerised accounting system speeds up the process to the point, in some cases, where it is done automatically without any need for human intervention, thus reducing the monotony of producing lengthy reports requiring extensive preparatory analysis of data. In many cases, such as VAT Returns and payslips, businesses find that they can use computer printouts or electronic output, e.g. on computer disks, instead of having to manually complete official or standard forms.

23.3   Computerised accounting books

Many businesses now make good use of accounting packages which are readily available and have been well tested. Such packages are commonly modularised with, typically, the Sales Ledger, Purchase Ledger, General Ledger, stock control, sales invoicing, sales order processing, purchases order processing, fixed assets, payroll, bill of materials, and job costing all being offered as separate modules in their own right. When a business decides to computerise its accounting system, it acquires only those modules it needs rather than a complete range of modules. For example, a sole trader would have no use for a payroll module.

The various ledgers and accounts maintained in a computerised accounting system mimic those kept in a manual system. The General Ledger, for example, will adhere to the basic rules of double entry bookkeeping in that each debit entry has a corresponding credit entry – if a customer is issued with an invoice, the transaction giving precise details of the invoice will be stored in the credit sales records to form part of the customer history and then the double entry is made by crediting sales accounts and debiting a debtor's account.

The difference lies in the method of entry – each transaction is entered only once (accountants refer to this as a 'single entry' system) and the software automatically completes the double entry. This has a down side, however, in that some computerised accounting packages will post various amounts into suspense accounts when it is unclear as to where postings are to be made. These require manual intervention and journal entries to remove the items from the suspense account and complete the original double entry. (Suspense accounts are the topic of Chapter 33.)

Flexibility

The information stored is available instantly and can be used to produce statements, ledger account details, analysis of how long debts have been outstanding, etc. immediately it is requested. For example, the computerised Sales Ledger will hold all details about customers. The starting point would be to enter the details concerning the customer (name, address, etc.) along with the balance brought forward from the manual system (if such a transfer is occurring; otherwise, if it is a new customer, an opening zero balance will be created automatically by the software). All transactions that correspond to a customer, such as the issue of an invoice or receipt of payment, are entered into the system and automatically posted to the customer's account. Customers can, at any time, be issued with a statement of their account, and the business can always obtain an up-to-date and complete history of trading with any particular customer. The purchase ledger will operate exactly the same way in that supplier details are held and, once entered through the purchases module, all transactions relating to individual purchasers will automatically be posted to the appropriate creditor account.

Bank payments and receipts are a central feature of computerised accounting systems. The modules can be operated by someone with virtually no bookkeeping knowledge. For example, if an electricity bill is paid, the system will prompt for the details required in order to process and record the double entry.

Account codes

In order to use a computerised accounting system efficiently and effectively, someone with both accounting skills and a good knowledge of the business will be required to organise the accounts and ledgers in the first instance. Some of these packages are written for no specific business and need to be 'tailored' to the one that is going to use it. Most require businesses to define what accounts they are to have in their general ledger and how such accounts are to be grouped. For example, fixed asset accounts may have account references commencing with 'F', while expense accounts commence with 'E'; the package will probably have its own default set of **account codes** (the computerised equivalent of the folio in a manual system), and it may be necessary to override the defaults in the accounting package in order to use the business's own account code list. In addition, part of the setting up of a computer system will require the tailoring of the package for certain reports such as the profit and loss account and balance sheet.

Knowledge of double entry

Most packages are capable of allowing businesses to set up their preferred methods for dealing with depreciation of fixed assets and regular payments of, for example, rent and rates. However, as you saw with the need to correct entries to a suspense account arising from the computer not knowing how to complete a double entry, such packages do require a good 'knowledge' of double entry so that adjustments can be made through their journal entries. For example, the computer will not overcome some errors and omissions such as the operator misreading an amount on an invoice or crediting a payment to a wrong customer account. Anyone correcting these errors will require a full knowledge of the relevant part of the accounting system as well as bookkeeping and accounting principles.

23.4 Computerised stock control and modular integration

Automation of much of the data processing can be taken further when integrating other modules. Stock control offers the benefit of keeping very close tabs on stock levels. If an invoicing package is also in use, then an invoice can be generated in such a way that an operator can collect the details of the business or person to invoice from the sales ledger and details of all stock to be invoiced from the stock files. Once the invoice has been raised, the recorded stock levels fall accordingly, the sales ledger is updated and the nominal entries are made by crediting sales and debiting debtors' control (a topic which will be covered in Chapter 31).

Sales order processing

Sales order processing allows an order to be placed into the system and can then be used at a later stage to generate an invoice. Sales order processing is important to many businesses as it gives them an indication about what stock levels are required. Having sales orders on computer also offers the advantage of being able to avoid any orders being left overdue and late. Computers can produce outstanding order reports and such things as 'picking lists' (a list of items to be taken out of storage and given or shipped to customers) very quickly.

Purchase order processing

Purchase order processing allows an operator to print an order to send off to a supplier or, in some more advanced systems, it may be transmitted over a direct link into the supplier's accounting system where it will be recorded and converted into an issue from stock. The computerised purchase order system also serves the useful purpose of allowing instant access to information about what is on order. By entering stock on order against various stock records, it reduces the likelihood of issuing multiple orders for stock unnecessarily.

Modular integration

The full use of all modules in this integrated manner allows a business to access stock details and get a complete profile on its status in terms of what is left in stock, what is on order, what has been ordered by customers. Furthermore, most packages keep a history of stock movements so helping the business to analyse specific stock turnovers. When integrated in this fashion, the processing structure may be as depicted in Exhibit 23.3.

Exhibit 23.3 An integrated computerised accounting system

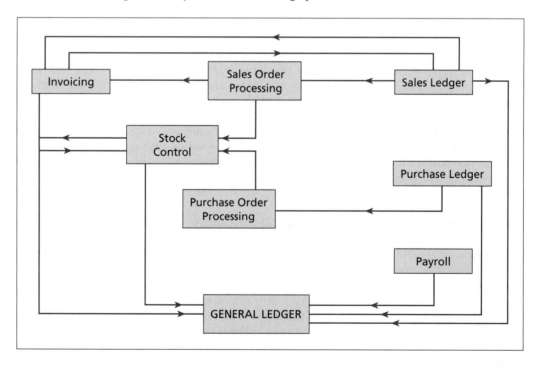

Exhibit 23.3 includes a payroll module. Businesses with a large number of employees would find this particularly useful as payroll systems require a good deal of regular processing. Again, a reasonable knowledge of payroll is required in order to set up the system in the first place.

23.5   Accounting information systems

An **accounting information system (AIS)** is the total suite of components that, together, comprise all the inputs, storage, transaction processing, collating, and reporting of financial transaction data. It is, in effect, the infrastructure that supports the production and delivery of accounting information.

The objective of an accounting information system is to collect and store data about accounting transactions in order to generate meaningful output for decision-making. The shoebox containing receipts for all purchases and a cheque book kept by the corner shopkeeper is, in itself, an accounting system, as is the set of day books and ledgers kept by the local department store and the integrated computerised accounting system of a company such as Ford, BT, or British Airways.

There is no need for an AIS to be computerised in order to be described in this way. Computerisation may only have been introduced on some of the accounting tasks, such as the accounting books, the payroll system, or the stock control system. When the entire suite of accounting tasks and records is computerised, the benefits are clearly greater than when only parts of the AIS are computerised. Most people assume you are talking about a *fully* computerised accounting system when you refer to an AIS and *this is how we shall use the term in the rest of this chapter.* However, much of what follows, apart from the benefits of full integration, is also applicable to partially computerised AISs.

Full integration and compatibility

For an AIS to be fully effective, *all* the components need to be integrated with each other, otherwise information gets lost, misentered from one record to another, or duplicated (often incorrectly as each version of it is updated at different times). Major errors may ultimately arise if integration is not 100 per cent. In a computerised AIS, there is the added problem that some of the components or modules may be written for use in a different operating system and may not be immediately compatible with the other modules with which data is to be exchanged, retrieved, or transferred. This was a major problem until the late 1980s, since when much of the difficulty of operating system incompatibility has been eradicated.

However, with software the problem still remains – even documents prepared on one version of word processing software may not transfer with 100 per cent accuracy to an earlier or later version of the same software, never mind to other word processing packages. The same holds for spreadsheets and database files. Therefore, at the planning stage, it is important to ensure that all hardware and software that is to be used is 100 per cent compatible and that, where it is not, steps are taken to ensure that a workable alternative way of communicating data and information between modules is found.

> ### Activity 23.3
> If there is not full integration of an AIS, what examples can you think of where data may need to be entered more than once and maintained in two or more different records simultaneously? What problems may result from this?

Outputs

An AIS, computerised or manual, can, of course, produce whatever reports you wish, so long as the relevant data is stored within or accessible to the AIS. Where a fully computerised AIS is clearly superior is in the range of reports it can produce virtually instantly and in the way it can be programmed to produce periodic reports precisely when they are scheduled to be available. No longer is there any need for decision-makers to wait two weeks for the summary of the previous month's business activities. It is now available as soon as business closes at the end of the last day of the month.

Some of the other reports produced by most manual AISs can also take a very long time to produce. Some, however, only take an hour or two to prepare manually. However, a computerised AIS can produce these reports in seconds, and as often as the decision-makers wish. These include aged debtors reports (a list of debtors showing how much they each owe, and for how long the amounts have been outstanding); price lists; stock levels and reordering stock quantities; lists of invoices and credit notes; and audit trail information to enable errors to be traced and corrected (whereby the route a transaction took through the accounting records to the financial statements is revealed). The savings in personnel and time and, therefore, costs that can result from fully computerising the AIS cannot be understated, even for smaller businesses who wish to maximise their efficiency.

Activity 23.4

When computers were first used in this way, many decision-makers were far from pleased. Why?

In the early days of computerised AISs, the output was all on paper. Now, much of it is electronic.

Electronic dissemination

One of the major benefits of a computerised AIS is that output generated from it need not be in hard copy. It can be visual on a computer screen, or distributed electronically on CD or floppy disk, or by direct file transfer to another computer over a LAN, WAN, Intranet, Extranet or the Internet.

While many organisations still require that information be passed to them on their own forms, the IT revolution of the last few years has led to many organisations being willing to accept printout generated from a computer, or even floppy disks containing the document, instead of having their own forms completed and returned. For example, fairly standard and repetitive information generation, such as VAT receipts and payments, are common to most businesses, and Customs and Excise will accept computer-generated VAT returns. The Inland Revenue will accept computer-generated payroll data.

There is also an increasing use of email to transmit documents and the Inland Revenue now accepts personal income tax forms in this way. In fact, the Inland Revenue currently (2001) accepts all the following documents electronically:

- starter/leaver details (forms P45, P46, P160)
- daily coding (form P6)
- annual and budget code number updates (form P9)
- pension and works number updates
- end of year returns (form P14)
- expenses and benefits (form P11D)
- construction industry vouchers CIS23 and CIS25

Benefits of electronic submission of documents

Among the recognised benefits of electronic submission of documents and hence, potentially, of a computerised AIS are:

- speed
- improved accuracy in that what is sent is what was intended to be sent
- improved accuracy in that what is sent is received, and in the form intended
- lower administration costs
- greater security
- less use of paper
- immediate acknowledgement of receipt

Benefits of electronic transmission of funds

Of course, if electronic submission of documents is a recent phenomenon, electronic transmission of funds has been around a good deal longer. Among the benefits attributed to it and again, potentially, to a computerised AIS are:

- certainty of payment on a specific date
- certainty that exactly the amount due to be paid is paid
- immediate acknowledgement of receipt
- lower administration costs
- lower bank charges
- greater security

Benefits of linking AISs

Another significant recent change brought about by computerisation of AISs is the growth in electronic data exchange between supplier and customer. Some very large companies now insist that their suppliers link their stock systems to the customer's AIS. The customer can then interrogate the stock records of the supplier to see if items are available and place orders directly into the supplier's AIS without any need for physical transmission of an order document. This has helped the growth of just-in-time stock keeping by customers who, rather than holding their own stock, simply order it from their suppliers when required.

Among the benefits attributed to it and again, potentially, to a computerised AIS are:

- speed
- lower administration costs
- greater awareness of the current position
- improved control of related risks
- greater security of a continuing relationship between the parties

23.6 Issues to consider when introducing a fully computerised AIS

When you computerise an accounting system, you have some decisions to make. These include:

1 Deciding whether to mimic what you have been doing manually or start from scratch and redesign everything. For example, you may only have been using one ledger in the manual system, but may choose to use three or four in the computerised system. You may have had a two-column cash book in the manual system but decide to have a columnar cash book in the computerised system.
2 Deciding whether to buy a general accounting package 'off-the-shelf' or create one from scratch. Depending on the size of the business, creating one from scratch may be done using a spreadsheet and a database package or it may involve having computer programmers writing the entire system.

3 If you decide to buy one off-the-shelf, you need to decide how much to customise it, if at all.

4 If you decide not to customise it, or aren't able to customise parts of it, you may need to change the terminology you use when referring to parts of the accounting system. For example, you may need to refer to the Nominal Ledger rather than the General Ledger and to the Purchases Journal rather than the Purchases Day Book. For example, *Sage* uses the term 'Customers Module' rather than Sales Ledger and 'Suppliers Module' instead of a Purchases Ledger.

5 You need to decide who is going to be responsible for overseeing the project.

6 You need to decide how long you are going to allow for the new system to be developed and make plans to introduce it accordingly.

7 You need to decide who is to be trained in using it and when.

8 You need to decide how long you will run the new system in parallel with the existing manual system before you stop using the manual system.

9 You need to identify the hardware you will need and ensure that it is in place at the appropriate time.

10 You need to identify who is going to test the new system and what data is to be used to do so.

11 You need to weigh up the costs and benefits of computerising the accounting system and decide whether it is actually worth doing it.

These are just some of the issues you need to deal with. Many more will appear as each of these questions is answered and many more will materialise as the project proceeds.

The most popular software used by small and medium-sized businesses in the UK is *Sage*. However, you should look at a range of available alternatives, such as *Pegasus*, *Quickbooks*, and *Microsoft Great Plains*, before proceeding to purchase the package you intend using. Factors to consider obviously include price, but they also include capacity, hardware requirements, ease of use, reliability, appropriateness of the way data is entered, stored and secured, and the range and style of reports that can be produced. You also need to consider compatibility of the package with any other systems or packages you might wish to link it to if that is, in fact, a possibility in the first place. Accountants are not normally the most knowledgeable people to answer these technical questions and guidance from an IT specialist is often advisable.

Once the package is installed and fully operational, you need to monitor its effectiveness and reliability and need to have contingency plans in place should it ultimately prove to have been a mistake. (In other words, you need to ensure you can revert to the previous system if necessary.)

When you come to review your hardware or operating system with a view to upgrading it, you need to ensure the package will continue to run without any problems when you upgrade. You also need to consider carefully before committing to an upgrade of the accounting package, in case things that used to work no longer function or need to be done in very different ways.

You also need to ensure that the data stored in the system is backed up regularly and that password or other security devices are in place in order to prevent unauthorised access to it.

Overall, you need to think the whole thing out very carefully before committing to the switch and you need to ensure you have all the controls over the system in place before it starts to be used.

Nevertheless, although great care and a lot of effort must be expended when converting to a computerised accounting system, there is no doubt that the benefits of having an appropriate one will vastly improve the quality and reliability of the accounting data and information.

You should now have learnt that:

1 Bookkeeping and accounting skills and knowledge are more important than computing skills and knowledge when a switch is made from a manual accounting system to a computerised accounting system.

2 The user interface of an accounting package often looks similar to those of other frequently used Windows-based software packages.

3 Computerised accounting systems can do everything a manual accounting system can do, but does them quicker, more accurately, more consistently, and with greater flexibility.

4 A considerably enhanced ability to obtain reports is available from a computerised accounting system compared to a manual accounting system.

5 The various records maintained in a computerised accounting system mimic those in a manual accounting system, though the names of some of the records may be different.

6 Acccount codes are used in computerised accounting systems instead of folio numbers.

7 Maximised integration of the various components in a computerised accounting system generates the maximum benefits.

8 Compatibility between the various components in a computerised accounting system is essential if it is to operate effectively.

9 One of the major benefits of computerised accounting systems is the ability to generate electronic output.

10 Implementing a switch to a computerised accounting system is a non-trivial task that should never be done lightly and needs to be done with the greatest of care.

Answers to activities

23.1 This question can be answered from many perspectives including:

- vastly lower relative cost of computer technology and IT in general
- greater ease of use thanks to a graphical rather than a text-based visual interface (this only really became the norm in the mid 1990s)
- wide range of available software to choose from
- the current high flexibility in (even off-the-shelf) software enabling customisation to suit the needs of the business
- a vastly greater level of IT literacy
- pressure from accountants to modernise methods and so increase control over the accounting records
- greater financial awareness among business people generally (e.g. the enormous growth in MBA holders over the last twenty years)
- pressures from the authorities to maintain up-to-date accounting records (e.g. VAT)
- pressure from competitors (i.e. the need to keep up)
- deeper insight that can be gained by using computers and information technology (C&IT) to present views of the business and business opportunities virtually instantly when they could only be produced manually after weeks of effort
- a desire to appear 'modern and up-to-date'.

23.2 Most accountants would disagree with the comment in a general sense but agree with it in the context of (a) knowing the accounts to use (b) knowing whether an entry looks correct and, most importantly, (c) knowing how to make appropriate entries when an error has occurred.

23.3 One example would be where the stock control system is not integrated with the Sales Ledger. A customer could return goods that were recorded in the stock control system immediately. However, it might take a few hours, even days for the credit entry to be made in the customer's account in the Sales Ledger. During the delay period, the customer might be refused credit because the account showed that the customer's credit limit had been reached when, in fact, the customer had no outstanding debt to the business as a result of having returned the items purchased. The customer might also be sent a statement of the account that did not show the credit entry but was accompanied by a letter demanding immediate payment as the account was now overdue. If the reverse happened and the first entry was made in the Sales Ledger, orders from other customers for the same items might be rejected because the stock records showed a zero amount of those items in stock when, in fact, the ones returned by the customer were in the warehouse.

Another problem of non-integration relates to customer details. If they are changed, for example by a change of address, and only entered in the Sales Ledger and not in the records maintained by the delivery department, goods ordered by the customer could be sent to the wrong address.

If the cash book is not fully integrated with the Sales Ledger, customers may pay their accounts but still be shown as debtors when the system is asked to print an aged list of debtors in the middle of a month. Time and effort might then be expended chasing a debt that didn't exist and, of course, the customer would not be exactly pleased either.

23.4 There were a number of issues at that time:

- The output was sometimes inaccurate, mainly due to the inexperience of the people who were keying data into the AIS, but also due to errors in programming. Also, until the late 1970s, much of the input was by punched card and cards in a batch had to be entered into the computer in the same order as they were produced. If a batch of cards was dropped before being put into the card reader that then transferred the data into the computer, all sorts of nonsense could result. This type of situation gave rise to the phrase 'garbage in, garbage out' which was often used by those who favoured traditional manual systems when explaining why computers were 'useless'. It still applies today, but for different reasons, such as the original data being incorrect or out-of-date.
- Many early AISs were developed by computer specialists, not accountants. They often produced reports that were less meaningful than they might have been, frequently omitting key information. The decision-makers did not know what rules had been followed in generating numbers in the reports and so would sometimes reach a decision assuming the data meant one thing when, in fact, it meant something else. (For example, the scrap value of a fixed asset may have been ignored when calculating whether it should be used for one more year or replaced.) They also often gave everything possible to the decision-makers, resulting in huge piles of reports being received of which only a few pages were actually of any interest.

In other words, the output from early computerised AISs was often less than useful and often could not be relied upon.

REVIEW QUESTIONS

23.1 What benefits for the whole accounting system can follow from using a computer for accounting work?

23.2 Why is the need for accounting skills and knowledge important when the accounting system is computerised?

23.3 Why is the need to fully integrate a computerised accounting system so important?

23.4 What issues need to be considered when making the switch from a manual accounting system to a computerised accounting system?

PART 4

Adjustments for financial statements

Introduction

This part is concerned with all the adjustments that have to be made before financial statements can be prepared.

CHAPTER 24

Capital expenditure and revenue expenditure

Learning objectives

After you have studied this chapter, you should be able to:

- distinguish between expenditure that is capital in nature and that which is revenue expenditure
- explain why some expenditure is part capital expenditure and part revenue expenditure
- explain the effect on the financial statements, and the profits shown there, if revenue expenditure is wrongly treated as being capital expenditure, and vice versa

Introduction

In this chapter, you'll learn about the difference between capital expenditure and revenue expenditure. You will learn how to split expenditure that is part capital and part revenue and to make the appropriate entries in the ledgers and in the financial statements. You will also learn why organisations generally prefer to treat as much expenditure as possible as capital expenditure, how to deal with loan interest relating to acquisition of a fixed asset, and how to classify and deal with the income generated when a fixed asset is sold.

24.1 Capital expenditure

Before you start this topic, you need to be aware that 'capital expenditure' has nothing to do with the owner's Capital Account. The two terms happen to start with the same first word, and they are both things that are likely to be around the business for quite a long time. While both are, in a sense, long-term investments, one made by the business, the other made by the owner, they are, by definition, two very different things.

Capital expenditure is incurred when a business spends money either to

1 buy fixed assets, or
2 add to the value of an existing fixed asset.

Included in such amounts should be spending on

1 acquiring fixed assets
2 bringing them into the business
3 legal costs of buying buildings
4 carriage inwards on machinery bought
5 any other cost needed to get a fixed asset ready for use.

24.2   Revenue expenditure

Expenditure which is not spent on increasing the value of fixed assets, but on running the business on a day-to-day basis, is known as **revenue expenditure**.

The difference between revenue expenditure and capital expenditure can be seen clearly with the total cost of using a van for a business. To buy a van is capital expenditure. The van will be in use for several years and is, therefore, a fixed asset.

To pay for petrol to use in the van is revenue expenditure. This is because the expenditure is used up in a short time and does not add to the value of fixed assets.

> ### Activity 24.1
>
> Why do you think a business might want to treat an item of expenditure as capital rather than as revenue? (Hint: where does an item of capital expenditure *not* appear in the financial statements?)

24.3   Differences between capital and revenue expenditure

The examples listed in Exhibit 24.1 demonstrate the difference in classification.

Exhibit 24.1

Expenditure	Type of Expenditure
1 Buying van	Capital
2 Petrol costs for van	Revenue
3 Repairs to van	Revenue
4 Putting extra headlights on van	Capital
5 Buying machinery	Capital
6 Electricity costs of using machinery	Revenue
7 We spent £1,500 on machinery: £1,000 was for an item (improvement) added to the machine; and £500 was for repairs	Capital £1,000 Revenue £500
8 Painting outside of new building	Capital
9 Three years later – repainting outside of building in (8)	Revenue

You already know that revenue expenditure is chargeable to the Trading and Profit and Loss Account, while capital expenditure will result in increased figures for fixed assets in the Balance Sheet; and that getting the classification wrong affects the profits reported and the capital account and asset values in the financial statements. It is, therefore, important that this classification is correctly done.

24.4   Capital expenditure: further analysis

As mentioned earlier, capital expenditure not only consists of the cost of purchasing a fixed asset, but also includes other costs necessary to get the fixed asset operational.

> ### Activity 24.2
> Spend a minute listing some examples of these other costs like the ones you've already learnt about.

24.5 Joint expenditure

Sometimes one item of expenditure will need to be divided between capital and revenue expenditure – there was an example in Exhibit 24.1 when £1,500 was split between capital and revenue.

> ### Activity 24.3
> A builder was engaged to tackle some work on your premises, the total bill being for £3,000. If one-third of this was for repair work and two-thirds for improvements, where should the two parts be entered in the accounting books and where would they appear in the financial statements?

24.6 Incorrect treatment of expenditure

If one of the following occurs:

1 capital expenditure is incorrectly treated as revenue expenditure, or
2 revenue expenditure is incorrectly treated as capital expenditure,

then both the balance sheet figures and trading and profit and loss account figures will be incorrect.

This means that the net profit figure will also be incorrect and, if the expenditure affects items in the trading account part of that statement, the gross profit figure will also be incorrect.

> ### Activity 24.4
> Can you think of an example where an item may have been treated wrongly as revenue expenditure and charged in the trading account when it should have been treated as capital expenditure?

24.7 Treatment of loan interest

If money is borrowed to finance the purchase of a fixed asset, interest will have to be paid on the loan. Most accountants would argue that the loan interest is *not* a cost of acquiring the asset, but is simply a cost of *financing* its acquisition. This means that loan interest is revenue expenditure and *not* capital expenditure. In 1999, FRS 15 offered another view by making it acceptable to capitalise interest incurred in *constructing* a fixed asset.

> ### Activity 24.5
> Why shouldn't the interest on the funds borrowed to finance acquisition of a fixed asset be included in its cost?

24.8   Capital and revenue receipts

When an item of capital expenditure is sold, the receipt is called a capital receipt. Suppose a van is bought for £5,000, and sold five years later for £750. The £5,000 was treated as capital expenditure. The £750 received is treated as a capital receipt and credited to the fixed asset account in the General Ledger. (You will learn later in your studies that it is a bit more complicated than this, but this treatment is technically correct.)

Revenue receipts are sales and other revenue items that are added to gross profit, such as rent receivable and commissions receivable.

24.9   Finally

Students generally find this topic very difficult to grasp. Trying to remember when something should be treated as capital expenditure and when something should be treated as revenue expenditure just seems too difficult to remember correctly.

In fact, the rules are *very* simple:

1 If expenditure is directly incurred in bringing a fixed asset into use for the first time, it is capital expenditure.
2 If expenditure improves a fixed asset (by making it superior to what it was when it was first owned by the organisation, e.g. building an extension to a warehouse), it is capital expenditure.
3 All other expenditures are revenue expenditure.

So, faced with having to decide, ask if (1) is true in this case. If it isn't, ask if (2) is true in this case. If it isn't, it is revenue expenditure. If either (1) or (2) is true, it is capital expenditure – try it on the items in Exhibit 24.1, it works!

Learning outcomes

You should now have learnt:

1 How to distinguish between capital expenditure and revenue expenditure.
2 That some items are part capital expenditure and part revenue expenditure, and need to be apportioned accordingly.
3 That if capital expenditure or revenue expenditure is mistaken one for the other, then gross or net profit figures (or both) will be incorrectly stated, as will the capital account and fixed assets in the balance sheet.
4 That if capital receipts or revenue receipts are mistaken one for the other, then gross or net profit figures (or both) will be incorrectly stated, as will the capital account and fixed assets in the balance sheet.

Answers to activities

24.1   Capital expenditure appears in the balance sheet whereas revenue expenditure appears in the trading and profit and loss account. If expenditure is treated as revenue, it reduces profit immediately by the amount spend. If it is treated as capital, there is no immediate impact upon profit. Profit is only affected when a part of the expenditure is charged against income during the time the item purchased is in use, and those charges (called 'depreciation') spread the cost of the item over a number of years. As a result, profits are lower if an item of expenditure is treated as revenue.

Businesses like to show that they are being as profitable as possible, so they tend to want to treat everything possible as a capital expense. Doing this also makes the business look more wealthy as the fixed assets are at a higher value than they would have been had the expenditure been treated as revenue. (You'll learn about depreciation in Chapter 26.)

24.2 Some of the other possible additional costs are: (*a*) Installation costs (*b*) Inspection and testing the fixed asset before use (*c*) Architects' fees for building plans and for supervising construction of buildings (*d*) Demolition costs to remove something before new building can begin.

24.3 The debit entries would be Repairs £1,000 and Premises £2,000. The credit entry would be Creditor 'Builder' £3,000. The £1,000 will, therefore, appear in the trading and profit and loss account (in the profit and loss part) as revenue expenditure. The £2,000 identified as capital expenditure will appear in the balance sheet as part of the figure for Premises.

24.4 When goods are being maufactured from raw materials, employees will be being paid wages. Those wages will be part of the cost of the stock of finished goods. It sometimes happens that employees do other work in periods when their normal work is not keeping them busy. Imagine some employees were moved temporarily to help build an extension to the premises – for example, by helping to build a small garage to hold the company chairman's car while he was working in his office. If their wages for that period were mistakenly included as usual in the cost of goods produced, that would be an example of capital expenditure being wrongly classified as revenue expenditure that caused gross profit to be understated.

24.5 Organisations have a number of sources of funds, only one of which is borrowing. The fixed asset could have been paid for using existing funds already held by the organisation. The funds borrowed to pay for it could just as easily have been used to buy raw materials while the funds already available for purchase of raw materials could have been used to finance the new fixed asset. How could anyone be sure that the funds borrowed were actually used to purchase it, and why should they be tied so strongly to it when other funds could have been used instead? It is a very circuitous argument but, in the end, the funds borrowed entered the pool of all the organisation's funds. Just because an amount equal to the amount borrowed was then used to pay for the fixed asset is not sufficient reason to include the interest costs in the cost of the fixed asset. The interest costs are simply part of the costs of financing all the assets of the organisation. Until FRS 15 was issued in 1999, that is. FRS 15 allows interest directly attributable to the construction of a tangible fixed asset to be capitalised as part of the cost of that asset. Note that FRS 15 *does not* permit capitalisation of interest incurred on the funds used to purchase a fixed asset, only interest incurred on the construction of one.

REVIEW QUESTIONS

24.1

(*a*) What is meant by 'capital expenditure', and 'revenue expenditure'?

(*b*) Some of the following items should be treated as capital and some as revenue. For each of them state which classification applies:

(*i*)   The purchase of machinery for use in the business.
(*ii*) Carriage paid to bring the machinery in (*i*) above to the works.
(*iii*) Complete redecoration of the premises at a cost of £1,500.
(*iv*) A quarterly account for heating.
(*v*)   The purchase of a soft drinks vending machine for the canteen with a stock of soft drinks.
(*vi*) Wages paid by a building contractor to his own workmen for the erection of an office in the builder's stockyard.

24.2A Indicate which of the following would be revenue items and which would be capital items in a wholesale bakery:

(*a*) Purchase of a new van.
(*b*) Purchase of replacement engine for existing van.

(c) Cost of altering interior of new van to increase carrying capacity.
(d) Cost of motor tax for new van.
(e) Cost of motor tax for existing van.
(f) Cost of painting business's name on new van.
(g) Repair and maintenance of existing van.

24.3   Explain clearly the difference between capital expenditure and revenue expenditure. State which of the following you would classify as capital expenditure, giving your reasons:

(a) Cost of building extension to factory.
(b) Purchase of extra filing cabinets for sales office.
(c) Cost of repairs to accounting machine.
(d) Cost of installing reconditioned engine in delivery van.
(e) Legal fees paid in connection with factory extension.

24.4A   The data which follows was extracted from the books of account of H Kirk, an engineer, on 31 March 20X6, his financial year end.

	£
(a) Purchase of extra milling machine (includes £300 for repair of an old machine)	2,900
(b) Rent	750
(c) Electrical expenses (includes new wiring £600, part of premises improvement)	3,280
(d) Carriage inwards (includes £150 carriage on new cement mixer)	1,260
(e) Purchase of extra drilling machine	4,100

You are required to allocate each or part of the items above to either 'capital' or 'revenue' expenditure.

24.5   For the business of J Charles, wholesale chemist, classify the following between 'capital' and 'revenue' expenditure:

(a) Purchase of an extra van.
(b) Cost of rebuilding warehouse wall which had fallen down.
(c) Building extension to the warehouse.
(d) Painting extension to warehouse when it is first built.
(e) Repainting extension to warehouse three years later than that done in (d).
(f) Carriage costs on bricks for new warehouse extension.
(g) Carriage costs on purchases.
(h) Carriage costs on sales.
(i) Legal costs of collecting debts.
(j) Legal charges on acquiring new premises for office.
(k) Fire insurance premium.
(l) Costs of erecting new machine.

24.6A   For the business of H Ward, a food merchant, classify the following between 'capital' and 'revenue' expenditure:

(a) Repairs to meat slicer.
(b) New tyre for van.
(c) Additional shop counter.
(d) Renewing signwriting on shop.
(e) Fitting partitions in shop.
(f) Roof repairs.
(g) Installing thief detection equipment.
(h) Wages of shop assistant.
(i) Carriage on returns outwards.
(j) New cash register.
(k) Repairs to office safe.
(l) Installing extra toilet.

24.7

(a) Distinguish between capital and revenue expenditure.

(b) Napa Ltd took delivery of a microcomputer and printer on 1 July 20X6, the beginning of its financial year. The list price of the equipment was £4,999 but Napa Ltd was able to negotiate a price of £4,000 with the supplier. However, the supplier charged an additional £340 to install and test the equipment. The supplier offered a 5% discount if Napa Ltd paid for the equipment and the additional installation costs within seven days. Napa Ltd was able to take advantage of this additional discount. The installation of special electrical wiring for the computer cost £110. After initial testing certain modifications costing £199 proved necessary. Staff were sent on special training courses to operate the microcomputer and this cost £990. Napa Ltd insured the machine against fire and theft at a cost of £49 per annum. A maintenance agreement was entered into with Sonoma plc. Under this agreement Sonoma plc promised to provide 24 hour breakdown cover for one year. The cost of the maintenance agreement was £350.

Required:
Calculate the acquisition cost of the microcomputer to Napa Ltd.

(c) The following costs were also incurred by Napa Ltd during the financial year ended 30 June 20X7:

(1) Interest on loan to purchase microcomputer.
(2) Cost of software for use with the microcomputer.
(3) Cost of customising the software for use in Napa Ltd's business.
(4) Cost of paper used by the computer printer.
(5) Wages of computer operators.
(6) Cost of ribbons used by the computer printer.
(7) Cost of adding extra memory to the microcomputer.
(8) Cost of floppy disks used during the year.
(9) Costs of adding a manufacturer's upgrade to the microcomputer equipment.
(10) Cost of adding air conditioning to the computer room.

Required:
Classify each of the above as capital expenditure or revenue expenditure.

(*Association of Accounting Technicians*)

24.8 At the beginning of the financial year on 1 April 20X5, a company had a balance on plant account of £372,000 and on provision for depreciation of plant account of £205,400.

The company's policy is to provide depreciation using the reducing balance method applied to the fixed assets held at the end of the financial year at the rate of 20% per annum.

On 1 September 20X5 the company sold for £13,700 some plant which it had acquired on 31 October 20X1 at a cost of £36,000. Additionally, installation costs totalled £4,000. During 20X3 major repairs costing £6,300 had been carried out on this plant and, in order to increase the capacity of the plant, a new motor had been fitted in December 20X3 at a cost of £4,400. A further overhaul costing £2,700 had been carried out during 20X4.

The company acquired new replacement plant on 30 November 20X5 at a cost of £96,000, inclusive of installation charges of £7,000.

Required:
Calculate:
(a) the balance of plant at cost at 31 March 20X6
(b) the provision for depreciation of plant at 31 March 20X6
(c) the profit or loss on disposal of the plant.

(*Association of Chartered Certified Accountants*)

24.9A Sema plc, a company in the heavy engineering industry, carried out an expansion programme in the 20X6 financial year, in order to meet a permanent increase in contracts.

The company selected a suitable site and commissioned a survey and valuation report, for which the fee was £1,500. On the basis of the report the site was acquired for £90,000.

Solicitor's fees for drawing up the contract and conveyancing were £3,000.

Fees of £8,700 were paid to the architects for preparing the building plans and overseeing the building work. This was carried out partly by the company's own workforce (at a wages cost of £11,600), using company building materials (cost £76,800), and partly by subcontractors who charged £69,400, of which £4,700 related to the demolition of an existing building on the same site.

The completed building housed two hydraulic presses.

The cost of press A was £97,000 (ex works), payable in a single lump sum two months after installation. Sema was given a trade discount of 10% and a cash discount for prompt payment of 2%. Hire of a transporter to collect the press and to convey it to the new building was £2,900. Installation costs were £2,310, including hire of lifting gear, £1,400.

Press B would have cost £105,800 (delivered) if it had been paid in one lump sum. However, Sema opted to pay three equal annual instalments of £40,000, starting on the date of acquisition. Installation costs were £2,550, including hire of lifting gear, £1,750.

The whole of the above expenditure was financed by the issue of £500,000 7% Debentures (on which the annual interest payable was £35,000).

Before the above acquisitions were taken into account, the balances (at cost) on the fixed asset accounts for premises and plant were £521,100 and £407,500 respectively.

Required:
(a) Using such of the above information as is relevant, post and balance the premises and plant accounts for the 20X6 financial year.
(b) State, with reasons, which of the given information you have not used in your answer to (a) above.

(*Association of Chartered Certified Accountants*)

CHAPTER 25

Bad debts, provisions for doubtful debts, and provisions for discounts on debtors

Learning objectives

After you have studied this chapter, you should be able to:
- explain and show how bad debts are written off
- explain why provisions for doubtful debts are made
- make the necessary entries to record a provision for doubtful debts in the books
- calculate and make provisions for discounts on debtors
- make all the entries in the profit and loss account and balance sheet for bad debts, provisions for doubtful debts, and provisions for cash discount

Introduction

In this chapter, you'll learn how businesses deal with bad debts and how they provide for the possibility that other debts will not be paid. You'll learn how to record increases and decreases in the provision for doubtful debts. Finally, you'll learn how to make and adjust provisions for cash discounts.

25.1 Bad debts

With many businesses a large proportion, if not all, of the sales are on credit. The business is therefore taking the risk that some of the customers may never pay for the goods sold to them on credit. This is a normal business risk and such **bad debts** are a normal business expense. They must be charged to profit and loss as an expense when calculating the profit or loss for the period. The other thing that needs done is to remove the bad debt from the asset account. Usually, this will mean closing the debtor's account, but not always.

When a debt is found to be 'bad', the asset as shown by the debt in the debtor's account is worthless. It must be eliminated from the account.

This is done by crediting the debtor's account to cancel the asset and increasing the expense account of bad debts by debiting it there.

Activity 25.1
What circumstances might lead you to write off a debt as bad and *not* close the debtor's account?

There are a range of possible scenarios that may exist concerning a bad debt. The first two were discussed in the answer to Activity 25.1:

- the debtor may be refusing to pay one of a number of invoices;
- the debtor may be refusing to pay part of an invoice;
- the debtor may owe payment on a number of invoices and has indicated that only a proportion of the total amount due will ever be paid because the debtor's business has failed;
- the debtor's business has failed and nothing is ever likely to be received.

Whatever the reason, once a debt has been declared 'bad', the journal entry is the same. You debit the bad debt account with the amount of the bad debt and credit the debtor's account in the Sales Ledger to complete the double entry.

At the end of the period, the total of the bad debts account is transferred to the profit and loss account.

An example of debts being written off as bad is shown in Exhibit 25.1.

Exhibit 25.1

C Bloom

20X5			£	20X5				£
Jan	8	Sales	50	Dec	31	Bad debts		50

R Shaw

20X5			£	20X5				£
Feb	16	Sales	240	Aug	17	Cash		200
				Dec	31	Bad debts		40
			240					240

Bad Debts

20X5			£	20X5			£
Dec	31	C Bloom	50	Dec	31	Profit and loss	90
"	"	R Shaw	40				
			90				90

Profit and Loss Account (extract) for the year ended 31 December 20X5

	£
Gross profit	xxx
Less Expenses:	
Bad debts	(90)

25.2 Provisions for doubtful debts

Why provisions are needed

When we are drawing up our financial statements, we want to achieve the following objectives:

- to charge as an expense in the profit and loss account for that year an amount representing debts that will never be paid;
- to show in the balance sheet a debtors figure as close as possible to the true value of debtors at the balance sheet date.

Debts declared bad are usually debts that have existed for some time, perhaps even from earlier accounting periods.

However, how about other debts that have not been paid by the year end? These may not have been owing for so long, in which case it will be more difficult to determine which of them will be bad debts. Nevertheless, as all businesses experience bad debts at some time, it is likely that at least some of these other debts will ultimately prove to be bad. The prudence concept – you learnt about this in Chapter 10 – says that this possibility needs to be provided for in the current period, otherwise both the debtor balance reported in the balance sheet and the profit reported in the profit and loss account will almost certainly be overstated.

It is impossible to determine with absolute accuracy at the year end what the true amount is in respect of debtors who will never pay their accounts. So, how do you decide how much to provide as a provision against the possibility of some of the remaining debts (after removing those which have been written off as bad) proving bad in a future period?

In order to arrive at a figure for doubtful debts, a business must first consider that some debtors will never pay any of the amount they owe, while others will pay a part of the amount owing only, leaving the remainder permanently unpaid. The estimated figure can be made:

1 by looking at each debt, and deciding to what extent it will be bad;
2 by estimating, on the basis of experience, what percentage of the total amount due from the remaining debtors will ultimately prove to be bad debts.

It is well known that the longer a debt is owing, the more likely it is that it will become a bad debt. Some businesses draw up an ageing schedule, showing how long debts have been owing. Older debtors need higher percentage estimates of bad debts than do newer debtors. The percentages chosen should reflect the actual pattern of bad debts experienced in the past. Exhibit 25.2 gives an example of an ageing schedule.

Exhibit 25.2

Ageing Schedule for Doubtful Debts			
Period debt owing	Amount	Estimated percentage doubtful	Provision for doubtful debts
	£	%	£
Less than one month	5,000	1	50
1 month to 2 months	3,000	3	90
2 months to 3 months	800	4	32
3 months to 1 year	200	5	10
Over 1 year	160	20	32
	9,160		214

Most businesses don't go to this level of detail. Instead, they apply a percentage to the overall debtor balance (after deducting the bad debts). The percentage will be one the business has established over the years as being the most appropriate.

Now, let's look at how the provision for doubtful debts is entered in the books.

Accounting entries for provisions for doubtful debts

The accounting entries needed for the **provision for doubtful debts** are:
Year in which provision is *first* made:

1 Debit the profit and loss account with the amount of the provision (i.e. deduct it from gross profit as an expense).
2 Credit the *Provision for Doubtful Debts Account*.

Exhibit 25.3 shows the entries needed for a provision for doubtful debts.

Exhibit 25.3

At 31 December 20X3, the debtors figure after deducting bad debts was £10,000. It is estimated that 2 per cent of debts (i.e. £200) will eventually prove to be bad debts, and it is decided to make a provision for these. The accounts will appear as follows:

Profit and Loss Account (extract) for the year ended 31 December 20X3

	£
Gross profit	XXX
Less Expenses:	
Provision for doubtful debts	(200)

Provision for Doubtful Debts

		20X3	£
		Dec 31 Profit and loss	200

In the balance sheet, the balance on the provision for doubtful debts will be deducted from the total of debtors:

Balance Sheet (extract) as at 31 December 20X3

Current assets	£	£
Debtors	10,000	
Less Provision for doubtful debts	(200)	
		9,800

You'll have noticed that we are using two different accounts to make the two different debtor adjustments. This is done in order to make it clear how much is (*a*) being written off as bad and how much is (*b*) being treated as a provision for doubtful debts:

(*a*) **Bad debts expense account:** This is used only when the debt has been proved to be a bad debt and is written off.

(*b*) **Provision for doubtful debts account:** This account is used only for estimates of the amount of the debtors remaining at the year end *after the bad debts have been written off* that are likely to finish up as bad debts. (This account is also known as the 'provision for *bad* debts account'.)

By charging both (*a*) and (*b*) in the profit and loss account for the year, we present the full picture of the amounts provided for in respect of both bad and doubtful debts. As you've already seen in Exhibits 25.1 and 25.3, these amounts are shown as deductions from the gross profit.

By showing (*b*) as a deduction from the figure of debtors in the balance sheet at the year end, we then get a net figure, which represents a more accurate figure of the value of debtors than the total of all the debtor balances in the Sales Ledger. It may not be absolutely accurate – only time will tell which of the debtors will turn out to be bad debts – but it is better than not attempting to make an estimate.

When you look at depreciation in Chapter 26, you will see that it bears similarities to the provision for doubtful debts. Depreciation is charged as a debit to profit and loss and a credit against fixed asset accounts in the General Ledger. It represents an estimate of how much of the overall economic usefulness of a fixed asset has been used up in each accounting period. Like the provision for doubtful debts, it too can never be completely accurate since only in several years' time, when the asset is put out of use, can it be determined whether or not the provisions made have been appropriate. Having to make estimates where absolute accuracy is impossible is a part of accounting.

Activity 25.2
Why do accountants have to make these provisions?

25.3   Increasing the provision

Let us suppose that for the same business as in Exhibit 25.3, at the end of the following year, 31 December 20X4, the doubtful debts provision needed to be increased. This was because the provision was kept at 2 per cent, but the debtors had risen to £12,000. A provision of £200 had been brought forward from the *previous* year, but we now want a total provision of £240 (i.e. 2 per cent of £12,000). All that is now needed is a provision for an extra £40. The double entry will be:

1 Debit Profit and Loss Account (i.e. deduct it from gross profit as an expense).
2 Credit the Provision for Doubtful Debts Account.

These entries are illustrated in Exhibit 25.4.

Exhibit 25.4

Profit and Loss Account (extract) for the year ended 31 December 20X4

	£
Gross profit	xxx
Less Expenses	
Provision for doubtful debts (increase)	(40)

Provision for Doubtful Debts

20X4		£	20X4			£
Dec 31	Balance c/d	240	Jan	1	Balance b/d	200
			Dec	31	Profit and loss	40
		240				240
			20X5			
			Jan	1	Balance b/d	240

Balance Sheet (extract) as on 31 December 20X4

Current assets	£	£
Debtors	12,000	
Less Provision for doubtful debts	(240)	
		11,760

Activity 25.3
Why do you only need to create an expense for the difference between the provisions of the two years?

25.4   Reducing the provision

To reduce the provision, you simply do the opposite to what you did to increase it. The provision for doubtful debts has a credit balance. Therefore, to reduce it we would need a debit entry in the provision account. The credit would be in the profit and loss account. Let's assume that at 31 December 20X5, the debtors figure had fallen to £10,500 but the provision remained at 2 per cent, i.e. £210 (2 per cent of £10,500).

As the provision had previously been £240, it now needs to be reduced by £30. The double entry is:

1 Debit Provision for Doubtful Debts Account.
2 Credit Profit and Loss Account (i.e. add it as a gain to gross profit).

These entries are illustrated in Exhibit 25.5.

Exhibit 25.5

Provision for Doubtful Debts

20X5			£	20X5			£
Dec	31	Profit and loss	30	Jan	1	Balance b/d	240
''	31	Balance c/d	210				
			240				240
				20X6			
				Jan	1	Balance b/d	210

Profit and Loss Account (extract) for the year ended 31 December 20X5

	£
Gross profit	xxx
Add Reduction in provision for doubtful debts	30

Balance Sheet (extract) as on 31 December 20X5

Current assets	£	£
Debtors	10,500	
Less Provision for doubtful debts	(210)	
		10,290

You will have noticed that increases in the provision for doubtful debts increase the total of expenses. On the other hand, a reduction in the provision for doubtful debts will be added to the gross profit.

Activity 25.4

Without looking back in your textbook, write down the double entries for *(a)* an increase and *(b)* a decrease in the provision for doubtful debts.

Let us now look at a comprehensive example in Exhibit 25.6.

Exhibit 25.6

A business starts on 1 January 20X2 and its financial year end is 31 December annually. A table of the debtors, the bad debts written off and the estimated bad debts at the rate of 2 per cent of debtors at the end of each year is now given. The double entry accounts and the extracts from the final accounts follow.

Year to 31 December	Debtors at end of year (after bad debts written off)	Bad debts written off during year	Debts thought at end of year to be impossible to collect: 2% of debtors
	£	£	£
20X2	6,000	423	120 (2% of £6,000)
20X3	7,000	510	140 (2% of £7,000)
20X4	7,750	604	155 (2% of £7,750)
20X5	6,500	610	130 (2% of £6,500)

Bad Debts

20X2		£	20X2		£
Dec 31	Various debtors	423	Dec 31	Profit and loss	423
20X3			20X3		
Dec 31	Various debtors	510	Dec 31	Profit and loss	510
20X4			20X4		
Dec 31	Various debtors	604	Dec 31	Profit and loss	604
20X5			20X5		
Dec 31	Various debtors	610	Dec 31	Profit and loss	610

Provision for Doubtful Debts

20X2		£	20X2		£
Dec 31	Balance c/d	120	Dec 31	Profit and loss	120
20X3			20X3		
Dec 31	Balance c/d	140	Jan 1	Balance b/d	120
			Dec 31	Profit and loss	20
		140			140
20X4			20X4		
Dec 31	Balance c/d	155	Jan 1	Balance b/d	140
			Dec 31	Profit and loss	15
		155			155
20X5			20X5		
Dec 31	Profit and loss	25	Jan 1	Balance b/d	155
	Balance c/d	130			
		155			155
			20X6		
			Jan 1	Balance b/d	130

Profit and Loss Accounts (extracts) for the year ended 31 December

		£	£
Gross profit for 20X2, 20X3, 20X4, 20X5			xxx
20X2	*Less* Expenses:		
	Bad debts	423	
	Provision for doubtful debts (increase)	120	
			(543)
20X3	*Less* Expenses:		
	Bad debts	510	
	Provision for doubtful debts (increase)	20	
			(530)
20X4	*Less* Expenses:		
	Bad debts	604	
	Provision for doubtful debts (increase)	15	
			(619)
20X5	*Add* Reduction in provision for doubtful debts	25	
	Less Expenses:		
	Bad debts	(610)	
			(585)

Balance Sheets (extracts) as at 31 December

		£	£
20X2	Debtors	6,000	
	Less Provision for doubtful debts	(120)	
			5,880
20X3	Debtors	7,000	
	Less Provision for doubtful debts	(140)	
			6,860
20X4	Debtors	7,750	
	Less Provision for doubtful debts	(155)	
			7,595
20X5	Debtors	6,500	
	Less Provision for doubtful debts	(130)	
			6,370

25.5 Bad debts recovered

It is not uncommon for a debt written off in previous years to be recovered. When this happens, you

1 Reinstate the debt by making the following entries:

Dr Debtor's account
　Cr Bad debts recovered account

2 When payment is received from the debtor in settlement of all or part of the debt:

Dr Cash/bank
　Cr Debtor's account

with the amount received.

At the end of the financial year, the credit balance in the bad debts recovered account is transferred to either the bad debts account or direct to the credit side of the profit and loss account. The effect is the same, since the bad debts account will, in itself, be transferred to the profit and loss account at the end of the financial year.

> ### Activity 25.5
> Why do you think we reinstate the debt just to cancel it out again? Why don't we simply debit the bank account and credit the bad debts recovered account?

25.6 Provisions for cash discounts on debtors

Some businesses create provisions for cash discounts to be allowed on the debtors outstanding at the balance sheet date. This, they maintain, is quite legitimate, as the amount of debtors less any doubtful debt provision is not the best estimate of collectable debts, owing to cash discounts which will be given to debtors if they pay within a given time. The cost of discounts, it is argued, should be charged in the period when the sales were made. While this practice is of dubious merit (as cash discount is treated as a finance charge, not as an adjustment to sales revenue), it is one used in practice by some businesses.

The procedure for dealing with this is similar to the doubtful debts provision. It must be borne in mind that the estimate of discounts to be allowed should be based on the net figure of debtors less doubtful debts provision, as it is obvious that cash discounts are not allowed on bad debts! Let's look at an example in Exhibit 25.7.

Exhibit 25.7

Year ended 31 December	Debtors	Provision for doubtful debts	Provision for cash discounts allowed
	£	£	%
20X3	4,000	200	2
20X4	5,000	350	2
20X5	4,750	250	2

Provision for Cash Discounts on Debtors

		£			£
20X3			20X3		
Dec 31	Balance c/d	76	Dec 31 Profit and loss		76
20X4			20X4		
Dec 31	Balance c/d	93	Jan 1 Balance b/d		76
			Dec 31 Profit and loss		17
		93			93
20X5			20X5		
Dec 31	Profit and loss	3	Jan 1 Balance b/d		93
" "	Balance c/d	90			
		93			93
			20X6		
			Jan 1 Balance b/d		90

Profit and Loss Account (extracts) for the year ended 31 December

	£
Gross profits (20X3 and 20X4 and 20X5)	xxx
Less Expenses:	
(20X3) Provision for cash discounts on debtors	(76)
(20X4) Increase in provision for cash discounts on debtors	(17)
Add (20X5) Reduction in provision for cash discounts on debtors	3

Balance Sheets (extracts) as at 31 December

		£	£	£
20X3	Debtors		4,000	
	Less Provision for doubtful debts	200		
	" Provision for discounts on debtors	76		
			(276)	
				3,724
20X4	Debtors		5,000	
	Less Provision for doubtful debts	350		
	" Provision for discounts on debtors	93		
			(443)	
				4,557
20X5	Debtors		4,750	
	Less Provision for doubtful debts	250		
	" Provision for discounts on debtors	90		
			(340)	
				4,410

25.7 Finally

As with distinguishing capital expenditure and revenue expenditure, students generally find this topic very difficult to grasp. It seems to be too difficult for some students to remember the difference between the treatment of bad debts and provisions for doubtful debts. They also often struggle to make the correct adjustments when the provision changes, with the most common error being that they charge all the provision, instead of only the change, to profit and loss.

There is no shortcut to getting this right. You need to keep the difference between bad debts and provisions for doubtful debts very clearly in your mind. Learning them as two separate topics seems to help. So far as the treatment of the change in the provision is concerned, don't try calling it 'change in the provision for doubtful debts', you'll only get confused when you make the entry in the balance sheet. And there is where the difficulty lies. *In the balance sheet, the entire provision is deducted from the figure for debtors but, in the profit and loss account, you only include the change.* Try to memorise this last sentence. It may make all the difference.

Learning outcomes

You should now have learnt:

1 That debts we are unable to collect are called bad debts.

2 That bad debts are credited to the customer's account (to cancel them) and debited to a bad debts account.

3 That provisions for doubtful debts are needed, otherwise the value of the debtors on the balance sheet will be showing too high a value, and could mislead anyone looking at the balance sheet. Also, this allows for more accurate calculation of profits or losses.

4 That the provision for doubtful debts is calculated *after* bad debts have been deducted from the debtor balances.

5 That the amount of the provision for doubtful debts is based on the best estimate that can be made taking all the facts into account.

6 That an increase in the provision for doubtful debts will create a debit entry in the profit and loss account.

7 That a reduction in the provision for doubtful debts will create a credit entry in the profit and loss account.

8 That the provision for doubtful debts is shown as a deduction from the debtors in the balance sheet.

9 That provisions for cash discount are made in the same way as provisions for doubtful debts.

10 How to record bad debts, provisions for doubtful debts, and provisions for cash discounts in the accounting books and in the profit and loss account and balance sheet.

Answers to activities

25.1 Sometimes a debtor will contest an invoice and refuse to pay it while continuing to pay all other invoices. This may happen, for example, when the debtor claims the goods were delivered damaged and you have refused to issue a credit note because you believe the goods were delivered safely. Another example occurs when the debtor is refusing to pay part of an invoice. This may happen, for example, when the customer claims not to have received all the items on the invoice. In both those circumstances, many businesses will eventually write off the debt on the disputed invoice and continue to trade with the customer.

25.2   The prudence concept which you learnt about in Chapter 10 requires it.

25.3   During the year, some debts will have been written off as bad. They will include debts from the previous year which last year's provision was intended to cover. If last year's estimate was correct, you could add this year's bad debts to the change in the provision and the total would be the same as the total provision you want to make this year, not just the difference between the two years' provisions. So, in effect, you've converted last year's provision into this year's bad debts. All you need do now is adjust the balance on the provision for doubtful debts account to make it equal to the provision you want to make against this year's closing debtors balance.

25.4   (*a*) *Dr* Profit and loss account   *Cr* Provision for doubtful debts account
         (*b*) *Dr* Provision for doubtful debts account   *Cr* Profit and loss account

Note how they are the opposite of each other.

25.5   The reason for reinstating the debt in the ledger account of the debtor is to have a detailed history of the debtor's account as a guide for granting credit in future. When a debt is written off as bad, it is recorded in the debtor's ledger account. Therefore, when a bad debt is recovered, it should also be shown in the debtor's ledger account, so as to provide the full picture.

REVIEW QUESTIONS

25.1   In a new business during the year ended 31 December 20X8 the following debts are found to be bad, and are written off on the dates shown:

30 April	H Gordon	£110
31 August	D Bellamy Ltd	£ 64
31 October	J Alderton	£ 12

On 31 December 20X8 the schedule of remaining debtors, amounting in total to £6,850, is examined, and it is decided to make a provision for doubtful debts of £220.

You are required to show:
(*a*) The Bad Debts Account, and the Provision for Doubtful Debts Account.
(*b*) The charge to the Profit and Loss Account.
(*c*) The relevant extracts from the Balance Sheet as at 31 December 20X8.

25.2   A business had always made a provision for doubtful debts at the rate of 5% of debtors. On 1 January 20X7 the provision for this, brought forward from the previous year, was £260.
   During the year to 31 December 20X7 the bad debts written off amounted to £540.
   On 31 December 20X7 the remaining debtors totalled £6,200 and the usual provision for doubtful debts is to be made.

You are to show:
(*a*) The Bad Debts Account for the year ended 31 December 20X7.
(*b*) The Provision for Doubtful Debts Account for the year.
(*c*) Extract from the Profit and Loss Account for the year.
(*d*) The relevant extract from the Balance Sheet as at 31 December 20X7.

25.3   A business started trading on 1 January 20X6. During the two years ended 31 December 20X6 and 20X7 the following debts were written off to the Bad Debts Account on the dates stated:

31 August 20X6	W Best	£ 85
30 September 20X6	S Avon	£140
28 February 20X7	L J Friend	£180
31 August 20X7	N Kelly	£ 60
30 November 20X7	A Oliver	£250

On 31 December 20X6 there had been a total of debtors remaining of £40,500. It was decided to make a provision for doubtful debts of £550.

On 31 December 20X7 there had been a total of debtors remaining of £47,300. It was decided to make a provision for doubtful debts of £600.

You are required to show:

(*i*) The Bad Debts Account and the Provision for Doubtful Debts Account for each of the two years.

(*ii*) The relevant extracts from the Balance Sheets as at 31 December 20X6 and 20X7.

25.4A   A business, which started trading on 1 January 20X5, adjusted its doubtful debt provision at the end of each year on a percentage basis, but each year the percentage rate is adjusted in accordance with the current 'economic climate'. The following details are available for the three years ended 31 December 20X5, 20X6 and 20X7.

	Bad debts written off year to 31 December	Debtors at 31 December	Percentage provision for doubtful debts
	£	£	
20X5	656	22,000	5
20X6	1,805	40,000	7
20X7	3,847	60,000	6

You are required to show:

(*a*) Bad Debts Accounts for each of the three years.

(*b*) Provision for Doubtful Debts Accounts for each of the three years.

(*c*) Balance Sheet extracts as at 31 December 20X5, 20X6 and 20X7.

25.5A

(*a*) Businesses often create a provision for doubtful debts.

(*i*)   Of which concept (or convention) is this an example? Explain your answer.

(*ii*) What is the purpose of creating a provision for doubtful debts?

(*iii*) How might the amount of a provision for doubtful debts be calculated?

(*b*) On 1 January 20X8 there was a balance of £500 in the Provision for Doubtful Debts Account, and it was decided to maintain the provision at 5% of the debtors at each year end. The debtors on 31 December each year were:

	£
20X8	12,000
20X9	8,000
20X0	8,000

Show the necessary entries for the **three** years ended 31 December 20X8 to 31 December 20X0 inclusive in the following:

(*i*) the Provision for Doubtful Debts Account;

(*ii*) the Profit and Loss Accounts.

(*c*) What is the difference between bad debts and provision for doubtful debts?

(*d*) On 1 January 20X0 Warren Mair owed Jason Dalgleish £130. On 25 August 20X0 Mair was declared bankrupt. A payment of 30p in the £ was received in full settlement. The remaining balance was written off as a bad debt. Write up the account of Warren Mair in Jason Dalgleish's ledger.

(*Northern Examinations and Assessment Board: GCSE*)

25.6   The balance sheet as at 31 May 20X7 of Forest Traders Limited included a provision for doubtful debts of £2,300. The company's accounts for the year ended 31 May 20X8 are now being prepared. The company's policy now is to relate the provision for doubtful debts to the age of debts outstanding. The debts outstanding at 31 May 20X8 and the required provisions for doubtful debts are as follows:

Debts outstanding	Amount	Provision for doubtful debts
	£	%
Up to 1 month	24,000	1
More than 1 month and up to 2 months	10,000	2
More than 2 months and up to 3 months	8,000	4
More than 3 months	3,000	5

Customers are allowed a cash discount of 2$\frac{1}{2}$% for settlement of debts within one month. It is now proposed to make a provision for discounts to be allowed in the company's accounts for the year ended 31 May 20X8.

Required:
Prepare the following accounts for the year ended 31 May 20X8 in the books of Forest Traders Limited to record the above transactions:

(a) Provision for doubtful debts;
(b) Provision for discounts to be allowed on debtors.

(*Association of Accounting Technicians*)

25.7A A business makes a provision for doubtful debts of 5% of debtors, also a provision of 2$\frac{1}{2}$% for discount on debtors.

On 1 January 20X7 the balances brought forward on the relevant accounts were provision for doubtful debts £672 and provision for discounts on debtors £631.

You are required to:
(a) Enter the balances in the appropriate accounts, using a separate Provision for Doubtful Debts Account.
(b) During 20X7 the business incurred bad debts £2,960 and allowed discounts £6,578. On 31 December 20X7 debtors amounted to £25,600. Show the entries in the appropriate accounts for the year 20X7, assuming that the business's accounting year ends on 31 December 20X7, also balance sheet extracts at 31 December 20X7.

25.8 E Chivers commenced business on 1 January 20X7 and makes his accounts to 31 December every year. For the year ended 31 December 20X7, bad debts written off amounted to £1,200. It was also found necessary to create a provision for doubtful debts of £2,000.

In 20X8, debts amounting to £1,600 proved bad and were written off. Mrs P Iles, whose debt of £350 was written off as bad in 20X7, settled her account in full on 30 November 20X8. As at 31 December 20X8 total debts outstanding were £56,000. It was decided to bring the provision up to 5% of this figure on that date.

In 20X9, £2,350 debts were written off during the year, and another recovery of £150 was made in respect of debts written off in 20X7. As at 31 December 20X9, total debts outstanding were £42,000. The provision for doubtful debts is to be maintained at 5% of this figure.

You are required to show for the years 20X7, 20X8 and 20X9, the
(a) Bad Debts Account.
(b) Bad Debts Recovered Account.
(c) Provision for Doubtful Debts Account.
(d) Extract from the Profit and Loss Account.

25.9
(A) Explain why a provision may be made for doubtful debts.
(B) Explain the procedure to be followed when a customer whose debt has been written off as bad subsequently pays the amount originally owing.
(C) On 1 January 20X7 D Watson had debtors of £25,000 on which he had made a provision for doubtful debts of 3%.

During 20X7,
(*i*) A Stewart who owed D Watson £1,200 was declared bankrupt and a settlement of 25p in the £ was made, the balance being treated as a bad debt.
(*ii*) Other bad debts written off during the year amounted to £2,300.

On 31 December 20X7 total debtors amounted to £24,300 but this requires to be adjusted as follows:

(*a*) J Smith, a debtor owing £600, was known to be unable to pay and this amount was to be written off.
(*b*) A cheque for £200 from S McIntosh was returned from the bank unpaid.

D Watson maintained his provision for doubtful debts at 3% debtors.

Required:
(1) For the financial year ended 31 December 20X7, show the entries in the following accounts:
   (*i*) Provision for doubtful debts
   (*ii*) Bad debts
(2) What is the effect on net profit of the change in the provision for doubtful debts?

(*Scottish Qualifications Authority*)

CHAPTER 26

Depreciation of fixed assets: nature and calculations

After you have studied this chapter, you should be able to:
- define depreciation
- explain why depreciation is provided
- calculate depreciation using both the straight line and the reducing balance methods
- calculate depreciation on assets bought or sold within an accounting period

Introduction

In this chapter, you'll learn why depreciation must be provided and how to calculate it using the two most widely used methods, in the year of acquisition, year of disposal, and all the years in between.

26.1 Nature of fixed assets

Before going any further, you need to be sure that you know what a fixed asset is.

Activity 26.1
Write down the three characteristics that distinguish fixed assets from current assets.

If you don't or didn't know how to define fixed assets, be sure that you do before going on to look at the topic of depreciation.

26.2 Depreciation of fixed assets

Fixed assets such as machinery, motor vehicles, fixtures and even buildings do not last for ever. If the amount received (if any) on the disposal of a fixed asset is deducted from the cost of buying it, the value of the fixed asset can be said to have 'depreciated in value' by that amount over its period of usefulness to the business. For example, if a van was bought for £10,000 and sold five years later for £2,000 then its value has depreciated over the period of its use by £8,000.

This is the only time that depreciation can be calculated accurately. That is, you can only *estimate* what it should be each year while the fixed asset continues to be used.

26.3   Depreciation is an expense

Depreciation is that part of the original cost of a fixed asset that is consumed during its period of use by the business. The annual charge to profit and loss for depreciation is based upon an estimate of how much of the overall economic usefulness of a fixed asset has been used up in that accounting period. It is an expense for services consumed in the same way as expenses are incurred for items such as wages, rent or electricity. Because it is charged as an expense to the profit and loss account, depreciation reduces net profit.

For example, if a PC cost £1,200 and was expected to be used for three years, it might be estimated at the end of the first year that a third of its overall usefulness had been consumed. Depreciation would then be charged at an amount equal to one-third of the cost of the PC, i.e. £400. Profit would be reduced by £400 and the value of the PC in the balance sheet would be reduced from £1,200 to £800.

Using an example of a van and the petrol it consumes, you can see that the only real difference between the expense of depreciation for the van and the expense of petrol incurred in order to use the van, is that the petrol expense is used up in a day or two, whereas the expense for use of the van is spread over several years. Both expenses are expenses of the business.

> ### Activity 26.2
> If depreciation reduces profits and reduces the value of assets and so reduces the capital account of the owner, why do businesses bother providing for depreciation?

26.4   Causes of depreciation

These can be divided up between physical deterioration, economic factors, the time factor, and depletion. Let us look at these in more detail.

Physical deterioration

1 **Wear and tear.** When a motor vehicle or machinery or fixtures and fittings are used they eventually wear out. Some last many years, others last only a few years. This is also true of buildings, although some may last for a long time.
2 **Erosion, rust, rot and decay.** Land may be eroded or wasted away by the action of wind, rain, sun and other elements of nature. Similarly, the metals in motor vehicles or machinery will rust away. Wood will rot eventually. Decay is a process which will also be present due to the elements of nature and the lack of proper attention.

Economic factors

These may be said to be the reasons for an asset being put out of use even though it is in good physical condition. The two main factors are usually **obsolescence** and **inadequacy**.

1 **Obsolescence.** This is the process of becoming out-of-date. For instance, over the years there has been great progress in the development of synthesisers and electronic devices used by leading commercial musicians. The old equipment will therefore have become obsolete, and much of it will have been taken out of use by such musicians.

   This does not mean that the equipment is worn out. Other people may well buy the old equipment and use it, possibly because they cannot afford to buy new up-to-date equipment.

2 **Inadequacy**. This arises when an asset is no longer used because of the growth and changes in the size of the business. For instance, a small ferryboat that is operated by a business at a coastal resort will become entirely inadequate when the resort becomes more popular. Then it will be found that it would be more efficient and economical to operate a large ferryboat, and so the smaller boat will be put out of use by the business.

In this case also it does not mean that the ferryboat is no longer in good working order, nor that it is obsolete. It may be sold to a business at a smaller resort.

The time factor

Obviously time is needed for wear and tear, erosion, etc., and for obsolescence and inadequacy to take place. However, there are fixed assets to which the time factor is connected in a different way. These are assets which have a legal life fixed in terms of years.

For instance, you may agree to rent some buildings for ten years. This is normally called a lease. When the years have passed, the lease is worth nothing to you, as it has finished. Whatever you paid for the lease is now of no value.

A similar asset is where you buy a patent so that only you are able to produce something. When the patent's time has finished it then has no value. The usual length of life of a patent is sixteen years.

Instead of using the term depreciation, the term *amortisation* is often used for these assets.

Depletion

Other assets are of wasting character, perhaps due to the extraction of raw materials from them. These materials are then either used by the business to make something else, or are sold in their raw state to other businesses. Natural resources such as mines, quarries and oil wells come under this heading. To provide for the consumption of an asset of a wasting character is called provision for **depletion**.

26.5 | Land and buildings

Prior to the issue of SSAP 12 in 1977, freehold and long leasehold properties were very rarely subject to a charge for depreciation. It was contended that, as property values tended to rise rather than fall, it was inappropriate to charge depreciation.

SSAP 12 changed all that by requiring that depreciation be written off over the property's useful life, with the exception that freehold land does not normally require a provision for depreciation. This is because land does not normally depreciate. Buildings do, however, eventually fall into disrepair or become obsolete and must be subject to a charge for depreciation each year.

When FRS 15 replaced SSAP 12 in 1999, it repeated these requirements. It also dealt with the problem of the distinction between the cost of freehold land and the cost of the buildings upon it, by insisting that the two elements of the cost be separated.

26.6 | Appreciation

At this stage, you may be wondering what happens when fixed assets increase (appreciate) in value. The answer to this is that normal accounting procedure would be to ignore any such appreciation, as to bring appreciation into account would be to contravene both the historical cost concept and the prudence concept you learnt about in Chapter 10.

However, one of the problems when SSAP 12 was introduced was that the UK was in the middle of a boom in property prices which had been going on for some time and didn't really end until the early 1990s. Businesses could see that the market value of their properties was rising. At the same time, they were being instructed (by the accounting standard) to charge their profit and loss account with depreciation that represented a fall in the value of the property over the period. Not surprisingly, this didn't seem to make any sense. To address this, SSAP 12 allowed fixed assets to be revalued and for depreciation to then be calculated on the basis of the revalued amount. FRS 15 also permits this to be done.

26.7 Provision for depreciation as an allocation of cost

Depreciation in total over the life of a fixed asset can be calculated quite simply as cost less the amount receivable when the fixed asset is put out of use by the business. This amount receivable is normally referred to as the **residual value** of an asset. If the item is bought and sold for a lower amount within the same accounting period, then the difference in value is charged as depreciation in arriving at that period's net profit.

The difficulties start when the asset is used for more than one accounting period: an attempt has to be made to charge each period with the depreciation for that period.

Although depreciation provisions are intended to allocate the cost of a fixed asset to each accounting period in which it is in use, it does not follow that there is any truly accurate method of performing this task. All that can be said is that the cost should be allocated over the life of the fixed asset in such a way as to charge it as equitably as possible to the periods in which it is used. The difficulties involved are considerable and include:

1 Apart from a few assets, such as a lease, how accurately can a business assess an asset's useful life? Even a lease may be put out of use if the premises leased have become inadequate or inappropriate (e.g. after a change in the product being sold or unexpected growth in the size of the business).
2 How is 'use' measured? A car owned by a business for two years may have been driven one year by a very careful driver and another year by a reckless driver. The standard of driving will affect the car and also the amount of cash receivable on its disposal. How should such a business apportion the car's depreciation costs?
3 There are other expenses besides depreciation, such as repairs and maintenance of the fixed asset. As both of these affect the rate and amount of depreciation, should they not also affect the depreciation provision calculations?
4 How can a business possibly know the amount receivable in x years' time when the asset is put out of use?

These are only some of the difficulties. Accounting has developed some methods to make the depreciation calculation that are considered acceptable. However, you will see that none of them really manages to address these issues. Nevertheless, just as with provisions for doubtful debts, making some allowance for depreciation is better than making none at all.

26.8 Methods of calculating depreciation charges

The two main methods in use are the **straight line method** and the **reducing balance method**. Other methods may be used in certain cases, and some of them are covered in Chapter 37. Most accountants think that the straight line method is the one that is generally most suitable.

Straight line method

By this method, the number of years of use is estimated. The cost is then divided by the number of years, to give the depreciation charge each year.

For instance, if a lorry was bought for £22,000 and we thought we would keep it for four years and then sell it for £2,000 the depreciation to be charged each year would be:

$$\frac{\text{Cost (£22,000) – Estimated disposal value (£2,000)}}{\text{Number of expected years of use (4)}} = \frac{£20,000}{4}$$

= £5,000 depreciation each year for four years.

If, on the other hand, we thought that after four years the lorry would have no disposal value, the charge for depreciation would be:

$$\frac{\text{Cost (£22,000)}}{\text{Number of expected years of use (4)}} = \frac{£22,000}{4}$$

= £5,500 depreciation each year for four years.

Reducing balance method

In this method, a fixed percentage for depreciation is deducted from the cost in the first year. In the second or later years the same percentage is taken of the reduced balance (i.e. cost *less* depreciation already charged). This method is also known as the *diminishing balance method* or the *diminishing debit balance method*.

If a machine is bought for £10,000 and depreciation is to be charged at 20 per cent, the calculations for the first three years would be as follows:

	£
Cost	10,000
First year: depreciation (20%)	(2,000)
	8,000
Second year: depreciation (20% of £8,000)	(1,600)
	6,400
Third year: depreciation (20% of £6,400)	(1,280)
Cost not yet apportioned, end of Year 3	5,120

The basic formula used to find the percentage to apply with this method is:

$$r = 1 - \sqrt[n]{\frac{s}{c}}$$

where n = the number of years
         s = the net residual value (this must be a significant amount or the answers will be absurd, since the depreciation rate would amount to nearly one)
         c = the cost of the asset
         r = the rate of depreciation to be applied.

Using as an example the figures

         n = 4 years
         s = residual value £256
         c = cost £10,000

the calculations would appear as:

$$r = 1 - \sqrt[4]{\frac{256}{£10,000}} = 1 - \frac{4}{10} = 0.6 \text{ or } 60 \text{ per cent}$$

The depreciation calculation applied to each of the four years of use would be:

	£
Cost	10,000
Year 1: Depreciation provision 60% of £10,000	(6,000)
Cost not yet apportioned, end of Year 1	4,000
Year 2: Depreciation provision 60% of £4,000	(2,400)
Cost not yet apportioned, end of Year 2	1,600
Year 3: Depreciation provision 60% of £1,600	(960)
Cost not yet apportioned, end of Year 3	640
Year 4: Depreciation provision 60% of £640	(384)
Cost not yet apportioned, end of Year 4	256

In this case, the percentage to be applied worked out conveniently to a round figure of 60%. However, the answer will often come out to several decimal places, e.g. 59.846512. When it does, normal practice is to take the nearest whole figure as a percentage to be applied. However, nowadays, many of the businesses performing this calculation do so using a spreadsheet. They don't need to worry any more about the difficulties of performing calculations using numbers with lots of decimal places. They can simply build the formula into the calculation and don't need to worry about how many decimal places the depreciation rate may have.

Activity 26.3

What do you think you do when the *amount* of depreciation to be charged in a period is not a whole number?

The depreciation rate percentage to be applied under this method, assuming a significant amount for residual value, is usually between two and three times greater than under the straight line method.

The advocates of the reducing balance method usually argue that it helps to even out the total amount charged as expenses for the use of the asset each year. Provisions for depreciation are not the only costs charged. There are also the running costs and the repairs and maintenance element of running costs usually increases with age. Therefore, in order to equate total usage costs for each year of use, the depreciation provisions should fall over time, while the repairs and maintenance element increases. However, as can be seen from the figures in the example already given, the repairs and maintenance element would have to be comparatively large after the first year to bring about an equal total charge for each year of use.

To summarise, the people who favour this method say that:

In the early years A higher charge for depreciation + A lower charge for repairs and upkeep	will tend to be fairly equal to	*In the later years* A lower charge for depreciation + A higher charge for repairs and upkeep

---

26.9 Choice of method

The purpose of depreciation is to spread the total cost of a fixed asset over the periods in which it is to be used. The method chosen should be that which allocates cost to each period in accordance with the proportion of the overall economic benefit from using the fixed asset that was expended during that period.

If, therefore, the main value is to be obtained from the asset in its earliest years, it may be appropriate to use the reducing balance method, which charges more in the early years. If, on the other hand, the benefits are to be gained evenly over the years, then the straight line method would be more appropriate.

The repairs and maintenance factor also has to be taken into account. One argument supporting this was mentioned in the last section.

Exhibit 26.1 gives a comparison of the calculations using the two methods.

Exhibit 26.1

A business has just bought a machine for £8,000. It will be kept in use for four years, when it will be disposed of for an estimated amount of £500. The accountant has asked you to prepare a comparison of the amounts charged as depreciation using both methods.

For the straight line method, a figure of (£8,000 − £500) ÷ 4 = £7,500 ÷ 4 = £1,875 per annum is to be used. For the reducing balance method, a percentage figure of 50 per cent will be used.

	Method 1 Straight Line £		Method 2 Reducing Balance £
Cost	8,000		8,000
Depreciation: year 1	(1,875)	(50% of £8,000)	(4,000)
	6,125		4,000
Depreciation: year 2	(1,875)	(50% of £4,000)	(2,000)
	4,250		2,000
Depreciation: year 3	(1,875)	(50% of £2,000)	(1,000)
	2,375		1,000
Depreciation: year 4	(1,875)	(50% of £1,000)	(500)
Disposal value	500		500

This example illustrates the fact that using the reducing balance method has a much higher charge for depreciation in the early years, and lower charges in the later years.

26.10 Depreciation provisions and assets bought or sold

There are two main methods of calculating depreciation provisions for assets bought or sold during an accounting period.

1 Ignore the dates during the accounting period that the assets were bought or sold, and simply calculate a full period's depreciation on the assets in use at the end of the period. Thus, assets sold during the accounting period will have had no provision for depreciation made for that last period irrespective of how many months they were in use. Conversely, assets bought during the period will have a full period of depreciation provision calculated even though they may not have been owned throughout the whole of the period.

2 Provide for depreciation on the basis of 'one month's ownership = one month's provision for depreciation'. Fractions of months are usually ignored. This is obviously a more precise method than Method 1.

The first method is the one normally used in practice. However, for examination purposes, where the dates on which assets are bought and sold are shown, you should use Method 2. If no such dates are given then, obviously, Method 1 is the one to use, but you should indicate that you are assuming this is the method to be adopted.

26.11 Other methods of calculating depreciation

There are many more methods of calculating depreciation, some of which are used in particular industries, such as the hotel and catering industry, but they are outside the scope of this chapter. These are fully considered in Chapter 37. You will find the revaluation method, depletion unit method, machine hour method and the sum of the year's digits methods in that chapter.

Learning outcomes

You should now have learnt:

1 That depreciation is an expense of the business and has to be charged against any period during which a fixed asset has been in use.
2 That the main causes of depreciation are: physical deterioration, economic factors, the time factor and depletion.
3 How to calculate depreciation using the straight line method.
4 How to calculate depreciation using the reducing balance method.
5 How to calculate depreciation on assets bought or sold within an accounting period.
6 That there are other methods of calculating depreciation in addition to the straight line and reducing balance methods.

Answers to activities

26.1 Fixed assets are those assets of material value which are:

- of long life, and
- to be used in the business, and
- not bought with the main purpose of resale.

26.2 Firstly, financial statements must show a true and fair view of the financial performance and position of the business. If depreciation was not provided for, both fixed assets and profits would be stated in the financial statements at inflated amounts. This would only mislead the users of those financial statements and, so, depreciation must be charged. Secondly, FRS 15 requires that fixed assets are depreciated.

26.3 Just as with the depreciation percentage, you round it to the nearest whole number.

REVIEW QUESTIONS

26.1 D Sankey, a manufacturer, purchases a lathe for the sum of £4,000. It has an estimated life of five years and a scrap value of £500.

Sankey is not certain whether he should use the straight line or the reducing balance basis for the purpose of calculating depreciation on the machine.

You are required to calculate the depreciation on the lathe using both methods, showing clearly the balance remaining in the lathe account at the end of each of the five years for each method. (Assume that 40 per cent per annum is to be used for the reducing balance method.)

26.2 A machine costs £12,500. It will be kept for four years, and then sold for an estimated figure of £5,120. Show the calculations of the figures for depreciation (to nearest £) for each of the four years using (a) the straight line method, (b) the reducing balance method, for this method using a depreciation rate of 20 per cent.

26.3 A motor vehicle costs £6,400. It will be kept for five years, and then sold for scrap for £200. Calculate the depreciation for each year using (a) the reducing balance method, using a depreciation rate of 50 per cent, (b) the straight line method.

26.4A A machine costs £5,120. It will be kept for five years, and then sold at an estimated figure of £1,215. Show the calculations of the figures for depreciation for each year using (a) the straight line method, (b) the reducing balance method, for this method using a depreciation rate of 25 per cent.

26.5A A bulldozer costs £12,150. It will be kept for five years. At the end of that time agreement has already been made that it will be sold for £1,600. Show your calculations of the amount of depreciation each year if (a) the reducing balance method at a rate of $33\frac{1}{3}$ per cent was used, (b) the straight line method was used.

26.6A A tractor is bought for £6,000. It will be used for three years, and then sold back to the supplier for £3,072. Show the depreciation calculations for each year using (a) the reducing balance method with a rate of 20 per cent, (b) the straight line method.

26.7 A company, which makes up its accounts annually to 31 December, provides for depreciation of its machinery at the rate of 10 per cent per annum on the diminishing balance system.
   On 31 December 20X9, the machinery consisted of three items purchased as under:

	£
On 1 January 20X7 Machine A	Cost 3,000
On 1 April 20X8 Machine B	Cost 2,000
On 1 July 20X9 Machine C	Cost 1,000

Required:
Your calculations showing the depreciation provision for the year 20X9.

CHAPTER 27

Double entry records for depreciation

Learning objectives

After you have studied this chapter, you should be able to:

- incorporate depreciation calculations into the accounting records
- record the entries relating to disposal of fixed assets
- make depreciation entries using either a one-stage or a two-stage method of recording depreciation

Introduction

Now that you know what depreciation is and how it may be calculated, in this chapter you'll learn how to make the appropriate entries for depreciation in the accounting books. You'll also learn how to make the appropriate period-end entries in the financial statements.

27.1 Recording depreciation

Looking back quite a few years, the charge for depreciation on a fixed asset was recorded in the account for that fixed asset. This method has now fallen into disuse.

Activity 27.1
Why do you think this is no longer done?

The method now used involves maintaining each fixed asset at its cost in the ledger account while operating another ledger account where the depreciation to date is recorded. This account is known as the '**accumulated provision for depreciation account**', often shortened to the **accumulated depreciation account** (or sometimes, confusingly, known as the 'provision for depreciation account').

Activity 27.2
Why do you think it would be confusing to call the accumulated provision for depreciation account the 'provision for depreciation account'?

Let's look at how this method of recording depreciation is applied by first looking at the double entry required and then looking at it being used in the example shown in Exhibit 27.1.

The depreciation is posted directly into the cumulative provision for depreciation account. The double entry is:

> Debit the profit and loss account
> Credit the accumulated provision for depreciation account

Exhibit 27.1

In a business with financial years ended 31 December a machine is bought for £2,000 on 1 January 20X5. It is to be depreciated at the rate of 20 per cent using the reducing balance method. The records for the first three years are:

Machinery

20X5			£		
Jan	1	Cash	2,000		

Accumulated Provision for Depreciation – Machinery

20X5			£	20X5			£
Dec	31	Balance c/d	400	Dec	31	Profit and loss	400
20X6				20X6			
Dec	31	Balance c/d	720	Jan	1	Balance b/d	400
				Dec	31	Profit and loss	320
			720				720
20X7				20X7			
Dec	31	Balance c/d	976	Jan	1	Balance b/d	720
				Dec	31	Profit and loss	256
			976				976
				20X8			
				Jan	1	Balance b/d	976

Profit and Loss Account (extracts) for the year ended 31 December

		£
20X5	Depreciation	400
20X6	Depreciation	320
20X7	Depreciation	256

Note: In this case, the depreciation for the period being posted to the profit and loss account is being described as 'depreciation' and *not* by the name of the account it is being posted from. This clearly is not the convention usually adopted when posting entries between ledger accounts and is very much 'the exception that proves the rule'.

> ### Activity 27.3
> What advantages are there in making this exception to the rule by using 'depreciation' rather than 'accumulated provision for depreciation' in the profit and loss account entry?

Now the balance on the Machinery Account is shown on the balance sheet at the end of each year less the balance on the Cumulative Provision for Depreciation Account.

Balance Sheets (extracts)

	£	£
As at 31 December 20X5		
Machinery at cost	2,000	
Less Accumulated depreciation	(400)	
		1,600
As at 31 December 20X6		
Machinery at cost	2,000	
Less Accumulated depreciation	(720)	
		1,280
As at 31 December 20X7		
Machinery at cost	2,000	
Less Accumulated depreciation	(976)	
		1,024

27.2 The disposal of a fixed asset

Reason for accounting entries

Upon the sale of a fixed asset, we will want to remove it from our ledger accounts. This means that the cost of that asset needs to be taken out of the asset account. In addition, the accumulated depreciation on the asset which has been sold will have to be taken out of the accumulated provision. Finally, the profit and loss on sale, if any, will have to be calculated and posted to the profit and loss account.

When we charge depreciation on a fixed asset we are having to make an informed guess. We will not often guess correctly. This means that, when we dispose of an asset, the amount received for it is usually different from our estimate.

> **Activity 27.4**
> List as many things as you can think of in one minute that could cause the amount charged for depreciation to have been incorrect.

Accounting entries needed

On the sale of a fixed asset, in this example machinery, the following entries are needed:

(A) Transfer the cost price of the asset sold to an assets disposal account (in this case a machinery disposals account):

    Debit machinery disposals account
      Credit machinery account

(B) Transfer the depreciation already charged to the assets disposal account:

    Debit accumulated provision for depreciation: machinery
      Credit machinery disposals account

(C) For the amount received on disposal:

    Debit cash book
      Credit machinery disposals account

(D) Transfer the difference (i.e. the amount needed to balance the machinery disposals account) to the profit and loss account.

(i) If the machinery disposals account shows a credit balance (i.e. if more has been credited to the account than has been debited to it), there is a profit on the sale:

> Debit machinery disposals account
> Credit profit and loss account

(ii) If the machinery disposals account shows a debit balance, there is a loss on sale:

> Debit profit and loss account
> Credit machinery disposals account

These entries can be illustrated by looking at those needed if the machinery already shown in Exhibit 27.1 was sold. At 31 December 20X7, the cost was £2,000 and a total of £976 had been written off as depreciation leaving a book value of £2,000 – £976 = £1,024. If the machinery is sold in 20X8 for *more* than £1,024 a profit on sale will be made. If, on the other hand, the machinery is sold for *less* than £1,024 then a loss will be incurred.

Exhibit 27.2 shows the entries needed when the machinery has been sold for £1,070 and a profit of £46 on sale has, therefore, been made. Exhibit 27.3 shows where the machinery has been sold for £950, thus incurring a loss on sale of £74. In both cases, the sale is on 2 January 20X8 and no depreciation is to be charged for the two days' ownership in 20X8. (The letters in brackets refer to the accounting double entries, A–D, above.)

Exhibit 27.2 Fixed asset sold at a profit

Machinery

20X5				£	20X8				£
Jan	1	Cash		2,000	Jan	2	Machinery disposals	(A)	2,000

Accumulated Provision for Depreciation: Machinery

20X8				£	20X8			£
Jan	2	Machinery disposals	(B)	976	Jan	1	Balance b/d	976

Machinery Disposals

20X8				£	20X8				£
Jan	2	Machinery	(A)	2,000	Jan	2	Accumulated provision		
Dec	31	Profit and loss	(D)	46			for depreciation	(B)	976
					Jan	2	Cash	(C)	1,070
				2,046					2,046

Profit and Loss Account for the year ended 31 December 20X8

		£
Gross profit		xxx
Add Profit on sale of machinery	(D)	46

Exhibit 27.3 Fixed asset sold at a loss

Machinery

20X5				£	20X8				£
Jan	1	Cash		2,000	Jan	2	Machinery disposals	(A)	2,000

Accumulated Provision for Depreciation: Machinery

20X8				£	20X8			£
Jan	2	Machinery disposals	(B)	976	Jan	1	Balance b/d	976

Machinery Disposals

20X8				£	20X8				£
Jan	2	Machinery	(A)	2,000	Jan	2	Accumulated provision		
							for depreciation	(B)	976
					Jan	2	Cash	(C)	950
					Dec	31	Profit and loss	(D)	74
				2,000					2,000

Profit and Loss Account for the year ended 31 December 20X8

			£
Gross profit			xxx
Less Loss on sale of machinery		(D)	(74)

In many cases, the disposal of an asset will mean that we have sold it. This will not always be the case. For example, a car may be given up in part exchange against the purchase of a new car. Here the disposal value is the exchange value. If a new car costing £10,000 was to be paid for by £6,000 in cash and an allowance of £4,000 for the old car, then the disposal value of the old car is £4,000.

Similarly a car may have been in an accident and now be worthless. If it was insured, the disposal value will be the amount received from the insurance company. If an asset is scrapped, the disposal value is that received from the sale of the scrap, which may be nil.

27.3 Change of depreciation method

It is possible to make a change in the method of calculating depreciation. This should not be done frequently, and it should only be undertaken after a thorough review. Where a change is made, if material (*see* Chapter 10 on materiality), the effect of doing so upon the figures reported should be shown as a note to the financial statements in the year of change.

Further examples

So far, the examples have deliberately been kept simple. Only one fixed asset has been shown in each case. Exhibits 27.4 and 27.5 give examples of more complicated cases.

Exhibit 27.4

A machine is bought on 1 January 20X5 for £1,000 and another one on 1 October 20X6 for £1,200. The first machine is sold on 30 June 20X7 for £720. The business's financial year ends on 31 December. The machinery is to be depreciated at 10 per cent, using the straight line method. Machinery in existence at the end of each year is to be depreciated for a full year. No depreciation is to be charged on any machnery disposed of during the year.

Machinery

20X5			£	20X5			£
Jan	1	Cash	1,000	Dec	31	Balance c/d	1,000
20X6				20X6			
Jan	1	Balance b/d	1,000	Dec	31	Balance c/d	2,200
Oct	1	Cash	1,200				
			2,200				2,200
20X7				20X7			
Jan	1	Balance b/d	2,200	Jun	30	Disposals	1,000
				Dec	31	Balance c/d	1,200
			2,200				2,200
20X8							
Jan	1	Balance b/d	1,200				

Accumulated Provision for Depreciation: Machinery

20X5			£	20X5			£
Dec	31	Balance c/d	100	Dec	31	Profit and loss	100
20X6				20X6			
Dec	31	Balance c/d	320	Jan	1	Balance b/d	100
				Dec	31	Profit and loss	220
			320				320
20X7				20X7			
Jun	30	Disposals of machinery		Jan	1	Balance b/d	320
		(2 years × 10 per cent		Dec	31	Profit and loss	120
		× £1,000)	200				
Dec	31	Balance c/d	240				
			440				440
				20X8			
				Jan	1	Balance b/d	240

Disposals of Machinery

20X7			£	20X7			£
Jun	30	Machinery	1,000	Jun	30	Cash	720
				Jun	30	Accumulated provision	
						for depreciation	200
				Dec	31	Profit and loss	80
			1,000				1,000

Profit and Loss Account (extracts) for the year ended 31 December

	£
Gross profit	xxx
Less Expenses:	
20X5 Provision for depreciation: Machinery	(100)
20X6 Provision for depreciation: Machinery	(220)
20X7 Provision for depreciation: Machinery	(120)
Loss on machinery sold	(80)

Balance Sheet (extracts) as at 31 December

		£	£
20X5	Machinery at cost	1,000	
	Less Accumulated depreciation	(100)	
			900
20X6	Machinery at cost	2,200	
	Less Accumulated depreciation	(320)	
			1,880
20X7	Machinery at cost	1,200	
	Less Accumulated depreciation	(240)	
			960

Another example can now be given. This is somewhat more complicated. Firstly, it involves a greater number of items. Secondly, the depreciation provisions are calculated on a proportionate basis, i.e. one month's depreciation for one month's ownership.

Exhibit 27.5

A business with its financial year end being 31 December buys two vans on 1 January 20X1, No 1 for £8,000 and No 2 for £5,000. It also buys another van, No 3, on 1 July 20X3 for £9,000 and another, No 4, on 1 October 20X3 for £7,200. The first two vans are sold, No 1 for £2,290 on 30 September 20X4, and No 2 for scrap for £50 on 30 June 20X5.

Depreciation is on the straight line basis, 20 per cent per annum, ignoring scrap value in this particular case when calculating depreciation per annum. Show the extracts from the assets account, provision for depreciation account, disposal account and profit and loss account for the years ended 31 December 20X1, 20X2, 20X3, 20X4, and 20X5, and the balance sheets as at those dates.

Vans

20X1			£	20X1			£
Jan	1	Cash	13,000	Dec	31	Balance c/d	13,000
20X2				20X2			
Jan	1	Balance b/d	13,000	Dec	31	Balance c/d	13,000
20X3				20X3			
Jan	1	Balance b/d	13,000				
July	1	Cash	9,000				
Oct	1	Cash	7,200	Dec	31	Balance c/d	29,200
			29,200				29,200
20X4				20X4			
Jan	1	Balance b/d	29,200	Sept	30	Disposals	8,000
				Dec	31	Balance c/d	21,200
			29,200				29,200
20X5				20X5			
Jan	1	Balance b/d	21,200	June	30	Disposals	5,000
				Dec	31	Balance c/d	16,200
			21,200				21,200
20X6							
Jan	1	Balance b/d	16,200				

Accumulated Provision for Depreciation: Vans

20X1			£	20X1			£
Dec	31	Balance c/d	2,600	Dec	31	Profit and loss	2,600
20X2				20X2			
				Jan	1	Balance b/d	2,600
Dec	31	Balance c/d	5,200	Dec	31	Profit and loss	2,600
			5,200				5,200
20X3				20X3			
				Jan	1	Balance b/d	5,200
Dec	31	Balance c/d	9,060	Dec	31	Profit and loss	3,860
			9,060				9,060
20X4				20X4			
Sept	30	Disposals	6,000	Jan	1	Balance b/d	9,060
Dec	31	Balance c/d	8,500	Dec	31	Profit and loss	5,440
			14,500				14,500
20X5				20X5			
June	30	Disposals	4,500	Jan	1	Balance b/d	8,500
Dec	31	Balance c/d	7,740	Dec	31	Profit and loss	3,740
			12,240				12,240
				20X6			
				Jan	1	Balance b/d	7,740

Workings – depreciation provisions		£	£
20X1	20% of £13,000		2,600
20X2	20% of £13,000		2,600
20X3	20% of £13,000 × 12 months	2,600	
	20% of £9,000 × 6 months	900	
	20% of £7,200 × 3 months	360	
			3,860
20X4	20% of £21,200 × 12 months	4,240	
	20% of £8,000 × 9 months	1,200	
			5,440
20X5	20% of £16,200 × 12 months	3,240	
	20% of £5,000 × 6 months	500	
			3,740

Workings – transfers of depreciation provisions to disposal accounts

Van 1   Bought Jan 1 20X1 Cost £8,000
        Sold Sept 30 20X4
        Period of ownership 3³/₄ years
        Depreciation provisions 3³/₄ × 20% × £8,000 = £6,000
Van 2   Bought Jan 1 20X1 Cost £5,000
        Sold June 30 20X5
        Period of ownership 4¹/₂ years
        Depreciation provisions 4¹/₂ × 20% × £5,000 = £4,500

Disposals of Vans

20X4			£	20X4				£
Sept	30	Van	8,000	Sept	30	Accumulated provision for depreciation		6,000
Dec	31	Profit and loss	290	"	"	Cash		2,290
			8,290					8,290
20X5				20X5				
Jun	30	Van	5,000	Jun	30	Accumulated provision for depreciation		4,500
				"	"	Cash		50
				Dec	31	Profit and loss		450
			5,000					5,000

Profit and Loss Account (extracts) for the year ended 31 December

			£	£
Gross profit (each year 20X1, 20X2, 20X3)				xxx
	Less Expenses:			
20X1	Provision for depreciation: vans			(2,600)
20X2	Provision for depreciation: vans			(2,600)
20X3	Provision for depreciation: vans			(3,860)
20X4	Gross profit			x,xxx
	Add Profit on van sold			290
				x,xxx
	Less Expenses:			
	Provision for depreciation: vans			(5,440)
				x,xxx
20X5	Gross profit			x,xxx
	Less Expenses:			
	Provision for depreciation: vans		3,740	
	Loss on van sold		450	
				(4,190)

Balance Sheets (extracts) as at 31 December

		£	£
20X1	Vans at cost	13,000	
	Less Accumulated depreciation	(2,600)	
			10,400
20X2	Vans at cost	13,000	
	Less Accumulated depreciation	(5,200)	
			7,800
20X3	Vans at cost	29,200	
	Less Accumulated depreciation	(9,060)	
			20,140
20X4	Vans at cost	21,200	
	Less Accumulated depreciation	(8,500)	
			12,700
20X5	Vans at cost	16,200	
	Less Accumulated depreciation	(7,740)	
			8,460

27.4 Depreciation provisions and the replacement of assets

Making a provision for depreciation does not mean that money is invested somewhere to finance the replacement of the asset when it is put out of use. It is simply a bookkeeping entry, and the end result is that lower net profits are shown because the provisions have been charged to the profit and loss account.

It is not surprising to find that many people – especially students – who have not studied accounting, misunderstand the situation. They often think that a provision is the same as money kept somewhere with which to replace the asset eventually. Never make that mistake. It may cost you a lot of marks in an exam!

A cautious owner may take out less drawings if the net profit is lower, but that is no justification for arguing that depreciation results in funds being available to replace the fixed asset later!

27.5 Another approach

In this chapter, you've learnt how to perform the double entries necessary to record the periodic charge for depreciation. The method you learnt about was based upon the use of one double entry, a credit to the accumulated provision for depreciation account and a debit to the profit and loss account.

There is another method which is widely used in practice. It involves using a '**provision for depreciation account**', often shortened to '**depreciation account**', as well as the 'accumulated provision for depreciation account'. At the end of the period, you calculate the depreciation for the period and make the following double entry:

1 Debit the depreciation account
    Credit the cumulative provision for depreciation account
2 Debit the profit and loss account
    Credit the depreciation account

Compare this two-stage method to the one-stage method you learnt earlier:

> Debit the profit and loss account
> Credit the cumulative provision for depreciation account

Note how the double entry you learnt earlier combines the two entries used in the two-stage method by cancelling out the debit and credit to the depreciation account. This makes it much simpler to record the entries required, but adopting the two-stage approach has the advantage that it actually shows what has happened rather than compressing the two double entries that theory says should be used into one.

It also overcomes a theoretical difficulty inherent in the one-stage method – it forces the profit and loss account to be used like an expense account when all other expenses entered in the profit and loss account are entered from expense accounts in the General Ledger.

However, many accountants prefer to keep recording the entries as simple as possible and so use only the 'accumulated depreciation provision account'.

Nevertheless, you need to be aware of and able to do the two-stage method described above, just in case you should be asked to use it by an examiner. If you are *not* asked for two accounts (a depreciation account *plus* an accumulated provision for depreciation account) you should assume that the one-stage method is the one you are expected to use.

27.6 Finally

This chapter has covered all the principles involved. Obviously examiners can present their questions in their own way. In fact, in order to better test your understanding, examiners do tend to vary the way questions involving depreciation are presented. Practice all the questions in this book, including the exhibits, and compare them with the answers shown in full. Doing so will demonstrate the truth of this statement and prepare you better for your examination when you can be virtually guaranteed that you will need to be able to calculate and make appropriate entries for depreciation.

Learning outcomes

You should now have learnt:

1 That the method of showing depreciation in the asset account is now used only by some small organisations, and is outdated.

2 That using the modern methods, asset accounts are kept at cost price, while the depreciation is credited to an accumulated provision for depreciation account.

3 That when we sell a fixed asset, we must transfer both the cost and the accumulated depreciation to a separate disposal account.

4 That it is very rare for the depreciation provided to have been accurate.

5 That a profit on the disposal of a fixed asset is transferred to the credit of the profit and loss account.

6 That a loss on the disposal of a fixed asset is transferred to the debit of the profit and loss account.

7 That there are two methods of entering depreciation into the accounting books.

8 That the method you have learnt does so in one double entry and uses one ledger account for the accumulated provision for depreciation.

9 That the other, 'two-stage' method, uses two journal entries and two ledger accounts, one for the depreciation expense and the other to record the accumulated provision for depreciation.

10 That there are a number of alternatives for the names of the depreciation accounts involved under these two methods.

11 That the name 'provision for depreciation' is often used in place of 'accumulated provision for depreciation' in the balance sheet account that shows the depreciation accumulated to date.

Answers to activities

27.1 It has the effect of reducing the balance shown in the ledger for the fixed asset so that, over time, it may be very much less than the original cost. This makes it difficult to identify the original cost of fixed assets and means that, in the balance sheet, the only information that can be given is the value to which each fixed asset has been written down. Anyone looking at this information will have no way of assessing whether a fixed asset was originally very expensive (which may be relevant, for example, if it is a building) and so cannot arrive at a realistic view of what the fixed assets really comprise. Nor, especially in the case of smaller businesses, is it immediately obvious how long a fixed asset is likely to continue to be used or, in fact, whether there is actually an asset in current use – if the value has been written down to zero, it wouldn't have a balance, may have been written out of the ledger, and certainly wouldn't be included in the balance sheet.

27.2   Use of the term 'provision for depreciation account' can be very confusing as the name of the account used to record provisions for doubtful debts is the 'provision for doubtful debts account' and, as you know, that account is closed off at the end of the accounting period and the balance transferred to the debit side of the profit and loss account. In contrast, the balance on the 'accumulated provision for depreciation account' is shown in the balance sheet at the year end and carried forward to the next accounting period. The two treatments could hardly be more different. It is, therefore, asking for mistakes to be made if you use the same stem, 'provision for . . .', for them both. It must be said, however, that many people do, including some examiners. So, you need to be aware that when you see an account called the 'provision for depreciation account', it is referring to the account we shall call in this book the 'accumulated provision for depreciation account'. To help you get used to this, some of the multiple choice questions and review questions at the end of this chapter use the term 'provision for depreciation account'.

27.3   Doing so makes it clear that just one period's depreciation is being posted and *not* the entire accumulated depreciation to date.

27.4   We cannot be absolutely certain how long we will keep the asset in use, nor can we be certain how much the asset will be sold for when we dispose of it, or even that it will be possible to sell it at that time. We may also have chosen the wrong depreciation method causing the net book value of the asset (i.e. cost less accumulated depreciation) to have been reduced too quickly (reducing balance) or too slowly (straight line) in the event that it is disposed of earlier than expected.

MULTIPLE CHOICE QUESTIONS: SET 3

Now attempt Set 3 of multiple choice questions. (Answers to all the multiple choice questions are given in Appendix 2 at the end of this book.)

Each of these multiple choice questions has four suggested answers, (A), (B), (C) and (D). You should read each question and then decide which choice is best, either (A) or (B) or (C) or (D). *Write down your answers on a separate piece of paper.* You will then be able to redo the set of questions later without having to try to ignore your answers.

MC41   A cash discount is best described as a reduction in the sum to be paid

(A)   If payment is made within a previously agreed period
(B)   If payment is made by cash, not cheque
(C)   If payment is made either by cash or cheque
(D)   If purchases are made for cash, not on credit.

MC42   Discounts received are

(A)   Deducted when we receive cash
(B)   Given by us when we sell goods on credit
(C)   Deducted by us when we pay our accounts
(D)   None of these.

MC43   The total of the 'Discounts Allowed' column in the Cash Book is posted to

(A)   The debit of the Discounts Allowed account
(B)   The debit of the Discounts Received account
(C)   The credit of the Discounts Allowed account
(D)   The credit of the Discounts Received account.

MC44 Sales invoices are first entered in

(A) The Cash Book
(B) The Purchases Journal
(C) The Sales Account
(D) The Sales Journal.

MC45 The total of the Sales Journal is entered on

(A) The credit side of the Sales Account in the General Ledger
(B) The credit side of the General Account in the Sales Ledger
(C) The debit side of the Sales Account in the General Ledger
(D) The debit side of the Sales Day Book.

MC46 Given a purchases invoice showing 5 items of £80 each, less trade discount of 25 per cent and cash discount of 5 per cent, if paid within the credit period, your cheque would be made out for

(A) £285
(B) £280
(C) £260
(D) None of these.

MC47 An alternative name for a Sales Journal is

(A) Sales Invoice
(B) Sales Day Book
(C) Daily Sales
(D) Sales Ledger.

MC48 Entered in the Purchases Journal are

(A) Payments to suppliers
(B) Trade discounts
(C) Purchases invoices
(D) Discounts received.

MC49 The total of the Purchases Journal is transferred to the

(A) Credit side of the Purchases Account
(B) Debit side of the Purchases Day Book
(C) Credit side of the Purchases Book
(D) Debit side of the Purchases Account.

MC50 Credit notes issued by us will be entered in our

(A) Sales Account
(B) Returns Inwards Account
(C) Returns Inwards Journal
(D) Returns Outwards Journal.

MC51 The total of the Returns Outwards Journal is transferred to

(A) The credit side of the Returns Outwards Account
(B) The debit side of the Returns Outwards Account
(C) The credit side of the Returns Outwards Book
(D) The debit side of the Purchases Returns Book.

MC52 We originally sold 25 items at £12 each, less 33$\frac{1}{3}$ per cent trade discount. Our customer now returns 4 of them to us. What is the amount of credit note to be issued?

(A) £48
(B) £36

(C) £30

(D) £32.

MC53 Depreciation is

(A) The amount spent to buy a fixed asset

(B) The salvage value of a fixed asset

(C) The part of the cost of the fixed asset consumed during its period of use by the firm

(D) The amount of money spent in replacing assets.

MC54 A firm bought a machine for £3,200. It is to be depreciated at a rate of 25 per cent using the Reducing Balance Method. What would be the remaining book value after 2 years?

(A) £1,600

(B) £2,400

(C) £1,800

(D) Some other figure.

MC55 A firm bought a machine for £16,000. It is expected to be used for 5 years then sold for £1,000. What is the annual amount of depreciation if the straight line method is used?

(A) £3,200

(B) £3,100

(C) £3,750

(D) £3,000.

MC56 At the balance sheet date the balance on the Accumulated Provision for Depreciation Account is

(A) Transferred to Depreciation Account

(B) Transferred to Profit and Loss Account

(C) Simply deducted from the asset in the Balance Sheet

(D) Transferred to the Asset Account.

MC57 In the trial balance the balance on the Provision for Depreciation Account is

(A) Shown as a credit item

(B) Not shown, as it is part of depreciation

(C) Shown as a debit item

(D) Sometimes shown as a credit, sometimes as a debit.

MC58 If an accumulated provision for depreciation account is in use then the entries for the year's depreciation would be

(A) Credit Provision for Depreciation Account, debit Profit and Loss Account

(B) Debit Asset Account, credit Profit and Loss Account

(C) Credit Asset Account, debit Provision for Depreciation Account

(D) Credit Profit and Loss Account, debit Provision for Depreciation Account.

MC59 When the final accounts are prepared, the Bad Debts Account is closed by a transfer to the

(A) Balance Sheet

(B) Profit and Loss Account

(C) Trading Account

(D) Provision for Doubtful Debts Account.

MC60 A Provision for Doubtful Debts is created

(A) When debtors become bankrupt

(B) When debtors cease to be in business

(C) To provide for possible bad debts

(D) To write off bad debts.

REVIEW QUESTIONS

27.1 A company starts in business on 1 January 20X1. You are to write up the vans account and the provision for depreciation account for the year ended 31 December 20X1 from the information given below. Depreciation is at the rate of 20 per cent per annum, using the basis of one month's ownership needs one month's depreciation.

20X1   Bought two vans for £1,200 each on 1 January
          Bought one van for £1,400 on 1 July

27.2 A company starts in business on 1 January 20X3, the financial year end being 31 December. You are to show:

(*a*) The machinery account.
(*b*) The provision for depreciation account.
(*c*) The balance sheet extracts for each of the years 20X3, 20X4, 20X5, 20X6.

The machinery bought was:

20X3	1 January	1 machine costing £800
20X4	1 July	2 machines costing £500 each
	1 October	1 machine costing £600
20X6	1 April	1 machine costing £200

Depreciation is at the rate of 10 per cent per annum, using the straight line method, machines being depreciated for each proportion of a year.

27.3A A company maintains its fixed assets at cost. Depreciation provision accounts, one for each type of asset, are in use. Machinery is to be depreciated at the rate of 12½ per cent per annum, and fixtures at the rate of 10 per cent per annum, using the reducing balance method. Depreciation is to be calculated on assets in existence at the end of each year, giving a full year's depreciation even though the asset was bought part of the way through the year. The following transactions in assets have taken place:

20X5	1 January	Bought machinery £640, fixtures £100
	1 July	Bought fixtures £200
20X6	1 October	Bought machinery £720
	1 December	Bought fixtures £50

The financial year end of the business is 31 December.

You are to show:
(*a*) The machinery account.
(*b*) The fixtures account.
(*c*) The two separate provision for depreciation accounts.
(*d*) The fixed assets section of the balance sheet at the end of each year, for the years ended 31 December 20X5 and 20X6.

27.4 A company depreciates its plant at the rate of 20 per cent per annum, straight line method, for each month of ownership. From the following details draw up the plant account and the provision for depreciation account for each of the years 20X4, 20X5, 20X6 and 20X7.

20X4   Bought plant costing £900 on 1 January.
          Bought plant costing £600 on 1 October.
20X6   Bought plant costing £550 on 1 July.
20X7   Sold plant which had been bought for £900 on 1 January 20X4 for the sum of £275
          on 30 September 20X7.

You are also required to draw up the plant disposal account and the extracts from the balance sheet as at the end of each year.

27.5 A company maintains its fixed assets at cost. Depreciation provision accounts for each asset are kept.

At 31 December 20X8 the position was as follows:

	Total cost to date	Total depreciation to date
Machinery	52,590	25,670
Office furniture	2,860	1,490

The following additions were made during the financial year ended 31 December 20X9:
Machinery £2,480, office furniture £320.
Some old machines bought in 20X5 for £2,800 were sold for £800 during the year.
The rates of depreciation are:
Machinery 10 per cent, office furniture 5 per cent, using the straight line basis, calculated on the assets in existence at the end of each financial year irrespective of date of purchase.

You are required to show the asset and depreciation accounts for the year ended 31 December 20X9 and the balance sheet entries at that date.

27.6A
(a) What is the meaning of depreciation?
(b) Give **three** reasons why depreciation may occur.
(c) Name **two** methods of depreciation.
(d) In what way do you think the concept of consistency applies to depreciation?
(e) 'Since the calculation of depreciation is based on estimates, not facts, why bother to make the calculation?'
   Explain briefly why you think that the calculation of depreciation is based on estimates.
(f) If depreciation was omitted, what effects would this have on the final accounts?
(g) 'Some assets increase (appreciate) in value, but normal accounting procedure would be to ignore any such appreciation.'
   Explain why bringing appreciation into account would go against the prudence concept.
(h) A business whose financial year ends at 31 December purchased on 1 January 20X7 a machine for £5,000. The machine was to be depreciated by ten equal instalments. On 4 January 20X9 the machine was sold for £3,760.
   Ignoring any depreciation in the year of sale, show the relevant entries for each of the following accounts for the years ended 31 December 20X7, 20X8 and 20X9:
   (i) Machinery
   (ii) Provision for depreciation of machinery
   (iii) Machinery disposals
   (iv) Profit and loss

(*Northern Examinations and Assessment Board: GCSE*)

27.7
(a) Identify the four factors which cause fixed assets to depreciate.
(b) Which one of these factors is the most important for each of the following assets?
   (i) a gold mine,
   (ii) a lorry,
   (iii) a 50 year lease on a building,
   (iv) land,
   (v) a ship used to ferry passengers and vehicles across a river following the building of a bridge across the river,
   (vi) a franchise to market a new computer software package in a certain country.
(c) The financial year of Ochre Ltd will end on 31 December 20X6. At 1 January 20X6 the company had in use equipment with a total accumulated cost of £135,620 which had been depreciated by a total of £81,374. During the year ended 31 December 20X6 Ochre Ltd purchased new equipment costing £47,800 and sold off equipment which had originally cost £36,000, and which had been depreciated by £28,224, for £5,700. No further purchases or sales of equipment

are planned for December. The policy of the company is to depreciate equipment at 40% using the diminishing balance method. A full year's depreciation is provided for on all equipment in use by the company at the end of each year.

Required:
Show the following ledger accounts for the year ended 31 December 20X6:
(*i*) the Equipment Account;
(*ii*) the Provision for Depreciation on Equipment Account;
(*iii*) the Assets Disposals Account.

(*Association of Accounting Technicians*)

27.8A   Mavron plc owned the following motor vehicles as at 1 April 20X6:

Motor Vehicle	Date Acquired	Cost £	Estimated Residual Value £	Estimated Life (years)
AAT 101	1 October 20X3	8,500	2,500	5
DJH 202	1 April 20X4	12,000	2,000	8

Mavron plc's policy is to provide at the end of each financial year depreciation using the straight line method applied on a month-by-month basis on all motor vehicles used during the year.

During the financial year ended 31 March 20X7 the following occurred:

(*a*) On 30 June 20X6 AAT 101 was traded in and replaced by KGC 303. The trade-in allowance was £5,000. KGC 303 cost £15,000 and the balance due (after deducting the trade-in allowance) was paid partly in cash and partly by a loan of £6,000 from Pinot Finance. KGC 303 is expected to have a residual value of £4,000 after an estimated economic life of 5 years.
(*b*) The estimated remaining economic life of DJH 202 was reduced from 6 years to 4 years with no change in the estimated residual value.

Required:
(*a*) Show any Journal entries necessary to give effect to the above.
(*b*) Show the Journal entry necessary to record depreciation on Motor Vehicles for the year ended 31 March 20X7.
(*c*) Reconstruct the Motor Vehicles Account and the Provision for Depreciation Account for the year ended 31 March 20X7.

Show the necessary calculations clearly.

(*Association of Accounting Technicians*)

27.9   A business buys a fixed asset for £10,000. The business estimates that the asset will be used for 5 years. After exactly $2\frac{1}{2}$ years, however, the asset is suddenly sold for £5,000. The business always provides a full year's depreciation in the year of purchase and no depreciation in the year of disposal.

Required:
(*a*) Write up the relevant accounts (including disposal account but not profit and loss account) for each of Years 1, 2 and 3:
(*i*) Using the straight line depreciation method (assume 20% pa);
(*ii*) Using the reducing balance depreciation method (assume 40% pa).
(*b*) (*i*) What is the purpose of depreciation? In what circumstances would each of the two methods you have used be preferable?
(*ii*) What is the meaning of the net figure for the fixed asset in the balance sheet at the end of Year 2?
(*c*) If the asset was bought at the beginning of Year 1, but was not used at all until Year 2 (and it is confidently anticipated to last until Year 6), state under each method the appropriate depreciation charge in Year 1, and briefly justify your answer.

(*Association of Chartered Certified Accountants*)

27.10A   Contractors Ltd was formed on 1 January 20X6 and the following purchases and sales of machinery were made during the first 3 years of operations.

Date	Asset	Transaction	Price
1 January 20X6	Machines 1 and 2	purchase	£40,000 each
1 October 20X6	Machines 3 and 4	purchase	£15,200 each
30 June 20X8	Machine 3	sale	£12,640
1 July 20X8	Machine 5	purchase	£20,000

Each machine was estimated to last 10 years and to have a residual value of 5% of its cost price. Depreciation was by equal instalments, and it is company policy to charge depreciation for every month an asset is owned.

Required:
(*a*) Calculate
  (*i*) the total depreciation on Machinery for each of the years 20X6, 20X7, and 20X8;
  (*ii*) the profit or loss on the sale of Machine 3 in 20X8.
(*b*) Contractors Ltd depreciates its vehicles by 30% per annum using the diminishing balance method. What difference would it have made to annual reported profits over the life of a vehicle if it had decided instead to depreciate this asset by 20% straight line?

(*Scottish Qualifications Authority*)

CHAPTER 28

Accruals and prepayments and other adjustments for financial statements

Learning objectives

After you have studied this chapter, you should be able to:

- adjust expense accounts for accruals and prepayments
- adjust revenue accounts for amounts owing
- show accruals, prepayments and revenue debtors in the balance sheet
- ascertain the amounts of expense and revenue items to be shown in the profit and loss account after making adjustments for accruals and prepayments
- make the necessary end of period adjustments relating to drawings that have not yet been entered in the books
- explain what an extended trial balance is and describe what it looks like
- prepare accrual and prepayment entries to the accounts using two different methods

Introduction

In this chapter, you'll continue to learn about adjustments made to the ledger accounts at the end of a period. You'll learn how to make the appropriate entries in the accounts for outstanding balances on expense and income accounts and make the appropriate entries in the profit and loss account and balance sheet.

28.1 Financial statements so far

The trading and profit and loss accounts you have looked at have taken the sales for a period and deducted all the expenses for that period, the result being a net profit (or a net loss).

Up to this part of the book it has always been assumed that the expenses belonged exactly to the period of the trading and profit and loss account. If the trading and profit and loss account for the year ended 31 December 20X5 was being drawn up, then the rent paid as shown in the trial balance was exactly for 20X5. There was no rent owing at the beginning of 20X5 nor any owing at the end of 20X5, nor had any rent been paid in advance.

This was done to make your first meeting with financial statements much easier for you.

28.2 Adjustments needed

Let's look at two businesses which pay rent for buildings in Oxford. The rent for each building is £1,200 a year.

1 Business A pays £1,000 in the year. At the year end it owes £200 for rent.
Rent expense used up = £1,200
Rent paid for = £1,000

2 Business B pays £1,300 in the year. This figure includes £100 paid in advance for the following year.
Rent expense used up = £1,200
Rent paid for = £1,300

A profit and loss account for 12 months needs 12 months' rent as an expense = £1,200. This means that in both 1 and 2 the double entry accounts will have to be adjusted.

Activity 28.1

From your knowledge of double entry, you should be able to work out what the double entry required is in these two cases. What do you think it is? If you don't know what names to give the accounts, have a guess. (Hint: in the first case, there will be a creditor balance in the balance sheet and in the other, it will be a debtor balance.)

In all the examples following in this chapter the trading and profit and loss accounts are for the year ended 31 December 20X5.

28.3 Accrued expenses

Assume that rent of £1,000 per year is payable at the end of every three months. The rent was paid on time in March, but this is not always the case.

Amount	Rent due	Rent paid
£250	31 March 20X5	31 March 20X5
£250	30 June 20X5	2 July 20X5
£250	30 September 20X5	4 October 20X5
£250	31 December 20X5	5 January 20X6

Rent

20X5			£	
Mar	31	Cash	250	
Jul	2	"	250	
Oct	4	"	250	

The rent for the last quarter was paid on 5 January 20X6 and so will appear in the books of the year 20X6 as the result of a double entry made on that date.

The expense for 20X5 is obviously £1,000 as that is the year's rent, and this is the amount needed to be transferred to the profit and loss account. But, if £1,000 was put on the credit side of the rent account (the debit being in the profit and loss account) the account would be out of balance by £250 because the payment due on 31 December 20X5 was not made until 5 January 20X6. That is, if we posted £1,000 to profit and loss on 31 December, we would have £1,000 on the credit side of the account and only £750 on the debit side:

Rent

20X5			£	20X5			£
Mar	31	Cash	250	Dec	31	Profit and loss	1,000
Jul	2	''	250				
Oct	4	''	250				

This cannot be right.

To make the account balance the £250 rent owing for 20X5, but paid in 20X6, must be carried down to 20X6 as a credit balance because it is a liability on 31 December 20X5. Instead of rent owing it could be called rent accrued or just simply an 'accrual'.

The completed account can now be shown:

Rent

20X5			£	20X5			£
Mar	31	Cash	250	Dec	31	Profit and loss	1,000
Jul	2	''	250				
Oct	4	''	250				
Dec	31	Accrued c/d	250				
			1,000				1,000
				20X6			
				Jan	1	Accrued b/d	250

The balance c/d has been described as 'accrued c/d', rather than as 'balance c/d'. This is to explain what the balance is for. It is for an **accrued expense**.

28.4   Prepaid expenses

Insurance for a business is at the rate of £840 a year, starting from 1 January 20X5. The business has agreed to pay this at the rate of £210 every three months. However, payments were not made at the correct times. Details were:

Amount	Insurance due	Insurance paid
£210	31 March 20X5	£210 28 February 20X5
£210 £210	30 June 20X5 30 September 20X5	£420 31 August 20X5
£210	31 December 20X5	£420 18 November 20X5

The insurance account in the ledger for the year ended 31 December 20X5 is:

Insurance

20X5			£	20X5			£
Feb	28	Bank	210	Dec	31	Profit and loss	840
Aug	31	''	420				
Nov	18	''	420				

The last payment of £420 is not just for 20X5. It can be split as £210 for the three months to 31 December 20X5 and £210 for the three months ended 31 March 20X6. For a period of 12 months the cost of insurance is £840 and this is, therefore, the figure needing to be transferred to the profit and loss account.

If £840 is posted to the debit of profit and loss at 31 December 20X5, the insurance account will still have a debit balance of £210. This is a benefit paid for but not used up at the end of the period. It is an asset and needs carrying forward as such to 20X6, i.e. as a debit balance. Items like this are called **prepaid expenses**, 'prepayments', or 'amounts paid in advance'.

The account can now be completed:

Insurance

20X5			£	20X5			£
Feb	28	Bank	210	Dec	31	Profit and loss	840
Aug	31	''	420				
Nov	18	''	420	''	31	Prepaid c/d	210
			1,050				1,050
20X6							
Jan	1	Prepaid b/d	210				

Prepayment happens when items other than purchases are bought for use in the business, but are not fully used up in the period.

For instance, packing materials are normally not entirely used up over the period in which they are bought, there being a stock of packing materials in hand at the end of the period. This stock is, therefore, a form of prepayment and needs carrying down to the following period in which it will be used.

This can be seen in the following example:

> Year ended 31 December 20X5:
> Packing materials bought in the year = £2,200.
> Stock of packing materials in hand as at 31 December 20X5 = £400.

Looking at the example, it can be seen that in 20X5 the packing materials used up will have been £2,200 – £400 = £1,800. (We are assuming that there was no stock of packing materials at the start of 20X5.) We have a stock of £400 packing materials at 31 December 20X5 to be carried forward to 20X6. The £400 stock of packing materials will be carried forward as an asset balance (i.e. a debit balance) to 20X6:

Packing Materials

20X5			£	20X5			£
Dec	31	Bank	2,200	Dec	31	Profit and loss	1,800
				Dec	31	Stock c/d	400
			2,200				2,200
20X6							
Jan	1	Stock b/d	400				

The stock of packing materials is *not* added to the stock of unsold goods in hand in the balance sheet, but is added to the other prepayments of expenses.

28.5 Revenue owing at the end of period

The revenue owing for sales is already shown in the books. These are the debit balances on our customers' accounts, i.e. debtors. There may be other kinds of revenue, all of which has not been received by the end of the period, e.g. rent receivable. An example now follows.

Example

Our warehouse is larger than we need. We rent part of it to another business for £800 per annum. Details for the year ended 31 December were as follows:

Amount	Rent due	Rent received
£200	31 March 20X5	4 April 20X5
£200	30 June 20X5	6 July 20X5
£200	30 September 20X5	9 October 20X5
£200	31 December 20X5	7 January 20X6

The account for 20X5 will appear as:

Rent Receivable

			20X5			£
			Apr	4	Bank	200
			Jul	6	Bank	200
			Oct	9	Bank	200

The rent received of £200 on 7 January 20X6 will be entered in the books in 20X6.

Any rent paid by the business would be charged as a debit to the profit and loss account. Any rent received, being the opposite, is transferred to the credit of the profit and loss account, as it is a revenue.

The amount to be transferred for 20X5 is that earned for the 12 months, i.e. £800. The rent received account is completed by carrying down the balance owing as a debit balance to 20X6. The £200 owing is an asset on 31 December 20X5.

The rent receivable account can now be completed:

Rent Receivable

20X5			£	20X5			£
Dec	31	Profit and loss	800	Apr	4	Bank	200
				Jul	6	Bank	200
				Oct	9	Bank	200
				Dec	**31**	**Accrued c/d**	**200**
			800				800
20X6							
Jan	1	Accrued b/d	200				

28.6 Expenses and revenue account balances and the balance sheet

In all the cases listed dealing with adjustments in the financial statements, there will still be a balance on each account after the preparation of the trading and profit and loss accounts. All such balances remaining should appear in the balance sheet. The only question left is where and how they should be shown.

The amounts owing for expenses could be called expense creditors, expenses owing or accrued expenses. However, we'll use the term 'accruals'. They represent *very* current liabilities – they will have to be paid in the very near future.

The items prepaid could be called prepaid expenses or payments in advance, but we'll call them 'prepayments'. Similarly to accruals, they represent *very* current assets as they should be received very soon.

Activity 28.2

From your knowledge of accounting, how should all the expense account debit and credit balances appear in the balance sheet – as one debit entry and one credit entry or as an individual entry for each item? Why?

Activity 28.3

(a) where in the current asset sequence do you place prepayments?
(b) where in the current liability sequence do you place accruals?
(c) Why?

Amounts owing for rents receivable or other revenue owing are a special case. If you look back at the T-account in Section 28.5, you'll see that they are described as 'accrued'. However, they are not accrued expenses, as they represent amounts receivable. They are, therefore, **accrued income**.

Activity 28.4

Where do you think these items of accrued income go in the balance sheet?

The part of the balance sheet in respect of the accounts so far seen in this chapter is therefore:

Balance Sheet as at 31 December 20X5 (extract)

	£	£	£
Current assets			
Stock		xxx	
Debtors		200	
Prepayments (400 + 210)		610	
Bank		xxx	
Cash		xxx	
		x,xxx	
Less Current liabilities			
Trade creditors	xxx		
Accrued expenses	250		
		(xxx)	
Net current assets			x,xxx

28.7 Expenses and revenue accounts covering more than one period

So far we've only looked at accounts where there were closing accruals or prepayments. In real life, you will also expect to see some opening accruals and prepayments. This is something that students are often asked to deal with in examinations as it tests their knowledge and ability to distinguish the treatment of these items at the beginning and end of a period. Typically, they may be asked to draw up an expense or revenue account for a full year which has amounts owing or prepaid at both the beginning and end of the year. We can now see how this is done.

Example A

The following details are available:

(A) On 31 December 20X4, three months' rent amounting to a total of £3,000 was owing.
(B) The rent chargeable per year was £12,000.
(C) The following rent payments were made in the year 20X5:
    6 January £3,000; 4 April £3,000; 7 July £3,000; 18 October £3,000.
(D) The final three months' rent for 20X5 is still owing.

Now we can look at the completed rent account. The letters (A) to (D) give reference to the details above.

Rent

20X5				£	20X5				£
Jan	6	Bank	(C)	3,000	Jan	1	Accrued b/d	(A)	3,000
Apr	4	Bank	(C)	3,000	Dec	31	Profit and loss	(B)	12,000
Jul	7	Bank	(C)	3,000					
Oct	18	Bank	(C)	3,000					
Dec	31	Accrued c/d	(D)	3,000					
				15,000					15,000
					20X6				
					Jan	1	Accrued b/d		3,000

Example B

The following details are available:

(A) On 31 December 20X4, packing materials in hand amounted to £1,850.
(B) During the year to 31 December 20X5, we paid £27,480 for packing materials.
(C) There were no stocks of packing materials on 31 December 20X5.
(D) On 31 December 20X5, we still owed £2,750 for packing materials already received and used.

The packing materials account will appear as:

Packing Materials

20X5				£	20X5			£
Jan	1	Stocks b/d	(A)	1,850	Dec	31	Profit and loss	32,080
Dec	31	Bank	(B)	27,480				
Dec	31	Owing c/d	(D)	2,750				
				32,080				32,080
					20X6			
					Jan	1	Owing b/d	2,750

The figure of £32,080 is the difference on the account, and is transferred to the profit and loss account.

We can prove it is correct:

	£	£
Stock at start of year		1,850
Add Bought and used:		
Paid for	27,480	
Still owed for	2,750	
Cost of packing materials used in the year		30,230
		32,080

Example C

Where different expenses are put together in one account, it can get even more confusing. Let us look at where rent and rates are joined together. Here are the details for the year ended 31 December 20X5:

(A) Rent is payable of £6,000 per annum.
(B) Rates of £4,000 per annum are payable by instalments.
(C) At 1 January 20X5, rent of £1,000 had been prepaid in 20X4.
(D) On 1 January 20X5, rates of £400 were owed.
(E) During 20X5, rent of £4,500 was paid.
(F) During 20X5, rates of £5,000 were paid.
(G) On 31 December 20X5, rent of £500 was owing.
(H) On 31 December 20X5, rates of £600 had been prepaid.

A combined rent and rates account is to be drawn up for the year 20X5 showing the transfer to the profit and loss account, and balances are to be carried down to 20X6.

Rent and Rates

20X5				£	20X5				£
Jan	1	Rent prepaid b/d	(C)	1,000	Jan	1	Rates owing b/d	(D)	400
Dec	31	Bank: rent	(E)	4,500	Dec	31	Profit and loss a/c	(A) + (B)	10,000
Dec	31	Bank: rates	(F)	5,000					
Dec	**31**	**Rent accrued c/d**	**(G)**	**500**	**Dec**	**31**	**Rates prepaid c/d**	**(H)**	**600**
				11,000					11,000
20X6					20X6				
Jan	1	Rates prepaid b/d	(H)	600	Jan	1	Rent accrued b/d	(G)	500

To enter the correct figures, you need to keep the two items separate in your own mind. This is easiest if you produce a schedule like the one we produced above for packing materials stock. The one for rent would look like this:

	£	£
Rent due during the year		6,000
Less:		
Rent prepaid at start of year	1,000	
Rent paid during the year	4,500	
		(5,500)
Rent accrued at the end of the year		500

Activity 28.5
Prepare a similar schedule for rates.

28.8 Goods for own use

Traders will often take items out of their business stocks for their own use, without paying for them. There is nothing wrong about their doing this, but an entry should be made to record that this has happenned. This is done by:

1 Debit drawings account, to show that the proprietor has taken the goods for private use.
2 Credit purchases account, to reduce cost of goods available for sale.

In the United Kingdom, an adjustment may be needed for Value Added Tax. If goods supplied to a trader's customers have VAT added to their price, then any such goods taken for own use will need such an adjustment. This is because the VAT regulations state that VAT should be added to the cost of goods taken. The double entry for the VAT content would be:

1 Debit drawings account.
2 Credit VAT account.

Adjustments may also be needed for other private items. For instance, if a trader's private insurance had been incorrectly charged to the business insurance account, then the correction would be:

1 Debit drawings account.
2 Credit insurance account.

28.9 Distinctions between various kinds of capital

The capital account represents the claim of the proprietor against the assets of the business at a point in time. The word **capital** is, however, often used in a specific sense. The main meanings are listed below.

Capital invested

This means the total monetary value of everything brought into the business by the proprietors from their outside interests. The amount of capital invested is not disturbed by the amount of profits made by the business or losses incurred.

Capital employed

Students at an early stage in their studies are often asked to define this term. In fact, for those who progress to a more advanced stage, it will be seen in *Business Accounting 2* that capital employed could have several meanings as the term is often used quite loosely. At its simplest, it is taken to mean the monetary value of the resources that are being used in the business. Thus, if all the assets were added together and the liabilities of the business deducted, the answer would be that the difference is the amount of money employed in the business. You will by now realise that this is the same as the closing balance of the capital account. It is also sometimes called 'net assets' or 'net worth'.

Working capital

This is a term for the excess of the current assets over the current liabilities of a business and is the same as 'net current assets'.

28.10 Financial statements in the services sector

So far we have only looked at financial statements for businesses trading in some sort of goods. We drew up a trading account for some of these businesses because we wanted to identify the gross profit on goods sold.

There are, however, many businesses which do not deal in 'goods' but instead supply 'services'. This will include professional businesses such as accountants, solicitors, doctors, dentists, vets, management consultants, advertising agencies, estate agents, and internet service providers. Other examples include businesses specialising in computer repairs, window-cleaning, gardening, hairdressing, piano-tuning, and banks, football clubs, health clubs, gyms, and leisure centres.

As they do not deal in 'goods' there is no point in their attempting to draw up trading accounts. While it is quite possible for, say, a dentist to treat depreciation on equipment, the costs of materials consumed, and the dental assistant's salary as deductions from income in order to arrive at a figure for gross profit, such information is likely to be of little benefit in terms of decision-making. They will, however, prepare a profit and loss account and a balance sheet.

The first item in the profit and loss account will be the revenue which might be called 'work done', 'fees', 'charges', 'accounts rendered', 'takings', etc., depending on the nature of the organisation. Any other items of income will be added, e.g. rent receivable, and then the expenses will be listed and deducted to arrive at a net profit or net loss.

An example of the profit and loss account of a solicitor might be as per Exhibit 28.1.

Exhibit 28.1

J Plunkett, Solicitor
Profit and Loss Account for the year ended 31 December 20X5

	£	£
Revenue:		
Fees charged		87,500
Insurance commissions		1,300
		88,800
Less Expenses:		
Wages and salaries	29,470	
Rent and rates	11,290	
Office expenses	3,140	
Motor expenses	2,115	
General expenses	1,975	
Depreciation	2,720	
		(50,710)
Net profit		38,090

Other than for the descriptions given in the revenue section, it doesn't look very different from the ones you've prepared for traders. In effect, if you can prepare a trading and profit and loss account for a trader, you can do so for a service organisation. You just need to remember that there will be no trading account and that the income should be appropriately described.

28.11 Extended trial balances

Instead of drafting a set of financial statements in the way shown so far in this textbook, you could prepare an 'extended trial balance', or 'worksheet'. It can be very useful when there are a large number of adjustments to be made. Professional accountants use them a lot for that very reason.

Extended trial balances are usually drawn up on specially preprinted types of stationery with suitable vertical columns printed across the page. You start with the trial balance extracted from the ledgers and then enter adjustments in the columns to the right. Columns for the trading account, the profit and loss account, and the balance sheet then follow.

Exhibit 28.2 shows an example of the extended trial balance that could have been drawn up as an answer to Review Question 28.10. Once you have attempted the question yourself, compare your answer to the one shown in Exhibit 28.2. The gross profits and net profits are the same; it is simply the method of displaying the information that is different.

If you were an accountant, the financial statements you prepare and give to the owner and to anyone else who was an interested party, such as the Inspector of Taxes or the bank, would not be in the style of an extended trial balance. Instead, having completed the extended trial balance, the figures for the trading account, profit and loss account, and balance sheet would be transferred to financial statements prepared using the conventional style of presentation.

To provide such special stationery in an examination is unusual, though it has been known to happen. In addition, for students to draw up an extended trial balance from scratch could be very time-consuming. Therefore, it is very rare for examiners to ask for one to be prepared from scratch. However, the examiner may ask you something about extended trial balances (or worksheets), if this topic is included in the syllabus. You should note, however, that nowadays spreadsheets are often used to produce financial statements in this way. If your course includes use of spreadsheets to prepare financial statements, you are more likely to be asked to prepare an extended trial balance in your examination.

Exhibit 28.2

JOHN BROWN WORKSHEET

See Review Question 28.10

Account	Trial Balance 1 Dr	2 Cr	Adjustments 3 Dr	4 Cr	Trading Account 5 Dr	6 Cr	Profit and Loss Account 7 Dr	8 Cr	Balance Sheet 9 Dr	10 Cr
Sales		400,000				400,000				
Purchases	350,000				350,000					
Sales returns	5,000				5,000					
Purchases returns		6,200				6,200				
Stock 1.1.20X7	100,000				100,000					
Provision for bad debts		800		180 (iv)						980
Wages and salaries	30,000		5,000 (ii)				35,000			
Rates	6,000			500 (iii)			5,500			
Telephone	1,000		220 (v)				1,220			
Shop fittings	40,000			4,000 (vi)					36,000	
Van	30,000			6,000 (vi)					24,000	
Debtors	9,800								9,800	
Creditors		7,000								7,000
Bad debts	200						200			
Capital		179,000								179,000
Bank	3,000								3,000	
Drawings	18,000								18,000	
	593,000	593,000								
Stock 31.12.20X7 – Asset			120,000 (i)						120,000	
Stock 31.12.20X7 –				120,000 (i)		120,000				
Cost of goods sold										
Accrued expenses				5,000 (ii) 220 (v)						5,000 220
Provision for bad debts			180 (iv)				180			
Prepaid expenses			500 (iii)						500	
Depreciation shop fittings			4,000 (vi)				4,000			
Depreciation van			6,000 (vi)				6,000			
			135,900	135,900						
Gross profit (balancing figure)					71,200			71,200		
Net profit (balancing figure)							19,100			19,100
					71,200 526,200	526,200	19,100 71,200	71,200	211,300	19,100 211,300

28.12 Definition of accounting

In Chapter 1, you were given a definition of bookkeeping as being concerned with the work of entering information into accounting records and afterwards maintaining such records properly. This definition does not need to be amended.

However, accounting was not fully defined in Chapter 1. It would probably not have meant much to you at that stage in your studies. The following is the most widely used definition: '*The process of identifying, measuring, and communicating economic information to permit informed judgements and decisions by users of the information.*'

28.13 An alternative way to record accruals and prepayments

After learning in Chapter 27 that there was a second commonly used way to record provisions for depreciation, it will come as no surprise to you to learn that there is a second commonly used way to record accruals and prepayments. Just as with the two-stage method of recording depreciation provisions, the alternative way to record accruals and prepayments requires that you create additional ledger accounts. You open an accruals account and a prepayments account and post any balances on expense accounts at the period end to the appropriate one of the two new accounts.

The balance in an expense account under the method you learnt earlier in this chapter is described as either 'accrued c/d' or 'prepaid c/d'. Under the alternative method, there would be no balance in the expense account after the double entry to the accruals account or prepayments account. Instead, there will be a balance on these two accounts which is then entered in the balance sheet in exactly the same way as you did under the other method.

At the start of the next period, you reverse the entry by crediting the prepayments account and debiting each of the expense accounts that had debit balances. Similarly, the accruals account is debited and the expense accounts that had credit balances are credited with the appropriate amounts.

For example, taking the insurance account from Section 28.4, the entries in the the insurance account and prepayments account at the end of the year and at the start of the next year would be:

Insurance

20X5			£	20X5			£
Feb	28	Bank	210	Dec	31	Profit and loss	840
Aug	31	''	420				
Nov	18	''	420	''	31	Prepayments	210
			1,050				1,050
20X6							
Jan	1	Prepayments	210				

Prepayments

20X5			£	20X5			£
Dec	31	Insurance	210	Dec	31	Balance c/d	210
20X6				20X6			
Jan	1	Balance b/d	210	Jan	1	Insurance	210

In reality, it doesn't really matter which of these two methods you use. Examiners will accept them both unless they specifically ask for one of them to be used. Your teacher or lecturer will know whether this is likely to happen. Follow the guidance of your teacher or lecturer and use whichever method he or she indicates is more appropriate.

In order not to confuse things by switching back and forth between the two methods, all examples of accruals and prepayments and all questions involving accruals and prepayments in the rest of this textbook will use the method that has been covered in detail in this chapter. Should you be using the second method, as you will have seen above, it is very obvious what the equivalent entries would be when you look at examples prepared using the method adopted in this textbook.

Learning outcomes

You should now have learnt:

1 That adjustments are needed so that the expenses and income shown in the financial statements equal the expenses incurred in the period and the revenue that has arisen in the period.

2 That the balances relating to the adjustments will be shown on the balance sheet at the end of the period as current assets and current liabilities.

3 That goods taken for the owner's own use without anything being recorded in the books will necessitate a transfer from purchases to the drawings account, plus an adjustment for VAT if appropriate.

4 How to record appropriate entries in the accounts and financial statements at the end of a period for accrued expenses, prepaid expenses, accrued income, and drawings.

5 That private expenses should not be charged as an expense in the trading and profit and loss accounts, but should instead be charged to the drawings account.

6 That an extended trial balance is an alternative way of arriving at the figures to be included in the financial statements.

7 That there are two common ways to prepare accrual and prepayments.

Answers to activities

28.1 Don't worry if you didn't know what names to give the accounts other than the rent account. What is important is that you thought about it and that you knew which side the entries should be in the rent account.

   (a) *Dr* Rent account £200   *Cr* Accruals account £200
   (b) *Dr* Prepayments account £100   *Cr* Rent account £100

   Note how the two entries in the rent account are on opposite sides. The £200 rent owing at the end of the year is an expense that has not yet been entered in the books, but it must be as it relates to the current year. The £100 paid in advance for next year is not an expense of the current year, so you need to reduce the amount you have currently in the rent account so that the correct expense will be posted to the profit and loss account. The accruals account is similar to a creditor's account, but it is used for expenses unpaid at the year end. Similarly, the prepayments account is like a debtors account, but it is used to record amounts paid for expenses in advance of the accounting period in which the benefit (i.e. what was paid for) is received.

28.2 All the debit entries should be added together and shown as one entry called 'prepayments' within current assets. Similarly, all the credit entries should be added together and shown as one entry called 'accruals' under current liabilities. This is done so as to minimise the clutter in the balance sheet while providing enough information for anyone looking at the financial statement to be able to identify the figure for accruals and the figure for prepayments.

28.3 (a) between debtors and bank
     (b) between creditors and bank overdraft
     (c) their degree of liquidity.

28.4 They are usually added to debtors. This is because these represent a regular source of income and, even though the income has nothing to do with the goods or services that form the main activity of the business, they are in every other sense another form of customer account. It makes sense, therefore, to include them in the debtor balance shown in the balance sheet.

28.5

	£
Rates due during the year	4,000
Add: Rates accrued at the start of the year	400
	4,400
Less: Rates paid during the year	(5,000)
Rates prepaid at the end of the year	(600)

REVIEW QUESTIONS

28.1 The financial year of H Saunders ended on 31 December 20X6. Show the ledger accounts for the following items including the balance transferred to the necessary part of the financial statements, also the balances carried down to 20X7:

(*a*) Motor expenses: Paid in 20X6 £744; Owing at 31 December 20X6 £28.
(*b*) Insurance: Paid in 20X6 £420; Prepaid as at 31 December 20X6 £35.
(*c*) Stationery: Paid during 20X6 £1,800; Owing as at 31 December 20X5 £250; Owing as at 31 December 20X6 £490.
(*d*) Rates: Paid during 20X6 £950; Prepaid as at 31 December 20X5 £220; Prepaid as at 31 December 20X6 £290.
(*e*) Saunders sub-lets part of the premises. Receives £550 during the year ended 31 December 20X6. Tenant owed Saunders £180 on 31 December 20X5 and £210 on 31 December 20X6.

28.2A J Owen's year ended on 30 June 20X8. Write up the ledger accounts, showing the transfers to the financial statements and the balances carried down to the next year for the following:

(*a*) Stationery: Paid for the year to 30 June 20X8 £855; Stocks of stationery at 30 June 20X7 £290; at 30 June 20X8 £345.
(*b*) General expenses: Paid for the year to 30 June 20X8 £590; Owing at 30 June 20X7 £64; Owing at 30 June 20X8 £90.
(*c*) Rent and rates (combined account): Paid in the year to 30 June 20X8 £3,890; Rent owing at 30 June 20X7 £160; Rent paid in advance at 30 June 20X8 £250; Rates owing 30 June 20X7 £205; Rates owing 30 June 20X8 £360.
(*d*) Motor expenses: Paid in the year to 30 June 20X8 £4,750; Owing as at 30 June 20X7 £180; Owing as at 30 June 20X8 £375.
(*e*) Owen earns commission from the sales of one item. Received for the year to 30 June 20X8 £850; Owing at 30 June 20X7 £80; Owing at 30 June 20X8 £145.

28.3 On 1 January 20X8 the following balances, among others, stood in the books of M Baldock, a sole trader:

(*a*) Rates, £104 (Dr);
(*b*) Packing materials, £629 (Dr).

During the year ended 31 December 20X8 the information related to these two accounts is as follows:

(*i*) Rates of £1,500 were paid to cover the period 1 April 20X8 to 31 March 20X9;
(*ii*) £5,283 was paid for packing materials bought;
(*iii*) £357 was owing on 31 December 20X8 in respect of packing materials bought on credit;
(*iv*) Old materials amounting to £172 were sold as scrap for cash;
(*v*) Closing stock of packing materials was valued at £598.

You are required to write up the two accounts showing the appropriate amounts transferred to the Profit and Loss Account at 31 December 20X8, the end of the financial year of the trader.

Note: No separate accounts are opened for creditors for packing materials bought on credit.

28.4A On 1 January 20X6 the following balances, among others, stood in the books of T Thomas:

(a) Lighting and heating, (Dr) £277.
(b) Insurance, (Dr) £307.

During the year ended 31 December 20X6 the information related to these two accounts is as follows:

(i)   Fire insurance, £960, covering the year ended 31 April 20X7 was paid.
(ii)   General insurance, £630, covering the year ended 31 August 20X7 was paid.
(iii) An insurance rebate of £55 was received on 30 June 20X6.
(iv)   Electricity bills of £874 were paid.
(v)   An electricity bill of £83 for December 20X6 was unpaid as on 31 December 20X6.
(vi)   Oil bills of £1,260 were paid.
(vii) Stock of oil as on 31 December 20X6 was £92.

You are required to write up the accounts for lighting and heating, and for insurance, for the year to 31 December 20X6. Carry forward necessary balances to 20X7.

28.5 Three of the accounts in the ledger of Charlotte Williams indicated the following balances at 1 January 20X0:

Insurance paid in advance £562;
Wages outstanding £306;
Rent receivable, received in advance £36.

During 20X0 Charlotte:

Paid for insurance £1,019, by bank standing order;
Paid £15,000 wages, in cash;
Received £2,600 rent, by cheque, from the tenant.

At 31 December 20X0, insurance prepaid was £345. On the same day rent receivable in arrears was £105 and wages accrued amounted to £419.

(a) Prepare the insurance, wages and rent receivable accounts for the year ended 31 December 20X0, showing the year end transfers and the balances brought down.
(b) Prepare the profit and loss account extract showing clearly the amounts transferred from each of the above accounts for the year ended 31 December 20X0.
(c) Explain the effects on the financial statements of accounting for (i) expenses accrued and (ii) income received in advance at year end.
(d) What are the purposes of accounting for (i) expenses accrued and (ii) income received in advance at year end?

(Edexcel Foundation, London Examinations: GCSE)

28.6A The two accounts below were taken from the books of a retailer at the end of his financial year, 31 December 20X7.

Insurance Account

Dr			£			Cr £
20X7				**20X7**		
Jan 1	Balance		80	Dec 31	Profit and loss	530
Jan–Dec	Bank		540	Dec 31	Balance c/d	90
			620			620
Dec 31	Balance b/d		90			

Rent Receivable Account

Dr					Cr
20X7		£	20X7		£
Dec 31	Profit and loss	885	Jan 1	Balance	60
Dec 31	Balance c/d	75	Jan–Dec	Bank	900
		960			960
			Dec 31	Balance b/d	75

Required:

Answers to the following questions.

1 What type of account is the insurance account?
2 What type of account is the rent receivable account?
3 In which subdivision of the ledger will these accounts be found?
4 Under which heading will the closing balance of the insurance account be found on the balance sheet?
5 Under which heading will the closing balance of the rent receivable account be found on the balance sheet?
6 In which subsidiary book (book of prime entry) will the entries transferring amounts to the profit and loss account be found?
7 Which document will be the source of information for the entry in the insurance account 'bank £540'?
8 Which document will be the source of information for the entry in the rent receivable account 'bank £900'?
9 What amount for insurance will appear in the trial balance dated 31 December 20X7 prepared prior to the preparation of financial statements?
10 What amount for rent receivable will appear in the trial balance dated 31 December 20X7 prepared prior to the preparation of financial statements?
11 If the adjustment in the insurance account for £90 on 31 December had been overlooked, would the net profit have been under- or overstated and by how much?
12 If the adjustment in the rent receivable account for £75 on 31 December had been overlooked, would the net profit have been under- or overstated and by how much?

(Southern Examining Group: GCSE)

28.7A The owner of a small business selling and repairing cars which you patronise has just received a copy of his accounts for the current year.

He is rather baffled by some of the items and as he regards you as a financial expert, he has asked you to explain certain points of difficulty to him. This you have readily agreed to do. His questions are as follows:

(a) 'What is meant by the term "assets"? My mechanical knowledge and skill is an asset to the business but it does not seem to have been included.'
(b) 'The house I live in cost £30,000 five years ago and is now worth £60,000, but that is not included either.'
(c) 'What is the difference between "fixed assets" and "current assets"?'
(d) 'Why do amounts for "vehicles" appear under both fixed asset and current asset headings?'
(e) 'Why is the "bank and cash" figure in the balance sheet different from the profit for the year shown in the profit and loss account?'
(f) 'I see the profit and loss account has been charged with depreciation on equipment etc. I bought all these things several years ago and paid for them in cash. Does this mean that I am being charged for them again?'

Required:

Answer each of his questions in terms which he will be able to understand.

(Association of Chartered Certified Accountants)

28.8 The following trial balance was extracted from the books of A Scholes at the close of business on 28 February 20X7.

	Dr £	Cr £
Purchases and sales	11,280	19,740
Cash at bank	1,140	
Cash in hand	210	
Capital account 1 March 20X6		9,900
Drawings	2,850	
Office furniture	1,440	
Rent	1,020	
Wages and salaries	2,580	
Discounts	690	360
Debtors and creditors	4,920	2,490
Stock 1 March 20X6	2,970	
Provision for bad and doubtful debts 1 March 20X6		270
Delivery van	2,400	
Van running costs	450	
Bad debts written off	810	
	32,760	32,760

Notes:
(a) Stock 28 February 20X7 £3,510.
(b) Wages and salaries accrued at 28 February 20X7 £90.
(c) Rent prepaid at 28 February 20X7 £140.
(d) Van running costs owing at 28 February 20X7 £60.
(e) Increase the provision for bad and doubtful debts by £60.
(f) Provide for depreciation as follows: Office furniture £180; Delivery van £480.

Required:
Draw up the trading and profit and loss account for the year ending 28 February 20X7 together with a balance sheet as on 28 February 20X7.

28.9A T Morgan, a sole trader, extracted the following trial balance from his books at the close of business on 31 March 20X9:

	Dr £	Cr £
Purchases and sales	22,860	41,970
Stock 1 April 20X8	5,160	
Capital 1 April 20X8		7,200
Bank overdraft		4,350
Cash	90	
Discounts	1,440	930
Returns inwards	810	
Returns outwards		570
Carriage outwards	2,160	
Rent and insurance	1,740	
Provision for bad and doubtful debts		660
Fixtures and fittings	1,200	
Delivery van	2,100	
Debtors and creditors	11,910	6,060
Drawings	2,880	
Wages and salaries	8,940	
General office expenses	450	
	61,740	61,740

Notes:
(a) Stock 31 March 20X9 £4,290.
(b) Wages and salaries accrued at 31 March 20X9 £210; Office expenses owing £20.
(c) Rent prepaid 31 March 20X9 £180.
(d) Increase the provision for bad and doubtful debts by £150 to £810.
(e) Provide for depreciation as follows: Fixtures and fittings £120; Delivery van £300.

Required:

Prepare the trading and profit and loss accounts for the year ended 31 March 20X9 together with a balance sheet as at that date.

28.10 This question also relates to extended trial balances (*see* Exhibit 28.2)

From the following trial balance of John Brown, store owner, prepare a trading account and profit and loss account for the year ended 31 December 20X7, and a balance sheet as at that date, taking into consideration the adjustments shown below:

Trial Balance as at 31 December 20X7

	Dr £	Cr £
Sales		400,000
Purchases	350,000	
Sales returns	5,000	
Purchases returns		6,200
Opening stock at 1 January 20X7	100,000	
Provision for bad debts		800
Wages and salaries	30,000	
Rates	6,000	
Telephone	1,000	
Shop fittings at cost	40,000	
Van at cost	30,000	
Debtors and creditors	9,800	7,000
Bad debts	200	
Capital		179,000
Bank balance	3,000	
Drawings	18,000	
	593,000	593,000

(*i*)   Closing stock at 31 December 20X7 £120,000.
(*ii*) Accrued wages £5,000.
(*iii*) Rates prepaid £500.
(*iv*) The provision for bad debts to be increased to 10 per cent of debtors.
(*v*) Telephone account outstanding £220.
(*vi*) Depreciate shop fittings at 10 per cent per annum, and van at 20 per cent per annum, on cost.

28.11A The following trial balance has been extracted from the ledger of Mr Yousef, a sole trader.

Trial Balance as at 31 May 20X6

	Dr £	Cr £
Sales		138,078
Purchases	82,350	
Carriage	5,144	
Drawings	7,800	
Rent, rates and insurance	6,622	
Postage and stationery	3,001	
Advertising	1,330	
Salaries and wages	26,420	
Bad debts	877	
Provision for bad debts		130
Debtors	12,120	
Creditors		6,471
Cash in hand	177	
Cash at bank	1,002	
Stock as at 1 June 20X5	11,927	
Equipment		
at cost	58,000	
accumulated depreciation		19,000
Capital		53,091
	216,770	216,770

The following additional information as at 31 May 20X6 is available:

(a) Rent is accrued by £210.
(b) Rates have been prepaid by £880.
(c) £2,211 of carriage represents carriage inwards on purchases.
(d) Equipment is to be depreciated at 15% per annum using the straight line method.
(e) The provision for bad debts to be increased by £40.
(f) Stock at the close of business has been valued at £13,551.

Required:
Prepare a trading and profit and loss account for the year ended 31 May 20X6 and a balance sheet as at that date.

(*Association of Accounting Technicians*)

28.12   Mr Chai has been trading for some years as a wine merchant. The following list of balances has been extracted from his ledger as at 30 April 20X7, the end of his most recent financial year.

	£
Capital	83,887
Sales	259,870
Trade creditors	19,840
Returns out	13,407
Provision for bad debts	512
Discounts allowed	2,306
Discounts received	1,750
Purchases	135,680
Returns inwards	5,624
Carriage outwards	4,562
Drawings	18,440
Carriage inwards	11,830
Rent, rates and insurance	25,973
Heating and lighting	11,010
Postage, stationery and telephone	2,410
Advertising	5,980
Salaries and wages	38,521
Bad debts	2,008
Cash in hand	534
Cash at bank	4,440
Stock as at 1 May 20X6	15,654
Trade debtors	24,500
Fixtures and fittings – at cost	120,740
Provision for depreciation on fixtures and fittings – as at 30 April 20X7	63,020
Depreciation	12,074

The following additional information as at 30 April 20X7 is available:

(a) Stock at the close of business was valued at £17,750.
(b) Insurances have been prepaid by £1,120.
(c) Heating and lighting is accrued by £1,360.
(d) Rates have been prepaid by £5,435.
(e) The provision for bad debts is to be adjusted so that it is 3% of trade debtors.

Required:
Prepare Mr Chai's trading and profit and loss account for the year ended 30 April 20X7 and a balance sheet as at that date.

(*Association of Accounting Technicians*)

CHAPTER 29

The valuation of stock

Learning objectives

After you have studied this chapter, you should be able to:

- calculate the value of stock using three different methods
- explain why using the most appropriate method to value stock is important
- explain what effect changing prices has on stock valuation under each of three different methods
- explain why net realisable value is sometimes used instead of cost for stock valuation
- adjust stock valuations, where necessary, by a reduction to net realisable value
- explain how subjective factors influence the choice of stock valuation method
- explain why goods purchased on 'sale or return' are not included in the buyer's stock

Introduction

In this chapter, you will learn how to calculate the monetary value of stock using a variety of methods. You will learn why choosing the most appropriate method of stock valuation is important; and that a range of subjective factors can influence the choice of method, including the need to reflect how the stock is physically used. Finally, you'll learn how to treat goods sold on 'sale or return' and about the need to adjust stock levels identified in a stocktake to the level they would have been at the balance sheet date.

29.1 Different valuations of stock

Stock is the name given to the goods for resale, work in progress, and raw materials that are held at a point in time. Most people assume that when a value is placed upon stock, it is the only figure possible. This is not true.

Assume that a business has just completed its first financial year and is about to value stock at cost price. It has dealt in only one type of goods. A record of the transactions is now shown in Exhibit 29.1.

Exhibit 29.1

Bought			Sold		
20X5		£	**20X5**		£
January	10 at £30 each	300	May	8 for £50 each	400
April	10 at £34 each	340	November	24 for £60 each	1,440
October	20 at £40 each	800			
	40	1,440		32	1,840

A quick check by the storeman showed that there were still 8 units in stock at 31 December, which confirms what the records show above.

> ## Activity 29.1
> What valuation do you think should be placed on the 8 units of stock? Why?

The total figure of purchases is £1,440 and sales revenue during the year was £1,840. The trading account for the first year of trading can now be completed using the closing stock in the calculations.

Let's now look at the three most commonly used methods of valuing stock.

29.2 First in, first out method

This is usually known as **FIFO**, the first letters of each word. This method says that the first goods to be received are the first to be issued. Using the figures in Exhibit 29.1 we can now calculate the cost of closing stock on a FIFO basis as follows:

	Received	Issued	Stock after each transaction		
20X5				£	£
January	10 at £30 each		10 at £30 each		300
April	10 at £34 each		10 at £30 each	300	
			10 at £34 each	340	640
May		8 at £30 each	2 at £30 each	60	
			10 at £34 each	340	400
October	20 at £40 each		2 at £30 each	60	
			10 at £34 each	340	
			20 at £40 each	800	1,200
November		2 at £30 each			
		10 at £34 each			
		12 at £40 each			
		24	8 at £40 each		320

Thus, the closing stock at 31 December 20X5 at cost is valued under FIFO at £320.

> ## Activity 29.2
> Can you see another, simpler way of arriving at the same valuation under FIFO?

29.3 Last in, first out method

This is usually known as **LIFO**. As each issue of goods is made they are said to be from the last lot of goods received before that date. Where there is not enough left of the last lot of goods, then the balance of goods needed is said to come from the previous lot still unsold.

From the information shown in Exhibit 29.1 the calculation can now be shown.

	Received	Issued	Stock after each transaction		
20X5 January	10 at £30 each		10 at £30 each	£	£ 300
April	10 at £34 each		10 at £30 each 10 at £34 each	300 340	640
May		8 at £34 each	10 at £30 each 2 at £34 each	300 68	368
October	20 at £40 each		10 at £30 each 2 at £34 each 20 at £40 each	300 68 800	1,168
November		20 at £40 each 2 at £34 each 2 at £30 each 24	8 at £30 each		240

Thus, the closing stock at 31 December 20X5 at cost is valued under LIFO at £240.

Activity 29.3

Can you see another, simpler way of arriving at the same valuation under LIFO?

29.4 Average cost method (AVCO)

Using the **AVCO** method, with each receipt of goods the average cost for each item of stock is recalculated. Further issues of goods are then at that figure, until another receipt of goods means that another recalculation is needed. From the information in Exhibit 29.1 the calculation can be shown:

Received		Issued	Average cost per unit of stock held	Number of units in stock	Total value of stock
			£		£
January	10 at £30		30	10	300
April	10 at £34		32*	20	640
May		8 at £32	32	12	384
October	20 at £40		37**	32	1,184
November		24 at £37	37	8	296

The closing stock at 31 December 20X5 is therefore valued at £296.

* In April, this is calculated as follows: stock 10 × £30 = £300 + stock received (10 × £34) = £340 = total £640. You then divide the 20 units in stock into the total cost of that stock, i.e. £640 ÷ 20 = £32.
** In October, this is calculated as follows: stock 12 × £32 = £384 + stock received (20 × £40) = £800 = £1,184. There are 32 units in stock, so the average is £1,184 ÷ 32 = £37.

Note how under this approach you recalculate the average after every receipt of a batch of new stock and then use it as the cost of the next batch sold.

Activity 29.4

If 2 units had been sold in December, at what cost would they have been sold?

29.5 Stock valuation and the calculation of profits

Using the figures from Exhibit 29.1 with stock valuations shown by the three methods of FIFO, LIFO, and AVCO, the trading accounts would be:

Trading Account for the year ended 31 December 20X5							
	FIFO	LIFO	AVCO		FIFO	LIFO	AVCO
	£	£	£		£	£	£
Purchases	1,440	1,440	1,440	Sales	1,840	1,840	1,840
less Closing stock	(320)	(240)	(296)				
Cost of goods sold	1,120	1,200	1,144				
Gross profit	720	640	696				
	1,840	1,840	1,840		1,840	1,840	1,840

Activity 29.5

Which method has produced (*a*) the highest, (*b*) the middle, and (*c*) the lowest value for closing stock? Why do you think this has occurred?

As you can see, different methods of stock valuation result in different profits. It is, therefore, important that the method chosen is the one that is closest in its assumptions to the nature of the business.

29.6 Reduction to net realisable value

Having selected the most appropriate method to apply when determining the cost of closing stock, you next need to consider whether that value is realistic – that is, whether it is what the stock is *actually* worth at the end of the period. This is an example of application of the prudence concept that you learnt about in Chapter 10. Following the prudence concept, stock should never be undervalued or overvalued.

Activity 29.6

(*a*) What happens to gross profit if closing stock is undervalued? Why?
(*b*) What happens to gross profit if closing stock is overvalued? Why?

In order to check that stock is not overvalued, accountants calculate its **net realisable value**. This is done according to the formula:

Saleable value (i.e. what it can be sold for) – Expenses needed before completion of sale (such as costs of delivery to the seller's shops) = Net realisable value.

If the net realisable value of stock is less than the cost of the stock, then the figure to be used in the financial statements is net realisable value *not* cost.

A somewhat exaggerated example will show the necessity for this action. Assume that an art dealer has bought only two paintings during the financial year ended 31 December 20X8. She starts off the year without any stock, and then buys a genuine masterpiece for £6,000 and sells it later in the year for £11,500. The other is a fake, but she does not realise this when she buys it for £5,100, only to discover during the year that she made a terrible mistake and that its net realisable value is only £100. The fake remains unsold at the end of the year. The trading accounts, Exhibit 29.2, would appear as (*a*) if stock is valued at cost, and (*b*) if stock is valued at net realisable value.

Exhibit 29.2

Trading Account for the year ended 31 December 20X8

		(a)		(b)
		£		£
Sales		11,500		11,500
Purchases	11,100		11,100	
Less: Closing stock	(5,100)		(100)	
		(6,000)		(11,000)
Gross profit		5,500		500

Method (*a*) ignores the fact that the dealer had a bad trading year owing to her skill being found wanting in 20X8. If this method was used, then the loss on the fake would reveal itself in the following year's trading account. Method (*b*), however, recognises that the loss really occurred at the date of purchase rather than at the date of sale. Following the concept of prudence, accounting practice is to use method (*b*).

At one time, it was said that you should take the 'lower of cost or market value'. Changing it to 'lower of cost or net realisable value' gives a more precise description of what is to be done.

29.7 Stock groups and valuation

If there is only one sort of goods in stock, calculating the lower of cost or net realisable value is easy. If we have several or many types of goods in stock, we can use one of two ways of making the calculation – by category and by article.

Exhibit 29.3

Stock at 31 December 20X8			
Article	*Different categories*	*Cost*	*Net realisable value*
		£	£
1	A	100	80
2	A	120	150
3	A	300	400
4	B	180	170
5	B	150	130
6	B	260	210
7	C	410	540
8	C	360	410
9	C	420	310
		2,300	2,400

In Exhibit 29.3, Articles 1, 2 and 3 are televisions; Articles 4, 5 and 6 are radios; and Articles 7, 8 and 9 are videos. From the information given in the exhibit, we will calculate the stock using both these approaches.

The category method

The same sorts of items are put together in categories. Thus, televisions are in Category A, radios are in Category B, and Category C is videos.

A calculation showing a comparison of cost valuation and net realisable value for each category is now shown.

Category	Cost	Net realisable value
A	£100 + £120 + £300 = £520	£80 + £150 + £400 = £630
B	£180 + £150 + £260 = £590	£170 + £130 + £210 = £510
C	£410 + £360 + £420 = £1,190	£540 + £410 + £310 = £1,260

The lower of cost and net realisable value is, therefore:

		£
Category A: lower of £520 or £630	=	520
Category B: lower of £590 or £510	=	510
Category C: lower of £1,190 or £1,260	=	1,190
Stock is valued for final accounts at		2,220

The article method

By this method, the lower of cost or net realisable value for each article is compared and the lowest figure taken. From Exhibit 29.3 this gives us the following valuation:

Article	Valuation
	£
1	80
2	120
3	300
4	170
5	130
6	210
7	410
8	360
9	310
	£2,090

29.8 Some other bases in use

Retail businesses often estimate the cost of stock by calculating it in the first place at selling price, and then deducting the normal margin of gross profit on such stock. Adjustment is made for items which are to be sold at other than normal selling prices.

Where standard costing is in use, the figure of **standard cost** is frequently used. You'll learn about standard costing in *Business Accounting 2*. Standard cost is, effectively, what you would expect something to cost. When standard costing is in use, a standard cost will have been determined for purchases and it is that standard cost that would be used to value closing stock.

'Base stock' is a method used in industries where a minimum level of stock is always maintained. Power station fuel supplies, for example, may fall within this classification. The base stock is assumed to never deteriorate or be replaced and is valued at its original cost. Any other stock is valued using a 'normal' method, such as FIFO, LIFO or AVCO.

29.9 Periodic stock valuation

Some businesses do not keep detailed stock records like those shown in Exhibit 29.1. Instead, they wait until the end of a period before calculating the cost of their closing stock. In this case, AVCO is based upon the total cost of stock available for sale in the period divided by the number of units of stock available for sale in the period. You then multiply the closing stock by the overall average cost of the stock.

If you did this for the data in Exhibit 29.1 the closing stock value at cost would be (£1,440 ÷ 40 =) £36 × 8 = £288 (rather than £296, as calculated in Section 29.4). This method is also known as the 'weighted average cost method'.

If you used FIFO or LIFO in these circumstances, FIFO gives the same answer as under the method presented earlier. LIFO, on the other hand, would become the permanent opposite of FIFO, with all closing stock assumed to have come from the earliest batches of purchases.

> ### Activity 29.7
> If you have no detailed stock records, how could you use AVCO, FIFO, or LIFO?

You should assume that you are to calculate AVCO, FIFO and LIFO in the way they were presented earlier in this chapter *unless* an examiner asks you to calculate them on a periodic stock valuation basis.

29.10 Factors affecting the stock valuation decision

Obviously the overriding consideration applicable in all circumstances when valuing stock is the need to give a 'true and fair view' of the state of affairs of the undertaking as at the balance sheet date and of the trend of the business's trading results. There is, however, no precise definition of what constitutes a 'true and fair view' and it rests on the judgement of the persons concerned. It would be necessary to study the behavioural sciences to understand the factors that affect judgement. However, it should be possible to state that the judgement of any two persons will not always be the same in the differing circumstances of various businesses.

In fact, the only certain thing about stock valuation is that the concept of consistency (which you learnt about in Chapter 10) should be applied, i.e. once adopted, the same basis should be used in the financial statements until some good reason occurs to change it. A reference should then be made in the notes that accompany the financial statements as to the effect of the change on the reported profits, if the amount involved is material.

It will perhaps be useful to look at some of the factors which cause a particular basis to be chosen. The list is intended to be indicative rather than comprehensive, and is merely intended as a first brief look at matters which will have to be studied in depth by those intending to make a career in accountancy.

1 **Ignorance.** The personalities involved may not appreciate the fact that there is more than one possible way of valuing stock.
2 **Convenience.** The basis chosen may not be the best for the purposes of profit calculation but it may be the easiest to calculate. It must always be borne in mind that the benefits which flow from possessing information should be greater than the costs of obtaining it. The only difficulty with this is actually establishing when the benefits do exceed the cost but, in some circumstances, the decision not to adopt a given basis will be obvious.

3 **Custom.** It may be the particular method used in a certain trade or industry.

4 **Taxation.** The whole idea may be to defer the payment of tax for as long as possible. Because the stock figures affect the calculation of profits on which the tax is based the lowest possible stock figures may be taken to show the lowest profits up to the balance sheet date. (But doing this will result in a higher profit in the following period!)

5 **The capacity to borrow money or to sell the business at the highest possible price.** The higher the stock value shown, the higher will be the profits calculated to date and, therefore, at first sight the business looks more attractive to a buyer or lender. Either of these considerations may be more important to the owners than anything else. It may be thought that those in business are not so gullible, but all business people are not necessarily well acquainted with accounting customs. In fact, many small businesses are bought, or money is lent to them, without the expert advice of someone well versed in accounting.

6 **Remuneration purposes.** Where someone managing a business is paid in whole or in part by reference to the profits earned, then one basis may suit them better than others. They may therefore strive to have that basis used to suit their own ends. The owner, however, may try to follow another course to minimise the remuneration that he/she will have to pay out.

7 **Lack of information.** If proper stock records have not been kept, then such bases as the average cost method or the LIFO method may not be calculable using the approaches you learnt at the start of this chapter. Of course, a lack of proper stock records makes it very difficult to detect theft or losses of stock. If for no other reason than to enable these factors to be controlled, proper stock records should be kept by all trading businesses. As a result, this barrier to adopting AVCO and LIFO should not arise very often.

8 **Advice of the auditors.** Auditors are accountants who review the accounting records and the financial statements in order to report whether or not the financial statements present a true and fair view of the financial performance and financial position of a business. Many businesses use a particular basis because the auditors advised its use in the first instance. A different auditor may well advise that a different basis be used.

29.11 The conflict of aims

The list given in the previous section of some of the factors which affect decisions is certainly not exhaustive, but it does illustrate the fact that stock valuation is usually a compromise. There is not usually only one figure which is true and fair, there must be a variety of possibilities. Therefore the desire to borrow money and, in so doing, to paint a good picture by being reasonably optimistic in valuing stock will be tempered by the fact that this may increase the tax bill. Stock valuation is, therefore, a compromise between the various ends for which it is to be used.

29.12 Work in progress

The valuation of work in progress is subject to all the various criteria and methods used in valuing stock. Probably the cost element is more strongly pronounced than in stock valuation, as it is very often impossible or irrelevant to say what net realisable value or replacement price would be applicable to partly finished goods. Businesses operating in industries such as those which have contracts covering several years have evolved their own methods.

The valuation of long-term contract work in progress is regulated by SSAP 9 and is dealt with in *Business Accounting 2*.

29.13 Goods on sale or return

Goods received on sale or return

Sometimes goods may be received from a supplier on a **sale or return** basis. This is, for example, typically what happens when newsagents purchase newspapers. What this means is that the goods do not have to be paid for if they are not sold. If they cannot be sold, they are returned to the supplier. This means that until the goods are sold they belong to the seller, *not* the buyer.

The effect of an arrangement of this type is that there really isn't a liability to pay the seller until the goods have been sold on to a customer of the buyer. If there is no liability, the buyer cannot recognise the existence of the goods held on this basis when the buyer's financial statements are being prepared at the end of the accounting period. As a result, if goods on sale or return are held by the buyer at the stocktaking date, they should not be included in the buyer's stock valuation, nor in the figure for purchases.

Goods sent to our customers on sale or return

If a seller sends goods to a customer on a sale or return basis, the goods will continue to belong to the seller until they are sold on by the buyer. At the end of the supplier's accounting period, any goods held on this basis by its customers should be included in the seller's stock valuation, not in the figure for sales.

29.14 Stocktaking and the balance sheet date

All but the very smallest of trading businesses need to physically check that the stock their records tell them are held in stock actually exist. The process of doing so is called **stocktaking**. Students often think that all the counting and valuing of stock is done on the last day of the accounting period. This might be true in a small business, but it is often impossible in larger businesses. There may be too many items of stock to do it so quickly.

This means that stocktaking may take place over a period of days. To convert the physical stocktake stock levels to their actual levels at the balance sheet date, adjustments must be made to those stocktake levels of stock. Exhibit 29.4 gives an example of such adjustments.

Exhibit 29.4

Lee Ltd has a financial year which ends on 31 December 20X7. The stocktaking is not done until 8 January 20X8. When the items in stock on that date are priced out at cost, it is found that the stock value amounts to £28,850. The following information is available about transactions between 31 December 20X7 and 8 January 20X8:

1 Purchases since 31 December 20X7 amounted to £2,370 at cost.
2 Returns inwards since 31 December 20X7 were £350 at selling price.
3 Sales since 31 December 20X7 amounted to £3,800 at selling price.
4 The selling price is always cost price + 25 per cent.

Lee Ltd
Computation of stock as on 31 December 20X7

			£
Stock (at cost)			28,850
Add Items which were in stock on 31 December 20X7 (at cost)			
		£	
Sales		3,800	
Less Profit content (20 per cent of selling price)(note 1)		(760)	
			3,040
			31,890
Less Items which were not in stock on 31 December 20X7 (at cost)			
	£		
Returns inwards	350		
Less Profit content (20 per cent of selling price)(note 1)	(70)		
		280	
Purchases (at cost)		2,370	
			(2,650)
Stock in hand as on 31 December 20X7			29,240

Note 1: Stock is valued at cost (or net realisable value), and not at selling price. As this calculation has a sales figure in it which includes profit, we must deduct the profit part to get to the cost price. This is true also for returns inwards.

At one time, it was very rare for the auditors to attend at stocktaking time as observers. The professional accounting bodies now encourage the auditors to be present if at all possible.

29.15 Stock levels

One of the most common faults found in the running of a business is that too high a level of stock is maintained.

A considerable number of businesses that have problems with a shortage of finance will find that they can help matters by having a sensible look at the amounts of stock they hold. It would be a very rare business indeed which, if they had not investigated the matter previously, could not manage to let parts of their stock run down. As this would save spending cash on items that are not really needed, this cash could be better utilised elsewhere.

Learning outcomes

You should now have learnt:

1 That methods of valuing stocks, such as FIFO, LIFO, and AVCO, are only that – methods of *valuing* stocks. It does not mean that goods are *physically* sold on a FIFO or LIFO basis.

2 That because different methods of valuing stock result in different closing stock valuations, the amount of profit reported for a particular accounting period is affected by the method of stock valuation adopted.

3 That using net realisable when this is lower than cost, so that profits are not overstated, is an example of the prudence concept in accounting.

4 That many subjective factors may affect the choice of stock valuation method adopted.

5 That without stock records of quantities of items, it would be very difficult to track down theft or losses or to detect wastage of goods.

▶

6 That without proper stock records, it is unlikely that AVCO and LIFO can be applied in the way described at the start of this chapter.

7 That goods sold on sale or return should be included in the stock of the seller until the buyer has sold them.

8 That stocktaking is usually done over a period of time around the end of the accounting period.

9 That the stock levels identified at a stocktake need to be adjusted to the level they would have been at had the stocktake taken place on the balance sheet date.

Answers to activities

29.1 This is not as easy a question to answer as it first appears, especially if you have never studied this topic before. Firstly, applying the historic cost convention you learnt about in Chapter 10, we should value the stock at the cost of having it available for sale. That is, it should be valued at cost. If all purchases during the year cost the same per unit, arriving at the value to place on stock would be trivially easy. For example, if all of the units cost £30 each, the closing stock would be $8 \times £30 = £240$.

However, the goods in this example have been purchased at different prices. To cope with this, we look at it from the perspective of which of the goods purchased have been sold. Knowing which of them has been sold allows us to know which ones remain unsold, which will make valuing the stock very straightforward. In this case, purchases were made at £30, £34, and £40. If all the £34 and £40 purchases have been sold, we know to use £30 as the unit cost of the stock.

Unfortunately, many businesses do not know whether they have sold all the older units before they sell the newer units. For instance, a business selling spanners may not know if the older spanners had been sold before the newer ones were sold. A petrol station doesn't know whether all the fuel it has in stock was from one delivery or is a mixture of all the deliveries received from the supplier. Accounting deals with this by selecting the method of valuation that is most likely to fairly represent the cost of the goods sold and, hence, the value of the remaining stock.

To answer the question, you don't have enough information to decide what value to place on the 8 units of stock, but it should be based upon the best estimate you can make of the cost of those 8 units.

29.2 As at least 8 units were received in the last batch purchased, you can simply take the unit cost of that batch and multiply it by the units in stock. If you are asked to show your workings for calculation of closing stock under FIFO, this is a perfectly acceptable approach to adopt.

29.3 It's not so simple under LIFO. If you receive three batches of purchases of 10, 4, and 6 units respectively and you have 10 left in stock, there is no guarantee that they will all be from the first batch. You may have sold all 10 of the first batch before the second batch was received. Alternatively, you may have sold 3 before the second batch of 4 was delivered and then sold 6 before the last batch of 6 was received and then sold 1 before the year end. You do have 10 in stock, but 5 are from the first batch received and 5 from the last one. There is no shortcut available under for ascertaining in which batch the remaining stock was received.

29.4 There have been no further deliveries of new stock received so the average value of stock is still £37.

29.5 The AVCO stock valuation is between the values of FIFO and LIFO. FIFO has the highest value because the cost of purchases has been rising. Had they been falling, it would have been LIFO that had the greatest closing stock value. AVCO will lie between the other two whichever way prices are moving.

29.6 (a) Gross profit will be understated if closing stock is undervalued because the lower the value of closing stock, the higher the cost of goods sold.

(b) Gross profit will be overstated if closing stock is overvalued because the higher the value of closing stock, the lower the cost of goods sold.

29.7 It may be impossible. However, whatever the quality of your stock records, all businesses must retain evidence of their transactions. As a result, you could have a record of what was purchased, when, from whom, and for how much, but you may well have no record at all of what was sold, when, to whom, or for how much – if all sales are for cash, your only record may be the till receipt for each transaction, and that frequently shows no more than the date and value of the sale.

REVIEW QUESTIONS

29.1 From the following figures calculate the closing stock in trade that would be shown using (*i*) FIFO, (*ii*) LIFO, (*iii*) AVCO methods.

Bought		*Sold*	
March	10 at £34 each	December	12 for £56 each
September	20 at £40 each		

29.2 For question 29.1 draw up the trading account for the year showing the gross profits that would have been reported using (*i*) FIFO, (*ii*) LIFO, (*iii*) AVCO methods.

29.3A From the following figures calculate the closing stock-in-trade that would be shown using (*i*) FIFO, (*ii*) LIFO, (*iii*) AVCO methods on a perpetual inventory basis.

Bought		*Sold*	
January	24 at £10 each	June	30 at £16 each
April	16 at £12.50 each	November	34 at £18 each
October	30 at £13 each		

29.4A Draw up trading accounts using each of the three methods from the details in question 29.3A.

29.5 The sixth formers at the Broadway School run a tuck shop business. They began trading on 1 December 20X9 and sell two types of chocolate bar, 'Break' and 'Brunch'.

Their starting capital was a £200 loan from the School Fund.
Transactions are for cash only.
Each Break costs the sixth form 16p and each Brunch costs 12p.
25% is added to the cost to determine the selling price.
Transactions during December are summarised as follows:

December 6 Bought 5 boxes, each containing 48 bars, of Break; and 3 boxes, each containing 36 bars of Brunch.
December 20 The month's sales amounted to 200 Breaks and 90 Brunches.

(*a*) Record the above transactions in the cash, purchases and sales accounts. All calculations must be shown.
(*b*) On 20 December (the final day of term) a physical stocktaking showed 34 Break and 15 Brunch in stock. Using these figures calculate the value of the closing stock, and enter the amount in the stock account.
(*c*) Prepare a trading account for the tuck shop, calculating the gross profit/loss for the month of December 20X9.
(*d*) Calculate the number of each item that should have been in stock. Explain why this information should be a cause for concern.

(*Edexcel, London Examinations: GCSE*)

29.6 Thomas Brown and Partners, a business of practising accountants, have several clients who are retail distributors of the Allgush Paint Spray guns.

The current price list of Gushing Sprayers Limited, manufacturers, quotes the following wholesale prices for the Allgush Paint Spray guns:

Grade A distributors	£500 each
Grade B distributors	£560 each
Grade C distributors	£600 each

The current normal retail price of the Allgush Paint Spray gun is £750.

Thomas Brown and Partners are currently advising some of their clients concerning the valuation of stock in trade of Allgush Paint Spray guns.

1 Charles Gray – Grade B distributor

On 30 April 20X9, 15 Allgush Paint Spray guns were in stock, including 1 gun which was slightly damaged and expected to sell at half the normal retail price. Charles Gray considers that this gun should remain in stock at cost price until it is sold.

K. Peacock, a customer of Charles Gray, was expected to purchase a spray gun on 30 April 20X9, but no agreement was reached owing to the customer being involved in a road accident and expected to remain in hospital until late May 20X9.

Charles Gray argues that he is entitled to regard this as a sale during the year ended 30 April 20X9.

2 Jean Kim – Grade C distributor

On 31 May 20X9, 22 Allgush Paint Spray guns were in stock. Unfortunately Jean Kim's business is suffering a serious cash flow crisis. It is very doubtful that the business will survive and therefore a public auction of the stock in trade is likely. Reliable sources suggest that the spray guns may be auctioned for £510 each; auction fees and expenses are expected to total £300.

Jean Kim has requested advice as to the basis upon which her stock should be valued at 31 May 20X9.

3 Peter Fox – Grade A distributor

Peter Fox now considers that stock valuations should be related to selling prices because of the growing uncertainties of the market for spray guns.

Alternatively, Peter Fox has suggested that he uses the cost prices applicable to Grade C distributors as the basis for stock valuations – 'after all this will establish consistency with Grade C distributors'.

Required:

A brief report to each of Charles Gray, Jean Kim and Peter Fox concerning the valuation of their stocks in trade.

Note: Answers should include references to appropriate accounting concepts.

(*Association of Accounting Technicians*)

29.7A   Mary Smith commenced trading on 1 September 20X9 as a distributor of the Straight Cut garden lawn mower, a relatively new product which is now becoming increasingly popular.

Upon commencing trading, Mary Smith transferred £7,000 from her personal savings to open a business bank account.

Mary Smith's purchases and sales of the Straight Cut garden lawn mower during the three months ended 30 November 20X9 are as follows:

20X9	Bought	Sold
September	12 machines at £384 each	–
October	8 machines at £450 each	4 machines at £560 each
November	16 machines at £489 each	20 machines at £680 each

Assume all purchases are made in the first half of the month and all sales are in the second half of the month.

At the end of October 20X9, Mary Smith decided to take one Straight Cut garden lawn mower out of stock for cutting the lawn outside her showroom. It is estimated that this lawn mower will be used in Mary Smith's business for 8 years and have a nil estimated residual value. Mary Smith wishes to use the straight line basis of depreciation.

Additional information:

1 Overhead expenses paid during the three months ended 30 November 20X9 amounted to £1,520.

2 There were no amounts prepaid on 30 November 20X9, but sales commissions payable of $2\frac{1}{2}\%$ of the gross profit on sales were accrued due on 30 November 20X9.

3 Upon commencing trading, Mary Smith resigned a business appointment with a salary of £15,000 per annum.
4 Mary Smith is able to obtain interest of 10% per annum on her personal savings.
5 One of the lawn mowers not sold on 30 November 20X9 has been damaged in the showroom and is to be repaired in December 20X9 at a cost of £50 before being sold for an expected £400.

Note: Ignore taxation.

Required:
(a) Prepare, in as much detail as possible, Mary Smith's trading and profit and loss account for the quarter ended 30 November 20X9 using:
  (i) the first in first out basis of stock valuation, and
  (ii) the last in first out basis of stock valuation.
(b) Using the results in (a) (i) above, prepare a statement comparing Mary Smith's income for the quarter ended 30 November 20X9 with that for the quarter ended 31 August 20X9.
(c) Give one advantage and one disadvantage of each of the bases of stock valuations used in (a) above.

(*Association of Accounting Technicians*)

29.8 'The idea that stock should be included in accounts at the lower of historical cost and net realisable value follows the prudence convention but not the consistency convention.'

Required:
(a) Do you agree with the quotation?
(b) Explain, with reasons, whether you think this idea (that stocks should be included in accounts at the lower of historical cost and net realisable value) is a useful one. Refer to at least two classes of user of financial accounting reports in your answer.

(*Association of Chartered Certified Accountants*)

29.9A After stocktaking for the year ended 31 May 20X9 had taken place, the closing stock of Cobden Ltd was aggregated to a figure of £87,612.
  During the course of the audit which followed, the undernoted facts were discovered:

(a) Some goods stored outside had been included at their normal cost price of £570. They had, however, deteriorated and would require an estimated £120 to be spent to restore them to their original condition, after which they could be sold for £800.
(b) Some goods had been damaged and were now unsaleable. They could, however, be sold for £110 as spares after repairs estimated at £40 had been carried out. They had originally cost £200.
(c) One stock sheet had been over-added by £126 and another under-added by £72.
(d) Cobden Ltd had received goods costing £2,010 during the last week of May 20X9 but, because the invoices did not arrive until June 20X9, they have not been included in stock.
(e) A stock sheet total of £1,234 had been transferred to the summary sheet as £1,243.
(f) Invoices totalling £638 arrived during the last week of May 20X9 (and were included in purchases and in creditors) but, because of transport delays, the goods did not arrive until late June 20X9 and were not included in closing stock.
(g) Portable generators on hire from another company at a charge of £347 were included, at this figure, in stock.
(h) Free samples sent to Cobden Ltd by various suppliers had been included in stock at the catalogue price of £63.
(i) Goods costing £418 sent to customers on a sale or return basis had been included in stock by Cobden Ltd at their selling price, £602.
(j) Goods sent on a sale or return basis to Cobden Ltd had been included in stock at the amount payable (£267) if retained. No decision to retain had been made.

Required:
Using such of the above information as is relevant, prepare a schedule amending the stock figure as at 31 May 20X9. State your reason for each amendment or for not making an amendment.

(*Association of Chartered Certified Accountants*)

CHAPTER 30

Bank reconciliation statements

Learning objectives

After you have studied this chapter, you should be able to:
- explain why bank reconciliations are done
- reconcile Cash Book balances with bank statement balances
- reconcile ledger accounts to suppliers' statements
- make the necessary entries in the accounts for dishonoured cheques

Introduction

In this chapter, you'll learn how to prepare a bank reconciliation statement and why you need to do this when a bank statement is received from the bank. You also learn how to deal with dishonoured cheques in the accounts.

30.1 Completing entries in the cash book

In the books of a business, funds paid into and out of the bank are entered into the bank columns of the Cash Book. At the same time, the bank will also be recording the flows of funds into and out of the business bank account.

If all the items entered in the Cash Book were the same as those entered in the records held by the bank, the balance on the business bank account as shown in the Cash Book and the balance on the account as shown by the bank's records would be the same.

Unfortunately, it isn't usually that simple, particularly in the case of a current account. There may be items paid into or out of the business bank account which have not been recorded in the Cash Book. And there may be items entered in the Cash Book that have not yet been entered in the bank's records of the account. To see if any of these things have happened, the Cash Book entries need to be compared to the record of the account held by the bank. Banks usually send a copy of that record, called a **bank statement**, to their customers on a regular basis, but a bank statement can be requested by a customer of the bank at any time.

Bank statements should *always* be checked against the Cash Book entries! (And you would be wise to do so yourself with your own bank account.)

Activity 30.1
What might cause the two balances to be different? Spend two minutes making a list.

Let's look at an example of a cash book and a bank statement in Exhibit 30.1:

Exhibit 30.1

Cash Book (bank columns only: *before* balancing on 31.12.20X8)

20X8				£	20X8				£
Dec	1	Balance b/d	✔	250	Dec	5	J Gordon	✔	65
''	20	P Thomas	✔	100	''	27	K Hughes	✔	175
''	28	D Jones	✔	190					

Bank Statement

				Withdrawals £	Deposits £	Balance £
20X8						250
Dec	1	Balance b/d	✔			250
''	8	10625(note 1)	✔	65		185
''	21	Deposit	✔		100	285
''	28	Deposit	✔		190	475
''	29	10626(note 1)	✔	175		300
''	30	Bank Giro credit: P Smith			70	370
''	31	Bank charges		50		320

Note 1: 10625 and 10626 refer to the serial numbers on the cheques paid out.

It is now possible to see that the two items not shown in our Cash Book are:

Bank Giro credit: P Smith	£70
Bank charges	£50

P Smith had paid £70 but, instead of sending a cheque, he paid the money by bank giro credit transfer direct into the business bank account. The business did not know of this until it received the bank statement.

The other item was in respect of bank charges. The bank has charged £50 for keeping the bank account and all the work connected with it. Instead of sending an invoice, the bank has simply taken the money out of the bank account.

Activity 30.2

What sensible rule does this give you relating to when you should balance off the bank account in the Cash Book at the end of the accounting period?

As we have now identified the items missing from the Cash Book, we can now complete writing it up by entering the two items we have identified:

Cash Book (bank columns only: *after* balancing on 31.12.20X8)

20X8			£	20X8			£
Dec	1	Balance b/d	250	Dec	5	J Gordon	65
''	20	P Thomas	100	''	27	K Hughes	175
''	28	D Jones	190	''	**31**	**Bank charges**	**50**
''	**30**	**P Smith**	**70**	''	31	Balance c/d	320
			610				610
20X9							
Jan	1	Balance b/d	320				

Both the bank statement and Cash Book closing balances are now shown as being £320.

30.2   Where closing balances differ

Although a cash book may be kept up to date by a business, it obviously cannot alter the bank's own records. Even after writing up entries in the Cash Book, there may still be a difference between the Cash Book balance and the balance on the bank statement. Exhibit 30.2 shows such a case.

Exhibit 30.2

Cash Book (after being completed to date)

20X9			£	20X9			£
Jan	1	Balance b/d	320	Jan	10	C Morgan	110
''	16	R Lomas	160	''	20	M McCarthy	90
''	24	V Verity	140	''	28	Cheshire CC rates	180
''	31	J Soames	470	''	30	M Peck	200
''	31	R Johnson	90	''	31	Balance c/d	600
			1,180				1,180
Feb	1	Balance b/d	600				

Bank Statement

20X9			Withdrawals £	Deposits £	Balance £
Jan	1	Balance b/d			320
''	12	10627	110		210
''	16	Deposit		160	370
''	23	10628	90		280
''	24	Deposit		140	420
''	28	Direct debit: Cheshire CC	180		240
''	31	Bank Giro credit: R Johnson		90	330

Activity 30.3

Try to identify which items are causing the two balances to be different even after the bank statement has been checked against the Cash Book and the necessary additional entries have been made in the Cash Book. (Hint: there are two items involved.)

You can see that two items are in the Cash Book but are not shown on the bank statement. These are:

(i)   A cheque had been paid to M Peck on January 30. He deposited it in his bank on January 31 but his bank didn't collect the money from the business's bank until February 2. This is known as an **unpresented cheque**.

(ii)   Although a cheque for £470 was received from J Soames on January 31 and the business deposited it with the bank on that date, the bank did not receive the funds from Soames' bank until February. This is known as a 'bank lodgement not yet credited' to the business bank account.

The cash book balance on January 31 was £600, whereas the bank statement shows a balance of £330. To prove that although the balances are different they can be 'reconciled' (i.e. made to agree) with each other, a **bank reconciliation statement** is prepared. It will either start with the bank statement balance and then reconcile it to the Cash Book balance, or it will start with the Cash Book balance and then reconcile it to the bank statement balance. If the second approach is adopted, it would appear as:

Bank Reconciliation Statement as at 31 December 20X8

		£
Balance as per cash book		600
Add Unpresented cheque	(i)	200
		800
Less Bank lodgement not on statement	(ii)	(470)
Balance per bank statement		330

If the two balances cannot be reconciled then there will be an error somewhere. This will have to be located and then corrected.

This reconciliation technique is also used when dealing with other statements drawn up outside the firm: for example, when reconciling purchase ledger accounts to suppliers' statements.

30.3 The bank balance in the balance sheet

The balance to be shown in the balance sheet is that per the Cash Book after it has been written up to date. In Exhibit 30.2, the balance sheet figure would be £600.

This is an important point, and one that students often get wrong! The bank reconciliation shown in the last section is simply verifying that you know why there is a difference between the two balances. It is *not* calculating what the bank account figure in the balance sheet should be because it starts with the balance in the Cash Book *after* adjusting it for items revealed in the bank statement.

30.4 An alternative approach to bank reconciliations

In order to avoid the confusion that may arise concerning what figure to include in the balance sheet, many accountants use a slightly different form of bank reconciliation. In this approach, you take the balance as shown on the bank statement and the balance in the Cash Book *before* making any adjustments that are identified when it is compared to the bank statement. You then reconcile each of them in turn to arrive at the balance that should appear in the balance sheet.

Having completed the reconciliation, you then update the Cash Book so that it balances at the correct amount, i.e. the amount that will be shown in the balance sheet. An example is shown in Exhibit 30.3.

Exhibit 30.3

Cash Book (bank columns only: *before* balancing on 31.12.20X8)

20X8				£	20X8				£
Dec	1	Balance b/d	✔	160	Dec	8	V O'Connor	✔	115
''	12	D Tyrrall	✔	80	''	21	G Francis	✔	35
''	23	P McCarthy	✔	130	''	31	D Barnes		25
''	31	S Aisbitt		72					

Bank Statement

			Withdrawals	Deposits	Balance
20X8			£	£	£
Dec	1	Balance b/d	✔		160
"	11	24621	✔ 115		45
"	14	Deposit	✔	80	125
"	29	Deposit	✔	130	255
"	23	24622	✔ 35		220
"	30	Bank Giro credit: A Parkinson		24	244
"	31	Bank charges	40		204

You can see that the following are missing from the Cash Book:

(*a*) A bank giro credit of £24 made on December 30 by A Parkinson.
(*b*) Bank charges of £40.

And you can see that the following are missing from the bank statement:

(*c*) A cheque paid to D Barnes for £25 on December 31 has not yet been presented.
(*d*) A bank lodgement has not yet been credited – the cheque for £72 received from S Aisbitt on 31 December.

The bank reconciliation statement would be:

Bank Reconciliation Statement as at 31 December 20X8

		£
Balance as per cash book		267
Add Bank giro credit not yet entered	(*a*)	24
		291
Less Bank lodgement not on balance sheet	(*b*)	(40)
Balance in balance sheet		251
Add Cheque not yet presented	(*c*)	25
		276
Less Bank lodgement not on statement	(*d*)	(72)
Balance per bank statement		204

When you have adjustments to make to both the Cash Book and the bank account balances in order to reconcile them, this form of bank reconciliation statement is more useful than one that simply shows that you know why their balances are different (which is all the bank reconciliation statement in Section 30.2 shows).

(An alternative approach that is often used in practice is to start with the balance as per the Cash Book and adjust it to arrive at the balance per the balance sheet (i.e. the same as in the first half of the bank reconciliation statement shown above). You then have a second section that starts with the balance as per the bank statement and adjust it to once again to arrive at the balance per the balance sheet. Either of these two approaches is perfectly acceptable and both provide the same information.)

30.5 Other terms used in banking

1 **Standing Orders.** A firm can instruct its bank to pay regular amounts of money at stated dates to persons or firms. For instance, you may ask your bank to pay £200 a month to a building society to repay a mortgage.
2 **Direct Debits.** These are payments which have to be made, such as gas bills, electricity bills, telephone bills, rates, and insurance premiums. Instead of asking the bank to pay

the money, as with standing orders, you give permission to the creditor to obtain the money directly from your bank account. This is particularly useful if the amounts payable may vary from time to time, as it is the creditor who changes the payments, not you. With standing orders, if the amount is ever to be changed, *you* have to inform the bank. With direct debits it is *the creditor* who informs the bank.

Just as with anything else omitted from the Cash Book, items of these types need to be included in the reconciliation and entered in the Cash Book before balancing it off at the end of the period.

30.6 Bank overdrafts

The adjustment needed to reconcile a bank overdraft according to the firm's books (shown by a credit balance in the Cash Book) with that shown in the bank's records are the same as those needed when the account is not overdrawn.

Exhibit 30.4 is of a Cash Book and a bank statement both showing an overdraft. Only the cheque for G Cumberbatch (A) £106 and the cheque paid to J Kelly (B) £63 need adjusting. Work through the reconciliation statement and then see the note after it. Because the balance shown by the Cash Book is correct (and, therefore, the balance that will appear in the balance sheet), you can use the form of bank reconciliation statement shown in Section 30.2.

Exhibit 30.4

Cash Book

20X8				£	20X8					£
Dec	5	I Howe		308	Dec	1	Balance b/d			709
"	24	L Mason		120	"	9	P Davies			140
"	29	K King		124	"	27	J Kelly	(B)		63
"	31	G Cumberbatch	(A)	106	"	29	United Trust			77
"	31	Balance c/d		380	"	31	Bank charges			49
				1,038						1,038

Bank Statement

20X8			Dr £	Cr £	Balance £
Dec	1	Balance b/d			709 O/D
"	5	Cheque		308	401 O/D
"	14	P Davies	140		541 O/D
"	24	Cheque		120	421 O/D
"	29	K King: Credit transfer		124	297 O/D
"	29	United Trust: Standing order	77		374 O/D
"	31	Bank charges	49		423 O/D

Note: An overdraft is often shown with the letters 'O/D' following the amount. Alternatively, some banks use 'Dr' and 'Cr' after every balance entry to indicate whether the account is overdrawn.

Activity 30.4

Will the bank statement show 'Dr' or 'Cr' if an account is overdrawn?

Bank Reconciliation Statement as at 31 December 20X8

	£
Overdraft as per cash book	(380)
Add Unpresented cheque	63
	(317)
Less Bank lodgement not on bank statement	(106)
Overdraft per bank statement	(423)

Note: You may find it confusing looking at this bank reconciliation statement because the opening entry is an overdraft, i.e. a negative number. Don't be, the adjusting entries are the same as those you make when it is positive:

	£
Balance/overdraft per cash book	xxxx
Adjustments	
Unpresented cheque	Plus
Bank lodgement not on bank statement	Less
Balance/overdraft per bank statement	xxxx

30.7 Dishonoured cheques

When a cheque is received from a customer and paid into the bank, it is recorded on the debit side of the Cash Book. It is also shown on the bank statement as a deposit increasing the balance on the account. However, at a later date it may be found that the customer's bank will not pay the amount due on the cheque. The customer's bank has failed to 'honour' the cheque. The cheque is described as a **dishonoured cheque**.

There are several possible reasons for this. Imagine that K King paid a business with a cheque for £5,000 on 20 May 20X9. The business deposits it at the bank but, a few days later, the bank contacts the business and informs it that the cheque has been dishonoured. Typical reasons are:

1 King had put £5,000 in figures on the cheque, but had written it in words as 'five thousand *five hundred* pounds'. A new cheque correctly completed will need to be provided by King.
2 Normally cheques are considered *stale* six months after the date on the cheque. In other words, banks will not honour cheques over six months old. If King had put the year 20X8 on the cheque instead of 20X9, then King's bank would dishonour the cheque and King would need to be asked for a correctly dated replacement.
3 King simply did not have sufficient funds in her bank account. Suppose she had previously a balance of only £2,000 and yet she has made out a cheque for £5,000. Her bank has not allowed her an overdraft in order to honour the cheque. As a result, the cheque has been dishonoured. The bank inform the business that this has happened and the business would have to contact King, explain what has happened and ask for valid payment of the account.

In all of these cases, the bank would record the original entry in its records as being reversed. This is shown on the bank statement, for example, by the entry 'dishonoured cheque £5,000'. The business then makes the equivalent credit entry in the Cash Book while, at the same time, debiting King's account by the same amount.

When King originally paid the £5,000 the accounts in the ledger and Cash Book would have appeared as:

K King

20X9			£	20X9			£
May	1	Balance b/d	5,000	May	20	Bank	5,000

Bank Account

20X9			£		
May	20	K King	5,000		

After recording the dishonoured cheque, the accounts would be:

K King

20X9			£	20X9			£
May	1	Balance b/d	5,000	May	20	Bank	5,000
May	25	Bank: cheque dishonoured	5,000				

Bank Account

20X9			£	20X9			£
May	20	K King	5,000	May	25	K King: cheque dishonoured	5,000

In other words, King is once again shown as owing the business £5,000.

Learning outcomes

You should now have learnt:

1 Why it is important to perform a bank reconciliation when a bank statement is received.

2 That a bank reconciliation statement should show whether or not errors have been made either in the bank columns of the Cash Book or on the bank statement.

3 That a bank reconciliation statement can be prepared either before or after updating the Cash Book with items omitted from it that are shown on the bank statement.

4 That a bank reconciliation statement prepared after updating the Cash Book with items omitted from it that are shown on the bank statement shows that you know why the bank statement balance is different from that shown in the Cash Book and balance sheet.

5 That a bank reconciliation statement prepared before updating the Cash Book with items omitted from it that are shown on the bank statement is reconciled from Cash Book to balance sheet amount and then to the bank statement. It shows the amount to be entered in the balance sheet and also shows that you know why the bank statement balance is different from the balances shown in the Cash Book and in the balance sheet.

6 That in the case of bank overdrafts, the reconciliation statement adjustments are the same as those shown when there is a positive bank balance, but the opening and closing balances are negative.

7 How to prepare a bank reconciliation statement *after* updating the Cash Book with items omitted from it that are shown on the bank statement.

8 How to prepare a bank reconciliation statement *before* updating the Cash Book with items omitted from it that are shown on the bank statement.

9 Why cheques may be dishonoured and what the effect is upon the bank balance.

10 How to make the appropriate entries to the accounts when a cheque is dishonoured.

Answers to activities

30.1 There is quite a long list of possible causes, including:

- a business may take a day or two to deposit some cheques that it has already entered in the Cash Book
- a cheque may take a few days to be entered in the account of the business held at the bank after it is deposited (because the bank won't recognise the amount received until a few days later, in case there is a problem with it)
- bank interest paid and bank charges often aren't known by a business until a bank statement is received
- bank interest received won't be known by a business until it receives a bank statement
- standing orders may not be written up in the Cash Book of the business until they are identified on the bank statement
- the amount of a direct debit is sometimes not known and so should not be entered in the Cash Book until it is confirmed how much was paid out of the bank account
- customers may pay their accounts by direct transfer from their bank account or by paying cash directly into the business bank account and the business may only learn of their having done so some time later
- there may have been an error made in the Cash Book entries
- the bank may have made an error in operating the account, such as adding funds to it instead of to the account of the person depositing the funds
- a cheque paid into the bank may have 'bounced' (i.e. there were insufficient funds in the writer of the cheque's bank account to make the payment).

30.2 It is wise to wait until receiving the bank statement before balancing off the bank account in the Cash Book at the end of the accounting period. In a manual accounting system, if a Cash Book is balanced on a regular basis, balancing off is usually done at the end of the time period selected and any additional entries are recorded along with the other entries made in the following day, week, month, or quarter. However, at the end of the accounting year, the balancing off is often done in pencil (so that financial statements can be drafted) and then done in ink after any missing entries and corrections of errors have been entered following receipt of the bank statement.

30.3 M Peck £200 and J Soames £470.

30.4 'Dr' indicates an overdraft. The customer is a debtor of the bank. In the customer's balance sheet, the overdraft is included in the current liabilities, indicating that the bank is a creditor. Always remember that a bank is looking at the relationship from the opposite side to the view seen by the customer.

REVIEW QUESTIONS

30.1 From the following draw up a bank reconciliation statement from details as on 31 December 20X6:

	£
Cash at bank as per bank column of the cash book	678
Unpresented cheques	256
Cheques received and paid into the bank, but not yet entered on the bank statement	115
Credit transfers entered as banked on the bank statement but not entered in the cash book	56
Cash at bank as per bank statement	875

30.2A Draw up a bank reconciliation statement, after writing the cash book up to date, ascertaining the balance on the bank statement, from the following as on 31 March 20X9:

	£
Cash at bank as per bank column of the cash book (Dr)	3,896
Bankings made but not yet entered on bank statement	606
Bank charges on bank statement but not yet in cash book	28
Unpresented cheques C Clarke	117
Standing order to ABC Ltd entered on bank statement, but not in cash book	55
Credit transfer from A Wood entered on bank statement, but not yet in cash book	189

30.3 The following are extracts from the cash book and the bank statement of J Roche.

You are required to:
(*a*) Write the cash book up to date, and state the new balance as on 31 December 20X9, and
(*b*) Draw up a bank reconciliation statement as on 31 December 20X9.

Cash Book

20X9		Dr	£	20X9		Cr	£
Dec	1	Balance b/d	1,740	Dec	8	A Dailey	349
''	7	T J Masters	88	''	15	R Mason	33
''	22	J Ellis	73	''	28	G Small	115
''	31	K Wood	249	''	31	Balance c/d	1,831
''	31	M Barrett	178				
			2,328				2,328

Bank Statement

20X9			Dr £	Cr £	Balance £
Dec	1	Balance b/d			1,740
''	7	Cheque		88	1,828
''	11	A Dailey	349		1,479
''	20	R Mason	33		1,446
''	22	Cheque		73	1,519
''	31	Credit transfer: J Walters		54	1,573
''	31	Bank charges	22		1,551

30.4A The bank columns in the cash book for June 20X7 and the bank statement for that month for C Grant are as follows:

Cash Book

20X7		Dr	£	20X7		Cr	£
Jun	1	Balance b/d	2,379	Jun	5	D Blake	150
''	7	B Green	158	''	12	J Gray	433
''	16	A Silver	93	''	16	B Stephens	88
''	28	M Brown	307	''	29	Orange Club	57
''	30	K Black	624	''	30	Balance c/d	2,833
			3,561				3,561

Bank Statement

20X7			Dr £	Cr £	Balance £
Jun	1	Balance b/d			2,379
''	7	Cheque		158	2,537
''	8	D Blackness	150		2,387
''	16	Cheque		93	2,480
''	17	J Gray	433		2,047
''	18	B Stephens	88		1,959
''	28	Cheque		307	2,266
''	29	UDT standing order	44		2,222
''	30	Johnson: trader's credit		90	2,312
''	30	Bank charges	70		2,242

You are required to:

(a) Write the cash book up to date to take the above into account, and then

(b) Draw up a bank reconciliation statement as on 30 June 20X7.

30.5   Read the following and answer the questions below.

On 31 December 20X8 the bank column of C Tench's cash book showed a debit balance of £1,500.

The monthly bank statement written up to 31 December 20X8 showed a credit balance of £2,950.

On checking the cash book with the bank statement it was discovered that the following transactions had not been entered in the cash book:

Dividends of £240 had been paid directly to the bank.
A credit transfer – Customs and Excise VAT refund of £260 – had been collected by the bank.
Bank charges £30.
A direct debit of £70 for the RAC subscription had been paid by the bank.
A standing order of £200 for C Tench's loan repayment had been paid by the bank.
C Tench's deposit account balance of £1,400 was transferred into his bank current account.

A further check revealed the following items:

Two cheques drawn in favour of T Cod £250 and F Haddock £290 had been entered in the cash book but had not been presented for payment.
Cash and cheques amounting to £690 had been paid into the bank on 31 December 20X8 but were not credited by the bank until 2 January 20X9.

(a) Starting with the debit balance of £1,500, bring the cash book (bank columns) up to date and then balance the bank account.

(b) Prepare a bank reconciliation statement as at 31 December 20X8.

(*Midland Examining Group: GCSE*)

30.6A   In the draft accounts for the year ended 31 October 20X9 of Thomas P Lee, garage proprietor, the balance at bank according to the cash book was £894.68 in hand.

Subsequently the following discoveries were made:

(1) Cheque number 176276 dated 3 September 20X9 for £310.84 in favour of G Lowe Limited has been correctly recorded in the bank statement, but included in the cash book payments as £301.84.

(2) Bank commission charged of £169.56 and bank interest charged of £109.10 have been entered in the bank statement on 23 October 20X9, but not included in the cash book.

(3) The recently received bank statement shows that a cheque for £29.31 received from T Andrews and credited in the bank statements on 9 October 20X9 has now been dishonoured and debited in the bank statement on 26 October 20X9. The only entry in the cash book for this cheque records its receipt on 8 October 20X9.

(4) Cheque number 177145 for £15.10 has been recorded twice as a credit in the cash book.

(5) Amounts received in the last few days of October 20X9 totalling £1,895.60 and recorded in the cash book have not been included in the bank statements until 2 November 20X9.

(6) Cheques paid according to the cash book during October 20X9 and totalling £395.80 were not presented for payment to the bank until November 20X9.

(7) Traders' credits totalling £210.10 have been credited in the bank statement on 26 October 20X9, but not yet recorded in the cash book.

(8) A standing order payment of £15.00 on 17 October 20X9 to Countryside Publications has been recorded in the bank statement but is not mentioned in the cash book.

Required:

(a) Prepare a computation of the balance at bank to be included in Thomas P Lee's balance sheet as at 31 October 20X9.

(b) Prepare a bank reconciliation statement as at 31 October 20X9 for Thomas P Lee.

(c) Briefly explain why it is necessary to prepare bank reconciliation statements at accounting year ends.

(*Association of Accounting Technicians*)

30.7   The bank statement for G Greene for the month of March 20X6 is:

20X6			Dr	Cr	Balance
			£	£	£
Mar	1	Balance			5,197 O/D
ʺ	8	L Tulloch	122		5,319 O/D
ʺ	16	Cheque		244	5,075 O/D
ʺ	20	A Bennett	208		5,283 O/D
ʺ	21	Cheque		333	4,950 O/D
ʺ	31	M Turnbull: trader's credit		57	4,893 O/D
ʺ	31	BKS: standing order	49		4,942 O/D
ʺ	31	Bank charges	28		4,970 O/D

The cash book for March 20X6 is:

20X6		Dr	£	20X6		Cr	£
Mar	16	N Marsh	244	Mar	1	Balance b/d	5,197
ʺ	21	K Alexander	333	ʺ	6	L Tulloch	122
ʺ	31	U Sinclair	160	ʺ	30	A Bennett	208
ʺ	31	Balance c/d	5,280	ʺ	30	J Shaw	490
			6,017				6,017

You are to:
(a) Write the cash book up to date, and
(b) Draw up a bank reconciliation statement as on 31 March 20X6.

30.8A   Following is the cash book (bank columns) of E Flynn for December 20X7:

20X7		Dr	£	20X7		Cr	£
Dec	6	J Hall	155	Dec	1	Balance b/d	3,872
ʺ	20	C Walters	189	ʺ	10	P Wood	206
ʺ	31	P Miller	211	ʺ	19	M Roberts	315
ʺ	31	Balance c/d	3,922	ʺ	29	P Phillips	84
			4,477				4,477

The bank statement for the month is:

20X7			Dr	Cr	Balance
			£	£	£
Dec	1	Balance			3,872 O/D
ʺ	6	Cheque		155	3,717 O/D
ʺ	13	P Wood	206		3,923 O/D
ʺ	20	Cheque		189	3,734 O/D
ʺ	22	M Roberts	315		4,049 O/D
ʺ	30	Mercantile: standing order	200		4,249 O/D
ʺ	31	K Saunders: trader's credit		180	4,069 O/D
ʺ	31	Bank charges	65		4,134 O/D

You are required to:
(a) Write the cash book up to date to take the necessary items into account, and
(b) Draw up a bank reconciliation statement as on 31 December 20X7.

Control accounts

After you have studied this chapter, you should be able to:
- explain why control accounts can be useful
- draw up sales ledger control accounts
- draw up purchases ledger control accounts
- reconcile the Purchases Ledger and the Sales Ledger with their respective control accounts

Introduction

In this chapter, you'll learn about the benefits of using control accounts and the process involved in both preparing control accounts and reconciling them to the ledgers.

31.1 The benefits of accounting controls

In any but the smallest business, the accounting system is set up so as to embed controls that help ensure that errors are minimised and that nothing occurs that shouldn't, such as the cashier embezzling funds. One of the tasks undertaken by auditors is to check the various controls that are in place to ensure they are working satisfactorily and one of the things they will look out for is segregation of duties. So, for example, the same person will not both invoice customers and act as cashier when payment is received and, if someone claims reimbursement of an expense, it will be authorised for payment by someone else. Another form of control you've already learnt about involves whether or not customers are allowed to purchase goods on credit.

All these controls are 'organisational'. That is, they do not directly impose controls over the accounting data, nor do they ensure that accounting entries are correct. One control measure that does was covered in Chapter 30 – the process of bank reconciliation. In this chapter, we'll look at another accounting control, **control accounts**.

When all the accounts were kept in one ledger a trial balance could be drawn up as a test of the arithmetical accuracy of the accounts. If the trial balance totals disagree, the books of a small business could easily and quickly be checked so as to find the errors. Of course, as you know, even when the totals do agree, certain types of error may still have occurred, the nature of which makes it impossible for them to be detected in this way. Nevertheless, using a trial balance at least ensures that all the double entries appear, at least, to have been recorded correctly.

Activity 31.1
How do you find errors of the types that a trial balance cannot detect?

When a business has grown and the accounting work has been so divided up that there are several ledgers, any errors could be very difficult to find if a trial balance was the only device used to try to detect errors. Every item in every ledger may need to be checked just to find one error that caused the trial balance not to balance. What is required is a type of trial balance for each ledger, and this requirement is met by control accounts. A control account is a summary account that enables you to see at a glance whether the General Ledger balance for the ledger to which that control account belongs agrees with the total of all the individual accounts held within that ledger.

Using control accounts means that it is only the ledgers whose control accounts do not balance that need detailed checking to find errors.

31.2 Principle of control accounts

The principle on which the control account is based is simple and is as follows: if the opening balance of an account is known, together with information of the additions and deductions entered in the account, the closing balance can be calculated.

Applying this to a complete ledger, the total of opening balances together with the additions and deductions during the period should give the total of closing balances. This can be illustrated by reference to a Sales Ledger for entries for a month.

	£
Total of opening balances, 1 January 20X6	3,000
Add Total of entries which have increased the balances	9,500
	12,500
Less Total of entries which have reduced the balances	(8,000)
Total of closing balances should be	4,500

Because totals are used, control accounts are sometimes known as 'total accounts'. Thus, a control account for a Sales Ledger could be known as either a '**sales ledger control account**' or as a '**total debtors account**'.

Similarly, a control account for a Purchases Ledger could be known either as a '**purchases ledger control account**' or as a '**total creditors account**'.

In larger organisations, the control accounts are often part of the double entry system, with the individual personal accounts for debtors and creditors being treated as being for memorandum purposes only.

In smaller businesses, the control account may be a memorandum entry in the individual ledgers, resulting in a form of trial balance being held in each ledger.

A control account usually looks like any other T-account:

Sales Ledger Control

20X6			£	20X6			£
Jan	1	Balances b/d	x,xxx	Jan	31	Cash book (total of all cheques received from debtors in the period)	x,xxx
''	31	Sales day book (total of sales invoiced in the period)	xx,xxx	''	31	Cash book (total of all cheques received from debtors in the period)	xx,xxx
				''	31	Balances c/d	x,xxx
			xx,xxx				xx,xxx

31.3 Information for control accounts

Exhibits 31.1 and 31.2 list from where information is obtained with which to draw up control accounts.

Exhibit 31.1

Sales Ledger Control	Source
1 Opening debtors	List of debtors' balances drawn up at the end of the previous period
2 Credit sales	Total from the Sales Day Book
3 Returns inwards	Total of the Returns Inwards Day Book
4 Cheques received	Cash Book: bank column on received side. List extracted or the total of a special column for cheques which has been included in the Cash Book
5 Cash received	Cash Book: cash column on received side. List extracted or the total of a special column for cash which has been included in the Cash Book
6 Closing debtors	List of debtors' balances drawn up at the end of the period

Exhibit 31.2

Purchases Ledger Control	Source
1 Opening creditors	List of creditors' balances drawn up at the end of the previous period
2 Credit purchases	Total from Purchases Day Book
3 Returns outwards	Total of Returns Outwards Day Book
4 Cheques paid	Cash Book: bank column on payments side. List extracted or total of a special column for cheques which has been included in the Cash Book
5 Cash paid	Cash Book: cash column on payments side. List extracted or total of a special column for cash which has been included in the Cash Book
6 Closing creditors	List of creditors' balances drawn up at the end of the period

31.4 Form of control accounts

As shown in Section 31.2, control accounts kept in the General Ledger are normally prepared in the same form as an account, with the totals of the debit entries in the ledger on the left-hand side of the control account, and the totals of the various credit entries in the ledger on the right-hand side.

The process is very straightforward. Take the Sales Ledger as an example. The first two steps are identical to those you learnt in Chapters 13 (Cash Books) and 14 (Sales).

(i)   Individual amounts received from debtors are transferred from the Cash Book into the personal accounts in the Sales Ledger. (The double entry is completed automatically in the normal way, because the Cash Book is, in itself, a ledger account.)

(ii) Individual invoice amounts are transferred from the Sales Day Book into the personal accounts in the Sales Ledger. (You would complete the double entry in the normal way, by crediting the Sales Account.)

(iii) The Sales Ledger Control Account would open each period with the total of the debtor balances at the start of the period.

(iv) At the end of the period, you post the totals of all the payments from debtors received during the period from the Cash Book to the credit side of the Sales Ledger Control Account. (This is new.)

(v) This is followed by posting to the debit side of the Sales Ledger Control Account the totals of all new sales during the period shown in the Sales Day Book. (This is new.)

(vi) Balance off the control account.

(vii) Check whether the balance on the control account is equal to the total of all the balances in the Sales Ledger.

If the balance is not the same as the total of all the balances in the Sales Ledger, there is an error either in the totals entered in the control account from the books of original entry or, more likely, somewhere in the Sales Ledger.

Note: You do *not* enter the total of the balances from the Sales Ledger in the Control Account. Instead, you balance off the control account and check whether the balance c/d is the same as the total of all the individual balances in the Sales Ledger.

Activity 31.2

If you look at these seven steps, you can see that the first three are those you learnt to do earlier in the book, so you know that the other part of the double entry has been completed in the normal way. However, what about the double entries for (iv) and (v)? What is the other side of the double entry in each case?

Exhibit 31.3 shows an example of a sales ledger control account for a Sales Ledger in which all the entries are arithmetically correct and the totals transferred from the books of original entry are correct.

Exhibit 31.3

Sales Ledger Control Account data:	£
Debit balances on 1 January 20X6	1,894
Total credit sales for the month	10,290
Cheques received from customers in the month	7,284
Cash received from customers in the month	1,236
Returns inwards from customers during the month	296
Debit balances on 31 January as extracted from the Sales Ledger	3,368

Sales Ledger Control

20X6			£	20X6			£
Jan	1	Balances b/d	1,894	Jan	31	Bank	7,284
''	31	Sales	10,290	''	31	Cash	1,236
				''	31	Returns inwards	296
				''	31	Balances c/d	3,368
			12,184				12,184

We have proved the ledger to be arithmetically correct, because the control account balances with the amount equalling the total of the balances extracted from the Sales Ledger.

Like a trial balance, if the totals of a control account are not equal and the entries made to it were correct (i.e. the amounts transferred to it from the books of original entry have been corrrectly summed), this shows that there is an error somewhere in the ledger.

Exhibit 31.4 shows an example where an error is found to exist in a Purchases Ledger. The ledger will have to be checked in detail, the error found, and the control account then corrected.

Exhibit 31.4

Purchases Ledger Control Account data:	£
Credit balances on 1 January 20X6	3,890
Cheques paid to suppliers during the month	3,620
Returns outwards to suppliers in the month	95
Bought from suppliers in the month	4,936
Credit balances on 31 January as extracted from the Purchases Ledger	5,151

Purchases Ledger Control

20X6			£	20X6			£
Jan	31	Bank	3,620	Jan	1	Balances b/d	3,890
"	31	Returns outwards	95	"	31	Purchases	4,936
"	31	Balances c/d	5,151				
			8,866 (note 1)				8,826 (note 1)

Note 1: Providing all the totals transferred into the Purchases Ledger Control Account from the books of original entry were correct, there is a £40 difference between the debit and credit entries in the Purchases Ledger.

We will have to check the Purchases Ledger in detail to find the error. A double line has not yet been drawn under the totals. We will do this (known as 'ruling off the account') when the error has been found and the totals corrected.

Note: You need to be sure that the totals transferred from the books of original entry were correct before assuming that an out-of-balance control account means that the ledger is incorrect.

31.5 Other advantages of control accounts

Control accounts have merits other than that of locating errors. Normally the control accounts are under the charge of a responsible official, and fraud is made more difficult because transfers made (in an effort) to disguise frauds will have to pass the scrutiny of this person.

In a manual accounting system, the balances on the control account can always be taken to equal debtors and creditors without waiting for an extraction of individual balances. Management control is thereby aided, for the speed at which information is obtained is one of the prerequisites of efficient control.

31.6 Other sources of information for control accounts

With a large organisation there may well be more than one Sales Ledger or Purchases Ledger. The accounts in the Sales Ledgers may be divided up in ways such as:

● Alphabetically. Thus we may have three Sales Ledgers split A–F, G–O and P–Z.
● Geographically. This could be split: Europe, Far East, Africa, Australasia, North and South America.

For each ledger we must therefore have a separate control account. An example of a Columnar Sales Day Book is shown as Exhibit 31.5.

Exhibit 31.5

Columnar Sales Day Book

Date	Details	Total	A–F	G–O	P–Z
			Ledgers		
		£	£	£	£
20X6					
Feb 1	J Archer	58	58		
'' 3	G Gaunt	103		103	
'' 4	T Brown	116	116		
'' 8	C Dunn	205	205		
'' 10	A Smith	16			16
'' 12	P Smith	114			114
'' 15	D Owen	88		88	
'' 18	B Blake	17	17		
'' 22	T Green	1,396		1,396	
'' 27	C Males	48		48	
		2,161	396	1,635	130

The total of the A–F column will be the total sales figures for the Sales Ledger A–F control account, the total of the G–O column for the G–O control account, and so on.

A similar form of analysis can be used in the Purchases Day Book, Returns Inwards Day Book, Returns Outwards Day Book and the Cash Book. The *totals* necessary for each of the control accounts can be obtained from the appropriate columns in these books.

Other items, such as bad debts written off or transfers from one ledger to another, will be found in the Journal, where such items are recorded.

31.7 Other transfers

Transfers to bad debt accounts will have to be recorded in the sales ledger control account as they involve entries in the Sales Ledgers.

Similarly, a contra account, whereby the same entity is both a supplier and a customer, and inter-indebtedness is set off, will also need entering in the control accounts. An example of this follows:

(A) The business has sold A Hughes £600 goods.
(B) Hughes has supplied the business with £880 goods.
(C) The £600 owing by Hughes is set off against £880 owing to him.
(D) This leaves £280 owing to Hughes.

Sales Ledger
A Hughes

		£	
Sales	(A)	600	

Purchases Ledger
A Hughes

			£
	Purchases	(B)	880

The set-off now takes place following the preparation of a journal entry in the Journal:

Sales Ledger
A Hughes

		£			£
Sales	(A)	600	Set-off: Purchases ledger	(C)	600

Purchases Ledger
A Hughes

		£			£
Set-off: Sales ledger	(C)	600	Purchases	(B)	880
Balance c/d	(D)	280			
		880			880
			Balance b/d	(D)	280

The set-off will be posted from the Journal to the credit side of the sales ledger control account and to the debit side of the purchases ledger control account.

31.8 A more complicated example

Exhibit 31.6 shows a worked example of a more complicated control account.

You will see that there are sometimes credit balances in the Sales Ledger as well as debit balances. Suppose for instance we sold £500 goods to W Young, he then paid in full for them, and then afterwards he returned £40 goods to us. This would leave a credit balance of £40 on the account, whereas usually the balances in the Sales Ledger are debit balances.

Exhibit 31.6

20X6			£
Aug	1	Sales ledger – debit balances	3,816
''	1	Sales ledger – credit balances	22
''	31	Transactions for the month:	
		Cash received	104
		Cheques received	6,239
		Sales	7,090
		Bad debts written off	306
		Discounts allowed	298
		Returns inwards	664
		Cash refunded to a customer who had overpaid his account	37
		Dishonoured cheques	29
		Interest charged by us on overdue debt	50
		At the end of the month:	
		Sales ledger – debit balances	3,429
		Sales ledger – credit balances	40

Sales Ledger Control Account

20X6			£	20X6			£
Aug	1	Balances b/d	3,816	Aug	1	Balances b/d	22
''	31	Sales	7,090	''	31	Cash	104
		Cash refunded	37			Bank	6,239
		Bank: dishonoured cheques	29			Bad debts	306
		Interest on debt	50			Discounts allowed	298
		Balances c/d	40			Returns inwards	664
						Balances c/d	3,429
			11,062				11,062

Note that you do *not* net-off the debit and credit balances in the Sales Ledger.

31.9 Control accounts as part of double entry

In larger organisations, it would be normal to find that control accounts are an integral part of the double entry system, the balances of the control accounts being taken for the purpose of extracting a trial balance. The control accounts are kept in the General Ledger. In this case the personal accounts are being used as subsidiary records and the Sales and Purchases Ledgers are memorandum books lying outside the double entry system.

In organisations where the control accounts are not part of the double entry system, the control account is normally kept as a memorandum entry in the individual ledgers. The same entries are made to them at the end of the period as are made if they are part of the double entry system.

31.10 Self-balancing ledgers and adjustment accounts

Because ledgers which have a control account system are proved to be correct as far as the double entry is concerned they used to be called 'self-balancing ledgers'. The control accounts where such terminology were in use were then often called 'adjustment accounts'. These terms are very rarely used nowadays.

31.11 Reconciliation of control accounts

Errors and omissions can occur when entering information into the accounting records. We have seen in Chapter 30 how these are identified and used to reconcile differences between the bank account and the bank statement balances. When a ledger control account is not in balance, it indicates that something has gone wrong with the entries made to the accounting records. This leads to an investigation which (hopefully) reveals the cause(s). Then, in order to verify whether the identified item(s) caused the failure to balance the control account, a reconciliation is carried out.

Exhibit 31.7 shows an example of a **purchases ledger control account reconciliation**. It takes the original control account balance and adjusts it to arrive at an amended balance which should equal the revised total of the source amounts that, together, equal the control account balance.

It can be seen that the general approach is similar to that adopted for bank reconciliation statements. However, as each control account may be constructed using information from a number of sources (see Section 31.3) the extent of the investigation to identify the cause of the control account imbalance is likely to be far greater than that undertaken when performing a bank reconciliation.

Exhibit 31.7

An example of a Purchases Ledger Control Account Reconciliation

	£
Original purchases ledger control account balance	xxx
Add Invoice omitted from control account, but entered in Purchases Ledger	xxx
Supplier balance excluded from Purchases Ledger total because the account had been included in the Sales Ledger by mistake	xxx
Credit sale posted in error to the debit of a Purchases Ledger account instead of the debit of an account in the Sales Ledger	xxx
Under-casting error in calculation of total end of period creditors' balances	xxx
	xxx
Less Customer account with a credit balance included in the Purchases Ledger that should have been included in the Sales Ledger	(xxx)
Return inwards posted in error to the credit of a Purchases Ledger account instead of the credit of an account in the Sales Ledger	(xxx)
Credit note entered in error in the Returns Outwards Day Book as £223 instead of £332	(xxx)
Revised purchases ledger control account balance obtained from revised source amounts	xxx

31.12 Finally

Control accounts are mostly used in manual accounting systems. Most computerised accounting systems automatically provide all the benefits of using control accounts without the necessity of actually maintaining them. This is because computerised accounting systems automatically ensure that all double entries are completed, so ensuring that the ledgers all balance. Of course, errors can still arise, such as a posting made to the wrong ledger account, but not of the type that control accounts can detect.

Learning outcomes

You should now have learnt:

1 How to prepare control accounts.

2 How to prepare a control account reconciliation.

3 That control accounts enable errors to be traced down to the ledger that does not balance. Thus there will be no need to check all the books in full to find an error.

4 That transfers between Sales and Purchases Ledgers should be prepared in the Journal and shown in the control accounts.

5 That control accounts are often part of the double entry system, which means that the Sales Ledger and Purchases Ledger are treated as memorandum books outside the double entry system.

6 That when control accounts are outside the double entry system, they are kept as memorandum accounts in the individual ledgers. The entries to them are the same as for control accounts that lie within the double entry system.

7 That control accounts are normally only used in manual accounting systems.

Answers to activities

31.1 These errors tend to be detected either as the result of someone drawing attention to an entry that appears to be incorrect or as the result of sample checking of the entries that have been made in the accounting books. A debtor may, for example, question whether the amount on an invoice is correctly summed or suggest that one of the invoices listed in the debtor's monthly statement had nothing to do with the debtor. One of the tasks that auditors carry out involves checking a sample of the transactions during a period so as to determine the level of errors within the entries made relating to them. If the level of error detected is considered material, a more extensive check will be carried out.

31.2 (iv) The other side of the double entry was done earlier at the time when the individual amounts received from debtors were posted as credits to the individual debtor accounts in the Sales Ledger. That is, *the other side of this double entry was all the the debit entries to the Cash Book* (see Chapter 13). The posting of each receipt as a credit to the individual debtor accounts done in step (i) is actually a memorandum entry and does not form part of the double entry system. So, in effect, the Sales Ledger has been taken out of the double entry system and is now a Memorandum book. *To summarise, step (iv) is actually the credit side of the double entry whose debit side is all the debit entries in the Cash Book.*

(v) The other side of the double entry was done earlier at the time when each sale was posted from the Sales Day Book to the individual debtors accounts in the Sales Ledger. That is, *the other side of this double entry was the credit entry made when the total of the sales shown in the Sales Day Book was posted to the Sales Account in the General Ledger* (see Chapter 14). The posting of each sale as a debit to the individual debtor accounts done in step (ii) is actually a memorandum entry and does not form part of the double entry system. *To summarise, step (v) is actually the debit side of the double entry whose credit side is all the credit entries in the Sales Account.*

REVIEW QUESTIONS

31.1 You are required to prepare a sales ledger control account from the following for the month of May:

20X6			£
May	1	Sales ledger balances	4,936
		Totals for May:	
		Sales journal	49,916
		Returns inwards journal	1,139
		Cheques and cash received from customers	46,490
		Discounts allowed	1,455
May	31	Sales ledger balances	5,768

31.2A You are required to prepare a purchases ledger control account from the following for the month of June. The balance of the account is to be taken as the amount of creditors as on 30 June.

20X6			£
June	1	Purchases ledger balances	3,676
		Totals for June:	
		Purchases journal	42,257
		Returns outwards journal	1,098
		Cheques paid to suppliers	38,765
		Discounts received from suppliers	887
June	30	Purchases ledger balances	?

31.3 Prepare a sales ledger control account from the following:

20X5			£
May	1	Debit balances	6,420
		Totals for May:	
		Sales journal	12,800
		Cash and cheques received from debtors	10,370
		Discounts allowed	395
		Debit balances in the sales ledger set off against credit	
		balances in the purchases ledger	145
May	31	Debit balances	?
		Credit balances	50

31.4A Prepare a sales ledger control account from the following information for July 20X9, carrying down the balance at 31 July:

20X9			£
July	1	Sales ledger balances	9,700
July	31	Sales journal	99,280
		Bad debts written off	279
		Cheques received from debtors	95,120
		Discounts allowed	1,285
		Cheques dishonoured	226
		Returns inwards	3,170
		Set-offs against balances in purchases ledger	400

31.5 The trial balance of Queen and Square Ltd revealed a difference in the books. In order that the error(s) could be located it was decided to prepare purchases and sales ledger control accounts.

From the following prepare the control accounts and show where an error may have been made:

20X6			£
Jan	1	Purchases ledger balances	11,874
		Sales ledger balances	19,744
		Totals for the year 20X6	
		Purchases journal	154,562
		Sales journal	199,662
		Returns outwards journal	2,648
		Returns inwards journal	4,556
		Cheques paid to suppliers	146,100
		Petty cash paid to suppliers	78
		Cheques and cash received from customers	185,960
		Discounts allowed	5,830
		Discounts received	2,134
		Balances on the sales ledger set off against balances in the purchases ledger	1,036
Dec	31	The list of balances from the purchases ledger shows a total of £14,530 and that from the sales ledger a total of £22,024	

31.6A   The following extracts have been taken from the subsidiary books of the business owned by D Jenkinson for the month of April 20X0.

Purchases Day Book

			£
Apr	3	W Allen	480
	7	J Morris	270
	17	T Sage	410
	24	F Wilding	650

Returns Outwards Day Book

			£
Apr	14	W Allen	50
	29	T Sage	80

Cash Book (Credit side)

			Discounts received £	Bank £
Apr	9	T Sage	30	690
	18	F Wilding	5	195
	24	J Morris	31	389
	27	W Allen	18	322

Journal

			£	£
Apr	30	Creditor W Allen	180	
		Debtor W Allen		180
		being transfer from sales ledger to purchases ledger		

It should be noted that the balances in the accounts of D Jenkinson's suppliers on 1 April 20X0 were as follows:

	£
W Allen	360
J Morris	140
T Sage	720
F Wilding	310

Required:
(a) The name of the source document which will have been used for making entries in the
  (i) purchases day book
  (ii) returns outwards day book.
(b) The name of **two** subsidiary books (other than those shown in the extracts above) which could form part of D Jenkinson's accounting system. In the case of **one** of the subsidiary books chosen, explain its purpose.
(c) The account of T Sage in D Jenkinson's purchases ledger for the month of April 20X0. (The account should be balanced at the end of the month.)
(d) D Jenkinson's purchases ledger control account for the month of April 20X0. (The account should be balanced at the end of the month.)

(e) Advice for D Jenkinson on **two** ways in which he might find the purchases ledger control account useful.

(*Southern Examining Group: GCSE*)

31.7 The financial year of The Better Trading Company ended on 30 November 20X7. You have been asked to prepare a Total Debtors Account and a Total Creditors Account in order to produce end-of-year figures for Debtors and Creditors for the draft final accounts.

You are able to obtain the following information for the financial year from the books of original entry:

		£
Sales	– cash	344,890
	– credit	268,187
Purchases	– cash	14,440
	– credit	496,600
Total receipts from customers		600,570
Total payments to suppliers		503,970
Discounts allowed (all to credit customers)		5,520
Discounts received (all from credit suppliers)		3,510
Refunds given to cash customers		5,070
Balance in the sales ledger set off against balance in the purchases ledger		70
Bad debts written off		780
Increase in the provision for bad debts		90
Credit notes issued to credit customers		4,140
Credit notes received from credit suppliers		1,480

According to the audited financial statements for the previous year debtors and creditors as at 1 December 20X6 were £26,555 and £43,450 respectively.

Required:
Draw up the relevant Total Accounts entering end-of-year totals for debtors and creditors.

(*Association of Accounting Technicians*)

31.8
(a) Why are many accounting systems designed with a purchases ledger (creditors ledger) control account, as well as with a purchases ledger (creditors ledger)?
(b) The following errors have been discovered:
 (i) An invoice for £654 has been entered in the purchases day book as £456;
 (ii) A prompt payment discount of £100 from a creditor had been completely omitted from the accounting records;
 (iii) Purchases of £250 had been entered on the wrong side of a supplier's account in the purchases ledger;
 (iv) No entry had been made to record an agreement to contra an amount owed to X of £600 against an amount owed by X of £400;
 (v) A credit note for £60 had been entered as if it was an invoice.
 State the numerical effect on the purchases ledger control account balance of correcting each of these items (treating each item separately).
(c) Information technology and computerised systems are rapidly increasing in importance in data recording. Do you consider that this trend will eventually remove the need for control accounts to be incorporated in the design of accounting systems? Explain your answer briefly.

(*Association of Chartered Certified Accountants*)

CHAPTER 32

Errors not affecting trial balance agreement

Learning objectives

After you have studied this chapter, you should be able to:
- correct all errors which do not affect trial balance totals being equal
- distinguish between the different kinds of errors that may arise

Introduction

In this chapter, you'll learn how to identify and correct a range of errors that can arise when financial transactions are entered in the ledger accounts.

32.1 Types of error

In Chapter 6 it was seen that if we followed the rules

- every debit entry needs a corresponding credit entry
- every credit entry needs a corresponding debit entry

and entered up our books using these rules then, when we extracted the trial balance, its totals would agree, i.e. it would 'balance'.

Suppose we correctly entered cash sales £70 to the debit of the Cash Book, but did not enter the £70 to the credit of the sales account. If this were the only error in the books, the trial balance totals would differ by £70. However, there are certain kinds of error which would not affect the agreement of the trial balance totals, and we will now consider these:

1 **Errors of omission** – where a transaction is completely omitted from the books. If we sold £90 goods to J Brewer, but did not enter it in either the sales or Brewer's personal account, the trial balance would still 'balance'.

2 **Errors of commission** – this type of error occurs when the correct amount is entered but in the wrong person's account, e.g. where a sale of £11 to C Green is entered in the account of K Green. It will be noted that the correct class of account was used, both the accounts concerned being personal accounts.

3 **Errors of principle** – where an item is entered in the wrong class of account, e.g. if purchase of a fixed asset, such as a van, is debited to an expenses account, such as motor expenses account.

4 **Compensating errors** – where errors cancel each other out. If the sales account was added up to be £10 too much and the purchases account was also added up to be £10 too much, then these two errors would cancel out in the trial balance. This is because the totals of both the debit side and the credit side of the trial balance will be £10 too much.

5 **Errors of original entry** – where the original figure is incorrect, yet double entry is still observed using this incorrect figure. An instance of this could be where there were sales of £150 goods but an error is made in calculating the sales invoice. If it were calculated as £130, and £130 were credited as sales and £130 were debited to the personal account of the customer, the trial balance would still balance.

6 **Complete reversal of entries** – where the correct accounts are used but each item is shown on the wrong side of the account. Suppose we had paid a cheque to D Williams for £200, the double entry of which is Cr Bank £200, Dr D Williams £200. In error it is entered as Cr D Williams £200, Dr Bank £200. The trial balance totals will still agree.

7 **Transposition errors** – where the wrong sequence of the individual characters within a number was entered. For example, £142 entered instead of £124. This is quite a common error and is very difficult to spot when the error has occurred in both the debit and the credit entries, as the trial balance would still balance. (It is more common for this error to occur on one side of the double entry only.)

32.2 Correction of errors

Most errors are found at a date later than the one on which they are first made. When we correct them we should not do so by crossing out items, tearing out accounts and throwing them away, or using chemicals to make the writing disappear.

> *Activity 32.1*
> In which book should all the correcting double entries first be entered?

We make corrections to double entry accounts by preparing journal entries. We should:

1 Show the corrections by means of journal entries, and then
2 Show the corrections in the double entry set of accounts, by posting these journal entries to the ledger accounts affected.

1 Error of omission

The sale of goods, £59 to E George, has been completely omitted from the books. We must correct this by entering the sale in the books. The journal entries for the correction are now shown:[Note]

The Journal

	Dr	Cr
	£	£
E George	59	
Sales account		59
Correction of omission of Sales Invoice Number . . . from sales journal		

Note: in all these examples, the folio column has been omitted so as to make the example clearer.

2 Error of commission

A purchase of goods, £44 from C Simons, was entered in error in C Simpson's account. To correct this, it must be cancelled out of C Simpson's account, and then entered where it should be in C Simons' account. The double entry will be:

C Simpson

20X5	£	20X5	£
Sept 30 C Simons: Error corrected	44	Sept 30 Purchases	44

C Simons

		20X5	£
		Sept 30 Purchases:	
		Entered originally in	
		C Simpson's account	44

The Journal entry will be:

The Journal

	Dr	Cr
	£	£
C Simpson	44	
C Simons		44
Purchase Invoice Number . . . entered in wrong personal account, now corrected		

In fact, the journal entry should be made before the double entry in the accounts is completed. The example was shown as above to make it easier to understand.

3 Error of principle

The purchase of a machine, £200, is debited to the purchases account instead of being debited to a machinery account. We therefore cancel the item out of the purchases account by crediting that account. It is then entered where it should be by debiting the machinery account.

The Journal

	Dr	Cr
	£	£
Machinery account	200	
Purchases account		200
Correction of error: purchase of fixed asset debited to purchases account		

4 Compensating error

The sales account is overcast by £200, as also is the wages account. The trial balance therefore still balances. This assumes that these are the only two errors found in the books.

The Journal

	Dr	Cr
	£	£
Sales account	200	
Wages account		200
Correction of overcasts of £200 each in the sales account and the wages account which compensated for each other		

5 Error of original entry

A sale of £38 to A Smailes was entered in the books as £28. It needs another £10 of sales entering now.

The Journal

	Dr	Cr
	£	£
A Smailes	10	
Sales account		10
Correction of error whereby sales were understated by £10		

6 Complete reversal of entries

A payment of cash of £16 to M Dickson was entered on the receipts side of the Cash Book in error and credited to M Dickson's account. This is somewhat more difficult to adjust. First must come the amount needed to cancel the error, then comes the actual entry itself. Because of this, the correcting entry is double the actual amount first recorded. We can now look at why this is so:

What we should have had:

Cash

			£
		M Dickson	16

M Dickson

	£		
Cash	16		

was entered wrongly as:

Cash

	£		
M Dickson	16		

M Dickson

			£
		Cash	16

We can now see that we have to enter double the original amount to correct the error:

Cash

	£		£
M Dickson	16	M Dickson (error corrected)	32

M Dickson

	£		£
Cash (error corrected)	32	M Dickson	16

Overall, when corrected, the £16 debit and £32 credit in the cash account means there is a net credit of £16. Similarly, Dickson's account shows £32 debit and £16 credit, a net debit of £16. As the final (net) answer is the same as what should have been entered originally, the error is now corrected.

The Journal entry appears:

The Journal

	Dr	Cr
	£	£
M Dickson	32	
Cash		32
Payment of cash £16 debited to cash and credited to		
M Dickson in error on . . . Error now corrected		

7 Transposition error

A credit purchase from P Maclaran costing £56 was entered in the books as £65. The £9 error needs to be removed.

The Journal

	Dr	Cr
	£	£
P Maclaran	9	
Purchases account		9
<u>Correction of error whereby purchases were overstated by £9</u>		

32.3 Casting

You will often notice the use of the expression **casting**, which means adding up. Overcasting means incorrectly adding up a column of figures to give an answer which is greater than it should be. **Undercasting** means incorrectly adding up a column of figures to give an answer which is less than it should be.

Learning outcomes

You should now have learnt:

1 How to describe each of a range of possible errors that can be made when recording financial transactions in the accounts that will not be detected by producing a trial balance.

2 How to identify and correct each of these types of errors.

3 That when errors are found, they should be amended by using proper double entry procedures.

4 That all corrections of errors should take place via the Journal, where entries are first recorded before being posted to the appropriate ledger accounts.

Answer to activity

32.1   The Journal.

REVIEW QUESTIONS

32.1   Show the journal entries necessary to correct the following errors:

(a) A sale of goods £678 to J Harris had been entered in J Hart's account.

(b) The purchase of a machine on credit from L Pyle for £4,390 had been completely omitted from our books.

(c) The purchase of a van £3,800 had been entered in error in the Motor Expenses account.

(d) A sale of £221 to E Fitzwilliam had been entered in the books, both debit and credit, as £212.

(e) Commission received £257 had been entered in error in the Sales account.

(f) A receipt of cash from T Heath £77 had been entered on the credit side of the cash book and the debit side of T Heath's account.

(g) A purchase of goods £189 had been entered in error on the debit side of the Drawings account.

(h) Discounts Allowed £366 had been entered in error on the debit side of the Discounts Received account.

32.2A Show the journal entries needed to correct the following errors:

(a) Purchases £699 on credit from K Ward had been entered in H Wood's account.
(b) A cheque of £189 paid for advertisements had been entered in the cash column of the cash book instead of in the bank column.
(c) Sale of goods £443 on credit to B Gordon had been entered in error in B Gorton's account.
(d) Purchase of goods on credit K Isaacs £89 entered in two places in error as £99.
(e) Cash paid to H Moore £89 entered on the debit side of the cash book and the credit side of H Moore's account.
(f) A sale of fittings £500 had been entered in the Sales account.
(g) Cash withdrawn from bank £100 had been entered in the cash column on the credit side of the cash book, and in the bank column on the debit side.
(h) Purchase of goods £428 has been entered in error in the Fittings account.

32.3 After preparing its draft final accounts for the year ended 31 March 20X6 and its draft balance sheet as at 31 March 20X6 a business discovered that the stock lists used to compute the value of stock as at 31 March 20X6 contained the following entry:

Stock item	Number	Cost per unit	Total cost
Y 4003	100	£1.39	£1,390

Required:
(a) What is wrong with this particular entry?
(b) What would the effect of the error have been on
   (i)   the value of stock as at 31 March 20X6?
   (ii) the cost of goods sold for the year ended 31 March 20X6?
   (iii) the net profit for the year ended 31 March 20X6?
   (iv) the total for Current Assets as at 31 March 20X6?
   (v) the Owner's Capital as at 31 March 20X6?

(Association of Accounting Technicians)

32.4 Give the journal entries needed to record the corrections of the following. Narratives are not required.

(a) Extra capital of £10,000 paid into the bank had been credited to Sales account.
(b) Goods taken for own use £700 had been debited to General Expenses.
(c) Private insurance £89 had been debited to Insurance account.
(d) A purchase of goods from C Kelly £857 had been entered in the books as £587.
(e) Cash banked £390 had been credited to the bank column and debited to the cash column in the cash book.
(f) Cash drawings of £400 had been credited to the bank column of the cash book.
(g) Returns inwards £168 from M McCarthy had been entered in error in J Charlton's account.
(h) A sale of a van for £1,000 had been credited to Motor Expenses.

32.5A Journal entries to correct the following are required, but the narratives can be omitted.

(a) Commissions Received £880 have been credited to Rent Received account.
(b) Bank charges £77 have been debited to Rent account.
(c) Completely omitted from the books is a payment of Sundry Expenses by cheque £23.
(d) A purchase of fixtures £478 has been entered in Purchases account.
(e) Returns inwards £833 have been entered on the debit side of the Returns Outwards account.
(f) A loan from R Smiley £5,000 has been entered on the credit side of the Capital account.
(g) Loan interest of £500 has been debited to Premises account.
(h) Goods taken for own use £250 have been debited to Purchases account and credited to Drawings.

32.6A Thomas Smith, a retail trader, has very limited accounting knowledge. In the absence of his accounting technician, he extracted the following trial balance as at 31 March 20X8 from his business's accounting records:

	£	£
Stock in trade at 1 April 20X7		10,700
Stock in trade at 31 March 20X8	7,800	
Discounts allowed		310
Discounts received	450	
Provision for doubtful debts	960	
Purchases	94,000	
Purchases returns	1,400	
Sales		132,100
Sales returns	1,100	
Freehold property: at cost	70,000	
Provision for depreciation	3,500	
Motor vehicles: at cost	15,000	
Provision for depreciation	4,500	
Capital – Thomas Smith		84,600
Balance at bank	7,100	
Trade debtors		11,300
Trade creditors	7,600	
Establishment and administrative expenditure	16,600	
Drawings	9,000	
	£239,010	£239,010

Required:

(a) Prepare a corrected trial balance as at 31 March 20X8.

After the preparation of the above trial balance, but before the completion of the final accounts for the year ended 31 March 20X8, the following discoveries were made:

(i) The correct valuation of the stock in trade at 1 April 20X7 is £12,000; apparently some stock lists had been mislaid.

(ii) A credit note for £210 has now been received from J Hardwell Limited; this relates to goods returned in December 20X7 by Thomas Smith. However, up to now J Hardwell Limited had not accepted that the goods were not of merchantable quality and Thomas Smith's accounting records did not record the return of the goods.

(iii) Trade sample goods were sent to John Grey in February 20X8. These were free samples, but were charged wrongly at £1,000 to John Grey. A credit note is now being prepared to rectify the error.

(iv) In March 20X8, Thomas Smith painted the inside walls of his stockroom using materials costing £150 which were included in the purchases figure in the above trial balance. Thomas Smith estimates that he saved £800 by doing all the painting himself.

(b) Prepare the journal entries necessary to amend the accounts for the above discoveries. *Note:* narratives are required.

(*Association of Accounting Technicians*)

CHAPTER 33

Suspense accounts and errors

After you have studied this chapter, you should be able to:

- explain why a suspense account may be used
- create a suspense account in order to balance the trial balance
- correct errors using a suspense account
- recalculate profits after errors have been corrected
- explain why using a suspense account is generally inappropriate

Introduction

In this chapter, you'll learn how use suspense accounts to temporarily balance an out-of-balance trial balance. You'll also learn that it is not often a wise thing to do, even temporarily.

33.1 Errors and the trial balance

In the last chapter, we looked at errors that do not affect the trial balance. However, many errors will mean that trial balance totals will not be equal. These include:

- Incorrect additions in any account.
- Making an entry on only one side of the accounts, e.g. a debit but no credit; a credit but no debit.
- Entering a different amount on the debit side from the amount on the credit side.

33.2 Suspense account

We should try very hard to find errors when the trial balance totals are not equal. When they cannot be found, the trial balance totals can be made to agree with each other by inserting the amount of the difference between the two sides in a **suspense account**. This occurs in Exhibit 33.1 where there is a £40 difference.

Exhibit 33.1

Trial Balance as on 31 December 20X5

	Dr	Cr
	£	£
Totals after all the accounts have been listed	100,000	99,960
Suspense account		40
	100,000	100,000

To make the two totals the same, a figure of £40 for the suspense account has been shown on the credit side of the trial balance. A suspense account is opened and the £40 difference is also shown there on the credit side:

Suspense Account

			£
	20X5		
	Dec 31	Difference per trial balance	40

Activity 33.1

Where is the debit side of this entry made?

33.3 Suspense account and the balance sheet

If the errors are not found before the financial statements are prepared, the suspense account balance will be included in the balance sheet. Where the balance is a credit balance, it should be included on the capital and liabilities side of the balance sheet. When the balance is a debit balance it should be shown on the assets side of the balance sheet.

Activity 33.2

Does the use of a suspense account in financial statements affect the true and fair view that they are always meant to portray?

33.4 Correction of errors

When the errors are found they must be corrected, using double entry. Each correction must first have an entry in the journal describing it, and then be posted to the accounts concerned.

One error only

We will look at two examples:

1 Assume that the error of £40 as shown in Exhibit 33.1 is found in the following year on 31 March 20X6. The error was that the sales account was undercast by £40. The action taken to correct this is:

> Debit suspense account to close it: £40.
> Credit sales account to show item where it should have been: £40.

The accounts now appear as Exhibit 33.2.

Exhibit 33.2

Suspense Account

20X6		£	20X5		£
Mar 31	Sales	40	Dec 31	Difference per trial balance	40

Sales

	20X6		£
	Mar 31 Suspense		40

This can be shown in journal form as:

The Journal

		Dr	Cr
20X6		£	£
Mar 31	Suspense	40	
	Sales		40
	Correction of undercasting of sales by £40 in last year's accounts		

2 The trial balance on 31 December 20X6 had a difference of £168. It was a shortage on the debit side.

A suspense account is opened, and the difference of £168 is entered on the debit side. On 31 May 20X7 the error was found. We had made a payment of £168 to K Leek to close his account. It was correctly entered in the Cash Book, but was not entered in K Leek's account.

First of all (A), the account of K Leek is debited with £168, as it should have been in 20X6. Second (B), the suspense account is credited with £168 so that the account can be closed.

K Leek

20X7			£	20X7			£
May 31 Bank	(A)		168	Jan 1 Balance b/d			168

The account of K Leek is now correct.

Suspense Account

20X7		£	20X7			£
Jan 1 Difference per trial balance		168	May 31 K Leek	(B)		168

The Journal entry is:

The Journal

		Dr	Cr
20X7		£	£
May 31	K Leek	168	
	Suspense		168
	Correction of non-entry of payment last year in K Leek's account		

More than one error

We can now look at Exhibit 33.3 where the suspense account difference was caused by more than one error.

Exhibit 33.3

The trial balance at 31 December 20X7 showed a difference of £77, being a shortage on the debit side. A suspense account is opened, and the difference of £77 is entered on the debit side of the account.

On 28 February 20X8 all the errors from the previous year were found.

(A) A cheque of £150 paid to L Kent had been correctly entered in the Cash Book, but had not been entered in Kent's account.

(B) The purchases account had been undercast by £20.

(C) A cheque of £93 received from K Sand had been correctly entered in the Cash Book, but had not been entered in Sand's account.

These three errors resulted in a net error of £77, shown by a debit of £77 on the debit side of the suspense account. These are corrected as follows:

(a) Make correcting entries in accounts for (A), (B) and (C).

(b) Record double entry for these items in the suspense account.

L Kent

20X8			£	
Feb 28 Suspense	(A)		150	

Purchases

20X8			£	
Feb 28 Suspense	(B)		20	

K Sand

			20X8			£
			Feb 28 Suspense	(C)		93

Suspense Account

20X8			£	20X8			£
Jan 1 Balance b/d			77	Feb 28 L Kent	(A)		150
Feb 28 K Sand	(C)		93	Feb 28 Purchases	(B)		20
			170				170

The Journal

		Dr	Cr
20X8		£	£
Feb 28 L Kent		150	
Suspense			150
Cheque paid omitted from Kent's account			
Feb 28 Purchases		20	
Suspense			20
Undercasting of purchases by £20 in last year's accounts			
Feb 28 Suspense		93	
K Sand			93
Cheque received omitted from Sand's account			

Note: Only those errors which make the trial balance totals different from each other can be corrected via the suspense account.

33.5 The effect of errors on profits

Some of the errors will have meant that original profits calculated will be wrong. Other errors will have no effect upon profits. We will use Exhibit 33.4 to illustrate the different kinds of errors.

Exhibit 33.4 shows a set of accounts in which errors have been made.

Exhibit 33.4

K Davis

Trading and Profit and Loss Account for the year ended 31 December 20X5

		£	£
Sales			8,000
Less	Cost of goods sold:		
	Opening stock	500	
	Add Purchases	6,100	
		6,600	
	Less Closing stock	(700)	
			(5,900)
Gross profit			2,100
Add Discounts received			250
			2,350
Less	Expenses:		
	Rent	200	
	Insurance	120	
	Lighting	180	
	Depreciation	250	
			(750)
Net profit			1,600

Balance Sheet as at 31 December 20X5

	£	£
Fixed assets		
Fixtures at cost	2,200	
Less Depreciation to date	(800)	
		1,400
Current assets		
Stock	700	
Debtors	600	
Bank	340	
	1,640	
Less Current liabilities		
Creditors	(600)	
		1,040
Suspense account		60
		2,500
Capital		
Balance as at 1.1.20X5		1,800
Add Net profit		1,600
		3,400
Less Drawings		(900)
		2,500

1 Errors which do not affect profit calculations

If an error affects items only in the balance sheet, then the original calculated profit will not need altering. Exhibit 33.5 shows this.

Exhibit 33.5

Assume that in Exhibit 33.4 the £60 debit balance on the suspense account was because of the following error:

On 1 November 20X5 we paid £60 to a creditor T Monk. It was correctly entered in the Cash Book. It was not entered anywhere else. The error was found on 1 June 20X6.

The journal entries to correct it will be:

The Journal

	Dr	Cr
	£	£
20X6		
June 1 T Monk	60	
Suspense account		60
Payment to T Monk on 1 November 20X5 not		
entered in his account. Correction now made		

Both of these accounts appeared in the balance sheet only with T Monk as part of creditors. The net profit of £1,600 does not have to be changed.

2 Errors which do affect profit calculations

If the error is in one of the figures shown in the trading and profit and loss account, then the original profit will need altering. Exhibit 33.6 shows this.

Exhibit 33.6

Assume that in Exhibit 33.4 the £60 debit balance was because the rent account was added up incorrectly. It should be shown as £260 instead of £200. The error was found on 1 June 20X6. The journal entries to correct it are:

The Journal

	Dr	Cr
	£	£
20X6		
Jun 1 Rent	60	
Suspense		60
Correction of rent undercast last year		

Rent last year should have been increased by £60. This would have reduced net profit by £60. A statement of corrected profit for the year is now shown.

K Davis
Statement of Corrected Net Profit for the year ended 31 December 20X5

	£
Net profit per the accounts	1,600
Less Rent understated	(60)
	1,540

3 Where there have been several errors

If in Exhibit 33.4 there had been four errors in the accounts of K Davis, found on 31 March 20X6, their correction can now be seen. Assume that the net difference had also been £60.

(A) Sales overcast by	£70
(B) Insurance undercast by	£40
(C) Cash received from a debtor entered in the Cash Book only	£50
(D) A purchase of £59 is entered in the books, debit and credit entries as	£95

Note: Error (D) is known as an error of transposition, as the correct figures have been shown in the wrong order, i.e. they have been 'transposed'.

The entries in the suspense account and the journal entries will be as follows:

Suspense Account

20X6				£	20X6				£
Jan	1	Balance b/d		60	Mar	31	Sales	(A)	70
Mar	31	Debtor	(C)	50	''	31	Insurance	(B)	40
				110					110

The Journal

						Dr	Cr
						£	£
20X6							
1	Mar	31	Sales			70	
				Suspense			70
				Sales overcast of £70 in 20X5			
2	Mar	31	Insurance			40	
				Suspense			40
				Insurance expense undercast by £40 in 20X5			
3	Mar	31	Suspense			50	
				Debtor's account			50
				Cash received omitted from debtor's account in 20X5			
4	Mar	31	Creditor's account			36	
				Purchases			36
				Credit purchase of £59 entered both as debit and credit as £95 in 20X5			

Note: In (D), the correction of the overstatement of purchases does *not* pass through the suspense account.

Now we can calculate the corrected net profit for the year 20X5. Only items (A), (B) and (D) affect figures in the trading and profit and loss account. These are the only adjustments to be made to profit.

K Davis
Statement of corrected net profit for the year ended 31 December 20X5

			£
Net profit per the accounts			1,600
Add Purchases overstated	(D)		36
			1,636
Less Sales overcast	(A)	70	
Insurance undercast	(B)	40	
			(110)
Corrected net profit for the year			1,526

Error (C), the cash not posted to a debtor's account, did not affect profit calculations.

33.6 Suspense accounts: businesses and examinations

Businesses

Every attempt should be made to find errors. A suspense account should be opened only if all other efforts have failed, and they *never* should!

Examinations

Unless it is part of a question, *do not* make your balance sheet totals agree by using a suspense account. The same applies to trial balances. Examiners are very likely to penalise you for showing a suspense account when it should not be required.

Overall

Suspense accounts have probably been used ever since people first started keeping accounts and using them to produce financial statements. However, just because suspense accounts have been used for a very long time does not mean that they should still be used today.

Long ago, accounting records were very poorly maintained. The people maintaining them were frequently untrained and, very possibly, self-taught. Errors were fairly common, and no one was very concerned when it proved difficult to find out what had caused a trial balance not to balance, if they even went to the extent of preparing one.

Businesses were largely owned by one person who would often also prepare the financial statements, more out of interest than in order to make much use of what they showed which, before there was some regulation concerning what they presented, was frequently little more than the excess or shortfall of revenue over expenditure.

Nowadays, accounting is far more sophisticated and the people maintaining the accounting records are much better trained. Many organisations use computerised accounting systems and very few organisations of any complexity continue to do everything manually and, when they do, their records will be good enough to make tracing an error reasonably straightforward.

Errors of the types that cause trial balances not to balance are, therefore, much less common and much easier to detect. As a result, it is inconceivable that a suspense account will ever be needed in practice when an accountant is involved in preparing or auditing the financial statements.

Nevertheless, that does not mean it will never happen that circumstances may make it impossible for a sole trader's financial statements to be ready in time to show the bank manager when asking for a loan. It is probably only in circumstances of this type that you may find suspense accounts still in use, albeit rarely. An example may be when money is received by post with no explanation and no information. It needs to be put somewhere in the ledger accounts so a suspense account is used while the reason it was sent to the business is identified.

Learning outcomes

You should now have learnt:

1 How to make the appropriate entries in setting up a suspense account.

2 How to make the correcting entries involving the suspense account when the cause of an error is identified.

3 That some errors may cause the profits originally calculated to have been incorrect.

4 That errors that do not affect profit calculations will have an effect only on items in the balance sheet.

5 That nowadays suspense accounts very rarely need to be used, if at all.

Answers to activities

33.1 This is a major problem in the use of suspense accounts. There is no double entry and, therefore, no debit to match the credit of £40! The justification for this is that there is either a £40 hidden credit somewhere in the accounts that has been omitted when the balances were extracted for the trial balance, or that an extra £40 has been added by mistake to the debit entries in the trial balance. As a result, making this single entry is only completing the existing double entry, the other side being the mistake. Many accountants believe that it is bad practice to open a suspense account as it contravenes the basic principles of double entry. You would be wise to follow that advice and only open a suspense account if an examiner requires you to do so.

33.2   If it is material, definitely. If it is not material, it could be argued that no one will be concerned. However, the appearance of a suspense account in the balance sheet is, by definition, material – you don't include anything in the financial statements as a separate entry that is not of interest to the users of the financial statements. There has been *at least* one error made in the accounting entries and the fact that it cannot be found may indicate a much more serious problem with the accounting system. This is of concern to anyone with a knowledge of accounting, for nowadays when all complex accounting systems are computerised, *no* error should be that difficult to find, no matter how large or complicated the financial system or the organisation.

MULTIPLE CHOICE QUESTIONS: SET 4

Now attempt Set 4 of multiple choice questions. (Answers to all the multiple choice questions are given in Appendix 2 at the end of this book.)

Each of these multiple choice questions has four suggested answers, (A), (B), (C) and (D). You should read each question and then decide which choice is best, either (A) or (B) or (C) or (D). *Write down your answers on a separate piece of paper.* You will then be able to redo the set of questions later without having to try to ignore your answers.

MC61   Working Capital is a term meaning

(A) The amount of capital invested by the proprietor
(B) The excess of the current assets over the current liabilities
(C) The capital less drawings
(D) The total of Fixed Assets – Current Assets.

MC62   A credit balance brought down on a Rent Account means

(A) We owe that rent at that date
(B) We have paid that rent in advance at that date
(C) We have paid too much rent
(D) We have paid too little in rent.

MC63   A debit balance brought down on a Packing Materials Account means

(A) We owe for packing materials
(B) We are owed for packing materials
(C) We have lost money on packing materials
(D) We have a stock of packing materials unused.

MC64   If we take goods for own use we should

(A) Debit Drawings Account: Credit Purchases Account
(B) Debit Purchases Account: Credit Drawings Account
(C) Debit Drawings Account: Credit Stock Account
(D) Debit Sales Account: Credit Stock Account.

MC65   Capital Expenditure is

(A) The extra capital paid in by the proprietor
(B) The costs of running the business on a day-to-day basis
(C) Money spent on buying fixed assets or adding value to them
(D) Money spent on selling fixed assets.

MC66   In the business of C Sangster, who owns a clothing store, which of the following are Capital Expenditure?

(*i*)   Shop fixtures bought
(*ii*)   Wages of assistants
(*iii*)   New van bought
(*iv*)   Petrol for van.

(A)   (*i*) and (*iii*)
(B)   (*i*) and (*ii*)
(C)   (*ii*) and (*iii*)
(D)   (*ii*) and (*iv*).

MC67   If £500 was shown added to Purchases instead of being added to a fixed asset

(A)   Net profit only would be understated
(B)   Net profit only would be overstated
(C)   It would not affect net profit
(D)   Both gross and net profits would be understated.

MC68   A cheque paid by you, but not yet passed through the banking system, is

(A)   A standing order
(B)   A dishonoured cheque
(C)   A credit transfer
(D)   An unpresented cheque.

MC69   A Bank Reconciliation Statement is a statement

(A)   Sent by the bank when the account is overdrawn
(B)   Drawn up by us to verify our cash book balance with the bank statement balance
(C)   Drawn up by the bank to verify the cash book
(D)   Sent by the bank when we have made an error.

MC70   Which of the following are not true? A Bank Reconciliation Statement is

(*i*)   Part of the double entry system
(*ii*)   Not part of the double entry system
(*iii*)   Sent by the firm to the bank
(*iv*)   Posted to the ledger accounts.

(A)   (*i*), (*iii*) and (*iv*)
(B)   (*i*) and (*ii*)
(C)   (*i*), (*ii*) and (*iv*)
(D)   (*ii*), (*iii*) and (*iv*).

MC71   Which of the following should be entered in the Journal?

(*i*)   Payment for cash purchases
(*ii*)   Fixtures bought on credit
(*iii*)   Credit sale of goods
(*iv*)   Sale of surplus machinery.

(A)   (*i*) and (*iv*)
(B)   (*ii*) and (*iii*)
(C)   (*iii*) and (*iv*)
(D)   (*ii*) and (*iv*).

MC72   The Journal is

(A)   Part of the double entry system
(B)   A supplement to the Cash Book

(C) Not part of the double entry system

(D) Used when other journals have been mislaid.

MC73 Given a desired cash float of £200, if £146 is spent in the period, how much will be reimbursed at the end of the period?

(A) £200

(B) £54

(C) £254

(D) £146.

MC74 When a petty cash book is kept there will be

(A) More entries made in the general ledger

(B) Fewer entries made in the general ledger

(C) The same number of entries in the general ledger

(D) No entries made at all in the general ledger for items paid by petty cash.

MC75 Which of the following do *not* affect trial balance agreement?

(*i*)   Sales £105 to A Henry entered in P Henry's account

(*ii*) Cheque payment of £134 for Motor expenses entered only in Cash Book

(*iii*) Purchases £440 from C Browne entered in both accounts as £404

(*iv*) Wages account added up incorrectly, being totalled £10 too much.

(A) (*i*) and (*iv*)

(B) (*i*) and (*iii*)

(C) (*ii*) and (*iii*)

(D) (*iii*) and (*iv*).

MC76 Which of the following are *not* errors of principle?

(*i*)   Motor expenses entered in Motor Vehicles account

(*ii*) Purchases of machinery entered in Purchases account

(*iii*) Sale of £250 to C Phillips completely omitted from books

(*iv*) Sale to A Henriques entered in A Henry's account.

(A) (*ii*) and (*iii*)

(B) (*i*) and (*ii*)

(C) (*iii*) and (*iv*)

(D) (*i*) and (*iv*).

MC77 Errors are corrected via the Journal because

(A) It saves the bookkeeper's time

(B) It saves entering them in the ledger

(C) It is much easier to do

(D) It provides a good record explaining the double entry records.

MC78 Which of these errors would be disclosed by the trial balance?

(A) Cheque £95 from C Smith entered in Smith's account as £59

(B) Selling expenses had been debited to Sales Account

(C) Credit sales of £300 entered in both double entry accounts as £30

(D) A purchase of £250 was omitted entirely from the books.

MC79 If a trial balance totals do *not* agree, the difference must be entered in

(A) The Profit and Loss Account

(B) A Suspense Account

(C) A Nominal Account

(D) The Capital Account.

MC80   What should happen if the balance on a Suspense Account is of a material amount?

(A) Should be written off to the balance sheet
(B) Carry forward the balance to the next period
(C) Find the error(s) before publishing the final accounts
(D) Write it off to Profit and Loss Account.

REVIEW QUESTIONS

33.1   Your bookkeeper extracted a trial balance on 31 December 20X8 which failed to agree by £330, a shortage on the credit side of the trial balance. A suspense account was opened for the difference.

In January 20X9 the following errors made in 20X8 were found:

(*i*)   Sales day book had been undercast by £100.
(*ii*)   Sales of £250 to J Cantrell had been debited in error to J Cochrane's account.
(*iii*) Rent account had been undercast by £70.
(*iv*)   Discounts Received account had been undercast by £300.
(*v*)   The sale of a motor vehicle at book value had been credited in error to Sales account £360.

You are required to:
(*a*) Show the journal entries necessary to correct the errors.
(*b*) Draw up the suspense account after the errors described have been corrected.
(*c*) If the net profit had previously been calculated at £7,900 for the year ended 31 December 20X8, show the calculations of the corrected net profit.

33.2A   You have extracted a trial balance and drawn up accounts for the year ended 31 December 20X6. There was a shortage of £292 on the credit side of the trial balance, a suspense account being opened for that amount.

During 20X7 the following errors made in 20X6 were located:

(*i*)   £55 received from sales of old office equipment has been entered in the sales account.
(*ii*)   Purchases day book had been overcast by £60.
(*iii*) A private purchase of £115 had been included in the business purchases.
(*iv*)   Bank charges £38 entered in the cash book have not been posted to the bank charges account.
(*v*)   A sale of goods to B Cross £690 was correctly entered in the sales book but entered in the personal account as £960.

Required:
(*a*) Show the requisite journal entries to correct the errors.
(*b*) Write up the suspense account showing the correction of the errors.
(*c*) The net profit originally calculated for 20X6 was £11,370. Show your calculation of the correct figure.

33.3   Show how each of the following errors would affect trial balance agreement:

(*i*)   Equipment repairs £720 was debited to the equipment account.
(*ii*)   £1,700 discounts allowed credited to discounts received account.
(*iii*) Stock at close overvalued by £2,000.
(*iv*)   £750 commission received was debited to the sales account.
(*v*)   Drawings £305 credited to the capital account.
(*vi*)   Cheque paying £170 to C Charles entered in cash book but not in personal account.
(*vii*) Cheque £248 from L Barnes credited to L Barrett.

Format should be as follows:

Item	If no effect state 'No'	Debit side exceeds credit side by amount shown	Credit side exceeds debit side by amount shown
(i)			
(ii)			
(iii)			
(iv)			
(v)			
(vi)			
(vii)			

33.4 The following is a trial balance which has been incorrectly drawn up:

Trial Balance – 31 January 20X9

	£	£
Capital 1 February 20X8	5,500	
Drawings	2,800	
Stock 1 February 20X8		2,597
Trade debtors		2,130
Furniture and fittings	1,750	
Cash in hand	1,020	
Trade creditors		2,735
Sales		7,430
Returns inwards		85
Discount received	46	
Business expenses	950	
Purchases	4,380	
	16,446	14,977

In addition to the mistakes evident above, the following errors were also discovered:

1 A payment of £75 made to a creditor had not been posted from the cash book into the purchases ledger.
2 A cheque for £56 received from a customer had been correctly entered in the cash book but posted to the customer's account as £50.
3 A purchase of fittings £120 had been included in the purchases account.
4 The total of the discounts allowed column in the cash book of £38 had not been posted into the general ledger.
5 A page of the sales day book was correctly totalled as £564 but carried forward as £456.

Show the trial balance as it would appear after all the errors had been corrected. You are required to show all workings.

33.5 Study the following and answer the questions below.

The trial balance of Mary Harris (Gowns) as at 31 December 20X8 showed a difference which was posted to a suspense account. Draft final accounts for the year ended 31 December 20X8 were prepared showing a net profit of £47,240. The following errors were subsequently discovered:

● Sales of £450 to C Thomas had been debited to Thomasson Manufacturing Ltd.
● A payment of £275 for telephone charges had been entered on the debit side of the Telephone account as £375.
● The sales journal had been undercast by £2,000.
● Repairs to a machine, amounting to £390, had been charged to Machinery account.
● A cheque for £1,500, being rent received from Atlas Ltd, had only been entered in the cash book.
● Purchases from P Brooks, amounting to £765, had been received on 31 December 20X8 and included in the closing stock at that date, but the invoice had not been entered in the purchases journal.

Questions:
(a) (i) Give the journal entries, without narratives, necessary to correct the above errors.
   (ii) Show the effect of each of these adjustments on the net profit in the draft accounts and the correct profit for the year ended 31 December 20X8.
(b) (i) State briefly the purpose of the journal, giving a suitable example of its use.
   (ii) State why it is necessary to distinguish between capital and revenue expenditure.

(*Midland Examining Group: GCSE*)

33.6A Gail Dawson is the owner of a retail business. She has employed an inexperienced book-keeper to maintain her accounting records.

(a) On 31 March 20X9, the end of the business's accounting year, the bookkeeper extracted the following trial balance from the business's records:

Trial Balance at 31 March 20X9	Dr £	Cr £
Fixed assets at cost	18,300	
Provision for depreciation of fixed assets,		
1 April 20X8	2,800	
Stocks		
1 April 20X8	3,700	
31 March 20X9		2,960
Trade debtors		1,825
Trade creditors	864	
Balance at bank (overdrawn)	382	
Capital		26,860
Drawings	7,740	
Sales	26,080	
Purchases		18,327
Running expenses	6,904	
Provision for doubtful debts	90	
Suspense		16,888
	£66,860	£66,860

Required:
1 A corrected version of Gail Dawson's trial balance dated 31 March 20X9 based on the above information, but with an amended figure for the suspense account.

(b) The following errors were found in the accounting system after a corrected version of the trial balance above was prepared.

   (i)   The total of the sales day book for December 20X8 had been overstated by £120.
   (ii) In January 20X9 some new office equipment had been purchased for £360; this had been debited to the purchases account.
   (iii) A payment by cheque to a creditor, £216, had been entered in the books as £261.
   (iv) A credit note for £37 sent to a customer had been overlooked.
   (v)   The owner had withdrawn a cheque for £80 for private use in October 20X8; both the bank and drawings account had been credited with this amount.

Required:
In the books of Gail Dawson
2 Journal entries to correct each of these errors.
   (**Note:** narratives are NOT required.)
3 The suspense account. (Start with the amount in the corrected trial balance given in answer to Required 1 above, and include any entries arising from the correction of the errors.)
4 An explanation of the term 'error of commission'. (Give an example of such an error to illustrate your answer.)

(*Southern Examining Group: GCSE*)

33.7 The trial balance as at 30 April 20X7 of Timber Products Limited was balanced by the inclusion of the following debit balance:

Difference on trial balance suspense account £2,513.

Subsequent investigations revealed the following errors:

(i) Discounts received of £324 in January 20X7 have been posted to the debit of the discounts allowed account.
(ii) Wages of £2,963 paid in February 20X7 have not been posted from the cash book.
(iii) A remittance of £940 received from K Mitcham in November 20X6 has been posted to the credit of B Mansell Limited.
(iv) In December 20X6, the company took advantage of an opportunity to purchase a large quantity of stationery at a bargain price of £2,000. No adjustments have been made in the accounts for the fact that three-quarters, in value, of this stationery was in stock on 30 April 20X7.
(v) A payment of £341 to J Winters in January 20X7 has been posted in the personal account as £143.
(vi) A remittance of £3,000 received from D North, a credit customer, in April 20X7 has been credited to sales.

The draft accounts for the year ended 30 April 20X7 of Timber Products Limited show a net profit of £24,760.

Timber Products Limited has very few personal accounts and therefore does not maintain either a purchases ledger control account or a sales ledger control account.

Required:
(a) Prepare the difference on trial balance suspense account showing, where appropriate, the entries necessary to correct the accounting errors.
(b) Prepare a computation of the corrected net profit for the year ended 30 April 20X7 following corrections for the above accounting errors.
(c) Outline the principal uses of trial balances.

(*Association of Accounting Technicians*)

33.8A Chi Knitwear Ltd is an old-fashioned firm with a handwritten set of books. A trial balance is extracted at the end of each month, and a profit and loss account and balance sheet are computed. This month, however, the trial balance will not balance, the credits exceeding debits by £1,536.

You are asked to help and after inspection of the ledgers discover the following errors.

(i) A balance of £87 on a debtor's account has been omitted from the schedule of debtors, the total of which was entered as debtors in the trial balance.
(ii) A small piece of machinery purchased for £1,200 had been written off to repairs.
(iii) The receipts side of the cash book had been undercast by £720.
(iv) The total of one page of the sales day book had been carried forward as £8,154, whereas the correct amount was £8,514.
(v) A credit note for £179 received from a supplier had been posted to the wrong side of his account.
(vi) An electricity bill in the sum of £152, not yet accrued for, is discovered in a filing tray.
(vii) Mr Smith, whose past debts to the company had been the subject of a provision, at last paid £731 to clear his account. His personal account has been credited but the cheque has not yet passed through the cash book.

Required:
(a) Write up the suspense account to clear the difference, and
(b) State the effect on the accounts of correcting each error.

(*Association of Chartered Certified Accountants*)

33.9A The trial balance of Happy Bookkeeper Ltd, as produced by its bookkeeper, includes the following items:

Sales ledger control account	£110,172
Purchases ledger control account	£78,266
Suspense account (debit balance)	£2,315

You have been given the following information:

(*i*) The sales ledger debit balances total £111,111 and the credit balances total £1,234.

(*ii*) The purchases ledger credit balances total £77,777 and the debit balances total £1,111.

(*iii*) The sales ledger includes a debit balance of £700 for business X, and the purchases ledger includes a credit balance of £800 relating to the same business X. Only the net amount will eventually be paid.

(*iv*) Included in the credit balance on the sales ledger is a balance of £600 in the name of H Smith. This arose because a sales invoice for £600 had earlier been posted in error from the sales day book to the debit of the account of M Smith in the purchases ledger.

(*v*) An allowance of £300 against some damaged goods had been omitted from the appropriate account in the sales ledger. This allowance had been included in the control account.

(*vi*) An invoice for £456 had been entered in the purchases day book as £654.

(*vii*) A cash receipt from a credit customer for £345 had been entered in the cash book as £245.

(*viii*) The purchases day book had been overcast by £1,000.

(*ix*) The bank balance of £1,200 had been included in the trial balance, in error, as an overdraft.

(*x*) The bookkeeper had been instructed to write off £500 from customer Y's account as a bad debt, and to reduce the provision for doubtful debts by £700. By mistake, however, he had written off £700 from customer Y's account and *increased* the provision for doubtful debts by £500.

(*xi*) The debit balance on the insurance account in the nominal ledger of £3,456 had been included in the trial balance as £3,546.

Required:
Record corrections in the control and suspense accounts. Attempt to reconcile the sales ledger control account with the sales ledger balances, and the purchases ledger control account with the purchases ledger balances. What further action do you recommend?

(*Association of Chartered Certified Accountants*)

PART 5

Special accounting procedures

Introduction

This part is concerned with the accounting procedures that have to be followed with different forms of organisations, and commences with a chapter outlining the basic accounting ratios which may be found necessary at this stage.

CHAPTER 34

Introduction to accounting ratios

Learning objectives

After you have studied this chapter, you should be able to:
- calculate some basic accounting ratios
- use accounting ratios to calculate missing figures in financial statements
- offer some explanations for changes in these ratios over time

Introduction

In this chapter, you'll learn about the relationship between mark-up and margin and how to use the relationship between them and sales revenue and gross profit to find figures that are missing in the trading account. You will also learn how to calculate the stock turnover ratio and some explanations for why these ratios change over time.

34.1 The need for accounting ratios

We will see in, Chapter 47, that accounting ratios are used to enable us to analyse and interpret accounting statements.

This chapter has been inserted at this point in the book simply so that you will be able to deal with the material in Chapter 35 which includes the drawing up of accounts from incomplete records. The ratios described in this chapter will be sufficient for you to deduce the data needed to make the incomplete records into a complete set of records, so that you can then draw up the financial statements. Without the use of such accounting ratios, the construction of financial statements from incomplete records would often be impossible.

> *Activity 34.1*
> What do you think is meant by the term 'incomplete records'?

34.2 Mark-up and margin

The purchase cost, gross profit and selling price of goods or services may be shown as:

$$\boxed{\text{Cost Price} + \text{Gross Profit} = \text{Selling Price}}$$

When shown as a fraction or percentage of the cost price, the gross profit is known as the **mark-up**.

When shown as a fraction or percentage of the selling price, gross profit is known as the **margin**.

We can calculate margin and mark-up using this example:

$$\text{Cost Price} + \text{Gross Profit} = \text{Selling Price}$$
$$\text{£4} \quad + \quad \text{£1} \quad = \text{£5}$$

$\text{Mark-up} = \dfrac{\text{Gross Profit}}{\text{Cost Price}}$ as a fraction, or if required as a percentage, multiply by 100:

$$£\frac{1}{4} = \frac{1}{4}, \quad \text{or } \frac{1}{4} \times 100 = 25 \text{ per cent.}$$

$\text{Margin} = \dfrac{\text{Gross Profit}}{\text{Selling Price}}$ as a fraction, or if required as a percentage, multiply by 100:

$$£\frac{1}{5} = \frac{1}{5}, \quad \text{or } \frac{1}{5} \times 100 = 20 \text{ per cent.}$$

Activity 34.2
Can you see a simple rule connecting mark-up to margin?

34.3 Calculating missing figures

Now we can use these ratios to complete trading accounts where some of the figures are missing. In all the examples in this chapter, we shall

● assume that all the goods in a firm have the same rate of mark-up, and
● ignore wastages and theft of goods.

Example 1
The following figures are for the year 20X5:

	£
Stock 1.1.20X5	400
Stock 31.12.20X5	600
Purchases	5,200

A uniform rate of mark-up of 20% is applied.

Required: find the gross profit and the sales figures.

Firstly, you prepare a Trading Account with the various missing figures shown as blank (or highlighted with a highlight pen, or with '?' inserted where the missing number should go):

Trading Account for the year ended 31 December 20X5

	£	£
Sales		?
Less Cost of goods sold:		
Stock 1.1.20X5	400	
Add Purchases	5,200	
	5,600	
Less Stock 31.12.20X5	(600)	
		(5,000)
Gross profit		?

Answer:

It is known that:	Cost of goods sold + Gross Profit		= Sales
and you know that you can use			
mark-up to find the profit, because:	Cost of goods sold + Percentage Mark-up = Sales		
So:	£5,000	+ 20%	= Sales
So Sales =	£5,000	+ £1,000	= £6,000

The trading account can be completed by inserting the Gross Profit £1,000 and £6,000 for Sales.

Trading Account for the year ended 31 December 20X5

	£	£
Sales		6,000
Less Cost of goods sold:		
Stock 1.1.20X5	400	
Add Purchases	5,200	
	5,600	
Less Stock 31.12.20X5	(600)	
		(5,000)
Gross profit		1,000

Example 2

Another firm has the following figures for 20X6:

	£
Stock 1.1.20X6	500
Stock 31.12.20X6	800
Sales	6,400

A uniform rate of margin of 25% is in use.

Required: find the gross profit and the figure for purchases.

Trading Account for the year ended 31 December 20X6

	£	£
Sales		6,400
Less Cost of goods sold:		
Stock 1.1.20X6	500	
Add Purchases	?	
	?	
Less Stock 31.12.20X6	800	?
Gross profit		?

Answer:	Cost of goods sold + Gross profit = Sales	
Moving items about:	Sales	− Gross profit = Cost of goods sold
	Sales	− 25% margin = Cost of goods sold
	£6,400	− £1,600 = £4,800

Now the following figures are known:

		£	£
Sales			6,400
Less Cost of goods sold:			
Stock 1.1.20X6		500	
Add Purchases	(1)	?	
	(2)	?	
Less Stock 31.12.20X6		(800)	
			(4,800)
Gross profit			1,600

The two missing figures are found by normal arithmetical deduction:

	No (2) less £800	= £4,800
	Therefore No (2)	= £5,600
So that:	£500 opening stock + No (1)	= £5,600
	Therefore No (1)	= £5,100

The completed trading account can now be shown:

Trading Account for the year ended 31 December 20X6

	£	£
Sales		6,400
Less Cost of goods sold:		
Stock 1.1.20X6	500	
Add Purchases	5,100	
	5,600	
Less Stock 31.12.20X6	(800)	
		(4,800)
Gross profit		1,600

This technique is found very useful by retail stores when estimating the amount to be bought if a certain sales target is to be achieved. Alternatively, stock levels or sales figures can be estimated given information as to purchases and opening stock figures.

34.4 The relationship between mark-up and margin

As you learnt in Activity 34.2, both of these figures refer to the same gross profit, but express it as a fraction or a percentage of different figures. This connection through gross profit means that if you know one of the two (mark-up or margin) you will be able to determine the other.

You learnt a simple definition of this relationship in Activity 34.2. Now we'll take it further so that you can use the relationship in any situation.

If the mark-up is known, to find the margin take the same numerator to be numerator of the margin, then for the denominator of the margin take the total of the mark-up's denominator plus the numerator. For example:

Mark-up		*Margin*
$\dfrac{1}{4}$	$\dfrac{1}{4+1} =$	$\dfrac{1}{5}$
$\dfrac{2}{11}$	$\dfrac{2}{11+2} =$	$\dfrac{2}{13}$

If the margin is known, to find the mark-up take the same numerator to be the numerator of the mark-up, then for the denominator of the mark-up take the figure of the margin's denominator less the numerator:

Margin		*Mark-up*
$\dfrac{1}{6}$	$\dfrac{1}{6-1} =$	$\dfrac{1}{5}$
$\dfrac{3}{13}$	$\dfrac{3}{13-3} =$	$\dfrac{3}{10}$

Be sure that you learn this relationship. It is very commonly required in examinations.

34.5 Manager's commission

Managers of businesses are very often remunerated by a basic salary plus a percentage of profits. It is quite common to find the percentage expressed not as a percentage of profits before such commission has been deducted, but as a percentage of the amount remaining after deduction of the commission.

For example, assume that profits before the manager's commission was deducted amounted to £8,400 and that the manager was entitled to 5% of the profits remaining after such commission was deducted. If 5% of £8,400 was taken, this amounts to £420, and the profits remaining would amount to £7,980. However, 5% of £7,980 amounts to £399 so that the answer of £420 is wrong.

The formula to be used to arrive at the correct answer is:

$$\frac{\text{Percentage commission}}{100 + \text{Percentage commission}} \times \text{Profit before commission.}$$

In the above problem this would be used as follows:

$$\frac{5}{100 + 5} \times £8,400 = £400 \text{ manager's commission.}$$

The profits remaining are £8,000 and as £400 represents 5% of it the answer is verified.

> ### Activity 34.3
> The same approach is taken when you want to know the VAT included in a bill you've paid. Assuming a VAT rate of 17.5%, what is the VAT when the total bill is £235?

34.6 Commonly used accounting ratios

There are some ratios that are in common use for the purpose of comparing one period's results against those of a previous period. Two of those most in use are the ratio of gross profit to sales, and the rate of **stock turnover** or 'stockturn'.

Gross profit as percentage of sales

The basic formula is:

$$\frac{\text{Gross Profit}}{\text{Sales}} \times \frac{100}{1} = \text{Gross Profit as percentage of sales.}$$

Put another way, this represents the amount of gross profit for every £100 of sales revenue. If the answer turned out to be 15%, this would mean that for every £100 of sales revenue £15 gross profit was made before any expenses were paid.

This ratio is used as a test of the profitability of the sales. Just because sales revenue has increased does not, of itself, mean that the gross profit will increase.

Activity 34.4
Spend a minute thinking about this and then write down why you think gross profit won't always increase if sales revenue increases.

The trading accounts in Exhibit 34.1 illustrate this.

Exhibit 34.1

Trading Accounts for the year ended 31 December

		20X6		20X7
	£	£	£	£
Sales		7,000		8,000
Less Cost of goods sold:				
Opening stock	500		900	
Add Purchases	6,000		7,200	
	6,500		8,100	
Less Closing stock	(900)		(1,100)	
		(5,600)		(7,000)
Gross profit		1,400		1,000

In the year 20X6 the gross profit as a percentage of sales was

$$\frac{1,400}{7,000} \times \frac{100}{1} = 20 \text{ per cent.}$$

In the year 20X7 it became

$$\frac{1,000}{8,000} \times \frac{100}{1} = 12^{1}/_{2} \text{ per cent.}$$

Sales had increased but, as the gross profit percentage had fallen by a relatively greater amount, the gross profit has fallen. There can be many reasons for such a fall in the gross profit percentage, including:

1 Perhaps the goods being sold have cost more, but the selling price of the goods has not risen to the same extent.
2 There may have been a greater wastage or theft of goods.
3 There could be a difference in how much has been sold of each sort of goods, called the sales-mix, between this year and last, with different kinds of goods carrying different rates of gross profit per £100 of sales.
4 Perhaps in order to increase sales, reductions have been made in the selling price of goods.

(This last one was the example used in Activity 34.4, but any of these possible causes could have been used instead.) These are only some of the possible reasons for the decrease. The idea of calculating the ratio is to show that the profitability per £100 of sales has changed. The firm would then try to find out why and how such a change has taken place.

As the figure of sales revenue less returns inwards is also known as 'turnover', the ratio is sometimes referred to as 'gross profit percentage on turnover'. However, the most frequently used names for it are 'gross profit on sales' and 'gross margin'.

Stock turnover

If we always kept just £100 of stock at cost which, when we sold it, would always sell for £125, and we sold this amount eight times in a year, we would make $8 \times £25 = £200$ gross profit. The quicker we sell our stock (we could say the quicker we turn over our stock) the more the profit we will make, if our gross profit percentage stays the same.

To check on how quickly we are turning over our stock we can use the formula:

$$\frac{\text{Cost of goods sold}}{\text{Average stock}} = \text{Number of times stock is turned over within a period.}$$

Activity 34.5

Spend a minute thinking about this and then write down why you think it might be useful to know how many times we turn over our stock in a period.

It would be best if the average stock held could be calculated by valuing the stock quite a few times each year, then dividing the totals of the figures obtained by the number of valuations. For instance, monthly stock figures are added up and then divided by twelve. This would provide a far more meaningful figure for 'average' stock. However, it is quite common, especially in examinations or in cases where no other information is available, to calculate the average stock as the opening stock plus the closing stock and the answer divided by two. Using the figures in Exhibit 34.1 we can calculate the stock turnover for 20X6 and 20X7:

$$20X6 \qquad \frac{5,600}{(500 + 900) \div 2} = 8 \text{ times per annum}$$

$$20X7 \qquad \frac{7,000}{(900 + 1,100) \div 2} = 7 \text{ times per annum}$$

Instead of saying that the stock turnover is so many times per annum, we could say on average how long we keep stock before we sell it. We do this by the formula:

To express it in months: 12 ÷ Stock turnover = x months
To express it in days: 365 ÷ Stock turnover = x days

From Exhibit 34.1:

	20X6	*20X7*
In months	$\frac{12}{8} = 1.5$ months	$\frac{12}{7} = 1.7$ months
In days	$\frac{365}{8} = 45.6$ days	$\frac{365}{7} = 52.1$ days

All the above figures are rounded off to one decimal place.

When the rate of stock turnover is falling it can be due to such causes as a slowing down of sales activity, or to keeping a higher figure of stock than is really necessary. The ratio does not prove anything by itself, it merely prompts inquiries as to why it should be changing.

This chapter has introduced ratios so as to help you understand the material in the next chapter. In Chapter 47, we will return again to ratios, and cover the topic with a more advanced and detailed survey of what a range of ratios can be used for.

You should now have learnt:

1 That accounting ratios can be used to deduce missing figures, given certain assumptions.
2 That if the mark-up is known, the margin can easily be calculated.
3 That if the margin is known, the mark-up can easily be calculated.
4 How to calculate the gross profit on sales and stock turnover ratios.
5 What may cause these ratios to change over time.

Answers to activities

34.1 Incomplete records exist where a business does not keep detailed accounting records. Perhaps it only operates a cash book, maybe not even that. In these circumstances, accountants have to construct the records that would have existed had a proper set of books been maintained, so that they can then prepare the financial statements. This entails working through invoices, receipts, and bank records, plus any records the business actually kept and trying to identify and record what actually occurred during the period. Because of the logical relationships that exist between many of the items in financial statements, and because of the unambiguous rule of double entry, ratios defining the relationship between various items can be used to assist in this investigation. So, for example, if you know what stock was held at the start, what was purchased and you know what is left in stock at the end, you can easily work out what was sold.

34.2 If you take mark-up and add one to the denominator (the bottom part of the fraction), you get the margin. This is *always* the case when the numerator (the top line) is '1'.

34.3 You use the same formula but replace both the two '5s' in the example with '17.5' and 'Profit before commission' with the total amount of the bill:

$$\frac{17.5}{100 + 17.5} \times £235 = £35$$

This is a *very* useful formula to know. You would be wise to remember it.

34.4 Gross profit may increase at the same rate as sales revenue because demand absorbed more units at the original price. This is normally the case if you make relatively small increases in the volume offered for sale when demand is currently exceeding supply. However, when sales volume increases, it is often partly because selling price has been reduced. Even though total sales volume has increased, sales revenue per unit is less than previously and so gross profit as a percentage of sales revenue will be lower than previously. Unless enough additional units were sold to recover the profit lost as a result of cutting the selling price, total gross profit will fall, not increase.

When a business is in trouble and cutting selling prices to try to make more profits by selling more units, it can often look as if it is doing much better if you only look at the sales revenue and gross profit figures. However, when you calculate the gross profit as a percentage of sales (i.e. the gross margin) and compare it with the previous gross margin, you can see that the business is possibly doing less well than before in terms of overall profitability.

34.5 It is useful to know as you can compare how quickly stock is turning over now compared to the past. If it is turning over more slowly now (i.e. less times in a period than before), stock levels may have grown higher, which may mean that the costs of holding stocks have risen. This rise in stock levels may be due to our now buying more stock every time we place an order – perhaps suppliers are offering discounts for larger sized orders. This may be good, or it may be bad. You need to investigate the situation and find out. Hence, checking the trend in stock turnover alerts you to the possibility that costs may be rising and that they may exceed any savings being made. You can also check your rate of stock turnover with those of your competitors, enabling you to detect if your stock ordering and storing practices are significantly different from theirs. If they are, you would then investigate what is happening so as to ensure you are not wasting resources unnecessarily.

REVIEW QUESTIONS

34.1 R Stubbs is a trader who sells all of his goods at 25% above cost. His books give the following information at 31 December 20X9:

	£
Stock 1 January 20X9	9,872
Stock 31 December 20X9	12,620
Sales for year	60,000

You are required to:
(a) Ascertain cost of goods sold.
(b) Show the value of purchases during the year.
(c) Calculate the profit made by Stubbs.

Show your answer in the form of a trading account.

34.2A C White gives you the following information as at 30 June 20X7:

	£
Stock 1 July 20X6	6,000
Purchases	54,000

White's mark-up is 50% on 'cost of goods sold'. His average stock during the year was £12,000. Draw up a trading and profit and loss account for the year ended 30 June 20X7.

(a) Calculate the closing stock as at 30 June 20X7.
(b) State the total amount of profit and loss expenditure White must not exceed if he is to maintain a *net* profit on sales of 10%.

34.3 J Green's business has a rate of turnover of 7 times. Average stock is £12,600. Mark-up is 50%. Expenses are $66^2/_3$% of gross profit.

You are to calculate:
(a) Cost of goods sold.
(b) Gross profit.
(c) Turnover.
(d) Total expenses.
(e) Net profit.

34.4A The following figures relate to the retail business of J Clarke for the month of May 20X9. Goods which are on sale fall into two categories, A and B.

	Category A	Category B
Sales to the public at manufacturer's recommended list price	£6,000	£14,000
Trade discount allowed to retailers	20%	25%
Total expenses as a percentage of sales	10%	10%
Annual rate of stock turnover	12	20

Calculate for each category:
(a) Cost of goods sold
(b) Gross profit
(c) Total expenses
(d) Net profit
(e) Average stock at cost, assuming that sales are distributed evenly over the year, and that there are twelve equal months in the year.

34.5 The following trading account for the year ended 31 December 20X8 is given to you by H Rayner:

	£	£
Sales		150,000
Less Cost of goods sold:		
Opening stock	20,100	
Add Purchases	129,900	
	150,000	
Less Closing stock	(28,500)	
		(121,500)
Gross profit		28,500

Rayner says that normally he adds 25% to the cost of goods to fix the sales price. However, this year saw some arithmetical errors in these calculations.

(a) Calculate what his sales would have been if he had not made any errors.
(b) Given that his expenses remain constant at 7% of his sales, calculate his net profit for the year 20X8.
(c) Work out the rate of stock turnover for 20X8.
(d) He thinks that next year he can increase his mark-up to $27\frac{1}{2}$%, selling goods which will cost him £140,000. If he does not make any more errors in calculating selling prices, you are to calculate the expected gross and net profits for 20X9.

34.6A   *Trading Account for the year ended 31 December 20X9*

	£		£
Stock 1 January 20X9	3,000	Sales	60,000
Purchases	47,000		
	50,000		
Stock 31 December 20X9	(4,500)		
Cost of sales	45,500		
Gross profit	14,500		
	60,000		60,000

R Sheldon presents you with the trading account set out above.^Author's note He always calculates his selling price by adding $33\frac{1}{3}$% of cost on to the cost price.

(a) If he has adhered strictly to the statement above, what should be the percentage of gross profit to sales?
(b) Calculate his actual percentage of gross profit to sales.
(c) Give two reasons for the difference between the figures you have calculated above.
(d) His suppliers are proposing to increase their prices by 5%, but R Sheldon considers that he would be unwise to increase his selling price. To obtain some impression of the effect on gross profit if his costs should be increased by 5% he asks you to reconstruct his trading account to show the gross profit if the increase had applied from 1 January 20X9.
(e) Using the figures given in the trading account at the beginning of the question, calculate R Sheldon's rate of stock turnover.
(f) R Sheldon's expenses amount to 10% of his sales. Calculate his net profit for the year ended 31 December 20X9.
(g) If all expenses remained unchanged, but suppliers of stock increased their prices by 5% as in (d) above, calculate the percentage reduction in the amount of net profit which R Sheldon's accounts would have shown.

(*Edexcel, London Examinations: GCSE*)

Author's note: **This layout was used a lot in the past. It is not used very much nowadays. You should use the layout in Question 34.5 whenever asked to prepare a trading account.**

CHAPTER 35

Single entry and incomplete records

Learning objectives

After you have studied this chapter, you should be able to:

- deduce the figure of profits where only the increase in capital and details of drawings are known
- draw up a trading and profit and loss account and balance sheet from records not kept on a double entry system
- deduce the figure for cash drawings when all other cash receipts and cash payments are known
- deduce the figures of sales and purchases from incomplete records

Introduction

In this chapter, you'll learn about single entry and incomplete records. You will learn how to use the accounting equation to identify the profit for a period when only the opening and closing capital figures and drawings are known. You will also learn how to find the figure for cash drawings or the figure for cash expenses when all other cash receipts and payments are known. And you will learn how to find the figures for purchases and sales from incomplete records.

35.1 Why double entry is not used

For every small shopkeeper, market stall, Internet cafe, or other small business to keep its books using a full double entry system would be ridiculous. First of all, a large number of the owners of such firms would not know how to write up double entry records, even if they wanted to.

It is more likely that they would enter details of a transaction once only, using a single entry system. Many of them would fail to record every transaction, resulting in incomplete records.

It is, perhaps, only fair to remember that accounting is supposed to be an aid to management – accounting *is not* something to be done as an end in itself. Therefore, many small firms, especially retail shops, can have all the information they want by merely keeping a cash book and having some form of record, not necessarily in double entry form, of their debtors and creditors.

However, despite many small businesses not having any need for accounting records, most do have to prepare financial statements or, at least, calculate their sales or profits at least once a year. How can these be calculated if the bookkeeping records are inadequate or incomplete?

Activity 35.1

What may cause these accounting statements and figures to need to be calculated?

(*i*) profits
(*ii*) sales
(*iii*) financial statements

35.2 Profit as an increase in capital

From your knowledge of the accounting equation, you know that unless there has been an introduction of extra cash or resources into the firm, the only way that capital can be increased is by making profits.

Identifying profits when opening and closing capital are known

If you know the capital at the start of a period and the capital at the end of the period, profit is the figure found by subtracting capital at the start of the period from that at the end of the period.

Let's look at a firm where capital at the end of 20X4 was £2,000. During 20X5 there have been no drawings, and no extra capital has been brought in by the owner. At the end of 20X5 the capital was £3,000.

$$\text{Net profit} = \underset{\text{capital}}{\underset{\text{This year's}}{£3,000}} \ - \ \underset{\text{capital}}{\underset{\text{Last year's}}{£2,000}} \ = £1,000$$

If drawings had been £700, the profits must have been £1,700:

$$\underset{£2,000}{\text{Last year's Capital}} + \underset{?}{\text{Profits}} - \underset{£700}{\text{Drawings}} = \underset{£3,000}{\text{This year's Capital}}$$

We can see that £1,700 profits was the figure needed to complete the formula, filling in the missing figure by normal arithmetical deduction:

$$£2,000 + £1,700 - £700 = £3,000$$

Identifying profits when you only have a list of the opening and closing assets and liabilities

In this case, you use the accounting equation.

Activity 35.2

What is the formula for the accounting equation? Write down both (a) the normal form and (b) the alternate form.

Exhibit 35.1 shows the calculation of profit where insufficient information is available to draft a trading and profit and loss account. The only information available is about the assets and liabilities.

Exhibit 35.1

H Taylor has not kept proper bookkeeping records, but she has kept notes in diary form of the transactions of her business. She is able to give you details of her assets and liabilities as at 31 December 20X5 and 31 December 20X6:

At 31 December 20X5
    Assets: Van £1,000; Fixtures £700; Stock £850; Debtors £950; Bank £1,100; Cash £100.
    Liabilities: Creditors £200; Loan from J Ogden £600.

At 31 December 20X6
    Assets: Van (after depreciation) £800; Fixtures (after depreciation) £630; Stock £990; Debtors £1,240; Bank £1,700; Cash £200.
    Liabilities: Creditors £300; Loan from J Ogden £400; Drawings were £900.

You need to put all these figures into a format that will enable you to identify the profit. Firstly, you need to draw up a **Statement of Affairs** as at 31 December 20X5. This is really just a balance sheet, but is the name used when you are dealing with incomplete records.

From the accounting equation, you know that capital is the difference between the assets and liabilities.

H Taylor
Statement of Affairs as at 31 December 20X5

	£	£
Fixed assets		
Van		1,000
Fixtures		700
		1,700
Current assets		
Stock	850	
Debtors	950	
Bank	1,100	
Cash	100	
	3,000	
Less Current liabilities		
Creditors	(200)	
Net current assets		2,800
		4,500
Less: Long-term liability		
Loan from J Ogden		(600)
Net assets		3,900
Financed by:		
Capital[Note 1]		3,900

Note 1: the accounting equation tells you that this must be the figure to use.

You now draw up a second statement of affairs, this time as at the end of 20X6. The formula of Opening Capital + Profit – Drawings = Closing Capital is then used to deduce the figure of profit.

H Taylor
Statement of Affairs as at 31 December 20X6

	£	£
Fixed assets		
Van		800
Fixtures		630
		1,430
Current assets		
Stock	990	
Debtors	1,240	
Bank	1,700	
Cash	200	
	4,130	
Less Current liabilities		
Creditors	(300)	
Net current assets		3,830
		5,260
Less: Long-term liability		
Loan from J Ogden		(400)
Net assets		4,860
Financed by:		
Capital		
Balance at 1.1.20X6		3,900
Add Net profit	(C)	?
	(B)	?
Less Drawings		(900)
	(A)	

Deduction of net profit:
Opening Capital + Net Profit – Drawings = Closing Capital. Finding the missing figures (A), (B) and (C) by deduction:

(A) is the same as the total of the top half of the balance sheet, i.e. £4,860;
(B) is therefore £4,860 + £900 = £5,760;
(C) is therefore £5,760 – £3,900 = £1,860.

To check:

Capital		
Balance at 1.1.20X6		3,900
Add Net profit	(C)	1,860
	(B)	5,760
Less Drawings		(900)
	(A)	4,860

   Obviously, this method of calculating profit is very unsatisfactory. It is much more informative when a trading and profit and loss account can be drawn up. Therefore, whenever possible, this 'comparisons of capital method' of ascertaining profit should be avoided and a full set of financial statements drawn up from the available records.

   It is important to realise that a business would have exactly the same trading and profit and loss account and balance sheet whether they kept their books by single entry or double entry. However, as you will see, whereas the double entry system uses the trial balance in preparing the financial statements, the single entry system will have to arrive at the same answer by different means.

35.3 Drawing up the financial statements

The following example shows the various stages of drawing up final accounts from a single entry set of records.

The accountant has found the following details of transactions for J Frank's shop for the year ended 31 December 20X5.

(a) The sales are mostly on a credit basis. No record of sales has been made, but £10,000 has been received from persons to whom goods have been sold – £9,500 by cheque and £500 by cash.
(b) Amount paid by cheque to suppliers during the year = £7,200.
(c) Expenses paid during the year: by cheque: Rent £200, General Expenses £180; by cash: Rent £50.
(d) J Frank took £10 cash per week (for 52 weeks) as drawings.
(e) Other information is available:

	At 31.12.20X4	At 31.12.20X5
	£	£
Debtors	1,100	1,320
Creditors for goods	400	650
Rent owing	–	50
Bank balance	1,130	3,050
Cash balance	80	10
Stock	1,590	1,700

(f) The only fixed asset consists of fixtures which were valued at 31 December 20X4 at £800. These are to be depreciated at 10 per cent per annum.

Stage 1: Draw up a Statement of Affairs on the closing day of the previous accounting period:

J Frank
Statement of Affairs as at 31 December 20X4

	£	£
Fixed assets		
Fixtures		800
Current assets		
Stock	1,590	
Debtors	1,100	
Bank	1,130	
Cash	80	
	3,900	
Less Current liabilities		
Creditors	(400)	
Net current assets		3,500
		4,300
Financed by:		
Capital (difference)		4,300

All of these opening figures are then taken into account when drawing up the final accounts for 20X5.

Stage 2: A cash and bank summary, showing the totals of each separate item, plus opening and closing balances, is drawn up.

	Cash	Bank		Cash	Bank
	£	£		£	£
Balances 31.12.20X4	80	1,130	Suppliers		7,200
Receipts from debtors	500	9,500	Rent	50	200
			General Expenses		180
			Drawings	520	
			Balances 31.12.20X5	10	3,050
	580	10,630		580	10,630

Stage 3: Calculate the figures for purchases and sales to be shown in the trading account. Remember that the figures needed are the same as those which would have been found if double entry records had been kept.

Purchases: In double entry, purchases means the goods that have been bought in the period irrespective of whether they have been paid for or not during the period. The figure of payments to suppliers must, therefore, be adjusted to find the figure for purchases.

	£
Paid during the year	7,200
Less Payments made, but which were for goods purchased in a previous year	
(creditors 31.12.20X4)	(400)
	6,800
Add Purchases made in this year for which payment has not yet been made	
(creditors 31.12.20X5)	650
Goods bought in this year, i.e. purchases	7,450

The same answer could have been obtained if the information had been shown in the form of a total creditors account, the figure for purchases being the amount required to make the account totals agree.

Total Creditors

	£		£
Cash paid to suppliers	7,200	Balances b/d	400
Balances c/d	650	Purchases (missing figure)	7,450
	7,850		7,850

Sales: The sales figure will only equal receipts where all the sales are for cash. Therefore, the receipts figures need adjusting to find sales. This can only be done by constructing a total debtors account, the sales figure being the one needed to make the totals agree.

Total Debtors

	£		£
Balances b/d	1,100	Receipts: Cash	500
		Cheque	9,500
Sales (missing figure)	10,220	Balances c/d	1,320
	11,320		11,320

Stage 4: Expenses. Where there are no accruals or prepayments either at the beginning or end of the accounting period, then expenses paid will equal expenses used up during the period. These figures will be charged to the trading and profit and loss account.

On the other hand, where such prepayments or accruals exist, then an expense account should be drawn up for that particular item. When all known items are entered, the missing figure will be the expenses to be charged for the accounting period. In this case, only the rent account needs to be drawn up.

Rent Account

	£		£
Cheques	200	Rent (missing figure)	300
Cash	50		
Accrued c/d	50		
	300		300

Stage 5: Now draw up the financial statements.

J Frank
Trading and Profit and Loss Account for the year ended 31 December 20X5

	£	£
Sales (stage 3)		10,220
Less Cost of goods sold:		
Stock at 1.1.20X5	1,590	
Add Purchases (stage 3)	7,450	
	9,040	
Less Stock at 31.12.20X5	(1,700)	
		(7,340)
Gross profit		2,880
Less Expenses:		
Rent (stage 4)	300	
General expenses	180	
Depreciation: Fixtures	80	
		(560)
Net profit		2,320

Balance Sheet as at 31 December 20X5

	£	£	£
Fixed assets			
Fixtures at 1.1.20X5			800
Less Depreciation			(80)
			720
Current assets			
Stock		1,700	
Debtors		1,320	
Bank		3,050	
Cash		10	
		6,080	
Less Current liabilities			
Creditors	650		
Rent owing	50		
		(700)	
Net current assets			5,380
			6,100
Financed by:			
Capital			
Balance 1.1.20X5 (per Opening Statement of Affairs)			4,300
Add Net profit			2,320
			6,620
Less Drawings			(520)
			6,100

35.4 Incomplete records and missing figures

In practice, part of the information relating to *cash* receipts or payments is often missing. If the missing information is in respect of one type of payment, then it is normal to assume that the missing figure is the amount required to make both totals agree in the *cash* column of the cash and bank summary. (This does not happen with bank items owing to the fact that another copy of the bank statement can always be obtained from the bank.)

Exhibit 35.2 shows an example where the figure for Drawings is unknown. The exhibit also shows the contra entry made in the cash book when cash receipts are banked.

Exhibit 35.2

The following information on cash and bank receipts and payments is available:

	Cash	Bank
	£	£
Cash paid into the bank during the year	5,500	
Receipts from debtors	7,250	800
Paid to suppliers	320	4,930
Drawings during the year	?	–
Expenses paid	150	900
Balances at 1.1.20X5	35	1,200
Balances at 31.12.20X5	50	1,670

Now, you need to enter this information in a cash book:

	Cash	Bank		Cash	Bank
	£	£		£	£
Balances 1.1.20X5	35	1,200	Bankings C (contra entry)	5,500	
Received from debtors	7,250	800	Suppliers	320	4,930
Bankings C (contra entry)		5,500	Expenses	150	900
			Drawings	?	
			Balances 31.12.20X5	50	1,670
	7,285	7,500		7,285	7,500

The amount needed to make the two sides of the cash columns agree is £1,265. This is the figure for drawings.

Exhibit 35.3

Information on cash and bank transactions is available as follows:

	Cash	Bank
	£	£
Receipts from debtors	?	6,080
Cash withdrawn from the bank for business use (this is the amount which is used besides cash receipts from debtors to pay drawings and expenses)		920
Paid to suppliers		5,800
Expenses paid	640	230
Drawings	1,180	315
Balances at 1.1.20X7	40	1,560
Balances at 31.12.20X7	70	375

	Cash	Bank		Cash	Bank
	£	£		£	£
Balances 1.1.20X7	40	1,560	Suppliers		5,800
Received from debtors	?	6,080	Expenses	640	230
Withdrawn from Bank C	920		Withdrawn from Bank C		920
			Drawings	1,180	315
			Balances 31.12.20X7	70	375
	1,890	7,640		1,890	7,640

As it is the only missing item, receipts from debtors is, therefore, the amount needed to make each side of the cash column agree, £930.

It must be emphasised that balancing figures are acceptable *only* when all the other figures have been verified. Should, for instance, a cash expense be omitted when cash received from debtors is being calculated, then this would result in an understatement not only of expenses but also, ultimately, of sales.

35.5 | Where there are two missing pieces of information

Quite often, the only cash expense item for which there is some doubt is drawings. Receipts will normally have been retained for all the others.

If both cash drawings and cash receipts from debtors (or from cash sales) were not known, it would not be possible to deduce both of these figures separately. The only course available would be to estimate whichever figure was more capable of being accurately assessed, use this as a 'known' figure, then deduce the other figure. However, this is a most unsatisfactory position as both of the figures are estimates, the accuracy of each one relying entirely upon the accuracy of the other.

> *Activity 35.3*
> Why is arriving at a figure for drawings that is as accurate as possible *very* important for the owner of a business?

35.6 | Cash sales and purchases for cash

Where there are cash sales as well as sales on credit terms, then the cash sales must be added to sales on credit to give the total sales for the year. This total figure of sales will be the one shown in the trading account.

Similarly, purchases for cash will need to be added to credit purchases in order to produce the figure of total purchases for the trading account.

35.7 | Goods stolen or lost by fire, etc.

When goods are stolen, destroyed by fire, or lost in some other way, their value will have to be calculated. This could be needed to justify an insurance claim or to settle problems concerning taxation, etc.

If the stock had been valued immediately before the fire, burglary, etc, then the value of the stock lost would obviously be known. Also, if a full and detailed system of stock records were kept, then the value would also be known. However, as the occurrence of fires or burglaries cannot be foreseen, and many small businesses do not keep full and proper stock records, the value of the stock lost has to be calculated in some other way.

The methods described in this chapter and in Chapter 34 are used. Bear in mind that you are going to be calculating figures as at the time of the fire or theft, not at the end of the accounting period.

Exhibits 35.4 and 35.5 will now be looked at. The first exhibit involves a very simple case, where figures of purchases and sales are known and all goods are sold at the same gross profit margin. The second exhibit is rather more complicated.

Exhibit 35.4

J Collins lost the whole of his stock in a fire on 17 March 20X9. The last time that a stock-taking had been done was on 31 December 20X8, the last balance sheet date, when stock was valued at cost at £1,950. Purchases from then until 17 March 20X9 amounted to £6,870 and sales in that period were £9,600. All sales were made at a uniform gross profit margin of 20 per cent.

First, the trading account can be drawn up with the known figures included. Then the missing figures can be deduced.

J Collins
Trading Account for the period 1 January 20X9 to 17 March 20X9

		£	£
Sales			9,600
Less Cost of goods sold:			
Opening stock		1,950	
Add Purchases		6,870	
		8,820	
Less Closing stock	(C)	(?)	
	(B)		(?)
Gross profit	(A)		?

Now the missing figures can be deduced:

It is known that the gross profit margin is 20 per cent, therefore gross profit (A) is 20% of £9,600 = £1,920.

Now (B) ? + (A) £1,920 = £9,600, so that (B) is the difference, i.e. £7,680.

Now that (B) is known, (C) can be deduced: £8,820 – (C) ? = £7,680, so (C) is the difference, i.e. £1,140.

The figure for goods destroyed by fire, at cost, is therefore £1,140.

Note: you should always do this calculation in the sequence shown (i.e. A then B then C)

Exhibit 35.5

T Scott had the whole of his stock stolen from his warehouse on the night of 20 August 20X6. Also destroyed were his sales and purchases journals, but the sales and purchases ledgers were salvaged. The following facts are known:

(a) Stock was known at the last balance sheet date, 31 March 20X6, to be £12,480 at cost.
(b) Receipts from debtors during the period 1 April to 20 August 20X6 amounted to £31,745. Debtors were: at 31 March 20X6 £14,278, at 20 August 20X6 £12,333.
(c) Payments to creditors during the period 1 April to 20 August 20X6 amounted to £17,270. Creditors were: at 31 March 20X6 £7,633, at 20 August 20X6 £6,289.
(d) The gross profit margin on all sales has been constant at 25 per cent.

Before we can start to construct a trading account for the period, we need to find out the figures for sales and purchases. These can be found by drawing up total debtors and total creditors accounts, sales and purchases figures being the difference on the accounts.

Total Creditors

	£		£
Cash and bank	17,270	Balances b/d	7,633
Balances c/d	6,289	**Purchases (difference)**	**15,926**
	23,559		23,559

Total Debtors

	£		£
Balances b/d	14,278	Cash and bank	31,745
Sales (difference)	**29,800**	Balances c/d	12,333
	44,078		44,078

> *Activity 35.4*
>
> You already did this for another example earlier in this chapter. Where?

The trading account can now show the figures already known.

Trading Account for the period 1 April to 20 August 20X6

		£		£
Sales				29,800
Less Cost of goods sold:				
Opening stock		12,480		
Add Purchases		15,926		
		28,406		
Less Closing stock	(C)	(?)		
			(B)	(?)
Gross profit			(A)	?

Gross profit can be found, as the margin on sales is known to be 25%, therefore (A) = 25% of £29,800 = £7,450.
Cost of goods sold (B) ? + Gross profit £7,450 = £29,800, therefore (B) is £22,350.
£28,406 – (C) ? = (B) £22,350, therefore (C) is £6,056.
The figure for cost of goods stolen is therefore £6,056.

The completed trading account is, therefore:

Trading Account for the period 1 April to 20 August 20X6

		£		£
Sales				29,800
Less Cost of goods sold:				
Opening stock		12,480		
Add Purchases		15,926		
		28,406		
Less Closing stock	(C)	(6,056)		
			(B)	(22,350)
Gross profit			(A)	7,450

You should now have learnt:

1 The difference between a single entry system and a double entry system.

2 How to calculate net profit for a small trader when you know the change in capital over a period and the amount of drawings during the period.

3 How to prepare a trading and profit and loss account and balance sheet from records not kept on a double entry system.

4 How to deduce the figures for purchases and sales from a total creditors account and a total debtors account.

Answers to activities

35.1 There are a range of possible reasons. Of the three examples shown here, the first must be done once a year, the second must be done from time to time, and the third is done on demand:

(*i*) Profits need to be calculated for the purpose of determining the income tax payable.

(*ii*) Turnover (i.e. sales) needs to be calculated in order to know whether or not the business needs to register for VAT.

(*iii*) Financial statements may be required by the bank.

35.2 (*a*) Capital = Assets – Liabilities
(*b*) Assets = Capital + Liabilities

35.3 Normal practice would be to try to get the owner to list all the cash withdrawn as accurately as possible and then use that figure for drawings. However, care needs to be taken to make this as accurate as possible because the Inland Revenue (the UK tax authority) has very sophisticated data on the relationship between business income and expenditure and profitability, and also on level of income and standard of living enjoyed by a taxpayer. If the owner underestimates drawings this could have very serious repercussions for the owner.

35.4 This is exactly the same as what you did in Section 35.3 Stage 3.

REVIEW QUESTIONS

35.1 B Arkwright started in business on 1 January 20X5 with £10,000 in a bank account. Unfortunately he did not keep proper books of account.

He is forced to submit a calculation of profit for the year ended 31 December 20X5 to the Inspector of Taxes. He ascertains that at 31 December 20X5 he had stock valued at cost £3,950, a van which had cost £2,800 during the year and which had depreciated by £550, debtors of £4,970, expenses prepaid of £170, bank balance £2,564, cash balance £55, trade creditors £1,030, and expenses owing £470.

His drawings were: cash £100 per week for 50 weeks, cheque payments £673.

Draw up statements to show the profit or loss for the year.

35.2A J Kirkwood is a dealer who has not kept proper books of account. At 31 August 20X6 his state of affairs was as follows:

	£
Cash	115
Bank balance	2,209
Fixtures	4,000
Stock	16,740
Debtors	11,890
Creditors	9,052
Van (at valuation)	3,000

During the year to 31 August 20X7 his drawings amounted to £7,560. Winnings from a football pool £2,800 were put into the business. Extra fixtures were bought for £2,000.

At 31 August 20X7 his assets and liabilities were: Cash £84; Bank overdraft £165; Stock £21,491; Creditors for goods £6,002; Creditors for expenses £236; Fixtures to be depreciated £600; Van to be valued at £2,500; Debtors £15,821; Prepaid expenses £72.

Draw up a statement showing the profit and loss made by Kirkwood for the year ended 31 August 20X7.

35.3 Following is a summary of Kelly's bank account for the year ended 31 December 20X7:

	£		£
Balance 1.1.20X7	405	Payments to creditors for goods	29,487
Receipts from debtors	37,936	Rent	1,650
Balance 31.12.20X7	602	Rates	890
		Sundry expenses	375
		Drawings	6,541
	38,943		38,943

All of the business takings have been paid into the bank with the exception of £9,630. Out of this, Kelly has paid wages of £5,472, drawings of £1,164 and purchase of goods £2,994.
The following additional information is available:

	31.12.20X6	31.12.20X7
Stock	13,862	15,144
Creditors for goods	5,624	7,389
Debtors for goods	9,031	8,624
Rates prepaid	210	225
Rent owing	150	–
Fixtures at valuation	2,500	2,250

You are to draw up a set of final accounts for the year ended 31 December 20X7. Show all of your workings.

35.4A J Evans has kept records of his business transactions in a single entry form, but he did not realise that he had to record cash drawings. His bank account for the year 20X8 is as follows:

	£		£
Balance 1.1.20X8	1,890	Cash withdrawn from bank	5,400
Receipts from debtors	44,656	Trade creditors	31,695
Loan from T Hughes	2,000	Rent	2,750
		Rates	1,316
		Drawings	3,095
		Sundry expenses	1,642
		Balance 31.12.20X8	2,648
	48,546		48,546

Records of cash paid were: Sundry expenses £122; Trade creditors £642. Cash sales amounted to £698.
The following information is also available:

	31.12.20X7	31.12.20X8
	£	£
Cash in hand	48	93
Trade creditors	4,896	5,091
Debtors	6,013	7,132
Rent owing	–	250
Rates in advance	282	312
Van (at valuation)	2,800	2,400
Stock	11,163	13,021

You are to draw up a trading and profit and loss account for the year ended 31 December 20X8, and a balance sheet as at that date. Show all of your workings.

35.5 On 1 May 20X8 Jenny Barnes, who is a retailer, had the following balances in her books: Premises £70,000; Equipment £8,200; Vehicles £5,100; Stock £9,500; Trade debtors £150. Jenny does not keep proper books of account, but bank statements covering the 12 months from 1 May 20X8 to 30 April 20X9 were obtained from the bank and summarised as follows:

	£
Money paid into bank:	
Extra capital	8,000
Shop takings	96,500
Received from debtors	1,400
Payments made by cheque:	
Paid for stock purchased	70,500
Purchase of delivery van	6,200
Vehicle running expenses	1,020
Lighting and heating	940
Sales assistants' wages	5,260
Miscellaneous expenses	962

It has been discovered that, in the year ending 30 April 20X9, the owner had paid into the bank all shop takings apart from cash used to pay (*i*) £408 miscellaneous expenses and (*ii*) £500 per month drawings.

At 30 April 20X9:

£7,600 was owing to suppliers for stock bought on credit.
  The amount owed by trade debtors is to be treated as a bad debt. Assume that there had been no sales on credit during the year.
  Stock was valued at £13,620.

Depreciation for the year was calculated at £720 (equipment) and £1,000 (vehicles).

You are asked to prepare trading and profit and loss accounts for the year ended 30 April 20X9. (Show all necessary workings separately.)

(*Edexcel Foundation, London Examinations: GCSE*)

35.6A Bill Smithson runs a second-hand furniture business from a shop which he rents. He does not keep complete accounting records, but is able to provide you with the following information about his financial position at 1 April 20X8: Stock of furniture £3,210; Trade debtors £2,643; Trade creditors £1,598; Motor vehicle £5,100; Shop fittings £4,200; Motor vehicle expenses owing £432.
  He has also provided the following summary of his bank account for the year ended 31 March 20X9:

	£		£
Balance at 1 Apr 20X8	2,420	Payments of trade creditors	22,177
Cheques received from trade debtors	44,846	Electricity	1,090
Cash sales	3,921	Telephone	360
		Rent	2,000
		Advertising	1,430
		Shop fittings	2,550
		Insurance	946
		Motor vehicle expenses	2,116
		Drawings	16,743
		Balance at 31 Mar 20X9	1,775
	£51,187		£51,187

All cash and cheques received were paid into the bank account immediately.
  You find that the following must also be taken into account:

- Depreciation is to be written off the motor vehicle at 20% and off the shop fittings at 10%, calculated on the book values at 1 April 20X8 plus additions during the year.
- At 31 March 20X9 motor vehicle expenses owing were £291 and insurance paid in advance was £177.

- Included in the amount paid for shop fittings were:
  a table bought for £300, which Smithson resold during the year at cost,
  some wooden shelving (cost £250), which Smithson used in building an extension to his house.
  Other balances at 31 March 20X9 were:

	£
Trade debtors	4,012
Trade creditors	2,445
Stock of furniture	4,063

Required:

(a) For the year ended 31 March 20X9
  (i) calculate Smithson's sales and purchases,
  (ii) prepare his trading and profit and loss account.
(b) Prepare Smithson's balance sheet as at 31 March 20X9.

(*Midland Examining Group: GCSE*)

35.7   Although Janet Lambert has run a small business for many years, she has never kept adequate accounting records. However, a need to obtain a bank loan for the expansion of the business has necessitated the preparation of 'final' accounts for the year ended 31 August 20X9. As a result, the following information has been obtained after much careful research:

1 Janet Lambert's business assets and liabilities are as follows:

As at	1 September 20X8	31 August 20X9
	£	£
Stock in trade	8,600	16,800
Debtors for sales	3,900	4,300
Creditors for purchases	7,400	8,900
Rent prepaid	300	420
Electricity accrued due	210	160
Balance at bank	2,300	1,650
Cash in hand	360	330

2 All takings have been banked after deducting the following payments:

Cash drawings – Janet Lambert has not kept a record of cash drawings, but suggests these will be in the region of	£8,000
Casual labour	£1,200
Purchase of goods for resale	£1,800

Note: Takings have been the source of all amounts banked.

3 Bank payments during the year ended 31 August 20X9 have been summarised as follows:

	£
Purchases	101,500
Rent	5,040
Electricity	1,390
Delivery costs (to customers)	3,000
Casual labour	6,620

4 It has been established that a gross profit of 33⅓% on cost has been obtained on all goods sold.

5 Despite her apparent lack of precise accounting records, Janet Lambert is able to confirm that she has taken out of the business during the year under review goods for her own use costing £600.

Required:

(a) Prepare a computation of total purchases for the year ended 31 August 20X9.
(b) Prepare a trading and profit and loss account for the year ended 31 August 20X9 and a balance sheet as at that date, both in as much detail as possible.
(c) Explain why it is necessary to introduce accruals and prepayments into accounting.

(*Association of Accounting Technicians*)

35.8A   Jean Smith, who retails wooden ornaments, has been so busy since she commenced business on 1 April 20X5 that she has neglected to keep adequate accounting records. Jean's opening capital consisted of her life savings of £15,000 which she used to open a business bank account. The transactions in this bank account during the year ended 31 March 20X6 have been summarised from the bank account as follows:

	£
Receipts:	
Loan from John Peacock, uncle	10,000
Takings	42,000
Payments:	
Purchases of goods for resale	26,400
Electricity for period to 31 December 20X5	760
Rent of premises for 15 months to 30 June 20X6	3,500
Rates of premises for the year ended 31 March 20X6	1,200
Wages of assistants	14,700
Purchase of van, 1 October 20X5	7,600
Purchase of holiday caravan for Jean Smith's private use	8,500
Van licence and insurance, payments covering a year	250

According to the bank account, the balance in hand on 31 March 20X6 was £4,090 in Jean Smith's favour.

While the intention was to bank all takings intact, it now transpires that, in addition to cash drawings, the following payments were made out of takings before bankings:

	£
Van running expenses	890
Postages, stationery and other sundry expenses	355

On 31 March 20X6, takings of £640 awaited banking; this was done on 1 April 20X6. It has been discovered that amounts paid into the bank of £340 on 29 March 20X6 were not credited to Jean's bank account until 2 April 20X6 and a cheque of £120, drawn on 28 March 20X6 for purchases, was not paid until 10 April 20X6. The normal rate of gross profit on the goods sold by Jean Smith is 50% on sales. However, during the year a purchase of ornamental goldfish costing £600 proved to be unpopular with customers and therefore the entire stock bought had to be sold at cost price.

Interest at the rate of 5% per annum is payable on each anniversary of the loan from John Peacock on 1 January 20X6.

Depreciation is to be provided on the van on the straight line basis; it is estimated that the van will be disposed of after five years' use for £100.

The stock of goods for resale at 31 March 20X6 has been valued at cost at £1,900.

Creditors for purchases at 31 March 20X6 amounted to £880 and electricity charges accrued due at that date were £180.

Trade debtors at 31 March 20X6 totalled £2,300.

Required:
Prepare a trading and profit and loss account for the year ended 31 March 20X6 and a balance sheet as at that date.

(*Association of Accounting Technicians*)

35.9   David Denton set up in business as a plumber a year ago, and he has asked you to act as his accountant. His instructions to you are in the form of the following letter.

Dear Henry,

I was pleased when you agreed to act as my accountant and look forward to your first visit to check my records. The proposed fee of £250 p.a. is acceptable. I regret that the paperwork for the work done during the year is incomplete. I started my business on 1 January last, and put £6,500 into a business bank account on that date. I brought my van into the firm at that time, and reckon that it was worth £3,600 then. I think it will last another three years after the end of the first year of business use.

I have drawn £90 per week from the business bank account during the year. In my trade it is difficult to take a holiday, but my wife managed to get away for a while. The travel agent's bill for £280 was paid out of the business account. I bought the lease of the yard and office for £6,500. The lease has ten years to run, and the rent is only £300 a year payable in advance on the anniversary of the date of purchase, which was 1 April. I borrowed £4,000 on that day from Aunt Jane to help pay for the lease. I have agreed to pay her 10% interest per annum, but have been too busy to do anything about this yet.

I was lucky enough to meet Miss Prism shortly before I set up on my own, and she has worked for me as an office organiser right from the start. She is paid a salary of £3,000 p.a. All the bills for the year have been carefully preserved in a tool box, and we analysed them last week. The materials I have bought cost me £9,600, but I reckon there was £580 worth left in the yard on 31 December. I have not yet paid for them all yet, I think we owed £714 to the suppliers on 31 December. I was surprised to see that I had spent £4,800 on plumbing equipment, but it should last me five years or so. Electricity bills received up to 30 September came to £1,122; but motor expenses were £912, and general expenses £1,349 for the year. The insurance premium for the year to 31 March next was £800. All these have been paid by cheque but Miss Prism has lost the rate demand. I expect the Local Authority will send a reminder soon since I have not yet paid. I seem to remember that rates came to £180 for the year to 31 March next.

Miss Prism sent out bills to my customers for work done, but some of them are very slow to pay. Altogether the charges made were £29,863, but only £25,613 had been received by 31 December. Miss Prism thinks that 10% of the remaining bills are not likely to be paid. Other customers for jobs too small to bill have paid £3,418 in cash for work done, but I only managed to bank £2,600 of this money. I used £400 of the difference to pay the family's grocery bills, and Miss Prism used the rest for general expenses, except for £123 which was left over in a drawer in the office on 31 December.
Kind regards,
Yours sincerely,
David.

You are required to draw up a profit and loss account for the year ended 31 December, and a balance sheet as at that date.

(*Association of Chartered Certified Accountants*)

35.10   The following are summaries of the cash book and bank accounts of J Duncan who does not keep his books using the double entry system.

Bank Summary	£	£
Balance on 1 January 20X8		8,000
Receipts		
Debtors	26,000	
Cash banked	4,100	30,100
		38,100
Payments		
Trade creditors	18,500	
Rent	1,400	
Machinery	7,500	
Wages	6,100	
Insurance	1,450	
Debtors (dishonoured cheque)	250	
Loan interest	300	35,500
Balance on 31 December 20X8		2,600

Cash Summary	£	£
Balance on 1 January 20X8		300
Receipts		
Cash sales	14,000	
Debtors	400	14,400
		14,700
Payments		
Drawings	9,500	
Repairs	300	
Electricity	750	
Cash banked	4,100	14,650
Balance on 31 December 20X8		50

The following referred to 20X8	£
Bad debts written off	400
Discount received	350
Goods withdrawn by J Duncan for own use	300
Credit note issued	1,200

The following additional information is available.	1 January 20X8	31 December 20X8
	£	£
Stocks	4,100	3,200
Machinery	12,600	15,900
Rent prepaid	200	
Rent owing		250
Debtors	6,300	5,000
Creditors	2,400	2,500
Loan from bank at 8%	5,000	5,000
Loan interest owing		100

You are required to:
(a) Calculate the value of J Duncan's capital on 1 January 20X8.
(b) Prepare the Trading and Profit and Loss Accounts for the year ended 31 December 20X8.

(*Scottish Qualifications Authority*)

35.11   Using the information in Review Question 35.10, prepare J Duncan's Balance Sheet as at 31 December 20X8.

35.12A   The following are summaries of the cash book and bank accounts of P Maclaran who does not keep her books using the double entry system.

Bank Summary	£	£
Balance on 1 January 20X8		6,000
Receipts		
Debtors	35,000	
Cash banked	2,200	37,200
		43,200
Payments		
Trade creditors	31,000	
Rent	1,100	
Machinery	3,400	
Wages	9,200	
Insurance	850	
Debtors (dishonoured cheque)	80	
Loan interest	500	(46,130)
Balance on 31 December 20X8		(2,930)

Cash Summary	£	£
Balance on 1 January 20X8		60
Receipts		
Cash sales	9,700	
Debtors	1,100	10,800
		10,860
Payments		
Drawings	6,600	
Repairs	1,400	
Electricity	570	
Cash banked	2,200	(10,770)
Balance on 31 December 20X8		90

The following referred to 20X8	£
Bad debts written off	240
Discount received	600
Goods withdrawn by P Maclaran for own use	1,200
Credit note issued	640

The following additional information is available.	*1 January 20X8*	*31 December 20X8*
	£	£
Stocks	2,300	5,400
Machinery	9,800	10,400
Rent prepaid		100
Rent owing	150	
Debtors	8,100	9,200
Creditors	5,700	4,800
Loan from bank at 10%	7,000	7,000
Loan interest owing		200

You are required to:
(*a*) Calculate the value of P Maclaran's capital on 1 January 20X8.
(*b*) Prepare the Trading and Profit and Loss Accounts for the year ended 31 December 20X8.

35.13A Using the information in Question 35.12, prepare P Maclaran's Balance Sheet as at 31 December 20X8.

CHAPTER 36

Receipts and payments accounts and income and expenditure accounts

Learning objectives

After you have studied this chapter, you should be able to:

- explain the main differences between the financial statements of non-profit-oriented organisations and those of profit-oriented organisations
- prepare receipts and payments accounts
- prepare income and expenditure accounts and balance sheets for non-profit-oriented organisations
- calculate profit and losses from special activities and incorporate them into the financial statements
- make appropriate entries relating to subscriptions, life membership, and donations

Introduction

In this chapter, you'll learn about the financial statements prepared by non-profit-oriented organisations, and about how they differ from those prepared for profit-oriented organisations.

36.1 Non-profit-oriented organisations

As their main purpose is not trading or profit-making, charities, clubs, associations and other non-profit-oriented organisations do not prepare trading and profit and loss accounts. They are run so that their members can do things such as play football, chess or dungeons and dragons. Rather than producing trading and profit and loss accounts, they prepare either 'receipts and payments accounts' or 'income and expenditure accounts'.

36.2 Receipts and payments accounts

Receipts and payments accounts are a summary of the Cash Book for the period. For an organisation with no assets (other than cash) and no liabilities, a summary of the Cash Book reveals everything about what has happened financially during a period.

Exhibit 36.1 is an example.

Exhibit 36.1

The Homers Running Club
Receipts and Payments Account for the year ended 31 December 20X5

Receipts	£	Payments	£
Bank balance 1.1.20X5	236	Groundsman's wages	728
Subscriptions received in 20X5	1,148	Sports ground rental	296
Rent received	116	Committee expenses	58
		Printing and stationery	33
		Bank balance 31.12.20X5	385
	1,500		1,500

> **Activity 36.1**
>
> Why do you think non-profit-oriented organisations prepare receipts and payments accounts when they have all this information in the Cash Book already?

36.3 Income and expenditure accounts

When assets are owned and/or there are liabilities, the receipts and payments account is not a good way of drawing up financial statements. Other than the cash received and paid out, it shows only the cash balances. The other assets and liabilities are not shown at all. What is required is:

1 a balance sheet, and
2 an account showing whether the association's capital has increased.

In a profit-oriented organisation, 2 would be a trading and profit and loss account. In a non-profit-oriented organisation, 2 would be an **income and expenditure account**.

An income and expenditure account follows the same rules as a trading and profit and loss account. The only differences are the terms used.

A comparison between the terminology of financial statements produced by profit-oriented and non-profit-oriented organisations now follows.

Terms used

Profit-oriented organisation	Non-profit-oriented organisation
1 Trading and Profit and Loss Account	1 Income and Expenditure Account
2 Net Profit	2 Surplus of Income over Expenditure
3 Net Loss	3 Excess of Expenditure over Income

36.4 Profit or loss for a special purpose

Sometimes there are reasons why a non-profit-oriented organisation would want a profit and loss account.

This is where something is done to make a profit. The profit is not to be kept, but used to pay for the main purpose of the organisation.

For instance, a football club may have discos or dances which people pay to go to. Any profit from these helps to pay football expenses. For these discos and dances a trading and profit and loss account would be drawn up. Any profit (or loss) would be transferred to the income and expenditure account.

36.5 Accumulated fund

A sole trader or a partnership would have capital accounts. A non-profit-oriented organisation would instead have an **accumulated fund**. In effect, it is the same as a capital account, as it is the difference between assets and liabilities.

For a sole trader or partnership

Capital = Assets − Liabilities

In a non-profit-oriented organisation

Accumulated Fund = Assets − Liabilities

36.6 Drawing up income and expenditure accounts

We can now look at the preparation of an income and expenditure account and a balance sheet of a club in Exhibit 36.2. A separate trading account is to be prepared for a bar, where refreshments are sold to make a profit.

The majority of clubs and associations keep their accounts using single entry methods. This example will therefore be from single entry records, using the principles described in the last chapter.

Exhibit 36.2

The treasurer of the Long Lane Football Club has prepared a receipts and payments account, but members have complained about the inadequacy of such an account. She therefore asks an accountant to prepare a trading account for the bar, and an income and expenditure account and a balance sheet. The treasurer gives the accountant a copy of the receipts and payments account together with information on assets and liabilities at the beginning and end of the year:

Long Lane Football Club
Receipts and Payments Account for the year ended 31 December 20X6

Receipts	£	Payments	£
Bank balance 1.1.20X6	524	Payment for bar supplies	3,962
Subscriptions received for		Wages:	
20X5 (arrears)	55	Groundsman and assistant	939
20X6	1,236	Barman	624
20X7 (in advance)	40	Bar expenses	234
Bar sales	5,628	Repairs to stands	119
Donations received	120	Ground upkeep	229
		Secretary's expenses	138
		Transport costs	305
		Bank balance 31.12.20X6	1,053
	7,603		7,603

Additional information:	31.12.20X5	31.12.20X6
1	£	£
Stocks in the bar – at cost	496	558
Owing for bar supplies	294	340
Bar expenses owing	25	36
Transport costs	–	65

2 The land and football stands were valued at 31 December 20X5 at: land £4,000; football stands £2,000; the stands are to be depreciated by 10 per cent per annum.

3 The equipment at 31 December 20X5 was valued at £550, and is to be depreciated at 20 per cent per annum.

4 Subscriptions owing by members amounted to £55 on 31 December 20X5, and £66 on 31 December 20X6.

From this information, in the following three stages, the accountant drew up the appropriate accounts and statements:

Stage 1: Draw up a Statement of Affairs at the end of the previous period.

Statement of Affairs as at 31 December 20X5

	£	£	£
Fixed assets			
Land			4,000
Stands			2,000
Equipment			550
Current assets			6,550
Stock in bar		496	
Debtors for subscriptions		55	
Cash at bank		524	
Less Current liabilities		1,075	
Creditors	294		
Bar expenses owing	25		
		(319)	
Net current assets			756
			7,306
Financed by:			
Accumulated fund (difference)			7,306

Activity 36.2

Why do you think this statement was described as being a 'statement of affairs' rather than a 'balance sheet'?

Stage 2: Draw up a Bar Trading Account.

Long Lane Football Club
Bar Trading Account for the year ended 31 December 20X6

	£	£
Sales		5,628
Less Cost of goods sold:		
Stock 1.1.20X6	496	
Add Purchases[1]	4,008	
	4,504	
Less Stock 31.12.20X6	(558)	
		(3,946)
Gross profit		1,682
Less Bar expenses[2]	245	
Barman's wages	624	
		(869)
Net profit to income and expenditure account		813

Notes:

1   **Purchases Control**

	£		£
Cash	3,962	Balances (creditors) b/d	294
Balances c/d	340	Trading account (difference)	4,008
	4,302		4,302

2   **Bar Expenses**

	£		£
Cash	234	Balance b/d	25
Balance c/d	36	Trading account (difference)	245
	270		270

Stage 3: Draw up the financial statements.

Long Lane Football Club
Income and Expenditure Account for the year ended 31 December 20X6

Income	£	£	£
Subscriptions for 20X6[1]			1,302
Profit from the bar			813
Donations received			120
			2,235
Less Expenditure			
Wages – Groundsman and assistant		939	
Repairs to stands		119	
Ground upkeep		229	
Secretary's expenses		138	
Transport costs[2]		370	
Depreciation			
Stands	200		
Equipment	110		
		310	
			(2,105)
Surplus of income over expenditure			130

Notes:

1   **Subscriptions Received**

	£		£
Balance (debtors) b/d	55	Cash 20X5	55
Income and expenditure		20X6	1,236
account (difference)	1,302	20X7	40
Balance (in advance) c/d	40	Balance (owing) c/d	66
	1,397		1,397

2   **Transport Costs**

	£		£
Cash	305	Income and expenditure	
Accrued c/d	65	account (difference)	370
	370		370

It will be noted that subscriptions received in advance are carried down as a credit balance to the following period.

The Long Lane Football Club
Balance Sheet as at 31 December 20X6

	£	£	£
Fixed assets			
Land at valuation			4,000
Pavilion at valuation		2,000	
Less Depreciation		(200)	
			1,800
Equipment at valuation		550	
Less Depreciation		(110)	
			440
			6,240
Current assets			
Stock of bar supplies		558	
Debtors for subscriptions		66	
Cash at bank		1,053	
		1,677	
Less Current liabilities			
Creditors for bar supplies	340		
Bar expenses owing	36		
Transport costs owing	65		
Subscriptions received in advance	40		
		(481)	
Net current assets			1,196
			7,436
Financed by:			
Accumulated fund			
Balance as at 1.1.20X6			7,306
Add Surplus of income over expenditure			130
			7,436

36.7 Outstanding subscriptions and the prudence concept

So far we have treated subscriptions owing as being an asset. However, as any treasurer of a club would tell you, most subscriptions that have been owing for a long time are never paid – members lose interest or simply go somewhere else. As a result, many clubs do not include unpaid subscriptions as an asset in the balance sheet.

Activity 36.3

Does this policy of ignoring subscriptions due when preparing the financial statements comply with the prudence concept? Why/Why not?

In an examination, you should assume that subscriptions owing are to be brought into the financial statements, unless instructions to the contrary are given.

Exhibit 36.3 shows an instance where subscriptions in arrears and in advance occur at the beginning and end of a period.

Exhibit 36.3

An amateur theatrical group charges its members an annual subscription of £20 per member. It accrues for subscriptions owing at the end of each year and also adjusts for subscriptions received in advance.

(A) On 1 January 20X2, 18 members owed £360 for the year 20X1.
(B) In December 20X1, 4 members paid £80 for the year 20X2.
(C) During the year 20X2 it received cash for subscriptions £7,420.

	£
For 20X1	360
For 20X2	6,920
For 20X3	140
	7,420

(D) At 31 December 20X2, 11 members had not paid their 20X2 subscriptions.

Subscriptions

20X2			£	20X2			£
Jan	1	Owing b/d (A)	360	Jan	1	Prepaid b/d (B)	80
Dec	31	Income and expenditure[1]	7,220	Dec	31	Bank (C)	7,420
Dec	31	Prepaid c/d (C)	140	Dec	31	Owing c/d (D)	220
			7,720				7,720
20X3				20X3			
Jan	1	Owing b/d (D)	220	Jan	1	Prepaid b/d (C)	140

1 This is the difference between the two sides of the account.

36.8 Life membership

In some clubs and societies, members can make a payment for life membership. This means that by paying a fairly substantial amount now members can enjoy the facilities of the club for the rest of their lives.

Such a receipt should not be treated as income in the income and expenditure account solely in the year in which the member paid the money. It should be credited to a life membership account, and transfers should be made from that account to the credit of the income and expenditure account of an appropriate amount annually.

Exactly what is meant by an appropriate amount to transfer each year is decided by the committee of the club or society. The usual basis is to establish, on average, how long members will continue to use the benefits of the club. To take an extreme case, if a club was in existence which could not be joined until one achieved the age of 70, then the expected number of years' use of the club on average per member would be relatively few. Another club, such as a golf club, where a fair proportion of the members joined when reasonably young, and where the game is capable of being played by members until and during old age, would expect a much higher average of years of use per member. In the end, the club has to decide for itself.

As a club has to provide amenities for life members without any further payment, the credit balance remaining on the account, after the transfer of the agreed amount has been made to the credit of the income and expenditure account, should be shown on the balance sheet as a liability.

In an examination, be sure to follow the instructions set by the examiner.

36.9 Donations

Any donations received are usually shown as income in the year that they are received.

36.10 Entrance fees

When they first join a club, in addition to the membership fee for that year, new members often have to pay an entrance fee. Entrance fees are normally included as income in the year that they are received. A club could, however, decide to treat them differently, perhaps by spreading the income over a number of years. It all depends on the circumstances.

Learning outcomes

You should now have learnt:

1 That a receipts and payments account does not show the full financial position of an organisation, except for one where the only asset is cash and there are no liabilities.

2 That an income and expenditure account is drawn up to show either the surplus of income over expenditure or the excess of expenditure over income. These are the same as 'profit' or 'loss' in a profit-oriented organisation.

3 That the accumulated fund is basically the same as a capital account.

4 That although the main object of the organisation is non-profit-oriented, certain activities may be run at a profit (or may lose money) in order to help finance the main objectives of the organisation.

5 That in an examination you should treat subscriptions owing at the end of a period in the same way as debtors, unless told otherwise.

6 That donations are usually treated as income in the period in which they are received.

7 That entrance fees are usually treated as income in the year in which they are received.

8 That the treatment of life membership fees is purely at the discretion of the organisation, but that they are usually amortised over an appropriate period.

Answers to activities

36.1 Just as you would prepare a balance sheet for a profit-oriented organisation in order to summarise its financial position at a specific point in time, so non-profit-oriented organisations that deal only in cash, own no assets and have no liabilities, may prepare a receipts and payments account in order to show what happened over a period and the amount of funds left at the end. Non-profit-oriented organisations with assets and liabilities also use them, but normally in order to help prepare their main financial statements.

36.2 You could just as easily draw up a balance sheet but you're trying to summarise the financial statement even more than in a balance sheet. You would not, for example, show provision for doubtful debts being subtracted from debtors in a statement of affairs, but you would in the balance sheet of a sole trader. To avoid confusion, the title 'statement of affairs' is used when performing any preparatory work prior to preparing the balance sheet. (It must be said, however, that you would not be wrong if you called the statement of affairs a balance sheet.)

36.3 It does not comply with the prudence concept. You will remember from your coverage of the prudence concept in Chapter 10 that you should not overstate *or* understate income and expenditure. While this practice ensures the figure for subscriptions due is not overstated, it does understate them.

REVIEW QUESTIONS

36.1 A summary of the Uppertown Football Club is shown below. From it, and the additional information, you are to construct an income and expenditure account for the year ended 31 December 20X4, and a balance sheet as at that date.

Cash Book Summary

	£		£
Balance 1.1.20X4	180	Purchase of equipment	125
Collections at matches	1,650	Rent for football pitch	300
Profit on sale of refreshments	315	Printing and stationery	65
		Secretary's expenses	144
		Repairs to equipment	46
		Groundsman's wages	520
		Miscellaneous expenses	66
		Balance 31.12.20X4	879
	2,145		2,145

Further information:
(*i*)   At 1.1.20X4 equipment was valued at £500.
(*ii*) Depreciate all equipment 20 per cent for the year 20X4.
(*iii*) At 31.12.20X4 rent paid in advance was £60.
(*iv*) At 31.12.20X4 there was £33 owing for printing.

36.2A The following trial balance of Haven Golf Club was extracted from the books as on 31 December 20X8:

	Dr	Cr
	£	£
Clubhouse	21,000	
Equipment	6,809	
Profits from raffles		4,980
Subscriptions received		18,760
Wages of bar staff	2,809	
Bar stocks 1 January 20X8	1,764	
Bar purchases and sales	11,658	17,973
Greenkeepers' wages	7,698	
Golf professional's salary	6,000	
General expenses	580	
Cash at bank	1,570	
Accumulated fund at 1 January 20X8		18,175
	59,888	59,888

Notes:
(*i*)   Bar purchases and sales were on a cash basis. Bar stocks at 31 December 20X8 were valued at £989.
(*ii*) Subscriptions paid in advance by members at 31 December 20X8 amounted to £180.
(*iii*) Provide for depreciation of equipment £760.

You are required to:
(*a*) Draw up the bar trading account for the year ended 31 December 20X8.
(*b*) Draw up the income and expenditure account for the year ended 31 December 20X8, and a balance sheet as at 31 December 20X8.

36.3 Read the following and answer the questions below.

On 1 January 20X8 The Happy Haddock Angling Club had the following assets:

	£
Cash at bank	200
Snack bar stocks	800
Club house buildings	12,500

During the year to 31 December 20X8 the Club received and paid the following amounts:

Receipts	£	Payments	£
Subscriptions 20X8	3,500	Rent and rates	1,500
Subscriptions 20X9	380	Extension to club house	8,000
Snack bar income	6,000	Snack bar purchases	3,750
Visitors' fees	650	Secretarial expenses	240
Loan from bank	5,500	Interest on loan	260
Competition fees	820	Snack bar expenses	600
		Games equipment	2,000

Notes: The snack bar stock on 31 December 20X8 was £900.
The games equipment should be depreciated by 20%.

(a) Prepare an income and expenditure account for the year ended 31 December 20X8. Show, either in this account or separately, the snack bar profit or loss.
(b) Prepare a balance sheet as at 31 December 20X8.

(*Midland Examining Group: GCSE*)

36.4A   The treasurer of the City Sports Club has produced the following receipts and payments account for the year ended 31 December 20X7:

Receipts	£	Payments	£
Balance at bank 1 January 20X7	1,298	Coffee supplies bought	1,456
Subscriptions received	3,790	Wages of attendants and cleaners	1,776
Profits and dances	186	Rent of rooms	887
Profit on exhibition	112	New equipment bought	565
Coffee bar takings	2,798	Travelling expenses of teams	673
Sale of equipment	66	Balance at bank 31 December 20X7	2,893
	8,250		8,250

Notes:
(*i*)   Coffee bar stocks were valued: 31 December 20X6 £59, 31 December 20X7 £103. There was nothing owing for coffee bar stocks on either of these dates.
(*ii*) On 1 January 20X7 the club's equipment was valued at £2,788. Included in this figure, valued at £77, was the equipment sold during the year for £66.
(*iii*) The amount to be charged for depreciation of equipment for the year is £279. This is in addition to the loss on equipment sold during the year.
(*iv*) Subscriptions owing by members 31 December 20X6 nil, at 31 December 20X7 £29.

You are required to:
(a) Draw up the coffee bar trading account for the year ended 31 December 20X7. For this purpose £650 of the wages is to be charged to this account; the remainder will be charged in the income and expenditure account.
(b) Calculate the accumulated fund as at 1 January 20X7.
(c) Draw up the income and expenditure account for the year ended 31 December 20X7, and a balance sheet as at 31 December 20X7.

36.5   The following is a summary of the receipts and payments of the Miniville Rotary Club during the year ended 31 July 20X9.

Miniville Rotary Club
Receipts and Payments Account for the year ended 31 July 20X9

	£		£
Cash and bank balances b/d	210	Secretarial expenses	163
Sales of competition tickets	437	Rent	1,402
Members' subscriptions	1,987	Visiting speakers' expenses	1,275
Donations	177	Donations to charities	35
Refund of rent	500	Prizes for competitions	270
Balance c/d	13	Stationery and printing	179
	£3,324		£3,324

The following valuations are also available:

as at 31 July	20X8	20X9
	£	£
Equipment (original cost £1,420)	975	780
Subscriptions in arrears	65	85
Subscriptions in advance	10	37
Owing to suppliers of competition prizes	58	68
Stocks of competition prizes	38	46

Required:
(a) Calculate the value of the accumulated fund of the Miniville Rotary Club as at 1 August 20X8.
(b) Reconstruct the following accounts for the year ended 31 July 20X9:
   (i) the subscriptions account,
   (ii) the competition prizes account.
(c) Prepare an income and expenditure account for the Miniville Rotary Club for the year ended 31 July 20X9 and a balance sheet as at that date.

(*Association of Accounting Technicians*)

36.6A The Milham Theatre Club has been in existence for a number of years. Members pay an annual subscription of £15 which entitles them to join trips to professional productions at a reduced rate.

On 1 February 20X7 the Club's assets and liabilities were as follows:

Cash in hand £80, Bank balance (overdrawn) £180, Subscriptions in arrears £150, Savings account with local building society £1,950, Amount owing for coach hire £60.

Required:
(a) A *detailed* calculation of the Milham Theatre Club's accumulated fund at 1 February 20X7.

The Club's treasurer was able to present the following information at 31 January 20X8:

Receipts and Payments Accounts for year ended 31 January 20X8

	£	£
Opening balances		
Cash in hand	80	
Cash at bank (overdrawn)*	(180)	
		(100)
Receipts		
Subscriptions		
for year ended 31 January 20X7	120	
for year ended 31 January 20X8	1,620	
for year ended 31 January 20X9	165	
Gift from member	1,000	
Interest on building society account	140	
Theatre outings		
receipts from members for theatre tickets	2,720	
receipts from members for coach travel	1,240	
		7,005
		6,905
Payments		
Transfer to building society account	1,210	
Theatre trips		
tickets	3,120	
coach hire	1,540	
Secretarial and administrative expenses	55	
		(5,925)
		980
Closing balances		
cash in hand	35	
cash at bank	945	
		980

- On 31 January 20X8 the club committee decided to write off any arrears of subscriptions for the year ended 31 January 20X7; the membership secretary reported that £75 is due for subscriptions for the year ended 31 January 20X8.
- The treasurer has calculated that the full amount of interest receivable on the building society account for the year ended 31 January 20X8 is £155.
- The club committee has decided that the gift should be capitalised.

Required:
(b) An account showing the surplus or deficit made by the Milham Theatre Club on theatre trips.
(c) An income and expenditure account for the Milham Theatre Club for the year ended 31 January 20X8.
(d) An *extract* from the Milham Theatre Club's balance sheet as at 31 January 20X8, showing the accumulated fund and current liability sections only.

The club committee have been concerned by the fact that the club's income has been steadily declining over recent years.

Required:
(e) Advice for the committee on *four* ways in which they could improve the club's income.

(*Southern Examining Group: GCSE*)

Note: Figures in brackets represent minus amounts.

36.7 The accounting records of the Happy Tickers Sports and Social Club are in a mess. You manage to find the following information to help you prepare the accounts for the year to 31 December 20X8.

Summarised Balance Sheet as at 31 December 20X7

	£
Half-share in motorised roller	600
New sports equipment unsold	1,000
Used sports equipment at valuation	700
Rent prepaid (2 months)	200
Subscriptions 20X7	60
Café stocks	800
Cash and bank	1,210
	4,570
Life subscriptions	1,400
Subscriptions 20X8	120
Insurance accrued (3 months)	150
Accumulated fund	2,900
	4,570

Receipts in the year to 31 December 20X8:	£
Subscriptions – 20X7	40
– 20X8	1,100
– 20X9	80
– Life	200
From sales of new sports equipment	900
From sales of used sports equipment	14
Café takings	4,660
	6,994

Payments in the year to 31 December 20X8:	
Rent (for 12 months)	1,200
Insurance (for 18 months)	900
To suppliers of sports equipment	1,000
To café suppliers	1,900
Wages of café manager	2,000
Total cost of repairing motorised roller	450
	7,450

Notes:
(*i*) Ownership and all expenses of the motorised roller are agreed to be shared equally with the Carefree Conveyancers Sports and Social Club which occupies a nearby site. The roller cost a total of £2,000 on 1 January 20X6 and had an estimated life of 10 years.
(*ii*) Life subscriptions are brought into income equally over 10 years, in a scheme begun 5 years ago in 20X3. Since the scheme began the cost of £200 per person has been constant. Prior to 31 December 20X7 10 life subscriptions had been received.
(*iii*) Four more annual subscriptions of £20 each had been promised relating to 20X8, but not yet received. Annual subscriptions promised but unpaid are carried forward for a maximum of 12 months.
(*iv*) New sports equipment is sold to members at cost plus 50%. Used equipment is sold off to members at book valuation. Half the sports equipment bought in the year (all from a cash and carry supplier) has been used within the club, and half made available for sale, new, to members. The 'used equipment at valuation' figure in the 31 December 20X8 balance sheet is to remain at £700.
(*v*) Closing café stocks are £850, and £80 is owed to suppliers at 31 December 20X8.

Required:
(*a*) Calculate the profit on café operations and the profit on sale of sports equipment.
(*b*) Prepare a statement of subscription income for 20X8.
(*c*) Prepare an income and expenditure statement for the year to 31 December 20X8, and balance sheet as at 31 December 20X8.
(*d*) Why do life subscriptions appear as a liability?

(*Association of Chartered Certified Accountants*)

CHAPTER 37

Manufacturing accounts

Learning objectives

After you have studied this chapter, you should be able to:

- calculate prime cost and production cost of goods manufactured
- draw up manufacturing accounts, and appropriate trading and profit and loss accounts
- adjust the manufacturing account in respect of work in progress
- explain and calculate a further five methods of providing for depreciation

Introduction

In this chapter, you'll learn how to prepare manufacturing accounts and the reasons for doing so. You'll also learn five further methods that can be used for calculating depreciation and the circumstances in which each of them may be used.

37.1 Manufacturing: not retailing

We now have to deal with businesses which are manufacturers. For these businesses, a **manufacturing account** is prepared in addition to the trading and profit and loss accounts. It is produced for internal use only. People other than the owners and managers of the organisation rarely see a manufacturing account.

If a business is using manufacturing accounts, the trading account will contain the cost of manufacturing the goods manufactured during the period instead of a figure for purchases (of finished goods). The manufacturing account is used to calculate and show the cost of manufacturing those goods. The figure it produces that is used in the trading account is known as the **production cost**.

37.2 Divisions of costs

In a manufacturing business the costs are divided into different types. These may be summarised in chart form as follows:

37.3 Direct and indirect costs

With reference to the above chart, when you see the word *direct* followed by a type of cost, you know that it has been possible to trace the costs of making an item to the item being manufactured. The sum of all the **direct costs** is known as the **prime cost**. If a cost cannot easily be traced to the item being manufactured, then it is an indirect cost and will be included under **indirect manufacturing costs** (which are also sometimes known as 'factory overhead expenses'). 'Production cost' is the sum of prime cost plus the indirect manufacturing costs.

For example, the wages of a machine operator making a particular item will be direct labour. The wages of a foreman in charge of many men on different jobs will be indirect labour, and will be part of the indirect manufacturing costs. Other examples of costs being direct costs would be:

1 Cost of raw materials including carriage inwards on those raw materials.
2 Hire of special machinery for a job.

Activity 37.1
Think about it for a minute and then list five costs you think are direct and five that you think are indirect.

37.4 Indirect manufacturing costs

'Indirect manufacturing costs' are all those costs which occur in the factory or other place where production is being done, but which cannot easily be traced to the items being manufactured. Examples are:

- wages of cleaners
- wages of crane drivers
- rent and rates of the factory
- depreciation of plant and machinery
- costs of operating forklift trucks
- factory power
- factory lighting

37.5 Administration expenses

'Administration expenses' consist of such items as managers' salaries, legal and accountancy charges, the depreciation of accounting machinery and secretarial salaries.

37.6 Selling and distribution expenses

'Selling and distribution expenses' are items such as sales staff's salaries and commission, carriage outwards, depreciation of delivery vans, advertising and display expenses.

37.7 Financial charges

'Financial charges' are expense items such as bank charges and discounts allowed.

37.8 Format of financial statements

Manufacturing account part

This is debited with the production cost of goods completed during the accounting period. It contains costs of:

- Direct materials.
- Direct labour.
- Direct expenses.
- Indirect manufacturing costs.

The manufacturing account includes all purchases of raw materials, including the stock adjustments for raw materials. It also includes stock adjustments for **work in progress** (goods that are part-completed at the end of a period). Let's put this into a series of steps:

1 Add opening stock of raw materials to purchases and subtract the closing stock of raw materials.
2 Add in all the direct costs to get the prime cost.
3 Add in all the indirect manufacturing costs.
4 Add the opening stock of work in progress and subtract the closing stock of work in progress to get the production cost of all goods completed in the period.

Thus, when completed, the manufacturing account shows the total of production cost that relates to those manufactured goods that have been available for sale during the period. This figure will then be transferred down to the profit and loss account where it will replace the entry for purchases.

Trading account part

This account includes:

- Production cost brought down from the manufacturing account.
- Opening and closing stocks of finished goods.
- Sales.

When completed this account will disclose the gross profit. This will then be carried down to the profit and loss account part.

The manufacturing account and the trading account can be shown in the form of a diagram:

Manufacturing Account

	£
Production costs for the period:	
Direct materials	xxx
Direct labour	xxx
Direct expenses	xxx
Production cost of goods completed c/d to trading account	xxx

Trading Account

		£	£
Sales			xxx
Less Production cost of goods sold:			
Opening stock of finished goods	(A)	xxx	
Add Production costs of goods completed b/d		xxx	
Less Closing stock of finished goods		xxx	
	(B)	(xxx)	
Gross profit			(xxx)
			xxx

(A) is production costs of goods unsold in previous period.
(B) is production costs of goods unsold at end of the current period.

Profit and loss account part

This is prepared in the way you learnt in earlier chapters in this book. You know, therefore, that it includes:

● Gross profit brought down from the trading account.
● All administration expenses.
● All selling and distribution expenses
● All financial charges.

However, some of the items you would normally put in the profit and loss account part are already included in the manufacturing account, e.g. depreciation on machines, and canteen wages. When completed, this account will show the net profit.

> *Activity 37.2*
> Why do you think some expenses have been moved to the manufacturing account?

37.9 A worked example of a manufacturing account

Exhibit 37.1 shows the necessary details for a manufacturing account. It has been assumed that there were no partly completed units (work in progress) either at the beginning or end of the period.

Exhibit 37.1

Details of production cost for the year ended 31 December 20X7:

	£
1 January 20X7, stock of raw materials	500
31 December 20X7, stock of raw materials	700
Raw materials purchased	8,000
Manufacturing (direct) wages	21,000
Royalties	150
Indirect wages	9,000
Rent of factory – excluding administration and selling and distribution blocks	440
Depreciation of plant and machinery in factory	400
General indirect expenses	310

Manufacturing Account for the year ended 31 December 20X7

	£	£
Stock of raw materials 1.1.20X7		500
Add Purchases		8,000
		8,500
Less Stock of raw materials 31.12.20X7		(700)
Cost of raw materials consumed		7,800
Manufacturing wages		21,000
Royalties		150
Prime cost		28,950
Indirect manufacturing costs		
Rent	440	
Indirect wages	9,000	
General expenses	310	
Depreciation of plant and machinery	400	
Production cost of goods completed c/d		10,150
		39,100

Sometimes, if a business has produced less than the customers have demanded, then the business may well have bought an outside supply of finished goods. In this case, the trading account will have both a figure for purchases and a figure for production cost of goods completed.

37.10 Work in progress

The production cost to be carried down to the trading account is that of production cost of goods completed during the period. If items have not been completed, they cannot be sold. Therefore, they should not appear in the trading account.

For instance, if we have the following information, we can calculate the transfer to the trading account:

	£
Total production costs expended during the year	5,000
Production costs last year on goods not completed last year, but completed in this year (work in progress)	300
Production costs this year on goods which were not completed by the year end (work in progress)	440

The calculation is:

	£
Total production costs expended this year	5,000
Add Costs from last year, in respect of goods completed in this year (work in progress)	300
	5,300
Less Costs in this year, for goods to be completed next year (work in progress)	(440)
Production costs expended on goods completed this year	4,860

37.11 Another worked example

Exhibit 37.2

	£
1 January 20X7, Stock of raw materials	800
31 December 20X7, Stock of raw materials	1,050
1 January 20X7, Work in progress	350
31 December 20X7, Work in progress	420
Year to 31 December 20X7:	
Wages: Direct	3,960
Indirect	2,550
Purchase of raw materials	8,700
Fuel and power	990
Direct expenses	140
Lubricants	300
Carriage inwards on raw materials	200
Rent of factory	720
Depreciation of factory plant and machinery	420
Internal transport expenses	180
Insurance of factory buildings and plant	150
General factory expenses	330

This information produces the following manufacturing account:

Manufacturing Account for the year ended 31 December 20X7

	£	£
Stock of raw materials 1.1.20X7		800
Add Purchases		8,700
″ Carriage inwards		200
		9,700
Less Stock of raw materials 31.12.20X7		(1,050)
Cost of raw materials consumed		8,650
Direct wages		3,960
Direct expenses		140
Prime cost		12,750
Indirect manufacturing costs:		
Fuel and power	990	
Indirect wages	2,550	
Lubricants	300	
Rent	720	
Depreciation of plant	420	
Internal transport expenses	180	
Insurance	150	
General factory expenses	330	
		5,640
		18,390
Add Work in progress 1.1.20X7		350
		18,740
Less Work in progress 31.12.20X7		(420)
Production cost of goods completed c/d		18,320

The trading account is concerned with finished goods. If in the foregoing exhibit there had been £3,500 stock of finished goods at 1 January 20X7 and £4,400 at 31 December 20X7, and the sales of finished goods amounted to £25,000 then the trading account would appear:

Trading Account for the year ended 31 December 20X7

	£	£
Sales		25,000
Less Cost of goods sold:		
Stock of finished goods 1.1.20X7	3,500	
Add Production cost of goods completed b/d	18,320	
	21,820	
Less Stock of finished goods 31.12.20X7	(4,400)	
		(17,420)
Gross profit c/d		7,580

The profit and loss account is then constructed in the normal way.

37.12 Apportionment of expenses

Quite often expenses will have to be split between

- Indirect manufacturing costs: to be charged in the manufacturing account part
- Administration expenses:
- Selling and distribution expenses: } to be charged in the profit and loss account part
- Financial charges:

An instance of this could be the rent expense. If the rent is paid separately for each part of the organisation, then it is easy to charge the rent to each sort of expense. However, only one figure of rent may be paid, without any indication as to how much is for the factory part, how much is for the selling and distribution part and how much is for the administration buildings.

How the rent expense will be apportioned in the latter case will depend on circumstances, using the most equitable way of doing it. A range of methods may be used, including ones based upon:

- floor area;
- property valuations of each part of the buildings and land.

37.13 Full set of financial statements

A complete worked example is now given. Note that in the profit and loss account the expenses have been separated so as to show whether they are administration expenses, selling and distribution expenses, or financial charges.

The trial balance in Exhibit 37.3 has been extracted from the books of J Jarvis, Toy Manufacturer, as on 31 December 20X7.

Exhibit 37.3

J Jarvis
Trial Balance as on 31 December 20X7

	Dr	Cr
	£	£
Stock of raw materials 1.1.20X7	2,100	
Stock of finished goods 1.1.20X7	3,890	
Work in progress 1.1.20X7	1,350	
Wages (direct £18,000; factory indirect £14,500)	32,500	
Royalties	700	
Carriage inwards (on raw materials)	350	
Purchases of raw materials	37,000	
Productive machinery (cost £28,000)	23,000	
Accounting machinery (cost £2,000)	1,200	
General factory expenses	3,100	
Lighting	750	
Factory power	1,370	
Administrative salaries	4,400	
Sales reps' salaries	3,000	
Commission on sales	1,150	
Rent	1,200	
Insurance	420	
General administration expenses	1,340	
Bank charges	230	
Discounts allowed	480	
Carriage outwards	590	
Sales		100,000
Debtors and creditors	14,230	12,500
Bank	5,680	
Cash	150	
Drawings	2,000	
Capital as at 1.1.20X7		29,680
	142,180	142,180

Notes at 31.12.20X7:

1 Stock of raw materials £2,400, stock of finished goods £4,000, work in progress £1,500.
2 Lighting, rent and insurance are to be apportioned: factory $5/6$, administration $1/6$.
3 Depreciation on productive and accounting machinery at 10 per cent per annum on cost.

J Jarvis
Manufacturing, Trading and Profit and Loss Account for the year ended 31 December 20X7

	£	£	£
Stock of raw materials 1.1.20X7			2,100
Add Purchases			37,000
'' Carriage inwards			350
			39,450
Less Stock raw materials 31.12.20X7			(2,400)
Cost of raw materials consumed			37,050
Direct labour			18,000
Royalties			700
Prime cost			55,750
Indirect manufacturing costs:			
General factory expenses		3,100	
Lighting $^5/_6$		625	
Power		1,370	
Rent $^5/_6$		1,000	
Insurance $^5/_6$		350	
Depreciation of plant		2,800	
Indirect labour		14,500	
			23,745
			79,495
Add Work in progress 1.1.20X7			1,350
			80,845
Less Work in progress 31.12.20X7			(1,500)
Production cost of goods completed c/d			79,345
Sales			100,000
Less Cost of goods sold:			
Stock of finished goods 1.1.20X7		3,890	
Add Production cost of goods completed		79,345	
		83,235	
Less Stock of finished goods 31.12.20X7		(4,000)	
			(79,235)
Gross profit			20,765
Administration expenses			
Administrative salaries	4,400		
Rent $^1/_6$	200		
Insurance $^1/_6$	70		
General expenses	1,340		
Lighting $^1/_6$	125		
Depreciation of accounting machinery	200		
		6,335	
Selling and distribution expenses			
Sales reps' salaries	3,000		
Commission on sales	1,150		
Carriage outwards	590		
		4,740	
Financial charges			
Bank charges	230		
Discounts allowed	480		
		710	
			(11,785)
Net profit			8,980

J Jarvis
Balance Sheet as at 31 December 20X7

	£	£
Fixed assets		
Productive machinery at cost	28,000	
Less Depreciation to date	(7,800)	
		20,200
Accounting machinery at cost	2,000	
Less Depreciation to date	(1,000)	
		1,000
		21,200
Current assets		
Stock		
Raw materials	2,400	
Finished goods	4,000	
Work in progress	1,500	
Debtors	14,230	
Bank	5,680	
Cash	150	
	27,960	
Less Current liabilities		
Creditors	(12,500)	
Net current assets		15,460
		36,660
Financed by		
Capital		
Balance as at 1.1.20X7		29,680
Add Net profit		8,980
		38,660
Less Drawings		(2,000)
		36,660

37.14 Market value of goods manufactured

The financial statements of Jarvis, just illustrated, are subject to the limitation that the respective amounts of the gross profit which are attributable to the manufacturing side or to the selling side of the business are not known. A technique is sometimes used to bring out this additional information. By this method, the cost which would have been involved if the goods had been bought in their finished state instead of being manufactured by the business is brought into account. This is credited to the manufacturing account and debited to the trading account so as to throw up two figures of gross profit instead of one. It should be pointed out that the net profit will remain unaffected. All that will have happened will be that the figure of £20,765 gross profit will be shown as two figures instead of one. When added together, they will total £20,765.

The financial statements in summarised form will appear:

Manufacturing, Trading and Profit and Loss Account for the year ended
31 December 20X7

	£	£
Market value of goods completed c/d		95,000
Less Production cost of goods completed (as before)		79,345
Gross profit on manufacture c/d		15,655
Sales		100,000
Stock of finished goods 1.1.20X7	3,890	
Add Market value of goods completed b/d	95,000	
	98,890	
Less Stock of finished goods 31.12.20X7	(4,000)	
		(94,890)
Gross profit on trading c/d		5,110
Gross profit		
On manufacturing	15,655	
On trading	5,110	
		20,765

37.15 Further methods of providing for depreciation

In Chapter 26, the straight line and reducing balance methods for calculating depreciation were examined. We can now look at some further methods.

There is no information easily available to show how many organisations are using each method. It is possible to devise one's own special method. If it brings about an equitable charge for depreciation for the organisation, then the method will be suitable.

The revaluation method

When there are a few expensive items of fixed assets, it is not difficult to draw up the necessary accounts for depreciation. For each item we:

(*a*) Find its cost.
(*b*) Estimate its years of use to the business.
(*c*) Calculate and provide depreciation.
(*d*) Make the adjustments when the asset is disposed of.
(*e*) Calculate profit or loss on disposal.

This is worth doing for expensive items. There are, however, many examples of fixed assets for which the calculation would not be worth doing and, in fact, may be impossible. Some businesses will have many low cost fixed assets. Garages or engineering works will have a lot of spanners, screwdrivers and other small tools; brewers will have crates; laboratories will have many small, low cost glass instruments.

It would be impossible to follow procedures (*a*) to (*e*) above for every screwdriver or crate. Instead the revaluation method is used.

The method is not difficult to use. An example is shown in Exhibit 37.4:

Exhibit 37.4

A business has a lot of steel containers. These are not sold but are used by the business.

	£
On 1 January 20X6 the containers were valued at	3,500
During the year to 31 December containers were purchased costing	1,300
On 31 December 20X6 the containers were valued at	3,800

The depreciation is calculated:

	£
Value at start of period	3,500
Add Cost of items bought during period	1,300
	4,800
Less Value at close of period	(3,800)
Depreciation for year to 31 December 20X6	1,000

The depreciation figure £1,000 will be charged as an expense. Using this approach, we can look at Exhibit 37.5, where depreciation is entered in the books for the first three years of a business starting trading.

Exhibit 37.5

The business starts in business on 1 January 20X6.

	£
In its first year it buys crates costing	800
Their estimated value at 31 December 20X6	540
Crates bought in the year ended 31 December 20X7	320
Estimated value of all crates in hand on 31 December 20X7	530
Crates bought in the year ended 31 December 20X8	590
Estimated value of all crates in hand on 31 December 20X8	700

Crates

20X6			£	20X6			£
Dec	31	Cash (during the year)	800	Dec	31	Profit and loss	260
				''	31	Stock c/d	540
			800				800
20X7				20X7			
Jan	1	Stock b/d	540	Dec	31	Profit and loss	330
Dec	31	Cash (during the year)	320	''	31	Stock c/d	530
			860				860
20X8				20X8			
Jan	1	Stock b/d	530	Dec	31	Profit and loss	420
Dec	31	Cash (during the year)	590	''	31	Stock c/d	700
			1,120				1,120
20X9							
Jan	1	Stock b/d	700				

Profit and Loss Account for the year ended 31 December

		£	
20X6	Use of crates	260	
20X7	Use of crates	330	
20X8	Use of crates	420	

The balance of the crates account at the end of each year is shown as a fixed asset in the balance sheet.

Sometimes the business may make its own items such as tools or crates. In these instances the tools account or crates account should be debited with labour costs and material costs.

Revaluation is also used, for instance, by farmers for their cattle. Like other fixed assets depreciation should be provided for, but during the early life of an animal it will be appreciating in value, only to depreciate later. The task of calculating the cost of an animal becomes virtually impossible if it has been born on the farm, and reared on the farm by grazing on the pasture land and being fed on other foodstuffs, some grown on the farm and others bought by the farmer.

To get over this problem the revaluation method is used. Because of the difficulty of calculating the cost of the animals, they are valued at the price which they would fetch if sold at market. This is an exception to the general rule of assets being shown at cost price.

Depletion unit method

With fixed assets such as a quarry from which raw materials are dug out to be sold to the building industry, a different method is needed.

If a quarry was bought for £5,000 and it was expected to contain 1,000 tonnes of saleable materials, then for each tonne taken out we would depreciate it by £5, i.e. £5,000 ÷ 1,000 = £5.

This can be shown as:

$$\frac{\text{Cost of fixed asset}}{\text{Expected total contents in units}} \times \text{Number of units taken in period}$$

$$= \text{Depreciation for that period.}$$

Machine hour method

With a machine the depreciation provision may be based on the number of hours that the machine was operated during the period compared with the total expected running hours during the machine's life with the business. A business which bought a machine costing £2,000 having an expected running life of 1,000 hours, and no scrap value, could provide for depreciation of the machine at the rate of £2 for every hour it was operated during a particular accounting period.

Sum of the years' digits method

This method is popular in the USA but not common in the UK. It provides for higher depreciation to be charged early in the life of an asset with lower depreciation in later years.

Given an asset costing £3,000 which will be in use for 5 years, the calculations will be:

From purchase the asset will last for	5 years
From the second year the asset will last for	4 years
From the third year the asset will last for	3 years
From the fourth year the asset will last for	2 years
From the fifth year the asset will last for	1 year
Sum of these digits	15

	£
1st year 5/15 of £3,000 is charged =	1,000
2nd year 4/15 of £3,000 is charged =	800
3rd year 3/15 of £3,000 is charged =	600
4th year 2/15 of £3,000 is charged =	400
5th year 1/15 of £3,000 is charged =	200
	3,000

Units of output method

This method establishes the total expected units of output expected from the asset. Depreciation, based on cost less salvage value, is then calculated for the period by taking that period's units of output as a proportion of the total expected output over the life of the asset.

An instance of this could be a machine which is expected to be able to produce 10,000 widgets over its useful life. It has cost £6,000 and has an expected salvage value of £1,000. In year 1 a total of 1,500 widgets are produced, and in year 2 the production is 2,500 widgets.

The depreciation per period is calculated:

$$(\text{Cost} - \text{salvage value}) \times \left(\frac{\text{period's production}}{\text{total expected production}} \right)$$

$$\text{Year 1:} \quad £5,000 \times \frac{1,500}{10,000} = £750 \text{ depreciation}$$

$$\text{Year 2:} \quad £5,000 \times \frac{2,500}{10,000} = £1,250 \text{ depreciation}$$

Learning outcomes

You should now have learnt:

1 Why manufacturing accounts are used.

2 How to prepare manufacturing accounts and appropriate trading and profit and loss accounts.

3 That the trading account is used for calculating the gross profit made by selling the goods manufactured.

4 That the profit and loss account shows as net profit what is left of gross profit after all administration, selling and distribution and finance costs incurred have been deducted.

5 That work in progress, both at the start and the close of a period, must be adjusted to ascertain the production costs of goods completed in the period.

6 How to calculate depreciation using five more methods.

7 The reasons why each of these five depreciation methods may be used.

Answers to activities

37.1   You may have included some of the following:

Direct costs	Indirect costs
(1) raw materials	canteen wages
(2) machine operator's wages	rates
(3) packer's wages	rent
(4) machine set-up costs	insurance
(5) crane hire for building contract	storage of finished goods costs

However, you can only really do a split like this if you have a specific job or product in mind. You must first identify the 'cost object', that is, the item you are making or providing. Taking the example of a construction company building a hotel (it is engaged in other similar projects at the same time). The direct and indirect costs may include:

Direct costs	*Indirect costs*
(1) concrete	site canteen wages
(2) forklift truck operator's wages	company lawyer's salary
(3) bricklayer's wages	company architect's salary
(4) steel girders	company headquarters insurance
(5) windows	company warehousing costs

Now you should see that the indirect costs are not solely incurred in order to build the hotel. This is the key. Direct costs are those costs you can specifically link to a specific job. All the other costs of a job are indirect.

37.2   Because only administration expenses, selling and distribution expenses and financial charges appear in the profit and loss account part when a manufacturing account is being used. The rest all arose because manufacturing was taking place and can be directly or indirectly attributed to the products being produced, so they appear in the manufacturing account.

REVIEW QUESTIONS

37.1   A business both buys loose tools and also makes some itself. The following data is available concerning the years ended 31 December 20X4, 20X5 and 20X6.

20X4		£
Jan 1	Stock of loose tools	1,250
	During the year:	
	Bought loose tools from suppliers	2,000
	Made own loose tools: the cost of wages of employees being £275 and the materials cost £169	
Dec 31	Loose tools valued at	2,700
20X5		
	During the year:	
	Loose tools bought from suppliers	1,450
	Made own loose tools: the cost of wages of employees being £495 and the materials cost £390	
Dec 31	Loose tools valued at	3,340
20X6		
	During the year:	
	Loose tools bought from suppliers	1,890
	Made own loose tools: the cost of wages of employees being £145 and the materials cost £290. Received refund from a supplier for faulty tools returned to him	88
Dec 31	Loose tools valued at	3,680

You are to draw up the Loose Tools Account for the three years, showing the amount transferred as an expense in each year to the Manufacturing Account.

37.2   On 1 April 20X6 a business purchased a machine costing £112,000. The machine can be used for a total of 20,000 hours over an estimated life of 48 months. At the end of that time the machine is expected to have a trade-in value of £12,000.

The financial year of the business ends on 31 December each year. It is expected that the machine will be used for:

4,000 hours during the financial year ending 31 December 20X6
5,000 hours during the financial year ending 31 December 20X7
5,000 hours during the financial year ending 31 December 20X8
5,000 hours during the financial year ending 31 December 20X9
1,000 hours during the financial year ending 31 December 20Y0

Required:

(a) Calculate the annual depreciation charges on the machine on each of the following bases for each of the financial years ending on 31 December 20X6, 20X7, 20X8, 20X9 and 20Y0:
  (i)   the straight line method applied on a month for month basis,
  (ii) the diminishing balance method at 40% per annum applied on a full year basis, and
  (iii) the units of output method.

(b) Suppose that during the financial year ended 31 December 20X7 the machine was used for only 1,500 hours before being sold for £80,000 on 30 June.
  Assuming that the business has chosen to apply the straight line method on a month for month basis, show the following accounts for 20X7 only:
  (i)   the Machine account,
  (ii) the Provision for Depreciation – Machine account, and
  (iii) the Assets Disposals account.

(*Association of Accounting Technicians*)

37.3A On 1 January 20X1 a business purchased a laser printer costing £1,800. The printer has an estimated life of 4 years after which it will have no residual value.
  It is expected that the output from the printer will be:

Year	Sheets printed
20X1	35,000
20X2	45,000
20X3	45,000
20X4	55,000
	180,000

Required:

(a) Calculate the annual depreciation charges for 20X1, 20X2, 20X3 and 20X4 on the laser printer on the following bases:
  (i)   the straight line basis,
  (ii) the diminishing balance method at 60% per annum, and
  (iii) the units of output method.

  Note: Your workings should be to the nearest £.

(b) Suppose that in 20X4 the laser printer were to be sold on 1 July for £200 and that the business had chosen to depreciate it at 60% per annum using the diminishing balance method applied on a month for month basis.
  Reconstruct the following accounts for 20X4 only:
  (i)   the Laser Printer account,
  (ii) the Provision for Depreciation – Laser Printer account, and
  (iii) the Assets Disposals account.

(*Association of Accounting Technicians*)

37.4 Prepare manufacturing, trading and profit and loss accounts from the following balances of T Jackson for the year ended 31 December 20X7.

	£
Stocks at 1 January 20X7:	
Raw materials	18,450
Work in progress	23,600
Finished goods	17,470
Purchases: Raw materials	64,300
Carriage on raw materials	1,605
Direct labour	65,810
Office salaries	16,920
Rent	2,700
Office lighting and heating	5,760
Depreciation: Works machinery	8,300
Office equipment	1,950
Sales	200,600
Factory fuel and power	5,920

Rent is to be apportioned: Factory $^2/_3$; Office $^1/_3$. Stocks at 31 December 20X7 were: Raw materials £20,210, Work in progress £17,390, Finished goods £21,485.

37.5A   Chesterton Plc are manufacturers. At the end of their accounting year, 30 April 20X9, the following information was available:

	£
Stocks at 1 May 20X8:	
Raw materials	17,500
Finished goods	24,800
Work in progress	15,270
Wages and salaries	
Factory direct	138,500
Factory indirect	27,200
Purchases of raw materials	95,600
Power and fuel (indirect)	18,260
Sales	410,400
Insurance	3,680
Returns inwards (finished goods)	5,200
Stocks at 30 April 20X9:	
Raw materials	13,200
Finished goods	14,600
Work in progress	15,700

Notes:
- The company's machinery cost £82,000 and the provision for depreciation on 1 May 20X8 was £27,000. Machinery is to be depreciated by 20% per annum using reducing balance method.
- Fuel and power £390 in arrears at 30 April 20X9; at the same date insurance £240 is prepaid.
- Insurance is to be allocated: $^5/_8$ factory; $^3/_8$ administration.

Required:
For Chesterton Plc
(a) A manufacturing account for the year ended 30 April 20X9, showing clearly:
    (i)   cost of raw materials consumed
    (ii) prime cost
    (iii) total cost of production.
(b) A trading account for the year ended 30 April 20X9 showing clearly:
    (i)   cost of sales of finished goods
    (ii) gross profit.

(*Southern Examining Group: GCSE*)

37.6 D Saunders is a manufacturer. His trial balance at 31 December 20X6 is as follows:

	£	£
Delivery van expenses	2,500	
Lighting and heating: Factory	2,859	
Office	1,110	
Manufacturing wages	45,470	
General expenses: Factory	5,640	
Office	3,816	
Sales reps: commission	7,860	
Purchase of raw materials	39,054	
Rent: Factory	4,800	
Office	2,200	
Machinery (cost £50,000)	32,500	
Office equipment (cost £15,000)	11,000	
Office salaries	6,285	
Debtors	28,370	
Creditors		19,450
Bank	13,337	
Sales		136,500
Premises (cost £50,000)	40,000	
Stocks at 31 December 20X5:		
Raw materials	8,565	
Finished goods	29,480	
Drawings	8,560	
Capital		137,456
	293,406	293,406

Prepare the manufacturing, trading and profit and loss accounts for the year ended 31 December 20X6 and a balance sheet as at that date. Give effect to the following adjustments:

1 Stocks at 31 December 20X6: raw materials £9,050, finished goods £31,200. There is no work in progress.
2 Depreciate machinery £2,000, office equipment £1,500, premises £1,000.
3 Manufacturing wages due but unpaid at 31 December 20X6 £305, office rent prepaid £108.

37.7A Jean Marsh owns a small business making and selling children's toys. The following trial balance was extracted from her books on 31 December 20X9.

	Dr £	Cr £
Capital		15,000
Drawings	2,000	
Sales		90,000
Stocks at 1 January 20X9:		
Raw materials	3,400	
Finished goods	6,100	
Purchases of raw materials	18,000	
Carriage inwards	800	
Factory wages	18,500	
Office salaries	16,900	
J Marsh: salary and expenses	10,400	
General expenses:		
Factory	1,200	
Office	750	
Lighting	2,500	
Rent	3,750	
Insurance	950	
Advertising	1,400	
Bad debts	650	
Discount received		1,600
Carriage outwards	375	
Plant and machinery, at cost less depreciation	9,100	
Car, at cost less depreciation	4,200	
Bank	3,600	
Cash in hand	325	
Debtors and creditors	7,700	6,000
	112,600	112,600

You are given the following additional information.

1 Stocks at 31 December 20X9

    Raw materials   £2,900

    Finished goods   £8,200

    There was no work in progress.

2 Depreciation for the year is to be charged as follows:

    Plant and machinery   £1,500

    Car   £ 500

3 At 31 December 20X9 Insurance paid in advance was £150 and Office general expenses unpaid were £75.

4 Lighting and rent are to be apportioned: $^4/_5$ Factory, $^1/_5$ Office

    Insurance is to be apportioned: $^3/_4$ Factory, $^1/_4$ Office

5 Jean is the business's salesperson and her salary and expenses are to be treated as a selling expense. She has sole use of the business's car.

Questions:

For the year ended 31 December 20X9 prepare

(*a*) a manufacturing account showing prime cost and factory cost of production.

(*b*) a trading account.

(*c*) a profit and loss account, distinguishing between administrative and selling costs.

(*d*) a balance sheet as at 31 December 20X9.*

(*Midland Examining Group: GCSE*)

*Part (*d*) of the question was not in the original examination question. It has been added to give you further practice.

37.8 The following list of balances as at 31 July 20X6 has been extracted from the books of Jane Seymour who commenced business on 1 August 20X5 as a designer and manufacturer of kitchen furniture:

	£
Plant and machinery, at cost on 1 August 20X5	60,000
Motor vehicles, at cost on 1 August 20X5	30,000
Loose tools, at cost	9,000
Sales	170,000
Raw materials purchased	43,000
Direct factory wages	39,000
Light and power	5,000
Indirect factory wages	8,000
Machinery repairs	1,600
Motor vehicle running expenses	12,000
Rent and insurances	11,600
Administrative staff salaries	31,000
Administrative expenses	9,000
Sales and distribution staff salaries	13,000
Capital at 1 August 20X5	122,000
Sundry debtors	16,500
Sundry creditors	11,200
Balance at bank	8,500
Drawings	6,000

Additional information for the year ended 31 July 20X6:

(*i*)   It is estimated that the plant and machinery will be used in the business for 10 years and the motor vehicles used for 4 years: in both cases it is estimated that the residual value will be nil. The straight line method of providing for depreciation is to be used.

(*ii*)   Light and power charges accrued due at 31 July 20X6 amounted to £1,000 and insurances prepaid at 31 July 20X6 totalled £800.

(*iii*)   Stocks were valued at cost at 31 July 20X6 as follows:

Raw materials   £ 7,000
Finished goods   £10,000

(*iv*)   The valuation of work in progress at 31 July 20X6 included variable and fixed factory over-heads and amounted to £12,300.

(*v*)   Two-thirds of the light and power and rent and insurances costs are to be allocated to the factory costs and one-third to general administration costs.

(*vi*)   Motor vehicle costs are to be allocated equally to factory costs and general administration costs.

(*vii*)   Goods manufactured during the year are to be transferred to the trading account at £95,000.

(*viii*)   Loose tools in hand on 31 July 20X6 were valued at £5,000.

Required:

(*a*)   Prepare a manufacturing, trading and profit and loss account for the year ended 31 July 20X6 of Jane Seymour.

(*b*)   An explanation of how each of the following accounting concepts have affected the preparation of the above accounts:

• conservatism,
• matching,
• going concern.

(*Association of Accounting Technicians*)

Departmental accounts

Introduction

In this chapter, you'll learn how to prepare departmental trading and profit and loss accounts and about how they can be used in order to inform decision-makers considering the closure of a department. You'll learn how to apportion indirect costs and, finally, you'll learn that basing departmental trading and profit and loss accounts on contribution is both more helpful and informative and less misleading than when they are prepared on the gross profit basis.

38.1 Use of departmental accounts

Some items of accounting information are more useful than others. For a retail store with five departments, it is better to know that the store has made £10,000 gross profit than not to know what the gross profit was. However, it would obviously be better if we knew how much gross profit was made in each department.

Assume that the gross profits and losses of a business's departments were as follows:

Department	Gross profit	Gross loss
	£	£
A	4,000	
B	3,000	
C	5,000	
D		8,000
E	6,000	
	18,000	8,000

Gross profit of the business, £10,000.

If we knew the above information, we could see how well, or how badly, each part of the business was doing. If we closed down Department D we could make a greater total gross profit of £18,000. Perhaps we could replace Department D with a department which would make a gross profit instead of a loss.

> ### Activity 38.1
> Why do you think we have only mentioned gross profit and haven't referred to net profit?

You would have to know more about the business before you could be certain what the figures mean. For example, some stores deliberately allow parts of their business to lose money, so that customers come to the store to buy the cheap goods and then spend money in the other departments.

Accounting information seldom tells all the story. It serves as one measure, but there are other non-accounting factors to be considered before a relevant decision for action can be made.

The various pros and cons of the actions to be taken to increase the overall profitability of a business cannot therefore be properly considered until the departmental gross profits or losses are known. It must not be thought that departmental accounts refer only to departmental stores. They refer to the various facets of a business.

The reputation of many a successful business person has been built up on an ability to utilise the departmental account principle to guide their actions to increase the profitability of a business. The lesson still has to be learned by many medium-sized and small businesses. It is one of accounting's greatest and simplest aids to business efficiency.

To find out how profitable each part of the business is, we have to prepare departmental accounts to give us the facts for each department.

38.2 Allocation of expenses

The expenses of the business are often split between the various departments, and the net profit for each department then calculated. Each expense is divided between the departments on what is considered to be the most logical basis. This will differ considerably between businesses. An example of a trading and profit and loss account drawn up in such a manner is shown in Exhibit 38.1.

Exhibit 38.1

Northern Stores has three departments:

	(a) Jewellery £	(b) Hairdressing £	(c) Clothing £
Stock of goods or materials, 1 January 20X8	2,000	1,500	3,000
Purchases	11,000	3,000	15,000
Stock of goods or materials, 31 December 20X8	3,000	2,500	4,000
Sales and work done	18,000	9,000	27,000
Wages of assistants in each department	2,800	5,000	6,000

The following expenses cannot be traced to any particular department:

	£
Rent	3,500
Administration expenses	4,800
Air conditioning and lighting	2,000
General expenses	1,200

It is decided to apportion (i.e. spread) the cost of rent together with air conditioning and lighting in accordance with the floor space occupied by each department. These were taken up in the ratios of (a) one-fifth, (b) half, (c) three-tenths. Administration expenses and general expenses are to be split in the ratio of sales and work done.

Northern Stores
Departmental Trading and Profit and Loss Accounts for the year ended 31 December 20X8

	(a) Jewellery		(b) Hairdressing		(c) Clothing	
	£	£	£	£	£	£
Sales and work done		18,000		9,000		27,000
Cost of goods or materials:						
Stock 1.1.20X8	2,000		1,500		3,000	
Add Purchases	11,000		3,000		15,000	
	13,000		4,500		18,000	
Less Stock 31.12.20X8	(3,000)		(2,500)		(4,000)	
		(10,000)		(2,000)		(14,000)
Gross profit		8,000		7,000		13,000
Less Expenses:						
Wages	2,800		5,000		6,000	
Rent	700		1,750		1,050	
Administration expenses	1,600		800		2,400	
Air conditioning and lighting	400		1,000		600	
General expenses	400		200		600	
		(5,900)		(8,750)		(10,650)
Net profit/(loss)		2,100		(1,750)		2,350

This way of calculating net profits and losses seems to imply a precision that is, in fact, lacking, and can often lead to the mistaken interpretation that the Hairdressing Department has lost £1,750 this year, and that this amount would be saved if the department were closed down. It has already been stated that different departments are very often dependent on one another, and the answer to Activity 38.1 explained why. Therefore, you should realise that this amount of loss would not necessarily be be saved by closing the Hairdressing Department.

To explain this further, the calculation of departmental net profits and losses is dependent on the arbitrary division of indirect costs. It is by no means certain that the indirect costs of the Hairdressing Department would be avoided if it were closed down. Assuming that the sales staff of the department could be discharged without compensation, then £5,000 would be saved in wages. The other expenses shown under the Hairdressing Department would not, however, necessarily disappear.

The rent may still be payable in full even if the department were closed down. The administration expenses may turn out to be only slightly down, say from £4,800 to £4,600 – a saving of £200; air conditioning and lighting may fall by £500 to £1,500; general expenses may be reduced by £100 to £1,100. None of these reductions are obvious from the Departmental Trading and Profit and Loss Accounts.

Taking these cost reductions as what would actually happen were the Hairdressing Department to be closed, indicates that there would be a saving of £5,800:

	£
Administration expenses	200
Air conditioning and lighting	500
General expenses	100
Wages	5,000
	5,800

But when open, assuming this year is typical, the Hairdressing Department makes £7,000 gross profit. The business is therefore £1,200 a year better off when the department is open than when it is closed, subject to certain assumptions, such as:

(a) That the remaining departments would not be profitably expanded into the space vacated to give greater proportionate benefits than the Hairdressing Department.
(b) That a new type of department which would be more profitable than hairdressing could not be set up.
(c) That the floor space could not be leased to another business at a more profitable figure than that shown by hairdressing – you can see examples of this in many large stores where a part of the store has been leased to a coffee house like Starbucks or Costa Coffee.

Activity 38.2

What other possible events that can only occur if the department is closed could make it profitable to close the Hairdressing Department?

There are also other factors which, though not easily seen in an accounting context, are still extremely pertinent. They are concerned with the possible loss of confidence in the business by customers generally – what appears to be an ailing business does not usually attract large numbers of customers.

Also, the effect on the remaining staff should not be ignored. The fear that the dismissal of the hairdressing staff may also happen to them may result in the loss of other staff, especially the most competent members who could easily find work elsewhere, and so the general quality of the staff may decline with serious consequences for the business.

38.3 Allocation of expenses: a better method

It is less misleading to show costs split as follows:

First section of trading and profit and loss account	Direct costs allocated entirely to the department which would *not* be paid if the department closed down
Second section of trading and profit and loss account	Costs not directly traceable to the department or which would still be payable even if the department closed down (i.e. indirect costs and fixed costs)

The *surpluses* brought down from the first section represent the **contribution** that each department has made to cover the remaining costs, the remainder being the net profit for the whole of the business. If direct costs of a department were greater than the sales figure then the result would be a **negative contribution**.

From the figures given in Exhibit 38.1 the departmental trading and profit and loss accounts prepared on the basis of contribution rather than gross profit would appear as in Exhibit 38.2:

Exhibit 38.2

Northern Stores

Departmental Trading and Profit and Loss Accounts for the year ended 31 December 20X8

	(a) Jewellery		(b) Hairdressing		(c) Clothing	
	£	£	£	£	£	£
Sales and work done		18,000		9,000		27,000
Less cost of goods or materials:						
Stock 1.1.20X8	2,000		1,500		3,000	
Add Purchases	11,000		3,000		15,000	
	13,000		4,500		18,000	
Less Stock 31.12.20X8	(3,000)		(2,500)		(4,000)	
	10,000		2,000		14,000	
Wages	2,800		5,000		6,000	
		(12,800)		(7,000)		(20,000)
Surpluses c/d		5,200		2,000		7,000

All Departments

	£	£
Surpluses b/d:		
Jewellery	5,200	
Hairdressing	2,000	
Clothing	7,000	
		14,200
Less		
Rent	3,500	
Administration expenses	4,800	
Air conditioning and lighting	2,000	
General expenses	1,200	
		(11,500)
Net profit		2,700

The contribution of a department is the result of activities which are under the control of a departmental manager. The efficiency of their control will affect the amount of the contribution.

The costs in the second section, such as rent, insurance or lighting, cannot be affected by the departmental manager. It is therefore only fair if the departmental manager is judged by the *contribution* of his or her department rather than the net profit of the department.

In examinations, students must answer the questions as set, and not give their own interpretations of what the question should be. Therefore, if examiners give details of the methods of apportionment of expenses, then they are really looking for an answer in the same style as Exhibit 38.1.

38.4 The balance sheet

The balance sheet does not usually show assets and liabilities split between different departments.

38.5 Inter-departmental transfers

Purchases made for one department may be subsequently sold in another department. In such a case, the items should be deducted from the figure for purchases of the original purchasing department, and added to the figure for purchases for the subsequent selling department.

Learning outcomes

You should now have learnt:

1 How to prepare departmental trading and profit and loss accounts on the gross profit basis.

2 How to prepare departmental trading and profit and loss accounts on the contribution basis.

3 That it is desirable for the contribution of each section of a business to be calculated to aid management decisions and that the contribution-based trading and profit and loss account is more appropriate for departmental closure decisions than the gross-profit-based statement.

4 That costs should be divided between those which can logically be allocated to departments and those which cannot.

5 That a negative contribution is only one guide as to whether a section of a business should be closed. There may be other factors which would go against such a closure, and others that would suggest that even departments with positive contributions should be closed.

Answers to activities

38.1 Indirect costs and fixed costs. Net profit includes them. Unlike a manufacturing company, in a trading company, the only costs that are included in the calculation of gross profit are the purchase costs of the items that were sold.

Indirect costs and direct wages and direct expenses appear in the profit and loss account as deductions from gross profit. So far as the direct costs are concerned, it would be appropriate to include them in any comparison between departments because they were definitely incurred for and by the department to which their cost is charged. However, it is not appropriate to include the indirect costs because they have to be spread across all the departments on a basis that is subjective rather than objective. That is, you cannot be certain that they were incurred in respect of the department to which they are charged.

Fixed costs can be direct expenses (e.g. lease of a cash register) or indirect expenses (e.g. rates). They are period costs of the business. They cannot be changed in the timescale you are looking at. If you wanted to know the net profit of a department, you would need to spread the indirect fixed costs across all the departments. This results in charges that are, at best, a close approximation to the extent to which each department merits that level of indirect fixed cost. Often it has very little to do with appropriateness of the charge made on each department. If you tried to use net profit to make comparisons, you would be basing any conclusion on figures that could easily have been very different had a different and, possibly, more appropriate method of spreading the indirect fixed costs been used. In addition to all this, there is also the question of what happens to the fixed costs, both direct and indirect, that you have charged to a department that you have decided to close because it is making a net loss. Perhaps the other departments are only profitable because the loss-making department is absorbing some of the fixed costs.

38.2 There is a large range of possibilities. You may have suggested some of the following:

- a restaurant could be opened by the store, attracting more shoppers and, therefore, boosting the sales of the remaining departments;
- the floor space could be used for a children's play area, thereby making the store more attractive to families with young children;
- the floor space could be converted to contain chairs, tables, plants and sculptures where shoppers can relax and chat to each other during the time they are in the store – you can see examples of this in many modern shopping centres.

REVIEW QUESTIONS

38.1 From the following you are to draw up the trading account for Charnley's Department Store for the year ended 31 December 20X8.

Stocks:	1.1.20X8		31.12.20X8
	£		£
Electrical Department	6,080		7,920
Furniture Department	17,298		16,150
Leisure Goods Department	14,370		22,395
Sales for the year:		£	
Electrical Department		29,840	
Furniture Department		73,060	
Leisure Goods Department		39,581	
Purchases for the year:			
Electrical Department		18,195	
Furniture Department		54,632	
Leisure Goods Department		27,388	

38.2 J Spratt is the proprietor of a shop selling books, periodicals, newspapers and children's games and toys. For the purposes of his accounts he wishes the business to be divided into two departments:

Department A   Books, periodicals and newspapers.
Department B   Games, toys and fancy goods.

The following balances have been extracted from his nominal ledger at 31 March 20X9:

	Dr	Cr
	£	£
Sales Department A		15,000
Sales Department B		10,000
Stocks Department A, 1 April 20X8	250	
Stocks Department B, 1 April 20X8	200	
Purchases Department A	11,800	
Purchases Department B	8,200	
Wages of sales assistants Department A	1,000	
Wages of sales assistants Department B	750	
Newspaper delivery wages	150	
General office salaries	750	
Rates	130	
Fire insurance – buildings	50	
Lighting and air conditioning	120	
Repairs to premises	25	
Internal telephone	25	
Cleaning	30	
Accountancy and audit charges	120	
General office expenses	60	

Stocks at 31 March 20X9 were valued at:
Department A £300
Department B £150

The proportion of the total floor area occupied by each department was:
Department A one-fifth
Department B four-fifths

Prepare J Spratt's trading and profit and loss account for the year ended 31 March 20X9, apportioning the costs, where necessary, to show the Department profit or loss. The apportionment should be made by using the methods as shown:

Area – Rates, Fire insurance, Lighting and air conditioning, Repairs, Telephone, Cleaning; Turnover – General office salaries, Accountancy, General office expenses.

38.3A   From the following list of balances you are required to prepare a departmental trading and profit and loss account in columnar form for the year ended 31 March 20X9, in respect of the business carried on under the name of Ivor's Superstores:

			£	£
Rent and rates				4,200
Delivery expenses				2,400
Commission				3,840
Insurance				900
Purchases:	Dept.	A	52,800	
		B	43,600	
		C	34,800	
				131,200
Discounts received				1,968
Salaries and wages				31,500
Advertising				1,944
Sales:	Dept.	A	80,000	
		B	64,000	
		C	48,000	
				192,000
Depreciation				2,940
Opening stock:	Dept.	A	14,600	
		B	11,240	
		C	9,120	
				34,960
Administration and general expenses				7,890
Closing stock:	Dept.	A	12,400	
		B	8,654	
		C	9,746	
				30,800

Except as follows, expenses are to be apportioned equally between the departments.

Delivery expenses – proportionate to sales.
Commission – 2 per cent of sales.
Salaries and wages; Insurance – in the proportion of 6:5:4.
Discounts received – 1.5 per cent of purchases.

Cash flow statements

Introduction

In this chapter, you'll learn about cash flow statements, how to prepare them and the requirements of FRS 1, the accounting standard that regulates their preparation.

39.1 Need for cash flow statements

For any business it is important to ensure that:

- Sufficient profits are made to finance the business activities.
- Sufficient cash funds are available as and when needed.

Activity 39.1
What do you think is meant by 'cash' in this context? (Hint: what are truly liquid assets?)

We ascertain the amount of profits in a profit and loss account. We also show what the assets, capital and liabilities are at a given date by drawing up a balance sheet. Although the balance sheet shows the cash balance (see definition later) at a given date, it does not show us how we have used our cash funds during the accounting period.

What we really need, to help throw some light on to the cash situation, is some form of statement which shows us exactly where the cash has come from during the year, and exactly what we have done with it. The statement that fulfils these needs is called a **cash flow statement**.

39.2 Financial Reporting Standard 1: Cash Flow Statements

In 1991, the Accounting Standards Board issued the first Financial Reporting Standard (FRS 1). It was revised and reissued in 1996. The standard, as its title suggests, concerns the preparation of cash flow statements.

This focus on cash flow has not always been considered of such importance. An earlier SSAP (which FRS 1 replaced) had favoured the use of 'source and application of funds statements'. These funds were concerned with working capital and not cash. FRS 1 changed all of this, with cash as the central item.

The Accounting Standards Board requires all but the smallest comapnies to include cash flow statements with their published financial statements. It does, however, encourage all other organisations preparing financial statements to use them.

39.3 Businesses other than companies

Although small companies, partnerships and sole traders do not have to prepare them, cash flow statements can be of considerable use to all organisations.

FRS 1 prescribes a format for cash flow statements. An example is shown later in Exhibit 39.6. This is suitable for a company but, obviously, there are factors concerning partnerships and sole traders which do not occur in companies. It will be of help to students if the cash flow statements for sole traders and partnerships are fashioned to be as like those for companies as is possible. Consequently, the layouts for cash flow statements of sole traders and partnerships in this book will follow the style of layout as laid down in FRS 1.

39.4 Profit and liquidity not directly related

Many people think that if we are making profits then there should be no shortage of cash. As you have learnt earlier in this book, this is not necessarily so. Let's look at a few instances where, although reasonable profits are being made by each of the following businesses, they could find themselves short of cash, maybe not now, but at some time in the future.

- A sole trader is making £40,000 a year profits. However, his drawings have been over £60,000 a year for some time.
- A company has been over-generous with credit terms to debtors, and last year extended the time in which debtors could pay from one month to three months. In addition it has taken on quite a few extra customers who are not creditworthy and such sales may result in bad debts in the future.
- A partnership whose products will not be on the market for quite a long time has invested in some very expensive machinery. A lot of money has been spent now, but no income will result in the near future.

In all of these cases, each of the businesses could easily run out of cash. In fact many businesses fail and are wound up because of cash shortages, despite adequate profits being made. Cash flow statements can help to signal the development of such problems.

Activity 39.2
Can you think of any more examples? Spend a minute thinking about this and then write down any you come up with.

39.5 Where from: where to

Basically a cash flow statement shows where the cash funds came from, and where they have gone to. Exhibit 39.1 shows details of such cash flows.

Exhibit 39.1

Cash comes from	Cash funds		Cash goes to
	In	Out	
1 Profits			1 Losses
2 Sales of Fixed Assets			2 Purchase of Fixed Assets
3 Decrease in Stock			3 Increase in Stock
4 Decrease in Debtors			4 Increase in Debtors
5 Capital Introduced			5 Drawings/Dividends
6 Loans Received			6 Loans Repaid
7 Increase in Creditors			7 Decrease in Creditors

These can be explained as follow:

1 Profits bring a flow of cash into the business. Losses take cash out of it.
2 The cash received from sales of fixed assets comes into the business. A purchase of fixed assets takes it out.
3 Reducing stock in the normal course of business means turning it into cash. An increase in stock ties up cash funds.
4 A reduction in debtors means that the extra amount paid comes into the business as cash. Letting debtors increase stops that extra amount of cash coming in.
5 An increase in a sole proprietor's capital, or issues of shares in a company, brings cash in. Drawings or dividends take it out.
6 Loans received bring in cash, while their repayment reduces cash.
7 An increase in creditors keeps the extra cash in the business. A decrease in creditors means that the extra payments take cash out.

If, therefore, we take the cash (and bank) balances at the start of a financial period, and adjust for cash flows in and out during the financial period, then we should arrive at the cash (and bank) balances at the end of the period. This can be shown as:

$$\left.\begin{array}{l}\text{Cash per}\\\text{balance}\\\text{sheet at the}\\\text{end of the}\\\text{previous}\\\text{period}\end{array}\right\} + \boxed{\begin{array}{l}\text{Changes – which must be because of}\\\text{cash flows during intervening period}\end{array}} = \left\{\begin{array}{l}\text{Cash per}\\\text{balance}\\\text{sheet at the}\\\text{end of the}\\\text{current}\\\text{period}\end{array}\right.$$

39.6 Construction of a cash flow statement

We will first of all look at a cash flow statement drawn up for a sole trader's business, as this will be easier than looking at the more complicated example of a limited company.

We will start from Exhibit 39.2 and construct Exhibit 39.3, a cash flow statement.

Exhibit 39.2

The following are the balance sheets of T Holmes as at 31 December 20X6 and 31 December 20X7:

	31.12.20X6		31.12.20X7	
Fixed assets	£	£	£	£
Premises at cost		25,000		28,800
Current assets				
Stock	12,500		12,850	
Debtors	21,650		23,140	
Cash and bank balances	4,300		5,620	
	38,450		41,610	
Less Current liabilities				
Creditors	(11,350)		(11,120)	
Working capital		27,100		30,490
		52,100		59,290
Financed by:				
Capital				
Opening balances b/fwd		52,660		52,100
Add Net profit for year		16,550		25,440
		69,210		77,540
Less Drawings		(17,110)		(18,250)
		52,100		59,290

Note: For simplicity, no depreciation has been charged in the accounts.

Exhibit 39.3

T Holmes
Cash Flow Statement for the year ended 31 December 20X7

	£
Net cash flow from operating activities (*see* Note 1)	23,370
Capital expenditure and financial investment	
Payment to acquire extra premises	(3,800)
Financing	
Drawings	(18,250)
Increase in cash	1,320

Notes:
1 Reconciliation of net profit to net cash inflow:

	£	£
Net profit		25,440
Less cash used for:		
Increase in stock	350	
Increase in debtors	1,490	
Decrease in creditors	230	
		(2,070)
Net cash flow from operating activities		23,370

2 Analysis of changes in cash during the year:

	£
Balance at 1 January 20X7	4,300
Net cash inflow	1,320
Balance at 31 December 20X7	5,620

39.7 Note on the use of brackets

As you know, in accounting it is customary to show a figure in brackets if it is a minus figure. This would be deducted from the other figures to arrive at the total of the column. These are seen very frequently in cash flow statements. For example, instead of bringing out a sub-total of the deductions, Note 1 accompanying Exhibit 39.3 would normally be shown as:

	£
Net profit	25,440
Increase in stock	(350)
Increase in debtors	(1,490)
Decrease in creditors	(230)
	23,370

39.8 Adjustments needed to net profit

You saw in the cash flow statement in Exhibit 39.3 that when net profit is included as a source of cash funds, the net profit figure has to be adjusted to take account of items included which do not involve a movement of cash *in the period covered by the cash flow statement*. The most common examples are depreciation, provisions for doubtful debts, and book profits and losses on the sale or disposal of fixed assets.

Depreciation

For instance, suppose we bought equipment costing £3,000 in the year ended 31 December 20X6. It is depreciated at £1,000 per annum for 3 years and then scrapped, disposal value being nil. This would result in the following:

	Years to 31 December		
	20X6	20X7	20X8
	£	£	£
(i) Item involving flow of cash:			
Cost of equipment (as this is purchase of an asset this is not part of the net profit calculation)	3,000		
(ii) Net profit before depreciation	12,000	13,000	15,000
(iii) Items not involving flow of cash:			
Depreciation	(1,000)	(1,000)	(1,000)
(iv) Net profit after depreciation	11,000	12,000	14,000

Now the question arises as to which of figures (*i*) to (*iv*) are the ones to be used in cash flow statements. Let us examine items (*i*) to (*iv*) accordingly.

(*i*)   A payment of £3,000 is made to buy equipment. This *does* involve a flow of cash and should therefore be included in the cash flow statement for 20X6.

(*ii*) Depreciation is represented by a bookkeeping entry:
Debit profit and loss: Credit provision for depreciation.
This does not involve any outflow of cash and *should not* be shown in a cash flow statement.

(*iii*) Net profit before depreciation. This brings cash flowing into the business and therefore *should* be shown in cash flow statements.

(*iv*) Net profit after depreciation. Depreciation does not involve cash flow, and therefore (*iii*) is the net profit we need.

In most examination questions (*iii*) will not be shown. As we will show you, the figure for net profit before depreciation will be calculated in the cash flow statement itself.

Doubtful debts provisions

A provision for doubtful debts is similar to a provision for depreciation. The cash flow occurs when a debt is paid, *not* when provisions are made in case there may be bad debts in the future. As a result, when preparing the cash flow statement, you need to add back to net profit any increase in doubtful debt provision or deduct from net profit any decrease in the doubtful debt provision.

If an examination question gives you the net profits *after* doubtful debts provision, then the provision has to be added back to exclude it from the profit calculations.

Activity 39.3
What about bad debts? Should you make similar adjustments in the cash flow statement for them? Why/why not?

Book profit/loss on sales of fixed assets

If a fixed asset with a book value (after depreciation) of £5,000 is sold for £6,400 cash, then the flow of cash is £6,400. The fact that there has been a book profit of £1,400 does not provide any more cash above the figure of £6,400. Similarly, the sale of an asset with a book value of £3,000 for £2,200 cash produces a flow of cash of £2,200. Book profits and losses of this type need to be eliminated by adjusting the net profit when preparing the cash flow statement.

39.9 Example of adjustments

As the net profit figure in accounts is

(*i*) *after* adjustments for depreciation,
(*ii*) *after* adjustment to provisions for doubtful debts, and
(*iii*) *after* book profits/losses on sales of fixed assets,

net profit needs to be adjusted in cash flow statements for these three events. However, the adjustments are only for depreciation in *that period*, and for fixed asset book profits/losses for *that period*. No adjustments are needed with reference to previous periods. Exhibit 39.4 shows examples of three businesses.

Exhibit 39.4

	Business A £	Business B £	Business C £
Depreciation for year	2,690	4,120	6,640
Increases in doubtful debt provision	540	360	
Decrease in doubtful debt provision			200
Book loss on sale of fixed assets	1,200		490
Book profit on sale of fixed assets		750	
Net profit after the above items are included	16,270	21,390	32,410

Reconciliation of net profit to net cash inflow

	£	£	£
Net profit	16,270	21,390	32,410
Adjustment for items not involving the movement of funds:			
Depreciation	2,690	4,120	6,640
Book profit on sale of fixed assets		(750)	
Book loss on sale of fixed assets	1,200		490
Increase in doubtful debt provision	540	360	
Decrease in doubtful debt provision			(200)
Net cash flow from operating activities	20,700	25,120	39,340

You will notice that the items in brackets, i.e. (750) and (200), had been credits in the profit and loss accounts and need deducting, while the other items were debits and need adding back.

39.10 A comprehensive example

Exhibit 39.5

The balance sheets of R Lester are as follows:

		31.12.20X7				31.12.20X8	
	£	£	£	£	£	£	£
Fixed assets							
Equipment at cost		28,500				26,100	
Less Depreciation to date		(11,450)				(13,010)	
			17,050				13,090
Current assets							
Stock		18,570				16,250	
Debtors	8,470			14,190			
Less Bad debts provision	(420)			(800)			
		8,050				13,390	
Cash and bank balances		4,060				3,700	
		30,680				33,340	
Less Current liabilities							
Creditors		(4,140)				(5,730)	
Net current assets			26,540				27,610
			43,590				40,700
Loan from J Gorsey			(10,000)				(4,000)
			33,590				36,700
Financed by:							
Capital							
Opening balances b/d			35,760				33,590
Add Net profit			10,240				11,070
Add Cash introduced			–				600
			46,000				45,260
Less Drawings			(12,410)				(8,560)
			33,590				36,700

Note: Equipment with a book value of £1,350 was sold for £900. Depreciation written off equipment during the year was £2,610.

The cash flow statement will be as follows:

R Lester
Cash Flow Statement for the year ended 31 December 20X8

	£	£
Net cash flow from operating activities (*see* Note 1)		12,700
Capital expenditure and financial investment		
Receipts from sale of fixed assets		900
Financing		
Capital introduced	600	
Loan repaid to J Gorsey	(6,000)	
Drawings	(8,560)	
		(13,960)
Decrease in cash		(360)

Notes:

1 Reconciliation of net profit to net cash inflow:

	£	£
Net profit		11,070
Depreciation	2,610	
Loss on sale of fixed assets	450	
Increase in bad debts provision	380	
Decrease in stock	2,320	
Increase in creditors	1,590	
Increase in debtors	(5,720)	
		1,630
Net cash flow from operating activities		12,700

2 Analysis of changes in cash during the year:

	£
Balance at 1 January 20X8	4,060
Net cash inflow	(360)
Balance at 31 December 20X8	3,700

39.11 UK companies and FRS 1

We have already stated that UK companies, except the very smallest, have to publish a cash flow statement for each accounting period. Students whose level of studies terminates with the conclusion of *Business Accounting 1* will not normally need to know more than has already been written in this chapter. However, some will need to know the basic layout given in FRS 1.

There are two approaches available under the standard: the 'direct' method, which shows the operating cash receipts and payments summing to the net cash flow from operating activities – in effect, it summarises the Cash Book; and the 'indirect' method, which identifies the net cash flow via a reconciliation to operating profit. As the reconciliation has also to be shown when the direct method is used, it is hardly surprising that the indirect method is the more commonly adopted one, it is also the method that the ASB recommend (because the cost of producing the data required for the direct method is likely to be greater than the benefit of doing so, in most cases).

It is the indirect method that most examining bodies wish you to know. The basic layout is shown in Exhibit 39.6.

Exhibit 39.6

X LIMITED
Cash Flow Statement for the year ended 31 December 20X7

	£000	£000
1 **Net cash inflow/(outflow) from operating activities** (*see* Note 1)		XXX
2 *Dividends from joint ventures and associates*		XXX
3 *Returns on investments and servicing of finance*		
Interest received	XXX	
Interest paid	(XXX)	
Preference dividends paid	(XXX)	
Net cash inflow/(outflow) from returns on investments and servicing of finance		XXX
4 *Taxation*		XXX
5 *Capital expenditure and financial investment*		
Payments to acquire intangible fixed assets	XXX	
Payments to acquire tangible fixed assets	XXX	
Receipts from sales of tangible fixed assets	XXX	
Net cash inflow/(outflow) from capital expenditure and financial investment		XXX
6 *Acquisitions and disposals*		
Purchase of subsidiary undertaking	(XXX)	
Sale of business	XXX	
Net cash inflow/(outflow) from acquisitions and disposals		XXX
7 *Equity dividends paid*		(XXX)
8 *Management of liquid resources*		
Cash withdrawn from 7 day deposit	XXX	
Purchase of government securities	(XXX)	
Sale of corporate bonds	XXX	
Net cash inflow/(outflow) from management of liquid resources		XXX
9 *Financing*		
Issue of ordinary share capital	XXX	
Repurchase of debenture loan	(XXX)	
Expenses paid in connection with share issues	(XXX)	
		XXX
Increase/(decrease) in cash in the period		XXX

Reconciliation of net cash flow to movement in net debt/funds

	£000	£000
Increase/(decrease) in cash in the period	XXX	
Cash inflow/(outflow) from increase/decrease in debt and lease financing	XXX	
Cash inflow/(outflow) from decrease/increase in liquid resources	XXX	
Change in net debt resulting from cash flows		XXX
Loans and finance leases acquired with subsidiary		(XXX)
New finance leases		(XXX)
Exchange rate translation differences		XXX
Movement in net debt in the period		XXX
Net debt at 1 January 20X7		XXX
Net debt at 31 December 20X7		XXX

Note to the cash flow statement

1 *Reconciliation of operating profit to net cash inflow/(outflow) from operating activities*

	£000
Operating profit	XXX
Depreciation charges	XXX
(Profit)/Loss on sale of tangible fixed assets	XXX
(Increase)/Decrease in stocks	XXX
(Increase)/Decrease in debtors	XXX
Increase/(Decrease) in creditors	XXX
Net cash inflow/(outflow) from operating activities	XXX

Each of the nine headings of the cash flow statement can be shown as one line in the statement and the detail in a note. (The numbers have been shown in Exhibit 39.6 in order to make it clear what the nine headings are. These line numbers would not normally be included in the cash flow statement.)

The first seven headings should be in the sequence shown. The eighth and ninth can be combined under one heading, so long as their cash flows are shown separately and separate sub-totals are given for each of them within it.

The reconciliation to net debt does not form part of the cash flow statement, nor does the reconciliation of operating profit to net cash flow from operating activities. Either can be shown in a separate note (as the reconciliation of operating profit to net cash flow from operating activities is shown above) or adjoining the cash flow statement (as in the case of the reconciliation of the movement of cash to net debt above).

39.12 Uses of cash flow statements

Cash flow statements have many uses other than the legal need for some companies to prepare them.

Let us first of all list a few cases where a business might find them useful in helping to answer their queries:

(a) One small businessman wants to know why he now has an overdraft. He started off the year with money in the bank, he has made profits, and yet he now has a bank overdraft.
(b) Another businessman wants to know why the bank balance has risen even though the business is losing money.
(c) The partners in a business have put in additional capital during the year. Even so, the bank balance has fallen dramatically. They want an explanation as to how this has happened.

A study of the final accounts themselves would not give them the information that they needed. However, a study of the cash flow statement in each case will reveal the answers to their questions.

Besides the answers to such specific queries, cash flow statements should also help businesses to assess the following:

- the cash flows which the business may be able to generate in the future;
- how far the business will be able to meet future commitments, e.g. tax due, loan repayments, interest payments, contracts that could possibly lose quite a lot of money;
- how far future share issues may be needed, or additional capital in the case of sole traders or partnerships;
- a valuation of the business.

You should now have learnt:

1 Why cash flow statements provide useful information for decision-making.

2 A range of sources and applications of cash.

3 How to adjust net profit for non-cash items to find the net cash flow from operating activities.

4 How to prepare a cash flow statement as defined by FRS 1.

5 How to present the net cash flow from operating activities using the indirect method.

6 Some of the uses that can be made of cash flow statements.

Answers to activities

39.1   Liquidity is the key. Nowadays, something is generally considered as sufficiently liquid to be described as 'cash' in this context if it can definitely be turned into cash within three months. Not only does **cash** in this sense include the obvious – cash balances and bank balances – it also includes funds invested in **cash equivalents**. These cash equivalents consist of the temporary investments of cash not required at present by the business, such as funds put on short-term deposit with a bank. Such investments must be readily convertible into cash, or available as cash within three months.

   This is an important definition and is one you should memorise if cash flow statements are examinable under the syllabus of your course.

39.2   Other examples include:

   • The bank overdraft has been growing steadily and is now greater than the amount owed by debtors.
   • A major supplier is experiencing cash flow problems and is threatening not to provide any further goods unless all bills are paid within 5 working days. Your business has no other sources of supply for these goods and the bank has indicated that it will not advance any further loans or increase the overdraft facility.
   • A seriously dangerous defect has been identified in the sole product manufactured by the business. This could lead to all items sold in the last year having to be replaced with newly produced replacements. The faulty items cannot be repaired. The business has already borrowed as much as it is allowed by the bank.

39.3   A bad debt that is written off represents an expense that *does not* involve a flow of cash during the period. A debt becomes cash when paid, and only does so at the time payment is received. In writing off the debt, you are saying that cash will not be received and have written the debt off to the profit and loss account. In theory, you need to adjust both the profit (by adding it back) and the change in the debtor balance. *However, these adjustments cancel each other out, so you need to do nothing when preparing the cash flow statement.*

REVIEW QUESTIONS

39.1   The balance sheets of M Daly, a sole trader, for two successive years are shown below. You are required to draw up a cash flow statement for the year ended 31 December 20X4.

Balance Sheets as at 31 December

	20X3			20X4		
	£	£	£	£	£	£
Fixed assets						
Land and premises (cost £3,000)			2,600			2,340
Plant and machinery						
(cost £2,000)			1,500			–
(cost £3,000)			–			2,300
			4,100			4,640
Current Assets						
Stocks		660			630	
Trade debtors		1,780			1,260	
Bank		–			710	
		2,440			2,600	
Current Liabilities						
Trade creditors	1,200			840		
Bank overdraft	640			–		
		(1,840)			(840)	
			600			1,760
			4,700			6,400
Loan (repayable December 20X9)			–			(1,000)
			4,700			5,400
Represented by						
Capital account:						
Balance at 1 January			4,200			4,700
Add Net profit for the year			1,800			2,200
			6,000			6,900
Less drawings			(1,300)			(1,500)
			4,700			5,400

39.2A

John Flynn

Balance Sheets as at 31 December

	20X8			20X9		
	£	£	£	£	£	£
Fixed assets						
Buildings			5,000			5,000
Fixtures *less* Depreciation			1,800			2,000
Van *less* Depreciation			2,890			5,470
			9,690			12,470
Current Assets						
Stocks		3,000			8,410	
Trade debtors		4,860			5,970	
Bank		3,100			–	
Cash		350			150	
		11,310			14,530	
Current Liabilities						
Creditors	2,900			2,040		
Bank overdraft	–			1,260		
		(2,900)			(3,300)	
			8,410			11,230
			18,100			23,700
Loan (repayable in 10 years' time)			(2,000)			(5,000)
			16,100			18,700
Represented by						
Capital account:						
Balance at 1 January			15,500			16,100
Add Net profit for the year			6,800			7,900
Cash introduced			–			2,500
			22,300			26,500
Less Drawings			(6,200)			(7,800)
			16,100			18,700

Draw up a cash flow statement for John Flynn for the year ended 31 December 20X9. You are told that fixtures bought in 20X9 cost £400, whilst a van was bought for £4,000.

39.3 Malcolm Phillips is a sole trader who prepares his accounts annually to 30 April. His summarised balance sheets for the last two years are shown below.

Balance Sheets as at 31 April

	20X8			20X9		
	£	£	£	£	£	£
Fixed assets			15,500			18,500
Less Provision for depreciation			(1,500)			(1,700)
			14,000			16,800
Current assets						
Stocks		3,100			5,900	
Trade debtors		3,900			3,400	
Bank		1,500			–	
		8,500			9,300	
Current liabilities						
Trade creditors	2,000			2,200		
Bank overdraft	–			900		
		(2,000)			(3,100)	
			6,500			6,200
			20,500			23,000
Represented by						
Capital account:						
Balance at 1 May			20,000			20,500
Add Net profit for the year			7,000			8,500
Additional capital introduced			–			2,000
			27,000			31,000
Less Drawings			(6,500)			(8,000)
			20,500			23,000

Malcolm is surprised to see that he now has an overdraft, in spite of making a profit and bringing in additional capital during the year.

Questions:
(a) Draw up a suitable financial statement which will explain to Malcolm how his overdraft has arisen.
(b) The following further information relates to the year ended 30 April 20X9.

	£
Sales (all on credit)	30,000
Cost of sales	22,500

Calculate Malcolm's
(i) gross profit margin
(ii) rate of stock turnover.

(Midland Examining Group: GCSE)

39.4   From the following details you are to draft a cash flow statement for C Willis for the year ended 31 December 20X8:

C Willis

Profit and Loss Account for the year ended 31 December 20X8

	£	£
Gross profit		29,328
Add Discounts received	298	
Profit on sale of van	570	868
		30,196
Less Expenses		
Motor expenses	1,590	
Wages	8,790	
General expenses	2,144	
Bad debts	340	
Increase in bad debt provision	120	
Depreciation: Van	1,090	14,074
		16,122

Balance Sheets at 31 December

	20X7		20X8	
	£	£	£	£
Fixed assets				
Vans at cost		11,200		7,200
Less Depreciation to date		(4,160)		(2,980)
		7,040		4,220
Current assets				
Stock	10,295		17,150	
Debtors *less* provision*	5,190		3,380	
Bank	1,568		2,115	
	17,053		22,645	
Less Current liabilities				
Creditors	(2,770)		(2,920)	
		14,283		19,725
		21,323		23,945
Less Long-term liability				
Loan from P Bond		(6,000)		(5,000)
		15,323		18,945
Capital				
Opening balance b/d		12,243		15,323
Add Net profit		14,080		16,122
		26,323		31,445
Less Drawings		(11,000)		(12,500)
		15,323		18,945

*Debtors 20X7 £5,490 – provision £300.
 Debtors 20X8 £3,800 – provision £420.

Note: The van was sold for £2,300 during 20X8.

39.5A You are required to draw up a cash flow statement for S Markham for the year ended 30 June 20X8 from the following information:

S Markham
Profit and Loss Account for the year ended 30 June 20X8

	£	£
Gross profit		139,940
Add Reduction in bad debt provision		170
		140,110
Less Expenses:		
Wages and salaries	49,220	
General trading expenses	14,125	
Equipment running costs	16,040	
Motor vehicle expenses	8,110	
Depreciation: Motor vehicles	3,090	
Equipment	2,195	
Loss on sale of equipment	560	
		(93,340)
Net profit		46,770

Balance Sheets at 30 June

	20X7		20X8	
	£	£	£	£
Fixed assets				
Equipment at cost	31,150		20,100	
Less Depreciation to date	(18,395)		(14,600)	
		12,755		5,500
Motor vehicles at cost	22,510		22,510	
Less Depreciation to date	(7,080)		(10,170)	
		15,430		12,340
		28,185		17,840
Current assets				
Stock	28,970		32,005	
Debtors *less* provision*	16,320		15,050	
Bank	9,050		28,225	
	54,340		75,280	
Less Current liabilities				
Creditors	(11,350)		(14,360)	
		42,990		60,920
		71,175		78,760
Less Long-term liability				
Loan from A White		(21,185)		(10,000)
		49,990		68,760
Capital				
Opening balance		38,340		49,990
Add Net profit		36,150		46,770
		74,490		96,760
Less Drawings		(24,500)		(28,000)
		49,990		68,760

*Debtors 20X7 £17,000 – provision £680.
  Debtors 20X8 £15,560 – provision £510.

Note: The equipment was sold for £4,500.

Joint venture accounts

Introduction

Joint ventures are becoming increasingly common. In this chapter, you'll learn how to record joint ventures in the books of the parties to a joint venture. You'll learn how to calculate profits and identify how much each of the parties must pay to the other parties at the end of the joint venture. Finally you'll learn that an accounting standard has been issued to regulate accounting for longer-term and larger joint ventures.

40.1 Nature of joint ventures

Sometimes a particular business venture can best be done by two or more businesses joining together to do it instead of doing it separately. The joining together is for that one venture only, it is not joining together to make a continuing business.

Such projects are known as **joint ventures**. For instance, a merchant might provide the capital, the transport to the markets and the selling skills. The farmer grows the produce. The profits or losses are then shared between them in agreed ratios. It is like a partnership, but only for this one transaction. There may be several joint ventures between the same businesses, but each one is a separate venture. The agreements for each venture may be different from each other.

40.2 Accounting for large joint ventures

For large-scale or long-term joint ventures, a separate bank account and separate set of books are kept. In such cases the calculation of profit is not difficult. It is similar to preparing a set of financial statements in an ordinary business.

40.3 Accounting for smaller joint ventures

No separate set of books or separate bank accounts are kept for smaller joint ventures. Each of the parties will record in their own books only those transactions with which they have been concerned. Exhibit 40.1 gives an example of such a joint venture.

Exhibit 40.1

White of London and Green of Glasgow enter into a joint venture. White is to supply the goods and pay some of the expenses. Green is to sell the goods and receive the cash, and pay the remainder of the expenses. Profits are to be shared equally.

Details of the transactions are as follows:

	£
White supplied the goods costing	1,800
White paid wages	200
White paid for storage expenses	160
Green paid transport expenses	120
Green paid selling expenses	320
Green received cash from sales of all the goods	3,200

Stage 1

White and Green will each have entered up their own part of the transactions. White will have opened an account named 'Joint Venture with Green'. Similarly, Green will have opened a 'Joint Venture with White' account. The double entry to these joint venture accounts will be:

In White's books:

Payments by White:	Debit joint venture with Green
	Credit Cash Book
Goods supplied to Green:	Debit joint venture with Green
	Credit purchases

In Green's books:

Payments by Green:	Debit joint venture with White
	Credit Cash Book
Cash received by Green:	Debit Cash Book
	Credit joint venture with White

At this point the joint venture accounts in each of their books will appear as follows:

White's books (in London)

Joint Venture with Green

	£		
Purchases	1,800		
Cash: wages	200		
Cash: storage expenses	160		

Green's books (in Glasgow)

Joint Venture with White

	£		£
Cash: transport expenses	120	Cash: sales	3,200
Cash: selling expenses	320		

Stage 2

At this stage, White and Green know only the details in their own set of books. They do not yet know what the details are in the other person's books.

This means that they cannot yet calculate profits, or find out how much cash has to be paid or received to close the venture. To do this they must each send a copy of their joint venture accounts to the other person.

Each person will then draw up a **memorandum joint venture account**, to include all the details from each joint venture account. The memorandum joint venture account is not a double entry account. It is drawn up only (*a*) to find out the shares of net profit or loss, and (*b*) to help calculate the amounts payable and receivable to close the venture. White and Green's memorandum joint venture account is now shown:

White and Green
Memorandum Joint Venture Account

	£	£		£
Purchases		1,800	Sales	3,200
Wages		200		
Storage expenses		160		
Transport expenses		120		
Selling expenses		320		
Net profit:				
White (one-half)	300			
Green (one-half)	300			
		600		
		3,200		3,200

Note: The profit is the difference between the two sides of the account. You find out what the balancing figure is; in this case, it is £600. Then you split it in the profit sharing ratio. In this case, profits are shared equally. White and Green, therefore, each receive half the profit, £300 each. Now you enter the figures, £300 to White, £300 to Green, and the total of £600, which balances and closes off the account.

Activity 40.1

Look closely at the Memorandum Joint Venture account. Where does each entry in the Memorandum Joint Venture account appear in the Joint Venture with Green and Joint Venture with White T-accounts? Are they on the same side in each case, or the opposite side? What does this tell you about making entries in the Memorandum Joint Venture account?

Stage 3

The net profit shares for White and Green need to be brought into their own books. This is done as follows:

White's books
Debit share of profit to Joint Venture with Green account
   Credit White's profit and loss account

The Joint Venture account in White's books now looks like this:

White's books (in London)

Joint Venture with Green

	£		
Purchases	1,800		
Cash: wages	200		
Cash: storage expenses	160		
Share of profit transferred			
to profit and loss account	300		

You then do the same in Green's books:

Green's books
   Debit share of profit to Joint Venture with White account
      Credit Green's profit and loss account

Green's books (in Glasgow)

Joint Venture with White

	£		£
Cash: transport expenses	120	Cash: sales	3,200
Cash: selling expenses	320		
Share of profit transferred			
to profit and loss account	300		

It won't come as a surprise to see that you have now copied the profit share entries from the Memorandum Joint Venture account into the Joint Venture accounts held by White and Green. Now you need to balance off the two Joint Venture accounts:

White's books (in London)

Joint Venture with Green

	£		£
Purchases	1,800	Balance c/d	2,460
Cash: wages	200		
Cash: storage expenses	160		
Share of profit transferred			
to profit and loss account	300		
	2,460		2,460
Balance b/d	2,460		

Green's books (in Glasgow)

Joint Venture with White

	£		£
Cash: transport expenses	120	Cash: sales	3,200
Cash: selling expenses	320		
Share of profit transferred			
to profit and loss account	300		
Balance c/d	**2,460**		
	3,200		3,200
		Balance b/d	2,460

> ### Activity 40.2
> Can you remember what is meant by a debit balance? Is it where the balance c/d is a debit or where the balance b/d is a debit?

Finally, the parties in the joint venture need to settle their debts to each other. They know whether they are to pay money or receive money when they look at the side of their copy of the joint venture account and see whether the balance is a debit or a credit:

(a) If the balance brought down is a credit balance, money is owing to the other party in the joint venture. In this case, Green owes White the amount shown by the credit balance, £2,460.

(b) If the balance brought down is a debit balance, money is due from the other party in the joint venture. In this case White is owed the amount of the balance, £2,460 by Green.

The payment is now made by Green to White and the final entry is made in each of the joint venture accounts, closing off the accounts.

White's books (in London)

Joint Venture with Green

	£		£
Purchases	1,800	Balance c/d	2,460
Cash: wages	200		
Cash: storage expenses	160		
Share of profit transferred			
to profit and loss account	300		
	2,460		2,460
Balance b/d	2,460	Cash in settlement from Green	2,460

Green's books (in Glasgow)

Joint Venture with White

	£		£
Cash: transport expenses	120	Cash: sales	3,200
Cash: selling expenses	320		
Share of profit transferred			
to profit and loss account	300		
Balance c/d	2,460		
	3,200		3,200
Cash in settlement to White	2,460	Balance b/d	2,460

40.4 FRS 9: Associates and Joint Ventures

In 1997, in response to a growing number of joint ventures, the ASB issued FRS 9. For the first time, an accounting standard existed laying out the accounting treatment for joint ventures. It was aimed more at accounting for long-term joint ventures, which were mentioned briefly in Section 40.2. However, it confirmed that the above treatment of short-term joint ventures is appropriate by stating that participants should account for their own assets, liabilities and cash flows measured according to the agreement governing the arangement.

You should now have learnt:

1 That when two or more businesses join together for a particular business venture, and do not form a permanent business entity, they have entered into a joint venture.

2 That larger and long-term joint ventures operate a separate bank account and books dedicated to the project.

3 That the participants in smaller joint ventures rely on their own bank accounts and books to run and record their part of the project, using a *memorandum joint venture account* to pass the details of their part of the project to the other participant(s).

4 Why separate joint venture accounts are kept by each party to smaller and short-term joint ventures.

5 How to make the appropriate entries in the books of the parties to the joint venture, calculate the profit, share that profit among the parties to the joint ventures and close off the joint venture accounts at the end of the joint venture.

6 That FRS 9 regulates accounting for long-term and larger joint ventures.

Answers to activities

40.1 It's quite simple really, isn't it? You take each debit entry in the first of the T-accounts (Joint Venture with Green) and copy it as a debit entry into the Memorandum Joint Venture account. You then do the same with the debits in the second T-account (Joint Venture with White). Then you do exactly the same with the credit entries. The order you do this in doesn't matter. All you need to ensure is that you have replicated all the T-account entries in the Memorandum Joint Venture account.

40.2 An account with a debit balance has more value on the debit side. That is, it is the side on which the balance b/d figure lies that tells you whether the balance is a debit or a credit. In this case, the Joint Venture account in White's books has a debit balance. The one in Green's books has a credit balance. Therefore, Green owes White.

REVIEW QUESTIONS

40.1 Ollier and Avon enter a joint venture, to share profits or losses equally, resulting from dealings in second-hand cars. Both parties take an active part in the business, each recording his own transactions. They have no joint banking account or separate set of books.

20X9
Jan	1	Ollier buys three cars for £900.
"	31	Ollier pays for repairs and respraying of vehicles £60.
Mar	1	Avon pays garage rental £20 and advertising expenses £10.
Apr	12	Avon pays for licence and insurance renewal of vehicles £36.
Aug	10	Avon buys a vehicle in excellent condition for £100.
"	31	Ollier sells the four vehicles, to various clients, the sales being completed on this date, totalling £1,600.

Show the relevant accounts in the books of both partners.

40.2A Mr Carter entered into a joint venture with Mr Thomas for the purchase and sale of bicycles. They agreed that profits and losses should be shared equally.
The following transactions took place:

(*a*) Mr Carter purchased bicycles for £88,900 and paid carriage £273.

(*b*) Mr Thomas purchased bicycles for £7,560 and paid carriage £51.

(*c*) Mr Thomas paid to Mr Carter £40,000.

(*d*) Mr Carter sold bicycles for £73,400 and sent a cheque for £30,000 to Mr Thomas.

(*e*) Mr Thomas sold for £10,230 all the bicycles he had purchased.

(*f*) The unsold bicycles in the possession of Mr Carter were taken over by him at a valuation of £26,000.

(*g*) The amount due from one venturer to the other was paid and the joint venture was dissolved.

You are required to prepare:

(*i*) a statement to show the net profit or loss of the joint venture, and

(*ii*) the accounts for the joint venture in the books of Mr Carter and Mr Thomas.

40.3 Plant, Hoe & Reap entered into a joint venture for dealing in carrots. The transactions connected with this venture were:

20X9

Jan	8	Plant rented land cost £156.
"	10	Hoe supplied seeds cost £48.
"	17	Plant employed labour for planting £105.
"	19	Hoe charged motor expenses £17.
"	30	Plant employed labour for fertilising £36.
Feb	28	Plant paid the following expenses: Sundries £10, Labour £18, Fertiliser £29.
Mar	17	Reap employed labour for lifting carrots £73.
"	30	Sale expenses London paid by Reap £39.
"	31	Reap received cash from sale proceeds gross £987.

Required:

Show the joint venture accounts in the books of Plant, Hoe & Reap. Also show in full the method of arriving at the profit on the venture which is to be apportioned: Plant seven-twelfths; Hoe three-twelfths; Reap two-twelfths.

Any outstanding balances between the parties are settled by cheque on 30 April.

40.4A Wild, Wood and Bine enter into a joint venture for dealing in antique brass figures. The following transactions took place:

20X8

Mar	1	Wild rented a shop, paying 3 months' rent £150.
"	2	Wood bought a van for £2,700.
"	4	Wood bought antiques for £650.
"	15	Bine received cash from sale proceeds of antiques £3,790.
"	28	Wild bought antiques for £1,200.
Apr	11	Van broke down. Bine agreed to use his own van for the job, until cessation of the joint venture, at an agreed charge of £400.
"	13	Van bought on Mar 2 was sold for £2,100. Proceeds were kept by Wild.
"	15	Sales of antiques, cash being kept by Wood £780.
"	18	Lighting bills paid for shop by Bine £120.
"	30	Bine bought antiques for £440.
May	4	General expenses of shop paid for £800, Bine and Wild paying half each.
"	19	Antiques sold by Bine £990, proceeds being kept by him.
"	31	Joint venture ended. The antiques still in stock were taken over at an agreed valuation of £2,100 by Wood.

Required:

Show the joint venture accounts in the books of each of the three parties. Show in full the workings needed to arrive at the profit on the venture. The profit or loss was to be split: Wood one-half; Wild one-third; Bine one-sixth. Any outstanding balances between the parties were settled on 31 May 20X8.

PART 6

Partnership accounts and company accounts

Introduction

This part is concerned with accounting procedures, particularly those affecting partnerships; gives an introduction to goodwill in relation to partnerships and other business organisations; and introduces the accounts of limited liability companies.

Partnership accounts: an introduction

After you have studied this chapter, you should be able to:

- explain what a partnership is and how it differs from a joint venture
- explain the rules relating to the number of partners
- distinguish between limited partners and general partners
- describe the main features of a partnership agreement
- explain what will happen if no agreement exists on how to share profits or losses
- draw up the the ledger accounts and financial statements for a partnership

Introduction

In this chapter, you'll learn about the nature of partnerships and the regulations governing them. You'll learn that there are two types of partner, limited and general, and about the difference between them, and about the difference between those that are limited partnerships and those that are not. Finally, you'll learn how to prepare partnership ledger accounts and how to prepare partnership financial statements.

41.1 The need for partnerships

So far we have mainly considered businesses owned by only one person. We've also looked at joint ventures, which are temporary projects involving two or more parties where they work together to make a profit and then disband the joint venture. When a more permanent possibility exists, two or more people may form themselves into a **partnership**. This is a long-term commitment to operate in business together. The people who own a partnership are called **partners**. They do not have to be based or work in the same place, though most do. However, they maintain one set of accounting records and share the profits and losses.

Activity 41.1
From your general knowledge, can you think of any well-known partnerships where the partners are located, not just in different cities, but in different countries? What line of business are they in?

There are various reasons for multiple ownership of a business.

Activity 41.2
Think about this for a minute and then write down as many reasons as you can for people wanting to form a partnership.

In addition to the reasons suggested in the answer, there is also the fact that many business ventures carry financial risk should they fail. By forming a partnership, the level of risk is reduced. Firstly, any loss can be shared by all the partners and, secondly, by involving more than one person's expertise, the chances of failure are reduced.

There are two types of multiple ownership: partnerships and limited companies. This chapter deals only with partnerships. Limited companies will be the subject of Chapter 45.

41.2 Nature of a partnership

A partnership has the following characteristics:

1 It is formed to make profits.
2 It must obey the law as given in the Partnership Act 1890. If there is a **limited partner**, as described in 41.3, there is also the Limited Partnership Act of 1907 to comply with as well.
3 Normally there can be a minimum of two partners and a maximum of twenty partners. Exceptions are banks, where there cannot be more than ten partners; and there is no maximum for firms of accountants, solicitors, stock exchange members, surveyors, auctioneers, valuers, estate agents, land agents, estate managers, or insurance brokers.
4 Each partner (except for limited partners described below) must pay their share of any debts that the partnership could not pay. If necessary, they could be forced to sell all their private possessions to pay their share of the debts. This can be said to be unlimited liability.
5 Partners who are not limited partners are known as **general partners**.

41.3 Limited partnerships

Limited partnerships are partnerships containing one or more **limited partner**. Limited partnerships must be registered with the Registrar of Companies. Limited partners are not liable for the debts as in section 41.2 (4) above. Limited partners have the following characteristics and restrictions on their role in the partnership:

1 Their liability for the debts of the partnership is limited to the capital they have put in. They can lose that capital, but they cannot be asked for any more money to pay the debts unless they contravene the regulations relating to their involvement in the partnership (see 2 and 3 below).
2 They are not allowed to take out or receive back any part of their contribution to the partnership during its lifetime.
3 They are not allowed to take part in the management of the partnership or to have the power to make the partnership take a decision. If they do, they become liable for all the debts and obligations of the partnership up to the amount taken out or received back or incurred while taking part in the management of the partnership.
4 All the partners cannot be limited partners, so there must be at least one general partner with unlimited liability.

Activity 41.3
What advantages do you think there might be to general partners in having a limited partner?

41.4 Partnership agreements

Agreements in writing are not necessary. However, it is better if a proper written agreement is drawn up by a lawyer or accountant. Where there is a proper written agreement there will be fewer problems between partners. A written agreement means less confusion about what has been agreed.

41.5 Contents of partnership agreements

The written agreement can contain as much, or as little, as the partners want. The law does not say what it must contain. The usual accounting contents are:

1 The capital to be contributed by each partner.
2 The ratio in which profits (or losses) are to be shared.
3 The rate of interest, if any, to be paid on capital before the profits are shared.
4 The rate of interest, if any, to be charged on partners' drawings.
5 Salaries to be paid to partners.
6 Arrangements for the admission of new partners.
7 Procedures to be carried out when a partner retires or dies.

> ### Activity 41.4
> Some partnerships don't bother drawing up a partnership agreement. How do the partners in those partnerships know what rights and responsibiities they have?

Points 1 to 5 in the list above are now examined in detail. Points 6 and 7 will be taken up in later chapters.

1 Capital contributions

Partners need not contribute equal amounts of capital. What matters is how much capital each partner *agrees* to contribute. It is not unusual for partners to increase the amount of capital they have invested in the partnership.

2 Profit (or loss) sharing ratios

Partners can agree to share profits/losses in any ratio or any way that they may wish. However, it is often thought by students that profits should be shared in the same ratio as that in which capital is contributed. For example, suppose the capitals were Allen £2,000 and Beet £1,000, many people would share the profits in the ratio of two-thirds to one-third, even though the work to be done by each partner is similar. A look at the division of the first few years' profits on such a basis would be:

Years	1	2	3	4	5	Total
	£	£	£	£	£	£
Net profits	1,800	2,400	3,000	3,000	3,600	13,800
Shared:						
Allen $^2/_3$	1,200	1,600	2,000	2,000	2,400	9,200
Beet $^1/_3$	600	800	1,000	1,000	1,200	4,600

It can now be seen that Allen would receive £9,200, or £4,600 more than Beet. To treat each partner fairly, the difference between the two shares of profit in this case, as the duties of the partners are the same, should be adequate to compensate Allen for putting extra capital into the firm. It is obvious that £4,600 extra profits is more than adequate for this purpose, as Allen only put in an extra £1,000 as capital.

Consider too the position of capital ratio sharing of profits if one partner put in £99,000 and the other put in £1,000 as capital.

To overcome the difficulty of compensating for the investment of extra capital, the concept of **interest on capital** was devised.

3 Interest on capitals

If the work to be done by each partner is of equal value but the capital contributed is unequal, it is reasonable to grant interest on the partners' capitals. This interest is treated as a deduction prior to the calculation of profits and their distribution according to the profit sharing ratio.

The rate of interest is a matter of agreement between the partners, but it should equal the return which they would have received if they had invested the capital elsewhere.

Taking Allen and Beet's firm again, but sharing the profits equally after charging 5 per cent per annum interest on capital, the division of profits would become:

Years	1	2	3	4	5		Total
	£	£	£	£	£		£
Net profit	1,800	2,400	3,000	3,000	3,600		13,800
Interest on capitals							
Allen	100	100	100	100	100	=	500
Beet	50	50	50	50	50	=	250
Remainder shared:							
Allen ½	825	1,125	1,425	1,425	1,725	=	6,525
Beet ½	825	1,125	1,425	1,425	1,725	=	6,525

Summary	Allen	Beet
	£	£
Interest on capital	500	250
Balance of profits	6,525	6,525
	7,025	6,775

Allen has thus received £250 more than Beet, this being adequate return (in the partners' estimation) for having invested an extra £1,000 in the firm for five years.

4 Interest on drawings

It is obviously in the best interests of the firm if cash is withdrawn from the firm by the partners in accordance with the two basic principles of: (*a*) as little as possible, and (*b*) as late as possible. The more cash that is left in the firm the more expansion can be financed, the greater the economies of having ample cash to take advantage of bargains and of not missing cash discounts because cash is not available and so on.

To deter the partners from taking out cash unnecessarily the concept can be used of charging the partners interest on each withdrawal, calculated from the date of withdrawal to the end of the financial year. The amount charged to them helps to swell the profits divisible between the partners. The rate of interest should be sufficient to achieve this without being too harsh.

Suppose that Allen and Beet have decided to charge **interest on drawings** at 5 per cent per annum, and that their year end was 31 December. The following drawings are made:

Allen

Drawings		Interest		
				£
1 January	£100	£100 × 5% × 12 months	=	5
1 March	£240	£240 × 5% ×10 months	=	10
1 May	£120	£120 × 5% × 8 months	=	4
1 July	£240	£240 × 5% × 6 months	=	6
1 October	£ 80	£ 80 × 5% × 3 months	=	1
		Interest charged to Allen	=	26

Beet

Drawings		Interest		
				£
1 January	£ 60	£ 60 × 5% ×12 months	=	3
1 August	£480	£480 × 5% × 5 months	=	10
1 December	£240	£240 × 5% × 1 month	=	1
		Interest charged to Beet	=	14

5 Partnership salaries

One partner may have more responsibility or tasks than the others. As a reward for this, rather than change the profit and loss sharing ratio, the partner may have a **partnership salary** which is deducted before sharing the balance of profits.

6 Performance-related payments to partners

Partners may agree that commission or performance-related bonuses be payable to some or all the partners linked to their individual performance. As with salaries, these would be deducted before sharing the balance of profits.

41.6 An example of the distribution of profits

Taylor and Clarke have been in partnership for one year sharing profits and losses in the ratio of Taylor $^3/_5$, Clarke $^2/_5$. They are entitled to 5 per cent per annum interest on capitals, Taylor having £2,000 capital and Clarke £6,000. Clarke is to have a salary of £500. They charge interest on drawings, Taylor being charged £50 and Clarke £100. The net profit, before any distributions to the partners, amounted to £5,000 for the year ended 31 December 20X7.

	£	£	£
Net profit			5,000
Add Charged for interest on drawings:			
Taylor		50	
Clarke		100	
			150
			5,150
Less Salary: Clarke		500	
Interest on capital:			
Taylor	100		
Clarke	300		
		400	
			(900)
Balance of profits			4,250
Shared:			
Taylor $^3/_5$		2,550	
Clarke $^2/_5$		1,700	
			4,250

The £5,000 net profits have therefore been shared:

	Taylor	Clarke
	£	£
Balance of profits	2,550	1,700
Interest on capital	100	300
Salary	–	500
	2,650	2,500
Less Interest on drawings	(50)	(100)
	2,600	2,400

£5,000

41.7 The financial statements

If the sales, stock and expenses of a partnership were exactly the same as that of a sole trader, then the trading and profit and loss account would be identical with that as prepared for the sole trader. However, a partnership would have an extra section shown under the profit and loss account. This section is called the profit and loss appropriation account, and it is in this account that the distribution of profits is shown. The heading to the trading and profit and loss account does not include the words 'appropriation account'. It is purely an accounting custom not to include it in the heading. (Sometimes examiners ask for it to be included in the heading, in which case, you need to do so!)

The trading and profit and loss account and the profit and loss appropriation account of Taylor and Clarke from the details given would appear:

Taylor and Clarke
Trading and Profit and Loss Account for the year ended 31 December 20X7

(Trading Account – same as for sole trader)

(Profit and Loss Account – same as for sole trader)

Profit and Loss Appropriation Account

	£	£	£
Net profit (from the Profit and Loss Account)			5,000
Interest on drawings:			
Taylor		50	
Clarke		100	
			150
			5,150
Less: Interest on capitals			
Taylor	100		
Clarke	300		
Salary: Clarke		400	
		500	(900)
			4,250
Balance of profits shared:			
Taylor ³/₅		2,550	
Clarke ²/₅		1,700	
			4,250

41.8 Fixed and fluctuating capital accounts

There are two choices open to partnerships: **fixed capital accounts** plus current accounts, and **fluctuating capital accounts**.

1 Fixed capital accounts plus current accounts

The capital account for each partner remains year by year at the figure of capital put into the firm by the partners. The profits, interest on capital and the salaries to which the partner may be entitled are then credited to a separate current account for the partner, and the drawings and the interest on drawings are debited to it. The balance of the current account at the end of each financial year will then represent the amount of undrawn (or withdrawn) profits. A credit balance will be undrawn profits, while a debit balance will be drawings in excess of the profits to which the partner was entitled.

For Taylor and Clarke, capital and current accounts, assuming drawings of £2,000 each, will appear:

Taylor – *Capital*

			20X7				£
			Jan	1	Bank		2,000

Clarke – *Capital*

			20X7				£
			Jan	1	Bank		6,000

Taylor – *Current Account*

20X7			£	20X7			£
Dec	31	Cash: Drawings	2,000	Dec	31	Profit and loss	
''	31	Profit and loss				appropriation account:	
		appropriation account:				Interest on capital	100
		Interest on drawings	50			Share of profits	2,550
''	31	Balance c/d	600				
			2,650				2,650
				20X8			
				Jan	1	Balance b/d	600

Clarke – *Current Account*

20X7			£	20X7			£
Dec	31	Cash: Drawings	2,000	Dec	31	Profit and loss	
''	31	Profit and loss				appropriation account:	
		appropriation account:				Interest on capital	300
		Interest on drawings	100			Share of profits	1,700
''	31	Balance c/d	400			Salary	500
			2,500				2,500
				20X8			
				Jan	1	Balance b/d	400

Notice that the salary of Clarke was not paid to him, it was merely credited to his account. If in fact it was paid in addition to his drawings, the £500 cash paid would have been debited to the current account, changing the £400 credit balance into a £100 debit balance.

Examiners often ask for the capital accounts and current accounts to be shown in columnar form. For the previous accounts of Taylor and Clarke these would appear as follows:

Capital Accounts

	Taylor	Clarke				Taylor	Clarke
	£	£	20X7			£	£
			Jan	1	Bank	2,000	6,000

Current Accounts

			Taylor	Clarke				Taylor	Clarke
20X7			£	£	20X7			£	£
Dec	31	Cash: Drawings	2,000	2,000	Dec	31	Interest on capital	100	300
''	31	Interest on drawings	50	100	''	31	Share of profits	2,550	1,700
''	31	Balances c/d	600	400	''	31	Salary		500
			2,650	2,500				2,650	2,500
					20X8				
					Jan	1	Balances b/d	600	400

2 Fluctuating capital accounts

The distribution of profits would be credited to the capital account, and the drawings and interest on drawings debited. Therefore the balance on the capital account will change each year, i.e. it will fluctuate.

If fluctuating capital accounts had been kept for Taylor and Clarke they would have appeared:

Taylor – Capital

20X7			£	20X7			£
Dec	31	Cash: Drawings	2,000	Jan	1	Bank	2,000
''	31	Profit and loss		Dec	31	Profit and loss	
		appropriation account:				appropriation account:	
		Interest on drawings	50			Interest on capital	100
''	31	Balance c/d	2,600			Share of profits	2,550
			4,650				4,650
				20X8			
				Jan	1	Balance b/d	2,600

Clarke – Capital

20X7			£	20X7			£
Dec	31	Cash: Drawings	2,000	Jan	1	Bank	6,000
''	31	Profit and loss		Dec	31	Profit and loss	
		appropriation account:				appropriation account:	
		Interest on				Interest on capital	300
		drawings	100			Salary	500
''	31	Balance c/d	6,400			Share of profit	1,700
			8,500				8,500
				20X8			
				Jan	1	Balance b/d	6,400

Fixed capital accounts preferred

The keeping of fixed capital accounts plus current accounts is considered preferable to fluctuating capital accounts. When partners are taking out greater amounts than the share of the profits that they are entitled to, this is shown up by a debit balance on the current account and so acts as a warning.

41.9 Where no partnership agreement exists

As mentioned in the answer to Activity 41.4, where no partnership agreement exists, express or implied, Section 24 of the Partnership Act 1890 governs the situation. The accounting content of this section states:

(a) Profits and losses are to be shared equally.
(b) There is to be no interest allowed on capital.
(c) No interest is to be charged on drawings.
(d) Salaries are not allowed.
(e) Partners who put a sum of money into a partnership in excess of the capital they have agreed to subscribe are entitled to interest at the rate of 5 per cent per annum on such an advance.

Section 24 applies where there is no agreement. There may be an agreement not by a partnership deed but in a letter, or it may be implied by conduct, for instance when a partner signs a balance sheet which shows profits shared in some other ratio than equally. Where a dispute arises as to whether an agreement exists or not, and this cannot be resolved by the partners, only the courts are competent to decide.

41.10 The balance sheet

The capital part side of the balance sheet will appear:

Balance Sheet as at 31 December 20X7 (extract)

					£	£
Capital accounts				Taylor	2,000	
				Clarke	6,000	
						8,000
Current accounts	*Taylor*		*Clarke*			
	£	£	£	£		
Interest on capital		100		300		
Share of profits		2,550		1,700		
Salary		–		500		
		2,650		2,500		
Less Drawings	2,000		2,000			
Interest on drawings	50		100			
		(2,050)		(2,100)		
		600		400		
						1,000

If one of the current accounts had finished in debit, for instance if the current account of Clarke had finished up as £400 debit, the figure of £400 would appear in brackets and the balances would appear net in the totals column:

	Taylor	*Clarke*	
	£	£	£
Closing balance	600	(400)	200

If the net figure turned out to be a debit figure then this would be deducted from the total of the capital accounts.

You should now have learnt:

1 That there is no limited liability in partnerships except for 'limited partners'.

2 That limited partners cannot withdraw any of the capital they invested in the partnership or take part in the management of the partnership.

3 That apart from some professions, if more than twenty owners of an organisation are needed, a limited company would need to be formed, not a partnership.

4 That the contents of a partnership agreement will override anything written in this chapter. Partners can agree to anything they want to, in as much or as little detail as they wish.

5 That if there is no partnership agreement, then the provisions of the Partnership Act 1890 (details shown in section 41.9) will apply.

6 That partners can agree to show their capital accounts using either the fixed capital or fluctuating capital methods.

7 How to prepare the ledger accounts and financial statements of partnerships.

Answers to activities

41.1 The best example is accounting partnerships. Some of them have offices all over the world.

41.2 Your answer could have included some of the following:
- The capital required is more than one person can provide.
- The experience or ability required to manage the business cannot be found in one person alone.
- Many people want to share management instead of doing everything on their own.
- Very often the partners will be members of the same family.

41.3 Limited partners contribute capital. They may also contribute expertise. Either of these is a benefit to the general partners – they have to contribute less capital and they can rely on the additional expertise when appropriate without needing to seek assistance from people outside the partnership. Also, because limited partners cannot be involved in the management of the partnership, general partners can take decisions without consulting a limited partner, thus saving time and effort when, in many instances, the limited partner will be busy doing other things that have nothing to do with the partnership business.

41.4 The Partnership Act 1890 imposes a standard partnership agreement upon partnerships that do not draw up a partnership agreement. See Section 41.9.

REVIEW QUESTIONS

41.1 Stephens, Owen and Jones are partners. They share profits and losses in the ratios of $^2/_5$, $^2/_5$ and $^1/_5$ respectively.

For the year ended 31 December 20X6, their capital accounts remained fixed at the following amounts:

	£
Stephens	6,000
Owen	4,000
Jones	2,000

They have agreed to give each other 10 per cent interest per annum on their capital accounts.

In addition to the above, partnership salaries of £3,000 for Owen and £1,000 for Jones are to be charged.

The net profit of the partnership, before taking any of the above into account was £25,200.

You are required to draw up the appropriation account of the partnership for the year ended 31 December 20X6.

41.2 Read the following and answer the questions below.

Roach and Salmon own a grocery shop. Their first financial year ended on 31 December 20X9.

The following balances were taken from the books on that date:

Capital:	Roach – £60,000;	Salmon – £48,000.
Partnership salaries:	Roach – £9,000;	Salmon – £6,000.
Drawings:	Roach – £12,860;	Salmon – £13,400.

The firm's net profit for the year was £32,840.
Interest on capital is to be allowed at 10% per year.
Profits and losses are to be shared equally.

(a) From the information above prepare the firm's appropriation account and the partners' current accounts.

(b) If there is no partnership agreement, to which Act of Parliament do the partners then refer?

(*Midland Examining Group: GCSE*)

41.3 Draw up a profit and loss appropriation account for the year ended 31 December 20X7 and balance sheet extracts at that date, from the following:

(*i*) Net profits £30,350.
(*ii*) Interest to be charged on capitals: Williams £2,000; Powell £1,500; Howe £900.
(*iii*) Interest to be charged on drawings: Williams £240; Powell £180; Howe £130.
(*iv*) Salaries to be credited: Powell £2,000; Howe £3,500.
(*v*) Profits to be shared: Williams 50%; Powell 30%; Howe 20%.
(*vi*) Current accounts: balances b/fwd Williams £1,860; Powell £946; Howe £717.
(*vii*) Capital accounts: balances b/fwd Williams £40,000; Powell £30,000; Howe £18,000.
(*viii*) Drawings: Williams £9,200; Powell £7,100; Howe £6,900.

41.4A Penrose and Wilcox are in partnership, sharing profits and losses in the ratio 3 : 2. The following information was taken from their books for the year ended 31 December 20X9, before the completion of their profit and loss appropriation account.

		£	
Current accounts (1 January 20X9)			
	Penrose	640	(*Dr*)
	Wilcox	330	(*Cr*)
Drawings	Penrose	3,000	
	Wilcox	2,000	
Net trading profit		6,810	
Interest on capital	Penrose	540	
	Wilcox	720	
Salary	Penrose	2,000	
Interest on drawings	Penrose	270	
	Wilcox	180	

(a) Prepare, for the year ended 31 December 20X9:
    (*i*) the profit and loss appropriation account of Penrose and Wilcox;
    (*ii*) the current accounts in the ledger for Penrose and Wilcox.
(b) Why in many partnerships are current accounts prepared as well as capital accounts?
(c) At 1 January 20X9 Penrose had a debit balance in his current account. What does this mean?

(d) In partnership accounts what is the purpose of preparing:
    (i) a profit and loss account?
    (ii) a profit and loss appropriation account?
(e) In partnership accounts why is:
    (i) interest allowed on capital?
    (ii) interest charged on drawings?

(*Northern Examinations and Assessment Board: GCSE*)

41.5 Bee, Cee and Dee have been holding preliminary discussions with a view to forming a partnership to buy and sell antiques.

The position has now been reached where the prospective partners have agreed the basic arrangements under which the partnership will operate.

Bee will contribute £40,000 as capital, and up to £10,000 as a long-term loan to the partnership, if needed. He has extensive other business interests and will not therefore be taking an active part in the running of the business.

Cee is unable to bring in more than £2,000 as capital initially, but, because he has an expert knowledge of the antique trade, will act as the manager of the business on a full-time basis.

Dee is willing to contribute £10,000 as capital. He will also assist in running the business as the need arises. In particular, he is prepared to attend auctions anywhere within the United Kingdom in order to acquire trading stock which he will transport back to the firm's premises in his van. On occasions he may also help Cee to restore the articles prior to sale to the public.

At the meeting, the three prospective partners intend to decide upon the financial arrangements for sharing out the profits (or losses) made by the firm, and have approached you for advice.

You are required to prepare a set of explanatory notes, under suitable headings, of the considerations which the prospective partners should take into account in arriving at their decisions at the next meeting.

(*Association of Chartered Certified Accountants*)

41.6 Mendez and Marshall are in partnership sharing profits and losses equally. The following is their trial balance as at 30 June 20X9.

	Dr £	Cr £
Buildings (cost £75,000)	50,000	
Fixtures at cost	11,000	
Provision for depreciation: Fixtures		3,300
Debtors	16,243	
Creditors		11,150
Cash at bank	677	
Stock at 30 June 20X8	41,979	
Sales		123,650
Purchases	85,416	
Carriage outwards	1,288	
Discounts allowed	115	
Loan interest: King	4,000	
Office expenses	2,416	
Salaries and wages	18,917	
Bad debts	503	
Provision for bad debts		400
Loan from J King		40,000
Capitals: Mendez		35,000
Marshall		29,500
Current accounts: Mendez		1,306
Marshall		298
Drawings: Mendez	6,400	
Marshall	5,650	
	244,604	244,604

Required:
Prepare a trading and profit and loss appropriation account for the year ended 30 June 20X9, and a balance sheet as at that date.

(a) Stock, 30 June 20X9, £56,340.
(b) Expenses to be accrued: Office Expenses £96; Wages £200.
(c) Depreciate fixtures 10 per cent on reducing balance basis, buildings £1,000.
(d) Reduce provision for bad debts to £320.
(e) Partnership salary: £800 to Mendez. Not yet entered.
(f) Interest on drawings: Mendez £180; Marshall £120.
(g) Interest on capital account balances at 10 per cent.

41.7A Oscar and Felix are in partnership. They share profits in the ratio: Oscar 60 per cent; Felix 40 per cent. The following trial balance was extracted as at 31 March 20X9.

	Dr £	Cr £
Office equipment at cost	6,500	
Motor vehicles at cost	9,200	
Provision for depreciation at 31.3.20X8:		
Motor vehicles		3,680
Office equipment		1,950
Stock at 31 March 20X8	24,970	
Debtors and creditors	20,960	16,275
Cash at bank	615	
Cash in hand	140	
Sales		90,370
Purchases	71,630	
Salaries	8,417	
Office expenses	1,370	
Discounts allowed	563	
Current accounts at 31.3.20X8		
Oscar		1,379
Felix		1,211
Capital accounts: Oscar		27,000
Felix		12,000
Drawings: Oscar	5,500	
Felix	4,000	
	153,865	153,865

Required:
Draw up a set of final accounts for the year ended 31 March 20X9 for the partnership. The following notes are applicable at 31 March 20X9.

(a) Stock 31 March 20X9 £27,340.
(b) Office expenses owing £110.
(c) Provide for depreciation: motor 20 per cent of cost, office equipment 10 per cent of cost.
(d) Charge interest on capitals at 10 per cent.
(e) Charge interest on drawings: Oscar £180; Felix £210.

41.8 The following list of balances as at 30 September 20X9 has been extracted from the books of Brick and Stone, trading in partnership, sharing the balance of profits and losses in the proportions 3:2 respectively.

	£	
Printing, stationery and postages	3,500	
Sales	322,100	
Stock in hand at 1 October 20X8	23,000	
Purchases	208,200	
Rent and rates	10,300	
Heat and light	8,700	
Staff salaries	36,100	
Telephone charges	2,900	
Motor vehicle running costs	5,620	
Discounts allowable	950	
Discounts receivable	370	
Sales returns	2,100	
Purchases returns	6,100	
Carriage inwards	1,700	
Carriage outwards	2,400	
Fixtures and fittings: at cost	26,000	
provision for depreciation	11,200	
Motor vehicles: at cost	46,000	
provision for depreciation	25,000	
Provision for doubtful debts	300	
Drawings: Brick	24,000	
Stone	11,000	
Current account balances at 1 October 20X8:		
Brick	3,600	credit
Stone	2,400	credit
Capital account balances at 1 October 20X8:		
Brick	33,000	
Stone	17,000	
Debtors	9,300	
Creditors	8,400	
Balance at bank	7,700	

Additional information:

1 £10,000 is to be transferred from Brick's capital account to a newly opened Brick Loan Account on 1 July 20X9.
   Interest at 10 per cent per annum on the loan is to be credited to Brick.
2 Stone is to be credited with a salary at the rate of £12,000 per annum from 1 April 20X9.
3 Stock in hand at 30 September 20X9 has been valued at cost at £32,000.
4 Telephone charges accrued due at 30 September 20X9 amounted to £400 and rent of £600 pre-paid at that date.
5 During the year ended 30 September 20X9 Stone has taken goods costing £1,000 for his own use.
6 Depreciation is to be provided at the following annual rates on the straight line basis:

Fixtures and fittings	10%
Motor vehicles	20%

Required:
(a) Prepare a trading and profit and loss account for the year ended 30 September 20X9.
(b) Prepare a balance sheet as at 30 September 20X9 which should include summaries of the partners' capital and current accounts for the year ended on that date.

Note: In both (a) and (b) vertical forms of presentation should be used.

(Association of Accounting Technicians)

41.9A Menzies, Whitlam and Gough share profits and losses in the ratios 5:3:2 respectively. Their trial balance as at 30 September 20X9 was as follows:

	Dr £	Cr £
Sales		210,500
Returns inwards	6,800	
Purchases	137,190	
Carriage inwards	1,500	
Stock 30 September 20X8	42,850	
Discounts allowed	110	
Salaries and wages	18,296	
Bad debts	1,234	
Provision for bad debts 30.9.20X8		800
General expenses	945	
Rent and rates	2,565	
Postages	2,450	
Motor expenses	3,940	
Vans at cost	12,500	
Office equipment at cost	8,400	
Provisions for depreciation at 30.9.20X8:		
Vans		4,200
Office equipment		2,700
Creditors		24,356
Debtors	37,178	
Cash at bank	666	
Drawings: Menzies	12,610	
Whitlam	8,417	
Gough	6,216	
Current accounts: Menzies		1,390
Whitlam	153	
Gough		2,074
Capital accounts: Menzies		30,000
Whitlam		16,000
Gough		12,000
	304,020	304,020

Draw up a set of final accounts for the year ended 30 September 20X9. The following notes are relevant at 30 September 20X9:

(*i*)   Stock 30 September 20X9, £51,060.
(*ii*)   Rates in advance £120; Stock of postage stamps £190.
(*iii*)   Increase provision for bad debts to £870.
(*iv*)   Salaries: Whitlam £1,200; Gough £700. Not yet recorded.
(*v*)   Interest on Drawings: Menzies £170; Whitlam £110; Gough £120.
(*vi*)   Interest on Capitals at 10 per cent.
(*vii*)   Depreciate Vans £2,500, Office equipment £1,680.

Goodwill for sole traders and partnerships

After you have studied this chapter, you should be able to:

- describe a range of methods for arriving at the selling price of a business
- explain and calculate super profits
- explain why goodwill exists
- explain why goodwill has a monetary value
- distinguish between purchased and non-purchased goodwill
- calculate purchased goodwill
- calculate the adjustments needed when there is some form of change in a partnership

Introduction

In this chapter, you'll learn about purchased goodwill and its treatment in the books and financial statements of sole traders and partnerships. You will also learn how to make adjustments to the partnership capital accounts when circumstances change.

42.1 Nature of goodwill

Suppose you have been running a business for some years and you wanted to sell it. How much would you ask as the total sale price of the business? You decide to list how much you could get for each asset if sold separately. This list might be as follows:

	£
Buildings	225,000
Machinery	75,000
Debtors	60,000
Stock	40,000
	400,000

Note: if there are any liabilities, you would deduct them from the total value of the assets to arrive at the value of the net assets, which is the net amount you would have left if you sold all the assets and paid off all the creditors.

So, if you sold off everything separately, you would expect to receive £400,000.

Activity 42.1

If you were running a successful business, would you be willing to sell it for the value of its net assets? Why/why not?

As the business is successful, a prospective buyer has been found who is willing to pay more than the £400,000 net asset value. As a result, you sell the whole of the business as a going concern to Mr Lee for £450,000. He has, therefore, paid £50,000 more than the total value of all the assets. This extra payment of £50,000 is called **goodwill**. He has paid this because he wanted to take over the business as a going concern, and so benefit from the product and customer base that already exists. Thus:

Purchased Goodwill = Total Price *less* value of net identifiable assets.

42.2 Reasons for payment of goodwill

In buying an existing business which has been established for some time there may be quite a few possible advantages. Some of them are listed here:

- A large number of regular customers who will continue to deal with the new owner.
- The business has a good reputation.
- It has experienced, efficient and reliable employees.
- The business is situated in a good location.
- It has good contacts with suppliers.
- It has well-known brand names that have not been valued and included as assets.

None of these advantages is available to completely new businesses. For this reason, many people are willing to pay an additional amount for goodwill when they buy an existing business.

42.3 Existence of goodwill

Goodwill does not necessarily exist in a business. If the business had a bad reputation, an inefficient labour force or other negative factors, the owner might be unlikely to be paid for goodwill on selling the business.

> *Activity 42.2*
> In the earlier example, goodwill was a positive figure of £50,000. If, instead, it had been a negative figure of £100,000 (being the estimated cost of a marketing campaign that would be necessary to restore customers' faith in the business) at what price would the business be most likely to be sold? Why?

42.4 Methods of calculating goodwill

There is no single way of calculating goodwill to which everyone can agree. The seller will probably want more for the goodwill than the buyer will want to pay. All that is certain is that when agreement is reached between buyer and seller concerning how much is to be paid for a business, the amount by which the figure agreed exceeds the net assets represents the goodwill. Various methods are used to help buyer and seller come to an agreed figure for a business. The calculations give buyer and seller a figure with which to begin discussions of the value.

Very often each industry or occupation has its own customary way of calculating goodwill:

(a) In more than one type of retail business it has been the custom to value goodwill at the average weekly sales for the past year multiplied by a given figure. The given figure will, of course, differ between different types of businesses, and often changes gradually in the same types of business in the long term.

(b) With many professional firms, such as accountants in public practice, it is the custom to value goodwill as being the gross annual fees times a given number. For instance, what is termed a two years' purchase of a firm with gross fees of £300,000 means goodwill = $2 \times £300,000 = £600,000$.

(c) The average net annual profit for a specified past number of years multiplied by an agreed number. This is often said to be x years' purchase of the net profits.

(d) The super-profits method.

Let's consider the last of these, the super-profits method. It may be argued, as in the case of a sole trader for example, that the net profits are not 'true profits'. This is because the sole trader has not charged for the following expenses:

(a) Services of the proprietor. He has worked in the business, but he has not charged for such services. Any drawings he makes are charged to a capital account, not to the profit and loss account.

(b) The use of the money he has invested in the business. If he had invested his money elsewhere he would have earned interest or dividends on such investments.

Super profits are what an accountant would call what is left of the net profits after allowances have been made for (a) services of the proprietor and (b) the use of the capital. They are usually calculated as:

	£	£
Annual net profits		80,000
Less (i) Remuneration proprietor would have earned for similar work elsewhere	20,000	
(ii) Interest that would have been earned if capital had been invested elsewhere	10,000	
		(30,000)
Annual super profits		50,000

The annual super profits are then multiplied by a number agreed by seller and purchaser of the business in order to arrive at the selling price.

42.5 Sole traders' books

Goodwill is only entered in a sole trader's accounts when it has been purchased. The existence of goodwill in the financial statements usually means that the business was purchased as a going concern by the owner. That is, the owner did not start the business from scratch.

> **Activity 42.3**
> There is another possible explanation for purchased goodwill appearing in a sole trader's balance sheet. What do you think it might be?

42.6 Partnership books

Although goodwill is not *normally* entered in the financial statements unless it has been purchased, sometimes it is necessary where partnerships are concerned.

Unless it has been agreed differently, partners own a share in the goodwill in the same ratio in which they share profits. For instance, if A takes one-quarter of the profits, A will be the owner of one-quarter of the goodwill. This is true even if there is no goodwill account.

This means that when something happens such as:

(a) existing partners decide to change profit and loss sharing ratios, or
(b) a new partner is introduced, or
(c) a partner retires or dies,

then the ownership of goodwill by partners changes in some way.

The change may involve cash passing from one partner to another, or an adjustment in the books, so that the changes in ownership do not lead to a partner (or partners) giving away their share of ownership for nothing.

42.7 Change in profit sharing ratios of existing partners

Sometimes the profit and loss sharing ratios have to be changed. Typical reasons are:

- A partner may now not work as much as in the past, possibly because of old age or ill-health.
- A partner's skills and ability may have changed, perhaps after attending a course or following an illness.
- A partner may now be doing much more for the business than in the past.

If the partners decide to change their profit sharing ratios, an adjustment will be needed.

To illustrate why this is so, let's look at the following example of a partnership in which goodwill is not already shown in a goodwill account at its correct value.

(a) A, B and C are in partnership, sharing profits and losses equally.
(b) On 31 December 20X5 they decide to change this to A one-half, B one-quarter and C one-quarter.
(c) On 31 December 20X5 the goodwill, which had never been shown in the books, was valued at £60,000. If, just before the profit-sharing change, the firm had been sold and £60,000 received for goodwill, then each partner would have received £20,000 as they shared profits equally.
(d) At any time after 31 December 20X5, once the profit sharing has changed, their ownership of goodwill is worth A £30,000, B £15,000 and C £15,000. If goodwill is sold for that amount then those figures will be received by the partners for goodwill.
(e) If, when (b) above happened, there had been no change made to A by B and C, or no other form of adjustment, then B and C would each have given away a £5,000 share of the goodwill for nothing. This would not be sensible.

We can now look at how the adjustments can be made when a goodwill account with the correct valuation does not already exist.

Exhibit 42.1

E, F and G have been in business for ten years. They have always shared profits equally. No goodwill account has ever existed in the books. On 31 December 20X6 they agree that G will take only a one-fifth share of the profits as from 1 January 20X7, because he will be devoting less of his time to the business in the future. E and F will each take two-fifths of the profits. The summarised balance sheet of the business on 31 December 20X6 appears as follows:

Balance Sheet as at 31 December 20X6

	£
Net Assets	7,000
Capital: E	3,000
F	1,800
G	2,200
	7,000

The partners agree that the goodwill should be valued at £3,000. Answer (1) shows the solution when a goodwill account is opened. Answer (2) is the solution when a goodwill account is not opened.

1 Goodwill account opened. Open a goodwill account. Then make the following entries: Debit goodwill account: total value of goodwill.

Credit partners' capital accounts: each one with his share of goodwill in old profit sharing ratio.

The goodwill account will appear as:

Goodwill

	£		£
Capitals: valuation shared		Balance c/d	3,000
E	1,000		
F	1,000		
G	1,000		
	3,000		3,000

The capital accounts may be shown in columnar fashion as:

Capital Accounts

	E £	F £	G £		E £	F £	G £
Balances c/d	4,000	2,800	3,200	Balances b/d	3,000	1,800	2,200
				Goodwill: old ratios	1,000	1,000	1,000
	4,000	2,800	3,200		4,000	2,800	3,200

The balance sheet items before and after the adjustments will appear as:

	Before £	After £		Before £	After £
Goodwill	–	3,000	Capitals: E	3,000	4,000
Other assets	7,000	7,000	F	1,800	2,800
			G	2,200	3,200
	7,000	10,000		7,000	10,000

2 Goodwill account not opened. The effect of the change of ownership of goodwill may be shown in the following form:

Before		After		Loss or Gain		Action Required
	£		£			
E One-third	1,000	Two-fifths	1,200	Gain	£200	Debit E's capital account £200
F One-third	1,000	Two-fifths	1,200	Gain	£200	Debit F's capital account £200
G One-third	1,000	One-fifth	600	Loss	£400	Credit G's capital account £400
	3,000		3,000			

The column headed '*Action Required*' shows that a partner who has gained goodwill because of the change must be charged for it by having his capital account debited with the value of the gain. A partner who has lost goodwill must be compensated for it by having his capital account credited.

The capital accounts will appear as:

Capital Accounts

	E £	F £	G £		E £	F £	G £
Goodwill adjustments	200	200		Balances b/d	3,000	1,800	2,200
Balances c/d	2,800	1,600	2,600	Goodwill adjustments			400
	3,000	1,800	2,600		3,000	1,800	2,600

As there is no goodwill account the balance sheet items before and after the adjustments will therefore appear as:

	Before £	After £		Before £	After £
Net assets	7,000	7,000	Capitals: E	3,000	2,800
			F	1,800	1,600
			G	2,200	2,600
	7,000	7,000		7,000	7,000

Comparison of methods 1 and 2

Let us see how the methods compare. Assume that shortly afterwards the assets in 1 and 2 are sold for £7,000 and the goodwill for £3,000. The total of £10,000 would be distributed as follows, using each of the methods:

Method 1 The £10,000 is exactly the amount needed to pay the partners according to the balances on their capital accounts. The payments are therefore made of

		£
Capitals paid to	E	4,000
	F	2,800
	G	3,200
Total cash paid		10,000

Method 2 First of all the balances on capital accounts, totalling £7,000, are to be paid. Then the £3,000 received for goodwill will be split between the partners in their profit and loss ratios. This will result in payments as follows:

	Capitals £	Goodwill Shared	£	Total Paid £
E	2,800	(^{2}/$_5$)	1,200	4,000
F	1,600	(^{2}/$_5$)	1,200	2,800
G	2,600	(^{1}/$_5$)	600	3,200
	7,000		3,000	10,000

You can see that the final amounts paid to the partners are the same whether a goodwill account is opened or not.

42.8   Admission of new partners

New partners may be admitted, usually for one of two reasons:

1 As an extra partner, either because the firm has grown or because someone is needed with different skills.
2 To replace partners who are leaving the firm. This might be because of retirement or death of a partner.

42.9   Goodwill on admission of new partners

The new partner will be entitled to a share in the profits. Normally, he will also be entitled to the same share of the value of goodwill. It is correct to charge him for his taking over that share of the goodwill.

42.10   Goodwill adjustments when new partners admitted

This calculation is done in four stages:

1 Show value of goodwill divided between old partners in old profit and loss sharing ratios.
2 Then show value of goodwill divided between partners (including new partner) in new profit and loss sharing ratio.
3 Goodwill gain shown: charge these partners for the gain.
4 Goodwill loss shown: give these partners an allowance for their losses.

This is illustrated in Exhibits 42.2 and 42.3.

Exhibit 42.2

A and B are in partnership, sharing profits and losses equally. C is admitted as a new partner. The three partners will share profits and losses one-third each.
    Total goodwill is valued at £60,000.

	Stage 1		Stage 2		Stage 3	
Partners	Old profit shares	Share of goodwill £	New profit shares	Share of goodwill £	Gain or loss £	Adjustment needed
A	1/2	30,000	1/3	20,000	10,000 Loss	Cr A Capital
B	1/2	30,000	1/3	20,000	10,000 Loss	Cr B Capital
C		–	1/3	20,000	20,000 Gain	Dr C Capital
		60,000		60,000		

This means that A and B need to have their capitals increased by £10,000 each. C needs his capital reducing by £20,000.
    Note that A and B have kept their profits in the same ratio to each other. While they used to have one-half each, now they have one-third each.
    We will now see in Exhibit 42.3 that the method shown is the same even when existing partners take a different share of the profit to that before the change.

Exhibit 42.3

D and E are in partnership sharing profits one-half each. A new partner F is admitted. Profits will now be shared D one-fifth, and E and F two-fifths each. D and E have therefore not kept their shares equal to each other. Goodwill is valued at £60,000.

	Stage 1		Stage 2		Stage 3	
Partners	Old profit shares	Share of goodwill £	New profit shares	Share of goodwill £	Gain or loss £	Adjustment needed
D	1/2	30,000	1/5	12,000	18,000 Loss	Cr D Capital
E	1/2	30,000	2/5	24,000	6,000 Loss	Cr E Capital
F		–	2/5	24,000	24,000 Gain	Dr F Capital
		60,000		60,000		

D needs his capital increased by £18,000. E's capital is to be increased by £6,000. F needs his capital reduced by £24,000.

42.11 Accounting entries for goodwill adjustments

These depend on how the partners wish to arrange the adjustment. Three methods are usually used:

1 Cash is paid by the new partner privately to the old partners for his/her share of the goodwill. No goodwill account is to be opened.

   In Exhibit 42.3, F would therefore give £24,000 in cash, being £18,000 to D and £6,000 to E. They would bank these amounts in their private bank accounts. No entry is made for this in the accounts of the partnership.

2 Cash is paid by the new partner into the business bank account for his/her share of the goodwill. No goodwill account is to be opened. Assume that the capital balances before F was admitted were D £50,000, E £50,000, and F was to pay in £50,000 as capital plus £24,000 for goodwill.

   The £24,000 payment is made in order to secure a share of the £60,000 existing goodwill. The £24,000 is shared between the two existing partners by increasing their capital accounts by the amounts shown in Stage 3 of Exhibit 43.3. The debit entry is to the bank account. The entries in the capital accounts are:

Capital Accounts

	D £	E £	F £		D £	E £	F £
Adjustments for goodwill			24,000	Balances b/d	50,000	50,000	
				Cash for capital			50,000
				Cash for goodwill			24,000
Balances c/d	68,000	56,000	50,000	Loss of goodwill	18,000	6,000	
	68,000	56,000	74,000		68,000	56,000	74,000

3 Goodwill account to be opened. No extra cash to be paid in by the new partner for goodwill.

In Exhibit 42.3, the opening capitals were D £50,000, E £50,000. F paid in £50,000 as capital.

Here, the situation is different from under the second method. The new partner is not paying anything in order to secure a share of the £60,000 of existing goodwill. As a result, it is shared now among the two original partners in their original profit sharing ratios ($\frac{1}{2}$: $\frac{1}{2}$) and the new partner's capital account is credited only with the £50,000 s/he is investing. This is done because the new partner is not entitled to any of the previously established goodwill and the only way to prevent that permanently is to recognise all the goodwill now and credit it to the existing partners' capital accounts.

The action required is:

• Debit goodwill account: with total value of goodwill.
• Credit capitals of old partners: with their shares of goodwill in old profit sharing ratios.

No adjustments for goodwill gains and losses are required as the capital accounts of D and E have been increased by the full value of the goodwill at the time of F's admission to partnership.

For Exhibit 42.3, the entries would appear as:

Goodwill

	£		£
Value divided: D Capital	30,000	Balance c/d	60,000
E Capital	30,000		
	60,000		60,000

Capital Accounts

	D £	E £	F £		D £	E £	F £
				Balances b/d	50,000	50,000	
				Cash for capital			50,000
Balances c/d	80,000	80,000	50,000	Goodwill	30,000	30,000	
	80,000	80,000	50,000		80,000	80,000	50,000

As stated in Section 42.7, if the partnership were dissolved and realised the £210,000 it was valued at when F was admitted, this would first be used to repay the capital account balances. D and F would, therefore, be fully compensated for the value of the goodwill at the time of F's admission to partnership, and F would receive exactly the amount of her/his investment.

42.12 Where new partners pay for share of goodwill

The last section looked at how the partners' capital accounts are adjusted to account for goodwill when a new partner is admitted. In the second case, £24,000 was paid for goodwill by the new partner. Total goodwill at that time was £60,000. The profit share of the new partner is 2/5. If you divide £24,000 by 2/5 you get £60,000. Therefore, if you didn't know that the total goodwill was £60,000 you can calculate it by dividing the amount a new partner pays for goodwill by that new partner's profit sharing ratio.

Unless otherwise agreed, the assumption is that the total value of goodwill is directly proportionate to the amount paid by the new partner for the share of profit the new partner will receive in future. If a new partner pays £1,200 for a one-fifth share of future profits, goodwill is taken to be £6,000. A sum of £800 for a one-quarter share of future profits would, therefore, be taken to imply a total value of £3,200 for goodwill.

42.13 Goodwill on withdrawal or death of partners

This depends on whether or not a goodwill account exists.

If there was no goodwill account

If no goodwill account already existed the partnership goodwill should be valued because the outgoing partner is entitled to his share of its value. This value is entered in double entry accounts:

● Debit goodwill account with valuation.
● Credit each old partner's capital account in profit sharing ratios.

Exhibit 42.4

H, I and J have been in partnership for many years sharing profit and losses equally. No goodwill account has ever existed.

J is leaving the partnership. The other two partners are to take over his share of profits equally. Capitals entered before goodwill were £50,000 each. The goodwill is valued at £45,000.

Goodwill

		£		£
Valuation:	Capital H	15,000	Balance c/d	45,000
	Capital I	15,000		
	Capital J	15,000		
		45,000		45,000
Balance b/d		45,000		

Capital Accounts

	H £	I £	J £		H £	I £	J £
Balances c/d	65,000	65,000	65,000	Balances b/d	50,000	50,000	50,000
				Goodwill shares	15,000	15,000	15,000
	65,000	65,000	65,000		65,000	65,000	65,000
				Balances b/d	65,000	65,000	65,000

When J leaves the partnership, his capital balance of £65,000 will be paid to him.

If a goodwill account exists

1 If a goodwill account exists with the correct valuation of goodwill entered in it, no further action is needed.
2 If the valuation in the goodwill account needs to be changed, the following will apply:
  Goodwill undervalued: Debit increase needed to goodwill account.
                         Credit increase to old partners' capital accounts in their old profit sharing ratios.
  Goodwill overvalued: Debit reduction to old partners' capital accounts in their old profit sharing ratios.
                         Credit reduction needed to goodwill account.

You should now have learnt:

1 What is meant by the term 'goodwill'.

2 What is meant by the term 'purchased goodwill', and how to calculate it.

3 How to calculate super profits.

4 How to record goodwill in the accounts of a partnership.

5 That the true value of goodwill can be established only when the business is sold, but for various reasons of fairness between partners it is valued the best way possible when there is no imminent sale of a business.

6 That if the old partners agree, a new partner can be admitted without paying anything in as capital.

7 That goodwill is usually owned by the partners in the ratio in which they share profits.

8 That if there is a change in partnership without adjustments for goodwill, then some partners will make an unfair gain while others will quite unfairly lose money.

9 That if a new partner pays a specific amount for his or her share of the goodwill, then that payment is said to be a 'premium'.

Answers to activities

42.1 What if someone wanted to buy the business so that they could run it for themselves? Would they not be willing to pay a bit extra so as to benefit from the customer and product base you've built up? When a business is sold as a 'going concern', the owners can usually receive more than simply the value of the assets or, to be more accurate, the value of its net assets (i.e. all assets less all liabilities). This difference is known as 'goodwill'.

42.2 It is unlikely that a potential buyer would be willing to pay more than £300,000 for the business and so it would most likely be sold, asset by asset, for £400,000.

42.3 The business may have been founded by the present owner who, at some time after starting the business, bought another business and combined the two businesses into one. For example, a newsagent may take over another newsagent and run both shops as one business. The purchased goodwill included in the amount paid for the second business would appear in the balance sheet of the combined business.

REVIEW QUESTIONS

42.1 The partners have always shared their profits in the ratios of Dinho 4: Manueli 3: Joana 1. They are to alter their profit ratios to Dinho 3: Manueli 5: Joana 2. The last balance sheet before the change was:

Balance Sheet as at 31 December 20X7

	£
Net Assets (not including goodwill)	14,000
	14,000
Capitals:	
Dinho	6,000
Manueli	4,800
Joana	3,200
	14,000

The partners agree to bring in goodwill, being valued at £12,000 on the change.

Show the balance sheets on 1 January 20X8 after goodwill has been taken into account if:

(a) Goodwill account was opened.
(b) Goodwill account was not opened.

42.2A The partners are to change their profit ratios as shown:

	Old ratio	New ratio
A	2	3
B	3	4
C	4	3
D	1	2

They decide to bring in a goodwill amount of £18,000 on the change. The last balance sheet before any element of goodwill has been introduced was:

Balance Sheet as at 30 June 20X8

	£
Net assets (not including goodwill)	18,800
	18,800
Capitals:	
A	7,000
B	3,200
C	5,000
D	3,600
	18,800

Show the balance sheets on 1 July 20X8 after necessary adjustments have been made if:

(a) Goodwill account was opened.
(b) Goodwill account was not opened.

42.3 Rupert and Linda are in partnership, sharing profits and losses equally. They decide to admit Emma. By agreement, goodwill valued at £6,000 is to be introduced into the business books. Emma is required to provide capital equal to that of Linda after she has been credited with her share of goodwill. The new profit sharing ratio is to be 4:3:3 respectively for Rupert, Linda and Emma.

The balance sheet before admission of Emma showed:

	£
Fixed and current assets	15,000
Cash	2,000
	17,000
Current liabilities	(5,000)
	12,000
Capital Rupert	8,000
Capital Linda	4,000
	12,000

Show:
(a) Journal entries for admission of Emma.
(b) Opening balance sheet of new business.
(c) Journal entries for writing off the goodwill which the new partners decided to do soon after the start of the new business.

42.4A Larry, Mary and Simon are in partnership. They shared profits in the ratio 2:5:3. It is decided to admit Roger. It is agreed that goodwill was worth £10,000, but that this is not to be brought into the business records. Roger will bring £4,000 cash into the business for capital. The new profit sharing ratio is to be Larry 3: Mary 4: Simon 2: Roger 1.

The balance sheet before Roger was introduced was as follows:

	£
	£
Assets (other than in cash)	11,000
Cash	2,500
	13,500
Creditors	(1,500)
	12,000
Capitals: Larry	3,000
Mary	5,000
Simon	4,000
	12,000

Show:

(a) The entries in the capital accounts of Larry, Mary, Simon and Roger, the accounts to be in columnar form.

(b) The balance sheet after Roger has been introduced.

42.5 Tom, Una and Viv are in partnership. They shared profits in the ratio 4:5:1. It is decided to admit Willie. It is agreed that goodwill was worth £30,000 and that it was to be brought into the business records. Willie will bring £20,000 cash into the business for capital. The new profit-sharing ratio is to be Tom 6: Una 7: Viv 2: Willie 5.

The balance sheet before Willie was introduced was as follows:

	£
Assets (other than in cash)	40,000
Cash	6,000
	46,000
Liabilities	(9,000)
	37,000
Capitals: Tom	14,000
Una	18,000
Viv	5,000
	37,000

Show:

(a) The entries in the capital accounts of Tom, Una, Viv, and Willie, the accounts to be in columnar form.

(b) The balance sheet after Willie has been introduced.

42.6 A new partner has joined the business during the year and has paid in £10,000 for 'goodwill'. This £10,000 has been credited by the bookkeeper to the account of the new partner. The senior partner had objected to this, but the bookkeeper had replied: 'Why not credit the £10,000 to the account of the new partner? It is his money after all.'

Required:

Give your advice as to the proper treatment of this £10,000. Explain your reasons fully.

(*Association of Chartered Certified Accountants*)

42.7 Owing to staff illnesses, the draft final accounts for the year ended 31 March 20X9 of Messrs Stone, Pebble and Brick, trading in partnership as the Bigtime Building Supply Company, have been prepared by an inexperienced, but keen, clerk. The draft summarised balance sheet as at 31 March 20X9 is as follows:

	£	£
Tangible fixed assets: At cost less depreciation to date		45,400
Current assets	32,290	
Less: Trade creditors	(6,390)	
		25,900
		71,300

Represented by:	Stone	Pebble	Brick	Total
	£	£	£	£
Capital accounts: at 1 April 20X8	26,000	18,000	16,000	60,000
Current accounts:				
Share of net profit for the year ended 31 March 20X9	12,100	12,100	12,100	
Drawings year ended 31 March 20X9	(8,200)	(9,600)	(7,200)	
At 31 March 20X9	3,900	2,500	4,900	11,300
				71,300

The partnership commenced on 1 April 20X8 when each of the partners introduced, as their partnership capital, the net tangible fixed and current assets of their previously separate businesses. However, it has now been discovered that, contrary to what was agreed, no adjustments were made in the partnership books for the goodwill of the partners' former businesses now incorporated in the partnership. The agreed valuations of goodwill at 1 April 20X8 are as follows:

	£
Stone's business	30,000
Pebble's business	20,000
Brick's business	16,000

It is agreed that a goodwill account should not be opened in the partnership's books.

It has now been discovered that effect has not been given in the accounts to the following provisions in the partnership agreement effective from 1 January 20X9:

1 Stone's capital to be reduced to £20,000, the balance being transferred to a loan account upon which interest at the rate of 11% per annum will be paid on 31 December each year.
2 Partners to be credited with interest on their capital account balances at the rate of 5% per annum.
3 Brick to be credited with a partner's salary at the rate of £8,500 per annum.
4 The balance of the net profit or loss to be shared between Stone, Pebble and Brick in the ratio 5:3:2 respectively.

Notes:
1 It can be assumed that the net profit indicated in the draft accounts accrued uniformly throughout the year.
2 It has been agreed between the partners that no adjustments should be made for any partnership goodwill as at 1 January 20X9.

Required:
(a) Prepare the profit and loss appropriation account for the year ended 31 March 20X9.
(b) Prepare a corrected statement of the partners' capital and current accounts for inclusion in the partnership balance sheet as at 31 March 20X9.

(*Association of Accounting Technicians*)

CHAPTER 43

Revaluation of partnership assets

Learning objectives

After you have studied this chapter, you should be able to:
- explain why there may be a the need for revaluation of assets in a partnership
- calculate the amount of asset revaluation gain or loss attributable to each partner
- make the necessary entries to the ledger accounts when assets are revalued

Introduction

In this chapter, you'll learn about the events that make it necessary to revalue the assets of a partnership. You'll learn the journal entries required to record asset revaluations in the ledger accounts of the partnership and how to apportion gains and losses on revaluation between the partners.

43.1 Need for revaluation

When a business is sold, and the sale price of the assets differs from their book values, there will be a profit or loss on the sale. This profit or loss will be shared between the partners in their profit and loss sharing ratios.

This sharing of profits and losses on changing asset values doesn't just need to be done when a partnership is sold. It should also be done whenever any of the following happens:

- a new partner is admitted;
- a partner leaves the firm;
- the partners change profit and loss sharing ratios.

As no sale has taken place in any of these circumstances, the assets will have to be revalued to reflect what they are worth at the date when the change occurs, in order for the gains and losses to be identified.

Activity 43.1
Why do the assets need to be revalued in these cases? The business has not been sold. (Hint: there is no legal requirement to do so; and consider this question in the light of what you learnt in the last chapter about goodwill when new partners are admitted.)

Once the assets have been revalued, you need to record the changes and gains and losses in the ledger accounts of the partnership.

43.2   Profit or loss on revaluation

If the revaluation shows no difference in asset values, no further action is needed. This will not happen very often, especially if assets include buildings. These are normally shown at cost less accumulated depreciation, but this is very rarely the actual value of buildings after they have been owned for a few years.

		£
If:	New total valuation of assets	90,000
Is *more* than:	Old total valuation of assets	(60,000)
The result is:	Gain on revaluation	30,000

		£
If:	New total valuation of assets	40,000
Is *less* than:	Old total valuation of assets	(50,000)
The result is:	Loss on revaluation	(10,000)

43.3   Accounting for revaluation

Revaluation account is opened

The first thing you do upon revaluing partnership assets is to open a **revaluation account** and make the appropriate entries:

1 *For each asset showing a gain on revaluation:*
   Debit asset account with gain.
      Credit revaluation account.
2 *For each asset showing a loss on revaluation:*
   Debit revaluation account.
      Credit asset account with loss.
3 *If there is an increase in total valuation of assets:*
   Debit profit to revaluation account.
      Credit old partners' capital accounts in old profit and loss sharing ratios.*
4 *If there is a fall in total valuations of assets:*
   Debit old partners' capital accounts in old profit and loss sharing ratios.*
      Credit loss to revaluation account.

*If current accounts are kept for the partners, the entries should be made in their current accounts.

> ### Activity 43.2
> When you were looking at goodwill in the last chapter, you were interested in the difference between the amount received and the value of *net* assets. Why do we consider *only the assets* when there is a change in partners or a change in the profit sharing ratio?

Exhibit 43.1

Following is the balance sheet as at 31 December 20X5 of W and Y, who shared profit and losses in the ratios W two-thirds; Y one-third. From 1 January 20X6 the profit and loss sharing ratios are to be altered to W one-half; Y one-half.

Balance Sheet as at 31 December 20X5

	£	£
Premises at cost		6,500
Fixtures (at cost less depreciation)		1,500
		8,000
Stock	2,000	
Debtors	1,200	
Bank	800	
		4,000
		12,000
Capitals: W		7,000
Y		5,000
		12,000

The assets were revalued on 1 January 20X6 to be: Premises £9,000, Fixtures £1,100. Other assets remained at the same values.

Accounts to show the assets at revalued amounts follow:

Revaluation

	£	£		£
Assets reduced in value:			Assets increased in value:	
Fixtures		400	Premises	2,500
Gain on revaluation carried to				
Capital accounts:				
W two-thirds	1,400			
Y one-third	700			
		2,100		
		2,500		2,500

Premises

	£		£
Balance b/d	6,500	Balance c/d	9,000
Revaluation: Increase	2,500		
	9,000		9,000
Balance b/d	9,000		

Fixtures

	£		£
Balance b/d	1,500	Revaluation: Reduction	400
		Balance c/d	1,100
	1,500		1,500
Balance b/d	1,100		

Capital: W

	£		£
Balance c/d	8,400	Balance b/d	7,000
		Revaluation: Share of gain	1,400
	8,400		8,400
		Balance b/d	8,400

Capital: Y

	£		£
Balance c/d	5,700	Balance b/d	5,000
		Revaluation: Share of gain	700
	5,700		5,700
		Balance b/d	5,700

43.4 Revaluation of goodwill

This chapter deals with the revaluation of all assets other than goodwill. The revaluation of goodwill has already been dealt with in Chapter 42.

Learning outcomes

You should now have learnt:

1 How to make the entries arising from revaluations of partnership assets.

2 That when a new partner joins a firm, or a partner retires or dies, the partnership assets should be revalued.

3 That revaluation of assets should also occur when there is a change in the profit and loss sharing ratios of partners.

4 That profits on revaluation of assets are credited to the old partners' capital accounts in the old profit and loss sharing ratios.

5 That losses on revaluation of assets are debited to the old partners' capital accounts in the old profit and loss sharing ratios.

6 That the asset accounts also show the revalued amounts. Losses will have been credited to them and profits debited.

Answers to activities

43.1 When partners join or partners leave a partnership, there is, in effect, a new partnership. You learnt in the last chapter about goodwill that, when a new partner is admitted, the existing partners generally seek to ensure that they retain their share of the goodwill that has built up to that date. It should be fairly obvious, therefore, that the existing partners will also want to maintain the true value of their share of the business at that date in their capital accounts, rather than some historically-based figure.

If this were not done, new partners admitted would benefit from increases in value before they joined the firm, without having to pay anything for them. Similarly, if the value of assets had fallen before they had joined the firm, and no revaluation took place, they would share that loss of value without any adjustment being made for it. Partners who leave or change their profit and loss sharing ratios would also be affected if there were no payments or allowances for such gains or losses.

43.2 In this case, you are only concerned about whether the assets are stated at their true values. You assume that the liabilities are correctly stated and ignore them because they are already included in the calculation of capital. In other words, when considering goodwill, you are comparing the amount received with the total of the partners' account balances, i.e. the net worth of the business (assets less liabilities). In this case, you are only concerned in the first instance with what the true value is of *part* of the other side of the accounting equation, assets, and not with the true value of the net worth. When you make the entries in the ledger accounts, you effectively bring in the liabilities and calculate a new net worth, which is reflected in the new balances on the partners' account balances. The overall effect is the same, only you don't need to calculate net worth to know whether there has been a gain or loss on revaluation of the assets. You do need to do that in order to calculate goodwill.

REVIEW QUESTIONS

43.1

Hughes, Allen and Elliott
Balance Sheet as at 31 December 20X8

		£
Buildings at cost		8,000
Motor vehicles (at cost *less* depreciation)		3,550
Office fittings (at cost *less* depreciation)		1,310
		12,860
Stock	2,040	
Debtors	4,530	
Bank	1,390	
		7,960
		20,820
Capitals:		£
Hughes		9,560
Allen		6,420
Elliott		4,840
		20,820

The above partners have always shared profits and losses in the ratio: Hughes 5, Allen 3, Elliott 2.

From 1 January the assets were to be revalued as the profit sharing ratios are to be altered soon. The following assets are to be revalued to the figures shown: Buildings £17,500, Motor vehicles £2,600, Stock £1,890, Office fittings £1,090.

Required:
(a) You are required to show all the ledger accounts necessary to record the revaluation.
(b) Draw up a balance sheet as at 1 January 20X9.

43.2A Avon and Brown have been in partnership for many years sharing profits and losses in the ratio 3 : 2 respectively. The following was their balance sheet as at 31 December 20X6.

	£	£
Goodwill		2,000
Plant and machinery		1,800
Stock	1,960	
Debtors	2,130	
Cash at bank	90	
	4,180	
Sundry creditors	(980)	
		3,200
		7,000
Capital: Avon		4,000
Brown		3,000
		7,000

On 1 January 20X7, they decided to admit Charles as a partner on the condition that he contributed £2,000 as his capital but that the plant and machinery and stock should be revalued at £2,000 and £1,900 respectively, the other assets, excepting goodwill, remaining at their present book values. The goodwill was agreed to be valueless.

You are required to show:

(a) The ledger entries dealing with the above in the following accounts:

    (i)   Goodwill account,

    (ii) Revaluation accounts,

    (iii) Capital accounts;

(b) The balance sheet of the partnership immediately after the admission of Charles.

43.3   Alan, Bob and Charles are in partnership sharing profits and losses in the ratio 3:2:1 respectively. The balance sheet for the partnership as at 30 June 20X6 is as follows:

	£	£	£
Fixed assets			
Premises			90,000
Plant			37,000
Vehicles			15,000
Fixtures			2,000
			144,000
Current assets			
Stock		62,379	
Debtors		34,980	
Cash		760	
		98,119	
Current liabilities			
Creditors	19,036		
Bank overdraft	4,200		
		(23,236)	
			74,883
			218,883
Loan – Charles			(28,000)
			190,883
Capital			
Alan			85,000
Bob			65,000
Charles			35,000
			185,000
Current account			
Alan		3,714	
Bob		(2,509)	
Charles		4,678	
			5,883
			190,883

Charles decides to retire from the business on 30 June 20X6, and Don is admitted as a partner on that date. The following matters are agreed:

(a) Certain assets were revalued: Premises £120,000; Plant £35,000; Stock £54,179.

(b) Provision is to be made for doubtful debts in the sum of £3,000.

(c) Goodwill is to be recorded in the books on the day Charles retires in the sum of £42,000. The partners in the new firm do not wish to maintain a goodwill account so that amount is to be written back against the new partners' capital accounts.

(d) Alan and Bob are to share profits in the same ratio as before, and Don is to have the same share of profits as Bob.

(e) Charles is to take his car at its book value of £3,900 in part payment, and the balance of all he is owed by the firm in cash except £20,000 which he is willing to leave as a loan account.

(f) The partners in the new firm are to start on an equal footing so far as capital and current accounts are concerned. Don is to contribute cash to bring his capital and current accounts to the same amount as the original partner from the old firm who has the lower investment in the business.

The original partner in the old firm who has the higher investment will draw out cash so that his capital and current account balances equal those of his new partners.

Required:

(a) Account for the above transactions, including goodwill and retiring partners' accounts.

(b) Draft a balance sheet for the partnership of Alan, Bob and Don as at 30 June 20X6.

(*Association of Accounting Technicians*)

CHAPTER 44

Partnership dissolution

Learning objectives

After you have studied this chapter, you should be able to:

- explain what happens upon dissolution of a partnership
- record the entries relating to the dissolution of a partnership
- explain the differences between recording a partnership dissolution and making the entries when one partner leaves a partnership
- explain the Partnership Act 1890 rules relating to partnership dissolution
- explain the *Garner* v *Murray* rule

Introduction

In this chapter, you'll learn how to calculate and record the necessary entries when a partnership is dissolved. You'll learn that the process is laid down in the Partnership Act 1890 and what to do under the *Garner* v *Murray rule* when partners are unable to pay the amount they owe the partnership. Finally, you'll learn how to deal with a situation where the partnership assets are being disposed of over a long period of time.

44.1 Need for dissolution

You will recall from Chapter 40 that joint ventures are often short-term and that when the project they were formed to do has ended, the joint venture is terminated. You learnt in Chapter 41 that partnerships are long-term ventures that are formed with a long-term commitment on the part of the partners to operate in business together. In Chapter 42, you learnt that new partners are admitted from time to time; and, in Chapter 43, you learnt that partners can also leave partnerships. So partnerships really are not as permanent as they may at first appear.

Activity 44.1
Can you think of any partnership you know of where a partner left? How do you think the change in the partnership was treated in the ledgers?

In fact, so far as the UK tax authorities are concerned, every time a partner joins or leaves a partnership, a new partnership is brought into existence. Intuitively, this does make sense. Partnerships exist because of the desire to merge the skills, resources and expertise of the partners. Imagine a rock group whose lead guitarist leaves. The replacement is never quite the same. As another example, if two people are in a partnership running a restaurant and the one that does the cooking leaves, the replacement isn't going to want to prepare exactly the same meals.

Partnerships do change when a partner leaves. And they do change when a new partner joins. However, for accounting purposes, we only consider partnerships as changing sufficiently to merit treating them as ceasing to exist when the partners go their separate ways. When they do, this is known as partnership **dissolution** – the partnership has been dissolved.

Reasons for dissolution include the following:

(a) The partnership is no longer profitable, and there is no longer any reason to carry on trading.
(b) The partners cannot agree between themselves how to operate the partnership. They therefore decide to finish the partnership.
(c) Factors such as ill-health or old age may bring about the close of the partnership.

> *Activity 44.2*
>
> What is the difference between these events and partners simply leaving a partnership? For example, if there are three partners in a dental practice and two leave, why can't the third continue the business with new partners?

44.2 What happens upon dissolution

Upon **dissolution** the partnership firm stops trading or operating. Then, in accordance with the Partnership Act 1890:

(a) the assets are disposed of;
(b) the liabilities of the firm are paid to everyone other than partners;
(c) the partners are repaid their advances and current balances – advances are the amounts they have put in above and beyond the capital;
(d) the partners are paid the final amounts due to them on their capital accounts.

Any profit or loss on dissolution would be shared by all the partners in their profit and loss sharing ratios. Profits would increase capitals repayable to partners. Losses would reduce the capitals repayable.

If a partner's final balance on his capital and current accounts is in deficit, he will have to pay that amount into the partnership bank account.

44.3 Disposal of assets

The assets do not have to be sold to external parties. Quite often one or more existing partners will take assets at values agreed by all the partners. In such a case the partner may not pay in cash for such assets; instead they will be charged to his capital account.

44.4 Accounting for partnership dissolution

The main account around which the dissolution entries are made is known as the realisation account. It is this account in which it is calculated whether the realisation of the assets is at a profit or at a loss.

Exhibit 44.1 shows the simplest of partnership dissolutions. We will then look at a more difficult example in Exhibit 44.2.

Exhibit 44.1

The last balance sheet of A and B, who share profits A two-thirds : B one-third is shown below. On this date they are to dissolve the partnership.

Balance Sheet at 31 December 20X9

	£	£
Fixed assets		
Buildings		10,000
Motor vehicle		2,000
		12,000
Current assets		
Stock	3,000	
Debtors	4,000	
Bank	1,000	
	8,000	
Current liabilities		
Creditors	(2,000)	
		6,000
		18,000
Capitals: A		12,000
B		6,000
		18,000

The buildings were sold for £10,500 and the stock for £2,600. £3,500 was collected from debtors. The motor vehicle was taken over by A at an agreed value of £1,700, but he did not pay any cash for it. £2,000 was paid to creditors. The costs of the dissolution were paid which were £200.

The accounting entries needed are:

(A) Transfer book values of all assets to the realisation account:
  Debit realisation account
    Credit asset accounts
(B) Amounts received from disposal of assets:
  Debit bank
    Credit realisation account
(C) Values of assets taken over by partner without payment:
  Debit partner's capital account
    Credit realisation account
(D) Creditors paid:
  Debit creditors' accounts
    Credit bank
(E) Costs of dissolution:
  Debit realisation account
    Credit bank
(F) Profit or loss on realisation to be shared between partners in profit and loss sharing ratios:
  If a profit: Debit realisation account
      Credit partners' capital accounts
  If a loss: Debit partners' capital accounts
      Credit realisation account
(G) Pay to the partners their final balances on their capital accounts:
  Debit capital accounts
    Credit bank

The entries are now shown. The letters (A) to (G) as above are shown against each entry:

Buildings

		£			£
Balance b/d		10,000	Realisation	(A)	10,000

Motor Vehicle

		£			£
Balance b/d		2,000	Realisation	(A)	2,000

Stock

		£			£
Balance b/d		3,000	Realisation	(A)	3,000

Debtors

		£			£
Balance b/d		4,000	Realisation	(A)	4,000

Realisation

		£				£
Assets to be realised:			Bank: Assets sold			
Buildings	(A)	10,000	Buildings	(B)		10,500
Motor vehicle	(A)	2,000	Stock	(B)		2,600
Stock	(A)	3,000	Debtors	(B)		3,500
Debtors	(A)	4,000	Taken over by partner A:			
Bank:			Motor vehicle	(C)		1,700
Dissolution costs	(E)	200	Loss on realisation		£	
			A $^2/_3$	(F)	600	
			B $^1/_3$	(F)	300	
						900
		19,200				19,200

Bank

		£			£
Balance b/d		1,000	Creditors	(D)	2,000
Realisation: Assets sold			Realisation: Costs	(E)	200
Buildings	(B)	10,500	Capitals: to clear		
Stock	(B)	2,600	A	(G)	9,700
Debtors	(B)	3,500	B	(G)	5,700
		17,600			17,600

Creditors

		£		£
Bank	(D)	2,000	Balance b/d	2,000

A: Capital

		£		£
Realisation: Motor	(C)	1,700	Balance b/d	12,000
Realisation: Share of loss	(F)	600		
Bank: to close	(G)	9,700		
		12,000		12,000

B: Capital

		£		£
Realisation: Share of loss	(F)	300	Balance b/d	6,000
Bank: to close	(G)	5,700		
		6,000		6,000

The final balances on the partners' capital accounts should always equal the amount in the bank account from which they are to be paid. For instance, in the above exhibit there was £15,400 in the bank from which to pay A £9,700 and B £5,700. If the final bank balance does not pay out the partners' capital accounts exactly, you will have made a mistake somewhere.

44.5 A more detailed example

Exhibit 44.1 did not show the more difficult accounting entries. A more difficult example appears in Exhibit 44.2.

The extra information is:

(*a*) Any provision such as bad debts or depreciation is to be transferred to the credit of the asset account: see entries (A) in Exhibit 44.2.
(*b*) Discounts on creditors – to balance the creditors' account, transfer the discounts on creditors to the credit of the realisation account: see entries (F) in the exhibit.
(*c*) Transfer the balances on the partners' current accounts to their capital accounts: see entries (I) of the exhibit.
(*d*) A partner who owes the firm money because his capital account is in deficit must now pay the money owing: see entries (J) of the exhibit.

Exhibit 44.2

On 31 December 20X8, P, Q and R decided to dissolve their partnership. They had always shared profits in the ratio of P3 : Q2 : R1.

Their goodwill was sold for £3,000, the machinery for £1,800 and the stock for £1,900. There were three cars, all taken over by the partners at agreed values, P taking one for £800, Q one for £1,000 and R one for £500. The premises were taken over by R at an agreed value of £5,500. The amounts collected from debtors amounted to £2,700 after bad debts and discounts had been deducted. The creditors were discharged for £1,600, the difference being due to discounts received. The costs of dissolution amounted to £1,000.

Their last balance sheet is summarised as:

Balance Sheet as at 31 December 20X8

	£	£	£
Fixed assets			
Premises			5,000
Machinery			3,000
Motor vehicles			2,500
			10,500
Current assets			
Stock		1,800	
Debtors	3,000		
Less Provision for doubtful debts	(200)		
		2,800	
Bank		1,400	
		6,000	
Current liabilities			
Creditors		(1,700)	
			4,300
			14,800
Capital accounts: P			6,000
Q			5,000
R			3,000
			14,000
Current accounts: P		200	
Q		100	
R		500	
			800
			14,800

The accounts recording the dissolution are shown below. A description of each entry follows the accounts, the letters (A) to (K) against each entry indicating the relevant descriptions.

Premises

	£			£
Balance b/d	5,000	Realisation	(B)	5,000

Machinery

	£			£
Balance b/d	3,000	Realisation	(B)	3,000

Motor Vehicles

	£			£
Balance b/d	2,500	Realisation	(B)	2,500

Stock

	£			£
Balance b/d	1,800	Realisation	(B)	1,800

Debtors

	£			£
Balance b/d	3,000	Provision for doubtful debts	(A)	200
		Realisation	(B)	2,800
	3,000			3,000

Realisation

		£			£
Assets to be realised:			Bank: Assets sold		
Premises	(B)	5,000	Goodwill	(C)	3,000
Machinery	(B)	3,000	Machinery	(C)	1,800
Motor vehicles	(B)	2,500	Stock	(C)	1,900
Stock	(B)	1,800	Debtors	(C)	2,700
Debtors	(B)	2,800	Taken over by partners:		
Bank: Costs	(G)	1,000	P: Car	(D)	800
Profit on realisation:	(H)		Q: Car	(D)	1,000
	£		R: Car	(D)	500
P	600		R: Premises	(D)	5,500
Q	400		Creditors: Discounts	(F)	100
R	200				
		1,200			
		17,300			17,300

Creditors

		£		£
Bank	(E)	1,600	Balance b/d	1,700
Realisation (Discounts)	(F)	100		
		1,700		1,700

Bank

		£			£
Balance b/d		1,400	Creditors	(E)	1,600
Realisation: Assets sold			Realisation: Costs	(G)	1,000
Goodwill	(C)	3,000	P: Capital	(K)	6,000
Machinery	(C)	1,800	Q: Capital	(K)	4,500
Stock	(C)	1,900			
Debtors	(C)	2,700			
R: Capital	(J)	2,300			
		13,100			13,100

P Capital

		£		£
Realisation: Car	(D)	800	Balance b/d	6,000
Bank	(K)	6,000	Current account transferred (I)	200
			Realisation: Share of profit (H)	600
		6,800		6,800

Provision for Doubtful Debts

		£		£
Debtors	(A)	200	Balance b/d	200

P Current Account

		£		£
P: Capital	(I)	200	Balance b/d	200

Q Current Account

		£		£
Q: Capital	(I)	100	Balance b/d	100

Q Capital

		£		£
Realisation: Car	(D)	1,000	Balance b/d	5,000
Bank	(K)	4,500	Current account transferred (I)	100
			Realisation: Share of profit (H)	400
		5,500		5,500

R Capital

		£			£
Realisation: Car	(D)	500	Balance b/d		3,000
Realisation: Premises	(D)	5,500	Current account transferred (I)		500
			Realisation: Share of profit (H)		200
			Bank	(J)	2,300
		6,000			6,000

R Current Account

		£		£
R: Capital	(I)	500	Balance b/d	500

Description of transactions:

(A) The provision accounts are transferred to the relevant asset accounts so that the net balance on the asset accounts may be transferred to the realisation account. Debit provision accounts. Credit asset accounts.

(B) The net book values of the assets are transferred to the realisation account. Debit realisation account. Credit asset accounts.

(C) Assets sold. Debit bank account. Credit realisation account.

(D) Assets taken over by partners. Debit partners' capital accounts. Credit realisation account.

(E) Liabilities discharged. Credit bank account. Debit liability accounts.

(F) Discounts on creditors. Debit creditors' account. Credit realisation account.

(G) Costs of dissolution. Credit bank account. Debit realisation account.

(H) Profit or loss split in profit/loss sharing ratio. Profit – debit realisation account. Credit partners' capital accounts. The opposite if a loss.

(I) Transfer the balances on the partners' current accounts to their capital accounts.

(J) Any partner with a capital account in deficit, i.e. debits exceeding credits, must now pay in the amount needed to cancel his indebtedness to the partnership firm. Debit bank account. Credit capital account.

(K) The credit balances on the partners' capital accounts can now be paid to them. Credit bank account. Debit partners' capital accounts.

The payments made under (K) should complete the payment of all the balances in the partnership books.

44.6 The rule in *Garner* v *Murray*

It sometimes happens that a partner's capital account finishes up with a debit balance. Normally the partner will pay in an amount to clear his indebtedness to the firm. However, sometimes he will be unable to pay all, or part, of such a balance. In the case of **Garner v Murray** in 1904 (a case in England) the court ruled that, subject to any agreement to the contrary, such a deficiency was to be shared by the other partners *not* in their profit and loss sharing ratios but in the ratio of their 'last agreed capitals'. By 'their last agreed capitals' is meant the credit balances on their capital accounts in the normal balance sheet drawn up at the end of their last accounting period.

It must be borne in mind that the balances on their capital accounts after the assets have been realised may be far different from those on the last balance sheet. Where a partnership deed is drawn up it is commonly found that agreement is made to use normal profit and loss sharing ratios instead, thus rendering the *Garner* v *Murray* rule inoperative. **The Garner v Murray rule does not apply to partnerships in Scotland.**

Before reading further you should check whether or not this topic is in the requirements for your examinations.

Exhibit 44.3

After completing the realisation of all the assets, in respect of which a loss of £4,200 was incurred, but before making the final payments to the partners, the balance sheet appears:

Balance Sheet

	£	£
Cash at bank		6,400
		6,400
Capitals: R	5,800	
S	1,400	
T	400	
	7,600	
Less Q (debit balance)	(1,200)	
		6,400
		6,400

According to the last balance sheet drawn up before the dissolution, the partners' capital account credit balances were: Q £600; R £7,000; S £2,000; T £1,000; while the profits and losses were shared Q3 : R2 : S1 : T1.

Q is unable to meet any part of his deficiency. Each of the other partners therefore suffer the deficiency as follows:

$$\frac{\text{Own capital per balance sheet before dissolution}}{\text{Total of all solvent partners' capitals per same balance sheet}} \times \text{Deficiency}$$

This can now be calculated.

$$R \quad \frac{£7,000}{£7,000 + £2,000 + £1,000} \times 1,200 = £840$$

$$S \quad \frac{£2,000}{£7,000 + £2,000 + £1,000} \times 1,200 = £240$$

$$T \quad \frac{£1,000}{£7,000 + £2,000 + £1,000} \times 1,200 = \underline{£120}$$
$$\underline{£1,200}$$

When these amounts have been charged to the capital accounts, then the balances remaining on them will equal the amount of the bank balance. Payments may therefore be made to clear their capital accounts.

	Credit balance b/d £		Share of deficiency now debited £		Final credit balances £
R	5,800	–	840	=	4,960
S	1,400	–	240	=	1,160
T	400	–	120	=	280
Equals the bank balance					6,400

44.7 Piecemeal realisation of assets

Frequently the assets may take a long time to realise. The partners will naturally want payments made to them on account as cash is received. They will not want to wait for payments until the dissolution is completed just for the convenience of the accountant. There is, however, a danger that if too much is paid to a partner, and he is unable to repay it, then the person handling the dissolution could be placed in a very awkward position.

To counteract this, the concept of prudence is brought into play. This is done as follows:

(a) Each receipt of sale money is treated as being the final receipt, even though more could be received.
(b) Any loss then calculated so far to be shared between partners in profit and loss sharing ratios.
(c) Should any partner's capital account after each receipt show a debit balance, then he is assumed to be unable to pay in the deficiency. This deficit will be shared (failing any other agreement) between the partners using the *Garner* v *Murray* rule.
(d) After payments of liabilities and the costs of dissolution the remainder of the cash is then paid to the partners.

(e) In this manner, even if no further money were received, or should a partner become insolvent, the division of the available cash would be strictly in accordance with the legal requirements. Exhibit 44.4 shows such a series of calculations.

Exhibit 44.4

The following is the summarised balance sheet of H, I, J and K as at 31 December 20X8. The partners had shared profits in the ratios H6 : I4 : J1 : K1.

Balance Sheet as at 31 December 20X8

	£
Assets	8,400
Creditors	(1,800)
	6,600
Capitals:	
H	600
I	3,000
J	2,000
K	1,000
	6,600

On 1 March 20X9 some of the assets were sold for cash £5,000. Out of this the creditors' £1,800 and the cost of dissolution £200 are paid, leaving £3,000 distributable to the partners.

On 1 July 20X9 some more assets are sold for £2,100. As all of the liabilities and the costs of dissolution have already been paid, then the whole of the £2,100 is available for distribution between the partners.

On 1 October 20X9 the final sale of the assets realised £1,200.

First distribution: 1 March 20X9	H	I	J	K
	£	£	£	£
Capital balances before dissolution	600	3,000	2,000	1,000
Loss if no further assets realised: Assets £8,400 – Sales £5,000 = £3,400 + Costs £200 = £3,600 loss				
Loss shared in profit/loss ratios	1,800	1,200	300	300
	1,200Dr	1,800Cr	1,700Cr	700Cr
H's deficiency shared in *Garner* v *Murray* ratios		³/₆ 600	²/₆ 400	¹/₆ 200
Cash paid to partners (£3,000)		1,200	1,300	500

Second distribution: 1 July 20X9	H	I	J	K
	£	£	£	£
Capital balances before dissolution	600	3,000	2,000	1,000
Loss if no further assets realised: Assets £8,400 – Sales (£5,000 + £2,100) = £1,300 + Costs £200 = £1,500 loss				
Loss shared in profit/loss ratios	(750)	(500)	(125)	(125)
	150Dr	2,500Cr	1,875Cr	875Cr
H's deficiency shared in *Garner* v *Murray* ratios		(75)	(50)	(25)
		2,425	1,825	850
Less First distribution already paid		(1,200)	(1,300)	(500)
Cash now paid to partners (£2,100)		1,225	525	350

Third and find distribution: 1 October 20X9	H	I	J	K
	£	£	£	£
Capital balances before dissolution	600	3,000	2,000	1,000
Loss finally ascertained:				
Assets £8,400 – Sales (£5,000 + £2,100				
+ £1,200) = £100 + Costs £200 = £300 loss				
Loss shared in profit/loss ratios	(150)	(100)	(25)	(25)
	450Cr	2,900Cr	1,975Cr	975Cr
(No deficiency now exists on any				
capital account)				
Less First and second distributions	–	(2,425)	(1,825)	(850)
Cash now paid to partners (£1,200)	450	475	150	125

In any subsequent distribution following that in which all the partners have shared (i.e. no partners could then have had a deficiency left on their capital accounts) all receipts of cash are divided between the partners in their profit and loss sharing ratios. Following the above method would give the same answer for these subsequent distributions but obviously an immediate division in the profit and loss sharing ratios would be quicker. Try it for yourself and you'll see that the same answer would result.

Learning outcomes

You should now have learnt:

1 How to calculate the amounts due to and from each partner when a partnership is dissolved.

2 How to record partnership dissolution in the ledger accounts.

3 That upon dissolution, a partnership firm stops trading or operating, any profit or loss on dissolution being shared by the partners in their profit sharing ratio.

4 That the *Garner* v *Murray* rule does not apply to partnerships in Scotland.

Answers to activities

44.1   There is obviously no 'right' answer to this question. You may have noticed partnership changes at your local doctor's or dental practice. They can have quite an impact upon some of the patients. Similarly, there have been famous partnerships in ice skating, the theatre, music, and in sport, especially tennis, where switching partners creates a very different visual effect and level of satisfaction for the audience.

Many of these examples are really short-term joint ventures rather than partnerships. The doctors and dentists are most definitely partnerships. In many cases where one of *these* examples of joint ventures or partnerships change, a new one tends to develop in its place. In the case of those that are partnerships where the business is continuing with new partners, you can apply the techniques you've already learnt to apply when a partner leaves a partnership and when a partner joins and make the necessary entries in the partnership ledger accounts.

44.2   That may happen, in which case it could be argued that it should be treated as simply a change of membership of the partnership. There's nothing wrong with doing so if the business is continuing as before but, even in those cases, you will probably find it easier to treat it as a partnership dissolution, close off all the books and start afresh with the new partnership. This is because if only one partner is left in the business, you would need to remove each of the partners from the accounts anyway before adding in the new one(s).

REVIEW QUESTIONS

44.1   S, W and M are partners. They share profits and losses in the ratios of $^2/_5$, $^2/_5$ and $^1/_5$ respectively.

For the year ended 31 December 20X9 their capital accounts remained fixed at the following amounts:

	£
S	6,000
W	4,000
M	2,000

They have agreed to give each other 10 per cent interest per annum on their capital accounts.

In addition to the above, partnership salaries of £3,000 for W and £1,000 for M are to be charged.

The net profit of the partnership before taking any of the above into account was £25,200.

You are required to draw up the appropriation account of the partnership for the year ended 31 December 20X9.

44.2A   Draw up a profit and loss appropriation account for Winn, Pool and Howe for the year ended 31 December 20X7, and balance sheet extracts at that date, from the following:

(*i*)   Net profits £30,350.
(*ii*)   Interest to be charged on capitals: Winn £2,000; Pool £1,500; Howe £900.
(*iii*)   Interest to be charged on drawings: Winn £240; Pool £180; Howe £130.
(*iv*)   Salaries to be credited: Pool £2,000; Howe £3,500.
(*v*)   Profits to be shared: Winn 50%; Pool 30%; Howe 20%.
(*vi*)   Current accounts: Winn £1,860; Pool £946; Howe £717.
(*vii*)   Capital accounts: Winn £40,000; Pool £30,000; Howe £18,000.
(*viii*) Drawings: Winn £9,200; Pool £7,100; Howe £6,900.

44.3   Moore and Stephens, who share profits and losses equally, decide to dissolve their partnership as at 31 March 20X9. Their balance sheet on that date was as follows:

	£	£
Buildings		800
Tools and fixtures		850
		1,650
Debtors	2,800	
Cash	1,800	
	4,600	
Sundry creditors	(2,750)	
		1,850
		3,500
Capital account: Moore		2,000
Stephens		1,500
		3,500

The debtors realised £2,700, the buildings £400 and the tools and fixtures £950. The expenses of dissolution were £100 and discounts totalling £200 were received from creditors.

Required:
Prepare the accounts necessary to show the results of the realisation and of the disposal of the cash.

44.4   X, Y and Z have been in partnership for several years, sharing profits and losses in the ratio 3 : 2 : 1. Their last balance sheet which was prepared on 31 October 20X9 is as follows:

Balance Sheet of X, Y and Z
as at 31 October 20X9

	£	£	£
Fixed assets			
At cost			20,000
Less Depreciation			(6,000)
			14,000
Current assets			
Stock		5,000	
Debtors		21,000	
		26,000	
Current liabilities			
Bank	13,000		
Creditors	17,000		
		(30,000)	
			(4,000)
			10,000
Capital			
X			4,000
Y			4,000
Z			2,000
			10,000

Despite making good profits during recent years they had become increasingly dependent on one credit customer, Smithson, and in order to retain his custom they had gradually increased his credit limit until he owed the partnership £18,000. It has now been discovered that Smithson is insolvent and that he is unlikely to repay any of the money owed by him to the partnership. Reluctantly X, Y and Z have agreed to dissolve the partnership on the following terms:

(i) The stock is to be sold to Nelson Ltd for £4,000.
(ii) The fixed assets will be sold for £8,000 except for certain items with a book value of £5,000 which will be taken over by X at an agreed valuation of £7,000.
(iii) The debtors, except for Smithson, are expected to pay their accounts in full.
(iv) The costs of dissolution will be £800 and discounts received from creditors will be £500. Z is unable to meet his liability to the partnership out of his personal funds.

Required:
(a) the realisation account;
(b) the capital accounts to the partners recording the dissolution of the partnership.

(*Associated Examining Board*)

44.5A The following trial balance has been extracted from the books of Gain and Main as at 31 March 20X8; Gain and Main are in partnership sharing profits and losses in the ratio 3 to 2:

	£	£
Capital accounts:		
Gain		10,000
Main		5,000
Cash at bank	1,550	
Creditors		500
Current accounts:		
Gain		1,000
Main	2,000	
Debtors	2,000	
Depreciation: Fixtures and fittings		1,000
Motor vehicles		1,300
Fixtures and fittings	2,000	
Land and buildings	30,000	
Motor vehicles	4,500	
Net profit (for the year to 31 March 20X8)		26,250
Stock, at cost	3,000	
	£45,050	£45,050

In appropriating the net profit for the year, it has been agreed that Main should be entitled to a salary of £9,750. Each partner is also entitled to interest on his opening capital account balance at the rate of 10 per cent per annum.

Gain and Main have decided to convert the partnership into a limited company, Plain Limited, as from 1 April 20X8. The company is to take over all the assets and liabilities of the partnership, except that Gain is to retain for his personal use one of the motor vehicles at an agreed transfer price of £1,000.

The purchase consideration will consist of 40,000 ordinary shares of £1 each in Plain Limited, to be divided between the partners in profit-sharing ratio. Any balance on the partners' current accounts is to be settled in cash.

You are required to:
Prepare the main ledger accounts of the partnership in order to close off the books as at 31 March 20X8.

(Association of Accounting Technicians)

44.6A   A, B & C are partners sharing profits and losses in the ratio 2 : 2 : 1. The balance sheet of the partnership as at 30 September 20X7 was as follows:

	£	£
Freehold premises		18,000
Equipment and machinery		12,000
Cars		3,000
		33,000
Inventory^{Authors' note}	11,000	
Debtors	14,000	
Bank	9,000	
	34,000	
Creditors	(10,000)	
		24,000
		57,000
Loan account – A		(7,000)
		50,000
Capital accounts		
A		22,000
B		18,000
C		10,000
		50,000

Authors' note: Inventory is another word for stock.

The partners agreed to dispose of the business to CNO Limited with effect from 1 October 20X7 under the following conditions and terms:

(*i*)   CNO Limited will acquire the goodwill, all fixed assets and the inventory for the purchase consideration of £58,000. This consideration will include a payment of £10,000 in cash and the issue of 12,000 10 per cent preference shares of £1 each at par, and the balance by the issue of £1 ordinary shares at £1.25 per share.
(*ii*) The partnership business will settle amounts owing to creditors.
(*iii*) CNO Limited will collect the debts on behalf of the vendors.

Purchase consideration payments and allotments of shares were made on 1 October 20X7.

The partnership creditors were paid off by 31 October 20X7 after the taking of cash discounts of £190.

CNO Limited collected and paid over all partnership debts by 30 November 20X7 except for bad debts amounting to £800. Discounts allowed to debtors amounted to £400.

Required:
(*a*) Journal entries (including those relating to cash) necessary to close the books of the partnership, and

(*b*) Set out the basis on which the shares in CNO Limited are allotted to partners. Ignore interest.

(*Institute of Chartered Secretaries and Administrators*)

44.7   Amis, Lodge and Pym were in partnership sharing profits and losses in the ratio 5 : 3 : 2. The following trial balance has been extracted from their books of account as at 31 March 20X8:

	£	£
Bank interest received		750
Capital accounts (as at 1 April 20X7):		
Amis		80,000
Lodge		15,000
Pym		5,000
Carriage inwards	4,000	
Carriage outwards	12,000	
Cash at bank	4,900	
Current accounts:		
Amis	1,000	
Lodge	500	
Pym	400	
Discounts allowed	10,000	
Discounts received		4,530
Drawings:		
Amis	25,000	
Lodge	22,000	
Pym	15,000	
Motor vehicles:		
at cost	80,000	
accumulated depreciation (at 1 April 20X7)		20,000
Office expenses	30,400	
Plant and machinery:		
at cost	100,000	
accumulated depreciation (at 1 April 20X7)		36,600
Provision for bad and doubtful debts (at 1 April 20X7)		420
Purchases	225,000	
Rent, rates, heat and light	8,800	
Sales		404,500
Stock (at 1 April 20X7)	30,000	
Trade creditors		16,500
Trade debtors	14,300	
	£583,300	£583,300

Additional information:
(*a*) Stock at 31 March 20X8 was valued at £35,000.
(*b*) Depreciation on the fixed assets is to be charged as follows:
       Motor vehicles – 25 per cent on the reduced balance.
       Plant and machinery – 20 per cent on the original cost.
     There were no purchases or sales of fixed assets during the year to 31 March 20X8.
(*c*) The provision for bad and doubtful debts is to be maintained at a level equivalent to 5 per cent of the total trade debtors as at 31 March 20X8.
(*d*) An office expense of £405 was owing at 31 March 20X8, and some rent amounting to £1,500 had been paid in advance as at that date. These items had not been included in the list of balances shown in the trial balance.
(*e*) Interest on drawings and on the debit balance on each partner's current account is to be charged as follows:

	£
Amis	1,000
Lodge	900
Pym	720

(f) According to the partnership agreement, Pym is allowed a salary of £13,000 per annum. This amount was owing to Pym for the year to 31 March 20X8, and needs to be accounted for.

(g) The partnership agreement also allows each partner interest on his capital account at a rate of 10 per cent per annum. There were no movements on the respective partners' capital accounts during the year to 31 March 20X8, and the interest had not been credited to them as at that date.

Note: The information given above is sufficient to answer part (a) (i) and (ii) of the question, and notes (h) and (i) below are pertinent to requirements (b) (i), (ii) and (iii) of the question.

(h) On 1 April 20X8, Fowles Limited agreed to purchase the business on the following terms:
   (i) Amis to purchase one of the partnership's motor vehicles at an agreed value of £5,000, the remaining vehicles being taken over by the company at an agreed value of £30,000;
   (ii) the company agreed to purchase the plant and machinery at a value of £35,000 and the stock at a value of £38,500;
   (iii) the partners to settle the trade creditors: the total amount agreed with the creditors being £16,000;
   (iv) the trade debtors were not to be taken over by the company, the partners receiving cheques on 1 April 20X8 amounting to £12,985 in total from the trade debtors in settlement of the outstanding debts;
   (v) the partners paid the outstanding office expense on 1 April 20X8, and the landlord returned the rent paid in advance by cheque on the same day;
   (vi) as consideration for the sale of the partnership, the partners were to be paid £63,500 in cash by Fowles Limited, and to receive 75,000 in £1 ordinary shares in the company, the shares to be apportioned equally amongst the partners.

(i) Assume that all the matters relating to the dissolution of the partnership and its sales to the company took place on 1 April 20X8.

Required:

(a) Prepare:
   (i) Amis, Lodge and Pym's trading, profit and loss and profit and loss appropriation account for the year to 31 March 20X8;
   (ii) Amis, Lodge and Pym's current accounts (in columnar format) for the year to 31 March 20X8 (the final balance on each account is to be then transferred to each partner's respective capital account);
   and

(b) Compile the following accounts:
   (i) the partnership realisation account for the period up to and including 1 April 20X8;
   (ii) the partners' bank account for the period up to and including 1 April 20X8; and
   (iii) the partners' capital accounts (in columnar format) for the period up to and including 1 April 20X8.

Note: Detailed workings should be submitted with your answer.

(*Association of Accounting Technicians*)

44.8A Proudie, Slope and Thorne were in partnership sharing profits and losses in the ratio 3 : 1 : 1. The draft balance sheet of the partnership as at 31 May 20X9 is shown below:

	£000 Cost	£000 Depreciation	£000 Net book value
Fixed assets			
Land and buildings	200	40	160
Furniture	30	18	12
Motor vehicles	60	40	20
	290	98	192
Current assets			
Stocks		23	
Trade debtors	42		
Less Provision for doubtful debts	(1)		
		41	
Prepayments		2	
Cash		10	
		76	
Less Current liabilities			
Trade creditors	15		
Accruals	3		
		(18)	
			58
			250
Loan			
Proudie			(8)
			242
Financed by:			
Capital accounts			
Proudie		100	
Slope		60	
Thorne		40	
			200
Current accounts			
Proudie		24	
Slope		10	
Thorne		8	
			42
			242

Additional information:

1 Proudie decided to retire on 31 May 20X9. However, Slope and Thorne agreed to form a new partnership out of the old one, as from 1 June 20X9. They agreed to share profits and losses in the same ratio as in the old partnership.

2 Upon the dissolution of the old partnership, it was agreed that the following adjustments were to be made to the partnership balance sheet as at 31 May 20X9.

(a) Land and buildings were to be revalued at £200,000.

(b) Furniture was to be revalued at £5,000.

(c) Proudie agreed to take over one of the motor vehicles at a value of £4,000, the remaining motor vehicles being revalued at £10,000.

(d) Stocks were to be written down by £5,000.

(e) A bad debt of £2,000 was to be written off, and the provision for doubtful debts was then to be adjusted so that it represented 5 per cent of the then outstanding trade debtors as at 31 May 20X9.

(f) A further accrual of £3,000 for office expenses was to be made.

(g) Professional charges relating to the dissolution were estimated to be £1,000.

3 It has not been the practice of the partners to carry goodwill in the books of the partnership, but on the retirement of a partner it had been agreed that goodwill should be taken into account.

Goodwill was to be valued at an amount equal to the average annual profits of the three years expiring on the retirement. For the purpose of including goodwill in the dissolution arrangement when Proudie retired, the net profits for the last three years were as follows:

	£000
Year to 31 May 20X7	130
Year to 31 May 20X8	150
Year to 31 May 20X9	181

The net profit for the year to 31 May 20X9 had been calculated before any of the items listed in 2 above were taken into account. The net profit was only to be adjusted for items listed in 2(d), 2(e) and 2(f) above.

4 Goodwill is not to be carried in the books of the new partnership.
5 It was agreed that Proudie's old loan of £8,000 should be repaid to him on 31 May 20X9, but any further amount owing to him as a result of the dissolution of the partnership should be left as a long-term loan in the books of the new partnership.
6 The partners' current accounts were to be closed and any balances on them as at 31 May 20X9 were to be transferred to their respective capital accounts.

Required:
(a) Prepare the revaluation account as at 31 May 20X9.
(b) Prepare the partners' capital accounts as at the date of dissolution of the partnership, and bring down any balances on them in the books of the new partnership.
(c) Prepare Slope and Thorne's balance sheet as at 1 June 20X9.

(*Association of Accounting Technicians*)

44.9 Lock, Stock and Barrel have been in partnership as builders and contractors for many years. Owing to adverse trading conditions it has been decided to dissolve the partnership. Profits are shared Lock 40 per cent, Stock 30 per cent, Barrel 30 per cent. The partnership deed also provides that in the event of a partner being unable to pay off a debit balance the remaining partners will treat this as a trading loss.
    The latest partnership balance sheet was as follows:

	Cost	Depreciation	
Fixed tangible assets	£	£	£
Freehold yard and buildings	20,000	3,000	17,000
Plant and equipment	150,000	82,000	68,000
Motor vehicles	36,000	23,000	13,000
	206,000	108,000	98,000
Current assets			
Stock of land for building		75,000	
Houses in course of construction		115,000	
Stocks of materials		23,000	
Debtors for completed houses		62,000	
		275,000	
Current liabilities			
Trade creditors	77,000		
Deposits and progress payments	82,000		
Bank overdraft	132,500		
	(291,500)		
Excess of current liabilities over current assets			
			(16,500)
			81,500
Partners' capital accounts			
Lock		52,000	
Stock		26,000	
Barrel		3,500	
			81,500

During the six months from the date of the latest balance sheet to the date of dissolution the following transactions have taken place:

	£
Purchase of materials	20,250
Materials used for houses in course of construction	35,750
Payments for wages and subcontractors on building sites	78,000
Payments to trade creditors for materials	45,000
Sales of completed houses	280,000
Cash received from customers for houses	225,000
Payments for various general expenses	12,500
Payments for administration salaries	17,250
Cash withdrawn by partners: Lock	6,000
Stock	5,000
Barrel	4,000

All deposits and progress payments have been used for completed transactions.

Depreciation is normally provided each year at £600 on the freehold yard and buildings, at 10 per cent on cost for plant and equipment and 25 per cent on cost for motor vehicles.

The partners decide to dissolve the partnership on 1 February 20X7 and wish to take out the maximum cash possible, as items are sold. At this date there are no houses in course of construction and one-third of the stock of land had been used for building.

It is agreed that Barrel is insolvent and cannot bring any money into the partnership. The partners take over the partnership cars at an agreed figure of £2,000 each. All other vehicles were sold on 28 February 20X7 for £6,200. At the same date stocks of materials were sold for £7,000, and the stock of the land realised £72,500. On 30 April 20X7 the debtors paid in full and all the plant and equipment was sold for £50,000.

The freehold yard and buildings realised £100,000 on 1 June 20X7, on which date all remaining cash was distributed.

There are no costs of realisation or distribution.

Required:
(a) Prepare a partnership profit and loss account for the six months to 1 February 20X7, partners' capital accounts for the same period and a balance sheet at 1 February 20X7.
(b) Show calculations of the amounts distributable to the partners.
(c) Prepare a realisation account and the capital accounts of the partners to the final distribution.

(*Association of Chartered Certified Accountants*)

44.10A Grant and Herd are in partnership sharing profits and losses in the ratio 3 to 2. The following information relates to the year to 31 December 20X8:

	Dr	Cr
	£000	£000
Capital accounts (at 1 January 20X8):		
Grant		300
Herd		100
Cash at bank	5	
Creditors and accruals		25
Debtors and prepayments	18	
Drawings during the year: Grant (all at 30 June 20X8)	40	
Herd (all at 31 March 20X8)	40	
Fixed assets: at cost	300	
accumulated depreciation (at 31 December 20X8)		100
Herd – salary	10	
Net profit (for the year to 31 December 20X8)		60
Stocks at cost (at 31 December 20X8)	90	
Trade creditors		141
Trade debtors	223	
	726	726

Additional information:

1 The partnership agreement allows for Herd to be paid a salary of £20,000 per annum, and for interest of 5 per cent per annum to be paid on the partners' capital account balances as at 1 January in each year. Interest at a rate of 10 per cent per annum is charged on the partners' drawings.

2 The partners decide to dissolve the partnership as at 31 December 20X8, and the business was then sold to Valley Limited. The purchase consideration was to be 400,000 £1 ordinary shares in Valley at a premium of 25p per share. The shares were to be issued to the partners on 31 December 20X8, and they were to be shared between them in their profit-sharing ratio.

The sale agreement allowed Grant to take over one of the business cars at an agreed valuation of £10,000. Apart from the car and the cash and bank balances, the company took over all the other partnership assets and liabilities at their book values as at 31 December 20X8.

3 Matters relating to the appropriation of profit for the year to 31 December 20X8 are to be dealt with in the partners' capital accounts, including any arrears of salary owing to Herd.

Required:

(*a*) Write up the following accounts for the year to 31 December 20X8:
    (*i*)   the profit and loss appropriation account;
    (*ii*) Grant and Herd's capital accounts; and
    (*iii*) the realisation account.

(*b*) Prepare Valley's balance sheet as at 1 January 20X9 immediately after the acquisition of the partnership and assuming that no further transactions have taken place in the meantime.

(Association of Accounting Technicians)

CHAPTER 45

An introduction to the financial statements of limited liability companies

Learning objectives

After you have studied this chapter, you should be able to:
- explain how limited companies differ from sole traders and partnerships
- explain the differences between different classes of shares
- calculate how distributable profits available for dividends are divided between the different classes of shares
- explain the differences between shares and debentures
- prepare the trading and profit and loss accounts for a company for internal purposes
- prepare the balance sheet for a company for internal purposes
- explain what an audit report is
- explain the treatment of goodwill in company financial statements

Introduction

In this chapter, you'll learn about the different types of companies that can exist and about the different types of long-term funds they can raise in order to finance their activities. You'll learn how to prepare the financial statements for companies and about the differences between the treatment of goodwill in company accounts and its treatment in the accounts of sole traders and partnerships.

45.1 Need for limited companies

Limited liability companies, more commonly referred to as **limited companies**, came into existence originally because of the growth in the size of businesses, and the need to have a lot of people investing in the business who would not be able to take part in its management.

Activity 45.1
Why do you think a partnership was an inappropriate form of business in this case?

The law governing the preparation and publication of the financial statements of limited companies in the United Kingdom is contained in two Acts of Parliament. These are the Companies Acts of 1985 and 1989. Both Acts are in force for this purpose, the 1989 Act adding to and amending the 1985 Act.

45.2   Limited liability

The capital of a limited company is divided into **shares**. Shares can be of any nominal value – 10p, 25p, £1, £5, £10, or any other amount per share. To become a member of a limited company, or a **shareholder**, a person must buy one or more of the shares.

If shareholders have paid in full for their shares, their liability is limited to what they have already paid for those shares. If a company loses all its assets, all those shareholders can lose is their shares. They cannot be forced to pay anything more in respect of the company's losses.

Shareholders who have only partly paid for their shares can be forced to pay the balance owing on the shares, but nothing else.

Shareholders are therefore said to have 'limited liability' and this is why companies are known as 'limited liability' or, more usually, simply 'limited' companies. By addressing the need for investors to have limited risk of financial loss, the existence of limited liability encourages individuals to invest in these companies and makes it possible to have both a large number of owners and a large amount of capital invested in the company.

There are, in fact, a few companies which have unlimited liability, but these are outside the scope of this book.

45.3   Public and private companies

There are two classes of company, the **public company** and the **private company**. In the UK, private companies far outnumber public companies. In the Companies Acts, a public company is defined as one which fulfils the following conditions:

- Its memorandum (a document that describes the company) states that it is a public company, and that it has registered as such.
- It has an authorised share capital of at least £50,000.
- Minimum membership is two. There is no maximum.
- Its name must end with the words 'public limited company' or the abbreviation 'PLC'. It can have the Welsh equivalent if registered in Wales.

PLCs can, but don't have to offer their shares for sale on the Stock Exchange. It is through the Stock Exhange that a large ownership base can be established.

A private company is usually, but not always, a smaller business, and may be formed by one or more persons. It is defined by the Act as a company which is not a public company. The main differences between a private company and a public company are that a private company

- can have an authorised capital of less than £50,000, and
- cannot offer its shares for subscription to the public at large, whereas public companies can.

This means that if you were to walk into a bank, or similar public place, and see a prospectus offering anyone the chance to take up shares in a company, then that company would be a public company, i.e. a PLC.

The shares that are dealt in on the Stock Exchange are all of public limited companies. This does not mean that all public companies' shares are traded on the Stock Exchange, as, for various reasons, some public companies have either chosen not to, or not been allowed to have their shares traded there. The ones whose shares are traded are known as 'quoted companies' meaning that their shares have prices quoted on the Stock Exchange. They have to comply with Stock Exchange requirements in addition to those laid down by the Companies Acts and accounting standards.

> **Activity 45.2**
> Apart from not having to worry about complying with the Stock Exchange requirements, what other reasons can you think of that would explain why some PLCs do not wish to offer their shares on the Stock Market?

45.4 Directors of the company

The day-to-day business of a company is *not* carried out by the shareholders. The possession of a share normally confers voting rights on the holder, who is then able to attend general meetings of the company. At one of these general meetings, normally the **Annual General Meeting** or AGM, the shareholders vote for **directors**, these being the people who will be entrusted with the running of the business. At each AGM, the directors report on their stewardship, and this report is accompanied by a set of financial statements for the year – the 'annual report'.

45.5 Legal status of a limited company

A limited company is said to possess a 'separate legal identity' from that of its shareholders. Put simply, this means that a company is not seen as being exactly the same as its shareholders. For instance, a company can sue one or more of its shareholders, and similarly, a shareholder can sue the company. This would not be the case if the company and its shareholders were exactly the same thing, as one cannot sue oneself. This concept is often referred to as the **veil of incorporation**.

Note: This is an extremely important concept. The most frequently cited example of the strength of the veil of incorporation is a case that went to the House of Lords in 1897. The case is known as *Saloman* v *Saloman & Co Ltd*. It involved a company formed by a Mr Saloman. The company was run by Mr Saloman in the same way as when he was operating as a sole trader. He received all the profits and made all the decisions. However, the *veil of incorporation* meant that the company was treated as completely separate from him. When the business failed owing a large amount of money, Mr Saloman did not have to pay for the business debts personally. The debts were the responsibility of the company, not of Mr Saloman. This was held to be the case even though Mr Saloman had lent some money to the company in the form of secured debentures. This meant that any funds left in the company when it failed were first used to repay *those* debentures (because they were 'secured') and the rest of the creditors (who were not 'secured') received nothing.

45.6 Share capital

Shareholders of a limited company obtain their reward in the form of a share of the profits, known as a **dividend**. The directors consider the amount of profits and decide on the amount of profits which are placed to reserves. Out of the profits remaining the directors then propose the payment of a certain amount of dividend. It is important to note that the shareholders cannot propose a higher dividend for themselves than that already proposed by the directors. They can, however, propose that a lesser dividend should be paid, although this action is very rare indeed. If the directors propose that no dividend be paid, then the shareholders are powerless to alter the decision.

The decision by the directors as to the amount proposed as dividends is a very complex one and cannot be fully discussed here. Such points as government directives to reduce dividends, the effect of taxation, the availability of bank balances to pay the dividends, the possibility of takeover bids and so on will all be taken into account.

The dividend is usually expressed as a percentage. Ignoring income tax, a dividend of 10 per cent in Business A on 500,000 ordinary shares of £1 each will amount to £50,000, or a dividend of 6 per cent in Business B on 200,000 ordinary shares of £2 each will amount to £24,000. A shareholder having 100 shares in each business would receive £10 from Business A and £12 from Business B. There are two main types of shares:

1 **Preference shares**. These get an agreed percentage rate of dividend before the ordinary shareholders receive anything.
2 **Ordinary shares**. These receive the remainder of the total profits available for dividends. There is no upper limit to the amounts of dividends they can receive.

For example, if a company had 10,000 5 per cent preference shares of £1 each and 20,000 ordinary shares of £1 each, then the dividends would be payable as in Exhibit 45.1.

Exhibit 45.1

Year	1	2	3	4	5
	£	£	£	£	£
Profits appropriated for dividends	900	1,300	1,600	3,100	2,000
Preference dividends (5%)	500	500	500	500	500
Ordinary dividends	(2%)400	(4%)800	(5½%)1,100	(13%)2,600	(7½%)1,500

The two main types of preference shares are non-cumulative preference shares and cumulative preference shares:

1 **Non-cumulative preference shares**
These can receive a dividend up to an agreed percentage each year. If the amount paid is less than the maximum agreed amount, the shortfall is lost by the shareholder. The short-fall cannot be carried forward and paid in a future year.
2 **Cumulative preference shares**
These also have an agreed maximum percentage dividend. However, any shortfall of dividend paid in a year can be carried forward. These arrears of preference dividends will have to be paid before the ordinary shareholders receive anything.

Activity 45.3

Why do you think an investor might purchase preference shares rather than ordinary shares in a company?

Exhibit 45.2

A company has 5,000 £1 ordinary shares and 2,000 5 per cent non-cumulative preference shares of £1 each. The profits available for dividends are: year 1 £150, year 2 £80, year 3 £250, year 4 £60, year 5 £500.

Year	1	2	3	4	5
	£	£	£	£	£
Profits	150	80	250	60	500
Preference dividend (non-cumulative)					
(limited in years 2 and 4)	100	80	100	60	100
Dividends on ordinary shares	50	–	150	–	400

Exhibit 45.3

Assume that the preference shares in Exhibit 45.2 had been cumulative. The dividends would have been:

Year	1	2	3	4	5
	£	£	£	£	£
Profits	150	80	250	60	500
Preference dividend	100	80	120*	60	140*
Dividends on ordinary shares	50	–	130	–	360

*including arrears.

45.7 Share capital: different meanings

The term 'share capital' can have any of the following meanings:

1 **Authorised share capital.** Sometimes known as registered capital or nominal capital. This is the total of the share capital which the company is allowed to issue to shareholders.
2 **Issued share capital.** This is the total of the share capital actually issued to shareholders.

Note: Some students mix up these two terms and throw away marks in examinations as a result. In order to remember which is which, you only need to think about what the words 'authorised' and 'issued' mean.

If all of the authorised share capital has been issued, then 1 and 2 above would be the same amount.

3 **Called-up capital.** Where only part of the amount payable on each issued share has been asked for, the total amount asked for on all the issued shares is known as the called-up capital.
4 **Uncalled capital.** This is the total amount which is to be received in future relating to issued share capital, but which has not yet been asked for.
5 **Calls in arrears.** The total amount for which payment has been asked for (i.e. 'called for'), but has not yet been paid by shareholders.
6 **Paid-up capital.** This is the total of the amount of share capital which has been paid for by shareholders.

Exhibit 45.4 illustrates these different meanings.

Exhibit 45.4

1 Better Enterprises Ltd was formed with the legal right to be able to issue 100,000 shares of £1 each.
2 The company has actually issued 75,000 shares.
3 None of the shares has yet been fully paid up. So far the company has made calls of 80p (£0.80) per share.
4 All the calls have been paid by shareholders except for £200 owing from one shareholder.

(a) Authorised or nominal share capital is:	1	£100,000.
(b) Issued share capital is:	2	£75,000.
(c) Called-up capital is:	3	75,000 × £0.80 = £60,000.
(d) Calls in arrears amounted to:	4	£200.
(e) Paid-up capital is:	(c)	£60,000 less (d) £200 = £59,800.

45.8   Bonus shares

The issue of **bonus shares** would appear to be outside the scope of syllabuses at this level. However, some examinations have included a minor part of a question concerned with bonus shares. All that is needed here is a very brief explanation only, leaving further explanations for a later stage in your studies.

Bonus shares are 'free' shares issued to shareholders without their having to pay anything for them. The reserves (e.g. accumulated profits held in the profit and loss account and shown in the balance sheet) are utilised for the purpose. Thus, if before the bonus issue there were £20,000 of issued share capital and £12,000 reserves, and a bonus issue of 1 for 4 was then made (i.e. 1 bonus share for every 4 shares already held) the bonus issue would amount to £5,000. The share capital then becomes £25,000 and the reserves become £7,000.

A proper and fuller explanation appears in *Business Accounting 2*. An issue of bonus shares is often referred to as a **scrip issue**.

45.9   Debentures

You will recall the note about the veil of incorporation where debentures had been issued to the owner of company. The term **debenture** is used when a limited company receives money on loan, and certificates called debenture certificates are issued to the lender. Interest will be paid to the holder, the rate of interest being shown on the certificate. They are not always called debentures; they are often known as loan stock or as loan capital.

Debenture interest has to be paid whether profits are made or not. They are, therefore, different from shares, where dividends depend on profits being made. A debenture may be either:

● Redeemable, i.e. repayable at or by a particular date, or
● Irredeemable, normally repayable only when the company is officially terminated by its going into liquidation. (Also sometimes referred to as 'perpetual' debentures.)

If a date is shown behind a debenture, e.g. 2001/2008, it means that the company can redeem it in any of the years 2001 to 2008 inclusive.

People lending money to companies in the form of debentures will be interested in how safe their investment will be. Some debentures are given the legal right that on certain happenings the debenture holders will be able to take control of specific assets, or of the whole of the assets. They can then sell the assets and recoup the amount due under their debentures, or deal with the assets in ways specified in the deed under which the debentures were issued. Such debentures are known as being 'secured' against the assets – this was the case in the veil of incorporation note. (The term 'mortgage' debenture is sometimes used instead of 'secured'.) Other debentures have no prior right to control the assets under any circumstances. These are known as 'simple' or 'naked' debentures.

> *Activity 45.4*
> Why do you think a debenture might be 'secured' rather than being designated as a 'simple' debenture? (Hint: think about Mr Saloman.)

45.10   Trading and profit and loss accounts of companies

The trading and profit and loss accounts for both private and public companies are drawn up in exactly the same way.

The trading account of a limited company is no different from that of a sole trader or a partnership. However, some differences may be found in the profit and loss account. The two main expenses that would be found only in company accounts are directors' remuneration and debenture interest.

Directors' remuneration

As directors exist only in companies, this type of expense is found only in company accounts.

Directors are legally employees of the company, appointed by the shareholders. Their remuneration is charged to the profit and loss account.

Debenture interest

The interest payable for the use of the money is an expense of the company, and is payable whether profits are made or not. This means that debenture interest is charged as an expense in the profit and loss account itself. Contrast this with dividends which are dependent on profits having been made.

45.11 The appropriation account

Next under the profit and loss account is a section called the 'profit and loss appropriation account'. The appropriation account shows how the net profits are to be appropriated, i.e. how the profits are to be used. This is similar in nature to the appropriation account you learnt about when you looked at partnership accounts, in that it involves distributing the profit. However, that is as far as the similarity goes.

We may find any of the following in the appropriation account:

Credit side

1 **Net profit for the year**
   This is the net profit brought down from the main profit and loss account.
2 **Balance brought forward from last year**
   As you will see, all the profits may not be appropriated during a period. This then will be the balance on the appropriation account, as brought forward from the previous year. It is usually called retained profits.

Debit side

3 **Transfers to reserves**
   The directors may decide that some of the profits should not be included in the calculation of how much should be paid out as dividends. These profits are transferred to **reserve accounts**.

   There may be a specific reason for the transfer such as a need to replace fixed assets. In this case an amount would be transferred to a fixed assets replacement reserve.

   Or the reason may not be specific. In this case an amount would be transferred to a general reserve account.
4 **Amounts written off as goodwill**
   Goodwill, in a company, may have amounts written off it from time to time. When this is done the amount written off should be shown in the appropriation account and not in the main profit and loss account. (See also Section 45.16.)

5 Preliminary expenses

When a company is formed, there are many kinds of expenses concerned with its formation. These include, for example, legal expenses and various government taxes. Since 1981 these cannot be shown as an asset in the balance sheet, and can be charged to the appropriation account.

6 Taxation payable on profits

At this point in your studies you do not need to know very much about taxation. However, it does affect the preparation of accounts, and so we will tell you here as much as you need to know now. Sole traders and partnerships pay income tax based on their profits. Such income tax, when paid, is simply charged as drawings – it is not an expense.

In the case of companies, the taxation levied upon them is called **corporation tax**. It is also based on the amount of profits made. In the later stages of your examinations you will learn how to calculate it. At this point you will be told how much it is, or be given a simple arithmetical way of ascertaining the amount.

Corporation tax is *not* an expense, it is an appropriation of profits. This was established by two legal cases many years ago. However, for the sake of presentation and to make the accounts more understandable to the general reader, it is not shown with the other appropriations. Instead, as in Exhibit 45.5 it is shown as a deduction from profit for the year before taxation (i.e. this is the net profit figure) to show the net result, i.e. profit for the year after taxation.

7 Dividends

Out of the remainder of the profits the directors propose what dividends should be paid.

8 Balance carried forward to next year

After the dividends have been proposed there will probably be some profits that have not been appropriated. These retained profits will be carried forward to the following year.

Exhibit 45.5 shows the profit and loss appropriation account of a new business for its first three years of trading.

Exhibit 45.5

IDC Ltd has an ordinary share capital of 40,000 ordinary shares of £1 each and 20,000 5 per cent preference shares of £1 each.

- The net profits for the first three years of business ended 31 December are: 20X4, £10,967; 20X5, £14,864; and 20X6, £15,822.
- Transfers to reserves are made as follows: 20X4 nil; 20X5, general reserve, £1,000; and 20X6, fixed assets replacement reserve, £2,250.
- Dividends were proposed for each year on the preference shares at 5 per cent and on the ordinary shares at: 20X4, 10 per cent; 20X5, 12.5 per cent; 20X6, 15 per cent.
- Corporation tax, based on the net profits of each year, is 20X4 £4,100; 20X5 £5,250; 20X6 £6,300.

IDC Ltd
Profit and Loss Appropriation Accounts
(1) For the year ended 31 December 20X4

	£	£
Profit for the year before taxation		10,967
Less Corporation tax		(4,100)
Profit for the year after taxation		6,867
Less Proposed dividends:		
Preference dividend of 5%	1,000	
Ordinary dividend of 10%	4,000	
		(5,000)
Retained profits carried forward to next year		1,867

(2) For the year ended 31 December 20X5

	£	£	£
Profit for the year before taxation			14,864
Less Corporation tax			(5,250)
Profit for the year after taxation			9,614
Add Retained profits from last year			1,867
			11,481
Less Transfer to general reserve		1,000	
Proposed dividends:			
Preference dividend of 5%	1,000		
Ordinary dividend of 12½%	5,000		
		6,000	
			(7,000)
Retained profits carried forward to next year			4,481

(3) For the year ended 31 December 20X6

	£	£	£
Profit for the year before taxation			15,822
Less Corporation tax			(6,300)
Profit for the year after taxation			9,522
Add Retained profits from last year			4,481
			14,003
Less Transfer to fixed assets			
replacement reserve		2,250	
Proposed dividends:			
Preference dividend of 5%	1,000		
Ordinary dividend of 15%	6,000		
		7,000	
			(9,250)
Retained profits carried forward to next year			4,753

In the balance sheet, corporation tax owing can normally be found as a current liability.

45.12 The balance sheet

Prior to the UK Companies Act 1981, provided it disclosed the necessary information, a company could draw up its balance sheet and profit and loss account for publication in any way that it wished. The 1981 Act, however, stopped such freedom of display, and laid down the precise details to be shown. These were repeated in the Companies Acts of 1985 and 1989.

As many of the readers of this book will not be sitting UK examinations they will not have to comply with the UK Companies Acts. We are therefore showing two specimen balance sheets containing the same facts, one for students sitting UK examinations and the other for students sitting overseas examinations not based on UK legislation:

1 Exhibit 45.6 is for students sitting examinations based on UK laws. The specimen shown does not contain all the possible items which could be shown, as this chapter is an introduction to the topic only. *Business Accounting 2* gives a greater insight into company accounts.
2 Exhibit 45.7 is for students sitting local overseas examinations not based on UK legislation.

Exhibit 45.6 (for students sitting examinations based on UK company legislation)

Letters in brackets (A) to (G) refer to notes following the balance sheet.

Balance Sheet as at 31 December 20X7

		£	£	£
Fixed assets				
Intangible assets	(A)			
Goodwill				10,000
Tangible assets	(B)			
Buildings			9,000	
Machinery			5,600	
Motor vehicles			2,400	
				17,000
				27,000
Current assets				
Stock			6,000	
Debtors			3,000	
Bank			4,000	
			13,000	
Creditors: Amounts falling due within one year	(C)			
Proposed dividend		1,000		
Creditors		3,000		
Corporation tax owing		2,000		
			(6,000)	
Net current assets	(D)			7,000
Total assets less current liabilities				34,000
Creditors: amounts falling due after more than one year	(E)			
Debenture loans				(8,000)
				26,000
Capital and reserves				
Called-up share capital	(F)			20,000
Share premium account	(G)			1,200
Other reserves				
General reserve				3,800
Profit and loss account				1,000
				26,000

Notes:

(A) Intangible assets are those not having a 'physical' existence; for instance, you can see and touch tangible assets under (B), i.e. buildings, machinery etc., but you cannot see and touch goodwill.

(B) Tangible fixed assets under a separate heading. Note that figures are shown net after depreciation. In a note accompanying the accounts the cost and depreciation on these assets would be given.

(C) Only items payable within one year go under this heading.

(D) The term 'net current assets' replaces the more familiar term of 'working capital'.

(E) These particular debentures are repayable several years hence. If they had been payable within one year they would have been shown under (C).

(F) An analysis of share capital will be given in supplementary notes to the balance sheet.

(G) One reserve that is in fact not labelled with the word 'reserve' in its title is the share premium account. For various reasons (discussed fully in *Business Accounting 2*) shares can be issued for more than their face or nominal value. The excess of the price at which they are issued over the nominal value of the shares is credited to a share premium account. This is then shown with the other reserves in the balance sheet.

Exhibit 45.7 (for local overseas examinations)

Balance Sheet as at 31 December 20X7

		Cost	Depreciation to date (**b**)	Net book value
Fixed assets	(**a**)	£	£	£
Goodwill		15,000	5,000	10,000
Buildings		15,000	6,000	9,000
Machinery		8,000	2,400	5,600
Motor vehicles		4,000	1,600	2,400
		42,000	15,000	27,000
Current assets				
Stock			6,000	
Debtors			3,000	
Bank			4,000	
			13,000	
Less Current liabilities				
Proposed dividend		1,000		
Creditors		3,000		
Corporation tax owing		2,000		
			(6,000)	
Net current assets				7,000
				34,000
Debentures				
Six per cent debentures: repayable 20X9				(8,000)
				26,000
Financed by:				
Share capital				
Authorised 30,000 shares of £1 each	(**c**)			30,000
Issued 20,000 ordinary shares of £1 each, fully paid	(**d**)			20,000
Reserves	(**e**)			
Share premium			1,200	
General reserve			3,800	
Profit and loss account			1,000	
				6,000
	(**f**)			26,000

Notes:
(a) Fixed assets should normally be shown either at cost or alternatively at some other valuation. In either case, the method chosen should be clearly stated.
(b) The total depreciation from date of purchase to the date of the balance sheet should be shown.
(c) The authorised share capital, where it is different from the issued share capital, is shown as a note.
(d) Where shares are only partly called up, then it is the amount actually called up that appears in the balance sheet and not the full amount.
(e) Reserves consist either of those unused profits remaining in the appropriation account, or those transferred to a reserve account appropriately titled, e.g. general reserve, fixed assets replacement reserve. At this juncture all that needs to be said is that any account labelled as a reserve has originated by being charged as a debit in the appropriation account and credited to a reserve account with an appropriate title. These reserves are shown in the balance sheet after share capital under the heading of 'Reserves'.
(f) The share capital and reserves should be totalled so as to show the book value of all the shares in the company. Either the term 'shareholders' funds' or 'members' equity' is often given to the total of share capital plus reserves.

In *Business Accounting 2* you will be told more about the differences between 'revenue reserves' and 'capital reserves'. The main importance about the distinction is for deciding how much can be treated as being available for paying out to shareholders by cheque in the form of dividends. 'Revenue reserves', which include the appropriation account balance and the general reserve, can be treated as available for such dividends. 'Capital reserves', which will include revaluation reserves on property and land, also some reserves (which you have not yet met) which have to be created to meet some legal statutory need, cannot be treated as available for payment out as dividends.

A term which sometimes appears in examinations is that of 'fungible assets'. Fungible assets are assets which are substantially indistinguishable one from another.

A fully worked example

Exhibit 45.8

The following trial balance is extracted from the books of F W Ltd as on 31 December 20X5:

Trial balance as on 31 December 20X5

	Dr £	Cr £
10% preference share capital		20,000
Ordinary share capital		70,000
10% debentures (repayable 20X9)		30,000
Goodwill at cost	15,500	
Buildings at cost	95,000	
Equipment at cost	8,000	
Motor vehicles at cost	17,200	
Provision for depreciation: equipment 1.1.20X5		2,400
Provision for depreciation: motors 1.1.20X5		5,160
Stock 1.1.20X5	22,690	
Sales		98,200
Purchases	53,910	
Carriage inwards	1,620	
Salaries and wages	9,240	
Directors' remuneration	6,300	
Motor expenses	8,120	
Rates and insurances	2,930	
General expenses	560	
Debenture interest	1,500	
Debtors	18,610	
Creditors		11,370
Bank	8,390	
General reserve		5,000
Share premium account		14,000
Interim ordinary dividend paid	3,500	
Profit and loss account 31.12.20X4		16,940
	273,070	273,070

The following adjustments are needed:

(*i*)   Stock at 31.12.20X5 was £27,220.
(*ii*)   Depreciate motors £3,000, equipment £1,200.
(*iii*) Accrue debenture interest £1,500.
(*iv*)   Provide for preference dividend £2,000 and final ordinary dividend of 10 per cent.
(*v*)   Transfer £2,000 to general reserve.

(*vi*) Write off goodwill £3,000.
(*vii*) Authorised share capital is £20,000 in preference shares and £100,000 in ordinary shares.
(*viii*) Provide for corporation tax £5,000.

The financial statements will now be shown using a vertical form. The profit and loss account will be suitable both for those sitting UK examinations, and those sitting local overseas examinations. The balance sheets will be shown separately for both kinds of students.

Note that the profit and loss account is not restricted to that which must be published by companies.

(*a*) Trading and profit and loss accounts suitable both for UK and overseas examinations. For internal use only, not for publication.

F W Ltd
Trading & Profit & Loss Account for the year ended 31 December 20X5

		£	£	£
Sales				98,200
Less Cost of goods sold:				
Opening stock			22,690	
Add Purchases			53,910	
Add Carriage inwards			1,620	
			78,220	
Less Closing stock			(27,220)	
				(51,000)
Gross profit				47,200
Less Expenses:				
Salaries and wages			9,240	
Motor expenses			8,120	
Rates and insurances			2,930	
General expenses			560	
Directors' remuneration	(A)		6,300	
Debenture interest	(B)		3,000	
Depreciation: Motors			3,000	
Equipment			1,200	
				(34,350)
Profit for the year before taxation				12,850
Less Corporation tax				(5,000)
Profit for the year after taxation				7,850
Add Retained profits from last year				16,940
				24,790
Less Appropriations:				
Transfer to general reserve			2,000	
Goodwill part written off			3,000	
Preference share dividend			2,000	
Ordinary share dividends:				
Interim		3,500		
Final	(C)	7,000		
			10,500	
				(17,500)
Retained profits carried forward to next year				7,290

Notes:
(A) As stated earlier, directors' remuneration is shown as an expense in the profit and loss account itself.

(B) As stated earlier, debenture interest is an expense to be shown in the profit and loss account itself.

(C) The final dividend of 10 per cent is based on the issued ordinary share capital and *not* on the authorised ordinary share capital.

(*b*) Balance sheet based on UK legislation

F W Ltd
Balance Sheet as at 31 December 20X5

		£	£	£
Fixed assets				
Intangible assets				
Goodwill				12,500
Tangible assets	(A)			
Buildings			95,000	
Equipment			4,400	
Motors			9,040	
				108,440
				120,940
Current assets				
Stock			27,220	
Debtors			18,610	
Bank			8,390	
			54,220	
Creditors: amounts falling due within one year				
Creditors		11,370		
Proposed dividend		9,000		
Debenture interest accrued		1,500		
Taxation		5,000		
			(26,870)	
Net current assets				27,350
Total assets less current liabilities				148,290
Creditors: amounts falling due after more than one year				
10% Debentures				(30,000)
				118,290
Capital and reserves	(B)			
Called-up share capital	(C)			90,000
Share premium account				14,000
Other reserves				
General reserve				7,000
Profit and loss account				7,290
				118,290

(A) Notes to be given in an appendix as to cost, acquisitions and sales in the year and depreciation.

(B) Reserves consist either of those unused profits remaining in the appropriation account, or those transferred to a reserve account appropriately titled, e.g. general reserve, fixed assets replacement reserve, etc.

One reserve that is in fact not labelled with the word 'reserve' in its title is the share premium account. This is shown with the other reserves in the balance sheet.

The closing balance on the profit and loss appropriation account is shown under reserves. These are profits not already appropriated, and therefore 'reserved' for future use.

(C) The authorised share capital, where it is different from the issued share capital, is shown as a note. Notice that the total figure of £120,000 for authorised capital is not included when adding up the balance sheet sides. Only the issued capital figures are included in balance sheet totals.

(c) Balance sheet for students sitting local overseas examinations.

Balance Sheet as at 31 December 20X5

	Cost	Depreciation to date	Net book value
Fixed assets	£	£	£
Goodwill	15,500	3,000	12,500
Buildings	95,000	–	95,000
Equipment	8,000	3,600	4,400
Motors	17,200	8,160	9,040
	135,700	14,760	120,940
Current assets			
Stock		27,220	
Debtors		18,610	
Bank		8,390	
		54,220	
Less Current liabilities			
Creditors	11,370		
Dividends owing	9,000		
Debenture interest owing	1,500		
Taxation	5,000		
		(26,870)	
Net current assets			27,350
			148,290
Loan capital			
10% debentures			(30,000)
			118,290

	Authorised	Issued
Financed by:		
Share Capital	£	£
Preference shares	20,000	20,000
Ordinary shares	100,000	70,000
	120,000	90,000
Reserves		
Share premium	14,000	
General reserve	7,000	
Profit and loss	7,290	
		28,290
		118,290

45.13 True and fair view

When the financial statements of a company are published no one, neither the directors nor the auditors, ever states that 'the financial statements are correct'. This is because in preparing company financial statements many subjective estimates and judgements affect the figures. The valuation of stock, or the estimates of depreciation cannot be said to be 'correct', just as it is impossible to say that the provision for doubtful debts is 'correct'. Only time will tell whether these estimates and judgements will turn out to have been 'correct'.

The expression that is used is that, in the opinion of the auditors, the financial statements give a ***true and fair view*** of the state of affairs and financial performance of the company.

45.14   FRS 3: Reporting Financial Performance

Accounting is not a static subject. Changes occur over the years as they are seen to be necessary, and also get general agreement as to their usefulness. Since the advent of SSAPs (Statements of Standard Accounting Practice) and FRSs (Financial Reporting Standards), the number of changes that practitioners and students have had to learn has increased at a very fast rate. A prime example of this is the introduction of FRS 3, which necessitates changes to the formats of company profit and loss accounts when certain events have occurred.

Suppose that you are considering the affairs of a business over the years. The business has not changed significantly, there have been no acquisitions, no discontinued operations, no fundamental reorganisation or restructuring of the business, nor have there been any extraordinary items affecting the accounts. In these circumstances, when comparing the accounts over the years, you are comparing like with like, subject to the problem of the effects of inflation or deflation.

On the other hand, suppose that some of the things mentioned have occurred. When trying to see what the future might hold for the company, simply basing your opinions on what has happened in the past can be very confusing.

To help you to distinguish the past and the future, and to give you some idea as to what changes have occurred, FRS 3 requires that the following are highlighted in the profit and loss account if they are material in amount:

(a) *What the results of continuing operations are, including the results of acquisitions.* Obviously acquisitions affect future results, and are therefore included in continuing operations.
(b) *What the results have been of discontinued operations.* This should help distinguish the past from the future.
(c) *The profits or losses on the sale or termination of an operation, the costs of fundamental reorganisation or restructuring* and *the profits and losses on the disposal of fixed assets.* The profits and losses concerning these matters are not going to happen again, and so this also helps us distinguish the past from the future.

We can see in Exhibit 45.9 how FRS 3 requires (a), (b) and (c) to be shown on the face of the profit and loss account. Not only is the turnover split to show the figures relevant to continuing operations, acquisitions and discontinued operations, the operating profit is split in a similar fashion. In addition any profit or loss on the disposal of the discontinued operations would also be shown.

Exhibit 45.9

Block PLC
Profit and Loss Account for the year ending 31 December 20X6 (extract)

		£000	£000
1	Turnover		
	Continuing operations	520	
	Acquisitions	110	
		630	
	Discontinued operations	170	
			800
2	Cost of sales		(500)
3	Gross profit		300
4	Distribution costs	60	
5	Administrative expenses	40	
	Operating profit		(100)
	Continuing operations	160	
	Acquisitions	60	
	(A)	220	
	Discontinued operations (loss) (B)	(20)	
			200
	Profit on disposal of discontinued operations (C)		10
			210
6	Other operating income		20
	Profit or loss on ordinary activities before interest		230

The items marked (A), (B) and (C) can be described as exceptional items. They are material in amount, they fall within the ordinary activities of the business, and need to be shown so that the accounts will give a 'true and fair view'.

They are exceptional in that they are not the ordinary daily occurrence, but remember that they fall within the ordinary activities of the company. FRS 3 requires that three categories of exceptional items be shown separately on the face of the profit and loss account after operating profit and before interest, and included under the appropriate heading of continued or discontinued operations:

- profits or losses on the sale or termination of an operation;
- costs of a fundamental reorganisation or restructuring having a material effect on the nature and focus of the reporting entity's operations;
- profits or losses on the disposal of fixed assets.

Other exceptional items should be credited or charged in arriving at the profit or loss on ordinary activities by inclusion under the heading to which they relate. The amount of each exceptional item should be disclosed in a note, or on the face of the profit and loss account, if necessary, in order to give a true and fair view.

Some other items are also contained in FRS 3. These are:

(*a*) Where assets have been revalued there may be a material difference in the results shown in the accounts using such revalued figures, which obviously affects depreciation. If this is the case, then FRS 3 requires that there should also be shown as a note what the profit and loss account would have been if the account had been shown using historical (i.e. not revalued) figures.

There should also be a statement which shows how the reported profit on ordinary activities (using accounts with revalued assets) can be reconciled with that calculated using historical figures.

(b) A note should be given reconciling the opening and closing totals of shareholders' funds of the period. This shows how such items as the profit for the year or a new share issue have increased the funds, whereas dividends and items written off capital reserves have reduced the funds.

45.15 The Audit Report

The Companies Act requires that all companies other than dormant companies (i.e. companies that have not traded during the year) and small companies be audited every year. ('Small' is currently defined as having a turnover of not more than £1 million and a balance sheet total of not more than £1.4 million.)

The auditors are appointed each year by the shareholders at the company annual general meeting (AGM). The auditors complete the report after examining the books and accounts and, in the report, they must say whether or not they agree that the accounts give a true and fair view. The report is presented to the shareholders at the same time as the financial statements are presented to them at the AGM.

In preparing the audit report, the auditor must consider whether

- the accounts have been prepared in accordance with the Companies Act;
- the balance sheet shows a true and fair view of the state of the company's affairs at the end of the period and the profit and loss account shows a true and fair view of the results for the period;
- proper accounting records have been kept and proper returns received from parts of the company not visited by the auditor;
- the accounts are in agreement with the accounting records;
- the directors' report is consistent with the accounts.

Smaller companies (those with turnover below £1 million) are exempt from the requirement to have their financial statements audited. However, they may still do so, if they wish.

Organisations that are not required to have their financial statements audited, such as sole traders, partnerships, clubs and societies, can still have their accounts audited. In this case, the audit is described as a *non statutory audit*.

A qualified audit report indicates that the auditor is not satisfied that the financial statements present a true and fair view. When a company receives a qualified audit report, it acts as a signal to all stakeholders that something may be amiss. As such, it is a vitally important safeguard of the interests of the shareholders.

Contrary to what most of the public think, auditors do not guarantee to discover any fraud that may have occurred. That is not what the audit is for. Following such immense financial scandals as the Maxwell affair, the BCCI bank, Polly Peck and Barlow Clowes there has been pressure exerted upon the accounting profession to reconsider its position regarding the discovery of fraud when auditing the accounts of a company.

45.16 FRS 10: Goodwill and Intangible Assets (Companies)

This standard was issued in December 1997, replacing SSAP 22. It applies to companies, not to partnerships or sole traders.

1 Purchased goodwill and purchased intangible assets (e.g. patents, trade marks, etc.) should be capitalised as assets.

2 If goodwill has not been purchased then there should not be any entry of it in the company's books. (This is different from the situation applicable to partnerships.)

3 Internally developed intangible assets should be capitalised (i.e. entered in the company's books as an asset) only when they have a readily ascertainable market value.

4 The calculation of goodwill should be the excess of the value of the consideration given (the price paid) over the total of the fair values of the net assets acquired.

FRS 10 requires that goodwill and intangible assets are amortised (i.e. depreciated) over their useful economic life. However, when goodwill or intangible assets are regarded as having indefinite useful economic lives, they should not be amortised.

Learning outcomes

You should now have learnt:

1 That limited companies exist because of the disadvantages and constraints arising from partnerships.

2 That a fully paid-up shareholder's liability is limited to the shares he or she holds in the company. Shareholders cannot then be asked to pay any other company debt from their private resources.

3 The difference between public and private companies.

4 That there are far more private companies than public companies.

5 The difference between a PLC and a company that is not a PLC.

6 That a limited company has a 'separate legal entity' from that of its members.

7 The difference between ordinary shares and preference shares.

8 How dividends are calculated.

9 The difference between shares and debentures.

10 The contents of and purpose of a company's appropriation account.

11 That directors' remuneration is charged to the main part of the profit and loss account.

12 That debenture interest is charged to the main part of the profit and loss account.

13 That transfers to reserves, dividends and taxation are charged to the appropriation part of the profit and loss account.

14 That any balance of profits unappropriated at the end of a period is carried forward as a balance to the next period.

15 How to prepare company profit and loss accounts for internal purposes.

16 How to prepare company balance sheets for internal purposes.

17 How goodwill is treated in company financial statements.

Answers to activities

45.1 Partnerships were not suitable for such businesses because:

- normally they cannot have more than twenty partners, not counting limited partners.
- if a partnership business fails, partners could lose part, or all, of their private assets to pay the debts of the business.

Limited companies do not have restrictions on the number of owners. Nor do the owners of limited companies generally run the risk of losing everything they own if the company fails.

45.2 There may be any number of explanations, including:

- they may not wish a wide ownership base
- they may feel the costs of doing so are prohibitive
- they may feel there would not be sufficient demand for the shares to make it worthwhile
- the directors may be concerned that it would make it easier for the company to be taken over
- they may wish to wait until the Stock Market is at a higher level, i.e. they wish to wait until they can maximise the amount they can sell the shares for when they first offer them for sale on the Stock Market
- the Stock Market may be very volatile, making choosing a price at which to sell the shares very difficult – if the company gets it wrong, they may not sell all the shares they wanted to sell or they may not receive as much for each share as they could have done had they waited for the Stock Market to stabilise.

45.3 There is less risk for the investor. The annual preference dividend is known and it will be paid before any funds left over are used to pay a dividend on the ordinary shares. Even when an ordinary dividend is paid, it is not known in advance how much this will be, as it depends on how profitable the business has been over the financial period. It could be more than the preference dividend (which is normally the case) or it could be less. Although the preference dividend will often be at a lower rate than an ordinary dividend (i.e. a preference shareholder will receive less of a dividend for the same investment as an ordinary shareholder) the reduced risk results in some people preferring to purchase preference shares.

45.4 The lender may require it or the company may offer secured debenture status in order to attract funds at a more favourable rate of interest.

MULTIPLE CHOICE QUESTIONS: SET 5

Now attempt Set 5 of multiple choice questions. (**Answers to all the multiple choice questions are given in Appendix 2 at the end of this book.**)

Each of these multiple choice questions has four suggested answers, (A), (B), (C) and (D). You should read each question and then decide which choice is best, either (A) or (B) or (C) or (D). *Write down your answers on a separate piece of paper.* You will then be able to redo the set of questions later without having to try to ignore your answers.

MC81 Given opening debtors of £11,500, Sales £48,000 and receipts from debtors £45,000, the closing debtors should total

(A) £8,500
(B) £14,500
(C) £83,500
(D) £18,500

MC82 In a Sales Ledger Control Account the Bad Debts written off should be shown in the account

(A) As a debit
(B) As a credit
(C) Both as a debit and as a credit
(D) As a balance carried down

MC83 If cost price is £90 and selling price is £120, then

(*i*) Mark-up is 25 per cent
(*ii*) Margin is 33^1/$_3$ per cent
(*iii*) Margin is 25 per cent
(*iv*) Mark-up is 33^1/$_3$ per cent

(A)   (*i*) and (*ii*)
(B)   (*i*) and (*iii*)
(C)   (*iii*) and (*iv*)
(D)   (*ii*) and (*iv*)

MC84   Given cost of goods sold £16,000 and margin of 20 per cent, then sales figure is

(A)   £20,160
(B)   £13,600
(C)   £21,000
(D)   £20,000

MC85   If opening stock is £3,000, closing stock £5,000, sales £40,000 and margin 20 per cent, then stockturn is

(A)   8 times
(B)   7¹/₂ times
(C)   5 times
(D)   6 times

MC86   If creditors at 1 January 20X3 were £2,500, creditors at 31 December 20X3 £4,200 and payments to creditors £32,000, then purchases for 20X3 are

(A)   £30,300
(B)   £33,700
(C)   £31,600
(D)   £38,700

MC87   Given opening capital of £16,500, closing capital as £11,350 and drawings were £3,300, then

(A)   Loss for the year was £1,850
(B)   Profit for the year was £1,850
(C)   Loss for the year was £8,450
(D)   Profit for the year was £8,450

MC88   A Receipts and Payments Account is one

(A)   Which is accompanied by a balance sheet
(B)   In which the profit is calculated
(C)   In which the opening and closing cash balances are shown
(D)   In which the surplus of income over expenditure is calculated

MC89   Prime cost includes

(*i*)   Direct labour
(*ii*)   Factory overhead expenses
(*iii*) Raw materials consumed
(*iv*)   Direct expenses

(A)   (*i*), (*ii*) and (*iii*)
(B)   (*ii*), (*iii*) and (*iv*)
(C)   (*i*), (*iii*) and (*iv*)
(D)   (*i*), (*ii*) and (*iv*)

MC90   Which of the following should be charged in the Profit and Loss Account?

(A)   Office rent
(B)   Work in progress
(C)   Direct materials
(D)   Carriage on raw materials

MC91   In the Manufacturing Account is calculated

(A)   The production costs paid in the year
(B)   The total cost of goods produced
(C)   The production cost of goods completed in the period
(D)   The gross profit on goods sold

MC92   The best method of departmental accounts is

(A)   To allocate expenses in proportion to sales
(B)   To charge against each department its controllable costs
(C)   To allocate expenses in proportion to purchases
(D)   To charge against each department its uncontrollable costs

MC93   Where there is no partnership agreement then profits and losses

(A)   Must be shared in same proportion as capitals
(B)   Must be shared equally
(C)   Must be shared equally after adjusting for interest on capital
(D)   None of these

MC94   If it is required to maintain fixed capitals then the partners' shares of profits must be

(A)   Debited to capital accounts
(B)   Credited to capital accounts
(C)   Debited to partners' current accounts
(D)   Credited to partners' current accounts

MC95   You are to buy an existing business which has assets valued at buildings £50,000, Motor vehicles £15,000, Fixtures £5,000 and Stock £40,000. You are to pay £140,000 for the business. This means that

(A)   You are paying £40,000 for Goodwill
(B)   Buildings are costing you £30,000 more than their value
(C)   You are paying £30,000 for Goodwill
(D)   You have made an arithmetical mistake

MC96   Assets can be revalued in a partnership change because

(A)   The law insists upon it
(B)   It helps prevent injustice to some partners
(C)   Inflation affects all values
(D)   The depreciation charged on them needs to be reversed

MC97   Any loss on revaluation is

(A)   Credited to old partners in old profit-sharing ratios
(B)   Credited to new partners in new profit-sharing ratios
(C)   Debited to old partners in old profit-sharing ratios
(D)   Debited to new partners in new profit-sharing ratios

MC98   In a limited company which of the following are shown in the Appropriation Account?

(*i*)   Debenture interest
(*ii*)   Proposed dividend
(*iii*)   Transfers to reserves
(*iv*)   Directors' remuneration

(A)   (*i*) and (*ii*)
(B)   (*ii*) and (*iii*)
(C)   (*i*) and (*iv*)
(D)   (*ii*) and (*iv*)

MC99   The Issued Capital of a company is

(A)   Always the same as the Authorised Capital
(B)   The same as Preference Share Capital
(C)   Equal to the reserves of the company
(D)   None of the above

MC100   A company wishes to pay out all available profits as dividends. Net profit is £26,600. There are 20,000 8% Preference shares of £1 each, and 50,000 Ordinary shares of £1 each. £5,000 is to be transferred to General Reserve. What Ordinary dividends are to be paid, in percentage terms?

(A)   20 per cent
(B)   40 per cent
(C)   10 per cent
(D)   60 per cent

REVIEW QUESTIONS

45.1   GWR Ltd started in business on 1 January 20X6. Its issued share capital was 100,000 ordinary shares of £1 each and 50,000 10 per cent preference shares of £1 each. The following information is available:

- Its net profits for the first two years of business were: 20X6 £42,005; 20X7 £34,831.
- Preference dividends were paid for each of these years, whilst ordinary dividends were proposed as 20X6 12 per cent and 20X7 9 per cent.
- Corporation tax, based on the profits of these two years, was: 20X6 £13,480; 20X7 £11,114.
- Transfers to general reserve took place as: 20X6 £6,000; 20X7 £4,000.

Draw up profit and loss appropriation accounts for each of the years ended 31 December 20X6 and 20X7.

45.2   LMS Ltd has an authorised capital of £200,000, consisting of 160,000 ordinary shares of £1 each and 40,000 8 per cent preference shares of £1 each. Of these, 120,000 ordinary shares and all the preference shares had been issued when the business first started trading. The following information is available:

- The business has a financial year end of 31 December. The first three years of business resulted in net profit as follows: 20X7 £27,929; 20X8 £32,440; 20X9 £36,891.
- Dividends were paid each year on the preference shares. Dividends on the ordinary shares were proposed as follows: 20X7 8 per cent; 20X8 10 per cent; 20X9 11 per cent.
- Corporation tax, based on the profits of each year, was: 20X7 £8,331; 20X8 £10,446; 20X9 £12,001.
- Transfers to reserves were made as: general reserve 20X7 £3,000, 20X8 £4,000, and foreign exchange reserve 20X9 £2,000.

You are to show the profit and loss appropriation accounts for each of the years 20X7, 20X8 and 20X9.

45.3   A balance sheet is to be drawn up from the following as at 30 June 20X6:

	£
Issued share capital: ordinary shares £1 each	100,000
Authorised share capital: ordinary shares of £1 each	200,000
10 per cent debentures (repayable 30 June 20X9)	40,000
Buildings at cost	105,000
Motor vehicles at cost	62,500
Fixtures at cost	11,500
Profit and loss account	5,163
Fixed assets replacement reserve	8,000
Stock	16,210
Debtors	14,175
General reserve	6,000
Creditors	9,120
Proposed dividend	5,000
Depreciation to date: Motor vehicles	15,350
Premises	22,000
Fixtures	3,750
Bank (balancing figure for you to ascertain)	?

45.4A   From the information given below you are required to prepare for Streamline PLC:

(a) a profit and loss appropriation account for the year ended 31 December 20X9;
(b) a balance sheet as at 31 December 20X9.

Streamline PLC has an authorised share capital of £520,000, divided into 500,000 £1 ordinary shares and 20,000 5% preference shares of £1 each. Of these shares, 300,000 ordinary shares and all of the 5% preference shares have been issued and are fully paid.

   In addition to the above information, the following balances remained in the accounts after the profit and loss account had been prepared for the year ended 31 December 20X9.

	Dr	Cr
	£	£
Plant and machinery, at cost	140,000	
Provision for depreciation on plant and machinery		50,000
Premises at cost	250,000	
Profit and loss account balance (1 January 20X9)		34,000
Net trading profit for year ended 31 December 20X9		15,000
Wages owing		3,900
Bank balance	15,280	
Stock (31 December 20X9)	16,540	
Trade debtors and creditors	12,080	3,000
Advertising prepaid	2,000	
General reserve		10,000

The directors have proposed the payment of the preference share dividend, and an ordinary share dividend of 6%. They also recommend a transfer of £20,000 to the general reserve.

(*Northern Examinations and Assessment Board: GCSE*)

45.5 The trial balance extracted from the books of Chang Ltd at 31 December 20X8 was as follows:

	£	£
Share capital		100,000
Profit and loss account 31 December 20X7		34,280
Freehold premises at cost	65,000	
Machinery at cost	55,000	
Provision for depreciation on machinery account as at 31 December 20X7		15,800
Purchases	201,698	
Sales		316,810
General expenses	32,168	
Wages and salaries	54,207	
Rent	4,300	
Lighting expenses	1,549	
Bad debts	748	
Provision for doubtful debts at 31 December 20X7		861
Debtors	21,784	
Creditors		17,493
Stock in trade 31 December 20X7	25,689	
Bank balance	23,101	
	485,244	485,244

You are given the following additional information:

(*i*) The authorised and issued share capital is divided into 100,000 shares of £1 each.
(*ii*) Stock in trade at 31 December 20X8, £29,142.
(*iii*) Wages and salaries due at 31 December 20X8 amounted to £581.
(*iv*) Rent paid in advance at 31 December 20X8 amounted to £300.
(*v*) A dividend of £10,000 is proposed for 20X8.
(*vi*) The provision for doubtful debts is to be increased to £938.
(*vii*) A depreciation charge is to be made on machinery at the rate of 10 per cent per annum on cost.

Required:
A trading and profit and loss account for 20X8 and a balance sheet as at 31 December 20X8.

45.6A The following is the trial balance of B.B.C. Ltd as on 31 December 20X7:

	Dr £	Cr £
Share capital issued: ordinary shares £1		75,000
Debtors and creditors	28,560	22,472
Stock 31 December 20X6	41,415	
Bank	16,255	
Machinery at cost	45,000	
Motor vehicles at cost	28,000	
Depreciation provisions at 31.12.20X6:		
Machinery		18,000
Motor vehicles		12,600
Sales		97,500
Purchases	51,380	
Motor expenses	8,144	
Repairs to machinery	2,308	
Sundry expenses	1,076	
Wages and salaries	11,372	
Directors' remuneration	6,200	
Profit and loss account as at 31.12.20X6		6,138
General reserve		8,000
	239,710	239,710

Given the following information, you are to draw up a trading and profit and loss account for the year ended 31 December 20X7, and a balance sheet as at that date:

(*i*) Authorised share capital: £100,000 in ordinary shares of £1.
(*ii*) Stock at 31 December 20X7 £54,300.
(*iii*) Motor expenses owing £445.
(*iv*) Ordinary dividend proposed of 20 per cent.
(*v*) Transfer £2,000 to general reserve.
(*vi*) Provide for depreciation of all fixed assets at 20 per cent reducing balance method.

Required:
A trading and profit and loss account for 20X7 and a balance sheet as at 31 December 20X7.

45.7 You are to draw up a trading and profit and loss account for the year ended 31 December 20X8, and a balance sheet as at that date from the following trial balance and details of T Howe Ltd:

	Dr £	Cr £
Bank	6,723	
Debtors	18,910	
Creditors		12,304
Stock at 31 December 20X7	40,360	
Buildings at cost	100,000	
Equipment at cost	45,000	
Profit and loss account as at 31.12.20X7		15,286
General reserve		8,000
Foreign exchange reserve		4,200
Authorised and issued share capital		100,000
Purchases	72,360	
Sales		135,486
Carriage inwards	1,570	
Carriage outwards	1,390	
Salaries	18,310	
Rates and occupancy expenses	4,235	
Office expenses	3,022	
Sundry expenses	1,896	
Provisions for depreciation at 31.12.20X7:		
Buildings		32,000
Equipment		16,000
Directors' remuneration	9,500	
	323,276	323,276

Notes at 31 December 20X8:

(*i*) Stock at 31 December 20X8 £52,360.
(*ii*) Rates owing £280; Office expenses owing £190.
(*iii*) Dividend of 10 per cent proposed.
(*iv*) Transfers to reserves: General £1,000; Foreign exchange £800.
(*v*) Depreciation on cost: Buildings 5 per cent; Equipment 20 per cent.

45.8A Here is the trial balance of RF Ltd as at 30 June 20X8:

	Dr £	Cr £
Share capital: authorised and issued		50,000
Stock as at 30 June 20X7	38,295	
Debtors	26,890	
Creditors		12,310
10% debentures		20,000
Fixed assets replacement reserve		10,000
General reserve		6,000
Profit and loss account as at 30 June 20X7		3,964
Debenture interest	1,000	
Equipment at cost	35,000	
Motor vehicles at cost	28,500	
Bank	3,643	
Cash	180	
Sales		99,500
Purchases	66,350	
Returns inwards	1,150	
Carriage inwards	240	
Wages and salaries	10,360	
Rent, rates and insurance	5,170	
Discounts allowed	1,246	
Directors' remuneration	2,500	
Provision for depreciation at 30 June 20X7:		
Equipment		8,400
Motors		10,350
	220,524	220,524

Given the following information as at 30 June 20X8, draw up a set of financial statements for the year to that date:

(*i*) Stock 30 June 20X8 £49,371.
(*ii*) The share capital consisted of 25,000 ordinary shares of £1 each and 25,000 10 per cent preference shares of £1 each. The dividend on the preference shares was proposed to be paid as well as a dividend of 20 per cent on the ordinary shares.
(*iii*) Accrued rent £700; Directors' remuneration £2,500.
(*iv*) Debenture interest $1/2$ year's interest owing.
(*v*) Depreciation on cost: Equipment 10 per cent; Motors 20 per cent.
(*vi*) Transfers to reserves: General reserve £2,000; Fixed assets replacement reserve £1,000.

45.9 Burden PLC has an authorised capital of 500,000 ordinary shares of £0.50 each.
(*a*) At the end of its financial year, 31 May 20X9, the following balances appeared in the company's books:

	£
Issued capital: 400,000 shares fully paid	200,000
Freehold land and buildings at cost	320,000
Stock in trade	17,800
10% debentures	30,000
Trade debtors	6,840
Trade creditors	8,500
Expenses prepaid	760
Share premium	25,000
General reserve	20,000
Expenses outstanding	430
Profit and loss account balance (1 June 20X8)	36,200
Bank overdrawn	3,700
Fixtures, fittings and equipment	
at cost	54,000
provision for depreciation	17,500

The company's trading and profit and loss accounts had been prepared and revealed a net profit of £58,070. However, this figure and certain balances shown above needed adjustment in view of the following details which had not been recorded in the company's books.

(*i*)   It appeared that a trade debtor who owed £300 would not be able to pay. It was decided to write his account off as a bad debt.

(*ii*) An examination of the company's stock on 31 May 20X9 revealed that some items shown in the accounts at a cost of £1,800 had deteriorated and had a resale value of only £1,100.

(*iii*) At the end of the financial year some equipment which had cost £3,600 and which had a net book value of £800 had been sold for £1,300. A cheque for this amount had been received on 31 May 20X9.

Required:

1 A statement which shows the changes which should be made to the net profit of £58,070 in view of these unrecorded details.

(*b*) The directors proposed to pay a final dividend of 10% and to transfer £50,000 to general reserve on 31 May 20X9.

Required:

For Burden PLC (taking account of *all* the available information)

2 The profit and loss appropriation account for the year ended 31 May 20X9.

3 Two *extracts* from the company's balance sheet as at 31 May 20X9, showing in detail:

(*i*) the current assets, current liabilities and working capital

(*ii*) the items which make up the shareholders' funds.

(*c*) The directors are concerned about the company's liquidity position.

Required:

4 **THREE** transactions which will increase the company's working capital. State which balance sheet items will change as a result of each transaction and whether the item will increase or decrease in value.

(*Southern Examining Group: GCSE*)

45.10A   The accountant of Fiddles PLC has begun preparing financial statements but the work is not yet complete. At this stage the items included in the trial balance are as follows:

	£000
Land	100
Buildings	120
Plant and machinery	170
Depreciation provision	120
Share capital	100
Profit and loss balance brought forward	200
Debtors	200
Creditors	110
Stock	190
Operating profit	80
Debentures (16%)	180
Provision for doubtful debts	3
Bank balance (asset)	12
Suspense	1

Notes (*i*) to (*vii*) below are to be taken into account:

(*i*)   The debtors control account figure, which is used in the trial balance, does not agree with the total of the debtors ledger. A contra of £5,000 has been entered correctly in the individual ledger accounts but has been entered on the wrong side of both control accounts.

A batch total of sales of £12,345 had been entered in the double entry system as £13,345, although individual ledger account entries for these sales were correct. The balance of £4,000 on sales returns account has inadvertently been omitted from the trial balance, though correctly entered in the ledger records.

(ii) A standing order received from a regular customer for £2,000, and bank charges of £1,000, have been completely omitted from the records.

(iii) A debtor for £1,000 is to be written off. The provision for doubtful debts balance is to be adjusted to 1% of debtors.

(iv) The opening stock figure had been overstated by £1,000 and the closing stock figure had been understated by £2,000.

(v) Any remaining balance on suspense account should be treated as purchases if a debit balance and as sales if a credit balance.

(vi) The debentures were issued three months before the year end. No entries have been made as regards interest.

(vii) A dividend of 10% of share capital is to be proposed.

Required:

(a) Prepare journal entries to cover items in notes (i) to (v) above. You are NOT to open any new accounts and may use only those accounts included in the trial balance as given.

(b) Prepare financial statements for internal use in good order within the limits of the available information. For presentation purposes all the items arising from notes (i) to (vii) above should be regarded as material.

(*Association of Chartered Certified Accountants*)

45.11 'The historical cost convention looks backwards but the going concern convention looks forwards.'

Required:

(a) Explain clearly what is meant by:
  (i) the historical cost convention;
  (ii) the going concern convention.

(b) Does traditional financial accounting, using the historical cost convention, make the going concern convention unnecessary? Explain your answer fully.

(c) Which do you think a shareholder is likely to find more useful – a report on the past or an estimate of the future? Why?

(*Association of Chartered Certified Accountants*)

45.12 The chairman of a public limited company has written his annual report to the shareholders, extracts of which are quoted below.

Extract 1

'In May 20X6, in order to provide a basis for more efficient operations, we acquired PAG Warehousing and Transport Ltd. The agreed valuation of the net tangible assets acquired was £1.4 million. The purchase consideration, £1.7 million, was satisfied by an issue of 6.4 million equity shares, of £0.25 per share, to PAG's shareholders. These shares do not rank for dividend until 20X7.'

Extract 2

'As a measure of confidence in our ability to expand operations in 20X7 and 20X8, and to provide the necessary financial base, we issued £0.5 million 8% Redeemable Debenture Stock, 20X1/20X7, 20 million 6% £1 Redeemable Preference Shares and 4 million £1 equity shares. The opportunity was also taken to redeem the whole of the 5 million 11% £1 Redeemable Preference Shares.'

Required:

Answer the following questions on the above extracts.

Extract 1

(a) What does the difference of £0.3 million between the purchase consideration (£1.7m) and the net tangible assets value (£1.4m) represent?

(b) What does the difference of £0.1 million between the purchase consideration (£1.7m) and the nominal value of the equity shares (£1.6m) represent?

(c) What is the meaning of the term 'equity shares'?

(d) What is the meaning of the phrase 'do not rank for dividend'?

Extract 2

(e) In the description of the debenture stock issue, what is the significance of

  (i) 8%?

  (ii) 20X1/20X7?

(f) In the description of the preference share issue, what is the significance of

  (i) 6%?

  (ii) Redeemable?

(g) What is the most likely explanation for the company to have redeemed existing preference shares but at the same time to have issued others?

(h) What effect will these structural changes have had on the gearing of the company?[Authors' Note]

(j) Contrast the accounting treatment, in the company's profit and loss accounts, of the interest due on the debentures with dividends proposed on the equity shares.

(k) Explain the reasons for the different treatments you have outlined in your answer to (j) above.

(Association of Chartered Certified Accountants)

Authors' Note: Part (h) of the question is covered in the text in Chapter 47, Section 47.4. You should defer answering (h) until you have covered that material in the textbook.

45.13   The directors of the company by which you are employed as an accountant have received the forecast profit and loss account for 20X9 which disclosed a net profit for the year of £36,000.

This is considered to be an unacceptably low figure and a working party has been set up to investigate ways and means of improving the forecast profit.

The following suggestions have been put forward by various members of the working party:

(a) 'Every six months we deduct income tax of £10,000 from the debenture interest and pay it over to the Inland Revenue. If we withhold these payments, the company's profit will be increased considerably.'

(b) 'I see that in the three months August to October 20X9 we have forecast a total amount of £40,000 for repainting the exterior of the company's premises. If, instead, we charge this amount as capital expenditure, the company's profit will be increased by £40,000.'

(c) 'In November 20X9, the replacement of a machine is forecast. The proceeds from the sale of the old machinery should be credited to profit and loss account.'

(d) 'There is a credit balance of £86,000 on general reserve account. We can transfer some of this to profit and loss account to increase the 20X9 profit.'

(e) 'The company's £1 ordinary shares, which were originally issued at £1 per share, currently have a market value of £1.60 per share and this price is likely to be maintained. We can credit the surplus £0.60 per share to the 20X9 profit and loss account.'

(f) 'The company's premises were bought many years ago for £68,000, but following the rise in property values, they are now worth at least £300,000. This enhancement in value can be utilised to increase the 20X9 profit.'

You are required, as the accounting member of the working party, to comment on the feasibility of each of the above suggestions for increasing the 20X9 forecast profit.

(Association of Chartered Certified Accountants)

45.14   Explain what you understand by the accounting term 'debentures' and indicate the circumstances under which a debenture issue would or would not be an appropriate form of financing.

(Scottish Qualifications Authority)

CHAPTER 46

Purchase of existing partnership and sole traders' businesses

Learning objectives

After you have studied this chapter, you should be able to:
- enter up the purchase of a business in the purchaser's books
- draw up the balance sheet of the purchaser after taking over the assets and liabilities of the vendor

Introduction

In this chapter, you'll learn how to record the entries in the accounting books when a sole trader or a partnership is taken over by individuals, sole trader businesses, partnerships, and companies.

46.1 Types of purchase

You learnt in Chapter 42 that a sole trader's business may be sold as a going concern, rather than being broken up and its assets sold off one by one. The seller normally prefers to sell the business as a going concern, as more money is usually generated arising from the goodwill of the business. Buyers often prefer to purchase a going concern as it saves them all the problems of building markets and reputation.

In that chapter we also looked at the calculation of partnership goodwill when there was a change in the partners. We didn't consider what happens when a partnership is sold as a going concern. This happens relatively frequently. Now that you've learnt how to maintain partnership accounts, we're going to look further at the accounting treatment of sole traders being taken over as going concerns. While we will focus on sole traders, everything you will learn in this chapter applies also to partnerships when they are taken over as going concerns.

There are many ways in which a sole trader or a partnership may be taken over as a going concern. For example, an individual may purchase the business of a sole trader (this was the example used at the start of Chapter 42) or a sole trader may take over a partnership.

Activity 46.1
Think about this for a minute and then write down as many different entities (i.e. a person or persons, or a type of business) as you can think of that might purchase a sole trader or a partnership as a going concern.

46.2 Value of assets bought in purchaser's books

It must not be thought that because the assets bought are shown in the selling firm's books at one value, that the purchaser must record the assets taken over in its own books at the same value – you learnt about recording changes in asset values in Chapter 43 when you looked at revaluation of partnership assets but, in that case, you were looking at what you do when you revalue the assets of a partnership that is continuing in business, not when it is sold.

When a business is sold, the seller has no need to revalue the assets and adjust the values shown in the balance sheet. However the buyer really ought to show the assets (and liabilities) of the business it has taken over at their current values.

Activity 46.2
Why does the seller not need to revalue the assets of the business and change the values shown in the balance sheet?

The values shown in the books of the purchaser are, therefore, those values at which it is buying the assets, such values being frequently quite different from those shown in the selling firm's books. As an instance of this, the selling firm may have bought premises many years ago for £10,000 which are now worth £50,000. The purchaser buying the premises will obviously have to pay £50,000 for them. It is, therefore, this value that is recorded in the books of the purchaser.

Activity 46.3
Why would an accounting firm want to purchase another accounting firm?

46.3 Goodwill on purchase

As you might have guessed, when the total purchase price is *greater* than the new valuation made by the purchaser of the assets taken over, the difference is goodwill in the eyes of the purchaser. (The seller may have a very different view concerning the value of the assets.) This can be shown as:

	£
Total purchase consideration	90,000
Less New valuation of assets taken over	
(not usually the same values as per the old balance sheet)	(75,000)
Goodwill	15,000

The revised balance sheet of the purchaser will include goodwill as an asset at the calculated figure. It will also include the assets bought at their new valuations.

46.4 Capital reserve on purchase

Where the total purchase price is *less* than the new valuations of the assets taken over, the difference can either be treated in the purchaser's sole trader or partnership books as

negative goodwill or as a **capital reserve**. (Companies *must* treat it as negative goodwill.) When treated as a capital reserve, it can be shown as:

	£
Total purchase consideration	55,000
Less New valuation of assets taken over	
(not usually the same values as per the old balance sheet)	(75,000)
Capital reserve	(20,000)

The new valuations of the assets will appear in the revised balance sheet of the purchaser. The capital reserve will be shown in the capital section of the balance sheet.

46.5 Taking over a sole trader's business

It is easier to start with the takeover of the simplest sort of business unit, that of a sole trader. Some of the balance sheets shown will be deliberately simplified so that the principles involved are not hidden behind a mass of complicated calculations.

To illustrate the takeover of a business, given varying circumstances, the same business will be assumed to be taken over in different ways. The balance sheet of this business is that of A Brown, as shown in Exhibit 46.1.

Exhibit 46.1

A Brown
Balance Sheet as at 31 December 20X6

	£	£
Fixed assets		
Fixtures		30,000
Current assets		
Stock	8,000	
Debtors	7,000	
Bank	1,000	
	16,000	
Less: Current liabilities		
Creditors	(3,000)	
		13,000
		43,000
Capital		43,000

1 An individual purchases the business of a sole trader

(a) Assume that the assets and liabilities of A Brown, with the exception of the bank balance, are taken over by D Towers. He is to take over the assets and liabilities at the valuations as shown in Brown's balance sheet. The price to be paid is £52,000.

The opening balance sheet of Towers will be as shown in Exhibit 46.2.

Exhibit 46.2

D Towers
Balance Sheet as at 1 January 20X7

	£	£
Fixed assets		
Goodwill		10,000
Fixtures		30,000
		40,000
Current assets		
Stock	8,000	
Debtors	7,000	
	15,000	
Less: Current liabilities		
Creditors	(3,000)	
		12,000
		52,000
Capital		52,000

As £52,000 has been paid for the net assets (assets less liabilities) valued at £30,000 + £8,000 + £7,000 − £3,000 = £42,000, the excess £10,000 represents the amount paid for goodwill.

(b) Suppose that, instead of the information just given, the same amount (£52,000) has been paid by Towers, but the assets were taken over at a value of Fixtures £37,000; Stock £7,500; Debtors £6,500.

The opening balance sheet of D Towers would be as shown in Exhibit 46.3.

Exhibit 46.3

D Towers
Balance Sheet as at 1 January 20X7

	£	£
Fixed assets		
Goodwill		4,000
Fixtures		37,000
		41,000
Current assets		
Stock	7,500	
Debtors	6,500	
	14,000	
Less: Current liabilities		
Creditors	(3,000)	
		11,000
		52,000
Capital		52,000

As £52,000 had been paid for net assets valued at £37,000 + £7,500 + £6,500 − £3,000 = £48,000, the excess £4,000 represents the amount paid for goodwill. The other assets are shown at their value to the purchaser, Towers.

2 A partnership acquires the business of a sole trader

Assume instead that the business of Brown had been taken over by M Ukridge and D Allen. The partners are to introduce £30,000 each as capital. The price to be paid for the net assets, other than the bank balance, is £52,000. The purchasers placed the following values on the assets taken over: Fixtures £40,000; Stock £7,000; Debtors £6,000.

The opening balance sheet of Ukridge and Allen will be as in Exhibit 46.4.

Exhibit 46.4

M Ukridge and D Allen
Balance Sheet as at 1 January 20X7

	£	£
Fixed assets		
Goodwill		2,000
Fixtures		40,000
		42,000
Current assets		
Stock	7,000	
Debtors	6,000	
Bank*	8,000	
	21,000	
Less: Current liabilities		
Creditors	(3,000)	
		18,000
		60,000
Capitals		
M Ukridge		30,000
D Allen		30,000
		60,000

* The bank balance is made up of £30,000 + £30,000 introduced by the partners, less £52,000 paid to Brown = £8,000.

The sum of £52,000 has been paid for net assets of £40,000 + £7,000 + £6,000 − £3,000 = £50,000. This makes goodwill to be the excess of £2,000.

3 Amalgamation of existing sole traders

Now assume that Brown was to enter into partnership with T Owens whose last balance sheet is shown in Exhibit 46.5.

Exhibit 46.5

T Owens
Balance Sheet as at 31 December 20X6

	£	£
Fixed assets		
Premises		20,000
Fixtures		5,000
		25,000
Current assets		
Stock	6,000	
Debtors	9,000	
Bank	2,000	
	17,000	
Less: Current liabilities		
Creditors	(5,000)	
		12,000
		37,000
Capital		37,000

(a) If the two traders were to amalgamate all their business assets and liabilities, at the values as shown, the opening balance sheet of the partnership would be as in Exhibit 46.6 (remember that Brown's balance sheet is shown above in Exhibit 46.1).

Exhibit 46.6

A Brown & T Owens
Balance Sheet as at 1 January 20X7

	£	£
Fixed assets		
Premises		20,000
Fixtures		35,000
		55,000
Current assets		
Stock	14,000	
Debtors	16,000	
Bank	3,000	
	33,000	
Less: Current liabilities		
Creditors	(8,000)	
		25,000
		80,000
Capitals		
Brown		43,000
Owens		37,000
		80,000

(b) Suppose that instead of both parties agreeing to amalgamation at the asset values as shown, the following values had been agreed to:

Owens' premises to be valued at £25,000 and his stock at £5,500; other items as per the balance sheet in Exhibit 46.6. Brown's fixtures to be valued at £33,000; his stock at £7,200 and debtors at £6,400. It is also to be taken that Brown has goodwill of £7,000 whereas Owens' goodwill was considered valueless. Other items are as per the balance sheet in Exhibit 46.6.

The opening balance sheet will be at the revised figures, and is shown as Exhibit 46.7.

Exhibit 46.7

A Brown & T Owens
Balance Sheet as at 1 January 20X7

	£	£
Fixed assets		
Goodwill		7,000
Premises		25,000
Fixtures		38,000
		70,000
Current assets		
Stock	12,700	
Debtors	15,400	
Bank	3,000	
	31,100	
Less: Current liabilities		
Creditors	(8,000)	
		23,100
		93,100
Capitals		
Brown		51,600
Owen		41,500
		93,100

Brown's capital can be seen to be £43,000 + £3,000 (fixtures) − £800 (stock) − £600 (debtors) + £7,000 (goodwill) = £51,600.

Owens' capital is £37,000 + £5,000 (premises) − £500 (stock) = £41,500.

4 A limited company acquires the business of a sole trader

In this book, only an elementary treatment of this topic will be considered. More complicated examples will be covered in *Business Accounting 2*.

This time, D Lucas Ltd is taking over Brown's business. For Brown, you need to use the balance sheet shown in Exhibit 46.1. Before the acquisition, the balance sheet of D Lucas Ltd was as shown in Exhibit 46.8.

Exhibit 46.8

D Lucas Ltd
Balance Sheet as at 1 January 20X7

	£	£
Fixed assets		
Fixtures		36,000
Current assets		
Stock	23,000	
Debtors	14,000	
Bank	6,000	
	43,000	
Less: Current liabilities		
Creditors	(11,000)	
		32,000
		68,000
Capital and reserves		
Preference shares		20,000
Ordinary shares		40,000
Profit and loss		8,000
		68,000

(a) Assume that Brown's business had been acquired, except for the bank balance, goodwill being valued at £8,000 and the other assets and liabilities at balance sheet values. D Lucas Ltd is to issue an extra 32,000 £1 ordinary shares at par and 18,000 £1 preference shares at par to Brown, in full settlement of the £50,000 net assets taken over.

Exhibit 46.9 presents the summarised balance sheet of the company before and after the acquisition. (Note that the increase in the creditors amount is shown as a minus adjustment as it increases the amount to be deducted from the assets.)

Exhibit 46.9

D Lucas Ltd
Summarised Balance Sheet

	Before £	+ or − £	After £
Goodwill	–	+8,000	8,000
Fixtures	36,000	+30,000	66,000
Stock	23,000	+8,000	31,000
Debtors	14,000	+7,000	21,000
Bank	6,000		6,000
	79,000		132,000
Creditors	(11,000)	−3,000	(14,000)
	68,000		118,000

	Before £	+ or − £	After £
Capital and reserves			
Preference shares	20,000	+18,000	38,000
Ordinary shares	40,000	+32,000	72,000
Profit and loss	8,000		8,000
	68,000		118,000

(b) If instead we assume that the business of Brown was acquired as follows:

The purchase price to be satisfied by Brown being given £5,000 cash and issue an extra 50,000 ordinary shares at par and £10,000 debentures at par. The assets taken over to be valued at Fixtures £28,000; Stock £7,500; Debtors £6,500. The bank balance is not taken over.

Exhibit 46.10 shows the summarised balance sheet of the company after the acquisition. (Note that both the increase in the creditors amount and the debentures are shown as minus adjustments as they increase the amount to be deducted from the assets.)

Exhibit 46.10

D Lucas Ltd
Summarised Balance Sheet

	Before £	+ or – £	After £
Goodwill		+26,000	26,000
Fixtures	36,000	+28,000	64,000
Stock	23,000	+7,500	30,500
Debtors	14,000	+6,500	20,500
Bank	6,000	–5,000	1,000
	79,000		142,000
Creditors	(11,000)	–3,000	(14,000)
	68,000		128,000
Debentures	–	–10,000	(10,000)
	68,000		118,000

	Before £	+ or – £	After £
Capital and reserves			
Preference shares	20,000		20,000
Ordinary shares	40,000	+50,000	90,000
Profit and loss	8,000		8,000
	68,000		118,000

Goodwill is calculated: Purchase consideration is made up of ordinary shares £50,000 + debentures £10,000 + bank £5,000 = £65,000.

Net assets bought are: Fixtures £28,000 + Stock £7,500 + Debtors £6,500 – Creditors £3,000 = £39,000.

Therefore, Goodwill is £65,000 – £39,000 = £26,000.

46.6 Business purchase account

In this chapter, to economise on space and descriptions, only the balance sheets have been shown. However, in the books of the purchaser the purchase of a business should pass through a Business Purchase Account.

This would be as follows:

Business Purchase Account

Debit		Credit	
Each liability taken over	(B)	Each asset taken over	
Vendor: net amount of		at values placed on it,	
purchase price	(C)	including goodwill	(A)

Vendor's Account (Name of seller/s)

Debit		Credit	
Bank (or share capital)		Amount to be paid	
Amount paid	(D)	for business	(C)

Various Asset Accounts

Debit			
Business purchase (value placed			
on asset taken over)	(A)		

Various Liability Accounts

		Credit	
		Amount of liability	
		taken over	(B)

Bank (or Share Capital)

		Credit	
		Amount paid to vendor	(D)

Learning outcomes

You should now have learnt:

1 That assets purchased when a business is taken over are shown in the purchaser's balance sheet at their valuation, not at the value per the closing balance sheet of the seller.

2 That where a greater price is paid than the total valuation of identifiable net assets then the difference is shown as goodwill.

3 That where the purchase price is less than the total valuation of identifiable net assets then the difference is shown as a capital reserve or as negative goodwill (except for limited companies, which must show it as negative goodwill).

4 That a limited company may use shares or debentures, as well as cash, to pay for the acquisition of another business.

5 How to enter up the purchase of a business in the purchaser's books.

6 How to draw up the balance sheet of the purchaser after taking over the assets and liabilities of the vendor.

Answers to activities

46.1   These include:

- an individual purchases the business of a sole trader
- an existing sole trader buys the business of another sole trader
- a partnership acquires the business of a sole trader
- a partnership acquires the business of another partnership (this happens quite a lot in accounting partnerships)
- existing businesses of sole traders join together to form a partnership
- a limited company takes over the business of a sole trader
- a limited company takes over the business of a partnership.

46.2   Goodwill. The total amount received less the value of net assets shown in the balance sheet represents the goodwill paid by the purchaser. Adjusting the asset values first simply increases the accounting work to be done by the seller (in a partnership, the change in value of the assets would need to be shared among the partners, only to be followed by a similar series of entries to account for the goodwill).

46.3 There could be many reasons, including:

- to gain the specialist expertise of the other firm – one may specialise in small business accounts and the other in tax. Combining them removes the need to pay a specialist when they need the expertise the other firm specialises in.
- to save money by relocating the staff of one firm into the offices of the other, enabling the existing offices of the other firm to be sold.

However, the most common reason is to achieve growth. The number of times over the last ten years or so that the list by size of the largest accounting firms in the UK has changed is testimony to this drive for market dominance through growth.

REVIEW QUESTIONS

46.1

C Allen
Balance Sheet as at 31 December 20X8

	£	£
Fixed assets		
Premises		21,000
Current assets		
Stock	9,600	
Debtors	6,300	
Bank	1,700	
	17,600	
Less: Current liabilities		
Creditors	(6,800)	
		10,800
		31,800
Capital		31,800

(a) The business of Allen is taken over by S Walters in its entirety. The assets are deemed to be worth the balance sheet values as shown. The price paid by Walters is £40,000. Show the opening balance sheet of Walters.

(b) Suppose instead that R Jones had taken over Allen's business. He does not take over the bank balance, and values premises at £28,000 and stock at £9,200. The price paid by him is £46,000. Show the opening balance sheet of Jones.

46.2A I Dodgem's balance sheet as at 31 December 20X8 was as follows:

	£	£	£
Fixed assets			
Premises			55,000
Plant and machinery at cost *less* depreciation			21,000
Fixtures and fittings at cost *less* depreciation			4,000
			80,000
Current assets			
Stock		17,000	
Trade debtors		9,500	
Cash		4,500	
		31,000	
Less Current liabilities			
Trade creditors	8,000		
Bank overdraft	15,800		
Expenses owing	200		
		(24,000)	
			7,000
			87,000
Capital			87,000

An opportunity had arisen for Dodgem to acquire the business of A Swing who is retiring.

A Swing
Balance Sheet as at 31 December 20X8

Fixed assets	£	£
Premises		25,000
Plant		9,000
Motor vehicle		3,500
		37,500
Current assets		
Stock	11,000	
Trade debtors	6,000	
Bank	8,000	
Cash	500	
	25,500	
Less Current liabilities		
Trade creditors	(9,000)	
		16,500
		54,000
Capital		54,000

Dodgem agreed to take over Swing's premises, plant, stock, trade debtors and trade creditors.

For the purpose of his own records Dodgem valued the premises at £35,000, plant at £6,000 and stock at £8,000.

The agreed purchase price was £50,000 and in order to finance the purchase Dodgem had obtained a fixed loan for 5 years from his bank, for one half of the purchase price on the condition that he contributed the same amount from his own private resources in cash. The purchase price was paid on 1 January 20X9.

Dodgem also decided to scrap some of his oldest plant and machinery which cost £9,000 with depreciation to date £8,000. This was sold for scrap for £300 cash on 1 January 20X9. On the same date he bought one new plant for £4,000, paying in cash.

Required:
(a) The purchase of business account in I Dodgem's books.
(b) I Dodgem's balance sheet as at 1 January 20X9 after all the above transactions have been completed.

(*Associated Examining Board*)

46.3 Spectrum Ltd is a private company with an authorised capital of £700,000 divided into shares of £1 each. 500,000 shares have been issued and are fully paid. The company has been formed to acquire small retail shops and establish a chain of outlets.

The company made offers to three sole traders and purchased the businesses run by Red, Yellow and Blue.

The assets acquired, liabilities taken over, and prices paid are listed below:

	Red	Yellow	Blue
	£	£	£
Premises	75,000	80,000	90,000
Delivery vans	7,000	–	10,000
Furniture and fittings	12,000	13,000	13,000
Stock	8,000	7,000	12,000
Creditors	6,000	8,000	7,000
Purchase price	120,000	130,000	150,000

The company also purchased a warehouse to be used as a central distribution store for £60,000. This has been paid.

Preliminary expenses (formation expenses) of £15,000 have also been paid.

The company took over the three shops outlined above and started trading on 1 January 20X2.

Approaches have also been made to Green for the purchase of his business for £100,000. Green has accepted the offer and the company will take over in the near future the following assets and liabilities:

	£
Premises	70,000
Stock	18,000
Creditors	3,000

The transaction had not been completed on 1 January 20X2 and Green was still running his own business.

(a) Prepare the opening balance sheet of Spectrum Ltd as at 1 January 20X2.
(b) How would you advise Spectrum Ltd to finance the purchase of Green's business when the deal is completed?

(*Edexcel Foundation, London Examinations (University of London)*)

46.4   Dinho and Manueli are in partnership sharing profits and losses equally after interest of 10% on each partner's capital account in excess of £100,000. At 31 December 20X8, the partnership trial balance was:

	Dr £	Cr £
Bank		56,700
Capital accounts: Dinho		194,000
Manueli		123,000
Creditors		85,800
Debtors	121,000	
Equipment, at cost	85,000	
Long-term loan		160,000
Freehold property	290,000	
Provision for depreciation on equipment		20,000
Stocks	143,500	
	639,500	639,500

On 31 December 20X8, the partnership was converted to a limited company, Bin Ltd. All the partnership assets and liabilities were taken over by the company in exchange for shares in Bin Ltd valued at £304,000. The share capital was allocated so as to preserve the rights previously enjoyed by the partners under their partnership agreement.

The assets and liabilities and shares issued were all entered in the books of Bin Ltd at 31 December. In the company's books, the debtors were recorded at £116,000 and the freehold property was valued at £260,000.

On 1 January 20X9, Pa invested £120,000 in the company and was issued shares on the same basis as had been applied when deciding the share allocations to Dinho and Manueli – i.e. as if he had been an equal partner in the partnership.

Pa had previously been an employee of the partnership earning £40,000 per annum. The £120,000 he invested in the company had been earning interest of 6% per annum from the bank. His salary will continue to be paid.

Assume that all profits will be paid as dividends. Ignore taxation.

Required:
(a) Prepare the partnership realisation account after the sale of the business to Bin Ltd had been completed and recorded in the partnership books.
(b) Prepare Bin Ltd's balance sheet as at 1 January 20X9 after the purchase of shares by Pa.
(c) Calculate the annual profit that Bin Ltd needs to make before it pays any dividends if Pa is to receive the same amount of income as he was receiving before buying shares in Bin Ltd.

PART 7

An introduction to financial analysis

47 An introduction to the analysis and interpretation of accounting statements

Introduction

This part deals with the interpretation of figures contained in financial statements using ratio analysis.

CHAPTER 47

An introduction to the analysis and interpretation of accounting statements

Learning objectives

After you have studied this chapter, you should be able to:

- explain how the use of ratios can help to analyse the profitability, liquidity, efficiency and capital structure of businesses
- calculate the main accounting ratios
- interpret the results of calculating accounting ratios
- explain the advantages and disadvantages of the gearing of an organisation being high or low
- explain how the proportion of costs that are fixed and variable impacts profit at different levels of activity
- explain the relevance of FRS 18 and accounting standards in general to the preparation of financial statements

Introduction

In this chapter, you'll learn how to calculate and interpret the most commonly used accounting ratios. You'll learn how to assess an organisation's profitability, liquidity, efficiency, and capital structure using ratio analysis. In addition, you'll learn more about FRS 18 and the importance of it and of accounting standards in general to the preparation of financial statements.

47.1 The need for ratios

Without ratios, financial statements would be largely uninformative to all but the very skilled. With ratios, financial statements can be interpreted and usefully applied to satisfy the needs of the reader.

For example, let's take the performance of four companies, all dealing in the same type of goods:

	Gross profit	Sales
	£	£
Company A	10,000	84,800
Company B	15,000	125,200
Company C	25,000	192,750
Company D	17,500	146,840

Suppose you want to know which company gets the 'best' profit. Simply inspecting these figures and trying to decide which performance was the best, and which was the worst, is virtually impossible. To bring the same basis of comparison to each company we need some form of common measure. As you have already seen earlier in Chapter 34, one measure commonly used is a ratio – the gross margin, i.e. the amount of gross profit on sales as a percentage. Applying this to these four companies finds their margins are:

	%
Company *A*	11.79
Company *B*	11.98
Company *C*	12.97
Company *D*	11.91

On this basis, Company C with a gross margin of 12.97% or, in other words, £12.97 gross profit per £100 sales, has performed better than the other companies.

47.2 How to use ratios

You can only sensibly compare like with like. There is not much point, for example, in comparing the gross profit percentage of a wholesale chemist with that of a restaurant.

Similarly, figures are only comparable if they have been built up on a similar basis. The sales figures of Company X, which treats items as sales *only when cash is received*, **cannot** be properly compared with those of Company Z, which treats items as sales *as soon as they are invoiced*.

Another instance of this could be that of stock turnover, which you learnt about in Chapter 34. Let's compare two companies, Company K and Company L. They are both toy shops so would seem to be comparable. Both companies have annual sales revenue of £100,000. However, the average stock of K is £40,000 whilst that of L is £10,000. Cost of sales is £50,000, so their stock turnover ratios are:

$$\frac{\text{Cost of sales}}{\text{Average stock}} \qquad \overset{K}{\frac{50,000}{40,000}} = 1.25 \qquad \overset{L}{\frac{50,000}{10,000}} = 5$$

It looks as though L has managed to turn its stock over five times during the year compared with K, 1.25 times. Is it true? Well, it depends. Let's imagine that K had a financial year end of 30 November, just before Christmas, so toy stocks would be extremely high; that L had a year end of 31 January when, following the Christmas sales, its stock had dropped to the year's lowest level; and that at 30 November L also had stock valued at £40,000. Can you see how the difference in the timing of the year end can affect this ratio significantly?

Ratios therefore need *very* careful handling. They are extremely useful if used properly, and very misleading otherwise.

47.3 Users of ratios

As you know, there are vast number of parties interested in analysing financial statements, including shareholders, lenders, customers, suppliers, employees, government agencies and competitors. Yet, in many respects, they will be interested in different things. There is not, therefore, any definitive, all-encompassing list of points for analysis that would be useful to all these stakeholder groups.

Nevertheless, it is possible to construct a series of ratios that together will provide all of them with something that they will find relevant and from which they can investigate further if necessary.

Ratio analysis is a first step in assessing an entity. It removes some of the mystique surrounding the financial statements and makes it easier to pinpoint items which it would be interesting to investigate further.

Exhibit 47.1 shows some categories of ratios and indicates some of the stakeholder groups that would be interested in them.

Exhibit 47.1

Ratio category	*Examples of interested groups*
Profitability	Shareholders, management, employees, creditors, competitors, potential investors
Liquidity	Shareholders, suppliers, creditors, competitors
Efficiency	Shareholders, potential purchasers, competitors
Shareholder	Shareholders, potential investors
Capital structure	Shareholders, lenders, creditors, potential investors

As you will see, some ratios belong in more than one of these categories.

47.4 Categories of ratio

Profitability ratios

1 Return on capital employed (ROCE)

This is one of the most important profitability ratios, as it encompasses all the other ratios, and an adequate return on capital employed is why people invested their money in a business in the first place.

(a) Sole traders

In this chapter, we will use the average of the capital account as the figure for capital employed, i.e. (opening balance + closing balance) ÷ 2.

In Businesses C and D in Exhibit 47.2 the same amount of net profits has been made, but the capitals employed are different.

Exhibit 47.2

Balance Sheets

	C	D
	£	£
Fixed + Current assets – Current liabilities	10,000	16,000
Capital accounts		
Opening balance	8,000	14,000
Add Net profit	3,600	3,600
	11,600	17,600
Less Drawings	(1,600)	(1,600)
	10,000	16,000

Return on capital employed (ROCE) is:

$$\frac{\text{Net Profit}}{\text{Capital employed}} \times 100$$

therefore,

$$\begin{array}{cc} C \\ \dfrac{3,600}{(8,000 + 10,000) \div 2} \times \dfrac{100}{1} = 40\% \end{array} \qquad \begin{array}{cc} D \\ \dfrac{3,600}{(14,000 + 16,000) \div 2} \times \dfrac{100}{1} = 24\% \end{array}$$

The ratio illustrates that what is important is not simply how much profit has been made but how well the capital has been employed. Business C has made far better use of its capital, achieving a return of £40 net profit for every £100 invested, whereas D has received only a net profit of £24 per £100.

(b) Limited companies

There is no universally agreed definition of return on capital employed for companies. The main ones used are:

(i) return on capital employed by ordinary shareholders
(ii) return on capital employed by all long-term suppliers of capital.

Let's now look at each of these:

(i) In a limited company this is known as **Return on Owners' Equity** (ROOE) or, more commonly, **Return on Shareholders' Funds** (ROSF). From now on, we shall use the second of these terms, 'Return on Shareholders' Funds', but you will need to remember that when you see 'Return on Owners' Equity', it is the same as ROSF.
   The 'Return' is the net profit for the period. The term 'Shareholders' Funds' means the book value of all things in the balance sheet that describe the owners' capital and reserves. 'Owners' are the holders of the **ordinary** share capital. This is calculated: Ordinary Share Capital + all Reserves including Profit and Loss Account.
(ii) This is often known simply as 'Return on Capital Employed' (ROCE). The word 'Return' in this case means net profit + any preference share dividends + debenture and long-term loan interest. The word 'Capital' means Ordinary Share Capital + Reserves including Profit and Loss Account + Preference Shares + Debentures and Long-term Loans.

Given the following balance sheets and profit and loss accounts of two companies, *P* Ltd and *Q* Ltd, the calculations of ROSF and ROCE can be attempted:

Balance Sheets as at 31 December

	P Ltd		Q Ltd	
	£	£	£	£
	20X8	*20X9*	*20X8*	*20X9*
Fixed assets	5,200	5,600	8,400	9,300
Net current assets	2,800	3,400	1,600	2,700
	8,000	9,000	10,000	12,000
10% debentures	–	–	(1,200)	(1,200)
	8,000	9,000	8,800	10,800
Share capital (ordinary)	3,000	3,000	5,000	5,000
Reserves	5,000	6,000	3,800	5,800
	8,000	9,000	8,800	10,800

Profit and Loss Accounts for year to 31 December 20X9

	P Ltd	Q Ltd
	£	£
Net profit	2,200	3,800
Dividends	(1,200)	(1,800)
	1,000	2,000

Return on Shareholders' Funds (ROSF)

P Ltd

$$\frac{2,200}{(8,000 + 9,000) \div 2} \times \frac{100}{1} = 25.9\%$$

Q Ltd

$$\frac{3,800}{(8,800 + 10,800) \div 2} \times \frac{100}{1} = 38.8\%$$

Return on Capital Employed (ROCE)

P Ltd	Q Ltd
Same as ROSF[(Note 1)] = 25.9%	$\dfrac{3{,}800 + 120^{(Note\ 2)}}{(10{,}000 + 12{,}000) \div 2} \times \dfrac{100}{1} = 35.6\%$

Note 1: The return on capital employed by all long-term sources of capital (in *Q Ltd's* case, the shareholders' funds and the debentures) is the same as the ROSF in the case of *P Ltd*, as it has no debentures.

Note 2: The debenture interest (i.e. 10% of £1,200 = £120) must be added back, as it was an expense in calculating the £3,800 net profit.

2 Gross profit as percentage of sales

The formula is

$$\frac{\text{Gross profit}}{\text{Sales}} \times 100$$

This was dealt with in Chapter 34.

3 Net profit as a percentage of sales

The formula is

$$\frac{\text{Net profit}}{\text{Sales}} \times 100$$

Liquidity ratios

You saw earlier in this section that the ratio called 'return on capital employed' is used to provide an overall picture of profitability. It cannot always be assumed, however, that profitability is everything that is desirable. It must be stressed that accounting is used, not just to calculate profitability, but also to provide information that indicates whether or not the business will be able to pay its creditors, expenses, loans falling due, etc. at the correct times. Failure to ensure that these payments are covered effectively could mean that the business would have to be closed down. Being able to pay one's debts as they fall due is known as being 'liquid'.

It is also essential that a business is aware if a customer or borrower is at risk of not repaying the amount due. New customers are usually vetted prior to being allowed to trade on credit rather than by cash. For private individuals, there are credit rating agencies with extensive records of the credit histories of many individuals. For a small fee, a company can receive a report indicating whether a new customer might be a credit risk. Similarly, information can be purchased concerning companies that indicates their solvency, i.e. whether they are liable to be bad credit risks.

The difference between these two sources of information is that, while the information on private individuals is based on their previous credit record, that of the companies is generally based on a ratio analysis of their financial statements.

When it comes to the liquidity of a business, both its own ability to pay its debts when due and the ability of its debtors to pay the amount they owe to the business are of great importance. Ratio analysis that focuses upon liquidity (or solvency) of the business generally starts with a look at two ratios (**liquidity ratios**) that are affected most by these two aspects of liquidity, the **current ratio** and the **acid test ratio**.

1 Current ratio

This compares assets which will become liquid within approximately twelve months (i.e. total current assets) with liabilities which will be due for payment in the same period (i.e. total current liabilities) and is intended to indicate whether there are sufficient short-term assets to meet the short-term liabilities.

$$\text{Current ratio} = \frac{\text{Current assets}}{\text{Current liabilities}}$$

When calculated, the ratio may be expressed as either a ratio to 1, with current liabilities being set to 1, or as a 'number of times', representing the relative size of the amount of total current assets compared with total current liabilities.

With *all* ratios, once you have performed the calculation, you need to decide what it tells you. To do so, there is no point in using a universal guide, such as *'the ratio should always lie between 1 : 1 and 2 : 1'*. Any such guidance is at best useless and at worst misleading. Instead, you need to consider the result in its context.

For example:

● What is the norm in this industrial sector? (For example, retailers are often below 1 : 1.)
● Is this company significantly above or below that norm?
● If so, can this be justified after an analysis of the nature of these assets and liabilities, and of the reasons for the amounts of each held?

You need to contextualise *every* ratio you calculate when you are trying to understand what the result means, not just this one.

2 Acid test ratio

This shows that, provided creditors and debtors are paid at approximately the same time, a view might be made as to whether the business has sufficient liquid resources to meet its current liabilities.

$$\text{Acid test ratio} = \frac{\text{Current assets} - \text{stock}}{\text{Current liabilities}}$$

Exhibit 47.3 shows how two businesses may have similar profitability, yet their liquidity positions may be quite different.

Activity 47.1

What is the difference between the formulae for the current ratio and the acid test ratio?

Exhibit 47.3

	E		F	
	£	£	£	£
Fixed assets		40,000		70,000
Current assets				
Stock	30,000		50,000	
Debtors	45,000		9,000	
Bank	15,000		1,000	
	90,000		60,000	
Less Current liabilities: creditors	(30,000)		(30,000)	
		60,000		30,000
		100,000		100,000
Capital				
Opening capital		80,000		80,000
Add Net profit		36,000		36,000
		116,000		116,000
Less Drawings		(16,000)		(16,000)
		100,000		100,000

Note: Sales for both *E* and *F* amounted to £144,000. Gross profits for *E* and *F* were identical at £48,000.

Profitability is the same for both businesses. However, there is a vast difference in the liquidity of the two businesses.

Current ratios

$$E = \frac{90,000}{30,000} = 3$$

$$F = \frac{60,000}{30,000} = 2$$

This looks adequate on the face of it, but let's look at the acid test ratio:

Acid test ratios

$$E = \frac{60,000}{30,000} = 2$$

$$F = \frac{10,000}{30,000} = 0.33$$

This reveals that *F* may be in trouble, as it will probably find it difficult to pay its current liabilities on time. No matter how profitable a business is, unless it is adequately liquid it may fail.

However, although a business should be adequately liquid, it is possible for it to have too high a current ratio or acid test ratio. If too many resources are being held as current assets, it would make these two ratios appear healthy, but those resources could have been used more profitably – you don't get any interest on stock! Too high a balance in a current account at the bank also means that resources are being wasted.

Activity 47.2
Why is stock omitted from the acid test ratio?

Efficiency ratios

1 Stock turnover

Stock turnover measures how efficient a business is at maintaining an appropriate level of stock. When it is not being as efficient as it used to be, or is being less efficient than its competitors, this may indicate that control over stock levels is being undermined.

A reduction in stock turnover can mean that the business is slowing down. Stocks may be piling up and not being sold. This could lead to a liquidity crisis, as money may be being taken out of the bank simply to increase stocks which are not then sold quickly enough.

Note: In this chapter, we are classifying stock turnover as an efficiency ratio. It is often also classified as a liquidity ratio.

For Exhibit 47.3 the cost of sales for each company was £144,000 – £48,000 = £96,000. If opening stocks had been *E* £34,000 and *F* £46,000 then, using the average of the opening and closing stocks, the stock turnovers would have been:

	E	F
$\dfrac{\text{Cost of sales}}{\text{Average stock}}$	$\dfrac{96{,}000}{(34{,}000 + 30{,}000) \div 2}$	$\dfrac{96{,}000}{(46{,}000 + 50{,}000) \div 2}$
	$= \dfrac{96{,}000}{32{,}000} = 3 \text{ times}$	$= \dfrac{96{,}000}{48{,}000} = 2 \text{ times}$

It appears that F's stock may be too high, perhaps because it is having difficulty selling it compared with E. Or perhaps it is E that has a problem obtaining enough stock. Either way, further investigation is needed.

2 Debtor/sales ratio

The resources tied up in debtors is an important ratio subject. Money tied up unnecessarily in debtors is unproductive money. In the example in Exhibit 47.3 the **debtor/sales ratio** can be calculated for the two companies as:

	E	F
Debtor/sales	$45{,}000/144{,}000 = 1 : 3.2$	$9{,}000/144{,}000 = 1 : 16$

This relationship is often translated into the length of time a debtor takes to pay:

$$\text{E} \qquad 365 \times \frac{1}{3.2} = 114 \text{ days} \qquad\qquad \text{F} \qquad 365 \times \frac{1}{16} = 22.8 \text{ days}$$

Why Company E should have allowed so much time for its debtors to pay is a matter for investigation. Possibly the company was finding it harder to sell goods, and to sell at all was eventually forced to sell to customers on long credit terms. It could well be that E has no proper credit control system, whereas F has an extremely efficient one.

When the ratio is deteriorating (i.e. it is rising) this may signal liquidity problems.

Note: In this chapter, we are classifying debtors/sales as an efficiency ratio. Like stock turnover, it is often also classified as a '*liquidity ratio*', as it can reveal both efficiency and liquidity issues. The next ratio, creditors/purchases, also provides this double aspect view.

3 Creditor/purchases ratio

Assuming that purchases for E amounted to £92,000 and for F £100,000 then the **creditor/purchases ratio** can be calculated for each as:

	E	F
Creditor/purchases	$30{,}000/92{,}000 = 1 : 3.07$	$30{,}000/100{,}000 = 1 : 3.3$

This also is often translated into the length of time we take to pay our creditors. This turns out to be:

$$\text{E} \qquad 365 \times \frac{1}{3.07} = 118.9 \text{ days} \qquad\qquad \text{F} \qquad 365 \times \frac{1}{3.3} = 110.6 \text{ days}$$

Shareholder ratios

These will include the following ratios. Note that 'price' means the price of the shares on the Stock Exchange.

1 Earnings per share (EPS)

The formula is:

$$\text{Earnings per share} = \frac{\text{Net profit after interest and tax and preference dividends}}{\text{Number of ordinary shares issued}}$$

This gives the shareholder (or prospective shareholder) a chance to compare one year's earnings with another in terms easily understood. Many people consider EPS to be *the* most important ratio that can be calculated from the financial statements.

2 Price/earnings ratio (P/E)

The formula is:

$$\text{Price/earnings ratio} = \frac{\text{Market price per share}}{\text{Earnings per share}}$$

This puts the price into context as a multiple of the earnings. The greater the P/E ratio, the greater the demand for the shares.

3 Dividend yield

This is found by the formula:

$$\text{Dividend yield} = \frac{\text{Gross dividend per share}}{\text{Market price per share}}$$

This measures the real rate of return by comparing the dividend paid to the market price of a share.

4 Dividend cover

This is found by the formula:

$$\text{Dividend cover} = \frac{\text{Net profit after tax and preference dividends}}{\text{Ordinary dividends paid and proposed}}$$

This gives the shareholder some idea as to the proportion that the ordinary dividends bear to the amount available for distribution to ordinary shareholders. Usually, the dividend is described as being so many times covered by profits made. If, therefore, the dividend is said to be *three times covered*, it means that one-third of the available profits is being distributed as dividends.

Capital structure ratios

Gearing

The relationship of equity shares (ordinary shares) to other forms of long-term financing (long-term loans plus preference shares) can be extremely important. Analysts are, therefore, keen to ascertain a ratio to express this relationship.

There is more than one way of calculating **gearing**. The most widely used method is as follows:

$$\frac{\text{Long-term loans} + \text{Preference shares}}{\text{Ordinary share capital} + \text{Reserves} + \text{Preference shares} + \text{Long-term liabilities}} \times 100$$

This formula is sometimes abbreviated to:

$$\frac{\text{Prior charge capital}}{\text{Total capital}} \times 100$$

which is exactly the same.

Long-term loans include debentures. Total capital includes preference shares and ordinary shares, all the reserves and long-term loans.

Let's look at the calculations of the gearing of two companies, A Ltd and B Ltd in Exhibit 47.4. Both have already been trading for five years.

Exhibit 47.4

Year 5: items per balance sheet	A Ltd £	B Ltd £
10% debentures	10,000	100,000
10% preference shares	20,000	50,000
Ordinary shares	100,000	20,000
Reserves	70,000	30,000
	200,000	200,000

Gearing ratios:

$$\text{A Ltd:} \quad \frac{10,000 + 20,000}{10,000 + 20,000 + 100,000 + 70,000} \times \frac{100}{1} = 15\% \text{ (low gearing)}$$

$$\text{B Ltd:} \quad \frac{100,000 + 50,000}{100,000 + 50,000 + 20,000 + 30,000} \times \frac{100}{1} = 75\% \text{ (high gearing)}$$

Now let us look at how dividends are affected, given the same level of profits made before payment of debenture interest and preference dividends. All the profits made in these years are to be distributed.

A Ltd: Low gearing		Year 6 £	Year 7 £	Year 8 £	Year 9 £
Profits before deducting the following:		20,000	15,000	30,000	40,000
Debenture interest	1,000				
Preference dividend	2,000				
		(3,000)	(3,000)	(3,000)	(3,000)
Profits left for ordinary dividend		17,000	12,000	27,000	37,000
Rate of ordinary dividend		17%	12%	27%	37%

B Ltd: High gearing		Year 6 £	Year 7 £	Year 8 £	Year 9 £
Profits before deducting the following:		20,000	15,000	30,000	40,000
Debenture interest	10,000				
Preference dividend	5,000				
		(15,000)	(15,000)	(15,000)	(15,000)
Profits left for ordinary dividend		5,000	–	15,000	25,000
Rate of ordinary dividend		25%	–	75%	125%

A company with a high percentage gearing ratio is said to be *high geared*, whereas one with a low percentage gearing is said to be *low geared*. As you can see from the above example, the proportionate effect gearing has upon ordinary shareholders is far greater in a high geared company, ranging from 0 to 125 per cent dividend for B Ltd, whilst the range of ordinary dividends for A Ltd varied far less and lay between 17 and 37 per cent.

A high rate of debt (i.e. long-term loans and preference shares) means that in bad times very little might be left over for ordinary shareholders after payment of interest on the debt items and also preference dividends. In good times, however, the ordinary shareholders will enjoy a far higher return than in a low geared company.

This means that people investing in ordinary shares in a high geared company are taking a far greater risk with their money than if they had invested instead in a low geared company. It would have only required a drop of profits of £5,000 in Year 6 for B Ltd to find that there would be no ordinary dividends at all for both Years 6 and 7. Such a drop in Year 6 for A Ltd would still have allowed a dividend of 12 per cent for both of Years 6 and 7. Investors therefore who are prepared to risk their money in the hope of large dividends would have chosen B Ltd, whilst those who wanted to cut down on their risk and be more certain about receiving dividends would choose A Ltd.

Changing the gearing of a company

The management might decide that for various reasons it would like to change the gearing of the company. It can do this as follows:

To reduce gearing	*To increase gearing*
1 By issuing new ordinary shares	1 By issuing debentures
2 By redeeming debentures	2 By buying back ordinary shares in issue
3 By retaining profits	3 By issuing new preference shares

Such changes will be influenced by what kinds of investors the company wishes to attract. A highly geared company will attract risk-taking buyers of ordinary shares, whilst a low geared company will be more attractive to potential ordinary shareholders who wish to minimise risk.

Other ratios

There are a large number of other ratios which could be used, far more than can be mentioned in a textbook such as this. It will depend on the type of company exactly which ratios are the most important and it is difficult to generalise too much.

Different users of the accounts will want to use the ratio analysis which is of vital concern to them. If we can take as an example a bank which lends money to a company, it will want to ensure two things:

(*a*) that the company will be able to pay interest on the loan as it falls due; *and*
(*b*) that it will be able to repay the loan on the agreed date.

The bank is therefore interested in:

(*a*) short-term liquidity, concerning payment of loan interest; and
(*b*) long-term solvency for eventual repayment of the loan.

Possible ratios for each of these could be:

(*a*) **Short-term liquidity ratios**, mainly the *acid test ratio* and the *current ratio*, already described.
(*b*) **Long-term solvency ratios**, which might include:
  (i) *Operating profit/loan interest*
  This indicates how much of the profits are taken up by paying loan interest. Too great a proportion would mean that the company was borrowing more than was sensible, as a small fall in profits could mean the company operating at a loss with the consequent effect upon long-term solvency.
  (ii) *Total external liabilities/shareholders' funds*
  This ratio measures how much financing is done via share capital and retained profits, and how much is from external sources. Too high a proportion of external liabilities

could bring about long-term solvency problems if the company's profit-making capacity falls by a relatively small amount, as outside liabilities still have to be met.

(iii) *Shareholders' funds/total assets (excluding intangibles)*

This highlights the proportion of assets financed by the company's own funds. Large falls in this ratio will tend to show a difficulty with long-term solvency. Similarly, investors will want to see ratios suitable for their purposes, which are not the same as those for the bank. These will not only be used on a single company comparison, but probably with the average of the same type of ratios for other companies in the same industry.

47.5 The investor: choosing between shares and debentures

The choice of an investor will always be related to the amount of acceptable risk. We can list the possible investments under the headings of risk.

Lowest risk

Debenture holders have their interest paid to them whether or not profits are made. This contrasts with shares, both preference and ordinary, where there have to be profits available for distribution as dividends.

In addition, should there be insufficient cash funds available to pay debenture dividends, many debentures give their holders the right to sell off some or all of the assets of the company, and to recoup the amount of their debentures before anyone else has a claim. Such an investment does not have as much security as, say, government stocks, but it certainly ranks above the shares of that same company.

Medium risk

Preference shareholders have their dividends paid after the debenture interest has been paid, but before the ordinary shareholders. They still are dependent upon profits being available for distribution. If they are of the cumulative variety then any shortfall can be carried forward to future years and paid before any ordinary dividends are taken.

Highest risk

Ordinary shareholders have the highest risk. They must give way to both debenture holders and to preference shares for interest and dividends. However, should the remaining profits for distribution be very high then they may get a high return on their money.

47.6 Trend figures

In examinations, a student is often given just one year's accounting figures and asked to comment on them. Obviously, lack of space on an examination paper may preclude several years' figures being given, also the student lacks the time to prepare a comprehensive survey of several years' accounts.

In real life, however, it would be extremely stupid for anyone to base decisions on just one year's accounts, if more information was available. What is important for a business is not just what, say, accounting ratios are for one year, but what the trend has been.

Given two similar types of businesses *G* and *H*, both having existed for five years, if both of them had exactly the same ratios in Year 5, are they both equally desirable as investments? Given one year's accounts it may appear so, but if one had all the five years' figures it may not give the same picture, as Exhibit 47.5 illustrates.

Exhibit 47.5

	Years					
		1	2	3	4	5 (current)
Gross profit as % of sales	G	40	38	36	35	34
	H	30	32	33	33	34
Net profit as % of sales	G	15	13	12	12	11
	H	10	10	10	11	11
Net profit as % of capital employed	G	13	12	11	11	10
	H	8	8	9	9	10
Current ratio	G	3	2.8	2.6	2.3	2.0
	H	1.5	1.7	1.9	1.0	2.0

From these figures G appears to be the worse investment for the future, as the trend appears to be downwards. If the trend for G is continued it could be in a very dangerous financial situation in a year or two. Business H, on the other hand, is strengthening its position all the time.

Of course, it would be ridiculous to assert that H will continue on an upward trend. One would have to know more about the business to be able to judge whether or not that could be true.

However, given all other desirable information, trend figures would be an extra important indicator.

47.7 Fixed and variable costs

Some costs will remain constant whether activity increases or falls, at least within a given range of change of activity. These costs are called **fixed costs**. An example of this would be the rent of a shop which would remain at the same figure whether sales increased 10 per cent or fell 10 per cent. The same would remain true of such things as rates, fire insurance and so on.

Wages of shop assistants could also remain constant in such a case. If, for instance, the shop employed two assistants, then it would probably keep the same two assistants, on the same wages, whether sales increased or fell by 10 per cent.

Of course, such fixed costs can only be viewed as fixed in the short term. If sales doubled, then the business might well need a larger shop or more assistants. A larger shop would also certainly mean higher rates, higher fire insurance and so on, and with more assistants the total wage bill would be larger.

Variable costs on the other hand will change with swings in activity. Suppose that wrapping materials are used in the shop, then it could well be that an increase in sales of 10 per cent may see 10 per cent more wrapping materials used. Similarly an increase of 10 per cent of sales, if all sales are despatched by parcel post, could well see delivery charges increase by 10 per cent.

Some costs could be part fixed and part variable. Suppose that because of an increase in sales of 10 per cent, telephone calls made increased by 10 per cent. With telephone bills the cost is in two parts, one for the rent of the phone and the second part corresponding to the actual number of calls made. The rent would not change in such a case, and therefore this part of telephone expense would be 'fixed' whereas the calls part of the cost could increase by 10 per cent.

This means that the effect of a percentage change in activity could have a more, or less, percentage change in net profit, because the fixed costs (within that range of activity) may not alter.

Exhibit 47.6 shows the change in net profit in Business *A* which has a low proportion of its expenses as 'fixed' costs, whereas in Business *B* the 'fixed' costs are a relatively high proportion of its expenses.

Exhibit 47.6

Business A

	£	£	(a) If sales fell 10% £	£	(b) If sales rose 10% £	£
Sales		50,000		45,000		55,000
Less Cost of goods sold		(30,000)		(27,000)		(33,000)
Gross profit		20,000		18,000		22,000
Less Expenses:						
Fixed	3,000		3,000		3,000	
Variable	13,000		11,700		14,300	
		(16,000)		(14,700)		(17,300)
Net profit		4,000		3,300		4,700

Business B

	£	£	(a) If sales fell 10% £	£	(b) If sales rose 10% £	£
Sales		50,000		45,000		55,000
Less Cost of goods sold		(30,000)		(27,000)		(33,000)
Gross profit		20,000		18,000		22,000
Less Expenses:						
Fixed	12,000		12,000		12,000	
Variable	4,000		3,600		4,400	
		(16,000)		(15,600)		(16,400)
Net profit		4,000		2,400		5,600

The comparison of percentage changes in net profit therefore works out as follows:

$$A \qquad\qquad\qquad\qquad B$$

Decrease of 10% sales:

$$\frac{\text{Reduction in profit}}{\text{Original profit}} \times \frac{100}{1} \qquad \frac{700}{4,000} \times \frac{100}{1} = 17.5\% \qquad \frac{1,600}{4,000} \times \frac{100}{1} = 40\%$$

Increase of 10% sales:

$$\frac{\text{Increase in profit}}{\text{Original profit}} \times \frac{100}{1} \qquad \frac{700}{4,000} \times \frac{100}{1} = 17.5\% \qquad \frac{1,600}{4,000} \times \frac{100}{1} = 40\%$$

It can be seen that a change in activity in Business *B*, which has a higher fixed expense content, will result in greater percentage changes in profit: 40% in *B* compared with 17.5% in *A*.

47.8 Limitations of accounting statements

Financial statements are only partial information. They show the reader of them, in financial terms, what has happened *in the past*. This is better than having no information at all, but much more information is needed to fully understand the present situation.

First, it is impossible to sensibly compare two businesses which are completely unlike one another. To compare a supermarket's figures with those of a chemical factory would be rather pointless. It would be like comparing a lion with a lizard.

Second, there are a whole lot of factors that the past-focused financial statements do not disclose. The desire to keep to the money measurement concept, and the desire to be objective, both dealt with in Chapter 10, exclude a great deal of desirable information. Some typical desirable information can be listed but, beware, the list is indicative rather than exhaustive.

(*a*) What are the future plans of the business? Without this an investment in a business would be sheer guesswork.

(*b*) Has the firm got good quality staff?

(*c*) Is the business situated in a location desirable for such a business? A shipbuilding business situated a long way up a river which was becoming unnavigable, to use an extreme example, could soon be in trouble.

(*d*) What is its position as compared with its competitors? A business manufacturing a single product, which has a foreign competitor which has just invented a much improved product which will capture the whole market, is obviously in for a bad time.

(*e*) Will future government regulations affect it? Suppose that a business which is an importer of goods from Country X, which is outside the EU, finds that the EU is to ban all imports from Country X?

(*f*) Is its plant and machinery obsolete? If so, the business may not have sufficient funds to be able to replace it.

(*g*) Is the business of a high-risk type or in a relatively stable industry?

(*h*) Has the business got good customers? A business selling largely to Country Y, which is getting into trouble because of shortage of foreign exchange, could soon lose most of its trade. Also if one customer was responsible for, say, 60 per cent of sales, then the loss of that one customer would be calamitous.

(*i*) Has the business got good suppliers of its needs? A business in wholesaling could, for example, be forced to close down if manufacturers decided to sell direct to the general public.

(*j*) Problems concerned with the effects of distortion of accounting figures caused by inflation (or deflation).

You can see that the list would have to be an extremely long one if it was intended to cover all possibilities.

47.9 FRS 18: Accounting Policies

Users of financial statements issued by organisations want to analyse and evaluate the figures contained within them. They cannot do this effectively unless they know which accounting policies have been used when preparing such statements. This FRS was issued to help continue the improvement in the quality of financial reporting that had been started in 1971 by the accounting standard it replaced, SSAP 2.

The FRS focuses upon **accounting policies** and considers the **estimation techniques** used in implementing them. It also looks in detail at the various accounting concepts that you covered earlier when you worked through Chapter 10.

Accounting policies

These are defined in FRS 18 as:

those principles, bases, conventions, rules and practices applied by an entity that specify how the effects of transactions and other events are to be reflected in its financial statements through:

(*i*)   *recognising,*
(*ii*) *selecting measurement basis for, and*
(*iii*) *presenting*

assets, liabilities, gains, losses and changes to shareholders' funds.

In other words, accounting policies define the processes whereby transactions and other events are reflected in the financial statements. The accounting policies selected should enable the financial statements to give a true and fair view and should be consistent with accounting standards, UITFs, and company legislation.

When selecting an accounting policy, its appropriateness should be considered in the context of four 'objectives':

- Relevance –   Does it produce information that is useful for assessing stewardship and for making economic decisions?
- Reliability –   Does it reflect the substance of the transaction and other events that have occurred? Is it free of bias, i.e. neutral? Is it free of material error? If produced under uncertainty, has prudence been exercised?
- Comparability –   Can it be compared with similar information about the entity for some other period or point in time?
- Understandability – Is it capable of being understood by users who have a reasonable knowledge of business and economic activities and accounting?

Estimation techniques

These are the methods adopted in order to arrive at estimated monetary amounts for items that appear in the financial statements.

> ### Activity 47.3
> From your knowledge of accounting, what do you think these methods may include? Think about this for a minute and then write down as many example of estimation techniques as you can think of.

Examples of accounting policies

- The treatment of gains and losses on disposals of fixed assets – they could be applied to adjust the depreciation charge for the period, or they may appear as separate items in the financial statements.
- The classification of overheads in the financial statements – for example, some indirect costs may be included in the trading account, or they may be included in administration costs in the profit and loss account.
- The treatment of interest costs incurred in connection with the construction of fixed assets – these could be charged to profit and loss as a finance cost, or they could be capitalised and added to the other costs of creating the fixed assets (this is allowed by FRS 15).

Identifying whether an accounting policy has changed

This is done by considering whether any of three aspects have changed:

- recognition –   some items may be recognised in more than one way. For example, SSAP 13 allows expenditure on developing new products to be recognised either as a profit and loss expense or as an asset in the balance sheet.
- presentation –   how something is presented in the financial statements. For example, where certain indirect costs appear in the profit and loss account.
- **measurement basis** – the monetary aspects of the items in the financial statements, such as the basis of the stock valuation, say FIFO or LIFO.

If any of these three aspects have changed, it represents a change in accounting policy. If they haven't, something else has occurred, for example, the estimation technique in use. If depreciation was changed from straight line to reducing balance this would be a change in estimation technique, not a change in accounting policy. On the other hand, a decision to switch from valuing stock using FIFO to LIFO would constitute a change in accounting policy as the measurement basis had changed.

47.10 Further thoughts on concepts and conventions

In Chapter 10, you were introduced to the concepts and conventions used in accounting. Since then further chapters have consolidated your knowledge on specific points.

In recent years there has been a considerable change in the style of examinations in accounting at all levels. At one time nearly every examination question was purely computational, requiring you to prepare financial statements, draft journal entries, extract a trial balance and so on. Now, *in addition* to all that (which is still important) there are quite a lot of questions asking such things as:

- Why do we do it?
- What does it mean?
- How does it relate to the concepts and conventions of accounting?

Such questions depend very much on the interests and ingenuity of examiners. They like to set questions worded to find out those who can understand and interpret financial information, and eliminate those who cannot and simply try to repeat information learned by rote.

The examiners will often draw on knowledge from any part of the syllabus. It is therefore impossible for a student (or an author) to guess exactly how an examiner will select a question and how he will word it.

An example of this is where the examiner could ask you to show how different concepts contradict one another. Someone who has just read about the concepts, and memorised them, could not answer this unless they had thought further about it. Think about whether or not you could have answered that question before you read further.

One instance is the use of the concept of consistency. Basically it says that one should keep to the same method of entering an item each year. Yet if the net realisable value of stock is less than cost, then the normal method of showing it at cost should be abandoned and the net realisable value used instead. Thus, at the end of one period, stock may be shown at cost and at the end of the next period it will be shown at net realisable value. In this case the concept of prudence has overridden the concept of consistency.

Another instance of this is that of calculating profit based on sales whether they have been paid for or not. If the prudence concept were taken to extremes, then profit would only be calculated on a sale when the sale had been paid for. Instead, the realisation concept has overridden the prudence concept so you recognise a sale when it is reasonably certain that it will be paid for.

Review questions 47.11 to 47.20 are typical examination questions which obviously relate to concepts and conventions, and to general understanding of the subject.

47.11 Other accounting standards

As well as the accounting standards that you have read about in this book, there are some other standards which may appear in your examinations. We will cover them briefly here.

SSAP 13: Research and Development

Money spent on research and development presents a problem for accountants. You could argue that:

- Such costs are incurred so that profits can be earned in the future, and should therefore be carried forward to those future periods.
- Just because you have incurred such costs, you cannot be certain about future profitability occurring. It should therefore be written off as an expense in the period when the costs are incurred.

The costs can be divided between:

- **Pure (basic) research.** This is carried out to advance scientific and technical knowledge, but without any specific objective.
- **Applied research.** This utilises pure research undertaken so that a specific objective can be attained.
- **Development.** Work undertaken to develop new or existing products or services. This has to be carried out before commercial operations can begin.

SSAP 13 requires that both pure research and applied research costs be written off in the year they are incurred.

However, with development costs, if certain conditions are met, then they may be carried forward to future periods.

SSAP 17: Accounting for Post Balance Sheet Events

The balance sheet is supposed to reflect the financial position of a business at the balance sheet date. However, between the balance sheet date and its later approval by the board of directors, certain events may occur. These may mean that the balance sheet figures need amending.

The events can be divided between:

- **Adjusting events.** When these happen the balance sheet needs to be amended.
- **Non-adjusting events.** These do not lead to amendments of the balance sheet, but they may be shown as notes accompanying the balance sheet.

FRS 12: Provisions, Contingent Liabilities and Contingent Assets

This FRS was issued in September 1998, replacing SSAP 18. FRS 12 defines a provision as

a liability that is of uncertain timing or amount, to be settled by the transfer of economic benefits.

A provision should only be recognised when it is probable that a transfer of economic benefits will have to occur and a reasonable estimate can be made of the amount involved.

FRS 12 defines a contingent liability as

either a possible obligation arising from past events whose existence will be confirmed only by the occurrence of one or more uncertain future events not wholly within the entity's control; or a present obligation that arises from past events but is not recognised because it is not probable that a transfer of economic benefits will be required to settle the obligation or because the amount of the obligation cannot be measured with sufficient reliability.

An example of this could be where a legal action is being carried on, but the case has not yet been decided. For instance, a company may have been sued for £10 million damages, but the case is not yet over. The company may or may not have to pay the damages, but the case is so complex that it has no way of knowing.

FRS 12 defines a contingent asset as

a possible asset arising from past events whose existence will be confirmed only by the occurrence of one or more uncertain events not wholly within the entity's control.

Neither contingent liabilities nor contingent assets should be recognised. This is consistent with the prudence concept, as defined in FRS 18.

FRSSE: Financial Reporting Standard for Smaller Entities

This accounting standard was issued in November 1997. It provides a simplified version of the body of accounting standards and is for use by 'smaller entities', i.e. small companies and other organisations that would be classified as 'small' were they companies. The standard quotes from sections 247–249 of the Companies Act 1985 in defining a 'small' company as one that does not exceed two or more of the following criteria:

Turnover	£2.8 million
Balance sheet total	£1.4 million
Average number of employees	50

The FRSSE is applicable to the great majority of companies and will, undoubtedly, feature increasingly in both examinations and in the work undertaken by accountants.

Learning outcomes

You should now have learnt:

1 That comparing the trends to see if the ratios are getting better or worse as each period passes is essential for proper control. Prompt action needs to be taken where the trend in a ratio is deteriorating.

2 The importance of interpreting ratios in their context: that is, against those of other similar businesses or against the same ratios calculated for the same organisation using data from other time periods.

3 That a business must be both profitable *and* sufficiently liquid to be successful. One factor without the other can lead to serious trouble.

4 That careful credit control to ensure that the debtor/sales ratio is not too high is usually essential to the well-being of any business.

5 That gearing affects the risk factor for ordinary share investors. High gearing means greater risk whilst low gearing means lower risks.

6 How to calculate and interpret the most commonly used ratios.

7 The relevance of ratio analysis to an assessment of liquidity, efficiency, profitability and capital structure.

8 That the relative amounts of fixed and variable costs can affect profit significantly when there are swings in business activity.

9 The importance of FRS 18 to the preparation of financial statements.

Answers to activities

47.1 The only difference in the items involved between the two ratios is that the acid test (or 'quick') ratio does not include stock. Otherwise, it is identical to the current ratio, comparing current assets *other than stock* to current liabilities.

47.2 Stock is omitted as it is considered to be relatively illiquid, because it depends upon prevailing and future market forces and may be impossible to convert to cash in a relatively short time.

47.3 All depreciation methods and methods used to estimate doubtful debts are the main ones we have encountered so far in this book. However, we've also looked at asset revaluation, another aspect of accounting for which the methods adopted in arriving at the valuation would be considered estimation techniques. Basically, any method used to arrive at an *estimated* figure shown in the financial statements is an estimation technique. So, to answer the question fully, you need to make a list of all those items that appear in financial statements that are estimates. The methods used to arrive at the value used for those figures are all estimation techniques. This would include, for example, the method used in order to arrive at the proportion of an electricity bill spanning the period end that belongs in the period for which the financial statements are being prepared.

REVIEW QUESTIONS

47.1 You are to study the following financial statements for two similar types of retail store and then answer the questions which follow.

Financial Statements

	A		B	
	£	£	£	£
Profit and loss accounts				
Sales		80,000		120,000
Less Cost of goods sold				
Opening stock	25,000		22,500	
Add Purchases	50,000		91,000	
	75,000		113,500	
Less Closing stock	(15,000)	(60,000)	(17,500)	(96,000)
Gross profit		20,000		24,000
Less Depreciation	1,000		3,000	
Other expenses	9,000	(10,000)	6,000	(9,000)
Net profit		10,000		15,000
Balance sheets				
Fixed assets				
Equipment at cost	10,000		20,000	
Less Depreciation to date	(8,000)	2,000	(6,000)	14,000
Current assets				
Stock	15,000		17,500	
Debtors	25,000		20,000	
Bank	5,000		2,500	
	45,000		40,000	
Less Current liabilities				
Creditors	(5,000)	40,000	(10,000)	30,000
		42,000		44,000
Financed by:				
Capitals				
Balance at start of year		38,000		36,000
Add Net profit		10,000		15,000
		48,000		51,000
Less Drawings		(6,000)		(7,000)
		42,000		44,000

Required:
(a) Calculate the following ratios:
  (*i*)   gross profit as percentage of sales;
  (*ii*) net profit as percentage of sales;
  (*iii*) expenses as percentage of sales;
  (*iv*) stock turnover;
  (*v*)   rate of return of net profit on capital employed (use the average of the capital account for this purpose);
  (*vi*) current ratio;
  (*vii*) acid test ratio;
  (*viii*) debtor/sales ratio;
  (*ix*) creditor/purchases ratio.

(b) Drawing upon all your knowledge of accounting, comment upon the differences and similarities of the accounting ratios for A and B. Which business seems to be the most efficient? Give possible reasons.

47.2A   Study the following financial statements of two companies and then answer the questions which follow. Both companies are stores selling textile goods.

	R Ltd		T Ltd	
	£	£	£	£
Profit and loss accounts				
Sales		250,000		160,000
Less Cost of goods sold				
Opening stock	90,000		30,000	
Add Purchases	210,000		120,000	
	300,000		150,000	
Less Closing stock	(110,000)		(50,000)	
		(190,000)		(100,000)
Gross profit		60,000		60,000
Less Expenses				
Wages and salaries	14,000		10,000	
Directors' remuneration	10,000		10,000	
Other expenses	11,000		8,000	
		(35,000)		(28,000)
Net profit		25,000		32,000
Add Balance from last year		15,000		8,000
		40,000		40,000
Less Appropriations				
General reserve	2,000		2,000	
Dividend	25,000		20,000	
		(27,000)		(22,000)
Balance carried forward to next year		13,000		18,000
Balance sheets				
Fixed assets				
Equipment at cost	20,000		5,000	
Less Depreciation to date	(8,000)		(2,000)	
		12,000		3,000
Motor lorries	30,000		20,000	
Less Depreciation to date	(12,000)		(7,000)	
		18,000		13,000
		30,000		16,000
Current assets				
Stock	110,000		50,000	
Debtors	62,500		20,000	
Bank	7,500		10,000	
	180,000		80,000	
Less Current liabilities				
Creditors	(90,000)		(16,000)	
		90,000		64,000
		120,000		80,000
Financed by:				
Issued share capital		100,000		50,000
Reserves				
General reserve	7,000		12,000	
Profit and loss	13,000		18,000	
		20,000		30,000
		120,000		80,000

Required:

(a) Calculate the following ratios for each of *R Ltd* and *T Ltd*:

   (i)   gross profit as percentage of sales;
   (ii) net profit as percentage of sales;
   (iii) expenses as percentage of sales;
   (iv) stock turnover;
   (v)   rate of return of net profit on capital employed
         (for the purpose of this question only, take
         capital as being total of share capitals + reserves
         at the balance sheet date);

   (vi) current ratio;
   (vii) acid test ratio;
   (viii) debtor/sales ratio;
   (ix) creditor/purchases ratio.

(b) Comment briefly on the comparison of each ratio as between the two companies. State which company appears to be the most efficient, giving what you consider to be possible reasons.

47.3   Durham Limited had an authorised capital of £200,000 divided into 100,000 ordinary shares of £1 each and 200,000 8% preference shares of 50p each. The following balances remained in the accounts of the company after the trading and profit and loss accounts had been prepared for the year ended 30 April 20X9.

	Debit £	Credit £
Premises at cost	86,000	
General reserve		4,000
Ordinary shares: fully paid		100,000
8% Preference shares: fully paid		50,000
Electricity		100
Cash at bank	13,100	
Profit and loss account balance 1 May 20X8		14,500
Debtors and creditors	20,000	12,900
Net profit (year ended 30 April 20X9)		16,500
Machinery and plant at cost	60,000	
Provision for depreciation on machinery and plant		40,000
Stock	60,000	
Provision for bad debts		4,000
Insurance	900	
Preference share dividend paid	2,000	
	242,000	242,000

The Directors have recommended:
   a transfer of £5,000 to general reserve;
   an ordinary dividend of £0.15p per share; and
   a provision for the unpaid preference share dividend.

(a) Prepare the profit and loss appropriation account for year ended 30 April 20X9.
(b) Prepare the balance sheet as at 30 April 20X9, in a form which shows clearly the **working capital** and the **shareholders' funds.**
(c) Identify and calculate:
   (i)   one ratio indicating the firm's profitability;
   (ii) two ratios indicating the firm's liquidity position.
(d) Make use of your calculations in (c) above to comment on the firm's financial position.
(e) Name two points of comparison which are not available from the information above in this question but which could make your comments in (d) above more meaningful.

(Edexcel Foundation, London Examinations: GCSE)

47.4   The summarised accounts of Hope (Eternal Springs) Ltd for the years 20X8 and 20X9 are given below.

Trading and Profit and Loss Accounts for the year ended 31 December

	20X8		20X9	
	£000	£000	£000	£000
Sales		200		280
Less Cost of sales		(150)		(210)
Gross profit		50		70
Less				
Administration expenses	38		46	
Debenture interest	–		4	
		(38)		(50)
Net profit		12		20

Balance Sheets as at 31 December

	20X8		20X9	
	£000	£000	£000	£000
Fixed assets at cost less depreciation		110		140
Stock	20		30	
Debtors	25		28	
Bank	–		5	
	45		63	
Creditors	(15)		(12)	
Bank	(10)		–	
		20		51
		130		191
8% Debentures		(–)		(50)
		130		141
Ordinary share capital		100		100
Profit and Loss Account		30		41
		130		141

Stock at 1 January 20X8 was £50,000.

Required:

(a) Calculate the following ratios for 20X8 **and** 20X9:
  (i)   Gross profit: Sales
  (ii) Stock turnover
  (iii) Net profit: Sales
  (iv) Quick ('acid test')
  (v) Working capital
  (vi) Net profit: Capital employed
(b) State the possible reasons for and significance of any changes in the ratios shown by your calculations.

(*Midland Examining Group: GCSE*)

47.5A   The following figures are for AB Engineering Supplies Ltd at 31 December 20X9:

	£000	£000
Turnover		160
Gross profit		40
Average stock at cost price		10
Expenses		8
Fixed assets		108
Current assets		
Stock	10	
Debtors	8	
Bank	2	
		20
		128
Current liabilities		(10)
		118
Capital		118

(a) Calculate:
  (i) gross profit as a percentage of the sales;
  (ii) rate of stock turnover;
  (iii) net profit as a percentage of sales;
  (iv) net profit as a percentage of total capital employed (fixed assets plus current assets);
  (v) current ratio;
  (vi) quick asset (acid test) ratio.

(b) The following figures are for another firm in the same line of business, CD Engineering Services Ltd, for the year ended 31 December 20X9.

	CD Engineering Services Ltd
Gross profit as a percentage of the sales	25%
Rate of stock turnover	9
Net profit as a percentage of sales	10%
Net profit as a percentage of total capital employed	$12\frac{1}{2}$%
Current ratio	1 : 1
Quick asset (acid test) ratio	0.5 : 1

Compare your results in (a) with those given for CD Engineering Services Ltd.
  As a result of your comparison, say which you think was the more successful business during 20X9, giving your reasons.

(*Northern Examinations and Assessment Board: GCSE*)

47.6A Galloway Ltd has an authorised capital of 250,000 ordinary shares of £1 each.

(a) At the end of its financial year, 30 April 20X8, the following balances remained in the company's books after preparation of trading and profit and loss accounts.

	£
Motor vehicles:	
at cost	38,400
provision for depreciation	16,300
Net profit for year	36,600
Freehold premises at cost	190,000
Stock in trade	32,124
Share capital: 200,000 ordinary shares of £1 each, fully paid	200,000
Insurance prepaid	280
Profit and loss account balance brought forward	3,950
Wages and salaries due	774
General reserve	24,000
Trade creditors	3,847
Trade debtors	4,782
8% debentures	15,000
Rent receivable outstanding	175
Bank overdraft	1,830
Furniture and equipment:	
at cost	44,000
provision for depreciation	7,460

The directors have proposed

  (i) the transfer of £5,000 to the general reserve
  (ii) a final dividend on the ordinary shares of 12.5%.

(b) Galloway Ltd's directors are making an assessment of the company's performance for the year. They are concerned by a decline in both profitability and liquidity despite an increase in turnover.

Required:

1 THREE significant differences between ordinary shares and debentures.

2 For Galloway Ltd
 (i) a profit and loss appropriation account for the year ended 30 April 20X8
 (ii) a balance sheet as at 30 April 20X8 in a form which shows clearly:
   total shareholders' funds
   working capital.

3 Concerning the company's performance
 (i) Name ONE ratio which could be used to assess profitability.
 (ii) State TWO possible reasons why the profitability ratio may have declined despite increased turnover.
 (iii) Name ONE ratio, other than working capital ratio, which could be used to assess liquidity.
 (iv) Give FOUR suggestions as to how working capital could be increased during the year ahead.

(*Southern Examining Group: GCSE*)

47.7 The trading stock of Joan Street, retailer, has been reduced during the year ended 31 March 20X8 by £6,000 from its commencing figure of £21,000.

A number of financial ratios and related statistics have been compiled relating to the business of Joan Street for the year ended 31 March 20X8. These are shown below alongside comparative figures for a number of retailers who are members of the trade association to which Joan Street belongs:

	Joan Street	Trade association
	%	%
Net profit as % net capital employed (see Authors' Note)	15	16
$\dfrac{\text{Net profit}}{\text{Sales}}$	9	8
$\dfrac{\text{Sales}}{\text{Net capital employed}}$	$166^2/_3$	200
$\dfrac{\text{Fixed assets}}{\text{Sales}}$	45	35
Working capital ratio: $\dfrac{\text{Current assets}}{\text{Current liabilities}}$	400	$287^1/_2$
Acid test ratio: $\dfrac{\text{Bank + Debtors}}{\text{Current liabilities}}$	275	$187^1/_2$
$\dfrac{\text{Gross profit}}{\text{Sales}}$	25	26
Debtors collection period: $\dfrac{\text{Debtors} \times 365}{\text{Sales}}$	$36^1/_2$ days	$32^{17}/_{20}$ days
Stock turnover (based on average stock for the year)	10 times	8 times

Joan Street has supplied all the capital for her business and has had no drawings from the business during the year ended 31 March 20X8.

Required:

(a) Prepare the trading and profit and loss account for the year ended 31 March 20X8 and balance sheet as at that date of Joan Street in as much detail as possible.

(b) Identify two aspects of Joan Street's results for the year ended 31 March 20X8 which compare favourably with the trade association's figures and identify two aspects which compare unfavourably.

(c) Outline two drawbacks of the type of comparison used in this question.

(*Association of Accounting Technicians*)

Authors' Note: take the closing figure at 31 March 20X8.

47.8A Harold Smart, who is a small manufacturer trading as Space Age Projects, is very pleased with his recently completed financial results which show that a planned 20% increase in turnover has been achieved in the last accounting year.

The summarised results relating to the last three financial years are as follows:

Year ended 30 September			20X7	20X8	20X9
			£	£	£
Sales			90,000	100,000	120,000
Cost of sales			(74,000)	(75,000)	(92,000)
Gross profit			16,000	25,000	28,000
Administrative overheads			(3,000)	(5,000)	(6,000)
Net profit			13,000	20,000	22,000

As at 30 September	20X6	20X7	20X8	20X9
	£	£	£	£
Fixed assets:				
At cost	155,000	165,000	190,000	206,000
Provision for depreciation	(42,000)	(45,000)	(49,000)	(53,000)
	113,000	120,000	141,000	153,000
Current assets:				
Stock	3,000	4,000	7,000	30,000
Debtors	14,000	19,000	15,000	10,000
Balance at bank	2,000	1,000	3,000	–
	19,000	24,000	25,000	40,000
Current liabilities:				
Creditors	5,000	4,000	6,000	9,000
Bank overdraft	–	–	–	2,000
	5,000	4,000	6,000	11,000

Since 30 September 20X6, Harold Smart has not taken any drawings from the business.

Harold Smart has been invited recently to invest £150,000 for a 5-year fixed term in government loan stock earning interest at 12¹/₂% per annum.

Note: Taxation is to be ignored.

Notwithstanding his response to these financial results, Harold Smart is a very cautious person and therefore has asked a financial consultant for a report.

Required:
(a) A schedule of six accounting ratios or measures of resource utilisation covering each of the three years ended 30 September 20X9 of Space Age Projects.
(b) As financial consultant prepare a report to Harold Smart on the financial results of Space Age Projects given above including comments on the alternative future actions that he might take.

Note: Reports should utilise the information given in answers to part (a) of this question.

(Association of Accounting Technicians)

47.9 Business A and Business B are both engaged in retailing, but seem to take a different approach to this trade according to the information available. This information consists of a table of ratios, shown below:

Ratio	Business A	Business B
Current ratio	2 : 1	1.5 : 1
Quick assets (acid test) ratio	1.7 : 1	0.7 : 1
Return on capital employed (ROCE)	20%	17%
Return on shareholders' funds (ROSF)	30%	18%
Debtors turnover	63 days	21 days
Creditors turnover	50 days	45 days
Gross profit percentage	40%	15%
Net profit percentage	10%	10%
Stock turnover	52 days	25 days

Required:

(a) Explain briefly how each ratio is calculated.

(b) Describe what this information indicates about the differences in approach between the two businesses. If one of them prides itself on personal service and one of them on competitive prices, which do you think is which and why?

(*Association of Chartered Certified Accountants*)

47.10A You are given summarised information about two firms in the same line of business, A and B, as follows.

Balance sheets at 30 June	£000	A £000	£000	£000	B £000	£000
Land			80			260
Buildings		120			200	
Less: Depreciation		(40)			–	
			80			200
Plant		90			150	
Less: Depreciation		(70)			(40)	
			20			110
			180			570
Stocks		80			100	
Debtors		100			90	
Bank		–			10	
		180			200	
Creditors	110			120		
Bank	50			–		
		(160)			(120)	
			20			80
			200			650
Capital at start of year			100			300
Add: Profit for year			30			100
			130			400
Less: Drawings			(30)			(40)
			100			360
Land revaluation			–			160
Loan (10% p.a.)			100			130
			200			650
Sales			1,000			3,000
Cost of sales			400			2,000

Required:

(a) Produce a table of eight ratios calculated for both businesses.

(b) Write a report briefly outlining the strengths and weaknesses of the two businesses. Include comment on any major areas where the simple use of the figures could be misleading.

(*Association of Chartered Certified Accountants*)

47.11 The following letter has been received from a client. 'I gave my bank manager those audited accounts you prepared for last year. But he says he needs more information before he will agree to increase my overdraft. What could he possibly want to know that he can't get from those accounts? If they are not good enough why bother to prepare them?'

Required:

Outline the major points which should be included in a reply to this letter.

(*Association of Chartered Certified Accountants*)

47.12 An acquaintance of yours, H Gee, has recently set up in business for the first time as a general dealer.

The majority of his sales will be on credit to trade buyers but he will sell some goods to the public for cash.

He is not sure at which point of the business cycle he can regard his cash and credit sales to have taken place.

After seeking guidance on this matter from his friends, he is thoroughly confused by the conflicting advice he has received. Samples of the advice he has been given include:

The sale takes place when:
(*i*)   'you have bought goods which you know you should be able to sell easily';
(*ii*) 'the customer places the order';
(*iii*) 'you deliver the goods to the customer';
(*iv*) 'you invoice the goods to the customer';
(*v*)   'the customer pays for the goods';
(*vi*) 'the customer's cheque has been cleared by the bank'.

He now asks you to clarify the position for him.

Required:
(*a*) Write notes for Gee, setting out, in as easily understood a manner as possible, the accounting conventions and principles which should generally be followed when recognising sales revenue.
(*b*) Examine each of the statements (*i*) to (*vi*) above and advise Gee (stating your reasons) whether the method advocated is appropriate to the particular circumstances of his business.

(*Association of Chartered Certified Accountants*)

47.13 The annual final accounts of businesses are normally prepared on the assumption that the business is a going concern.

Required:
Explain and give a simple illustration of

(*a*) the effect of this convention on the figures which appear in those final accounts.
(*b*) the implications for the final accounts figures if this convention were deemed to be inoperative.

(*Association of Chartered Certified Accountants*)

47.14 One of the well known accounting concepts is that of materiality.

Required:
(*a*) Explain what is meant by this concept.
(*b*) State and explain three types of situation to which this concept might be applicable.
(*c*) State and explain two specific difficulties in applying this concept.

(*Association of Chartered Certified Accountants*)

47.15 State three classes of people, other than managers and owners, who are likely to need to use financial accounting information. Discuss whether you think their requirements are compatible.

(*Association of Chartered Certified Accountants*)

47.16 A firm produces a standard manufactured product. The stages of the production and sale of the product may be summarised as follows:

Stage	A	B	C	D
Activity	Raw material	WIP-I	WIP-II	Finished product
	£	£	£	£
Costs to date	100	120	150	170
Net realisable value	80	130	190	300

Stage	E	F	G	H
Activity	For sale	Sale agreed	Delivered	Paid for
	£	£	£	£
Costs to date	170	170	180	180
Net realisable value	300	300	300	300

Required:
(a) What general rule do accountants apply when deciding when to recognise revenue on any particular transaction?
(b) Apply this rule to the above situation. State and explain the stage at which you think revenue will be recognised by accountants.
(c) How much would the gross profit on a unit of this product be? Why?
(d) Suggest arguments in favour of delaying the recognition of revenue until stage H.
(e) Suggest arguments in favour of recognising revenue in appropriate successive amounts at stages B, C and D.

(*Association of Chartered Certified Accountants*)

47.17
(a) In accounting practice a distinction is drawn between the terms 'reserves' and 'provisions' and between 'accrued expenses' and 'creditors'.

Required:
Briefly define each of the four terms quoted and explain the effect of each on the preparation of accounts.

(b) While preparing the final accounts for year ended 30 September 20X7, the accountant of Lanep Lighting Ltd had to deal with the following matters:
   (i) the exterior of the company's premises was being repaired. The contractors had started work in August but were unlikely to finish before the end of November 20X7. The total cost would not be known until after completion. Cost of work carried out to 30 September 20X7 was estimated at £21,000;
   (ii) the company rented a sales showroom from Commercial Properties plc at a rental of £6,000 per annum payable half yearly in arrears on 1 August and 1 February;
   (iii) on 3 October 20X7 an invoice was received for £2,500, less a trade discount of 30 per cent, from Lucifer Ltd for goods for resale supplied during September 20X7;
   (iv) the directors of Lanep Lighting Ltd have decided that an annual amount of £5,000 should be set aside, starting with year ended 30 Sept 20X7, for the purpose of plant replacement.

Required:
State the accounting treatment which should be accorded to each of the above matters in the Lanep Lighting Ltd profit and loss account for year ended 30 September 20X7 and balance sheet at that date.

(*Association of Chartered Certified Accountants*)

47.18 Bradwich plc is a medium-sized engineering company whose shares are listed on a major Stock Exchange.

It has recently applied to its bankers for a 7-year loan of £500,000 to finance a modernisation and expansion programme.

Mr Whitehall, a recently retired civil servant, is contemplating investing £10,000 of his lump sum pension in the company's ordinary shares in order to provide both an income during his retirement and a legacy to his grandchildren after his death.

The bank and Mr Whitehall have each acquired copies of the company's most recent annual report and accounts.

Required:
(a) State, separately for each of the two parties, those aspects of the company's performance and financial position which would be of particular interest and relevance to their respective interests.
(b) State, separately for each of the two parties, the formula of four ratios which would assist in measuring or assessing the matters raised in your answer to (a).

(*Association of Chartered Certified Accountants*)

47.19   Explain what you understand by the accounting term 'capital gearing', showing clearly the benefits of, and the potential problems associated with high gearing.

(*Scottish Qualifications Authority*)

47.20A   What benefits can result through the use of ratios and what limitations should be imposed on any conclusions drawn from their use?

PART 8

An introduction to management accounting

Introduction

This part introduces the management accounting side of accounting and looks at how costs can be gathered and utilised in decision-making within an organisation.

CHAPTER 48

An introduction to management accounting

After you have studied this chapter, you should be able to:

- explain why cost accounting is needed for there to be an effective management accounting system
- explain why the benefits of operating a costing system should always outweigh the costs of operating it
- explain what characteristic must exist before anything can be described as information
- explain why different costs are often needed when making decisions about the future compared to those that are used to calculate profit in the past
- explain which costing approach is the relevant one to use when considering a change in what and/or how much is produced
- explain what is meant by marginal cost and why selling prices should always exceed it
- explain why budgets are prepared
- describe the role of management accountants in the budgetary process
- describe the relationship between financial accounting data and management accounting data

Introduction

In this chapter, you'll learn about the importance of data being suitable for the purpose for which it is to be used and of the need for information to be useful. You'll learn how costs are recorded and of two of the most used approaches to costing. You'll also learn about systems of costing and of the importance of budgeting, not just to business but also to the role of the management accountant. Finally, you will learn about how management accounting data often forms the basis of data used in financial accounting.

48.1 Background

So far, you have learnt about bookkeeping and the preparation of financial statements. In accounting, these are the two components of what is known as **financial accounting**. The information that is produced by financial accounting is usually historical, backwards looking and, mainly, for the use of decision-makers external to the organisation to which the data relates. You learnt about the sort of things that are done with this information in Chapter 47.

There is a second side to accounting. This one looks forwards and the output from it is used by decision-makers within the organisation. It also consists of two components: one where costs are recorded and one where the data is processed and converted into reports for managers and other decision-makers. The cost recording component is called **cost account-ing** and the processing and reporting component is called '**management accounting**', which is also the name used to refer to this side of accounting. It is also sometimes referred to as 'managerial accounting'.

48.2 Cost accounting

Cost accounting is needed so that there can be an effective management accounting system. Without a study of costs such a system could not exist. Before entering into any detailed description of costs it is better if we first ask what use we are going to make of information about costs in the business.

This can best be done by referring to something which is not accounting, and then relat-ing it to accounting. Suppose that your employer asked you to 'measure the distance between Manchester and London', but walked away from you without giving any further information. As you thought about the request the following thoughts might go through your head:

1 *HOW* is the distance to be measured? – e.g. by road, rail, plane, or train.
2 The *COSTS* and *BENEFITS* of obtaining the information – how much can you spend finding out the information without making it cost more to find out than will be saved by knowing the information we seek?
3 What is the *PURPOSE* for which the measurement will be used? – e.g. to travel there by car, to walk there, to have goods shipped there by train or by road.

The lesson to be learned from this is that measurement depends entirely on the use that is to be made of the data. Too often businesses make measurements of financial and other data without looking first at the use that is going to be made of it. In fact, it could be said that 'information' is useful data that is provided for someone.

Data given to someone which is not relevant to the purpose required is just not informa-tion. Data which is provided for a particular purpose, and which is completely wrong for the purpose, is worse than having no data at all. At least when there is no data, the manager knows the best that can be done is to guess.

When useless data is collected it has cost money to collect, in itself a waste of money. Secondly, it is often assumed to be useful and so misleads a manager into taking decisions that are completely inappropriate. Third, it clogs up the communication system within a business, so that other data is not acted on properly because of the general confusion that has been caused.

When looking at costs, you need to consider the following:

1 What is the data on costs wanted for?
2 How are the costs to be measured? and
3 That the cost of obtaining costing data should not exceed the benefits to be gained from having it.

When it is known what the costs are for, and how much is to be spent on studying them, the appropriate method for measuring them can be decided.

48.3 Costs

There are many classifications of cost. Let's briefly summarise those that you already know about.

Historical costs

These are the foundation of financial accounting. Exhibit 48.1 shows costs flowing through the financial accounting system.

Exhibit 48.1

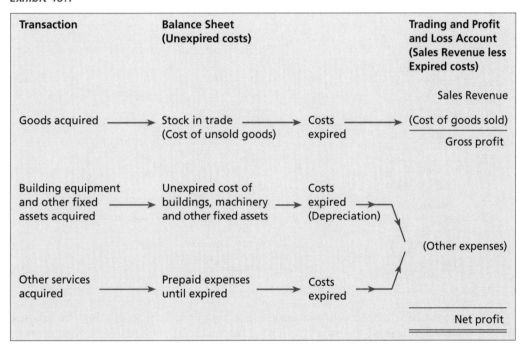

Product costs

These are the costs attributed to the units of goods manufactured. They are charged up to the cost of goods manufactured in the trading account, and would normally be part of the valuation of unsold goods if the goods to which they refer had not been sold by the end of the period. Product costs are therefore matched up against revenue as and when the goods are sold and not before.

Period costs

Period costs are those of a non-manufacturing nature and represent the selling and distribution, administration and financial expenses. They are treated as expenses of the period in which they were incurred irrespective of the volume of goods sold.

Combining all this, you arrive at the manufacturing accounts you covered in Chapter 37. Exhibit 48.2 shows the flow of costs through to finished products.

Exhibit 48.2

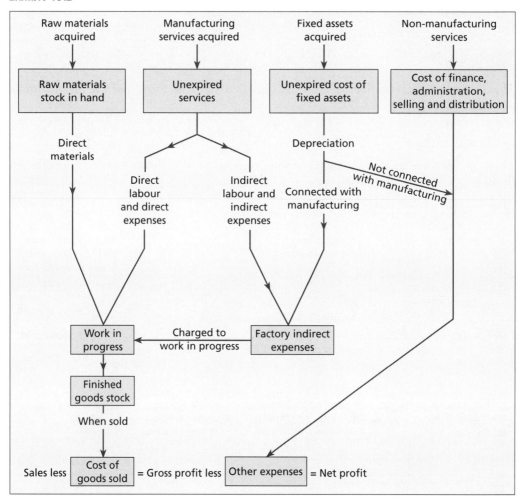

This, therefore, is what you use costs information for in financial accounting – to produce the information you need in order to prepare the financial statements. In management accounting, there is a different emphasis, some of which overlaps with the needs of financial accounting but some of which is for something quite different.

For example, most businesses want to know how much each item has cost to make. This means that the total costs for the whole business are not sufficient, and so these costs must be analysed further. They also want to know what costs are likely to be in the future. Again, more analysis is needed. Cost accounting is the process of measuring and recording all these costs.

Many advantages are gained by having a cost accounting system that provides this detail of cost information. When armed with the cost information that management accounting techniques can provide, managers and other internal decision-makers are far more able to make sensible decisions about what should be done to aid the progress of the business towards its objectives.

For example, imagine trying to decide which item to stop producing out of twelve items made by a business if you have little information as to the amount each item contributes towards the profitability of the business. Very often the solution will be that a new layout in the factory is needed; special training given to certain employees; changes made in the system of remunerating employees; and so on. The information provided by accounting is, therefore, only one part of the whole story for any problem requiring a decision to be made. Sometimes *it will be the least important information* available, as far as the decision-maker is concerned.

48.4 Cost control

One of the most important features of cost accounting is its use for control purposes, meaning, in this context, the control of expenditure. But control of expenditure is possible only if you can trace the costs down to employees who are responsible for such costs. A convenient and frequently adopted approach to collecting costs is through **cost centres** – production or service locations, functions, activities, or items of equipment. Costs are collected from cost centres for individual **cost units** – units of product or service. For example, in a manufacturing business, all direct materials, direct labour and direct expenses are traced to cost centres. (In this case, they may be known as 'product centres'.)

A cost centre may be a single machine used for jobbing work, i.e. quite a lot of separate jobs performed specially to conform with the customer's specifications. It could, however, be a group of similar machines or a production department. Thus, if a business makes metal boxes on one machine, all the costs incurred directly relating to that machine (cost centre) would be gathered and then shared (allocated) among all the metal boxes (cost units) made by that machine.

By comparison, factory indirect expenses are 'indirect' and so cannot be traced (or it is not worthwhile tracing them) to product centres. Instead, these are traced to cost centres which give service rather than being concerned with work directly on the products. Such cost centres are, therefore, known as 'service centres'. Examples of service centres would be the factory canteen or the maintenance department. The costs from these service centres will then need allocating to the product centres in a logical fashion – for example, canteen costs may be allocated to product cost centres according to the number of employees working at each of them.

In practice, there are a number of possible ways of allocating costs to cost centres. What must not be lost sight of is the endeavour to trace costs to a person responsible for the expenditure so that the costs can be controlled.

48.5 Costing approaches

There are a number of ways costs can be gathered and collated. The two most commonly used are **absorption costing** and **marginal costing**.

Absorption costing

This involves allocating all direct costs and factory indirect expenses to products. The factory indirect expenses are seen as adding to the value of work in progress and, therefore, to finished goods. The production cost of any article is thus comprised of direct materials, direct labour, any direct expenses and a share of factory indirect expense.

After the financial year end, it is possible to look back and calculate exactly what the factory indirect expenses were. This means that this figure is used when calculating the valuation of the closing stock. For a business which had produced 1,000 units, of which 200 units have not yet been sold, with a total production cost of £100,000, the closing stock valuation becomes:

$$\frac{\text{Unsold units}}{\text{Total units produced}} \times \text{Production cost of goods completed} = \frac{200}{1,000} \times £100,000$$

= £20,000 closing stock valuation

Cost data is, however, used for purposes other than that of valuing stock. The question is, therefore, often asked as to whether or not this method is suitable for all costing purposes. The short answer is that it is not. A fuller consideration of this question is beyond the scope of this book and is covered in *Business Accounting 2*.

Marginal costing

Where costing is used which takes account of only the variable cost of products rather than the full production cost, this is known as **marginal costing**. By ignoring the fixed costs, it is possible to see how much something contributes towards the profitability of a business. So, for example, if an order was received to buy 100 tables from a business for £65 each and the absorption cost of a table was £70, the order would be rejected but, if marginal costing was used and the marginal cost was £60, the order might be accepted as every table sold contributed £5 towards the overall profitability of the business. Whether it is or not will depend upon whether there is any spare production capacity.

When using marginal costing for decisions like this, care needs to be taken that over all the decisions taken, sufficient additional income is generated to pay for all the fixed costs that are ignored by marginal costing.

48.6 Costing systems

Having decided which costing approach to adopt, you then need to decide which costing system to adopt. The one you choose will depend upon how your products or services are produced. There are two main types of costing system, **job costing** and **process costing**.

Job costing

This is used when production consists of separate jobs. For instance, where a Rolls-Royce is made to each customer's specifications, each car can be regarded as a separate job. When a job is long-term, the term 'project costing' is often used.

Job costing also applies where batches of items are made. For example, a jam bottling company may make jam in batches of 10,000 bottles and then switch over to making a different type of jam for the next batch. A printer may print a batch of 2,000 copies of a book. The 'job' can thus be one item or a batch of similar items. When a batch is involved, it is usually referred to as 'batch costing'.

Process costing

Process costing is used where production is regarded as a continuous flow. It is applicable to industries such as oil, paint manufacturing, steel, textiles, and food processing, where production is repetitive and continuous. For example, an oil refinery where crude oil is processed continually, emerging as different grades of petrol, paraffin, motor oil, etc. would use process costing, as would a salt works where sea water is pumped into the works, and the resulting product is slabs or packets of salt. Another example would be a car manufacturer that produced one model of car for an extended period.

Overall

Job costing treats production as a number of separate jobs being performed, each of which needs to have costs allocated to it. Process costing, on the other hand, sees production as a continuous flow and no attempt is made to allocate costs to specific units being produced because the same thing is being produced continuously. As a result, costs per unit produced can always be calculated by dividing the costs for the period by the number of units produced.

Activity 48.2

For which of the following would you use job costing and for which would you use process costing? Split the job costing ones between job, batch, and project costing.

Newspaper printing
School meals
A film in a cinema
Making a film
Manufacturing computer memory chips
A play in a theatre
Egg production
Building a space satellite

48.7 | Budgeting and budgetary control

Management accounting is concerned with providing information for planning and control so that organisations can achieve their objectives. One of the central supporting devices of both of these aims is budgeting.

When a plan is expressed quantitatively it is known as a **budget** and the process of converting plans into budgets is known as **budgeting**.

The budgeting process may be quite formal in a large organisation with committees set up to perform the task. On the other hand in a very small business the owner may jot down the budget on a piece of scrap paper or even on the back of a used envelope. Some even manage without writing anything down at all – they have done the budgets in their heads and can easily remember them.

The methodology of budgetary control is probably accountancy's major contribution to management. Budgets are drawn up by management and recorded by management accountants. Actual results are compared against the budgets by the management accountants who pass reports to management concerning the extent to which budgets are being met. This enables managers to control activities and to step in and stop situations where the budget is being ignored or overlooked.

When budgets are being drawn up, two main objectives must be uppermost in the minds of management and management accountants – that budgets are for planning and for control. Management accountants must, therefore, operate a system of budgeting that enables these two aims to be achieved. They do so mainly through a system called variance analysis, which compares actual data to budgeted data and endeavours to identify what has given rise to any differences that are found. For example, if the gross profit on an item is lower than was budgeted, this could be because costs have risen or because the selling price has fallen. The management accountant uses special formulae to pinpoint the cause and passes the information to management so that they can exercise control if required.

48.8 Other aspects of management accounting

Management accounting is, therefore, all about gathering costs appropriately so that businesses can take appropriate decisions relating to manufacturing and selling their goods and services. Management accountants are primarily involved in establishing the costs incurred in producing the output of a business and in maintaining a budgeting system that provides managers with the capability to plan and control activity and so meet the objectives of the organisation.

Apart from the activities mentioned already in this chapter, management accountants are also involved in preparing any information of a financial nature that managers and other decision-makers require and which is not considered part of the role of the financial accountant. This can range from identifying the cost of a component part to the expected returns on a twenty-year project to build a chain of hotels. Their work can be very much more varied than that of a financial accountant, and they are not tied by any rules and regulations concerning either how they perform calculations or how they present information.

However, as much of the cost information they produce is also used in the financial accounting system, they do need to ensure that their cost data are capable of being used in that medium. As it is easier to simply have one set of costs for an entire business, rather than one calculated for the management accountants and one calculated for the financial accountants, most management accountants follow the rules relating to cost determination that financial accountants are obliged to follow.

This chapter has been very much an introduction to management accounting. The topic is covered in detail in *Business Accounting 2*.

Learning outcomes

You should now have learnt that:

1 Cost accounting is needed for there to be an effective management accounting system.

2 The benefits of operating a costing system should always outweigh the costs of operating it.

3 Information is data prepared for a purpose. To qualify as 'information', the 'information' must be useful.

4 Different costs will often be needed when making decisions about the future than were used when calculating profit in the past.

5 Marginal cost, not absorption cost, is the relevant cost when considering a change in what and/or how much is produced.

6 Selling prices should exceed marginal costs. (Almost the only exception to this would be where a product was being promoted as a 'loss leader'.)

7 In the long term, the total of all the differences between revenue and marginal cost must exceed the fixed costs of the business.

8 Budgets are prepared in order to guide the business towards its objectives.

9 Budgets should be drawn up within the context of *planning* and *control*.

Answers to activities

48.1 It is used for ratio analysis, particularly for trend analysis and benchmarking against appropriate comparators such as the previous year's figures or the equivalent figures relating to competitors.

48.2   *Job costing*
Newspaper printing (batch)
School meals (batch)
A film in a cinema (job)
Making a film (project)
A play in a theatre (job)
Building a space satellite (project)

Process costing
Egg production
Manufacturing computer memory chips

REVIEW QUESTIONS

48.1   What makes information useful?

48.2   What is the difference between absorption costing and marginal costing?

48.3   What is the difference between job costing, batch costing, project costing, and process costing?

48.4   What are the two main objectives of budgeting?

48.5   What role do management accountants play in the budgetary process?

Answers to review questions

Note: All the answers are the work of the author. None has been supplied by an examining body. The examining bodies accept no responsibility whatsoever for the accuracy or method of working in the answers given.

Note: In order to save space, in most cases brackets have not been entered to indicate negative numbers.

Also, £ signs have been omitted from columns of figures, except where the figures refer to £000, or where the denomination needs to be specified.

1.1

(a) 10,700	(b) 23,100	(c) 4,300	(d) 3,150
(e) 25,500	(f) 51,400		

1.3

(a) Asset	(b) Liability	(c) Asset
(d) Asset	(e) Liability	(f) Asset

1.5

Wrong: Assets: Loan from C Smith, Creditors; Liabilities: Stock of goods, Debtors.

1.7

Assets: Motor 2,000; Premises 5,000; Stock 1,000; Bank 700; Cash 100 = total 8,800.
Liabilities: Loan from Bevan 3,000; Creditors 400 = total 3,400.
Capital: 8,800 − 3,400 = 5,400.

1.9

A Foster
Balance Sheet as at 31 December 20X8

Fixed assets		
Fixtures	5,500	
Motor vehicles	5,700	11,200
Current assets		
Stock of goods	8,800	
Debtors	4,950	
Cash at bank	1,250	
	15,000	
Less Current liabilities		
Creditors	2,450	12,550
		23,750
Capital		23,750

1.11

	Assets	Liabilities	Capital
(a)	− Cash	− Creditors	
(b)	− Bank		
	+ Fixtures		
(c)	+ Stock	+ Creditors	
(d)	+ Cash		
(e)	+ Cash	+ Loan from J Walker	
(f)	+ Bank		
	− Debtors		
(g)	− Stock	− Creditors	
(h)	+ Premises		
	− Bank		

1.13

C Sangster
Balance Sheet as at 7 May 20X8

Fixed assets		
Fixtures	4,500	
Motor vehicle	4,200	8,700
Current assets		
Stock	5,720	
Debtors	3,000	
Bank	5,450	
Cash	400	
	14,570	
Less Current liabilities		
Creditors	2,370	12,200
		20,900
Capital		20,900

Appendix 1 • Answers to review questions

2.1

	Debited	Credited
(a)	Office machinery	D Isaacs Ltd
(b)	C Jones	Capital
(c)	Cash	N Fox
(d)	Loan: P Exeter	Bank
(e)	D Isaacs Ltd	Office machinery
(f)	Bank	N Lyn
(g)	Van	Cash

2.3

Bank
(1) Capital 2,500 | (2) Office furn. 150
| (5) Van 600
| (15) Planers 750
| (31) Machinery 280

Capital
| (1) Bank 2,500

Office furniture
(2) Bank 150 | (8) J Walker 60

Machinery
(3) Planers Ltd 750
(31) Bank 280

Cash
60 | (23) J Walker
(8) Off. furn. 60 |

Planers Ltd
(15) Bank 750 | (3) Machinery 750

Van
(5) Bank 600

J Walker & Sons
(8) Off. furn. 60 | (23) Cash 60

2.4

Cash
(1) Capital 2,000 | (2) Bank 1,800
(28) Bank 100 | (25) W Machinery 75

Bank
(2) Cash 1,800 | (8) Van 950
(30) J Smith 500 | (26) Betta-Built 500
| (28) Cash 100

Betta-Built Ltd
(18) Office furn. 62 | (5) Office furn. 120
(26) Bank 58 |

Capital
| (1) Cash 2,000

Office Furniture
(5) Betta-Built 120 | (18) Betta-Built 62

Van
(8) Bank 950

Works Machinery
(12) Evans & Sons 560
(25) Cash 75

Evans & Sons
| (12) Works machinery 560

J Smith (Loan)
| (30) Bank 500

3.1

	Debited	Credited
(a)	Purchases	J Reid
(b)	B Perkins	Sales
(c)	Van	H Thomas
(d)	Bank	Sales
(e)	Cash	Sales
(f)	H Hardy	Returns Outwards
(g)	Cash	Machinery
(h)	Returns Inwards	J Nelson
(i)	Purchases	D Simpson
(j)	H Forbes	Returns Outwards

3.3

Cash
(1) Capital 500 | (3) Purchases 85
(10) Sales 42 | (25) E Morgan 88
(31) A Knight 55 |

Purchases
(3) Cash 85
(7) E Morgan 116
(18) A Moses 98

Sales
| (10) Cash 42
| (24) A Knight 55

Returns Outwards
| (14) E Morgan 28
| (21) A Moses 19

A Knight
(24) Sales 55 | (31) Cash 55

E Morgan
(14) Returns 28 | (7) Purchases 116
(25) Cash 88 |

A Moses
(21) Returns 19 | (18) Purchases 98

Capital
| (1) Cash 500

3.5

Bank
(1) Capital 10,000 | (25) F Jones 1,070
(6) Cash 250 | (29) Manchester M 2,600

Cash
(2) T Cooper (Loan) 400 | (6) Bank 250
(4) Sales 200 | (20) Purchases 220
(24) Sales 70 | (31) Office Furn 100
(28) Capital 500 |

Sales
| (4) Cash 200
| (8) C Moody 180
| (10) J Newman 220
| (14) H Morgan 190
| (14) J Peat 320
| (24) Cash 70

Purchases
(3) F Jones 840
(3) S Charles 3,600
(11) F Jones 370
(20) Cash 220

Returns Inwards
(12) C Moody 40
(26) H Morgan 30

Returns Outwards
| (15) F Jones 140
| (19) S Charles 110

Van
(17) Manchester Motors 2,600

Manchester Motors
(29) Bank 2,600 | (17) Van 2,600

Office Furniture
(18) Faster S 600 | (27) Faster S 160
(31) Cash 100 |

Faster Supplies Ltd
(27) Office furn. 160 | (18) Office furn. 600

Capital
| (1) Bank 10,000
| (28) Cash 500

J Newman
(10) Sales 220

H Morgan
(26) Returns 30 | (14) Sales 190

C Moody
(12) Returns 40 | (8) Sales 180

F Jones
(15) Returns 140 | (3) Purchases 840
(25) Bank 1,070 | (11) Purchases 370

S Charles
(19) Returns 110 | (3) Purchases 3,600

J Peat
(14) Sales 320

T Cooper (Loan)
| (2) Cash 400

4.1

Bank

Debit	Credit
(1) Capital 2,000	(3) Fixtures 150
(21) Rent received 5	(24) Van 300

Cash

Debit	Credit
(5) Sales 275	(10) Rent 15
	(12) Stationery 27
	(30) Wages 117
	(31) Drawings 44

Purchases

Debit	Credit
(2) M Mills 175	
(6) S Waites 114	

Sales

Debit	Credit
	(5) Cash 275
	(23) U Henry 77

Fixtures

Debit	Credit
(3) Bank 150	

Rent

Debit	Credit
(10) Cash 15	

Capital

Debit	Credit
	(1) Bank 2,000

M Mills

Debit	Credit
(18) Returns out 23	(2) Purchases 175

S Waites

Debit	Credit
	(6) Purchases 114

U Henry

Debit	Credit
	(23) Sales 77

Rent Received

Debit	Credit
	(21) Bank 5

Stationery

Debit	Credit
(12) Cash 27	

Returns Out

Debit	Credit
	(18) M Mills 23

Van

Debit	Credit
(24) Bank 300	

Wages

Debit	Credit
(30) Cash 117	

Drawings

Debit	Credit
(31) Cash 44	

4.2

Cash

Debit	Credit
(1) Capital 1,500	(3) Rent 28
(11) Sales 49	(4) Bank 1,000
	(20) B Repairs 18
	(28) Purchases 125
	(30) Motor exps 15

Bank

Debit	Credit
(4) Cash 1,000	(7) Stationery 15
	(27) A Hanson 279
	(29) Van 395

Purchases

Debit	Credit
(2) A Hanson 296	
(28) Cash 125	

Sales

Debit	Credit
	(5) E Linton 54
	(11) Cash 49
	(17) S Morgan 29

Stationery

Debit	Credit
(7) Bank 15	

Returns Outwards

Debit	Credit
	(14) A Hanson 17

Fixtures

Debit	Credit
(31) A Webster 120	

Capital

Debit	Credit
	(1) Cash 1,500

Rent

Debit	Credit
(3) Cash 28	

Building Repairs

Debit	Credit
(20) Cash 18	

Motor Expenses

Debit	Credit
(30) Cash 15	

Van

Debit	Credit
(29) Bank 395	

A Hanson

Debit	Credit
(14) Returns out 17	(2) Purchases 296
(27) Bank 279	

E Linton

Debit	Credit
(5) Sales 54	(22) Returns in 14

S Morgan

Debit	Credit
(17) Sales 29	

Returns Inwards

Debit	Credit
(22) E Linton 14	

A Webster

Debit	Credit
	(31) Fixtures 120

4.5

(A) Bought motor vehicle £5,000, paying by bank.
(B) Paid off £4,000 creditors in cash.
(C) Lee lent us £150,000, this being paid into the bank.
(D) Bought land and buildings £125,000, paying by bank.
(E) Debtors paid cheques £80,000, being paid into bank.
(F) Land and buildings sold for £300,000, the proceeds being paid into the bank.
(G) Loan from Lee repaid out of the bank.
(H) Creditors £8,000 paid in cash.
(I) Stock costing £17,000 sold for £12,000 on credit. Loss of £5,000 shown deducted from Capital.

5.1

H Harvey

Debit	Credit
(1) Sales 690	(10) Returns 40
(4) Sales 66	(24) Cash 300
	(31) Balance c/d 416
756	756
(1) Balance b/d 416	

L Masters

Debit	Credit
(4) Sales 418	(31) Balance c/d 621
(31) Sales 203	
621	621
(1) Balance b/d 621	

N Morgan

Debit	Credit
(18) Bank 153	(1) Sales 153

J Lindo

Debit	Credit
(10) Returns 20	(1) Sales 420
(20) Bank 400	
420	420

5.2

J Young

Debit	Credit
(10) Returns 55	(1) Purchases 458
(28) Cash 250	(15) Purchases 80
(30) Balance c/d 233	
538	538
	(1) Balance b/d 233

L Williams

Debit	Credit
(30) Returns 17	(1) Purchases 120
(30) Balance c/d 180	(3) Purchases 77
197	197
	(1) Balance b/d 180

G Norman

Debit	Credit
(10) Returns 22	(1) Purchases 708
(30) Balance c/d 686	
708	708
	(1) Balance b/d 686

T Harris

Debit	Credit
(19) Bank 880	(3) Purchases 880

5.3

H Harvey

20X6		Dr	Cr	Balance
May 1	Sales	690		690 Dr
May 4	Sales	66		756 Dr
May 10	Returns		40	716 Dr
May 24	Cash		300	416 Dr

N Morgan

20X6		Dr	Cr	Balance
May 1	Sales	153		153 Dr
May 18	Bank		153	0

J Lindo

20X6		Dr	Cr	Balance
May 1	Sales	420		420 Dr
May 10	Returns		20	400 Dr
May 20	Bank		400	0

L Masters

20X6		Dr	Cr	Balance
May 4	Sales	418		418 Dr
May 31	Sales	203		621 Dr

5.4

J Young

20X8		Dr	Cr	Balance
Jun 1	Purchases		458	458 Cr
Jun 10	Returns	55		403 Cr
Jun 15	Purchases		80	483 Cr
Jun 28	Cash	250		233 Cr

L Williams

20X8		Dr	Cr	Balance
Jun 1	Purchases		120	120 Cr
Jun 3	Purchases		77	197 Cr
Jun 30	Returns	17		180 Cr

G Norman

20X8		Dr	Cr	Balance
Jun 1	Purchases		708	708 Cr
Jun 10	Returns	22		686 Cr

T Harris

20X8		Dr	Cr	Balance
Jun 3	Purchases		880	880 Cr
Jun 19	Bank	880		0

5.5

D Williams

(1)	Sales	458	(24)	Bank	300
			(28)	Cash	100
			(30)	Balance c/d	58
		458			458
(1)	Balance b/d	58			

J Moore

(1)	Sales	235	(12)	Returns	26
(8)	Sales	444	(20)	Balance c/d	653
		679			679
(1)	Balance b/d	653			

G Grant

(1)	Sales	98	(12)	Returns	9
			(30)	Balance c/d	89
		98			98
(1)	Balance b/d	89			

F Franklin

(8)	Sales	249	(30)	Bank	249

A White

(20)	Bank	77	(2)	Purchases	77

H Samuels

(17)	Returns	24	(2)	Purchases	231
(30)	Balance c/d	219	(10)	Purchases	12
		243			243
			(1)	Balance b/d	219

P Owen

			(2)	Purchases	65

O Oliver

(17)	Returns	12	(2)	Purchases	222
(26)	Cash	210			
		222			222

6.1

Cash

(1)	Capital	250	(6)	Rent	12
			(15)	Carriage	23
			(31)	Balance c/d	215
		250			250

Bank

(9)	C Bailey	43	(12)	K Gibson	25
(10)	H Spencer	150	(12)	D Ellis	54
			(31)	Rent	18
			(31)	Balance c/d	96
		193			193

Capital

			(1)	Cash	250

Rent

(6)	Cash	12			
(31)	Bank	18			

Purchases

(2)	D Ellis	54
(2)	C Mendez	87
(2)	K Gibson	25
(2)	D Booth	76
(2)	L Lowe	64
(18)	C Mendez	43
(18)	D Booth	110

Sales

			(4)	C Bailey	43
			(4)	B Hughes	62
			(4)	H Spencer	176
			(21)	B Hughes	67

B Hughes

(4)	Sales	62
(21)	Sales	67

H Spencer

(4)	Sales	176	(10)	Bank	150

6.1 (cont'd)

Carriage
(15) Cash	23	

D Ellis
(15) Cash	54	(2) Purchases		

C Mendez
(12) Bank	87	(2) Purchases	25	
		(18) Purchases		

K Gibson
(12) Bank	43	Rent	30	
		Carriage	23	

D Booth
(12) Bank	25	(2) Purchases	76	

L Lowe
(2) Purchases	76	(2) Purchases	110	
(18) Purchases				

C Bailey
(4) Sales	64	(2) Purchases		
(9) Bank	43			

Trial Balance as at 31 May 20X6

	Dr	Cr
Cash	215	
Bank	96	
Capital		250
Rent	30	
Carriage	23	
C Mendez		130
D Booth		186
L Lowe		64
B Hughes	129	
H Spencer	26	
Purchases	459	
Sales		348
	978	978

6.2

Sales
		(5) Cash	87	
		(7) H Elliott	35	
		(7) L Lane	42	
		(7) J Carlton	72	
		(13) L Lane	32	
		(13) J Carlton	23	

Purchases
(2) K Henriques	76		
(2) M Hyatt	27		
(2) T Braham	56		
(9) Cash	46		
(10) M Hyatt	57		
(10) T Braham	98		

Returns Outwards
		(18) T Braham	20	
		(27) K Henriques	24	

Bank
(1) Capital	800	(17) M Hyatt	84	
(24) J Carlton	95	(21) Betta Ltd	50	
		(31) Van	400	
		(31) Balance c/d	361	
	895		895	

Cash
(5) Sales	87	(6) Wages	14	
(30) J King (Loan)	60	(9) Purchases	46	
		(12) Wages	14	
		(31) Balance c/d	73	
	147		147	

Capital
		(1) Bank	800

Van
(31) Bank	400	

Wages
(6) Cash	14	
(12) Cash	14	

Shop Fixtures
(15) Betta Ltd	50	

J King (Loan)
		(30) Cash	60

Trial Balance as at 31 March 20X6

Bank	361	
Cash	73	
Capital		800
Van	400	
Wages	28	
Shop fixtures	50	
J King (Loan)		60
H Elliott	35	
L Lane	74	
K Henriques		52
T Braham		134
Sales		291
Purchases	360	
Returns outwards		44
	1,381	1,381

H Elliott
(7) Sales	35	

L Lane
(7) Sales	42	
(13) Sales	32	

J Carlton
(7) Sales	72	(24) Bank	95	
(13) Sales	23			

K Henriques
(27) Returns	24	(2) Purchases	76	

M Hyatt
(17) Bank	84	(2) Purchases	27	
		(10) Purchases	57	

T Braham
(18) Returns	20	(2) Purchases	56	
		(10) Purchases	98	

Betta Ltd
(21) Bank	50	(15) S. Fixtures	50	

B Webb

7.1   Trading and Profit and Loss Account for the year ended 31 December 20X6

Sales		18,462
Less Cost of goods sold:		
Purchases	14,629	
Less Closing stock	2,548	
		12,081
Gross profit		6,381
Less Expenses:		
Salaries	2,150	
Motor expenses	520	
Rent and rates	670	
Insurance	111	
General expenses	105	
		3,556
Net profit		2,825

7.2

C Worth

Trading and Profit and Loss Account for the year ended 30 June 20X8

Sales		28,794
Less Cost of goods sold:		
Purchases	23,803	
Less Closing stock	4,166	
		19,637
Gross profit c/d		9,157
Less Expenses:		
Salaries and wages	3,164	
Rent	854	
Lighting and heating	422	
Insurance	105	
Motor expenses	1,133	
Sundry expenses	506	
		6,184
Net profit		2,973

8.1

B Webb

Balance Sheet as at 31 December 20X6

Fixed assets		
Premises		1,500
Motors		1,200
		2,700
Current assets		
Stock	2,548	
Debtors	1,950	
Bank	1,654	
Cash	40	
	6,192	
Less Current liabilities		
Creditors	1,538	
		4,654
		7,354
Capital		
Balance at 1.1.20X6		5,424
Add Net profit		2,825
		8,249
Less Drawings		895
		7,354

8.2

C Worth

Balance Sheet as at 30 June 20X8

Fixed assets		
Buildings		50,000
Fixtures		1,000
Motors		5,500
		56,500
Current assets		
Stock	4,166	
Debtors	3,166	
Bank	3,847	
	11,179	
Less Current liabilities		
Creditors	1,206	
		9,973
		66,473
Capital		
Balance at 1.7.20X7		65,900
Add Net profit		2,973
		68,873
Less Drawings		2,400
		66,473

9.1

T Clarke

Trading Account for the year ended 31 December 20X7

Sales		38,742
Less Returns in		890
		37,852
Less Cost of goods sold:		
Purchases	33,333	
Less Returns out	495	
	32,838	
Carriage inwards	670	
	33,508	
Less Closing stock	7,489	
		26,019
Gross profit		11,833

9.3

R Graham

Trading and Profit and Loss Account for the year ended 30 September 20X9

Sales			18,600
Less Returns in			205
			18,395
Less Cost of goods sold:			
Opening stock			2,368
Add Purchases	11,874		
Less Returns out	322		
		11,552	
Carriage inwards		310	
		14,230	
Less Closing stock		2,946	
			11,284
Gross profit			7,111
Less Expenses:			
Salaries and wages		3,862	
Rent and rates		304	
Carriage out		200	
Insurance		78	
Motor expenses		664	
Office expenses		216	
Lighting and heating		166	
General expenses		314	
			5,804
Net profit			1,307

Balance Sheet as at 30 September 20X9

Fixed assets			
Premises			5,000
Fixtures			350
Motor vehicles			1,800
			7,150
Current assets			
Stock		2,946	
Debtors		3,896	
Bank		482	
		7,324	
Less Current liabilities			
Creditors		1,731	
			5,593
			12,743
Capital			
Balance at 1.10.20X8			12,636
Add Net profit			1,307
			13,943
Less Drawings			1,200
			12,743

9.4

B Jackson

Trading and Profit and Loss Account for the year ended 30 April 20X7

Sales			18,600
Less Returns in			440
			18,160
Less Cost of goods sold:			
Opening stock			3,776
Add Purchases		11,556	
Less Returns out		355	
		11,201	
Carriage inwards		234	
		15,211	
Less Closing stock		4,998	
			10,213
Gross profit			7,947
Less Expenses:			
Salaries and wages		2,447	
Motor expenses		664	
Rent		576	
Carriage out		326	
Sundry expenses		1,202	
			5,215
Net profit			2,732

Balance Sheet as at 30 April 20X7

Fixed assets			
Fixtures			600
Motors			2,400
			3,000
Current assets			
Stock		4,998	
Debtors		4,577	
Bank		3,876	
Cash		120	
		13,571	
Less Current liabilities			
Creditors		3,045	
			10,526
			13,526
Capital			
Balance as at 1.5.20X6			12,844
Add Net profit			2,732
			15,576
Less Drawings			2,050
			13,526

10.1
See text.

10.2
See text.

10.3
See text.

13.1

Cash Book

	Cash	Bank		Cash	Bank
(1) Capital	100		(2) Rent	10	
(3) F Lake (Loan)		500	(4) B McKenzie		65
(5) Sales	98		(9) B Burton	22	
(7) N Miller		62	(16) Bank C	50	
(11) Sales		53	(19) F Lake (Loan)		100
(15) G Moores	65		(26) Motor expenses		12
(16) Cash C		50	(30) Cash C		100
(22) Sales		66	(31) Wages	97	
(30) Bank C	100		(31) Balances c/d	184	454
	363	731		363	731

13.3

Cash Book

	Disct	Cash	Bank		Disct	Cash	Bank
(1) Balance b/d		230	4,756	(4) Rent			120
(2) R Burton	7		133	(8) N Black	9		351
(2) E Taylor	11		209	(8) P Towers	12		468
(2) R Harris	15		285	(8) C Rowse	20		780
(6) J Cotton: loan			1,000	(10) Motor expenses		44	
(12) H Hankins	3		74	(15) Wages		160	
(18) C Winston	13		247	(21) Cash			350
(18) R Wilson & Son	17		323	(24) Drawings		120	
(18) H Winter	23		437	(25) T Briers	7	133	
(21) Bank		350		(29) Fixtures			650
(31) Commission			88	(31) Balances c/d		123	4,833
	89	580	7,552		48	580	7,552

Discounts Received

(31) Total for month   48

Discounts Allowed

89

(31) Total for month

14.1

Sales Day Book

(1) J Gordon		187
(3) G Abrahams		166
(6) V White		12
(10) J Gordon		55
(17) F Williams		289
(19) U Richards		66
(27) V Wood		28
(31) L Simes		78
(31) Total for month		881

Sales Ledger

J Gordon	(1) Sales	187
	(10) Sales	55
G Abrahams	(3) Sales	166
V White	(6) Sales	12
F Williams	(17) Sales	289
U Richards	(19) Sales	66
V Wood	(27) Sales	28
L Simes	(31) Sales	78

General Ledger

Sales Account

(31) Total for month   881

14.3

Sales Day Book

(1) F Gray		60
(4) A Gray		120
(8) E Hines		20
(20) M Allen		180
(31) B Cooper		160
(31) Total for month		540

Workings of invoices:

(1) F Gray	3 rolls white tape × 10 =	30	
	5 sheets blue cotton × 6 =	30	
	1 dress length × 20 =	20	80
	Less trade discount 25%		20
			60
(4) A Gray	6 rolls white tape × 10 =	60	
	30 metres green felt × 4 =	120	180
	Less trade discount 33$\frac{1}{3}$%		60
			120
(8) E Hines	1 dress length black silk × 20 =		20
(20) M Allen	10 rolls white tape × 10 =	100	
	6 sheets blue cotton × 6 =	36	
	3 dress lengths black silk × 20 =	60	
	11 metres green felt × 4 =	44	240
	Less trade discount 25%		60
			180
(31) B Cooper	12 rolls white tape × 10 =	120	
	14 sheets blue cotton × 6 =	84	
	9 metres green felt × 4 =	36	240
	Less trade discount 33$\frac{1}{3}$%		80
			160

Sales Ledger

F Gray	(1) Sales	60
A Gray	(4) Sales	120
E Hines	(8) Sales	20
M Allen	(20) Sales	180
B Cooper	(31) Sales	160

General Ledger

Sales Account

(31) Total for month   540

15.1

Workings of purchases invoices

(1) K King
4 radios × 30 = 120
3 music centres × 160 = 480
600
Less trade discount 25% 150
450

(3) A Bell
2 washing machines × 200 = 400
5 vacuum cleaners × 60 = 300
2 dishwashers × 150 = 300
1,000
Less trade discount 20% 200
800

(15) J Kelly
1 music centre × 300 = 300
2 washing machines × 250 = 500
800
Less trade discount 25% 200
600

(20) B Powell
6 radios × 70 420
Less trade discount 33⅓% 140
280

(30) B Lewis
4 dishwashers × 200 800
Less trade discount 20% 160
640

Purchases Day Book
(1)	K King	450
(3)	A Bell	800
(15)	J Kelly	600
(20)	B Powell	280
(30)	B Lewis	640
		2,770

General Ledger
Purchases Account
(31) Total for month 2,770

Purchases Ledger
K King (1) Purchases 450
A Bell (3) Purchases 800
J Kelly (15) Purchases 600
B Powell (20) Purchases 280
B Lewis (30) Purchases 640

15.3

Purchases Day Book
(1)	Smith Stores	90
(23)	C Kelly	105
(31)	J Hamilton	180
		375

Purchases Ledger
Smith Stores (1) Purchases 90
C Kelly (23) Purchases 105
J Hamilton (31) Purchases 180

General Ledger
Purchases Account
(31) Total for month 375

Sales Day Book
(8)	A Grantley	72
(15)	A Henry	240
(24)	D Sangster	81
		393

Sales Ledger
A Grantley (8) Sales 72
A Henry (15) Sales 240
D Sangster (24) Sales 81

General Ledger
Sales Account
(31) Total for month 393

16.1

Purchases Day Book
(1)	H Lloyd	119
(4)	D Scott	98
(4)	A Simpson	114
(4)	A Williams	25
(4)	S Wood	56
(10)	A Simpson	59
(18)	M White	89
(18)	J Wong	67
(18)	H Miller	196
(18)	H Lewis	119
(31)	A Williams	56
(31)	C Cooper	98
		1,096

Returns Outwards Day Book
(7)	H Lloyd	16
(7)	D Scott	14
(25)	J Wong	5
(25)	A Simpson	11
		46

General Ledger
Purchases Account
(31) Total for month 1,096
Returns Outwards Account
(31) Total for month 46

Purchases Ledger
H Lloyd (7) Returns 16 | (1) Purchases 119
D Scott (7) Returns 14 | (4) Purchases 98
A Simpson (25) Returns 11 | (4) Purchases 114; (10) Purchases 59
A Williams (4) Purchases 25; (31) Purchases 56
S Wood (4) Purchases 56
M White (18) Purchases 89
J Wong (25) Returns 5 | (18) Purchases 67
H Miller (18) Purchases 196
H Lewis (18) Purchases 119
C Cooper (31) Purchases 98

16.3

Sales Day Book
(1)	T Thompson	56
(1)	L Rodriguez	148
(1)	K Barton	145
(7)	K Kelly	89
(7)	N Mendes	78
(7)	N Lee	257
(24)	K Mohammed	57
(24)	K Kelly	65
(24)	O Green	112
(31)	N Lee	55
		1,062

Purchases Day Book
(3)	P Potter	144
(3)	H Harris	25
(3)	B Spencer	76
(9)	B Perkins	24
(9)	H Harris	58
(9)	H Miles	123
(17)	H Harris	54
(17)	B Perkins	65
(17)	L Nixon	75
		644

Returns Inwards Day Book
(14)	T Thompson	5
(14)	K Barton	11
(14)	K Kelly	14
(28)	N Mendes	24
		54

Returns Outwards Day Book
(11)	P Potter	12
(11)	B Spencer	22
(20)	B Spencer	14
		48

Sales Ledger

T Thompson
(1) Sales 56 | (14) Returns 5

L Rodriguez
(1) Sales 148

K Barton
(1) Sales 145 | (14) Returns 11

K Kelly
(7) Sales 89 | (14) Returns 14
(24) Sales 65

N Mendes
(7) Sales 78 | (28) Returns 24

(7) Sales 257
(31) Sales 55

K Mohammed
(24) Sales 57

O Green
(24) Sales 112

Purchases Ledger

P Potter
(11) Returns 12 | (3) Purchases 144

H Harris
| (3) Purchases 25
| (9) Purchases 58
| (17) Purchases 54

B Spencer
(11) Returns 22 | (3) Purchases 76

B Perkins
(11) Returns 14 | (9) Purchases 24
(20) Returns 14 | (17) Purchases 65

H Miles
| (9) Purchases 123

L Nixon
| (17) Purchases 75

Returns Inwards Day Book

(11) K O'Connor 16
(11) L Staines 18
34

Returns Outwards Day Book

(19) N Lee 9

General Ledger

Purchases
(31) Total for month 644

Returns Inwards
(31) Total for month 54

Sales
(31) Total for month 1,062

Returns Outwards
(31) Total for month 48

T Best
(22) Purchases 72

N Hardy
(1) Balance 40 | (16) Bank & disc 40

M Nelson
(1) Balance 180 | (16) Bank & disc 40
(3) Sales 40 |
220 | 220

K O'Connor
(3) Sales 56 | (11) Returns 16
| (16) Bank & disc 40
56 | 56

J Johnson
(22) Purchases 89

Purchases Day Book

(2) B Blake 20
(2) C Harris 56
(2) H Gordon 38
(2) N Lee 69
(22) J Johnson 89
(22) T Best 72
344

Sales Day Book

(3) K O'Connor 56
(3) M Benjamin 78
(3) L Staines 98
(3) N Duffy 48
(3) B Green 118
(3) M Nelson 40
(9) M Benjamin 22
(9) L Pearson 67
527

The Journal

17.1

(1) Premises	2,000	
Van	450	
Fixtures	600	
Stock	1,289	
Debtors: N Hardy	40	
M Nelson	180	
Bank	1,254	
Cash	45	
Creditors: B Blake		60
V Reagan		200
Capital		5,598
	5,858	5,858
(14) Van	300	
Better Motors		300

Cash Book

	Disc	Cash	Bank		Disc	Cash	Bank
(1) Balances		45	1,254	(1) Rent			15
(16) N Hardy	2		38	(4) Motor expenses		13	
(16) M Nelson	11		209	(7) Drawings		20	
(16) K O'Connor	2		38	(24) B Blake	4		76
(16) L Staines	4		76	(24) V Reagan	10		190
				(24) N Lee	3		57
				(27) Salaries			56
				(30) Rates			66
				(31) Better Motors			300
				(31) Balance c/d		12	855
	19	45	1,615		17	45	1,615

Trial Balance as at 31 May 20X9

	Dr	Cr
C Harris		56
H Gordon		38
J Johnson		89
T Best		72
M Benjamin	100	
N Duffy	48	
B Green	118	
L Pearson	67	
Capital		5,598
Rent	15	
Motor expenses	13	
Drawings	20	
Salaries	56	
Rates	66	
Sales		527
Purchases	344	
Returns inwards	34	
Returns outwards		9
Premises	2,000	
Vans	750	
Fixtures	600	
Stock	1,289	
Discounts allowed	19	
Discounts received		17
Bank	855	
Cash	12	
	6,406	6,406

Purchases Ledger

B Blake

(24) Bank	76	(1) Balance	60
(24) Discount	4	(2) Purchases	20
	80		80

V Reagan

(24) Bank & disct.	200	(1) Balance b/d	200

C Harris

		(2) Purchases	56

H Gordon

		(2) Purchases	38

N Lee

(19) Returns	9	(2) Purchases	69
(24) Bank & disct	60		
	69		69

Sales Ledger

M Benjamin

(3) Sales	78
(9) Sales	22

L Staines

(3) Sales	98	(11) Returns	18
		(16) Bank & disct	80
	98		98

N Duffy

(3) Sales	48

B Green

(3) Sales	118

L Pearson

(9) Sales	67

General Ledger

Capital

(1) Balance	5,598

Rent

(1) Bank	15

Motor Expenses

(4) Cash	13

Drawings

(7) Cash	20

Salaries

(27) Bank	56

Rates

(30) Bank	66

Sales

(31) Total for month	527

Purchases

(31) Total for month	344

Returns Inwards

(31) Total for month	34

Returns Outwards

(31) Total for month	9

Premises

(1) Balance	2,000

Vans

(1) Balance	450
(14) Better Motors	300

Fixtures

(1) Balance	600

Stock

(1) Balance	1,289

Discounts Allowed

(31) Total for month	19

Discounts Received

(31) Total for month	17

Better Motors

(31) Bank	300	(14) Van	300

17.2

(a)	Motor vehicles	Dr	6,790	: Kingston	Cr	6,790
(b)	Bad debts	Dr	34	: H Newman	Cr	34
(c)	Unique Offices	Dr	490	: Office furniture	Cr	490
(d) (i)	Bank	Dr	39	: W Charles	Cr	39
(ii)	Bad debts	Dr	111	: W Charles	Cr	111
(e)	Drawings	Dr	45	: Purchases	Cr	45
(f)	Drawings	Dr	76	: Insurance	Cr	76
(g)	Machinery	Dr	980	: Systems Accelerated	Cr	980

18.1

(a)–(c)

Petty Cash Book

Receipts		Total	Cleaning	Motor Expenses	Postages	Stationery	Travelling
300	(1) Balance b/d						
	(2) Postages	18			18		
	(3) Travelling	12					12
	(4) Cleaning	15	15				
	(7) Petrol	22		22			
	(8) Travelling	25					25
	(9) Stationery	17				17	
	(11) Cleaning	18	18				
	(14) Postages	5			5		
	(15) Travelling	8					8
	(18) Stationery	9				9	
	(18) Cleaning	23	23				
	(20) Postages	13			13		
	(24) Motor service	43		43			
	(26) Petrol	18		18			
	(27) Cleaning	21	21				
	(29) Postages	5			5		
	(30) Petrol	14		14			
		286	77	97	41	26	45
286	(31) Cash						
	(31) Balance c/d	300					
586		586					

(d) See text.

18.2

(a) Briefly: To keep detail out of cash book.
To reduce postings to expense accounts.
To enable petty cash to be kept by someone other than main cashier.

(b)

Petty Cash Book

Receipts		Total	Post and stationery	Travel expenses	Ledger accounts
1.13	(1) Balance b/d				
23.87	(2) Cash				
	(4) Postages	8.50	8.50		
	(9) Courtney Bishop	2.35			2.35
	(11) Bus fares	1.72		1.72	
	(17) Envelopes	0.70	0.70		
0.68	(23) Telephone reimbursed				
	(26)	10.00		10.00	
		23.27	9.20	11.72	2.35
	(30) Balance c/d	2.41			
25.68		25.68			
2.41	(1) Balance b/d				
22.59	(1) Cash				

(c)

Post and Stationery
(30) Petty cash 9.20

Travel Expenses
(30) Petty cash 11.72

Courtney Bishop
(9) Petty cash 2.35

Telephone
(23) Petty cash 0.68

(b)

D Wilson Ltd Ledger
G Christie & Son

	£
20X7	
May 1 Sales	770

G Christie & Son Ledger
D Wilson Ltd

	£
20X7	
May 1 Purchases	770

19.3

Sales Day Book

		Net	VAT
20X9			
Aug	1 M Sinclair & Co	150	15
"	8 M Brown & Associates	260	26
"	19 A Axton Ltd	80	8
"	31 T Christie	30	3
		520	52

Sales Ledger
M Sinclair & Co
(1) Sales 165

M Brown & Associates
(8) Sales 286

A Axton Ltd
(19) Sales 88

T Christie
(31) Sales 33

General Ledger
Sales
(31) Credit sales for the month 520

Value Added Tax
(31) Sales Day Book: VAT content 52

19.4

Sales Day Book

	Net	VAT
(1) B Davies & Co	150	15
(4) C Grant Ltd	220	22
(16) C Grant Ltd	140	14
(31) B Karloff	80	8
	590	59

Purchases Day Book

	Net	VAT
(10) G Cooper & Son	400	40
(10) J Wayne Ltd	190	19
(14) B Lugosi	50	5
(23) S Hayward	60	6
	700	70

19.1

(a) Style of invoice will vary.
Calculations:

	£
3 sets of Boy Michael Golf Clubs × £270	810
150 Watson golf balls at £8 per 10 balls	120
4 Faldo golf bags at £30	120
	1,050
Less trade discount 33⅓%	350
	700
Add VAT 10%	70
	770

Sales Ledger

B Davies & Co
(1) Sales ... 165

C Grant Ltd
(4) Sales ... 242
(16) Sales ... 154

B Karloff
(31) Sales ... 88

Purchases Ledger

G Cooper & Son
(10) Purchases ... 440

J Wayne Ltd
(10) Purchases ... 209

B Lugosi
(14) Purchases ... 55

S Hayward
(23) Purchases ... 66

General Ledger

Sales
(31) Credit sales for month ... 590

Purchases
(31) Credit purchases for month ... 700

Value Added Tax
(31) VAT content in Purchases Day Book ... 70
(31) VAT content in Sales Day Book ... 59
(31) Balance c/d ... 11
70 / 70

19.6
(a)

Sales Day Book

Date	Name and Details	List price less trade discount £	p	VAT £	p	Total £	p
20X9							
Mar 9	Neville's Electrical	576	–	57	60	633	60
" 17	Maltby plc	3,000	–	300	–	3,300	–
" 29	Neville's Electrical	368	–	36	80	404	80
		3,944	–	394	40	4,338	40

(b)

Sales Ledger

Neville's Electrical
20X9
Mar 9 Sales ... 633.60
Mar 29 Sales ... 404.80

Maltby plc
20X9
Mar 17 Sales ... 3,300.00

(c)

General Ledger

Sales
20X9
Mar 31 Sales Day Book ... 3,944.00

Value Added Tax
20X9
Mar 31 Sales Day Book ... 394.40

Trial Balance as at 31 March 20X9

	Dr	Cr
Neville's Electrical	1,038.40	
Maltby plc	3,300.00	
Sales		3,944.00
Value Added Tax		394.40
	4,338.40	4,338.40

20.1

Columnar Sales Day Book

	Inv No	Total	VAT	Hi Fi Dept	TV Dept	Sundries Dept
20X7						
Feb 1 P Small	586	2,860	260		2,600	
" 2 L Goode	587	1,980	180	1,800		
" 3 R Daye	588	1,760	160		1,600	
" 5 B May	589	320	–			320
" 7 L Goode	590	990	90		900	
" 7 P Small	591	3,740	340	3,400		
		11,650	1,030	5,200	5,100	320

General Ledger

Sales
20X7
Feb 28 Total for month — Hi Fi 5,200 | TV 5,100 | Sundries 320

Value Added Tax
20X7
Feb 28 Total for month ... 1,030

P Small
2,860
3,740

L Goode
1,980
990

R Daye
1,760

B May
320

20.2

M Barber
Purchases Analysis Book

20X6	Total	Purchases	Light & Heat	Motor Exps	Stationery	Carriage Inwards
Jul 1 L Ogden	220	220				
" 3 E Evans	390	390				
" 4 North Electricity	88		88			
" 5 H Noone	110	110				
" 6 Kirk Motors	136			136		
" 8 Avon Enterprises	77				77	
" 10 Kirk Motors	55			55		
" 12 North Gas Board	134		134			
" 15 A Dodds	200	200				
" 17 O Aspinall	24		24			
" 18 J Kelly	310	310				
" 19 D Adams	85					85
" 21 J Moore	60				60	
" 23 H Noone	116	116				
" 27 D Flynn	62					62
" 31 Kirk Motors	185			185		
	2,252	1,346	246	376	137	147

20.3
General ledger: Purchases Dr 1,346; Lighting and heating Dr 246; Motor expenses Dr 376; Stationery Dr 137; Carriage inwards Dr 146.
Purchases ledger: Credits in personal accounts should be obvious.

21.1

Gross pay		200
Less: Income tax	27	
National Insurance	16	43
Net pay		157

21.2

Gross pay 40 × 4	160	
5 × 6	30	190
Less: Income tax*	25	
National Insurance	17	42
Net pay		148

*190 – 80 = 110. First 50 × 20% = 10 + (60 × 25%) 15 = total 25.

21.3

Salary		200
Commission		600
Gross pay		800
Less: Income tax*	85	
National Insurance	66	151
Net pay		649

*800 – 450 = 350. First 50 × 20% = 10 + (300 × 25%) 75 = total 85.

21.4

Salary		2,000
Bonus		400
		2,400
Less		
Superannuation	120	
Income tax*	450	
National Insurance	190	760
		1,640

*2,400 – 120 – 430 = 1,850. First 250 × 20% = 50 + (1,600 × 25%) 400 = 450.

22.1
See text.

22.2
See text.

22.3
See text.

23.1
See text.

23.2
See text.

23.3
See text.

23.4
See text.

24.1
(a) Per text.
(b) Capital: (i), (ii), machine part of (v), (vi).
Revenue: (iii), (iv), drinks part of (v).

24.3
Capital: (a), (b), (e).

24.5
Capital: (a), (c), (d), (f), (i), (l); Revenue: (b), (e), (g), (h), (i), (k).

24.7
(a) Per text.
(b) Microcomputer – acquisition cost

Basic cost	4,000
Installation and testing	340
	4,340
Less 5% discount	217
	4,123
Special wiring	110
Modifications	199
Staff training	990
Total cost	5,422

(c) 1. Revenue. 2. Capital. 3. Capital. 4. Revenue. 5. Revenue.
6. Revenue. 7. Capital. 8. Revenue. 9. Capital. 10. Capital.

24.8
(a)

Plant at Cost	
Balance 1 April 20X5	372,000
Add Acquisitions during year	96,000
	468,000
Less Disposals (36,000 + 4,000 + 4,400)	44,400
Balance 31 March 20X6	423,600

(b)

Provision for Depreciation of Plant	
Balance 1 April 20X5	205,400
Less Depreciation on disposals (W1)	25,200
	180,200
Add Provision for year 20% × (423,600 − 180,200)	48,680
Balance 31 March 20X6	228,880

Plant Sold		
Cost: year to 31 March 20X2		40,000
Depreciation: year to 31 March 20X2	20%	8,000
		32,000
Depreciation: year to 31 March 20X3	20%	6,400
		25,600
Addition		4,400
		30,000
Depreciation: year to 31 March 20X4	20%	6,000
		24,000
Depreciation: year to 31 March 20X5	20%	4,800
		19,200

(W1) Depreciation accumulated: 8,000 + 6,400 + 6,000 + 4,800 = 25,200.

(c) *Sale of plant*

Less Cost (40,000 + 4,400)		44,400
Depreciation		25,200
Book value at date of sale		19,200
Loss on disposal		5,500

25.1

Bad Debts			
20X8		20X8	
Apl 30 H Gordon	110	Dec 31 Profit and loss	186
Aug 31 D Bellamy	64		
Oct 31 J Alderton	12		
	186		186

Provision for doubtful debts		
	20X8	
	Dec 31 Profit and loss	220

Profit and Loss (extracts)	
Bad debts	186
Provision for doubtful debts	220

Balance Sheet as at 31 December 20X8 (extract)		
Debtors		6,850
Less: Provision for		
Bad debts	220	6,630

25.2

(a)

Bad debts			
20X7		20X7	
Dec 31 Various	540	Dec 31 Profit and loss	540

(b)

Provision for doubtful debts			
Dec 31 Balance c/d	310	Jan 1 Balance b/d	260
		Dec 31 Profit and loss	50
	310		310

(c)

Profit and Loss (extracts)	
Bad debts	540
Provision for doubtful debts	50

(d)

Balance Sheet (extract)		
Debtors		6,200
Less provision for doubtful debts	310	5,890

25.3

(i)

Bad Debts			
20X6		20X6	
Aug 31 W Best	85	Dec 31 Profit and loss	225
Sep 30 S Avon	140		
	225		225

20X7

Feb 28 L J Friend	180		**20X7**	
Aug 31 N Kelly	60		Dec 31 Profit and loss	490
Nov 30 A Oliver	250			
	490			490

Provision for Doubtful Debts

			20X6	
			Dec 31 Profit and loss	550
20X7			**20X7**	
Dec 31 Balance c/d	600		Dec 31 Profit and loss	50
	600			600

(ii)

Balance Sheet (extracts)

	20X6		**20X7**	
Debtors	40,500		47,300	
Less Provision for doubtful debts	550		600	
	39,950			

25.6

(a)

Provision for Doubtful Debts

20X8			**20X7**	
May 31 Profit and loss (W1)	1,390		Jun 1 Balance b/d	2,300
" 31 Balance c/d	910			
	2,300			2,300
			20X8	
			Jun 1 Balance b/d	910

(b)

Provision for Discounts Allowed

			20X8	
			May 31 Profit and loss (W2)	594

Workings

(W1) Provision 1.6.20X7		2,300
Less Provision 31.5.20X8	1% × 24,000	240
	2% × 10,000	200
	4% × 8,000	320
	5% × 3,000	150
		910
		1,390

Reduction in Provision

(W2) Debtors liable for discounts	24,000
Less Provision for doubtful debts	240
	23,760

Provision for discounts allowed 2½% × 23,760 = 594

25.8

(days and months omitted)

(a)

Bad Debts

20X7 Debtors	1,200	20X7 Profit and loss	1,200
20X8 Debtors	1,600	20X8 Profit and loss	1,600
20X9 Debtors	2,350	20X9 Profit and loss	2,350

(b)

20X8 Profit and loss	350		*Bad Debts Recovered*	
20X9 Profit and loss	150		20X8 Mrs P Iles	350
			20X9 Debtor	150

(c)

Provision for Doubtful Debts

			20X7 Profit and loss	2,000
20X8 Balance c/d	2,800		20X8 Profit and loss	800
	2,800			2,800
20X9 Profit and loss	700		20X9 Balance b/d	2,800
20X9 Balance c/d	2,100			
	2,800			2,800

(d)

Profit and Loss Account (extracts)

(20X7) Bad debts	1,200		
Provision for doubtful debts	2,000		
(20X8) Bad debts	1,600	(20X8) Bad debt	
Provision for doubtful debts	800	recovered	350
(20X9) Bad debts	2,350	(20X9) Reduction in provision	
		for bad debts	700
		Bad debt recovered	150

25.9

(A) See text.

(B) See text.

(C) (1) (i)

20X7

Dec 31 Profit and loss	33		*Provision for Doubtful Debts*	
" " Balance c/d	717**		**20X7**	
	750		Jan 1 Balance b/d	750*
				750

Bad Debts

20X7			
? Debtors – A Stewart	900	Dec 31 Profit and loss	3,800
? Debtors	2,300		
Dec 31 Debtors – J Smith	600		
	3,800		3,800

(2) the net profit will increase by £33.

*3% 25,000 = 750; **3% 23,900

26.1

Straight Line

Cost	4,000
Yr 1 Depreciation*	700
	3,300
Yr 2 Depreciation	700
	2,600
Yr 3 Depreciation	700
	1,900
Yr 4 Depreciation	700
	1,200
Yr 5 Depreciation	700
	500

Reducing Balance

Cost	4,000
Yr 1 Depn 40% of 4,000	1,600
	2,400
Yr 2 Depn 40% of 2,400	960
	1,440
Yr 3 Depn 40% of 1,440	576
	864
Yr 4 Depn 40% of 864	346
	518
Yr 5 Depn 40% of 518	207
	311

*$4,000 − 500 = 3,500 \div 5 = 700$

26.2

(a) Straight Line

Cost	12,500
Yr 1 Depreciation*	1,845
	10,655
Yr 2 Depreciation	1,845
	8,810
Yr 3 Depreciation	1,845
	6,965
Yr 4 Depreciation	1,845
	5,120

$$* \frac{12,500 - 5,120}{4} = 1,845$$

(b) Reducing Balance

Cost	12,500
Yr 1 Depn 20% of 12,500	2,500
	10,000
Yr 2 Depn 20% of 10,000	2,000
	8,000
Yr 3 Depn 20% of 8,000	1,600
	6,400
Yr 4 Depn 20% of 6,400	1,280
	5,120

26.3

(a) Reducing Balance

Cost	6,400
Yr 1 Depn 50% of 6,400	3,200
	3,200
Yr 2 Depn 50% of 3,200	1,600
	1,600
Yr 3 Depn 50% of 1,600	800
	800
Yr 4 Depn 50% of 800	400
	400
Yr 5 Depn 50% of 400	200
	200

(b) Straight Line

Cost	6,400
Yr 1 Depreciation*	1,240
	5,160
Yr 2 Depreciation	1,240
	3,920
Yr 3 Depreciation	1,240
	2,680
Yr 4 Depreciation	1,240
	1,440
Yr 5 Depreciation	1,240
	200

$$* \frac{6,400 - 200}{5} = 1,240$$

26.7

		Machines	
	A	B	C
Bought 1.1.20X7	3,000		
20X7 Depreciation 10% for 12 months	300		
	2,700		
Bought 1.4.20X8		2,000	
20X8 Depreciation 10% × 2,700	270		
" 10% for 9 months		150	
	2,430	1,850	
Bought 1.7.20X9			1,000
20X9 Depreciation 10% × 2,430	243		
" 10% × 1,850		185	
" 10% for 6 months			50
	2,187	1,665	950

20X9 Total Depreciation Provision $243 + 185 + 50 = 478$

27.1

Vans

20X1		20X1	
Jan 1 Bank	2,400	Dec 31 Balance c/d	3,800
Jul 1 Bank	1,400		
	3,800		3,800

Provision for Depreciation: Vans

20X1		20X1	
Dec 31 Balance c/d	620	Dec 31 Profit and loss	620

27.2

(a)

Machinery

20X3		20X3	
Jan 1 Bank	800	Dec 31 Balance c/d	800
20X4		**20X4**	
Jan 1 Balance b/d	800	Dec 31 Balance c/d	2,400
Jul 1 Bank	1,000		
Oct 1 Bank	600		
	2,400		2,400
20X5		**20X5**	
Jan 1 Balance b/d	2,400	Dec 31 Balance c/d	2,400
20X6		**20X6**	
Jan 1 Balance b/d	2,400	Dec 31 Balance c/d	2,600
Apr 1 Bank	200		
	2,600		2,600

(b)

Provision for Depreciation: Machinery

20X3	£	20X3	£
Dec 31 Balance c/d	80	Dec 31 Profit and loss	80
20X4		**20X4**	
Dec 31 Balance c/d	225	Jan 1 Balance b/d	80
		Dec 31 Profit and loss	145
			225
20X5		**20X5**	
Dec 31 Balance c/d	465	Jan 1 Balance b/d	225
		Dec 31 Profit and loss	240
			465
20X6		**20X6**	
Dec 31 Balance c/d	720	Jan 1 Balance b/d	465
		Dec 31 Profit and loss	255
			720

(c)

Balance Sheet Extracts

31 December 20X3		
Machinery at cost	800	
Less Depreciation	80	720
31 December 20X4		
Machinery at cost	2,400	
Less Depreciation to date	225	2,175
31 December 20X5		
Machinery at cost	2,400	
Less Depreciation to date	465	1,935
31 December 20X6		
Machinery at cost	2,600	
Less Depreciation to date	720	1,880

27.4

Plant

20X4	£	20X4	£
Jan 1 Bank	900	Dec 31 Balance c/d	1,500
Oct 1 Bank	600		
	1,500		1,500
20X6		**20X6**	
Jan 1 Balance b/d	1,500	Dec 31 Balance c/d	2,050
Jul 1 Bank	550		
	2,050		2,050
20X7		**20X7**	
Jan 1 Balance b/d	2,050	Sep 30 Disposals	900
		Dec 31 Balance c/d	1,150
	2,050		2,050

Provision for Depreciation: Plant

20X4	£	20X4	£
Dec 31 Balance c/d	210	Dec 31 Profit and loss	210
20X5		**20X5**	
Dec 31 Balance c/d	510	Jan 1 Balance b/d	210
		Dec 31 Profit and loss	300
	510		510
20X6		**20X6**	
Dec 31 Balance c/d	865	Jan 1 Balance b/d	510
		Dec 31 Profit and loss	355
	865		865
20X7		**20X7**	
Sep 30 Disposals	675	Jan 1 Balance b/d	865
Dec 31 Balance c/d	555	Dec 31 Profit and loss	365
	1,230		1,230

Plant Disposals

20X7	£	20X7	£
Sep 30 Plant	900	Sep 30 Provn for depn	675
Dec 31 Profit and loss	50	" 30 Bank	275
	950		950

Balance Sheets

	20X4	20X5	20X6	20X7
Plant at cost	1,500	1,500	2,050	1,150
Less depn to date	210	510	865	555
	1,290	990	1,185	595

27.5

Machinery

20X9	£	20X9	£
Jan 1 Balance b/d	52,590	Dec 31 Machinery disposals	2,800
Dec 31 Bank	2,480	" 31 Balance c/d	52,270
	55,070		55,070

Office Furniture

20X9	£	20X9	£
Jan 1 Balance b/d	2,860	Dec 31 Balance c/d	3,180
Dec 31 Bank	320		
	3,180		3,180

Provision for Depreciation: Machinery

20X9	£	20X9	£
Dec 31 Machinery disposals	1,120	Jan 1 Balance b/d	25,670
" 31 Balance c/d	29,777	Dec 31 Profit and loss	5,227
	30,897		30,897

Provision for Depreciation: Office Furniture

20X9	£	20X9	£
Dec 31 Balance c/d	1,649	Jan 1 Balance b/d	1,490
		Dec 31 Profit and loss	159
	1,649		1,649

Machinery Disposals

20X9			20X9		
Dec 31 Machinery	2,800		Dec 31 Provision for deprn		1,120
			" 31 Bank		800
			" 31 Profit and loss:		
			Loss on sale		880
		2,800			2,800

Balance Sheet as at 31 December 20X9

Machinery at cost	52,270	
Less Depreciation to date	29,777	22,493
Office furniture at cost	3,180	
Less Depreciation to date	1,649	1,531

27.7

(a) (i) Time factor (ii) Economic factors (iii) Deterioration physically (iv) Depletion.

(b) (i) Depletion (ii) Physical deterioration (iii) Time (iv) Not usually subject to depletion, but depends on circumstances (v) Economic factors, obsolescence for example (vi) Time factor.

(c)

Equipment

Balance b/d	135,620	Asset disposals		36,000
Bank	47,800	Balance c/d		147,420
	183,420			183,420
Balance b/d	147,420			

Provision for Depreciation – Equipment

Asset disposals	28,224	Balance b/d	81,374
Balance c/d	90,858	Profit and loss	37,708
	119,082		119,082
		Balance b/d	90,858

Asset Disposals

Equipment	36,000	Provision for depreciation	28,224
		Bank	5,700
		Profit and loss	2,076
	36,000		36,000

27.9

(a) (i) Straight line depreciation method

Fixed Asset

Year 1 Bank	10,000	Year 3 Asset disposals	10,000

Provision for Depreciation

		Year 1 Profit and loss	2,000
Year 2 Balance c/d	4,000	Year 2 Profit and loss	2,000
	4,000		4,000
Year 3 Asset disposals	4,000	Year 3 Balance b/d	4,000

Asset Disposals

Year 3 Fixed asset	10,000	Year 3 Bank	5,000
		" 3 Provision for depn.	4,000
		" 3 Profit and loss	1,000
	10,000		10,000

(ii) Reducing balance method

Fixed Asset

Year 1 Bank	10,000	Year 3 Asset disposals	10,000

Provision for Depreciation

		Year 1 Profit and loss	4,000
Year 2 Balance c/d	6,400	" 2 Profit and loss	2,400
	6,400		6,400
Year 3 Asset disposals	6,400	Year 3 Balance b/d	6,400

Asset Disposals

Year 3 Fixed asset	10,000	Year 3 Bank	5,000
" 3 Profit and loss	1,400	" 3 Provision for depn.	6,400
	11,400		11,400

(b) (i) The purpose of depreciation provisions is to apportion the cost of a fixed asset over the useful years of its life to the organisation.

The matching concept concerns the matching of costs against the revenues which those costs generate. If the benefit to be gained is equal in each year then the straight line method is to be preferred. If the benefits are greatest in year 1 and then falling year by year, then the reducing balance method would be preferred. The impact of maintenance costs of the fixed asset, if heavier in later years, may also give credence to the reducing balance method.

(ii) The net figure at the end of year 2 is the amount of original cost not yet expensed against revenue.

(c) The charge in year 1 should be nil in this case. The matching concept concerns matching costs against revenues. There have been no revenues in year 1, therefore there should be no costs.

28.1

(a)

Motor Expenses

20X6			20X6		
Dec 31	Cash and bank	744	Dec 31	Profit and loss	772
" 31	Owing c/d	28			
		772			772

(b)

Insurance

20X6			20X6		
Dec 31	Cash and bank	420	Dec 31	Prepaid c/d	35
			" 31	Profit and loss	385
		420			420

(c)

Stationery

20X6			20X6		
Dec 31	Cash and bank	1,800	Jan 1	Owing b/d	250
" 31	Owing c/d	490	Dec 31	Profit and loss	2,040
		2,290			2,290

(d)

Rates

20X6			20X6		
Jan 1	Prepaid b/d	220	Dec 31	Prepaid c/d	290
Dec 31	Cash and bank	950	" 31	Profit and loss	880
		1,170			1,170

(e)

Rent Received

20X6			20X6		
Jan 1	Owing b/d	180	Dec 31	Cash and bank	550
Dec 31	Profit and loss	580	" 31	Owing c/d	210
		760			760

28.3

Rates

20X8			20X8		
Jan 1	Balance b/d	104	Dec 31	Profit and loss	1,229
Dec 31	Bank	1,500	" 31	Prepaid c/d	375
		1,604			1,604

Packing Materials

20X8			20X8		
Jan 1	Balance b/d	629	Dec 31	Profit and loss	5,499
Dec 31	Bank	5,283	" 31	Cash: Scrap	172
" 31	Owing c/d	357	" 31	Stock c/d	598
		6,269			6,269

28.5

(a)

Insurance

20X0			20X0		
Jan 1	Prepaid b/d	562	Dec 31	Profit and loss	1,236
Dec 31	Bank	1,019	" 31	Prepaid c/d	345
		1,581			1,581
20X1					
Jan 1	Prepaid b/d	345			

Wages

20X0			20X0		
Dec 31	Cash	15,000	Jan 1	Accrued b/d	306
" 31	Accrued c/d	419	Dec 31	Profit and loss	15,113
		15,419			15,419
			20X1		
			Jan 1	Accrued b/d	419

Rent Receivable

20X0			20X0		
Dec 31	Profit and loss	2,741	Jan 1	In advance b/d	36
			Dec 31	Bank	2,600
			" 31	Arrears c/d	105
		2,741			2,741
20X1					
Jan 1	Arrears b/d	105			

(b)

Profit and Loss (extract)

Insurance	1,236	Rent receivable	2,741
Wages	15,113		

(c) (i) Expenses accrued increases the amount charged as expense for that period. It reduces the recorded net profit. It shows as a current liability in the balance sheet.

(ii) Income received in advance reduces the revenue to be recorded for that period. It reduces the recorded net profit. It shows as a current liability in the balance sheet.

(d) (i) To match up expenses charged in the profit and loss account with the expense cost used up in the period.

(ii) To match up revenue credited to profit and loss with revenue earned for the period.

28.8
A Scholes
Trading and Profit and Loss Account for the year ended 28 February 20X7

Sales		19,740
Less Cost of goods sold:		
Opening stock	2,970	
Add Purchases	11,280	
	14,250	
Less Closing stock	3,510	10,740
Gross profit		9,000
Add Discounts received		360
		9,360
Less Expenses:		
Wages and salaries (2,580 + 90)	2,670	
Rent (1,020 – 140)	880	
Discounts allowed	690	
Van running costs (450 + 60)	510	
Bad debts (810 + 60)	870	
Depreciation:		
Office furniture	180	
Delivery van	480	660
		6,280
Net profit		3,080

Balance Sheet as at 28 February 20X7

Fixed assets			
Office furniture		1,440	
Less Depreciation		180	1,260
Delivery van		2,400	
Less Depreciation		480	1,920
			3,180
Current assets			
Stock		3,510	
Debtors	4,920		
Less Provision for doubtful debts	330	4,590	
Prepaid expenses		140	
Cash at bank		1,140	
Cash in hand		210	
		9,590	
Less Current liabilities			
Creditors	2,490		
Expenses owing	150	2,640	
Net current assets			6,950
			10,130
Financed by:			
Capital			
Balance at 1.3.20X6			9,900
Add Net profit			3,080
			12,980
Less Drawings			2,850
			10,130

28.10
John Brown
Trading and Profit and Loss Account for the year ended 31 December 20X7

Sales			400,000
Less Returns in			5,000
			395,000
Less Cost of goods sold			
Stock at 1.1.20X7			100,000
Add Purchases	350,000		
Less Returns out	6,200	343,800	
		443,800	
Less Stock at 32.12.20X7		120,000	323,800
Gross profit			71,200
Less Wages		35,000	
Rates		5,500	
Telephone		1,220	
Bad debts		200	
Provision for doubtful debts		180	
Depreciation: Shop fittings		4,000	
Van		6,000	52,100
Net profit			19,100

Balance Sheet as at 31 December 20X7

Fixed assets			
Shop fittings at cost		40,000	
Less Depreciation		4,000	36,000
Van at cost		30,000	
Less Depreciation		6,000	24,000
			60,000
Current assets			
Stock		120,000	
Debtors	9,800		
Less Provision	980	8,820	
Prepayments		500	
Bank		3,000	
		132,320	
Less Current liabilities			
Creditors	7,000		
Expenses accrued	5,220	12,220	
Net current assets			120,100
			180,100
Financed by:			
Capital			
Balance as at 1.1.20X7			179,000
Add Net profit			19,100
			198,100
Less Drawings			18,000
			180,100

28.12

Mr Chai

Trading and Profit and Loss Account for the year ended 30 April 20X7

Sales (259,870 − 5,624)		254,246
Less Cost of goods sold		
Stock 1.5.20X6	15,654	
Purchases (135,680 − 13,407)	122,273	
Carriage inwards	11,830	
	149,757	
Less Stock 30.4.20X7	17,750	132,007
Gross profit		122,239
Discounts received		1,750
		123,989
Less Expenses		
Salaries and wages	38,521	
Rent, rates and insurances (25,973 − 1,120 − 5,435)	19,418	
Heating and lighting (11,010 + 1,360)	12,370	
Carriage out	4,562	
Advertising	5,980	
Postage, stationery and telephone	2,410	
Bad debts	2,008	
Provision for doubtful debts	223	
Discounts allowed	2,306	
Depreciation	12,074	99,872
Net profit		24,117

Balance Sheet as at 30 April 20X7

Fixed assets			
Fixtures and fittings at cost		120,740	
Less Depreciation to date		63,020	57,720
Current assets			
Stock		17,750	
Debtors	24,500		
Less Provision for doubtful debts	735	23,765	
Prepaid expenses		6,555	
Bank		4,440	
Cash		534	
		53,044	
Less Current liabilities			
Creditors	19,840		
Expenses accrued	1,360	21,200	
Net current assets			31,844
			89,564
Financed by:			
Capital: Balance as at 1.5.20X6			83,887
Add Net profit			24,117
			108,004
Less Drawings			18,440
			89,564

29.1

(i) FIFO Closing Stock 20 × £40 = £800

(ii)

	LIFO	Received	Issued	Stock after each transaction		
Jan		10 × £30		10 × £30	300	300
Mar		10 × £34		10 × £30	300	
				10 × £34	340	640
April			8 × £34	10 × £30	300	
				2 × £34	68	368
Sept		20 × £40		10 × £30	300	
				2 × £34	68	
				20 × £40	800	1,168
Dec			12 × £40	10 × £30	300	
				2 × £34	68	
				8 × £40	320	688

(iii)

	AVCO	Received	Issued	Average cost per unit stock held	No. of units in stock	Total value of stock
Jan		10 × £30		£30	10	£300
Mar		10 × £34		£32	20	£640
Apl			8	£32	12	£384
Sept		20 × £40		£37	32	£1,184
Dec			12	£37	20	£740

29.2

Trading Account for the year ended 31 December 20X0

	FIFO	LIFO	AVCO
Purchases	1,440	1,440	1,440
Less Closing stock	800	688	740
Cost of goods sold	640	752	700
Gross profit	400	288	340
	1,040	1,040	1,040

29.5

(a) (*dates and calculations omitted*)

Cash

Loan: School fund	200.00
Sales	53.50

Purchases

Cash	51.36

Sales

	Cash

(b) Stock valuation:

(All methods)			
Sales	8 × £46	368	
	12 × £56	672	1,040
			1,040
Purchases			51.36
	Break × 16p =	34	5.44
	Brunch × 12p =	15	1.80
			7.24

Stock

Trading account	7.24

		53.50

(c)

Broadway School
Trading Account for the month of December 20X9

Purchases	51.36	Sales	53.50
Less Closing stock	7.24		
	44.12		
Gross profit	9.38		
	53.50		53.50

(d)

	Break	*Brunch*
Purchases (units)	240	108
Less Sold	200	90
Stock should have been	40	18
Actual stock	34	15
Missing items	6	3

If there have been no arithmetical errors, one can only assume that someone has stolen 6 Breaks and 3 Brunches.

29.6

(This is a brief answer showing main points to be covered. In the examination the answer should be in report form and elaborated.)

1 For Charles Gray

(i) The concept of prudence says that stock should be valued at lower of cost or net realisable value. As 50% of the retail price £375 is lower than cost £560, then £375 will be taken as net realisable value and used for stock valuation.

(ii) The sale has not taken place by 30 April 20X9. The prudence concept does not anticipate profits and therefore the sale will not be assumed. The gun should therefore be included in stock, at cost price £560.

2 For Jean Kim

It appears that it is doubtful if the business can still be treated as a going concern. If the final decision is that the business cannot continue, then the stock valuation should be £510 each, as this is less than cost, with a further overall deduction of auction fees and expenses £300.

3 For Peter Fox

Stock must be valued at the lower of cost or net realisable value in this case. The cost to be used is the *cost* for Peter Fox. It is quite irrelevant what the cost may be for other distributors.

It would also be against the convention of consistency to adopt a different method. The consistency applies to Peter Fox, it is not a case of consistency with other businesses. Using selling prices as a basis is not acceptable to the vast majority of businesses.

29.8

(a) In one respect the consistency convention is not applied, as at one year end the stock may be shown at cost whereas the next year end may see stock valued at net realisable value.

On the other hand, as it is prudent to take the lower of cost or net realisable value, it can be said to be consistently prudent to consistently take the lower figure.

(b) Being prudent can be said to be an advantage. For instance, a shareholder can know that stocks are not overvalued: if they were, it would give him a false picture of his investment.

Someone to whom money is owed, such as a creditor, will know that the stocks in the balance sheet are realisable at least at that figure.

It is this knowledge that profits are not recorded because of excessive values placed on stocks that gives outside parties confidence to rely on reported profits.

30.1

Bank Reconciliation as on 31 December 20X6

Cash at bank as per cash book		678
Add Unpresented cheques	256	
Credit transfers	56	
		312
		990
Less Bank lodgements		115
Cash at bank as per bank statement		875

Note for students

Both in theory and in practice you can start with the cash book balance working to the bank statement balance, or you can reverse this method. Many teachers have their preferences, but this is a personal matter only. Examiners sometimes ask for them using one way, sometimes the other. Students should therefore be able to tackle them both ways.

30.3

(a)

Cash Book

20X9 (Totals so far)	2,328	20X9 (Totals so far)	497
Dec 31 J Walters	54	Dec 31 Bank Charges	22
		" 31 Balance c/d	1,863
	2,382		2,382

(b)

Bank Reconciliation Statement as on 31 December 20X9

Balance per cash book	1,863
Add Unpresented cheque	115
	1,978
Less Bankings not yet on bank statement (249 + 178)	427
Balance per bank statement	1,551

or

Bank Reconciliation Statement as on 31 December 20X9

Balance per bank statement	1,551
Add Bankings not yet on bank statement (249 + 178)	427
	1,978
Less Unpresented cheque	115
Balance per cash book	1,863

30.5

(a)

Cash Book (bank columns)

20X8			20X8		
Dec 31 Balance b/d	1,500		Dec 31 Bank charges		30
Dec 31 Dividends	240		Dec 31 RAC		70
Dec 31 Customs and Excise	260		Dec 31 Loan repayment		200
Dec 31 Deposit account	1,400		Dec 31 Balance c/d		3,100
	3,400				3,400

(b) *Bank Reconciliation Statement as on 31 December 20X8*

Balance per cash book	3,100
Add Unpresented cheques (250 + 290)	540
	3,640
Less Bankings not entered on statement	690
Balance per bank statement	2,950

30.7

Cash Book

20X6 (Totals so far)	737	20X6 (Totals so far)	6,017
Mar 31 M Turnbull	57	Mar 31 BKS	49
" 31 Balance c/d	5,300	" 31 Bank charges	28
	6,094		6,094

Bank Reconciliation Statement as at 31 March 20X6

Overdraft per cash book	5,300
Add Bankings not yet in bank statement	160
	5,460
Less Unpresented cheques	490
Overdraft per bank statement	4,970

31.1

Sales Ledger Control

Balances b/d	4,936	Returns inwards	1,139
Sales Day Book	49,916	Cheques and cash	46,490
		Discounts allowed	1,455
		Balances c/d	5,768
	54,852		54,852

31.3

Sales Ledger Control

20X5		20X5	
May 1 Balances b/d	6,420	May 31 Cash and bank	10,370
May 31 Sales	12,800	May 31 Discounts allowed	395
	50	May 31 Set-offs: purchases ledger	145
		May 31 Balances c/d	8,360
	19,270		19,270

31.5

Purchases Ledger Control

Returns outwards	2,648	Balances b/d	11,874
Bank	146,100	Purchases Day Book	154,562
Petty cash	78		
Discounts received	2,134		
Set-offs against sales ledger	1,036		
Balances c/d	14,530		
	*166,526		*166,436

*Difference between two sides 90

Sales Ledger Control

Balances b/d	3,100	Returns inwards	4,556
Sales Day Book	199,662	Bank and cash	185,960
		Discounts allowed	5,830
		Set-offs against purchase ledger	1,036
		Balances c/d	22,024
	219,406		219,406

31.7

Total Debtors Account

Balance b/d	26,555	Cash (600,570 − 344,890)	255,680
Credit sales	268,187	Discounts allowed	5,520
		Set-offs (Total debtors)	70
		Bad debts	780
		Returns inwards	4,140
		Balances c/d	28,552
	294,742		294,742
Balances b/d	28,552		

Total Creditors Account

Cash (503,970 − 14,440)	489,530	Balances b/d	43,450
Discounts received	3,510	Credit purchases	496,600
Set-offs (total creditors)	70		
Returns outwards	1,480		
Balances c/d	45,460		
	540,050		540,050
		Balances b/d	45,460

31.8

(a) To ensure an arithmetical check on the accounting records. The agreement of total of individual creditors balances with that of balance on control account provides that check.

If control account and ledger are kept by separate personnel, then a check on their work and honesty is provided.

(b) (i) Increase £198 (ii) Decrease £100 (iii) No effect (iv) Decrease £400 (v) Decrease £120.

(c) A computer will automatically enter two figures in different directions and will then confirm it in total fashion. As such there may seem at first sight for there to be no need for control accounts.

However, there is still the need to check on the accuracy of data input. It is important that both the skill and the honesty of the programmer are checked.

Accordingly there will still be a need for control accounts.

32.1

To economise on space, all narratives for journal entries are omitted.

(a)	J Harris	Dr	678	: L Hart	Cr 678
(b)	Machinery	Dr	4,390	: L Pyle	Cr 4,390
(c)	Van	Dr	3,800	: Motor expenses	Cr 3,800
(d)	E Fitzwilliam	Dr	9	: Sales	Cr 9
(e)	Sales	Dr	257	: Commissions rec'd	Cr 257
(f)	Cash needs double the amount.				
	T Heath	Dr	154	: T Heath	Cr 154
(g)	Purchases	Dr	189	: Drawings	Cr 189
(h)	Discounts allowed	Dr	366	: Discounts received	Cr 366

32.3

(a) 100 units × £1.39 = £139 *not* £1,390.

(b) (i) Stock overstated by £1,251 (i.e. 1,390 – 139).
    (ii) Cost of goods sold understated by £1,251.
    (iii) Net profit overstated by £1,251.
    (iv) Current Assets overstated by £1,251.
    (v) Owner's Capital overstated by £1,251.

32.4

(a)	Sales	Dr	10,000	: Capital	Cr 10,000
(b)	Drawings	Dr	700	: General expenses	Cr 700
(c)	Drawings	Dr	89	: Insurance	Cr 89
(d)	Purchases	Dr	270	: C Kelly	Cr 270
(e)	Bank	Dr	780	: Cash	Cr 780
(f)	Bank	Dr	400	: Cash	Cr 400
(g)	J Charlton	Dr	168	: M McCarthy	Cr 168
(h)	Motor expenses	Dr	1,000	: Motor disposals	Cr 1,000

33.1

(a)

The Journal (narratives omitted)

	Dr	Cr
(i) Suspense	100	
Sales		100
(ii) J Cantrell	250	
J Cochrane		250
(iii) Rent	70	
Suspense		70
(iv) Suspense	300	
Discounts received		300
(v) Sales	360	
Motor disposals		360

(b)

Suspense Account

Sales	100	Balance b/d	330
Discounts received	300	Rent	70
	400		400

(c)

Net profit per accounts		7,900
Add (i) Sales undercast	100	
(iv) Discounts undercast	300	400
		8,300
Less (iii) Rent undercast	70	
(v) Reduction in sales	360	430
Corrected net profit		7,870

33.3

Item	If no effect state 'No'	Debit side exceeds credit side by	Credit side exceeds debit side by
(i)	No		
(ii)			£3,400
(iii)	No		
(iv)		£1,500	
(v)			£610
(vi)			£170
(vii)	No		

33.4

Trial Balance as at 31 January 20X9

	Dr	Cr
Drawings	2,800	
Stock	2,597	
Debtors (2,130 – 6)	2,124	
Furniture (1,750 + 120)	1,870	
Cash	1,020	
Returns inwards	85	
Business expenses	950	
Purchases (4,380 – 120)	4,260	
Discounts allowed	38	
Capital		5,500
Creditors (2,735 – 75)		2,660
Sales (7,430 + 108)		7,538
Discounts received		46
	15,744	15,744

33.5

(a) (i)

The Journal

	Dr	Cr
C Thomas	450	
Thomasson Manufacturing Ltd		450
Suspense	100	
Telephone		100
Suspense	2,000	
Sales account		2,000
Machine repairs	390	
Machinery		390
Suspense	1,500	
Rent received*		1,500
Purchases account	765	
P Brooks		765

*Assumed not invoiced to Atlas Ltd

(ii) *Computation of Corrected Profit for year to 31 December 20X8*

Profit as originally reported		47,240
Add Telephone expense overstated	100	
Sales understated	2,000	
Rent received omitted	1,500	3,600
		50,840
Less Machinery repairs understated	390	
Purchases omitted	765	1,155
Corrected profit figure		49,685

(b) (i) Per text (ii) Per text

33.7

(a)

Difference on Trial Balance Suspense

Per trial balance	2,513		J Winters	198
Discounts received	324		Wages	2,963
Discounts allowed	324			
	3,161			3,161

(b) *Computation of Corrected Net Profit for year to 30 April 20X7*

Net profit per draft accounts			24,760
		–	+
(i) Discounts			648
(ii) Wages		2,963	
(iv) Stationery stock			1,500
(vi) Remittance		3,000	
		5,963	2,148
Correct net profit			3,815
(iii) and (v) did not affect profit			20,945

(c) Per text

R Stubbs

34.1

Trading Account for the year ended 31 December 20X9

Sales			60,000
Less Cost of goods sold:			
Stock 1.1.20X9		9,872	
Add Purchases	(D)	50,748	
		60,620	
Less Stock 32.12.20X9	(C)	12,620	
Gross profit	(B)		48,000
	(A)		12,000

Missing figures found in following order (A) to (D).
(A) Mark-up is 25%. Therefore Margin is 20%. Sales are 60,000 so Margin is 20%; 20% × 60,000 = 12,000 Gross Profit
(B) + (A) = 60,000. Therefore (B) + 12,000 = 60,000 and accordingly (B) is 48,000.
(C) – 12,620 = 48,000. Therefore (C) is 60,620.
(D) + 9,872 = 60,620. Therefore (D) is 50,748.

34.3

(a) We know that

$$\frac{\text{Cost of Goods Sold}}{\text{Average Stock}} = \text{Rate of Turnover}$$

Substituting $\dfrac{x}{12,600} = 7$

$x = $ Cost of Goods Sold = 88,200.

(b) If margin is 50%, gross profit is 50% of the cost of sales = 44,100.
(c) Turnover is (a) + (b) = 88,200 + 44,100 = 132,300.
(d) $66^{2}/_{3}$% × 44,100 = 29,400.
(e) Gross Profit – Expenses = Net Profit = 14,700.

34.5

(a) Sales = 121,500 + 25% (30,375) = 151,875.
(b) 28,500 – (7% × 150,000) 10,500 = 18,000.

(c) $\dfrac{121,500}{(20,100 + 28,500) \div 2} = \dfrac{121,500}{24,300} = 5$

(d) Gross profit is $27^{1}/_{2}$% × 140,000 = 38,500.
Sales are 140,000 + 38,500 = 178,500.
Expenses are 7% of sales = 12,495.
Net profit = 38,500 – 12,495 = 26,005.

35.1

B Arkwright
Statement of Affairs as at 31 December 20X5

Fixed assets			
Van at cost		2,800	
Less Depreciation		550	
			2,250
Current assets			
Stock		3,950	
Debtors		4,970	
Prepaid expenses		170	
Bank		2,564	
Cash		55	
		11,709	
Less Current liabilities			
Trade creditors	1,030		
Expenses owing	470		
		1,500	
Net current assets			10,209
			12,459
Capital			
Cash introduced		10,000	(C)
Add Net profit			(B)
Less Drawings			(A)
			5,673

Missing figures (A), (B) and (C) deduced in that order. (A) to balance is 12,459, thus (B) has to be 18,132 and (C) becomes 8,132.

35.3
Workings:

Purchases	Bank	29,487
	Cash	2,994
		32,481
− Creditors 31.12.20X6		5,624
		26,857
+ Creditors 31.12.20X7		7,389
Purchases for 20X7		34,246

Sales	Banked	37,936
	Cash	9,630
		47,566
− Debtors 31.12.20X6		9,031
		38,535
+ Debtors 31.12.20X7		8,624
Sales for 20X7		47,159

Opening Capital:			
	Bank	405	
	Stock	13,862	
	Debtors	9,031	
	Rates prepaid	210	
	Fixtures	2,500	26,008
	Less Creditors	5,624	
	Rent owing	150	
		5,774	
			20,234

Kelly
Trading and Profit and Loss Account for the year ended 31 December 20X7

Sales			47,159
Less Cost of goods sold:			
Opening stock		13,862	
Add Purchases		34,246	
		48,108	
Less Closing stock		15,144	
			32,964
Gross profit			14,195
Less Expenses:			
Wages		5,472	
Rent (1,650 − 150)		1,500	
Rates (890 + 210 − 225)		875	
Sundry expenses		375	
Depreciation: Fixtures		250	
			8,472
Net profit			5,723

Balance Sheet as at 31 December 20X7

Fixed assets			
Fixtures at valuation		2,500	
Less Depreciation		250	
			2,250
Current assets			
Stock		15,144	
Debtors		8,624	
Prepayments		225	
		23,993	
Less Current liabilities			
Trade creditors	7,389		
Bank overdraft	602		
		7,991	
Net current assets			16,002
			18,252
Capital			
Balance at 1.1.20X7			20,234
Add Net profit			5,723
			25,957
Less Drawings (1,164 + 6,541)			7,705
			18,252

35.5

Jenny Barnes
Trading and Profit and Loss Account for the year ended 30 April 20X9

Sales*		102,908
Opening stock	9,500	
Add Purchases (70,500 + 7,600)	78,100	
	87,600	
Less Closing stock	13,620	
Cost of goods sold	73,980	
Gross profit c/d	28,928	
	102,908	102,908
Gross profit b/d		28,928
Sales assistants' wages	5,260	
Vehicle running expenses	1,020	
Bad debts	150	
Miscellaneous expenses**	1,370	
Light and heat	940	
Depreciation: Equipment	720	
Vehicles	1,000	
Net profit	18,468	
	28,928	28,928

*Sales 96,500 + takings in cash later spent 6,408
(drawings 6,000 + expenses 408)
**Bank 962 + cash 408 = 1,370

35.7

(a)

Creditors Control

Bank	101,500	Balances b/d	7,400
Cash	1,800	Drawings: Goods	600
Balances c/d	8,900	Purchases (difference)	104,200
	112,200		112,200

(b)

Janet Lambert
Trading and Profit and Loss Account for the year ended 31 August 20X9

Sales (deduced – as margin is 25% = 4 × gross profit)		128,000
Opening stock	8,600	
Add Purchases	104,200	
	112,800	
Less Closing stock	16,800	
Cost of goods sold		96,000
Gross profit ($33\frac{1}{3}$% of Cost of goods sold)		32,000
Less: Casual labour (1,200 + 6,620)	7,820	
Rent (5,040 + 300 – 420)	4,920	
Delivery costs	3,000	
Electricity (1,390 + 160 – 210)	1,340	
		17,080
Net profit		14,920

Balance Sheet as at 31 August 20X9

Current assets			
Stock		16,800	
Debtors		4,300	
Prepayments		420	
Bank		1,650	
Cash		330	
			23,500
Less Current liabilities			
Creditors		8,900	
Expenses owing		160	9,060
			14,440
Capital:			
Balance as at 1 September 20X8 (Workings 1)			7,850
Add Net profit			14,920
			22,770
Less Drawings (Workings 2)			8,330
			14,440

Workings:

(1) Capital as on 1.9.20X8. Stock 8,600 + Debtors 3,900 + Bank 2,300 + Cash 360 = 15,460 – Creditors 7,400 – Accruals 210 = 7,850.

(2) Cash drawings. Step (A) find cash received from sales. Debtors b/d 3,900 + Sales 128,000 – Debtors c/d 4,300 = 127,600 cash received.

Step (B) find cash banked. Balance b/d 2,300 + cash received? – payments 117,550 = balance c/d 1,650. Therefore cash banked? = 116,900. Step (C) draw up cash account:

Balance b/d	360	Labour	1,200
Sales receipts	127,600	Purchases	1,800
		Banked	116,900
		Drawings (difference)	7,730
		Balance c/d	330
	127,960		127,960

(c) Per text.

35.9

David Denton
Profit and Loss Account for the year ended 31 December 20X0

Work done: Credit accounts	29,863	
For cash	3,418	
		33,281
Less Expenses:		
Materials (9,600 – 580)	9,020	
Secretarial salary	3,000	
Rent	225	
Rates (180 – 45)	135	
Insurance (800 – 200)	600	
Electricity (1,122 + 374 estimated)	1,496	
Motor expenses	912	
General expenses (1,349 + 295)	1,644	
Loan interest (4,000 × 10% × ³/₄)	300	
Provision for doubtful debts	425	
Accounting fee	250	
Amortisation of lease (650 × ³/₄)	487	
Depreciation: Equipment	960	
Van	900	1,860
		20,354
Net profit		12,927

Balance Sheet as at 31 December 20X0

	Cost	Depreciation	
Fixed assets			
Lease	6,500	487	
Equipment	4,800	960	
Vehicle	3,600	900	
	14,900	2,347	12,553
Current assets			
Stock		580	
Debtors	4,250		
Less Provision for doubtful debts	425	3,825	
Prepaid expenses (75 + 200)		275	
Bank (see workings)		6,084	
Cash		123	
		10,887	
Less Current liabilities			
Trade creditors	714		
Interest owing	300		
Accountancy fee owing	250		
Rates owing	135		
Electricity owing	374	1,773	
Net current assets			9,114
			21,667
Less Loan			(4,000)
			17,667
Financed by:			
Capital			
Introduced (6,500 + 3,600)		10,100	
Add Net profit		12,927	
		23,027	
Less Drawings (4,680 + 280 + 400)		5,360	
		17,667	

Workings:
Bank (6,500 + 25,613 + 2,600 + 4,000) = 38,713 – 4,680 – 280 – 6,500 – 300 –
3,000 – 8,886 – 4,800 – 1,122 – 912 – 800 = 6,084

35.10

(a)

J Duncan
Capital Account on 1 January 20X8

Bank		8,000
Cash		300
Stock		4,100
Machinery		12,600
Rent prepaid		200
Debtors		6,300
		31,500
Less: Creditors	2,400	
Loan	5,000	7,400
		24,100

(b)

J Duncan
Trading and Profit and Loss Account for the year ended 31 December 20X8

Sales			40,450
Less: Sales returns			1,200
			39,250
Less: Cost of Sales			
Opening Stock at 1 January 20X8		4,100	
Add: Purchases		18,950	
		23,050	
Less: Withdrawn by the owner	300		
Less: Closing stock at 31 December 20X8	3,200	3,500	
Gross profit			19,550
Add: Discount received			350
			20,050
Less: Expenses			
Rent		1,850	
Bad debts written off		400	
Wages		6,100	
Insurance		1,450	
Loan interest		400	
Depreciation		4,200	
Repairs		300	
Electricity		750	15,450
Net profit			4,600

Workings:
Sales 26,000 − 250 + 14,000 + 400 + 400 − 6,300 + 5,000 + 1,200 + 400 = 40,450
Purchases 18,500 − 2,400 + 2,500 + 350 = 18,950
Depreciation = balancing figure.

35.11   J Duncan
Balance Sheet as at 31 December 20X8

Fixed Assets			
Machinery at 1 January 20X8		12,600	
Add: Additions		7,500	
		20,100	
Less: Depreciation		4,200	15,900
Current assets			
Stock		3,200	
Debtors		5,000	
Bank		2,600	
Cash		50	
		10,850	
Current liabilities			
Creditors		2,500	
Accrued charges			
Loan interest	100		
Rent	250	350	
		2,850	8,000
			23,900
Less: Long-term liabilities			
Bank loan 8%			(5,000)
			18,900
Capital Account			
Balance at 1 January 20X8		24,100	
Add: Net profit		4,600	
		28,700	
Less: Drawings		9,800	
			18,900

36.1   Uppertown Football Club
Income and Expenditure Account for the year ended 31 December 20X4

Income		
Collections at matches		1,650
Profit on refreshments		315
		1,965
Less Expenditure		
Rent for pitch (300 − 60)	240	
Printing and stationery (65 + 33)	98	
Secretary's expenses	144	
Repairs to equipment	46	
Groundsman's wages	520	
Miscellaneous expenses	66	
Depreciation of equipment	125	1,239
Surplus of income over expenditure		726

Balance Sheet as at 31 December 20X4

Fixed assets		
Equipment	625	
Less Depreciation	125	500
Current assets		
Prepayment	60	
Cash	879	
	939	
Less *Current liabilities*		
Expenses owing	33	
Net current assets		906
		1,406
Financed by:		
Accumulated fund		
Balance at 1.1.20X4 (500 + 180)		680
Add Surplus of income over expenditure		726
		1,406

36.3

(a)

The Happy Haddock Angling Club
Income and Expenditure Account for the year ended 31 December 20X8

Income:		
Subscriptions		3,500
Visitors' fees		650
Competition fees		820
Snack bar profit (see workings)		1,750
		6,720
Less Expenditure:		
Rent and rates	1,500	
Secretarial expenses	240	
Loan interest	260	
Depreciation on games equipment	400	2,400
Surplus of income over expenditure		4,320

Workings: Snack bar profit: 6,000 − (800 + 3,750 − 900) − 600 = 1,750

(b)

Balance Sheet as at 31 December 20X8

Fixed assets			
Club house buildings			20,500
Games equipment		2,000	
Less Depreciation		400	1,600
			22,100
Current assets			
Snack bar stocks		900	
Bank		700	
		1,600	
Less Current liabilities			
Subscriptions received in advance		380	1,220
			23,320
Financed by:			
Accumulated fund			
Balance 1.1.20X8 (see workings)		13,500	
Add surplus for year		4,320	17,820
Loan from bank			5,500
			23,320

Workings: 200 + 800 + 12,500 = 13,500

36.5

(a)

Accumulated fund 1 August 20X8

Equipment		975
Stocks of prizes		38
Arrears of subscriptions		65
Cash and bank		210
		1,288
Less Subscriptions in advance	10	
Prizes suppliers	58	68
		1,220

(b)

(i)

Subscriptions

In arrears b/d	65	In advance b/d	10
In advance c/d	37	Cash	1,987
Income and expenditure	1,980	In arrears c/d	85
	2,082		2,082

(ii)

Competition prizes

Stocks b/d	38	Creditors b/d	58
Cash	270	Stock c/d	46
Creditors c/d	68	Cost of prizes given	272
	376		376

(c)

Miniville Rotary Club
Income and expenditure account for the year ended 31 July 20X9

Income		
Subscriptions		1,980
Ticket sales	437	
Less Cost of prizes	272	165
Donations received		177
		2,322
Less Expenditure		
Rent (1,402 − 500)	902	
Visiting speakers' expenses	1,275	
Secretarial expenses	163	
Stationery and printing	179	
Donations to charities	35	
Depreciation	195	2,749
Excess of expenditure over income		427

Balance sheet as at 31 July 20X9

Fixed assets			
Equipment at cost		1,420	
Less Depreciation		640	780
Current assets			
Stocks of prizes		46	
Arrears of subscriptions		85	
		131	
Less Current liabilities			
Creditors for prizes	68		
Advance subscriptions	37		
Bank overdraft	13	118	13
			793
Accumulated fund			
Balance 1.8.20X8			1,220
Less Excess of expenditure over income			427
			793

36.7

(a) Café operations:

Takings		4,660
Less Cost of supplies:		
Opening stock	800	
Add purchases (1,900 + 80)	1,980	
	2,780	
Less Closing stock	850	1,930
		2,730
Wages		2,000
Profit		730

Sports equipment:		
Sales		900
Less Cost of goods sold:		
Opening stock	1,000	
Add Purchases (1,000 × 50%)	500	
	1,500	
Less Closing stock (see note)	900	600
Profit		300

Note: To find closing stock 900 is sales at 50% on cost profit so cost of sales is 600. By arithmetical deduction closing stock is found to be 900.

(b)

Subscriptions

Owing b/d	60	In advance b/d		120
		Cash: 20X7		40
Income and expenditure	1,280	20X8		1,100
		20X9		80
In advance c/d	80	Owing c/d		80
	1,420			1,420

Life Subscriptions

Income and expenditure	220	Balance b/d	1,400
(11 × 20)		Cash	200
Balance c/d	1,380		
	1,600		1,600

(c)

Happy Tickers & Social Club
Income and Expenditure Account for the year ended 31 December 20X8

Income:		
Subscriptions (1,280 + 220)		1,500
Profit on café operations		730
Profit on sports equipment		300
		2,530
Less Expenditure		
Rent	1,200	
Insurance	600	
Repairs to roller (½ × 450)	225	
Sports equipment depreciation (see note 1)	486	
Depreciation of roller (½ × 200)	100	2,611
Excess of expenditure over income		81

Balance Sheet as at 31 December 20X8

Fixed assets		
Share in motor roller at cost	1,000	
Less Depreciation to date	500	500
Used sports equipment at valuation		700
		1,200
Current assets		
Stock of new sports equipment (*see note 2*)	900	
Stock of café supplies	850	
Subscriptions owing	80	
Carefree Conveyancers: owing for expenses	225	
Prepaid expenses	350	
Cash and bank (note 3)	754	
	3,159	
Less Current liabilities		
Café suppliers	80	
Advance subscriptions	80	160
		2,999
		4,199
Less Life subscriptions		1,380
		2,819
Accumulated fund		
Balance at 1.1.20X8		2,900
Less Excess of expenditure		(81)
		2,819

Notes:

1 Used Sports Equipment

Stock b/d	700	Cash	14
Transferred from		Income and expenditure a/c	486
purchases	500	Stock c/d	700
	1,200		1,200

2 b/d 1,000 + bought (1,000 × ½) 500 = 1,500 – sold 600 = 900

3 b/d 1,210 + receipts 6,994 – paid 7,450 = 754

(d) To most people probably the best description of the item would be as deferred income, i.e. income paid in advance for future benefits.

It could, however, be described as a liability of the club. The club in future will have to provide and finance amenities for life members, but they do not have to pay any more money for it. This is therefore the liability of the future to provide these services without further payment.

37.1

Loose Tools

20X4				20X4		
Jan 1	Stock	b/d	1,250	Dec 31	Manufacturing	994
Dec 31	Bank		2,000	" 31	Stock c/d	2,700
" 31	Wages		275			
" 31	Materials		169			
			3,694			3,694
20X5				20X5		
Jan 1	Stock	b/d	2,700	Dec 31	Manufacturing	1,695
Dec 31	Bank		1,450	" 31	Stock c/d	3,340
" 31	Wages		495			
" 31	Materials		390			
			5,035			5,035
20X6				20X6		
Jan 1	Stock	b/d	3,340	Dec 31	Bank: Refund	88
Dec 31	Bank		1,890	" 31	Manufacturing	1,897
" 31	Wages		145	" 31	Stock c/d	3,680
" 31	Materials		290			
			5,665			5,665

37.2

(a) (i) Straight line

Cost £112,000 − trade-in £12,000 = £100,000
Per month £100,000 ÷ 48 = 2,083.33

20X6	9 months	=	18,750
20X7	12 months	=	25,000
20X8	12 months	=	25,000
20X9	12 months	=	25,000
20X0	3 months	=	6,250
			100,000

(ii) Diminishing (Reducing) Balance:

Cost		112,000
Depreciation 20X6 (40%)		44,800
		67,200
Depreciation 20X7		26,880
		40,320
Depreciation 20X8		16,128
		24,192
Depreciation 20X9		9,677
		14,515
Depreciation 20X0		5,806
		8,709

(iii) Units of output (Total £100,000)

20X6	4,000/20,000	=	20,000
20X7	5,000/20,000	=	25,000
20X8	5,000/20,000	=	25,000
20X9	5,000/20,000	=	25,000
20X0	1,000/20,000	=	5,000

(b) (i)

Machine

20X7			20X7		
Jan 1	Balance b/d	112,000	Dec 31	Assets disposal	112,000

(ii) **Provision for Depreciation**

20X7			20X7		
Dec 31	Assets disposal	31,250	Jan 1	Balance b/d	18,750
			Dec 31	Profit and loss	12,500
		31,250			31,250

(iii) **Assets Disposals**

20X7			20X7		
Dec 31	Machine	112,000	Jun 30	Bank	80,000
			Dec 31	Depreciation	31,250
			" 31	Profit and loss	750
		112,000			112,000

37.4

T Jackson
Manufacturing, Trading and Profit and Loss Accounts
for the year ended 31 December 20X7

Stock raw materials 1.1.20X7			18,450
Add Purchases			64,300
Add Carriage inwards			1,605
			84,355
Less Stock raw materials 31.12.20X7			20,210
Cost of raw materials consumed			64,145
Direct labour			65,810
Prime cost			129,955
Factory overhead expenses			
Rent $^2/_3$		1,800	
Fuel and power		5,920	
Depreciation: Machinery		8,300	
			16,020
			145,975
Add Work in progress 1.1.20X7			23,600
			169,575
Less Work in progress 31.12.20X7			17,390
Production cost goods completed c/d			152,185
			200,600
Sales			200,600
Less Cost of goods sold			
Stock finished goods 1.1.20X7		17,470	
Add Production cost goods completed b/d		152,185	
		169,655	
Less Stock finished goods 31.12.20X7		21,485	
			148,170
Gross profit			52,430
Less Expenses:			
Office salaries		16,920	
Rent $^1/_3$		900	
Lighting and heating		5,760	
Depreciation: Office equipment		1,950	
			25,530
Net profit			26,900

37.6

D Saunders

Manufacturing Trading and Profit and Loss Account for the year ended 31 December 20X6

Stock of raw materials 1.1.20X6		8,565
Add Purchases		39,054
		47,619
Less Stock of raw materials 31.12.20X6		9,050
Cost of raw materials consumed		38,569
Manufacturing wages (45,470 + 305)		45,775
Prime cost		84,344
Factory overhead expenses:		
Factory lighting and heating	2,859	
General expenses: factory	5,640	
Rent of factory	4,800	
Depreciation: machinery	2,000	15,299
Production cost of goods completed c/d		99,643
Sales		136,500
Less Cost of goods sold:		
Stock finished goods 1.1.20X6	29,480	
Add Production cost of goods completed b/d	99,643	
	129,123	
Less stock finished goods 31.12.20X6	31,200	97,923
Gross profit		38,577
Less Expenses:		
Office salaries	6,285	
General expenses: office	3,816	
Office rent (2,200 – 108)	2,092	
Office heating and lighting	1,110	
Sales reps' commission	7,860	
Delivery van expenses	2,500	
Depreciation: Office equipment	1,500	
Premises	1,000	26,163
Net profit		12,414

Balance Sheet as at 31 December 20X6

	Cost	Depreciation	Net
Fixed assets			
Premises	50,000	11,000	39,000
Machinery	50,000	19,500	30,500
Office Equipment	15,000	5,500	9,500
	115,000	36,000	79,000
Current Assets			
Stocks: Finished goods		31,200	
Raw materials		9,050	
Debtors		28,370	
Prepaid expenses		108	
Bank		13,337	
		82,065	
Less current liabilities			
Creditors	19,450		
Expenses owing	305	19,755	
Net current assets			62,310
			141,310
Capital			
Balance 1.1.20X6			137,456
Add Net profit			12,414
			149,870
Less Drawings			8,560
			141,310

37.8

(a)

Jane Seymour

Manufacturing, Trading and Profit and Loss Account for the year ended 31 July 20X6

Direct materials purchased		43,000
Less Stock 31 July 20X6		7,000
		36,000
Direct factory wages		39,000
Prime cost		75,000
Factory overhead expenses:		
Indirect factory wages	8,000	
Machinery repairs	1,600	
Rent and insurance (11,600 – 800) × $\frac{2}{3}$	7,200	
Light and power (5,000 + 1,000) × $\frac{2}{3}$	4,000	
Loose tools (9,000 – 5,000)	4,000	
Motor vehicle running expenses (12,000 × $\frac{1}{2}$)	6,000	
Depreciation: Plant and machinery	6,000	
Motor vehicles (7,500 × $\frac{1}{2}$)	3,750	40,550
		115,550
Less Work in progress 31 July 20X6		12,300
		103,250
Transfer of goods manufactured to trading account		95,000
Loss on manufacturing		8,250

Sales		170,000
Less Goods manufactured transferred	95,000	
Stock at 31 July 20X6	10,000	
		85,000
Gross profit		85,000
Less Administrative staff salaries	31,000	
Administrative expenses	9,000	
Sales and distribution staff salaries	13,000	
Rent and insurance (11,600 − 800) × 1/3	3,600	
Motor vehicle running expenses (12,000 × 1/2)	6,000	
Light and power (5,000 + 1,000) × 1/3	2,000	
Depreciation: Motors (7,500 × 1/2)	3,750	
		68,350
Net profit in trading		16,650
Loss on manufacturing		8,250
Overall net profit		8,400

(b) *Conservatism.* The valuation of stock or work in progress does not include any element of expected future profit.

Matching. All of the prepayments and accruals adjusted for are examples of matching expenses against the time period, as also are the depreciation provisions.

Going Concern. When valuing stocks and work in progress, it has been assumed that the business is going to carry on indefinitely, and that they will be sold in the normal course of business rather than being sold because of cessation of activities.

38.1 Charnley's Department Store
Trading Account for the year ended 31 December 20X8

	Electrical	Furniture	Leisure Goods
Sales	29,840	73,060	39,581
Less Cost of goods sold:			
Stock 1.1.20X8	6,080	17,298	14,370
Add Purchases	18,195	54,632	27,388
	24,275	71,930	41,758
Less Stock 31.12.20X8	7,920	16,150	22,395
	16,355	55,780	19,363
Gross profit	13,485	17,280	20,218

38.2 J Spratt
Trading and Profit and Loss Account for the year ended 31 March 20X9

	A		B	
Sales		15,000		10,000
Less Cost of goods sold:				
Stock 1.4.20X8	250		200	
Add Purchases	11,800		8,200	
	12,050		8,400	
Less Stock 31.3.20X9	300	11,750	150	8,250
Gross profit		3,250		1,750
Less Expenses:				
Wages	1,000		750	
Newspapers: delivery	150			
General office salaries	450		300	
Rates	26		104	
Fire insurance	10		40	
Lighting and air conditioning	24		96	
Repairs to premises	5		20	
Internal telephone	5		20	
Cleaning	6		24	
Accounting and audit	72		48	
General office expenses	36	1,784	24	1,426
Net profits		1,466		324

39.1 M Daly
Cash Flow Statement for the year ended 31 December 20X3

Net cash flow from operating activities (note 1)		2,850
Returns on investments and servicing of finance		
Payments to acquire tangible fixed assets		(1,000)
Financing		
Loan received	1,000	
Drawings	(1,500)	
		(500)
Increase in cash		1,350

Notes:

1 Reconciliation of net profit to net cash inflow:

Net profit		2,200
Depreciation	460	
Decrease in stock	30	
Decrease in creditors	(360)	
Decrease in debtors	520	
Net cash flow from operating activities		2,850

2 Analysis of changes in cash during the year:

Balance at 1 January 20X3		(640)
Net cash inflow		1,350
Balance at 31 December 20X3		710

39.3

(a)

Malcolm Phillips
Cash Flow Statement for the year ended 30 April 20X9

Net cash flow from operating activities (note 1)		6,600
Returns on investments and servicing of finance		
Payments for fixed assets		(3,000)
Financing		
Capital introduced	2,000	
Drawings	(8,000)	
		(6,000)
Decrease in cash		(2,400)

Notes:

1 Reconciliation of net profit to net cash inflow:

Net profit		8,500
Depreciation	200	
Increase in creditors	200	
Increase in stock	(2,800)	
Decrease in debtors	500	
		(1,900)
		6,600

2 Analysis of changes in cash during the year:

Balance at 1.5.20X8	(900)
Net cash inflow	2,400
Balance at 30.4.20X9	1,500

(b) (i) $\dfrac{7,500}{30,000} \times \dfrac{100}{1} = 25\%$ (ii) $\dfrac{22,500}{(3,100 + 5,900) \div 2} = \dfrac{22,500}{4,500} = 5$

39.4

C Willis
Cash Flow Statement for the year ended 31 December 20X8

Net cash flow from operating activities (note 1)		11,747
Returns on investments and servicing of finance		
Receipts from sale of fixed assets		2,300
Financing		
Loan repaid to P Bond	(1,000)	
Drawings	(12,500)	
		(13,500)
Increase in cash		547

Notes:

1 Reconciliation of net profit to net cash inflow:

Net profit		16,122
Depreciation	1,090	
Profit on sale of van	(570)	
Increase in doubtful debt provision	120	
Increase in stock	(6,855)	
Decrease in debtors (5,490 – 3,800)	1,690	
Increase in creditors	150	
		(4,375)
		11,747

2 Analysis of changes in cash during the year:

Balance at 1 January 20X8	1,568
Net cash inflow	547
Balance at 31 December 20X8	2,115

40.1

Ollier's Books (dates ignored)

Joint Venture with Avon

Cars	900	Sales	1,600
Repairs and respraying	60		
Profit on venture	237		
Balance c/d	403		
	1,600		1,600
Cash to Avon	403	Balance b/d	403

Avon's Books

Joint Venture with Ollier

Garage rental	20	Balance c/d	403
Advertising	10		
Licence and insurance	36		
Car	100		
Profit on venture	237		
	403		403
Balance b/d	403	Cash from Ollier	403

Memorandum Joint Venture Account

Cars	1,000	Sales	1,600
Repairs and respraying	60		
Garage rental	20		
Advertising	10		
Licence and insurance	36		
Profit on venture			
Ollier ½	237		
Avon ½	237		
	474		
	1,600		1,600

40.3

Plant's Books

Joint Venture with Hoe and Reap

Rent	156	Balance c/d	620
Labour: Planting	105		
Labour: Fertilising	36		
Sundries	10		
Labour	18		
Fertiliser	29		
Share of profit	266		
	620		620
Balance b/d	620	Cash from Reap	620

Hoe's Books
Joint Venture with Plant and Reap

	£		£
Seeds	48	Balance c/d	179
Motor expenses	17		
Share of profit	114		
	179		179
Balance b/d	179	Cash from Reap	179

Reap's Books
Joint Venture with Plant and Hoe

	£		£
Lifting	73	Sales	987
Sale expenses	39		
Share of profit	76		
Balance c/d	799		
	987		987
Cash to Plant	620	Balance b/d	799
Cash to Hoe	179		
	799		799

Plant, Hoe and Reap, Memorandum Joint Venture Account

	£		£
Rent	156	Sales	987
Labour: Planting	105		
Labour: Fertilising	36		
Labour: sundry	18		
Labour: lifting	73		
Fertiliser	29		
Motor expenses	17		
Seeds	48		
Sale expenses	39		
Sundries	10		
Profit shared: Plant	266		
Hoe	114		
Reap	76		
	456		
	987		987

41.1
Stephens, Owen and Jones
Appropriation Account for the year ended 31 December 20X6

	£	£
Net profit b/d		25,200
Less Salaries: Owen	3,000	
Jones	1,000	4,000
Interest on capitals: Stephens	600	
Owen	400	
Jones	200	1,200
		5,200
		20,000
Balance of profits shared: Stephens $2/5$	8,000	
Owen $2/5$	8,000	
Jones $1/5$	4,000	
		20,000

41.2
(a)
Roach & Salmon
Profit and Loss Appropriation Account for the year ended 31 December 20X9

	£	£
Net profit brought down		32,840
Less: Salaries: Roach	9,000	
Salmon	6,000	15,000
Interest on capital:		
Roach	6,000	
Salmon	4,800	10,800
		25,800
		7,040
Balance of profits shared:		
Roach $1/2$	3,520	
Salmon $1/2$	3,520	7,040

Current Accounts (dates omitted)

	Roach	Salmon		Roach	Salmon
Drawings	12,860	13,400	Salaries	9,000	6,000
Balances c/d	5,660	920	Interest on capital	6,000	4,800
			Share of profits	3,520	3,520
	18,520	14,320		18,520	14,320

(b) Partnership Act 1890 (Section 24).

41.3
Williams, Powell and Howe
Appropriation Account for the year ended 31 December 20X7

	£	£
Net profit b/d		30,350
Add Interest on drawings: Williams	240	
Powell	180	
Howe	130	550
		30,900
Less Interest on Capitals: Williams	2,000	
Powell	1,500	
Howe	900	
	4,400	
Salaries: Powell	2,000	
Howe	3,500	
	5,500	9,900
		21,000
Balance of Profits Shared: Williams 50%	10,500	
Powell 30%	6,300	
Howe 20%	4,200	
		21,000

41.6

Mendez & Marshall
Trading and Profit and Loss Account for the year ended 30 June 20X9

Sales			123,650
Less Cost of goods sold:			
Opening stock		41,979	
Add Purchases		85,416	
		127,395	
Less Closing stock		56,340	
			71,055
Gross profit			52,595
Add Reduction in Provision for doubtful debts			80
			52,675
Less Salaries and wages (18,917 + 200)		19,117	
Office expenses (2,416 + 96)		2,512	
Carriage outwards		1,288	
Discounts allowed		115	
Bad debts		503	
Loan interest		4,000	
Depreciation: Fixtures	770		
Buildings	1,000	1,770	
			29,305
Net profit			23,370
Add Interest on drawings: Mendez		180	
Marshall		120	
			300
			23,670
Less Interest on capitals: Mendez	3,500		
Marshall	2,950		
		6,450	
Salary: Mendez		800	
			7,250
			16,420
Balance of profits shared: Mendez		8,210	
Marshall		8,210	
			16,420

Balance Sheet as at 31 December 20X7 (extracts)

Capitals: Williams		40,000	
Powell		30,000	
Howe		18,000	
			88,000

Current accounts:

	Williams	Powell	Howe
Balances 1.1.20X7	1,860	946	717
Add Share of profits	10,500	6,300	4,200
Salaries	2,000	2,000	3,500
Interest on capital		1,500	900
	14,360	10,746	9,317
Less Interest on drawings	240	180	130
Drawings	9,200	7,100	6,900
	4,920	3,466	2,287

	10,673

41.5
Considerations

(a) *Legal position re Partnership Act 1890*: Partners can agree to anything. The main thing is that of mutual agreement. The agreement can either be very formal in a partnership deed drawn up by a lawyer or else it can be evidenced in other ways.

The Act lays down the provisions for profit sharing if agreement has not been reached, written or otherwise.

(b) As Bee is not taking active part in the running of the business he could be registered as a limited partner under the 1907 Limited Partnership Act. This has the advantage that his liability is limited to the amount of capital invested by him; he can lose that but his personal possessions cannot be taken to pay any debts of the firm.

As Bee is a 'sleeping partner' you will have to decide whether his reward should be in the form of a fixed amount, or should vary according to the profits made. In this context you should also bear in mind whether or not he would suffer a share of losses if they occurred.

If he were to have a fixed amount, irrespective as to whether profits had been made or not, then the question arises as to the amount required. This is obviously a more risky investment than, say, government securities. He therefore would naturally expect to get a higher return.

Bee would probably feel aggrieved if the profits rose sharply, but he was still limited to the amounts already described. There could be an arrangement for extra payments if the profits exceeded a given figure.

Cee is the expert conducting the operations of the business. He will consequently expect a major share of the profits.

One possibility would be to give him a salary, similar to his current salary, before dividing whatever profits then remain.

(c) Dee is making himself available, as well as bringing in some capital. Because of this active involvement he will affect the profits made. It would seem appropriate to give him a salary commensurate with such work, plus a share of the profits.

(d) *Interest on capital*: Whatever is decided about profit-sharing, it would seem appropriate for each of the partners to be given interest on their capitals before sharing the balance of the profits.

41.8

Brick & Stone

(a) *Trading and Profit and Loss Account for the year ended 30 September 20X9*

Sales			322,100
Less Returns inwards			2,100
			320,000
Less Cost of goods sold			
Opening stock		23,000	
Purchases (208,200 – 1,000)	207,200		
Carriage inwards	1,700		
	208,900		
Less Returns outwards	6,100	202,800	
		225,800	
Less Closing stock		32,000	193,800
Gross profit			126,200
Less Establishment expenses:			
Rent and rates (10,300 – 600)	9,700		
Heat and light	8,700		
Depreciation: Fixtures	2,600	21,000	
Administrative Expenses:			
Staff salaries	36,100		
Telephone (2,900 + 400)	3,300		
Printing, stationery and postages	3,500	42,900	
Sales and distribution expenses:			
Motor expenses	5,620		
Carriage outwards	2,400		
Depreciation: Motors	9,200	17,220	
Financial expenses:			
Discounts allowable	950		
Loan interest	250		
	1,200		
	370	830	81,950
			44,250
Less Discounts receivable			
Net profit			
Less Salary: Stone		6,000	
Balance of profits shared:			
Brick ³/₅	22,950		
Stone ²/₅	15,300	38,250	44,250

Balance Sheet as at 30 June 20X9

	Cost	Depn	
Fixed assets			
Buildings	75,000	26,000	49,000
Fixtures	11,000	4,070	6,930
	86,000	30,070	55,930
Current assets			
Stock		56,340	
Debtors	16,243		
Less Provision for doubtful debts	320	15,923	
Bank		677	
		72,940	
Less Current liabilities			
Creditors	11,150		
Expenses owing	296	11,446	
Net current assets			61,494
			117,424
Less Loan from J King			(40,000)
			77,424

Financed by			
Capitals: Mendez		35,000	
Marshall		29,500	64,500

	Mendez	*Marshall*	
Current accounts			
Balance 1.7.20X8	1,306	298	
Add Interest on capital	3,500	2,950	
Add Salary	800		
Add Balance of profit	8,210	8,210	
	13,816	11,458	
Less Drawings	6,400	5,650	
Less Interest on drawings	180	120	
	7,236	5,688	12,924
			77,424

(b)

Brick & Stone
Balance Sheet as at 30 September 20X9

	Cost	Depn	Net
Fixed assets			
Fixtures and fittings	26,000	13,800	12,200
Motor vehicles	46,000	34,200	11,800
	72,000	48,000	24,000
Current assets			
Stock		32,000	
Debtors (9,300 – 300)		9,000	
Prepayments		600	
Bank		7,700	
		49,300	
Less Current liabilities			
Creditors	8,400		
Accrued expenses	400	8,800	40,500
			64,500
Financed by:			
Capitals: Brick (33,000 – 10,000)		23,000	
Stone		17,000	40,000
		Brick	Stone
Current accounts:			
Balances 1.10.20X8		3,600	2,400
Salary			6,000
Loan interest		250	
Share of profits		22,950	15,300
		26,800	23,700
		24,000	11,000
Less Drawings			
Goods for own use		2,800	1,000
			14,500
			54,500
Loan from Brick			10,000
			64,500

42.1

(a)

Balance Sheet as at 1 January 20X8

Goodwill		12,000
Other assets		14,000
		26,000
Capitals Dinho (6,000 + 6,000)		12,000
Manueli (4,800 + 4,500)		9,300
Joana (3,200 + 1,500)		4,700
		26,000

(b)

Goodwill Workings

	Before		After		Loss or Gain		Action needed	
Dinho	$4/8$	6,000	$3/10$	3,600	Loss	2,400	Credit Dinho	2,400
Manueli	$3/8$	4,500	$5/10$	6,000	Gain	1,500	Debit Manueli	1,500
Joana	$1/8$	1,500	$2/10$	2,400	Gain	900	Debit Joana	900
		12,000		12,000				

Balance Sheet as at 1 January 20X8

Net assets		14,000
		14,000
Capitals Dinho (6,000 + 2,400)		8,400
Manueli (4,800 – 1,500)		3,300
Joana (3,200 – 900)		2,300
		14,000

42.3

(a)

Goodwill				
Capitals	Rupert	6,000	Dr	3,000
	Linda			3,000
Cash				
	Capital Emma	7,000	Dr	7,000

(b)

Balance Sheet

Goodwill		6,000
Fixed and current assets		15,000
Cash		9,000
		30,000
Capitals	Rupert	11,000
	Linda	7,000
	Emma	7,000
Current liabilities		25,000
		5,000
		30,000

(c)

Capitals	Rupert	Dr	2,400
	Linda	Dr	1,800
	Emma	Dr	1,800
	Goodwill		6,000

42.5

(a)

Capital Accounts (£000)

	Tom	Una	Viv	Willie		Tom	Una	Viv	Willie
					Bal b/d	14	18	5	20
					Cash				
					Goodwill				
Bal c/d	26	33	8	20		12	15	3	
	26	33	8	20		26	33	8	20

(b) Goodwill 30,000; Other assets except cash 40,000; cash 26,000; Capitals as in (a); Creditors 9,000.

42.6

The senior partner's objection is a correct response. The money does not belong to the new partner once it has been paid.

This is because a new partner becomes an owner of part of the business, and this includes a part of the goodwill. This payment is specifically for that part of the goodwill. The goodwill was created by previous partners, and this is where the new partner buys his share from them. The £10,000 will be credited to the old partners in their old profit sharing ratio.

If C, the new partner, has paid £10,000 for one-fifth of the goodwill, then total goodwill is £50,000. Should the business be sold at a future date, and the goodwill realise £50,000, then C would receive one-fifth of the proceeds, i.e. £10,000, thus getting his money back. This illustrates the fairness of the accounting treatment of his original payment for goodwill. If anything had been credited to his account from this original payment for goodwill then he would have received that in addition. Obviously this would be unfair.

42.7

Stone, Pebble & Brick trading as Bigtime Building Supply Company

Profit and Loss Account for the year ended 31 March 20X9

	Apl–Dec	Jan–Mar
Net profit per accounts	27,225	9,075
Less Interest on Stone's Loan	—	385
	27,225	8,690
Interest on capitals: Stone		250
Pebble		200
Brick		125
Salary: Brick		2,125
Balance of profits shared:		
Stone	1/3 9,075	1/2 2,995
Pebble	1/3 9,075	3/10 1,797
Brick	1/3 9,075	2/10 1,198
	27,225	8,690

(b)

Capitals

	Stone	Pebble	Brick		Stone	Pebble	Brick
Goodwill adjustment		2,000	6,000	Balances b/d	26,000	18,000	16,000
Transfer to loan	14,000			Goodwill adjustment (see note)	8,000		
Balances c/d	20,000	16,000	10,000				
	34,000	18,000	16,000		34,000	18,000	16,000

Current Accounts

	Stone	Pebble	Brick		Stone	Pebble	Brick
Drawings	8,200	9,600	7,200	Interest on capital	250	200	125
Balances c/d	4,120	1,472	5,323	Salary			2,125
				Share of profits:			
				Apl–Dec	9,075	9,075	9,075
				Jan–Mar	2,995	1,797	1,198
	12,320	11,072	12,523		12,320	11,072	12,523

Note:

Goodwill:

	Value of goodwill taken over	Elimination of goodwill	Net effect
Stone	30,000	22,000	8,000 Cr
Pebble	20,000	22,000	2,000 Dr
Brick	16,000	22,000	6,000 Dr
	66,000	66,000	

43.1

(a)

Buildings

Balance b/d	8,000	Balance c/d	17,500
Revaluation: Increase	9,500		
	17,500		17,500

Motor Vehicles

Balance b/d	3,550	Revaluation: Reduction	950
		Balance c/d	2,600
	3,550		3,550

Stock

Balance b/d	2,040	Revaluation: Reduction	150
		Balance c/d	1,890
	2,040		2,040

Office Fittings

Balance b/d	1,310	Revaluation: Reduction	220
		Balance c/d	1,090
	1,310		1,310

Revaluation

Motor vehicles	950	Buildings	9,500
Stock	150		
Office fittings	220		
Profit on revaluation			
Hughes	4,090		
Allen	2,454		
Elliott	1,636		
	8,180		
	9,500		9,500

Capitals

	Hughes	Allen	Elliott
Balances c/d	13,650	8,874	6,476
	13,650	8,874	6,476
Balances b/d	9,560	6,420	4,840
Profit on revaluation	4,090	2,454	1,636
	13,650	8,874	6,476

(b)
Balance Sheet as at 1 January 20X9

Fixed assets		
Buildings at valuation		17,500
Motors at valuation		2,600
Office fittings at valuation		1,090
		21,190
Current assets		
Stock at valuation	1,890	
Debtors	4,530	
Bank	1,390	
		7,810
		29,000
Capitals:		
Hughes		13,650
Allen		8,874
Elliott		6,476
		29,000

43.3

(a)

Revaluation*

Premises	90,000	Premises	120,000
Plant	37,000	Plant	35,000
Stock	62,379	Stock	54,179
Provision doubtful debts	3,000		
Profit on revaluation			
Alan 3/6	8,400		
Bob 2/6	5,600		
Charles 1/6	2,800		
	16,800		
	209,179		209,179

*Just the net increases/decreases could have been recorded. Either method is acceptable.

Goodwill

Capitals: Alan	21,000	Goodwill cancelled	
Bob	14,000	Capitals: Alan 3/7	18,000
Don	7,000	Bob 2/7	12,000
	42,000	Don 2/7	12,000
			42,000

Capitals

	Alan	Bob	Charles	Don		Alan	Bob	Charles	Don
Goodwill	18,000	12,000	–	12,000	Balances b/d	85,000	65,000	35,000	–
Retirement	21,000		42,000		Goodwill	21,000	14,000	7,000	
Cash				67,000	Cash				79,000
Balances b/d	67,000	67,000							
	106,000	79,000	42,000	79,000		106,000	79,000	42,000	79,000

Current Accounts

	Alan	Bob	Charles	Don		Alan	Bob	Charles	Don
Balance b/d		2,509			Balance b/d	3,714		4,678	
Retirement			7,478		Profit on Revaluation				
Balances c/d	9,023	3,091		3,091	Cash	8,400	5,600	2,800	3,091
	12,114	5,600	7,478	3,091		12,114	5,600	7,478	3,091

Charles: Retirement

Car	3,900	Capital	42,000
Cash	53,578	Current	7,478
Balance c/d	20,000	Loan	28,000
	77,478		77,478

Bank

Balance b/d	79,000	Balance b/d	4,200
Don: Capital	3,091	Retirement – Charles	53,578
Don: Current	5,710	Repaid Alan – Capital	21,000
Balance c/d		Current	9,023
	87,801		87,801

(b) *Balance Sheet (summarised):*
Fixed assets total 168,100 + Current assets 86,919 – Current liabilities 24,746 = 230,273.
Capitals 67,000 each × 3 + Current accounts 3,091 × 3 = Total 230,273.

44.1

S, W and M

Appropriation Account for the year ended 31 December 20X9

Salaries: W	3,000		Net profit b/d		25,200
M	1,000				
		4,000			
Interest on capital					
S	600				
W	400				
M	200				
		1,200			
Balance of profits					
S 2/5	8,000				
W 2/5	8,000				
M 1/5	4,000				
		20,000			
		25,200			25,200

44.3

Realisation

Buildings	800	Cash: Debtors	2,700
Tools and fixtures	850	Buildings	400
Debtors	2,800	Tools etc.	950
Cash: Expenses	100	Discounts	200
		Loss on realisation: Moore	150
		Stephens	150
	4,550		4,550

Capital Accounts

	Moore	Stephens		Moore	Stephens
Loss on realisation	150	150	Balance b/d	2,000	1,500
Cash	1,850	1,350			
	2,000	1,500		2,000	1,500

Cash

Balance b/d	1,800	Expenses realisation	100
Debtors	2,700	Creditors	2,550
Buildings	400	Capitals: Moore	1,850
Tools	950	Stephens	1,350
	5,850		5,850

44.4

(a)

Realisation

Fixed assets	14,000	Bank: Fixed assets	8,000
Stock	5,000	X: Fixed assets	7,000
Debtors	21,000	Bank: Stock	4,000
Bank: Dissolution costs	800	Bank: Debtors	3,000
		Discounts on creditors	500
		Loss: X $3/6$	9,150
		Y $2/6$	6,100
		Z $1/6$	3,050
			18,300
	40,800		40,800

(b)

Capital Accounts

	X	Y	Z		X	Y	Z
Fixed assets taken over	7,000			Balances b/d	4,000	4,000	2,000
Loss shared	9,150	6,100	3,050	Deficiency shared:			
Deficiency		525		X		525	
				Y			525
				Bank to settle	12,675	2,625	
	16,675	6,625	3,050		16,675	6,625	3,050

Bank (as proof only)

Realisation: Fixed assets	8,000	Balance b/d	13,000
Stock	4,000	Creditors	16,500
Debtors	3,000	Realisation: Costs	800
Capital: X	12,675		
Y	2,625		
	30,300		30,300

44.7

(a) (i)

Amis, Lodge & Pym
Trading and Profit and Loss Account for the year ended 31 March 20X8

Sales		404,500
Less Cost of goods sold:		
Opening stock	30,000	
Add Purchases	225,000	
Add Carriage inwards	4,000	
	259,000	
Less Closing stock	35,000	224,000
Gross profit		180,500
Add Bank interest		750
Discounts received		4,530
		185,780
Less Office expenses (30,400 + 405)	30,805	
Rent, rates, light and heat (8,800 – 1,500)	7,300	
Carriage outwards	12,000	
Discounts allowed	10,000	
Provision for doubtful debts	295	
Depreciation: Motor	15,000	
Plant	20,000	95,400
Net profit		90,380
Add Interest on current accounts and drawings:		
Amis	1,000	
Lodge	900	
Pym	720	2,620
		93,000
Less Salary – Pym		13,000
Interest on capitals: Amis	8,000	
Lodge	1,500	
Pym	500	10,000
		23,000
		70,000
Balance of profit shared:		
Amis 50%	35,000	
Lodge 30%	21,000	
Pym 20%	14,000	
		70,000

(a) (ii)

Current Accounts

	Amis	Lodge	Pym		Amis	Lodge	Pym
Balances b/d	1,000	500	400	Salary			13,000
Drawings	25,000	22,000	15,000	Interest on capital	8,000	1,500	500
Interest on drawings	1,000	900	720	Balance on profits	35,000	21,000	14,000
Transfer to capital	16,000	–	11,380	Transfer to capital		900	
	43,000	23,400	27,500		43,000	23,400	27,500

(b) (i)

Realisation

Motors (80,000 − 35,000)	45,000	Discount on creditors		500
Plant (100,000 − 56,600)	43,400	Amis: Motor		5,000
Debtors (14,300 − 715)	13,585	Bank: Debtors		12,985
Stock	35,000	Fowles Ltd (75,000 + 63,500)		138,500
Profit on realisation				
Amis 50%	10,000			
Lodge 30%	6,000			
Pym 20%	4,000			
	20,000			
	156,985			156,985

(b) (ii)

Bank

Balance b/d	4,900	Office expenses	405
Realisation: Debtors	12,985	Creditors	16,000
Rent rebate	1,500	Capital: Amis	76,000
Fowles Ltd	63,500		
Capitals: Lodge	4,900		
Pym	4,620		
	92,405		92,405

(b) (iii)

Capital Accounts

	Amis	Lodge	Pym		Amis	Lodge	Pym
Current a/c		900		Balances b/d	80,000	15,000	5,000
Fowles Ltd	25,000	25,000	25,000	Current a/c	16,000		11,380
Realisation: Motor	5,000			Profit on realisation	10,000	6,000	4,000
Bank	76,000			Bank		4,900	4,620
	106,000	25,900	25,000		106,000	25,900	25,000

44.9

(a)

Lock, Stock and Barrel

Profit and Loss Account for the six months ended 1 February 20X7

Sales of completed houses		280,000
Less Costs of completing houses		
Houses in course of construction at start	115,000	
Materials used	35,750	
Land used (75,000 × 1/3)	25,000	
Wages and subcontractors	78,000	253,750
Gross profit		26,250
Less Administration salaries	17,250	
General expenses	12,500	
Depreciation: Freehold land	300	
Plant and equipment ($^6/_{12} \times 10\%$)	7,500	
Vehicles (25% × $^6/_{12}$)	4,500	42,050
Net loss		15,800
Shared: Lock 40%	6,320	
Stock 30%	4,740	
Barrel 30%	4,740	15,800

Capitals

	Lock	Stock	Barrel		Lock	Stock	Barrel
Drawings	6,000	5,000	4,000	Balances b/d	52,000	26,000	4,000
Loss shared	6,320	4,740	4,740	Balance c/d			4,740
Balances c/d	39,680	16,260					
	52,000	26,000	8,740		52,000	26,000	8,740

Lock, Stock and Barrel

Balance Sheet as at 1 February 20X7

	Cost	Depreciation	
Fixed tangible assets			
Freehold land and buildings	20,000	3,300	16,700
Plant and equipment	150,000	89,500	60,500
Motor vehicles	36,000	27,500	8,500
	206,000	120,300	85,700
Current assets			
Stock of land for building	50,000		
Stocks of materials	7,500		
Debtors for completed houses	35,000		
	92,500		
Less Current liabilities			
Trade creditors	52,250		
Bank overdraft	75,250	127,500	
Net current assets			(35,000)
Net assets			50,700
Financed by:			
Capitals: Lock			39,680
Stock			16,260
Barrel			(5,240)
			50,700

(b) Amounts distributable to partners:

On 28 February there was only (6,200 + 7,000 + 72,500 − 75,250) 10,450 hence there was nowhere near enough to pay off the creditors, and so payment to partners could not be made.

On 30 April we treat it as though no more cash will be received.

(c) *First distribution*

	Lock	Stock	Barrel
Capital balances before dissolution	39,680	16,260	(5,240)
Loss if no further assets realised			
(85,700 + 92,500 − 6,000 − 6,200 − 7,000 − 72,500 − 35,000 − 50,000) = 1,500			
Loss shared in profit/loss ratios	(600)	(450)	(450)
Cars taken over	(2,000)	(2,000)	(2,000)
	37,080	13,810	(7,690)
Barrel's deficiency shared profit/loss ratio	4,394	3,296	7,690
Paid to partners	32,686	10,514	—

Second and final distribution

	Lock	Stock	Barrel
Capital balances before dissolution	39,680	16,260	(5,240)
Profit finally ascertained			
100,000 − 1,500 = 98,500			
Shared	39,400	29,550	29,550
	79,080	45,810	24,310
Less Distribution and cars	34,686	12,514	2,000
Final distribution (100,000)	44,394	33,296	22,310

45.1

GWR Ltd

Profit and Loss Appropriation Accounts

(1) For the year ended 31 December 20X6

Profit for the year before taxation		42,005
Less Corporation tax		13,480
Profit for the year after taxation		28,525
Less: Transfer to general reserve	6,000	
Preference dividend of 10%	5,000	
Ordinary dividend of 12%	12,000	23,000
Retained profits carried forward to next year		5,525

(2) For the year ended 31 December 20X7

Profit for the tax year before taxation		34,831
Less Corporation tax		11,114
Profit for the year after taxation		23,717
Add Retained profits from last year		5,525
		29,242
Less: Transfer to general reserve	4,000	
Preference dividend of 10%	5,000	
Ordinary dividend of 9%	9,000	18,000
Retained profits carried forward to next year		11,242

45.2

LMS Ltd

Profit and Loss Appropriation accounts

(1) For the year ended 31 December 20X7

Profit for the year before taxation		27,929
Less Corporation tax		8,331
Profit for the year after taxation		19,598
Less: Transfer to general reserve	3,000	
Preference dividend 8%	3,200	
Ordinary dividend 8%	9,600	15,800
Retained profits carried forward to next year		3,798

(2) For the year ended 31 December 20X8

Profit for the year before taxation		32,440
Less Corporation tax		10,446
Profit for the year after taxation		21,994
Add Retained profits from last year		3,798
		25,792
Less: Transfer to general reserve	4,000	
Preference dividend 8%	3,200	
Ordinary dividend 10%	12,000	19,200
Retained profits carried forward to next year		6,592

(3) For the year ended 31 December 20X9

Profit for the year before taxation		36,891
Less Corporation tax		12,001
Profit for the year after taxation		24,890
Add Retained profits from last year		6,592
		31,482
Less: Transfer to foreign exchange reserve	2,000	
Preference dividend 8%	3,200	
Ordinary dividend 11%	13,200	18,400
Retained profits carried forward to next year		13,082

45.3

Balance Sheet as at 30 June 20X6

Fixed assets	Cost	Depn	
Buildings	105,000	22,000	83,000
Motors	62,500	15,350	47,150
Fixtures	11,500	3,750	7,750
	179,000	41,100	137,900

Current assets			
Stock		16,210	
Debtors		14,175	
Bank (difference)		4,998	
		35,383	

Less Current liabilities			
Creditors	9,120		
Proposed dividend	5,000		
		14,120	
Net current assets			21,263
Total assets *less* current liabilities			159,163
Less Debentures: repayable in 20X9			(40,000)
			119,163

Capital and reserves		
Called-up share capital		100,000
Fixed assets replacement reserve		8,000
General reserve		6,000
Profit and loss account		5,163
		119,163

Balance Sheet as at 31 December 20X8

Fixed assets			
Premises			65,000
Machinery		55,000	
Less Depreciation		21,300	
			33,700
			98,700

Current assets			
Stock		29,142	
Debtors	21,784		
Less Provision	938		
		20,846	
Prepayments		300	
Bank		23,101	
		73,389	

Less Current liabilities			
Proposed dividend	10,000		
Creditors	17,493		
Expenses owing	581		
		28,074	
Net current assets			45,315
			144,015

Financed by:		
Authorised and issued capital		100,000
Revenue reserves: Profit and loss account		44,015
		144,015

45.5 Chang Ltd

Trading and Profit and Loss Account for the year ended 31 December 20X8

Sales			316,810
Less Cost of goods sold			
Opening stock		25,689	
Add Purchases		201,698	
		227,387	
Less Closing stock		29,142	
			198,245
Gross profit			118,565
Less expenses			
Wages (54,207 + 581)		54,788	
Rent (4,300 – 300)		4,000	
Lighting		1,549	
Bad debts (748 + 77)		825	
General expenses		32,168	
Depreciation: Machinery		5,500	
			98,830
Net profit			19,735
Add Unappropriated profits from last year			34,280
			54,015
Less Proposed dividend			10,000
Unappropriated profits carried to next year			44,015

45.7 T Howe Ltd

Trading and Profit and Loss Account for the year ended 31 December 20X8

Sales			135,486
Less Cost of goods sold			
Opening stock		40,360	
Add Purchases		72,360	
Add Carriage inwards		1,570	
		114,290	
Less Closing stock		52,360	
			61,930
Gross profit			73,556
Less Expenses			
Salaries		18,310	
Rates and occupancy		4,515	
Carriage outwards		1,390	
Office expenses		3,212	
Sundry expenses		1,896	
Depreciation: Buildings		5,000	
Equipment		9,000	
Directors' remuneration		9,500	
			52,823
Net profit			20,733
Add Unappropriated profits from last year			15,286
			36,019

Less Appropriations

Proposed dividend	10,000	
General reserve	1,000	
Foreign exchange	800	
Unappropriated profits carried to next year		11,800
		24,219

Balance Sheet as at 31 December 20X8

	Cost	Depn	Net
Fixed assets			
Buildings	100,000	37,000	63,000
Equipment	45,000	25,000	20,000
	145,000	62,000	83,000
Current assets			
Stock		52,360	
Debtors		18,910	
Bank		6,723	
		77,993	
Less Current liabilities			
Creditors	12,304		
Expenses owing	470		
Proposed dividend	10,000		
	22,774		
Net current assets			55,219
			138,219

Financed by:

Share capital: authorised and issued		100,000
Reserves		
Foreign exchange	5,000	
General reserve	9,000	
Profit and loss	24,219	
		38,219
		138,219

45.9

1   *Burden plc: Computation of corrected net profit*

Recorded net profit		58,070
Add Profit on sale of equipment		500
		58,570
Less Bad debt written off	300	
Stock reduced to net realisable value	700	
		1,000
Correct figure of net profit		57,570

2   **Burden plc**
Profit and Loss Appropriation Account for the year ended 31 May 20X9

Net profit for the year brought down		57,570
Add Retained profits from last year		36,200
		93,770
Less Transfer to general reserve	50,000	
Proposed dividend of 10%	20,000	
		70,000
Retained profits carried forward to next year		23,770

3 (i)   *Current assets*

Stock		17,100
Debtors		6,540
Prepayments		760
		24,400
Less Current liabilities		
Trade creditors	8,500	
Accrued expenses	430	
Proposed dividend	20,000	
Bank overdraft	2,400	
		(31,330)
Net current assets deficit		(6,930)

Note: Figures in brackets are negative.

(ii)   *Capital and reserves*

Ordinary share capital: called up	200,000
Share premium	25,000
General reserve	70,000
Profit and loss account	23,770
Shareholders' funds	318,770

4   *Examples:*

Issue of shares: + Bank; + Share capital.
Sales of fixed assets: + Bank; − Fixed assets.
Debentures issued: + Bank; + Debentures.

45.11

(a) See text.
(b) The historical cost convention does not make the going concern convention unnecessary. Several instances illustrate this:
(i) Fixed assets are depreciated over the useful life of the assets. This presupposes that the business will continue to operate during the years of assumed useful life.
(ii) Prepayments also assume that the benefits available in the future will be able to be claimed, because the business is expected to continue.
(iii) Stocks are valued also on the basis that they will be disposed of during the future ordinary running of the business.
(iv) The accruals concept itself assumes that the business is to continue.
All of this shows that the two concepts complement each other.
(c) A shareholder wants accounts so that he can decide what to do with his shareholding, whether he should sell his shares or hold on to them.
To enable him to decide upon his actions, he would really like to know what is going to happen in the future. To help him in this he also would like information which shows him what happened in the past. Ideally therefore he would like both types of report, those on the past and on the future.
If he had a choice, the logical choice would be to receive a report on the future providing that it could be relied on.

45.12

Extract 1

(a) The amount paid for goodwill.

(b) The excess represents share premium.

(c) Equity shares generally means ordinary shares.

(d) That although issued in 20X6 a dividend will not be paid in that year. The first year that dividends *could* be paid is 20X7.

Extract 2

(e) (i) A rate of 8% per annum interest will be paid on them, irrespective of whether profits are made or not.

(ii) These are the years within which the debentures could be redeemed, if the company so wished.

(f) (i) This is the rate per annum at which preference dividends will be paid, subject to there being sufficient distributable profits.

(ii) That the shares could be bought back by the company.

(g) Probably because there was currently a lower interest rate prevailing at the time of redemption and the company took advantage of it.

(h) Large amounts of both fixed interest and fixed dividend funds have resulted in a raising of the gearing.

(i) Debenture interest gets charged before arriving at net profit. Dividends are an appropriation of profits.

(k) Shareholders are owners and help decide appropriations. Debenture holders are external lenders and interest expense has to be paid.

45.13

(a) This is incorrect. The tax portion has to be counted as part of the total cost, which is made up of debenture interest paid plus tax. Holding back payment will merely see legal action taken by the Inland Revenue to collect the tax.

(b) This cannot be done. The repainting of the exterior does not improve or enhance the original value of the premises. It cannot therefore be treated as capital expenditure.

(c) This is not feasible. Only the profit on the sale of the old machinery, found by deducting net book value from sales proceeds, can be so credited to the profit and loss account. The remainder is a capital receipt and should be treated as such.

(d) This is an incorrect view. Although some of the general reserve could, if circumstances allowed it, be transferred back to the profit and loss account, it could not be shown as affecting the operating profit for 20X9. This is because the reserve was built up over the years before 20X9.

(e) This is not feasible. The share capital has to be maintained at nominal value as per the Companies Act. A share premium cannot be created in this fashion, and even if it could, it would still have to be credited to the *share premium account* and not the profit and loss account.

(f) Incorrect. Although the premises could be revalued the credit for the increase has to be to a capital reserve account. This cannot then be transferred to the credit of the profit and loss account.

45.14

See text. Points to be made include that there must be an expectation that sufficient profits will be made in future to meet the debenture interest payments when due; also, there may be cheaper sources of finance available; also, if secured debentures are to be issued, there must be sufficient assets available to act as security over the issue. Gearing is also an issue to be considered – see text.

46.1

Balance Sheet as at 31 December 20X8

	(a) S Walters	(b) R Jones
Goodwill	8,200	9,300
Premises	21,000	28,000
Stock	9,600	9,200
Debtors	6,300	6,300
Bank	1,700	–
	46,800	52,800
Less Creditors	(6,800)	(6,800)
	40,000	46,000
Capital	40,000	46,000

46.3

(a)

Spectrum Ltd

Balance Sheet as at 1 January 20X2

Fixed assets		
Goodwill (note 1)		94,000
Premises (75,000 + 80,000 + 90,000 + 60,000)		305,000
Delivery vans (7,000 + 10,000)		17,000
Furniture and fittings (12,000 + 13,000 + 13,000)		38,000
		454,000
Current assets		
Stock (8,000 + 7,000 + 12,000)	27,000	
Bank (note 2)	25,000	
	52,000	
Less Current liabilities		
Creditors (6,000 + 8,000 + 7,000)	21,000	
Net current assets		31,000
		485,000
Financed by:		
Share capital		
Authorised 700,000 shares £1		700,000
Issued 500,000 shares £1		500,000
Reserves		
Profit and loss (note 3)		(15,000)
		485,000

Notes:

1 Goodwill: Red – paid   120,000

Net assets taken over		
75,000 + 7,000 + 12,000 + 8,000 – 6,000 =	96,000	
		24,000
Yellow – paid	130,000	
Net assets taken over		
80,000 + 13,000 + 7,000 – 8,000 =	92,000	
		38,000
Blue – paid	150,000	
Net assets taken over		
90,000 + 10,000 + 13,000 + 12,000 – 7,000 =	118,000	
		32,000
		94,000

2 Bank: Shares issued   500,000

Less: Preliminary expenses	15,000	
Warehouse	60,000	
Red	120,000	
Yellow	130,000	
Blue	150,000	475,000
		25,000

3 Prior to the 1981 Companies Act this could have been shown as an asset. It must now be written off immediately to profit and loss.

(b) Spectrum Ltd can issue part or the remainder of the authorised capital, i.e. 700,000 – 500,000 = £200,000. £100,000 will buy the business but some extra net current assets is also needed.

46.4

(a)

Dinho and Manueli
Realisation Account

Property	290,000	Creditors	85,800
Equipment	65,000	Bank	56,700
Stock	143,500	Loan	160,000
Debtors	121,000	Bin Ltd	304,000
		Loss: Dinho	6,500
		Manueli	6,500
	619,500		619,500

(b)

Bin Ltd

Goodwill [write downs (30,000 + 5,000) – realisation loss (13,000)]	22,000
Property	260,000
Equipment	65,000
Stocks	143,500
Debtors	116,000
Bank (120,000 – 56,700)	63,300
Creditors	(85,800)
	584,000
Ordinary Share Capital	300,000
10% Preference shares (D = 87,500; M = 16,500; P = 20,000)	124,000
Loan	160,000
	584,000

(c) (salary as before, therefore not relevant); earnings on savings were 120,000 @ 6% = 7,200; preference dividend will be 20,000 @ 10% = 2,000, therefore 5,200 needed from profit after preference dividend. Profit must be 3 × 5,200 = 15,600 + the total preference dividend of 12,400 = 28,000.

47.1

(a)

	A	B
(i) Gross profit as % of sales	$\frac{20,000}{80,000} \times \frac{100}{1} = 25\%$	$\frac{24,000}{120,000} \times \frac{100}{1} = 20\%$
(ii) Net profit as % of sales	$\frac{10,000}{80,000} \times \frac{100}{1} = 12.5\%$	$\frac{15,000}{120,000} \times \frac{100}{1} = 12.5\%$
(iii) Expenses as % of sales	$\frac{10,000}{80,000} \times \frac{100}{1} = 12.5\%$	$\frac{9,000}{120,000} \times \frac{100}{1} = 7.5\%$
(iv) Stock turnover	$\frac{60,000}{(25,000 + 15,000) \div 2} = 3$ times	$\frac{96,000}{(22,500 + 17,500) \div 2} = 4.8$ times
(v) Rate of return	$\frac{10,000}{(38,000 + 42,000) \div 2} \times \frac{100}{1} = 25\%$	$\frac{15,000}{(36,000 + 44,000) \div 2} \times \frac{100}{1} = 37.5\%$
(vi) Current ratio	$\frac{45,000}{5,000} = 9$	$\frac{40,000}{10,000} = 4$
(vii) Acid test ratio	$\frac{30,000}{5,000} = 6$	$\frac{22,500}{10,000} = 2.25$
(viii) Debtor/sales ratio	$\frac{25,000}{80,000} \times 12 = 3.75$ months	$\frac{20,000}{120,000} \times 12 = 2$ months
(ix) Creditor/purchases ratio	$\frac{5,000}{50,000} \times 12 = 1.2$ months	$\frac{10,000}{91,000} \times 12 = 1.3$ months approx.

(b) Business B is the most profitable, both in terms of actual net profits, £15,000 compared to £10,000, but also in terms of capital employed; B has managed to achieve a return of £37.50 for every £100 invested, i.e. 37.5%. A has managed a lower return of 25%. Reasons – possibly only – as not until you know more about the business could you give a definite answer:

(i) Possibly managed to sell far more merchandise because of lower prices, i.e. took only 20% margin as compared with A's 25% margin.

(ii) Maybe more efficient use of mechanised means in the business. Note B has more equipment, and perhaps as a consequence kept other expenses down to 6,000 as compared with A's 9,000.

(iii) Did not have as much stock lying idle. Turned over stock 4.8 times in the year as compared with 3 for *A*.

(iv) *A*'s current ratio of 9 far greater than normally needed. *B* kept it down to 4. *A* therefore had too much money lying idle and not doing anything.

(v) Following on from (iv) the Acid Test ratio for *A* also higher than necessary.

(vi) Part of the reasons for (iv) and (v) is that *A* waited (on average) 3.75 months to be paid by customers. *B* managed to collect them on a 2 months' average. Money represented by debts is money lying idle.

(vii) *A* also paid creditors quicker than did *B*, but not by much.

Put all these factors together, and it is obvious that *B* is being run far more efficiently, and is more profitable as a consequence.

47.3
(a)
Durham Limited

Profit and Loss Appropriation Account for the year ended 30.4.20X9

Net profit for the year b/d		16,500
Add Retained profits from last year		14,500
		31,000
Less Transfer to general reserve	5,000	
Preference dividend	4,000	
Proposed ordinary dividend	15,000	24,000
Retained profits carried forward to next year		7,000

(b)
Balance Sheet as at 30.4.20X9

Fixed assets			
Premises at cost		86,000	
Machinery and plant at cost	60,000		
Less Depreciation	40,000	20,000	106,000
Current assets			
Stock		60,000	
Debtors	20,000		
Less Provision	4,000	16,000	
Prepayments		900	
Bank		13,100	
		90,000	
Less Current liabilities			
Creditors	12,900		
Expenses owing	100		
Proposed dividends	17,000	30,000	
Working capital			60,000
			166,000
Capital and reserves			
8% preference shares		50,000	
Ordinary shares		100,000	150,000
General reserve			9,000
Profit and loss account			7,000
Shareholders' funds			166,000

(c) (i) *Return on Capital Employed (ROCE)*
This is the amount of profit earned compared with the amount of capital employed to earn it. Calculated:

$$\frac{\text{Net profit}}{\text{Average of shareholders' funds}} \times \frac{100}{1} = \frac{16,500}{(168,500 + 166,000) \div 2} \times \frac{100}{1}$$
$$= 9.87\%$$

(ii) *Current Ratio*
This calculates how well the current assets can finance current liabilities. Calculated:

$$\frac{\text{Current assets}}{\text{Current liabilities}} = \frac{90,000}{30,000} = 3:1$$

Acid Test Ratio
This calculates whether the business has sufficient liquid resources to meet its current liabilities. Calculated:

$$\frac{\text{Current assets} - \text{Stock}}{\text{Current liabilities}} = \frac{30,000}{30,000} = 1:1$$

(d) ROCE. The return of 9.87% would appear to be adequate, but we cannot really comment further without more information.
Current Ratio. A figure of 2:1 is often reckoned as adequate. In this case a 3:1 figure is more than adequate.
Acid Test Ratio. All current liabilities can be met and the return is therefore adequate.

(e) 1 Previous years' figures.
2 We would need to know ratios for other similar businesses.

47.4
(a) (i) Gross profit: Sales

20X8	20X9
$\dfrac{50}{200} \times \dfrac{100}{1} = 25\%$	$\dfrac{70}{280} \times \dfrac{100}{1} = 25\%$

(ii) Stock turnover

20X8	20X9
$\dfrac{150}{(50 + 20) \div 2} = 4.29$	$\dfrac{210}{(20 + 30) \div 2} = 8.4$

(iii) Net profit: Sales

20X8	20X9
$\dfrac{12}{200} \times \dfrac{100}{1} = 6\%$	$\dfrac{20}{280} \times \dfrac{100}{1} = 7.14\%$

(iv) Quick ratio

20X8	20X9
$\dfrac{25}{25} = 1$	$\dfrac{33}{12} = 2.75$

(v) Working capital (current ratio)

20X8	20X9
$\dfrac{45}{25} = 1.8$	$\dfrac{63}{12} = 5.25$

(vi) Net profit: Capital employed

20X8	20X9
$\dfrac{12}{130} \times \dfrac{100}{1} = 9.23\%$	$\dfrac{20}{191} \times \dfrac{100}{1} = 10.47\%$

(b) (Brief answer, but you should expand in an exam)

(i) No change.

(ii) Increase caused by lowering average stocks; also probably better sales management.

(iii) An increase in sales, without a larger increase in expenses, has led to a better return.

(iv) Issue of debentures has improved the cash situation and therefore a better quick ratio.

(v) Net current assets have increased largely due to issue of debentures, although partly offset by fixed assets bought.

(vi) Increasing sales and better stock turnover brought about better ROCE.

47.7

(a)

Joan Street

Trading and Profit and Loss Account for the year ended 31 March 20X8

Sales		(W3)	240,000
Cost of sales			
Opening stock		21,000	
Add Purchases	(W6)	174,000	
		195,000	
Less Closing stock	(W7)	15,000	
	(W1)		180,000
Gross profit	(W2)		60,000
Sundry expenses	(W5)		38,400
Net profit	(W4)		21,600

Balance Sheet as at 31 March 20X8

Fixed assets		(W9)	108,000
Current assets			
Stock		15,000	
Debtors	(W8)	24,000	
Bank	(W15)	9,000	
	(W14)	48,000	
Less Current liabilities	(W14)	12,000	
Net current assets		(W13)	36,000
		(W12)	144,000

Financed by:

Capital:		
Balance at 1.4.20X7	(W11)	122,400
Add Net profit	(W10)	21,600
		144,000

Workings (could possibly find alternatives)

(W1) As average stock $21,000 + 15,000 \div 2 = 18,000$ and stock turnover is 10, this means that cost of sales $= 18,000 \times 10 = 180,000$

(W2) As gross profit is 25% of sales, it must therefore be $33\frac{1}{3}\%$ of cost of sales

(W3) As (W1) is 180,000 & (W2) is 60,000 therefore sales $= (W1) + (W2) = 240,000$

(W4) Net profit $= 9\%$ of sales $= 21,600$

(W5) Missing figure, found by arithmetical deduction

(W6) & (W7) Missing figures – found by arithmetical deduction

(W8) $\dfrac{\text{Debtors (?)} \times 365}{\text{Sales}} = 36\frac{1}{2}$, i.e.

$\dfrac{? \times 365}{240,000} = 36\frac{1}{2}$, by arithmetic

debtors = 24,000. Proof $\dfrac{24,000 \times 365}{240,000} = 36\frac{1}{2}$

(W9) $45\% \times 240,000 = 108,000$

(W10) Knowing that net profit 21,600 is 15% of W10, so W10 $= 21,600 \times 100/15$ $= 144,000$

(W11) Missing figure

(W12) & (W13) Put in after (W11)

(W14) If Net current assets ratio is 4, it means a factor of current assets 4, current liabilities 1 = Net current assets 3. As (W13) is 36,000, current assets therefore:

$4/3 \times 36,000 = 48,000$

and current liabilities

$1/3 \times 36,000 = 12,000$

(W15) Is new missing figure.

(b) Question limited to two favourable and two unfavourable aspects (four given here for reader's benefit)

Favourable: Stock turnover, liquidity, net current assets, net profit on sales

Unfavourable: Gross profit to sales, debtors collection, return on capital employed, turnover to net capital employed.

(c) Drawbacks (more than two listed for reader's benefit)

(i) No access to trends over recent years.

(ii) No future plans etc. given.

(iii) Each business is often somewhat different.

(iv) Size of businesses not known.

The main points which could be covered are:

(i) The accounts are for last year, whereas in fact the bank is more interested in what might happen to the firm in the future.

(ii) The accounts are usually prepared on a historic cost basis. These therefore do not reflect current values.

(iii) The bank manager would want a cash budget to be drawn up for the ensuing periods. This would give the manager an indication as to whether or not the business will be able to meet its commitments as they fall due.

(iv) The bank manager wants to ensure that bank charges and interest can be paid promptly, also that a bank loan or overdraft will be able to be paid off. He will want to see that these commitments can still be met if the business has to cease operations. This means that the saleable value of assets on cessation, rather than the cost of them, is of much more interest to the bank manager.

To say that the accounts are 'not good enough' is misleading. What the manager is saying is that the accounts do not provide him with what he would really like to know. One could argue that there should be other types of final accounts drawn up in addition to those drawn up on a historic basis.

47.12

(a) The basis on which accounts are prepared is that of 'accruals'. By this it is meant that the recognition of revenue and expenditure takes place not at the point when cash is received or paid out, but instead at the point when the revenue is earned or the expenditure is incurred.

To establish the point of recognition of a sale, several criteria are necessary:

(i) The product, or the service, must have been supplied to the customer.

(ii) The buyer must have indicated his willingness to pay for the product or services and have accepted liability.

(iii) A monetary value of the goods or services must have been agreed to by the buyer.

(iv) Ownership of the goods must have passed to the buyer.

(b) (i) This cannot be recognised as a sale. It does not comply with any of the four criteria above.

(ii) This also cannot be recognised as a sale. Neither criterion (i) nor (iv) has been covered.

(iii) If this was a cash sale, all of the above criteria would probably be achieved on delivery, and therefore it could be appropriate to recognise the sale.

If it was a credit sale, if the invoice was sent with the goods and a delivery note stating satisfaction by the customer is signed by him, then it would also probably be appropriate to recognise the sale.

(iv) Usually takes place after the four criteria have been satisfied. If so, the sale should be recognised.

(v) In the case of cash sales this would be the point of recognition.

In the case of credit sales it would depend on whether or not criteria (a) (i) and (iv) had also been satisfied.

(vi) This would only influence recognition of sales if there was serious doubt about the ability of the customer to pay his debts.

47.9

(a)
(i) Current ratio: by dividing current assets by current liabilities.

(ii) Quick assets ratio: by dividing current assets less stock by current liabilities.

(iii) Return on capital employed (ROCE): can have more than one meaning. One in common use is net profit divided by capital plus long-term liabilities (e.g. loans), and shown as a percentage.

(iv) Return on shareholders' funds (ROSF): net profit divided by capital, shown as a percentage.

(v) Debtors turnover: Sales divided by average debtors, expressed in days or months.

(vi) Creditors turnover: Purchases divided by average creditors, expressed in days or months.

(vii) Gross profit percentage: Gross profit divided by sales, expressed as a percentage.

(viii) Net profit percentage: Net profit divided by sales.

(ix) Stock turnover: Cost of goods sold, divided by average stock, expressed in days.

(b) (This part of the question tests your ability to be able to deduce some conclusions from the information given. You have to use your imagination.)

First, an assumption, we do not know relative sizes of these two businesses. We will assume that they are approximately of the same size.

A has a higher current ratio, 2 to 1.5, but the quick assets ratio shows a much greater disparity, 1.7 to 0.7. As stock is not included in the quick assets ratio, it can be deduced that B has relatively greater stocks. Expected also from these ratios is that A has high amounts of debtors, this being seen because debtors turnover is 3 times as great for A as for B.

The return on shareholders' funds (ROSF) is much greater for A than for B, 30% to 18%, but the ROCE for A is not that different for B, 20% to 17%. This shows that A has far more in long-term borrowings than B. The ROCE indicates that A is somewhat more efficient than B, but not by a considerable amount.

Gross profit percentage is far greater for A than B, but net profit percentage is the same. Obviously A has extremely high operating expenses per £100 of sales.

The last ratio shows that stock in A lies unsold for twice as long a period as for B.

A summary of the above shows that A has lower stocks, greater debtors, sells at a slower rate, and has high operating expenses. B has greater stocks, sells its goods much quicker but at lower prices as shown by the gross profit percentage.

All the evidence points to A being a firm which gives emphasis to personal service to its customers. B on the other hand emphasises cheap prices and high turnover, with not as much concentration on personal service.

47.11

(There is no set answer. In addition, as a large number of points could be mentioned, the examiner cannot expect every aspect to be covered.)

47.13

Obviously there is no set answer to this question. However, the following may well be typical:

(a) If the business is going to carry on operating, then the going concern concept comes into operation. Consequently, fixed assets are valued at cost, less depreciation to date. Stocks will be valued at lower of cost or net realisable value. The 'net realisable value' will be that based on the business realising stock through normal operations.

(b) Should the business be deemed as a case for cessation, then the going concern concept could not be used. The values on fixed assets and stocks will be their disposal values. This should be affected by whether or not the business could be sold as a whole or whether it would have to be broken up. Similarly, figures would be affected by whether or not assets had to be sold off very quickly at low prices, or sold only when reasonable prices could be achieved.

It is not only the balance sheet that would be affected, as the profit and loss account would reflect the changes in values.

47.14

(a) See text, Chapter 10.

(b) Various illustrations are possible, but the following are examples:

(i) Apportionment of expenses between one period and another. For instance, very rarely would very small stocks of stationery be valued at the year end. This means that the stationery gets charged against one year's profits whereas in fact it may not all have been used up in that year.

(ii) Items expensed instead of being capitalised. Small items which are, in theory, capital expenditure will often be charged up to an expense account.

(iii) The value of assets approximated, instead of being measured with absolute precision.

(c) (i) An illustration could be made under (b) (iii). A stock of oil could well be estimated; the true figure, if known, might be one or two litres out. The cost of precise measurement would probably not be worth the benefit of having such information.

(ii) What is material in one company may not be material in another.

47.15

No set answer. Question is of a general nature rather than being specific. A variety of answers is therefore acceptable.

The examiner might expect to see the following covered (this is not a model answer):

(a) Different reports needed by different outside parties, as they have to meet different requirements. Might find they therefore include:

(i) for bankers – accounts based on 'break-up' value of the assets if they have to be sold off to repay loans or overdrafts;

(ii) for investors – to include how business has fared against budgets set for that year to see how successful business is at meeting targets;

(iii) for employees – include details of number of employees, wages and salaries paid, effect on pension funds;

(iv) for local community – to include reports showing amounts spent on pollution control, etc.

And any similar instances.

(b) The characteristics of useful information have been stated in *The Corporate Report* 1975, and the accounting reports should be measured against this.

(c) Presentation (additional) in form of pie charts, bar charts, etc., as these are often more easily understood by readers.

47.16

(a) Accountants follow the realisation concept when deciding when to recognise revenue on any particular transaction. This states that profit is normally regarded as being earned at the time when the goods or services are passed to the customer and he incurs liability for them. For a service business it means when the services have been performed.

(b) The stage at which revenue is recognised could be either F or G. The normal rule is that the goods have been despatched, not delivered. For instance the goods may be shipped to Australia and take several weeks to get there.

Exactly where this fits in with F or G in the question cannot be stipulated without further information.

(c) If F is accepted as point of recognition, then £130 will be gross profit. If G is accepted as point of recognition the gross profit recognised will be £120.

(d) The argument that can be advanced is to take the prudence concept to its final conclusion, in that the debtor should pay for the goods before the profit can be recognised.

Until H is reached there is always the possibility that the goods will not be paid for, or might be returned because of faults in the goods.

(e) If the goods are almost certain to be sold, it could give a better picture of the progress of the firm up to a particular point in time, if profit could be recognised in successive amounts at stages B, C and D.

47.17

(a) A 'provision' is an amount written off or retained by way of providing for depreciation, renewals or diminution in value of assets, or retained by way of providing for any known liability of which the amount cannot be determined with 'substantial' accuracy. This therefore covers such items as provisions for depreciation. A 'liability' is an amount owing which can be determined with substantial accuracy.

Sometimes, therefore, the difference between a provision and a liability hinges around what is meant by 'substantial' accuracy. Rent owing at the end of the financial year would normally be known with precision; this would obviously be a liability. Legal charges for a court case which has been heard, but for which the lawyers have not yet submitted their bill, would be a provision.

Accrued expenses are those accruing from one day to another, but not paid at the year end. Such items as rates, electricity, telephone charges will come under this heading.

Creditors are persons to whom money is owed for goods and services.

Reserves consist of either undistributed profits, or else sums that have been allocated originally from such profits or have been created to comply with the law. An example of the first kind is a *general reserve*, whilst a *share premium account* comes under the second heading.

Provisions, accrued expenses and creditors would all be taken into account before calculating net profit. Reserves do not interfere with the calculation of net profit, as they are appropriations of profit or in the case of capital reserves do not pass through the profit and loss account.

(b) (i) Provision made for £21,000. Charge to profit and loss and show in balance sheet under current liabilities.

(ii) Accrued expenses, $^2/_{12}$ £6,000 = £1,000. Charge against profit and loss account and show as current liability in balance sheet.

(iii) Creditor £2,500. Bring into purchases in trading account and show as current liability in balance sheet.

(iv) Reserve £5,000. Debit to profit and loss appropriation account as plant replacement reserve, and show in balance sheet under *reserves*.

47.18
(a) *The bank*

The bank will be interested in two main aspects. The first is the ability to repay the loan as and when it falls due. The second is the ability to pay interest on the due dates.

Mr Whitehall

He will be interested in the expected return on his investment. This means that recent performance of the company and its plans will be important to him. In addition the possible capital growth of his investment would be desirable.

(b) *Note*: More than four ratios for bank are given, but you should give four only as your answer.

Bank

Long-term ability to repay loan
(i) Members' equity/Total assets
(ii) Loan capital/Members' equity
(iii) Total liabilities/Members' equity
(iv) Operating profit/Loan interest.

Short-term liquidity
(i) Liquid assets/Current liabilities.
(ii) Current assets/Current liabilities.

Mr Whitehall

Return on investment
(i) Price per share/Earnings per share
(ii) Trends of (*i*) for past few years.
(iii) Net profit – Preference dividend/Ordinary dividend.
(iv) Trends of (*iii*) for past few years.

47.19
See text.

48.1
See text.

48.2
See text.

48.3
See text.

48.4
See text.

48.5
See text.

Answers to multiple choice questions

Set 1 (pages 56–60)

1	(C)	2	(D)	3	(B)	4	(C)	5	(A)
6	(C)	7	(C)	8	(A)	9	(C)	10	(A)
11	(B)	12	(D)	13	(B)	14	(D)	15	(B)
16	(C)	17	(C)	18	(A)	19	(D)	20	(C)

Set 2 (pages 134–7)

21	(A)	22	(B)	23	(A)	24	(D)	25	(C)
26	(A)	27	(D)	28	(A)	29	(C)	30	(A)
31	(C)	32	(D)	33	(C)	34	(C)	35	(D)
36	(B)	37	(A)	38	(B)	39	(C)	40	(C)

Set 3 (pages 282–4)

41	(A)	42	(C)	43	(A)	44	(D)	45	(A)
46	(A)	47	(B)	48	(C)	49	(D)	50	(C)
51	(A)	52	(D)	53	(C)	54	(C)	55	(D)
56	(C)	57	(A)	58	(A)	59	(B)	60	(C)

Set 4 (pages 361–4)

61	(B)	62	(A)	63	(D)	64	(A)	65	(C)
66	(A)	67	(D)	68	(D)	69	(B)	70	(A)
71	(D)	72	(C)	73	(D)	74	(B)	75	(B)
76	(C)	77	(D)	78	(A)	79	(B)	80	(C)

Set 5 (pages 540–3)

81	(B)	82	(B)	83	(C)	84	(D)	85	(A)
86	(B)	87	(A)	88	(C)	89	(C)	90	(A)
91	(C)	92	(B)	93	(B)	94	(D)	95	(C)
96	(B)	97	(C)	98	(B)	99	(D)	100	(B)

Glossary

Absorption costing (Chapter 48): The method of allocating all factory indirect expenses to products. (All fixed costs are allocated to cost units.)

Account (Chapter 2): Part of double entry records, containing details of transactions for a specific item.

Account codes (Chapter 23): The process of identifying, measuring and communicating economic information to permit informed judgements and decisions by users of the information.

Accounting (Chapter 28): The uses to which data recorded by bookkeeping can be put for various purposes.

Accounting cycle (Chapter 17): The sequence in which data is recorded and processed until it becomes part of the financial statements at the end of the period.

Accounting information system (AIS) (Chapter 23): The total suite of components that, together, comprise all the inputs, storage, transformation processing, collating, and reporting of financial transaction data. It is, in effect, the infrastructure that supports the production and delivery of accounting information.

Accounting policies (Chapter 47): Those principles, bases, conventions, rules and practices applied by an entity that specify how the effects of transactions and other events are to be reflected in its financial statements.

Accounts (or **Final Accounts**) (Chapter 9): This is a term previously used to refer to statements produced at the end of accounting periods, such as the trading and profit and loss account and the balance sheet. Nowadays, the term 'financial statements' is more commonly used.

Accruals concept (Chapter 10): The concept that profit is the difference between revenue and the expenses incurred in generating that revenue.

Accrued expense (Chapter 28): An expense for which the benefit has been received but which has not been paid for by the end of the period. It is included in the balance sheet under current liabilities as 'accruals'.

Accrued income (Chapter 28): Income (normally) from a source other than the main source of business income, such as rent receivable on an unused office in the company headquarters, that was due to be received by the end of the period but which has not been received by that date. It is added to debtors in the balance sheet.

Accumulated depreciation account (Chapter 27): The account where depreciation is accumulated for balance sheet purposes. It is used in order to leave the cost (or valuation) figure as the balance in the fixed asset account. (It is sometime confusingly referred to as the 'provision for depreciation account'.)

Accumulated fund (Chapter 36): A form of capital account for a non-profit-oriented organisation.

Acid test ratio (Chapter 47): A ratio comparing current assets less stock with current liabilities.

Amortisation (Chapter 26): A term used instead of depreciation when assets are used up simply because of the passing of time.

Assets (Chapter 1): Resources owned by a business.

AVCO (Chapter 29): A method by which the goods used are priced out at average cost.

Bad debt (Chapter 25): A debt that a business will not be able to collect.

Balance brought down (Chapter 5): The difference between both sides of an account that is entered below the totals on the opposite side to the one on which the balance carried down was entered. (This is normally abbreviated to 'balance b/d'.)

Balance carried down (Chapter 5): The difference between both sides of an account that is entered above the totals and makes the total of both sides equal each other. (This is normally abbreviated to 'balance c/d'.)

Balance off the account (Chapter 5): Insert the difference (called a 'balance') between the two sides of an account and then total and rule off the account. This is normally done at the end of a period (usually a month, a quarter, or a year).

Balance sheet (Chapter 1): A statement showing the assets, liabilities, and capital of a business.

Bank Cash Book (Chapter 18): A cash book that only contains entries relating to payments into and out of the bank.

Bank giro credit (Chapter 12): A type of pay-in slip usually used when the payment is into an account held in a different bank. The two types of form are virtually identical – a bank giro credit can be used instead of a pay-in slip, but not the other way around, as the details of the other bank need to be entered on the bank giro credit.

Bank Giro credit (Chapter 30): An amount paid by someone directly into someone else's bank account.

Bank loan (Chapter 12): An amount of money advanced by a bank that has a fixed rate of interest that is charged on the full amount and is repayable on a specified future date.

Bank reconciliation statement (Chapter 30): A calculation comparing the Cash Book balance with the bank statement balance.

Bank statement (Chapter 13): A copy issued by a bank to a customer showing the customer's current account maintained at the bank.

Bookkeeping (Chapter 1): The process of recording data relating to accounting transactions in the accounting books.

Books of original entry (Chapter 11): Books where the first entry recording a transaction is made. (These are sometimes referred to as 'Books of Prime Entry'.)

Bought Ledger (Chapter 20): A variant of a Purchases Ledger where the individual accounts of the creditors, whether they be for goods or for expenses such as stationery or motor expenses, can be kept together in a single ledger.

Budget (Chapters 1 and 48): A plan quantified in monetary terms in advance of a defined time period – usually showing planned income and expenditure and the capital employed to achieve a given objective.

Business entity concept (Chapter 10): Assumption that only transactions that affect the firm, and not the owner's private transactions, will be recorded.

Capital (Chapter 1): The total of resources invested and left in a business by its owner.

Capital expenditure (Chapter 24): When a business spends money to buy or add value to a fixed asset.

Capital reserve (Chapter 46): An account that can be used by sole traders and partnerships to place the amount by which the total purchase price paid for a business is less than the valuation of the net assets acquired. Limited companies cannot use a capital reserve for this purpose. Sole traders and partnerships can instead, if they wish, record the shortfall as negative goodwill.

Carriage inwards (Chapter 9): Cost of transport of goods into a business.

Carriage outwards (Chapter 9): Cost of transport of goods out to the customers of a business.

Cash (Chapter 39): Cash balances and bank balances, plus funds invested in 'cash equivalents'.

Cash Book (Chapter 11): A book of original entry for cash and bank receipts and payments.

Cash equivalents (Chapter 39): Temporary investments of cash not required at present by the business, such as funds put on short-term deposit with a bank. Such investments must be readily convertible into cash, or available as cash within three months.

Cash flow statement (Chapter 39): A statement showing how cash has been generated and disposed of by an organisation. The layout is regulated by FRS 1.

Casting (Chapter 32): Adding up figures.

Charge card (Chapter 12): A payment card that requires the cardholder to settle the account in full at the end of a specified period, e.g. American Express and Diners cards. Holders have to pay an annual fee for the card. (Compare this to a credit card.)

Cheque book (Chapter 12): Book containing forms (cheques) used to pay money out of a current account.

Clearing (Chapter 12): The process by which amounts paid by cheque from an account in one bank are transferred to the bank account of the payee.

Close off the account (Chapter 5): Totalling and ruling off an account on which there is no outstanding balance.

Columnar Purchases Day Book (Chapter 20): A Purchases Day Book used to record all items obtained on credit. It has analysis columns so that the various types of expenditure can be grouped together in a column. Also called a Purchases Analysis Book.

Columnar Sales Day Book (Chapter 20): A Sales Day Book used to show the sales for a period organised in analysis columns according to how the information recorded is to be analysed. Also called a Sales Analysis Book.

Compensating error (Chapter 32): Where two errors of equal amounts, but on opposite sides of the accounts, cancel each other out.

Consistency (Chapter 10): Keeping to the same method of recording and processing transactions.

Contra (Chapter 13): A contra, for Cash Book items, is where both the debit and the credit entries are shown in the Cash Book, such as when cash is paid into the bank.

Contribution (Chapter 38): The surplus of revenue over direct costs allocated to a section of a business.

Control account (Chapter 31): An account which checks the arithmetical accuracy of a ledger.

Cost centre (Chapter 48): A production or service location, function, activity, or item of equipment whose costs may be attributed to cost units.

Cost unit (Chapter 48): A unit of product or service in relation to which costs are ascertained.

Credit (Chapter 2): The right-hand side of the accounts in double entry.

Credit card (Chapter 12): A card enabling the holder to make purchases and to draw cash up to a pre-arranged limit. The credit granted in a period can be settled in full or in part by the end of a specified period. Many credit cards carry no annual fee. (Compare this to a charge card.)

Credit note (Chapter 16): A document sent to a customer showing allowance given by a supplier in respect of unsatisfactory goods.

Creditor (Chapter 1): A person to whom money is owed for goods or services.

Creditor/purchases ratio (Chapter 47): A ratio assessing how long a business takes to pay creditors.

Current account (Chapter 12): A bank account used for regular payments in and out of the bank.

Current assets (Chapter 8): Assets consisting of cash, goods for resale or items having a short life.

Current liabilities (Chapter 8): Liabilities to be paid for within a year of the balance sheet date.

Current ratio (Chapter 47): A ratio comparing current assets with current liabilities.

Day books (Chapter 11): Books in which credit sales, purchases, and returns inwards and outwards of goods are first recorded. The details are then posted from the day books to the ledger accounts.

Debenture (Chapter 45): Loan to a company.

Debit (Chapter 2): The left-hand side of the accounts in double entry.

Debit card (Chapter 12): A card linked to a bank or building society account and used to pay for goods and services by debiting the holder's account. Debit cards are usually combined with other facilities such as ATM and cheque guarantee functions.

Debit note (Chapter 16): A document sent to a supplier showing allowance to be given for unsatisfactory goods.

Debtor (Chapter 1): A person who owes money to a business for goods or services supplied to him.

Debtor/sales ratio (Chapter 47): A ratio assessing how long it takes debtors to pay their debts.

Depletion (Chapter 26): The wasting away of an asset as it is used up.

Deposit account (Chapter 12): A bank account for money to be kept in for a long time.

Depreciation (Chapter 26): The part of the cost of a fixed asset consumed during its period of use by the firm. It represents an estimate of how much of the overall economic usefulness of a fixed asset has been used up in each accounting period. It is charged as a debit to profit and loss and a credit against fixed asset accounts in the General Ledger.

Direct costs (Chapter 37): Costs that can be traced to the item being manufactured.

Direct debit (Chapter 12): A medium used to enable payments to be made automatically into a bank account for whatever amount the recipient requests.

Directors (Chapter 45): Officials appointed by shareholders to manage the company for them.

Discounts allowed (Chapter 13): A deduction from the amount due given to customers who pay their accounts within the time allowed.

Discounts received (Chapter 13): A deduction from the amount due given to a business by a supplier when their account is paid before the time allowed has elapsed. It appears as income in the profit and loss part of the trading and profit and loss account.

Dishonoured cheque (Chapter 30): A cheque which the writer's bank has refused to make payment upon.

Dissolution (Chapter 44): When a partnership firm ceases operations and its assets are disposed of.

Dividends (Chapter 45): The amount given to shareholders as their share of the profits of the company.

Double entry bookkeeping (Chapter 2): A system where each transaction is entered twice, once on the debit side and once on the credit side.

Drawer (Chapter 12): The person making out a cheque and using it for payment.

Drawings (Chapter 4): Funds or goods taken out of a business by the owners for their private use.

Dual aspect concept (Chapter 10): The concept of dealing with both aspects of a transaction.

Dumb terminal (Chapter 22): A computer screen with keyboard (and, perhaps, a mouse) that has no processing power of its own but uses the processing power of a central computer to carry out tasks involving the data held on that central computer.

Endorsement (Chapter 12): A means by which someone may pass the right to collect money due on a cheque.

Equity (Chapter 1): Another name for the capital of the owner.

Error of commission (Chapter 32): Where a correct amount is entered, but in the wrong person's account.

Error of omission (Chapter 32): Where a transaction is completely omitted from the books.

Error of original entry (Chapter 32): Where an item is entered, but both the debit and credit entries are of the same incorrect amount.

Error of principle (Chapter 32): Where an item is entered in the wrong type of account, e.g. a fixed asset in an expense account.

Estimation techniques (Chapter 47): The methods adopted in order to arrive at estimated monetary amounts for items that appear in the financial statements.

Exception reporting (Chapter 23): A process of issuing a warning message to decision-makers when something unexpected is happening: for example, when expenditure against a budget is higher than it should be.

Exempted businesses (Chapter 19): Businesses which do not have to add VAT to the price of goods and services supplied to them. They cannot obtain a refund of VAT paid on goods and services purchased by them.

Expenses (Chapter 4): The value of all the assets that have been used up to obtain revenues.

Extranet (Chapter 22): A network based on Internet technologies where data and information private to the business is made available to a specific group of outsiders, such as suppliers.

Factoring (Chapter 8): Selling the rights to the amounts owing by debtors to a finance company for an agreed amount (which is less than the figure at which they are recorded in the accounting books because the finance company needs to be paid for providing the service).

FIFO (Chapter 29): A method by which the first goods to be received are said to be the first to be sold.

Final accounts (or 'the Accounts') (Chapter 9): This is a term previously used to refer to statements produced at the end of accounting periods, such as the trading and profit and loss account and the balance sheet. Nowadays, the term 'financial statements' is more commonly used.

Financial modelling (Chapter 22): Manipulating accounting data to generate forecasts and perform sensitivity analysis.

Financial statements (Chapter 9): The more common term used to refer to statements produced at the end of accounting periods, such as the trading and profit and loss account and the balance sheet (sometimes referred to as 'final accounts' or simply 'the accounts').

Fixed assets (Chapter 8): Assets which have a long life bought with the intention to use them in the business and not with the intention to simply resell them.

Fixed capital accounts (Chapter 41): Capital accounts which consist only of the amounts of capital actually paid into the firm.

Fixed costs (Chapter 47): Expenses which remain constant whether activity rises or falls, within a given range of activity.

Float (Chapter 18): The amount at which the petty cash starts each period.

Fluctuating capital accounts (Chapter 41): Capital accounts whose balances change from one period to the next.

Folio columns (Chapter 13): Columns used for entering reference numbers.

Forecasting (Chapter 22): Taking present data and expected future trends, such as growth of a market and anticipated changes in price levels and demand, in order to arrive at a view of what the likely economic position of a business will be at some future date.

***Garner* v *Murrary* rule** (Chapter 44): If one partner is unable to make good a deficit on his capital account, the remaining partners will share the loss in proportion to their last agreed capitals, not in the profit/loss sharing ratio.

Gearing (Chapter 47): The ratio of long-term loans and preference shares shown as a percentage of total shareholders' funds, long-term loans, and preference shares.

General Ledger (Chapter 11): A ledger for all accounts other than those for customers and suppliers.

Going concern concept (Chapter 10): The assumption that a business is to continue for the foreseeable future.

Goodwill (Chapter 42): An amount representing the added value to a business of such factors as customer loyalty, reputation, market penetration, and expertise.

Gross loss (Chapter 7): Where the cost of goods sold exceeds the sales revenue.

Gross profit (Chapter 7): Where the sales revenue exceeds the cost of goods sold.

Historical cost concept (Chapter 10): Assets are normally shown at cost price.

Impersonal accounts (Chapter 11): All accounts other than debtors' and creditors' accounts.

Imprest system (Chapter 18): A system where a refund is made of the total paid out in a period in order to restore the float to its agreed level.

Income and expenditure account (Chapter 36): An account for a non-profit-oriented organisation to find the surplus or loss made during a period.

Indirect manufacturing costs (Chapter 37): Costs relating to manufacture that cannot be economically traced to the item being manufactured (also known as 'indirect costs' and, sometimes, as 'factory overhead expenses').

Input tax (Chapter 19): VAT added to the net price of inputs (i.e. purchases).

Inputs (Chapter 19): Purchases of goods and services.

Interest on capital (Chapter 41): An amount at an agreed rate of interest which is credited to a partner based on the amount of capital contributed by him/her.

Interest on drawings (Chapter 41): An amount at an agreed rate of interest, based on the drawings taken out, which is debited to the partners.

Intranet (Chapter 22): A network based on Internet technologies where data and information private to the business is made available to employees of the business.

Job costing (Chapter 48): A costing system that is applied when goods or services are produced in discrete jobs, either one item at a time, or in batches.

Joint ventures (Chapter 40): Business agreements under which two businesses join together for a set of activities and agree to share the profits.

Journal (Chapter 11): A book of original entry for all items not contained in the other books of original entry.

Liabilities (Chapter 1): Total of funds owed for assets supplied to a business or expenses incurred not yet paid.

LIFO (Chapter 29): A method by which the goods sold are said to have come from the last lot of goods received.

Limited company (Chapter 45): An organisation owned by its shareholders, whose liability is limited to their share capital.

Limited partner (Chapter 41): A partner whose liability is limited to the capital he or she has put into the firm.

Liquidity ratios (Chapter 47): Those ratios that relate to the cash position in an organisation and hence its ability to pay liabilities when due.

Local area network (LAN) (Chapter 22): A group of workstations linked together locally through wires.

Long-term liabilities (Chapter 8): Liabilities that do not have to be paid within twelve months of the balance sheet date.

Loss (Chapter 4): The result of selling goods for less than they cost.

Manufacturing account (Chapter 37): An account in which production cost is calculated.

Margin (Chapter 34): Profit shown as a percentage or fraction of selling price.

Marginal costing (Chapter 48): An approach to costing that takes account of the variable cost of products rather than the full production cost. It is particularly useful when considering utilisation of spare capacity.

Mark-up (Chapter 34): Profit shown as a percentage or fraction of cost price.

Materiality (Chapter 10): That something should only be included in the financial statements if it would be of interest to the stakeholders, i.e. to those people who make use of financial accounting statements. It need not be material to every stakeholder, but it must be material to a stakeholder before it merits inclusion.

Measurement basis (Chapter 47): The monetary aspects of the items in the financial statements, such as the basis of the stock valuation, say FIFO or LIFO.

Memorandum joint venture account (Chapter 40): A memorandum account outside the double entry system where the information contained in all the joint venture accounts held by the parties to the joint ventures are collated, the joint venture profit is calculated and the share of profit of each party is recorded in order to close off the account.

Money measurement concept (Chapter 10): The concept that accounting is concerned only with facts measurable in monetary terms, and for which purpose measurements can be used that obtain general agreement as to their suitability.

Narrative (Chapter 17): A description and explanation of the transaction recorded in the journal.

Negative contribution (Chapter 38): The excess of direct costs allocated to a section of a business over the revenue from that section.

Negative goodwill (Chapter 46): The name given to the amount by which the total purchase price for a business a limited company has taken over is less than the valuation of the assets at that time. The amount is entered at the top of the fixed assets in the balance sheet as a negative amount. (Sole traders and partnerships can use this approach instead of a capital reserve.)

Net current assets (Chapter 8): Current assets minus current liabilities. The figure represents the amount of resources the business has in a form that is readily convertible into cash. Same as working capital.

Net loss (Chapter 7): Where the cost of goods sold plus expenses is greater than the revenue.

Net profit (Chapter 7): Where sales revenue plus other income, such as rent received, exceeds the sum of cost of goods sold plus other expenses.

Net realisable value (Chapter 29): The value of goods calculated as their selling price less expenses before sale.

Nominal accounts (Chapter 11): Accounts in which expenses, revenue and capital are recorded.

Nominal Ledger (Chapter 11): Another name for the General Ledger.

Objectivity (Chapter 10): Using a method that everyone can agree to based on some clear and indisputable fact.

Obsolescence (Chapter 26): Becoming out of date.

Ordinary shares (Chapter 45): Shares entitled to dividends after the preference shareholders have been paid their dividends.

Output tax (Chapter 19): VAT added to the net price of outputs (i.e. sales).

Outputs (Chapter 19): Sales of goods and services.

Overdraft (Chapter 12): A facility granted by a bank that allows a customer holding a current account with the bank to spend more than the funds in the account. Interest is charged daily on the amount of the overdraft on that date and the overdraft is repayable at any time upon request from the bank.

Partnership (Chapter 41): A firm in which two or more people are working together as owners with a view to making profits.

Partnership salaries (Chapter 41): Agreed amounts payable to partners in respect of duties undertaken by them.

PAYE (Pay As You Earn) (Chapter 21): The system whereby income tax is deducted from wages and salaries by employers and sent to the Inland Revenue.

Payee (Chapter 12): The person to whom a cheque is paid.

Pay-in slip (Chapter 12): A form used for paying money into a bank account with the same bank.

Personal accounts (Chapter 11): Accounts for creditors and debtors.

Personal allowances (Chapter 21): Amounts each person may subtract from income in order to arrive at taxable income. The value of each allowance is set by Parliament following the Budget each year. They are for things like being married, caring for a dependent relative, etc.

Personal Identification Number or **PIN** (Chapter 12): A secret number issued by a bank to a customer so that the customer may use a debit card in an ATM.

Petty Cash Book (Chapter 18): A Cash Book for small payments.

Plastic card (Chapter 12): The generic name for the range of payment-related cards.

Posting (Chapter 13): The act of transferring information into ledger accounts from books of original entry.

Preference shares (Chapter 45): Shares that are entitled to an agreed rate of dividend before the ordinary shareholders receive anything.

Preliminary expenses (Chapter 45): All the costs that are incurred when a company is formed.

Prepaid expense (Chapter 28): An expense which has been paid in advance, the benefits from which will be received in the next period. It is included in the balance sheet under current assets as 'prepayments'.

Prime cost (Chapter 37): Direct materials plus direct labour plus direct expenses.

Private company (Chapter 45): A limited company that must issue its shares privately.

Private Ledger (Chapter 11): A ledger for capital and drawings accounts.

Process costing (Chapter 48): A costing system that is applied when goods or services are produced in a continuous flow.

Production cost (Chapter 37): Prime cost plus indirect manufacturing costs.

Profit (Chapter 4): The result of selling goods or services for more than they cost.

Profit and loss account (Chapter 7): An account in which net profit is calculated.

Provision for doubtful debts (Chapter 25): An account showing the expected amounts of debtors at the balance sheet date who will not be able to pay their accounts.

Prudence (Chapter 10): Ensuring that profit is not shown as being too high, or that assets are shown at too high a value and that the financial statements are neutral: that is, that neither gains nor losses are understated or overstated.

Public company (Chapter 45): A company that can issue its shares publicly, and for which there is no maximum number of shareholders.

Purchased goodwill (Chapter 42): The difference between the amount paid to acquire a part or the whole of a business as a going concern and the value of the net assets owned by the business.

Purchases (Chapter 3): Goods bought by the business for the prime purpose of selling them again.

Purchases Day Book (Chapter 11): Book of original entry for credit purchases. Also called the Purchases Journal.

Purchases invoice (Chapter 15): A document received by a purchaser showing details of goods bought and their prices.

Purchases Ledger (Chapter 11): A ledger for suppliers' personal accounts.

Real accounts (Chapter 11): Accounts in which property of all kinds is recorded.

Realisation concept (Chapter 10): Only profits and gains realised at the balance sheet date should be included in the profit and loss account. For a gain to be realised, it must be possible to be reasonably certain that it exists and that it can be measured with sufficient reliability.

Receipts and payments account (Chapter 36): A summary of the Cash Book of a non-profit-oriented organisation.

Reduced rate (of VAT) (Chapter 19): A lower VAT rate applicable to certain goods and services.

Reducing balance method (Chapter 26): A method of calculating depreciation based on the principle that you calculate annual depreciation as a percentage of the net-of-depreciation-to-date balance brought forward at the start of the period on the fixed asset.

Registered business (Chapter 19): A business that has registered for VAT. It must account for VAT and submit a VAT Return at the end of every VAT tax period.

Reserve accounts (Chapter 45): The transfer of apportioned profits to accounts for use in future years.

Residual value (Chapter 26): The net amount receivable when a fixed asset is put out of use by the business.

Return on capital employed (Chapter 47): Net profit as a percentage of capital employed, often abbreviated as ROCE.

Return on owners' equity (Chapter 47): Net profit as a percentage of ordinary share capital plus all reserves, often abbreviated as ROOE. The more common term in use for this is 'return on shareholders' funds'.

Return on shareholders' funds (Chapter 47): Net profit as a percentage of ordinary share capital plus all reserves, often abbreviated as ROSF and more commonly used than the alternative term, return on owners' equity.

Returns inwards (Chapter 9): Goods returned by customers. (Also known as 'sales returns'.)

Returns Inwards Day Book (Chapter 11): Book of original entry for goods returned by customers. Also called the Returns Inwards Journal or the Sales Returns Book.

Returns outwards (Chapter 9): Goods returned to suppliers. (Also known as 'purchases returns'.)

Returns Outwards Day Book (Chapter 11): Book of original entry for goods returned to suppliers. Also called the Returns Outwards Journal or the Purchases Returns Book.

Revaluation account (Chapter 43): An account used to record gains and losses when assets are revalued.

Revenue expenditure (Chapter 24): Expenses needed for the day-to-day running of the business.

Revenues (Chapter 4): The financial value of goods and services sold to customers.

Sale or return (Chapter 29): Goods passed to a customer on the understanding that a sale will not occur until they are paid for. As a result, these goods continue to belong to the seller.

Sales (Chapter 3): Goods sold by the business in which it normally deals which were bought with the prime intention of resale.

Sales Day Book (Chapter 11): Book of original entry for credit sales. Also called the Sales Journal.

Sales invoice (Chapter 14): A document showing details of goods sold and the prices of those goods.

Sales Ledger (Chapter 11): A ledger for customers' personal accounts.

Sensitivity analysis (Chapter 22): Altering volumes and amounts so as to see what would be likely to happen if they were changed. For example, a company may wish to know the financial effects of cutting its selling price by £1 a unit. Also called 'what if' analysis.

Separate determination concept (Chapter 10): The amount of each asset or liability should be determined separately.

Shares (Chapter 45): The division of the capital of a limited company into parts.

Smart card (Chapter 12): A card that holds details on a computer chip instead of a traditional magnetic stripe.

Standard cost (Chapter 29): What you would expect something to cost.

Standard rate (of VAT) (Chapter 19): The VAT rate usually used.

Standard-rated business (Chapter 19): A business that charges VAT at the standard rate on its sales.

Standing order (Chapter 12): A medium used to enable payments to be made automatically at given dates into a bank account for an amount agreed by the payer.

Statement (Chapter 16): A copy of a customer's personal account taken from the supplier's books.

Statement of Affairs (Chapter 35): A statement from which the capital of the owner can be found by estimating assets and liabilities. Then Capital = Assets − Liabilities. It is the equivalent of the balance sheet.

Stock (Chapter 1): Goods in which the business normally deals that are held with the intention of resale. They may be finished goods, partly finished goods, or raw materials awaiting conversion into finished goods which will then be sold. (Also known as inventory.)

Stock turnover (Chapter 34): The number of times stock is sold in an accounting period. (Also known as 'stockturn'.)

Stocktaking (Chapter 29): The process of physically identifying the stock on hand at a given point in time.

Straight line method (Chapter 26): A method of calculating depreciation that involves deducting the same amount every accounting period from the original cost of the fixed asset.

Subjectivity (Chapter 10): Using a method that other people may not agree to, derived from one's own personal preferences.

Substance over form (Chapter 10): Where real substance takes precedence over legal form.

Super profits (Chapter 42): Net profit less the opportunity costs of alternative earnings and alternative returns on capital invested that have been foregone.

Suspense account (Chapter 33): An account in which you can enter the amount equal to the difference in the trial balance while you try to find the cause of the error(s) that resulted in the failure of the trial balance to balance.

Switch (Chapter 12): A system that allows a debit card to be used to pay for goods and services in the UK. In effect, it is the electronic version of paying by cheque.

T-account (Chapter 2): The layout of accounts in the accounting books.

Tax code (Chapter 21): The number found by adding up an individual's personal allowances which is used to calculate that individual's tax liability.

Time interval concept (Chapter 10): Financial statements are prepared at regular intervals.

Total cost (Chapter 37): Production cost plus administration, selling and distribution expenses and finance expenses.

Trade discount (Chapter 14): A deduction in price given to a trade customer when calculating the price to be charged to that customer for some goods. It does not appear anywhere in the accounting books and so does not appear anywhere in the financial statements.

Trading account (Chapter 7): An account in which gross profit is calculated.

Trading and profit and loss account (Chapter 7): A financial statement in which both gross profit and net profit are calculated.

Transposition error (Chapter 32): Where the characters within a number are entered in the wrong sequence.

Trial balance (Chapter 6): A list of account titles and their balances in the ledgers, on a specific date, shown in debit and credit columns.

True and fair view (Chapter 45): The expression that is used by auditors to indicate whether, in their opinion, the financial statements fairly represent the state of affairs and financial performance of a company.

Unpresented cheque (Chapter 30): A cheque which has been given to a creditor but which has not yet been received and processed by the writer's bank.

Unregistered business (Chapter 19): A business that ignores VAT and treats it as part of the cost of purchases. It does not charge VAT on its outputs. It does not need to maintain any record of VAT paid.

Value Added Tax (VAT) (Chapter 19): A tax charged on the supply of most goods and services.

Variable costs (Chapter 47): Expenses which change in response to changes in the level of activity.

Website (of a business) (Chapter 22): A location on the Internet where businesses place information for the use of anyone who happens to want to look at it. In many cases, a business website contains copies of the latest financial statements of the business and a part of the website is devoted to promoting and selling goods and services.

'What if' analysis (Chapter 22): Altering volumes and amounts so as to see what would be likely to happen if they were changed. For example, a company may wish to know the financial effects of cutting its selling price by £1 a unit. Also called sensitivity analysis.

Wide area network (WAN) (Chapter 22): A group of workstations not all of which are based locally that are linked together by wires and over telephone lines.

Work in progress (Chapter 37): Items not completed at the end of a period.

Working capital (Chapter 8): Current assets minus current liabilities. The figure represents the amount of resources the business has in a form that is readily convertible into cash. Same as net current assets.

Workstation (Chapter 22): A dumb terminal or a PC that is used to access data held in a database on a central computer.

Zero rate (of VAT) (Chapter 19): The VAT rate (of zero) that applies to supply of certain goods and services.

Zero-rated business (Chapter 19): A business that only supplies zero-rated goods and services. It does not charge VAT to its customers but it receives a refund of VAT on goods and services it purchases.

Index

Note: This index does not include references to the glossary, but may be used in conjunction with it.